International Rare
Book Prices

SCIENCE &
MEDICINE

1992

International Rare
Book Prices

SCIENCE &
MEDICINE

Series Editor: Michael Cole

1992

The Clique

International Rare Book Prices – Science & Medicine
ISBN 1 870773 31 4

Typesetting by Maxiprint, York, England
Printed and bound by Biddles Ltd., Guildford, England

Contents

Introduction and Notes

The annual *IRBP* series, now in its sixth year, provides annual records of the pricing levels of out-of-print, rare or antiquarian books within a number of specialty subject areas and gives likely sources and suppliers for such books in Britain and the United States of America. It is intended to be used by both the experienced bookman and the newcomer to book-collecting.

Sources of information:

The books recorded each year in the various subject volumes of *IRBP* have been selected from catalogues of books for sale issued during the previous year by numerous bookselling firms in Britain and the United States. These firms, listed at the end of this volume, range in nature from the highly specialized, handling books solely within closely defined subject areas, through to large concerns with expertise across a broad spectrum of interests.

Extent of coverage:

IRBP concentrates exclusively on books published in the English language and, throughout the series as a whole, encompasses books published between the 16th century and the 1970s.

The 30,000 or so separate titles recorded in the annual volumes of *IRBP* vary greatly from year to year although naturally there is a degree of overlap, particularly of the more frequently found titles. Consecutive annual volumes do not, therefore, merely update pricings from earlier years; they give substantially different listings of books on each occasion. The value of the *IRBP* volumes lies in providing records of an ever-increasing range of individual titles which have appeared for sale on the antiquarian or rare book market.

Emphasis is placed throughout on books falling within the lower to middle range of the pricing scale (£10 - £250; $20 - $500) rather than restricting selection to the unusually fine or expensive. In so doing, *IRBP* provides a realistic overview of the norm, rather than the exception, within the booktrade.

Authorship and cross-references:

Authors are listed alphabetically by surname.

Whenever possible, the works of each author are grouped together under a single form of name irrespective of the various combinations of initials, forenames and surnames by which the author is known.

Works published anonymously, or where the name of the author is not recorded on the title-page, are suitably cross-referenced by providing the main entry under the name of the author (when mentioned by the bookseller) with a corresponding entry under the first appropriate word of the title. In cases of unknown, or unmentioned, authorship, entry is made solely under the title.

Full-titles:
Editorial policy is to eschew, whenever possible, short-title records in favour of full-, or at least more complete and explanatory, titles. Short-title listings do little to convey the flavour, or even the content, of many books - particularly those published prior to the nineteenth century.

Descriptions:
Books are listed alphabetically, using the first word of the title ignoring, for alphabetical purposes, the definite and indefinite articles *the, a* and *an.* Within this alphabetical grouping of titles, variant editions are not necessarily arranged in chronological order, i.e., a 2nd, 3rd or 4th edition might well be listed prior to an earlier edition.

Subject to restrictions of space and to the provisos set out below, the substance of each catalogue entry giving details of the particular copy offered for sale has been recorded in full.

The listings have been made so as to conform to a uniform order of presentation, viz: Title; place of publication; publisher or printer; date; edition; size; collation; elements of content worthy of note; description of contents including faults, if any; description and condition of binding; bookseller; price; approximate price conversion from dollars to sterling or vice versa.

Abbreviations of description customary within the booktrade have generally been used. A list of these abbreviations will be found on page *x.*

Collations:
Collations, when provided by the bookseller, are repeated in toto although it should be borne in mind that booksellers employ differing practices in this respect; some by providing complete collations and others by indicating merely the number of pages in the main body of the work concerned. The same edition of the same title catalogued by two booksellers could therefore have two apparently different collations and care should be taken not to regard any collation recorded in *IRBP* as being a definitive or absolute record of total content.

Currency conversion:
IRBP lists books offered for sale priced in either pounds sterling (£) or United States dollars ($). For the benefit of readers unaccustomed to one or other of these currencies, an approximate conversion figure in the alternative currency has been provided in parentheses after each entry, as, for example, "**£100** [≃ **$178]**", or, "**$60** [≃ **£34]**". The conversion is based upon an exchange rate of £1 sterling ≃ US $1.78 (US $1 ≃ £0.562 sterling), the approximate rate applicable at the date of going to press.

It must be stressed that the conversion figures in parentheses are provided merely as an indication of the approximate pricing level in the currency with which the reader may be most familiar and that fluctuations in exchange rates will make these approximations inaccurate to a greater or lesser degree.

Acknowledgements:
We are indebted to those booksellers who have provided their catalogues during 1991 for the purposes of *IRBP*. A list of the contributing booksellers forms an appendix at the rear of this volume.

This appendix forms a handy reference of contacts in Britain and the United States with proven experience of handling books within the individual specialist fields encompassed by the series. The booksellers listed therein are able, between them, to offer advice on any aspect of the rare and antiquarian booktrade.

Many of the listed books will still, at the time of publication, be available for purchase. Readers with a possible interest in acquiring any of the items may well find it worth their while communicating with the booksellers concerned to obtain further and complete details.

Caveat:
Whilst the greatest care has been taken in transcribing entries from catalogues, it should be understood that it is inevitable that an occasional error will have passed unnoticed. Obvious mistakes, usually typographical in nature, observed in catalogues have been corrected. We have not questioned the accuracy in bibliographical matters of the cataloguers concerned.

The Clique

Abbreviations

advt(s)	advertisement(s)	intl	initial
addtn(s)	addition(s)	iss	issue
a.e.g.	all edges gilt	jnt(s)	joint(s)
ALS	autograph letter signed	lge	large
altrtns	alterations	lea	leather
Amer	American	lib	library
bibliog(s)	bibliography(ies)	ltd	limited
b/w	black & white	litho(s)	lithograph(s)
bndg	binding	marg(s)	margin(s)
bd(s)	board(s)	ms(s)	manuscript(s)
b'plate	bookplate	mrbld	marbled
ctlg(s)	catalogue(s)	mod	modern
chromolitho(s)	chromo-lithograph(s)	mor	morocco
ca	circa	mtd	mounted
cold	coloured	n.d.	no date
coll	collected	n.p.	no place
contemp	contemporary	num	numerous
crnr(s)	corner(s)	obl	oblong
crrctd	corrected	occas	occasional(ly)
cvr(s)	cover(s)	orig	original
dec	decorated	p (pp)	page(s)
detchd	detached	perf	perforated
diag(s)	diagram(s)	pict	pictorial
dw(s)	dust wrapper(s)	port(s)	portrait(s)
edn(s)	edition(s)	pres	presentation
elab	elaborate	ptd	printed
engv(s)	engraving(s)	qtr	quarter
engvd	engraved	rebnd	rebind/rebound
enlgd	enlarged	rec	recent
esp	especially	repr(d)	repair(ed)
ex lib	ex library	rvsd	revised
f (ff)	leaf(ves)	roy	royal
f.e.p.	free end paper	sep	separate
facs	facsimile	sev	several
fig(s)	figure(s)	sgnd	signed
fldg	folding	sgntr	signature
ft	foot	sl	slight/slightly
frontis	frontispiece	sm	small
hand-cold	hand-coloured	t.e.g.	top edge gilt
hd	head	TLS	typed letter signed
ill(s)	illustration(s)	unif	uniform
illust	illustrated	v	very
imp	impression	vell	vellum
imprvd	improved	vol(s)	volume(s)
inc	including	w'engvd	wood-engraved
inscrbd	inscribed	w'cut(s)	woodcut(s)
inscrptn	inscription	wrap(s)	wrapper(s)

Science & Medicine
1991 Catalogue Prices

Abbatt, Richard
- A Treatise on the Calculus of Variations. London: 1836. 1st edn. Sm 8vo. xi,207 pp. Fldg plate (sl foxed). Mod cloth.
(Weiner) £60 [≈ $107]

Abbe, Cleveland
- The Mechanics of the Earth's Atmosphere. A Collection of Translations. Washington: Smithsonian, 1891. 1st edn. 8vo. 324 pp. Binder's cloth. *(Gaskell)* £30 [≈ $53]
- The Mechanics of the Earth's Atmosphere. A Collection of Translations. Third Collection. Washington: Smithsonian, 1891. 1st edn. 8vo. iv, 617 pp. Orig cloth.
(Gaskell) £20 [≈ $36]

Abbott, E. Abbott
- Flatland. A Romance of Many Dimensions. By A Square. London: 1884. Ills. Orig parchment wraps, sl soiled & worn.
(Blakeney) £75 [≈ $134]

Abbott, Maude
- Classified and Annotated Bibliography of Sir William Osler's Publications. Montreal: 1939. 2nd edn. 163 pp. Orig bndg.
(Fye) $100 [≈ £56]

Abercrombie, John
- The Garden Mushroom, its most effectual General Culture thoroughly displayed ... London: G. & J. Robinson, 1802. 70 pp. Sm repr hd of title. Disbound.
(Jarndyce) £85 [≈ $151]
- The Hot-House Gardener ... London: for John Stockdale, 1789. 1st edn. Roy 8vo. xvi, 238 pp. 5 hand cold plates inc frontis. Frontis lower marg sl trimmed. Contemp tree calf, rebacked. *(Vanbrugh)* £295 [≈ $525]
- Inquiries concerning the Intellectual Powers and the Investigation of Truth. London: 1830. 8vo. xv,435 pp. Lacks half-title. Contemp half calf, rubbed.
(Weiner) £100 [≈ $178]

Abercrombie, John & Mawe, Thomas
- Abercrombies and Mawe's Pocket Gardeners' Calendar; or, Monthly Journal in the Modern Practice of Gardening ... London: Orlando Hodgson, [ca 1835]. Frontis. Sl dusty, few pencil notes. Orig ptd wraps.
(Jarndyce) £32 [≈ $57]

Abercromby, Hon. Ralph
- Seas and Skies in Many Latitudes. or, Wanderings in Search of Weather. London: 1888. xvi,447 pp. 3 maps, 9 photos, 33 engvs. Orig pict cloth, rear inner hinge sl loose.
(Whitehart) £18 [≈ $32]

Abernethy, James
- The Hunterian Oration, for the Year 1819 ... Royal College of Surgeons ... London: 1819. 8vo. [1],66,[2 advt] pp. New mrbld bds, uncut. *(Goodrich)* $75 [≈ £42]

Abernethy, John
- The Surgical and Physiological Works ... London: Longman ..., 1830. 4 vols. 8vo. Lib marks, some foxing. Vols 1 & 2 early qtr sheep, vols 3 & 4 orig sheep, rebacked in cloth. *(Goodrich)* $250 [≈ £140]
- Surgical Observations on Diseases resembling Syphilis; and on Diseases of the Urethra. London: Longman ..., 1810. 8vo. 234 pp. Orig polished calf, rebacked.
(Goodrich) $250 [≈ £140]
- Surgical Observations on Diseases resembling Syphilis, and on Diseases of the Urethra. The Fourth Edition. London: Longman, 1822. 8vo. [iv],234,[spare label] pp. 8 advt pp inserted at start. 1 section roughly opened. Orig bds, extrs rubbed.
(Frew Mackenzie) £36 [≈ $64]
- Surgical Observations on the Constitutional Origin and Treatment of Local Diseases and on Aneurisms ... Ninth Edition. London: Longman, Rees ..., 1827. 8vo. xii,346 pp. Lacks front f.e.p. Orig bds, paper label, lower jnt split, tear in upper jnt.

(Gaskell) **£145 [≃ $258]**
- Surgical Observations on Tumours and on Lumbar Abscesses. London: Longman ..., 1811. 8vo. 222 pp. Occas foxing. Orig qtr calf, rebacked.   *(Goodrich)* **$295 [≃ £166]**

Abney, W. de W.
- Colour Vision being the Tyndall Lectures delivered in 1894 at the Royal Institution. London: 1895. ix,231 pp. Cold frontis, sev text diags. Ink inscrptns on half-title. Orig bndg.   *(Whitehart)* **£25 [≃ $45]**

Abney, W., & others
- Science Lectures at South Kensington. London: 1878-79. 2 vols. Text figs. Orig cloth.   *(Whitehart)* **£35 [≃ $62]**

Abraham, James Johnston
- Lettsom, His Life, Times, Friends and Descendants. London: Heinemann, 1933. 1st edn. Lge 8vo. xx,498 pp. Fldg table, num ills. Name. Orig cloth, upper cvr sl splashed.
        (Bow Windows) **£50 [≃ $89]**
- Lettsom: His Life, Times, Friends and Descendants. London: 1933. 1st edn. 498 pp. Ills. Orig bndg.   *(Fye)* **$60 [≃ £34]**

Abrahams, Harold
- Extinct Medical Schools of 19th-Century Philadelphia. Phila: 1966. 1st edn. 580 pp. Orig bndg.   *(Fye)* **$100 [≃ £56]**

Accum, Friedrich Christian
- A Practical Treatise on Gas-Light ... Fourth Edition. London: 1818. 8vo. xvii,194 pp. 7 cold plates (2 fldg). Lib perf stamp through plates, title & last leaf. Sl soiled. Half calf, worn, rebacked.   *(Weiner)* **£275 [≃ $490]**

Acheta Domestica (pseudonym)
- Episodes of Insect Life ... see Budgen, M.L.

Ackerknecht, Erwin
- Rudolf Virchow: Doctor, Statesman, Anthropologist. Madison: 1953. 1st edn. 304 pp. Orig bndg.   *(Fye)* **$75 [≃ £42]**

Ackermann, Rudolph
- Observations on Ackermann's Patent Moveable Axles for Four Wheeled Carriages ... London: 1819. 8vo. [ii],60 pp. 5 litho plates (lib stamp on blank margs). Cloth.
        (Weiner) **£325 [≃ $579]**

Acland, Henry W.
- The Harveian Oration. London: 1865. 8vo. 85 pp. Orig bndg. *(Goodrich)* **$45 [≃ £25]**
- Health in the Village. London: 1884. iv,88

pp. 52 ills inc 2 fldg maps. Orig bndg.
        (Whitehart) **£25 [≃ $45]**

Adami, J.G.
- Charles White of Manchester (1728-1813), and the Arrest of Puerperal Fever. New York: 1923. 1st Amer edn. 142 pp. Orig bndg.
        (Fye) **$50 [≃ £28]**

Adams, Daniel (editor)
- The Medical and Agricultural Register for the Years 1806 and 1807 ... Volume I [all published]. Boston: Manning & Loring, 1806-07. 24 numbers. 8vo. Contemp calf backed mrbld bds. *(Robertshaw)* **£70 [≃ $125]**

Adams, George, the elder, d. 1773
- A Treatise describing and explaining the Construction and Use of New Celestial and Terrestrial Globes ... London: for the author, 1766. 1st edn. 8vo. xxii,242,[8 advt] pp. 3 plates. Contemp calf, jnts cracked, hd of spine sl chipped.   *(Burmester)* **£750 [≃ $1,335]**

Adams, George, the younger, 1750-1795
- An Essay on Electricity, explaining the Theory and Practice of that useful Science ... Third Edition corrected and considerably enlarged. London: 1787. 8vo. 468 pp. Fldg frontis, title vignette, 7 plates. Mod half calf.
        (Robertshaw) **£180 [≃ $320]**
- Essays on the Microscope ... A General History of Insects ... Configuration of Salts ... London: for the author, by Robert Hindmarsh ..., 1787. 1st edn. Stout 4to. Half-title. Frontis (spotted, offset), 32 plates (1-31, 26 bis). Occas spot. New mrbld calf.
        (Georges) **£1,600 [≃ $2,848]**
- Geometrical and Graphical Essays ... Mathematical Instruments used in ... Surveying, Levelling, and Perspective ... Second Edition ... Enlarged by William Jones. London: 1797. 2 vols in one. 14 ctlg, 2 advt pp. Frontis, 34 fldg plates. Contemp calf, hd of spine v sl worn.
        (Weiner) **£175 [≃ $312]**
- Lectures on Natural and Experimental Philosophy ... Second Edition, with considerable Corrections and Additions, by William Jones ... London: 1799. 5 vols. 8vo. Frontis, 43 fldg plates. End ff sl foxed. Contemp half calf. *(Fenning)* **£450 [≃ $801]**
- Plates for the Essays on the Microscope. London: 1787. Oblong folio. 33 plates on 31 sheets. Sl water stain lower part of early plates. Few old marg notes. Orig bds, uncut, v worn, front bd detached.
        (Weiner) **£375 [≃ $668]**

Adams, H. & A.
- The Genera of Recent Mollusca. London: Van Voorst, 1853-58. 3 vols. 8vo. 138 plates. Orig cloth, sm tear hd of 1 spine.
(Egglishaw) **£120 [≈ $214]**

Adams, H. Isabel
- Wild Flowers of the British Isles. London: Heinemann, 1907. 1st edn. 2 vols. 4to. 137 cold plates. Orig dec green cloth gilt.
(Gough) **£50 [≈ $89]**

Adams, H.G.
- Beautiful Shells, their Nature, Structure and Uses familiarly explained. London: Groombridge, 1887. Cr 8vo. [ii],156 pp. 8 cold plates, num w'engvs. Orig dec cloth gilt, a.e.g. *(Egglishaw)* **£28 [≈ $50]**
- Beautiful Shells. London: 1871. 8vo. [ii], 156 pp. 8 cold plates, num engvs. Tear in 1 plate & 1 marg reprd. Orig dec cloth, rather worn.
(Wheldon & Wesley) **£20 [≈ $36]**
- Favourite Song Birds. New Edition. London: 1887. Sm 8vo. 6 cold plates. Name. Labels removed from endpapers. Orig illust cloth, a.e.g., sl marked, sl rubbed.
(Bow Windows) **£45 [≈ $80]**
- Humming Birds, Described and Illustrated. London: Groombridge, n.d. Sm 8vo. [iv], 144, [12 advt] pp. 8 plates containing 16 cold figs, text ills. Orig green cloth blocked in gilt & black, a.e.g., sl worn, upper hinge strained.
(Blackwell's) **£65 [≈ $116]**

Adams, H.G. & H.B.
- The Smaller British Birds ... London: George Bell, 1874. 1st edn. Lge 8vo. iv,252 pp. 16 cold plates of birds & 16 of eggs. 1 plate sl foxed. Orig dec cloth gilt, a.e.g.
(Blackwell's) **£150 [≈ $267]**
- The Smaller British Birds. London: George Bell & Sons, 1874. 1st edn. Cr 4to. iv,252 pp. 32 cold plates by Fawcett after Lydon. Few sl marks. Orig pict cloth gilt, sl shaken.
(Ash) **£125 [≈ $223]**

Adams, John Couch
- Lectures on the Lunar Theory. Cambridge: 1900. iv,88 pp. Some foxing. Cloth.
(Whitehart) **£18 [≈ $32]**
- Lectures on Lunar Theory. Edited by R.A. Sampson. Cambridge: UP, 1900. 1st edn. 8vo. viii, 88 pp. Orig dark green cloth, uncut.
(Gaskell) **£80 [≈ $142]**
- Lectures on Lunar Theory. Edited by R.A. Sampson. Cambridge: UP, 1900. 1st edn. 8vo. viii, 88 pp. Orig dark blue cloth, edges trimmed. *(Gaskell)* **£60 [≈ $107]**
- The Scientific Papers. Edited by William

Grylls Adams with a Memoir by J.W.L. Glaisher. Cambridge: UP, 1896-1900. 1st edn. 2 vols. 4to. 6 charts vol 2. Orig cloth, largely unopened. *(Gaskell)* **£200 [≈ $356]**

Adams, Lionel E.
- The Collector's Manual of British Land and Freshwater Shells ... Second Edition. Leeds: 1896. Cr 8vo. 11 plates (9 cold). Orig cloth gilt. *(Fenning)* **£28.50 [≈ $52]**

Adams, William
- Lectures on the Pathology and Treatment of Lateral and Other Forms of Curvature of the Spine. London: 1865. 1st edn. 334 pp. 5 litho plates, 61 w'cuts. Orig bndg, recased.
(Fye) **$450 [≈ £253]**

Adams, William Bridges
- English Pleasure Carriages; their Origin, History, Varieties, Materials, Construction, Defects, Improvements, and Capabilities ... London: Charles Knight, 1837. 1st edn. 8vo. 16 w'engvd plates, text ills. Few spots of foxing. Orig cloth, sl shaken, extrs rubbed.
(Georges) **£150 [≈ $267]**

Addison, Thomas
- A Collection of the Published Writings. London: 1868. 1st edn. 242 pp. Orig bndg.
(Fye) **$250 [≈ £140]**

Adelmann, Howard
- Marcello Malpighi and the Evolution of Embryology. Ithaca: 1966. 1st edn. 5 vols. 4to. 2475 pp. Orig bndg. *(Fye)* **$200 [≈ £112]**

Adrian, Lord
- The Physical Background of Perception. Being the Waynflete Lectures delivered in the College of St. Mary Magdalen, Oxford ... Oxford: 1946. 96 pp. 21 figs. Dw (sl faded).
(Whitehart) **£15 [≈ $27]**

Adye, E.H.
- Modern Lithology Illustrated and Defined ... Edinburgh & London: 1907. 1st edn. Sm 8vo. [iv],128 pp. 16 cold plates. Crnr cut from fly leaf. Orig cloth. *(Bow Windows)* **£36 [≈ $64]**

Afnan, Soheil
- Avicenna. His Life and Works. London: 1958. 1st edn. 298 pp. Orig bndg.
(Fye) **$50 [≈ £28]**

Agassi, J.
- Faraday as a Natural Philosopher. Chicago: 1971. xiv,359 pp. Frontis port. Orig bndg.
(Whitehart) **£18 [≈ $32]**

Agassiz, Alexander
- The Coral Reefs of the Tropical Pacific. Cambridge, Mass.: 1903. 3 vols. 4to. xxxiii, 410 pp. Atlas of 238 plates. Sections & text figs. Sl blind stamp on titles. Half buckram. *(Wheldon & Wesley)* **£180 [≈ $320]**
- Letters and Recollections. Boston: 1913. 8vo. 454 pp. 2 charts, 18 ills. Cloth. *(Wheldon & Wesley)* **£45 [≈ $80]**

Agassiz, J.L.R.
- Contributions to the Natural History of the United States of America. Boston: 1857-62. 4 vols (all published). Roy 4to. 77 plates (2 cold). 1 sm repr. Ink nos on titles. Half calf. *(Wheldon & Wesley)* **£250 [≈ $445]**

Agassiz, Louis
- Methods of Study in Natural History. Boston: 1875. 10th edn. 8vo. viii,319 pp. Cloth, trifle used & loose. *(Wheldon & Wesley)* **£28 [≈ $50]**

Agassiz, Louis & Gould, Augustus A.
- Outlines of Comparative Physiology, touching the Structure and Development of the Races of Animals ... Edited from the Revised Edition and greatly enlarged. London: Bohn, 1855. 8vo. xxiv,442 pp. Cold frontis, 390 figs. Cloth. *(Egglishaw)* **£24 [≈ $43]**
- Principles of Zoology ... Boston: Gould, Kendall & Lincoln, 1848. 1st edn. 8vo. 216, [16 ctlg] pp. Orig cloth, sm split hd of upper hinge. *(Hemlock)* **$175 [≈ £98]**

Agnew, H.C.
- A Letter from Alexandria on the Evidence of the Practical Application of the Quadrature of the Circle, in the Configuration of the Great Pyramids of Gizeh. London: 1838. 4to. 57 pp. 8 plates. Used & annotated. Orig cloth, sl worn. *(Weiner)* **£45 [≈ $80]**

Agricola, Georg
- De Re Metallica translated from the first Latin Edition of 1556 ... By C. Herbert and Lou H. Hoover. London: Mining Magazine, 1912. 1st edn in English. Folio. [iv],xxxii,540,[1] pp. Num ills. Orig vellum over bds, uncut & unopened. *(Gaskell)* **£550 [≈ $979]**

Agrippa, Henricus Cornelius
- The Vanity of Arts & Sciences. London: 1684. 4th edn (?). Orig calf, worn but sound. *(Deja Vu)* **£450 [≈ $801]**
- The Vanity of Arts and Sciences. London: R.E. for R.B. & sold by C. Blount, 1684. 8vo.

[10], 368 pp. Port frontis. Rec pigskin. Wing A.791. *(O'Neal)* **$400 [≈ £225]**

Ahrendt, William Robert
- Automatic Feedback. New York: McGraw Hill, 1951. 1st edn. Lib b'plate & pocket. Orig bndg. *(Schoen)* **$65 [≈ £37]**

Aichorn, August
- Wayward Youth. With a Foreword by Sigmund Freud ... London: Putnam, [1936]. 1st English edn. xi,[3],236 pp. Orig cloth. *(Caius)* **$125 [≈ £70]**

Aikin, J.
- Observations on the External Use of Preparations of Lead. With Some General Remarks on Topical Medicines. London: 1771. iv, 104 pp. Some foxing to endpapers & title. Contemp polished calf, front hinge cracked but firm. *(Whitehart)* **£150 [≈ $267]**

Ainslie, Whitelaw
- Materia Indica; or some Account of those Articles which are employed by the Hindoos, and other Eastern Nations, in their Medicine, Arts, and Agriculture ... London: 1826. 2 vols. 8vo. xxiv,654; xxxix,604 pp. Marg worming. Half calf, worn, rebacked. *(Weiner)* **£325 [≈ $579]**

Ainsworth, G.C.
- Introduction to the History of Mycology. London: 1976. 8vo. xi,359 pp. 18 plates, 8 tables, 90 text figs. Free endpapers removed. Cloth, ft of spine marked. *(Wheldon & Wesley)* **£30 [≈ $53]**

Airy, G.B.
- Six Lectures on Astronomy ... London: [ca 1860]. 4th edn. ix,222 pp. 7 fldg plates. Occas sl foxing. Orig cloth, rubbed. *(Whitehart)* **£20 [≈ $36]**

Aitken, G.A.
- The Life and Works of John Arbuthnot. Oxford: 1892. xii,516 pp. Port frontis. Half-title sl foxed. Orig cloth. *(Whitehart)* **£85 [≈ $151]**

Alanson, E.
- Practical Observations on Amputation and the After-Treatment ... London: 1782. 2nd edn. xxxii,296 pp. Occas sl foxing. Contemp leather, rebacked. *(Whitehart)* **£220 [≈ $392]**

Albee, Fred
- Bone-Graft Surgery. Phila: 1915. 1st edn. 417 pp. Orig bndg. *(Fye)* **$400 [≈ £225]**

- Bone-Graft Surgery in Disease, Injury and Deformity. Phila: 1940. 403 pp. Ex-lib. Orig bndg.   *(Fye)* **$75 [≈£42]**
- Orthopedic and Reconstructive Surgery. Phila: 1919. 1st edn. 1138 pp. Orig bndg.
                                  (Fye) **$250 [≈£140]**
- A Surgeon's Fight to Rebuild Men: An Autobiography. New York: 1943. 1st edn. 349 pp. Dw.   *(Fye)* **$45 [≈£25]**

Albee, Louelli
- Doctor and I. Detroit: 1951. 1st edn. 240 pp. Ills. Orig bndg. Dw.   *(Fye)* **$40 [≈£22]**

Albin, E.
- A Natural History of Spiders, and Other Curious Insects. London: 1736. 4to. [viii],76 pp. Frontis, 40 (of 53) plates. Sl foxing & off-setting. A few plate margs trifle frayed. New half calf. *(Wheldon & Wesley)* **£225 [≈$401]**

Albright, Fuller & Reifenstein, Edward
- The Parathyroid Glands and Metabolic Bone Disease. Baltimore: 1948. 1st edn. 393 pp. Orig bndg.   *(Fye)* **$40 [≈£22]**

Alder, Joshua & Hancock, Albany
- The British Tunicata. London: Ray Society, 1905-12. 3 vols. 8vo. 3 ports, 66 plates (many cold). Cloth.
                   (Wheldon & Wesley) **£75 [≈$134]**
- The British Tunicata, an unfinished Monograph ... London: Ray Society, 1905. 2 vols. 8vo. 2 ports, 50 plates (33 cold), 86 text figs. Sm snag vol 1 title. Orig cloth gilt, spines sl faded.   *(Blackwell's)* **£250 [≈$445]**

Alexander, Franz
- The Medical Value of Psychoanalysis. New York: Norton, [1936]. 278 pp. Orig cloth.
                                  (Caius) **$50 [≈£28]**

Alexander, Franz & Ross, Helen (editors)
- Dynamic Psychiatry. Chicago: UP, [1952]. 1st edn. xii,578 pp. Name. Lib stamp rear endpaper. Orig cloth.   *(Caius)* **$50 [≈£28]**

Alexander, William
- An Experimental Enquiry concerning the Causes which have generally been said to produce Putrid Diseases. London: Becket & De Hondt, 1771. 8vo. [8],256 pp. 1 clean tear. Orig bds, uncut, rebacked, crnrs worn.
                             (Spelman) **£120 [≈$214]**

Ali, Salim
- The Birds of Sikkim. OUP: 1962. 1st edn. Tall 8vo. xxx,404 pp. 26 cold plates. Orig blue cloth.   *(Gough)* **£50 [≈$89]**

- The Birds of Travancore and Cochin. London: 1953. Roy 8vo. xx,436 pp. 16 cold & 6 plain plates, 32 text figs. Cloth, sm tear hd of spine, inner jnts cracked.
                   (Wheldon & Wesley) **£50 [≈$89]**

Ali, Salim & Ripley, S.D.
- Handbook of the Birds of India and Pakistan, together with those of Nepal, Sikkim, Bhutan and Ceylon. London: 1978-83-72-74. 2nd edn vols 1-4. 10 vols. Roy 8vo. Cold plates. Cloth. Dws.   *(Wheldon & Wesley)* **£200 [≈$356]**

Aiken, Henry
- The Beauties & Defects of the Figure of the Horse. London: 1881. Thin roy 8vo. 29 pp. Addtnl dec title, 18 plates. Endpapers sl browned. Orig cloth backed bds, wear to extrs.   *(Francis Edwards)* **£45 [≈$80]**

Allegro, J.M.
- The Sacred Mushroom & The Cross. London: 1970. 1st edn. Thick 8vo. Cold frontis, ills. Dw.   *(Deja Vu)* **£25 [≈$45]**

Allen, H.S.
- Photo-Electricity. The Liberation of Electrons by Light ... London: 1913. xi,221 pp. 34 figs. Endpapers foxed. Orig bndg, spine sl worn.   *(Whitehart)* **£18 [≈$32]**

Allen, W.D.
- Neutron Detection. New York: Philosophical Library, 1960. 1st edn. 12mo. 260 pp. Orig black cloth.   *(Schoen)* **$60 [≈£34]**

Alley, G.
- Observations on the Hydragyria; or that Vesicular Disease arising from the Exhibition of Mercury. London: 1810. xx,104 pp. 3 cold plates. Sl dust stained cvr.
                             (Whitehart) **£200 [≈$356]**

Allis, Oscar
- An Inquiry into the Difficulties encountered in the Reduction of Dislocations of the Hip. Phila: 1896. 1st edn. 171 pp. Orig bndg. Inscribed by the author. *(Fye)* **$200 [≈£112]**
- Scoliosis: A New Study of an Old Problem. Phila: 1938. 1st edn. 168 pp. 102 ills. Orig wraps.   *(Fye)* **$100 [≈£56]**

Allman, G.J.
- A Monograph of the Freshwater Polyzoa, including all the known Species both British and Foreign. London: Ray Society, 1856. Folio. viii,119 pp. 1 plain & 10 hand cold plates. Occas sl foxing. Half calf, crnrs worn.
                             (Egglishaw) **£80 [≈$142]**

Allsop, Robert Owen
- The Turkish Bath: its Design and Construction ... London: 1890. 8vo. vii,152 pp. Illust advt endpapers. Few marks. Orig cloth gilt, sl discold.   *(Weiner)* **£50 [≈ $89]**

Alpheraky, S.
- The Geese of Europe and Asia being the Description of most of the Old World Species. London: Rowland Ward, 1905. 198 pp. 24 cold plates. Orig cloth.
    (Trophy Room Books) **$1,000 [≈ £562]**
- The Geese of Europe and Asia; Description of most of the Old World Species. London: 1905. 4to. ix,198 pp. 25 cold plates. Orig cloth.   *(Wheldon & Wesley)* **£300 [≈ $534]**
- The Geese of Europe and Asia; Description of most of the Old World Species. London: 1905. 4to. ix,198 pp. 25 cold plates. Sl foxing. Orig cloth, sl stained.
    (Wheldon & Wesley) **£270 [≈ $481]**

Alston, Charles
- A Third Dissertation on Quick-Lime and Lime-Water. Edinburgh: 1757. 8vo. iv,46 pp. Disbound.   *(Weiner)* **£100 [≈ $178]**

Amateur Work ...
- Amateur Work, Illustrated. A Practical Magazine of Constructive and Decorative Art and Manual Labour. Vols I & II New Series. London: 1888-90. 2 vols. Num fldg plates, ills. Some fldg plates torn. Half roan.
    (Whitehart) **£50 [≈ $89]**

Amory, Robert
- A Treatise on Electrolysis and its Applications to Therapeutical and Surgical Treatment in Disease. New York: Wood, 1886. Wood Library edn. 8vo. 8vo. vii,307 pp. Orig bndg.   *(Goodrich)* **$65 [≈ £37]**

Amphlett, John & Rea, Carleton
- The Botany of Worcestershire ... Birmingham: Cornish Bros., 1909. 1st edn. 8vo. xxxiii,651, subscribers pp. Fldg map in pocket. Orig cloth gilt, unopened.
    (Hollett) **£65 [≈ $116]**

Andersen, Knud
- Catalogue of the Chiroptera in the Collection of the British Museum. Vol 1: Megachiroptera. London: 1912. 2nd edn. Thick 8vo. ci,854 pp. 79 ills. Prelims sl foxed. Orig cloth, partly unopened.
    (Francis Edwards) **£45 [≈ $80]**

Anderson, B.W.
- Gem Testing. New York: Van Nostrand

Reinhold, 1980. 9th edn. 8vo. 434 pp. 6 cold plates, text ills. Orig cloth. Dw.
    (Gemmary) **$50 [≈ £28]**

Anderson, J.
- Dura Den, a Monograph of the Yellow Sandstone and its remarkable Fossil Remains. Edinburgh: Constable, 1859. Roy 8vo. 96 pp. Cold vignette, cold map, 1 plain & 7 cold plates. Orig cloth, partly faded.
    (Egglishaw) **£58 [≈ $103]**
- Zoology of Egypt. Vol. 1. Reptilia and Batrachia. London: (1898) 1965. Reprint. 4to. 436 pp. Map, 52 plates. Cloth.
    (Wheldon & Wesley) **£65 [≈ $116]**

Anderson, Thomas
- Researches on Some of the Crystalline Constituents of Opium. Edinburgh: Neill, 1852. Offprint from Transactions of the Royal Society of Edinburgh XX: 3. 4to. [2],347-375 pp. Few sm marg tears & nicks. Disbound.   *(Caius)* **$115 [≈ £65]**

Anderson, Thomas M'Call
- Contributions to Clinical Medicine. Edited by J. Hinshelwood. Edinburgh: 1898. xi,416 pp. 28 ills. Orig cloth. "With the author's compliments" on half-title.
    (Whitehart) **£28 [≈ $5,029]**
- On the Parasitic Affections of the Skin. London: 1868. 2nd edn. xi,250 pp. Frontis, 1 plate, 33 ills. Occas foxing. Orig cloth, worn, marked & dust stained.
    (Whitehart) **£25 [≈ $45]**

Andes, Louis Edgar
- Oil Colours and Printers' Inks. London: Scott, Greenwood, 1918. 2nd English edn, enlgd. 8vo. xvi,220,[4] pp. 57 ills. Cloth.
    (Bookpress) **$65 [≈ £37]**

Andral, G.
- Medical Clinic: Diseases of the Encephalon, with Extracts from Ollivier's Work on Diseases of the Spinal Cord and its Membranes. Condensed and Translated, with Observations by D. Spillan. Phila: Haswell, 1843. 8vo. 303 pp. Foxed. Orig sheep bds, rebacked.   *(Goodrich)* **$175 [≈ £98]**

Andrews, F.W.
- The Flowering Plants of the Anglo-Egyptian Sudan. London: 1950-56. 3 vols. 8vo. Map, 435 text figs. Endpapers sl marked. Cloth.
    (Wheldon & Wesley) **£60 [≈ $107]**

Andrews, George Henry
- Modern Husbandry. London: Nathaniel

Cooke, 1853. 1st edn. Demy 8vo. x,404 pp. W'engvd plates & ills. Orig dec cloth gilt, reprd. *(Ash)* **£75 [≈ $134]**

Andrews, J.
- The Parterre: or, Beauties of Flora. London: 1842. Folio. [iv],24 pp. 11 (of 12) hand cold plates. Lacks plate 5. Sl staining. Orig dec cloth gilt, a.e.g., reprd.
(Wheldon & Wesley) **£875 [≈ $1,558]**

Andrews, William
- Famous Frosts and Frost Fairs. London: George Redway, 1887. One of 400 signed by the author. 12mo. 91 pp. Frontis, ills. Orig gilt dec linen bds, upper jnt weak.
(Schoen) **$60 [≈ £34]**

Andry, Nicholas
- An Account of the Breeding of Worms in Human Bodies ... London: H. Rhodes, 1701. 1st edn in English. 8vo. xl,[iv],120 pp, 121-176 ff, 177-266,[xxvi] pp.. 5 plates. Later sheep. *(Bookpress)* **$600 [≈ £337]**
- Orthopaedia. Phila: 1961. Facsimile of London 1743 edn. 2 vols. Orig imitation leather. Slipcase. *(Fye)* **$225 [≈ £126]**

Annals of Natural History
- Annals of Natural History; or Magazine of Zoology, Botany and Geology, conducted by Sir W. Jardine ... Volume I. London: 1838. 8vo. viii, 488 pp. 15 plates (4 hand cold). Lib labels. Possibly lacks a plate. Contemp half calf, sl worn. *(Egglishaw)* **£48 [≈ $85]**

Annandale, Thomas
- The Malformations, Diseases, and Injuries of the Fingers and Toes and their Surgical Treatment. Edinburgh: 1865. 1st edn. 292 pp. 12 engvd plates. Orig bndg.
(Fye) **$750 [≈ £421]**
- Observations and Cases in Surgery. Edinburgh: 1865. 1st edn. 80 pp. Orig wraps.
(Fye) **$200 [≈ £112]**

Ansted, David T.
- The Applications of Geology to the Arts and Manufactures ... Lectures ... Delivered before the Society of Arts ... London: Robert Hardwicke, 1865. 1st coll edn. Sm 8vo. iv, [3], 300, [4 advt] pp. 18 ills. Orig cloth gilt, discold. *(Fenning)* **£45 [≈ $80]**
- Elementary Course of Geology, Mineralogy, and Physical Geography. Reissued with Notes and Additions. London: 1869. xvi,606 pp. 250 text figs. Sm lib stamp title verso. Orig cloth, spine ends sl worn.
(Whitehart) **£25 [≈ $45]**

- In Search of Minerals. London: SPCK, 1880. Cr 8vo. vi,282,4 pp. Text figs. Orig dec cloth.
(Gemmary) **$125 [≈ £70]**

Ansted, David T., & others
- Geology, Mineralogy, and Crystallography. London: Houlston & Stoneman, 1855. Cr 8vo. xvi, 587 pp. 396 text figs. Qtr leather, worn. *(Gemmary)* **$100 [≈ £56]**

Anstie, Francis E.
- Neuralgia and the Diseases that Resemble It. New York: Appleton, 1883. 362,[4 advt] pp. Lib marks. Contemp half calf, worn.
(Caius) **$85 [≈ £48]**

Antram, C.
- Butterflies of India. Calcutta & Simla: 1924. Roy 8vo. xvi,226 pp. Plate, 413 ills. Orig cloth, sl warped, trifle loose.
(Wheldon & Wesley) **£70 [≈ $125]**

Aplin, O.V.
- The Birds of Oxfordshire. Oxford: Clarendon Press, 1889. 1st edn. 8vo. [viii], 217 pp. Hand cold plate. Orig cloth, paper label.
(Bow Windows) **£50 [≈ $89]**

Apperley, C.J.
- See Nimrod (C.J. Apperley)

Appert, Nicholas
- The Art of Preserving all Kinds of Animal and Vegetable Substances for Several Years. London: 1811. 1st edn in English. 8vo. xxiii, 164 pp. Fldg plate (spotted). Explanation of plate bound in at end. Occas spotting. Bds.
(Weiner) **£200 [≈ $356]**

Arber, Agnes
- The Gramineae, a Study of Cereal, Bamboo and Grass. Cambridge: 1934. 1st edn. 8vo. xvii, 480 pp. Cold frontis, 212 text figs. Cloth. Author's pres copy.
(Wheldon & Wesley) **£40 [≈ $71]**
- The Natural Philosophy of Plant Form. Cambridge: 1950. 8vo. xiv,247 pp. 47 ills. Endpapers foxed. Cloth.
(Wheldon & Wesley) **£35 [≈ $62]**

Arbuthnot, John
- An Essay concerning the Nature of Aliments, and the Choice of Them, according to the Different Constitutions of Human Bodies ... Third Edition, to which are added, Practical Rules of Diet ... London: 1735. 8vo. 436 pp. Contemp calf, sl rubbed.
(Robertshaw) **£95 [≈ $169]**
- Miscellaneous Works. With an Account of

the Author's Life. London: 1770. 2nd edn. 2
vols. xvi,246; 310 pp. Half mor, a.e.g., rather
worn.   *(Whitehart)* **£140 [≈ $249]**

Archey, G.
- The Moa, a Study of the Dinornithiformes.
Auckland: 1941. 4to. 145 pp, inc 15 plates &
9 fldg tables. Wraps (sl foxed). Author's pres
copy.   *(Wheldon & Wesley)* **£50 [≈ $89]**

Aretaeus
- The Extant Works of Aretaeus, the
Cappadocian. Edited and Translated by
Francis Adams. London: The Sydenham
Society, 1856. 8vo. 510 pp. Orig cloth.
            (Robertshaw) **£18 [≈ $32]**

Argyll, Duke of
- Geology and the Deluge. Glasgow: 1885. 8vo.
47 pp. Sm lib stamp title verso. Orig cloth,
soiled.   *(Weiner)* **£20 [≈ $36]**

Aristotle
- The Metaphysics ... Translated from the
Greek: with Copious Notes ... by Thomas
Taylor. London: for the author, 1801. 1st
edn. 4to. [iv],[lvi],[468] pp. Sl foxing.
Contemp calf backed bds, jnts tender.
            (Gach) **$1,250 [≈ £702]**

Aristotle's Last Legacy ...
- Aristotle's Last Legacy: Unfolding the
Mysteries of Nature in the Generation of Man
... London: for R.G. & sold by the
booksellers, 1712. 1st edn. 12mo. [iv],112 pp.
Frontis. Sm repr 1 leaf. Last leaf sl stained.
Contemp sheep.
            (David White) **£150 [≈ $267]**

Arjunba, Sakharam
- Principles and Practice of Medicine designed
for the Students of the Vernacular Class,
Grant Medical College, Bombay. Indu
Prakash Press: 1869. 8vo. Panelled sheep, gilt
dentelles. Author's inscrptn to the dedicatee.
            (Goodrich) **$250 [≈ £140]**

Arkell, W.J.
- The Jurassic System in Great Britain.
Oxford: 1933. Roy 8vo. xii,681 pp. 45 plates,
text figs. Cloth.
            (Wheldon & Wesley) **£50 [≈ $89]**
- A Monograph of the Ammonites of the
English Corallian Beds. London: Pal. Soc.,
1935-48. 14 parts in 1 vol. 4to. 420 pp. 84
plates. Buckram, damp stained.
            (Wheldon & Wesley) **£100 [≈ $178]**

Armsby, Henry P.
- Manual of Cattle-Feeding. A Treatise on the
Laws of Animal Nutrition and the Chemistry
of Feeding-Stuffs ... New York: John Wiley,
1880. 1st edn. 8vo. x,525 pp. Occas stamp.
Orig cloth.   *(Fenning)* **£24.50 [≈ $45]**

Armstrong, Harry
- Principles and Practice of Aviation Medicine.
Baltimore: 1939. 1st edn, 3rd printing. 496
pp. Photo ills. Orig bndg.   *(Fye)* **$75 [≈ £42]**
- Principles and Practice of Aviation Medicine.
London: 1939. xii,496 pp. Frontis, 86 text
figs. Orig bndg.   *(Whitehart)* **£25 [≈ $45]**

Armstrong, John
- Practical Illustrations of the Scarlet Fever,
Measles and Pulmonary Consumptions. With
Observations on the Efficacy of Sulphureous
Waters in Chronic Complaints. London:
1818. 2nd edn. xii,468 pp. Page edges sl
dusty. Contemp cloth, rebacked.
            (Whitehart) **£80 [≈ $142]**
- Practical Illustrations of the Scarlet fever,
Measles, and Pulmonary Consumption: with
Observations on the Efficacy of Sulphurous
Waters in Chronic Complaints. Second
Edition. London: 1818. 8vo. 468 pp. Mod
bds.   *(Robertshaw)* **£45 [≈ $80]**

Armstrong, William George, 1st Lord
- Electric Movement in Air and Water with
Theoretical Inferences. London: 1897. Folio.
vii, 55 pp. 41 ills on 32 plates. Orig elab gilt
dec cloth, sl marked, backstrip relaid. Inscrbd
by the author.   *(Weiner)* **£200 [≈ $356]**

Arnold, E.C.
- British Waders ... Cambridge: UP, 1924. 1st
edn. 4to. vii,102 pp. 52 cold plates. Orig cloth
gilt, lower crnrs of bds bumped, sm repr
upper hinge.   *(Hollett)* **£60 [≈ $107]**
- British Waders. Illustrated in Water-Colour
with Descriptive Notes. Cambridge: 1924.
4to. vii,102 pp. 51 cold plates. Cloth.
            (Wheldon & Wesley) **£40 [≈ $71]**

Arnold, F.H.
- Flora of Sussex ... New Edition, with
Numerous Additions. London: 1907. Sm 8vo.
xxi, 154 pp. Cold frontis, map, ills. Sl foxing.
Orig cloth.   *(Bow Windows)* **£24 [≈ $43]**

Arnold, G.
- The Sphecidae of Madagascar. Bulawayo:
1944. One of 200. Roy 8vo. 193 pp. 140 text
figs. Cloth. *(Wheldon & Wesley)* **£25 [≈ $45]**

Arnold, Howard
- Memoir of Jonathan Mason Warren, M.D. Boston: 1886. 1st edn. 329 pp. Orig bndg.
(Fye) **$50 [≈ £28]**

Arnott, Neil
- Elements of Physics, or Natural Philosophy, General and Medical, explained independently of Technical Mathematics ... Fourth Edition. London: 1829. 2 vols. 8vo. Num text diags. Some marks, sm tears. Contemp half calf, jnts cracked, spine & crnrs worn & chipped *(Bow Windows)* **£48 [≈ $85]**

Art ...
- The Art of Cookery, made Plain and Easy ... see Glasse, Hannah.
- The Art of Invigorating and Prolonging Life ... see Kitchiner, William.
- The Art of Making Fireworks, improved to the Modern Practice ... Derby: Richardson; London: Simpkin Marshall; Portsea: S. Horsey, [ca 1820?]. 8vo. 24 pp. Hand cold fldg frontis (imprint cropped). Disbound. Anon. 2 authorities attribute to Christopher Grotz. *(Burmester)* **£150 [≈ $267]**
- The Art of Preserving the Feet; or Practical Instructions for the Prevention and Cure of Corns, Bunions, Chilblains ... By an Experienced Chiropodist. London: Colburn, 1818. 1st edn. xvi,239 pp. Contemp qtr calf, mrbld bds. *(C.R. Johnson)* **£285 [≈ $507]**

The Artificial Clock-Maker ...
- See Derham, William

Artis, Edmund Tyrell
- Ante Diluvian Phytology, illustrated by a Collection of the Fossil Remains of Plants peculiar to the Coal Formations. London: the author ..., 1825. 1st edn. 4to. xv,[24] pp. 24 engvs. Qtr linen over orig bds, sl worn & chipped, new endpapers.
(Blackwell's) **£150 [≈ $267]**
- Antediluvian Phytology, illustrated by a Collection of the Fossil Remains of Plants peculiar to the Coal Formations of Great Britain. London: 1838. 4to. xiv,24 pp. 25 plates. Cloth, rebacked, few minor stains.
(Wheldon & Wesley) **£120 [≈ $214]**

Artz, Curtis & Reiss, Eric
- The Treatment of Burns. Phila: 1957. 1st edn. 250 pp. 199 ills. Orig bndg.
(Fye) **$50 [≈ £28]**

Aschoff, Ludwig
- Lectures on Pathology delivered in the United States. New York: Hoeber, 1959. 8vo.

365 pp. Orig bndg, sl spotted.
(Goodrich) **$45 [≈ £25]**

Ashe, Thomas
- Memoirs of Mammoth, and various other extraordinary and stupendous Bones ... found in the vicinity of the Ohio, Wabash ... Rivers ... visit the Liverpool Museum. Liverpool: G.F. Harris, 1806. 1st edn. 8vo. 12, 60 pp. Disbound, untrimmed.
(Blackwell's) **£150 [≈ $267]**

Ashenhurst, Thomas R.
- Lectures on Practical Weaving: the Power Loom and Cloth Dissecting. Huddersfield & Bradford: 1895. 1st edn. 8vo. 611,[5],[10 advt] pp. Port, 3 cold plates, 326 ills. Orig cloth. *(Fenning)* **£48.50 [≈ $87]**

Astley, H.D.
- My Birds in Freedom and Captivity. London: 1900. One of 100 numbered Large Paper. Sm 4to. xvi,254 pp. Cold frontis, 21 gravure plates, 17 ills. Orig buckram, trifle used.
(Wheldon & Wesley) **£40 [≈ $71]**

Aston, F.W.
- Isotopes. London: Edward Arnold, 1922. 1st edn. 8vo. viii,152 pp. 4 plates. Some foxing. Orig bndg, hd of spine worn.
(Key Books) **$150 [≈ £84]**

Astruc, John
- A General and Compleat Treatise on all the Diseases incident to Children ... London: John Nourse, 1746. 1st English edn. 8vo. [x], 229, [1] pp. Edges on 2 ff reprd. Contemp calf, rebacked. *(Bookpress)* **$750 [≈ £421]**
- A Treatise of the Venereal Disease ... Translated from the Latin by William Barrow. London: for W. Innys, 1737. 1st English edn. 2 vols. 8vo. Contemp calf, backstrips relaid. *(Appelfeld)* **$275 [≈ £154]**

Atchley, S.C.
- Wild Flowers of Attica. Edited by W.B. Turill. London: 1938. 4to. xix,59 pp. 22 cold plates. Orig cloth. *(Henly)* **£68 [≈ $121]**

Atkinson, John
- A Compendium of the Ornithology of Great Britain. With a reference to the Anatomy and Physiology of Birds. London: 1820. xii,232 pp. Title soiled. Amateur half mor.
(Francis Edwards) **£35 [≈ $62]**

Atkinson, John C.
- British Birds' Eggs and Nests, Popularly Described. New Edition. London: Routledge,

1870. Lge 12mo. viii,182,[1 advt] pp. Fldg table in pocket, 12 cold plates. Orig cloth gilt, a.e.g., spine faded, inner hinges cracked.
(Fenning) **£24.50 [≈ $45]**

- British Birds' Eggs and Nests Popularly Described. London: Routledge, 1882. Sm 8vo. 182 pp. Frontis, 10 cold plates, fldg table. Red prize leather gilt, spine sl faded.
(Carol Howard) **£30 [≈ $53]**

- British Birds' Eggs and Nests, popularly described. Illustrated by W.S. Coleman. London: Routledge, [1880s]. 8vo. viii,182 pp, advt leaf. Fldg chart (torn without loss) in pocket, 12 chromolitho plates. Orig pict cloth.
(Claude Cox) **£20 [≈ $36]**

Audubon, John James
- Letters of John James Audubon 1826-1840. Edited by Howard Corning. Boston: Club of Odd Volumes, 1930. One of 225. 8vo. Orig cloth & bds. Slipcase.
(Dermont) **$250 [≈ £140]**

Audubon, John James & Bachman, J.
- The Quadrupeds of North America. New York: 1852-54. 1st 8vo edn. Vols 1 & 2 2nd issues. 3 vols. Roy 8vo. 155 hand cold litho plates. Occas sl spotting of text. Sm blind stamps on titles. Orig dark green mor, a.e.g., backstrips relaid.
(Wheldon & Wesley) **£2,500 [≈ $4,450]**

Austen, E.E.
- A Monograph of the Tsetse-Flies (Genus Glossina, Westwood) based on the Collection in the British Museum. London: 1903. Roy 8vo. ix, 319 pp. Fldg map, 7 cold plates, 2 litho plates. Cloth. *(Egglishaw)* **£25 [≈ $45]**

Aveling, James Hobson
- English Midwives, their History and Prospects. Reprint of the 1872 Edition with an Introduction ... by John L. Thornton. London: 1967. 186 pp. Orig bndg.
(Fye) **$60 [≈ £34]**

Axe, Wortley (editor)
- The Horse: Its Treatment in Health and Disease with a Complete Guide to Breaking, Training and Management. London: Gresham Pub. Co., 1906. 9 vols, 20 sections. 4to. Cold plates, ills. Orig dec green cloth, fine. *(Bookline)* **£70 [≈ $125]**

Ayre, Joseph
- Pathological Researches into the Nature and Treatment of Dropsy of the Brain, Chest, Abdomen, Ovarium, and Skin ... Second Edition ... London: Longman ..., 1829. 8vo. xii,287 pp. Sl foxing. Half roan.

(Goodrich) **$195 [≈ £110]**

Ayres, William & Henfrey, Arthur
- The Garden Companion, and Florist's Guide. January to October 1852. London: William S. Orr, 1852. 4to. 154 pp. 20 hand cold plates, many heightened with gum arabic. Contemp half calf gilt, sl rubbed, inner hinges cracked. *(Hollett)* **£250 [≈ $445]**

Ayres, William & Moore, Thomas
- The Florist's Guide, and Gardener's and Naturalist's Calendar. London: William S. Orr, 1850. 4to. 192,[ii] pp. 12 hand cold plates, mostly heightened with gum arabic. Contemp half calf gilt, sl worn.
(Hollett) **£180 [≈ $320]**

B., H.B.H.
- Journal during an Aerial Voyage ... see Beaufoy, H.B.H.

Baas, Joh. Hermann
- Outlines of the History of Medicine and the Medical Profession. Translated by H.E. Henderson, M.D. New York: Vail, 1889. 1st Amer edn. 8vo. 1173 pp. Orig bndg, shelf wear, jnts starting. *(Goodrich)* **$150 [≈ £84]**

Babbage, Charles
- The Ninth Bridgewater Treatise, A Fragment. London: Murray, 1837. 1st edn. 8vo. xxii, 23-240 pp. Ills. Blue stamp on title. Cloth. *(Key Books)* **$425 [≈ £239]**
- On the Economy of Machinery and Manufacture. London: Charles Knight, 1832. 1st edn. 8vo. xvi,320,[2 advt] pp. Engvd title. Orig cloth, sl rubbed, upper inner hinge strengthened. *(Gaskell)* **£850 [≈ $1,513]**
- On the Economy of Machinery and Manufactures. London: Charles Knight, 1833. 3rd edn, enlgd. 12mo. xxiv,392,[4 advt] pp. Title vignette. Backstrip relaid.
(Key Books) **$350 [≈ £197]**
- Passages from the Life of a Philosopher. London: Longman, 1864. 1st edn. 8vo. xii,496 pp. Frontis, w'engvd text ills. Orig cloth, recased, new endpapers.
(Gaskell) **£950 [≈ $1,691]**

Babington, C.C.
- Flora of Cambridgeshire ... London: 1860. lvi, 327 pp. Fldg map. Orig cloth, dull.
(Whitehart) **£18 [≈ $32]**
- Memorials, Journal and Botanical Correspondence. Cambridge: 1897. 8vo. xciv, 476 pp. Pedigree, 2 ports. Orig cloth, trifle used. *(Wheldon & Wesley)* **£28 [≈ $50]**

Babington, Matthew
- A Letter in reply to Observations on the Subject of the Midland Counties' Railway, by Mr. N.W. Cundy, Civil Engineer. Leicester: (1835). 8vo. 14 pp. New bds.
(Weiner) **£50 [≈ $89]**

Bacon, Sir Francis
- History Natural and Experimental, of Life and Death. Or of the Prolongation of Life ... London: John Haviland for William Lee, and Humphry Moseley, 1638. 24mo. Imprimatur leaf at beginning and at end. Some foxing & browning. New calf, old bds laid down.
(Goodrich) **$595 [≈ £334]**
- Of the Advancement and Proficience of Learning ... Oxford: Leon. Lichfield ..., 1640. 1st complete edn in English. Translated by G. Watts. Folio. Port frontis (altered by a Victorian hand), addtnl engvd title. Lacks colophon leaf. Contemp sheep. STC 1167.
(Vanbrugh) **£525 [≈ $935]**
- Of the Advancement and Proficience of Learning ... Interpreted by Gilbert Wats. London: for Thomas Williams, 1674. 2nd Watts edn. Folio. Port frontis. Contemp calf, rebacked. Wing B.312.
(Vanbrugh) **£375 [≈ $668]**
- Of the Advancement and Proficiencie of Learning: or the Partition of Sciences. Nine Books. London: for Thomas Williams, 1674. Folio. Frontis. Contemp calf, crnrs worn, front jnt cracked. Buckram slipcase. Wing B.312.
(Waterfield's) **£165 [≈ $294]**
- Of the Advancement and Proficiencie of Learning: or the Partitions of Sciences ... London: T. Williams, 1674. Sm folio. [32],38, [14], 322,[20] pp. Frontis port. Contemp speckled calf, rebacked. Cloth box. Wing B.312.
(O'Neal) **$450 [≈ £253]**
- Sylva Sylvarum: or, A Naturall History ... London: J.F. for William Lee, 1651. Folio. Port frontis, addtnl engvd title. Occas sl damp stain, edges of 1st 2 ff brittle. Contemp calf, Victorian reback. Wing B.327.
(Vanbrugh) **£425 [≈ $757]**
- The Two Books ... Of the Proficience and Advancement of Learning, Divine and Humane. Oxford: 1633. 3rd edn. 4to. [ii],335 pp. 19th c calf backed bds, rebacked. STC 1166.
(Vanbrugh) **£345 [≈ $614]**

Badger, John
- A Collection of Remarkable Cures of the King's Evil. Perfected by the Royal Touch collected from the Writings of many eminent Physicians and Surgeons ... London: Cooper, 1748. 8vo. Half-title, 64 pp. Some foxing, early underlining. New bds.

(Goodrich) **$135 [≈ £76]**

Badham, Charles David
- A Treatise on the Esculent Funguses of England. London: Reeve Bros., 1847. 1st edn. Cr 4to. x,138 pp. Hand cold frontis, 20 litho plates (17 hand cold). Orig dec cloth gilt, spine sl worn & sunned, sl shaken.
(Ash) **£450 [≈ $801]**
- A Treatise on the Esculent Funguses of England. Second Edition. London: Lovell Reeve, 1863. xvi,152,[16 advt] pp. 12 hand cold plates. Orig pict black cloth gilt, fine.
(Gough) **£195 [≈ $347]**

The Badianus Manuscript ...
- See de la Cruz, Martin

Baerwald, M. & Mahoney, T.
- The Story of Jewelry. New York: Abelard Schuman, 1960. 8vo. 222 pp. 98 text figs. Orig cloth.
(Gemmary) **$40 [≈ £22]**

Baetjer, Frederick & Waters, Charles
- Injuries & Diseases of the Bones and Joints: their Differential Diagnosis by Means of the Roentgen Rays. New York: 1921. 1st edn. 349 pp. Num plates. Orig bndg.
(Fye) **$125 [≈ £70]**

Baglivi, Girogi
- The Practice of Physick, Reduc'd to the ancient Way of Observations ... The Second Edition. London: Midwinter ..., 1723. 8vo. xvi, 431 pp. Occas browning. New qtr calf.
(Goodrich) **$250 [≈ £140]**

Bagnall, J.E.
- The Flora of Warwickshire ... London: 1891. One of 500 signed by the author. 8vo. xxxiv, 579 pp. Map in pocket. Cloth, trifle used.
(Wheldon & Wesley) **£50 [≈ $89]**

Bagster, S.
- The Management of Bees. London: 1834. 8vo. xx, 244 pp. Cold frontis, text figs. Cloth, rather used. *(Wheldon & Wesley)* **£45 [≈ $80]**

Bailey, E.B., & others
- Tertiary and Post-Tertiary Geology of Mull, Loch Aline, Oban. London: 1924. 8vo. x, 445 pp. 6 plates, 66 text figs. Cloth gilt.
(Henly) **£60 [≈ $107]**

Bailey, H. & Bishop, W.J.
- Notable Names in Medicine and Surgery. Springfield: 1959. 3rd edn. 216 pp. Orig bndg.
(Fye) **$75 [≈ £42]**

Bailey, Hamilton
- Emergency Surgery. Bristol: 1930-31. 1st edn. 2 vols. 380; 415 pp. 754 ills. Orig bndgs.
(Fye) **$175 [≃ £98]**
- Surgery of Modern Warfare. Baltimore: 1942. 2nd edn. 2 vols. 1000 pp. Num ills. Orig bndg., *(Fye)* **$75 [≃ £42]**

Bailey, L.H.
- The Standard Cyclopedia of Horticulture ... New York: 1917. 2nd edn, enlgd. 6 vols. 4to. Cold plates, num ills. Orig bndg, spines sl faded, v sl rubbed. *(Hortulus)* **$320 [≃ £180]**

Bailey, Percival
- Intracranial Tumors. Springfield: C.C. Thomas, 1933. 1st edn. xxii,[2],475,[3] pp. Frontis, text ills. Sm ownership marks. Orig blue cloth. *(Caius)* **$250 [≃ £140]**
- Intracranial Tumors. Springfield: 1948. 2nd edn. xxiv,478 pp. Frontis, 16 plates, text ills. Orig cloth, recased. *(Whitehart)* **£40 [≃ $71]**

Baillie, John
- A Letter to Dr. ------- in Answer to a Tract in the Bibliotheque Ancienne & Moderne, relating to some Passages in Dr. Freind's History of Physick ... London: J. Roberts, 1728. 8vo. [iv],80 pp. Half-title & title browned. Rec bds. *(Goodrich)* **$295 [≃ £160]**

Baillie, Matthew
- The Works of Matthew Baillie, M.D. To which is prefixed an Account of His Life, Collected from Authentic Sources. By J. Wardrop. London: 1825. 2 vols. lxxii,238; lxxii, 408 pp. Three qtr calf, backstrips relaid. *(Whitehart)* **£190 [≃ $338]**

Bain, Alexander
- The Senses and the Intellect. London: John W. Parker & Son, 1855. 1st edn. 8vo. [xxxii], 614 pp, advt leaf. Sl foxing. Orig cloth.
(Gach) **$285 [≃ £160]**

Baird, W.
- The Natural History of the British Entomostraca. London: Ray Society, 1850. 8vo. viii, 364 pp. 36 plates (17 cold). Occas sl foxing. Cloth, rebacked.
(Wheldon & Wesley) **£35 [≃ $62]**

Baker, E.C. Stuart
- Birds: Fauna of British India, including Ceylon and Burma. Second Edition. London: Taylor & Francis, 1922-24. 2 vols. 8vo. 17 cold plates, 179 text figs. Orig cloth gilt.
(Blackwell's) **£310 [≃ $552]**
- The Fauna of British India, Including Ceylon

and Burma - Birds. London: Taylor & Francis, 1922-30. 8 vols. Lge 8vo. Fldg map, 35 cold & 3 plain plates. Orig cloth gilt, extrs sl rubbed, crnrs bumped, few hinges sl tender. *(Hollett)* **£275 [≃ $490]**
- The Game-Birds of India, Burma and Ceylon. Vol II. Snipe, Bustards and Sand-Grouse. London: 1921. Roy 8vo. xvi,328 pp. 2 maps, 19 cold & 6 plain plates. Marg foxing. Orig half mor, trifle faded.
(Wheldon & Wesley) **£70 [≃ $125]**
- The Game-Birds of India, Burma and Ceylon. Vol III. Pheasants and Bustard-Quail. London: 1930. Roy 8vo. x,341 pp. 20 plates (11 cold). Orig half cloth.
(Wheldon & Wesley) **£100 [≃ $178]**
- The Indian Ducks and their Allies. Bombay: Bombay Natural History Soc., 1908. One of 1200. xi,292 pp. 30 chromolitho plates. Orig half mor, t.e.g., rear cvr sl stained.
(Egglishaw) **£300 [≃ $534]**

Baker, Henry
- The Microscope Made Easy ... London: Dodsley, 1745. 4th edn. 8vo. xvi,311,[13] pp. Fldg table, 15 plates (plate 13 defective). Contemp calf, hd of spine worn, jnts cracking. *(Egglishaw)* **£130 [≃ $231]**

Baker, Humfrey
- The Well-Spring of Sciences: which teacheth the perfect worke and practise of Arithmetick ... London: Thomas Purfoot, 1617. Sm 8vo. Title sl rubbed & soiled. Occas sl water stains. Contemp vellum, some soiling, lacks ties. STC 1217. *(Ximenes)* **$1,250 [≃ £702]**

Baker, J.G.
- Handbook of the Amaryllideae. London: 1888. 8vo. xii,216 pp. Cloth.
(Wheldon & Wesley) **£40 [≃ $71]**
- Handbook of the Bromeliaceae. London: 1889. 8vo. xi,243 pp. Orig cloth.
(Wheldon & Wesley) **£45 [≃ $80]**
- Handbook of the Fern-Allies: a Synopsis of the Genera and Species of the Natural Orders Equisetaceae, Lycopodiaceae, Selaginellaceae, Rhizocarpeae. London: 1887. 8vo. 159 pp. Cloth. *(Wheldon & Wesley)* **£35 [≃ $62]**
- Handbook of the Irideae. London: 1892. 8vo. xii,247 pp. Foxed. Orig cloth.
(Wheldon & Wesley) **£40 [≃ $71]**

Baker, R.T. & Smith, H.G.
- A Research on the Eucalypts, especially in regard to their Essential Oils. Sydney: 1920. 2nd edn. 4to. xv,470 pp. 2 maps, 50 cold & 70 plain plates. Cloth, rather used.
(Wheldon & Wesley) **£70 [≃ $125]**

Bakewell, Robert
- An Introduction to Geology ... London: 1815. 2nd edn. 8vo. xxviii,492 pp. Geological map, 4 sections, 2 plates (4 hand cold, 3 fldg). Contemp calf, rebacked.
(Henly) **£235 [≈ $418]**
- An Introduction to Geology ... The Fourth Edition, greatly enlarged. London: 1833. 8vo. xxxvi, 589,[1] pp. Errata slip. Frontis, 8 plates (2 hand cold). Half calf, jnts just beginning to crack.
(Bow Windows) **£135 [≈ $240]**

Baldwin, William
- Reliquiae Baldwinianae: Selections from the Correspondence of the late William Baldwin, compiled by W. Darlington. Phila: 1843. Post 8vo. 346,[1] pp. Port. Foxed. Orig cloth.
(Wheldon & Wesley) **£45 [≈ $80]**

Balfour, Francis
- A Collection of Treatises on the Effects of Sol-Lunar Influence on Fevers; with an Improved Method of Curing Them. Third Edition. Cupar: 1815. 8vo. [2],12,xxxii, [4], 383, [2], 354-359 [bis] pp. 2 fldg plates. Contemp tree calf gilt. Author's pres inscrptn.
(Spelman) **£280 [≈ $498]**

Balfour, J.H.
- The Plants of the Bible. New Edition. London: 1885. 8vo. 249 pp. Num ills. Red calf gilt.
(Wheldon & Wesley) **£35 [≈ $62]**

Balfour-Browne, F.
- British Water Beetles. London: Ray Society, 1940-58. 3 vols. 8vo. 67 maps, 5 plates, 266 text figs. Orig cloth.
(Wheldon & Wesley) **£90 [≈ $160]**

Ball, James Moores
- The Sack-'Em-Up Men. An Account of the Rise and Fall of the Modern Resurrectionists. London: 1928. xxxi,216 pp. Frontis, 60 plates, 18 text figs. Dw.
(Whitehart) **£40 [≈ $71]**

Ball, Sir Robert Stawell
- An Atlas of Astronomy. A Series of Seventy-Two Plates with Introduction and Index. London: George Phillip & Son, 1892. 8vo. Orig cloth gilt, sl shaken.
(Waterfield's) **£60 [≈ $107]**
- The Story of the Heavens. London: Cassell, (1905). 8vo. 24 cold plates, num ills. Orig dec blue cloth, t.e.g.   *(Appelfeld)* **$75 [≈£42]**
- A Treatise on Spherical Astronomy. Cambridge: UP, 1908. 1st edn. 8vo. xii,506 pp. Orig cloth.   *(Gaskell)* **£25 [≈ $45]**

Ball, S.H.
- A Roman Book on Precious Stones. Los Angeles: Gemological Institute of America, 1950. 8vo. xii,338 pp. Orig dec cloth, shaken.
(Gemmary) **$50 [≈ £28]**

Ball, W.W. Rouse
- An Essay on Newton's 'Principia'. London: 1893. 8vo. x,175 pp. Orig cloth.
(Weiner) **£75 [≈ $134]**

Ballance, Charles
- Some Points in the Surgery of the Brain and its Membranes. London: Macmillan, 1908. 1st edn. 8vo. xvi,451 pp. Lib marks inc perf stamp in title. Orig bndg, spine & foredges crudely taped.   *(Goodrich)* **$125 [≈ £70]**

Bampfield, R.W.
- An Essay on Curvatures and Diseases of the Spine, including all the Forms of Spinal Curvature. London: 1824. 1st edn. Lacks frontis. Orig cloth backed bds.
(Fye) **$350 [≈ £197]**

Bancroft, Frederic & Humphreys, George (editors)
- Surgical Treatment of the Soft Tissues. Phila: 1946. 1st edn. 520 pp. 244 ills. Orig bndg.
(Fye) **$100 [≈ £56]**

Bancroft, P.
- Gem & Crystal Treasures. Fallbrook: Western Enterprises, 1984. One of 300 sgnd. 4to. 488 pp. Num ills. Orig calf.
(Gemmary) **$275 [≈ £154]**

Bankoff, George
- The Story of Plastic Surgery. London: 1952. 1st edn. 224 pp. Orig bndg.
(Fye) **$100 [≈ £56]**

Banks, John, Lecturer in Experimental Philosophy
- A Treatise on Mills, in Four Parts ... Kendal: W. Richardson & W. Pennington, 1795. 1st edn. 8vo. [iii]-xxiv, 172,[iv] pp. Lacks half-title. 3 fldg plates. Sm stain ft of 1 leaf. Extreme margs dusty. Rec qtr calf, rough trimmed.   *(Blackwell's)* **£150 [≈ $267]**

Banks, Sam & Laufman, Harold
- An Atlas of Surgical Exposures of the Extremities. Phila: 1953. 1st edn. 4to. 391 pp. 552 ills. Orig bndg.   *(Fye)* **$50 [≈ £28]**

Bannerman, David Armitage
- The Birds of the British Isles. London: Oliver & Boyd, 1953. 1st edn. 12 vols. Sm 4to. Num

cold plates. Occas sl foxing. Dws (sl chipped).
(Carol Howard) **£330 [≃ $587]**
- The Birds of the British Isles. Edinburgh:
Oliver & Boyd, 1953-63. 12 vols. 4to. 386
cold & 2 plain plates. Orig buckram gilt. Dws.
(Blackwell's) **£500 [≃ $890]**
- Birds of the British Isles. Illustrated by G.E.
Lodge. London: 1953-63. 12 vols. Imperial
8vo. 386 cold & 2 plain plates. Orig cloth.
(Henly) **£285 [≃ $507]**
- The Birds of Tropical West Africa, with
special reference to those of Gambia, Sierra
Leone, the Gold Coast and Nigeria. London:
1930-51. 8 vols. Imperial 8vo. 7 maps, 83 cold
& 3 plain plates, 695 text figs. Orig cloth.
(Wheldon & Wesley) **£600 [≃ $1,068]**
- The Birds of West and Equatorial Africa.
London: 1953. 2 vols. 8vo. 1526 pp. 30 cold
& 24 plain plates, 433 text figs. Cloth, sm
stain back cvrs vol 2.
(Wheldon & Wesley) **£80 [≃ $142]**

Bannerman, David Armitage & W.M.
- Birds of Cyprus. London: 1958. Imperial
8vo. xxxix,384 pp. Fldg map, 17 cold & 14
plain plates, num text ills. Orig cloth. Dws.
Signed by the authors. *(Henly)* **£175 [≃ $312]**
- Birds of Cyprus. London: 1958. Imperial
8vo. lxix,384 pp. Map, 16 cold & 15 half-tone
plates, 2 line-drawings. Good ex-lib. Orig
cloth.   *(Wheldon & Wesley)* **£90 [≃ $160]**
- Birds of the Atlantic Islands. London:
1963-68. 4 vols. Roy 8vo. 11 maps, 47 cold &
54 plain plates, num text figs. Cloth. Dws.
(Wheldon & Wesley) **£475 [≃ $846]**
- The Birds of the Balearics. London: 1983. Cr
4to. xiii,230 pp. 12 cold plates, text ills. Orig
cloth. Dw.   *(Henly)* **£35 [≃ $62]**

Banyer, Henry
- Pharmacopoeia Pauperum: or, the Hospital
Dispensatory containing the chief Medicines
now used in the Hospitals of London ...
Second Edition much enlarged. London:
1721. 12mo. 128 pp. Lib stamp on title. Mod
calf.   *(Robertshaw)* **£65 [≃ $116]**

Barbette, Paul
- The Chirurgical and Anatomical Works ...
Together with a Treatise of the Plague ...
London: Carby for Pitt, 1672. 1st English
edn. [15], "342" [ie 346], 52, [16] pp. Addtnl
engvd title, ills. Sl browning. Upper margs
cropped. Contemp calf. Wing B.699.
(Hemlock) **$2,000 [≃ £1,124]**

Barker, Fordyce
- On Sea-Sickness. New York: Appleton, 1870.
8vo. 36 pp. Orig limp bds, a.e.g., stained.

(Goodrich) **$65 [≃ £37]**

Barlow, John
- On Man's Power over Himself to Prevent or
Control Insanity. London: W. Pickering,
1849. 2nd edn, enlgd. [2],vi, 123,[1] pp. Orig
green cloth, paper labels, some wear &
rubbing. Anon.   *(Caius)* **$200 [≃ £112]**

Barlow, P., & others
- A Treatise on the Strength of Materials.
London: 1867. xii,396 pp. 19 plates, num text
figs. Occas sl foxing on plates. Orig cloth,
new endpapers.   *(Whitehart)* **£50 [≃ $89]**

Barnard, J.E.
- Practical   Photo-Micrography.   London:
Edward Arnold, 1911. 1st edn. 8vo. xii,322
pp. 10 plates, 79 figs. Orig cloth, sl rubbed &
stained.   *(David White)* **£25 [≃ $45]**

Barnard, J.G.
- The   Phenomena   of   the   Gyroscope,
Analytically Examined. New York: Van
Nostrand, 1858. 1st edn. 8vo. [vi],537-560,
529-536, 299-304 pp. Contemp mor, a.e.g., sl
rubbed.   *(Bookpress)* **$425 [≃ £239]**

Barnhill, John & Mellinger, William
- Surgical Anatomy of the Head and Neck.
Baltimore: 1940. 2nd edn. 773 pp. Num ills.
Orig bndg.   *(Fye)* **$50 [≃ £28]**

Baronio, Giuseppe
- On Grafting in Animals (Degli Innesti
Animali). Boston: Bird & Bull Press, 1985.
Ltd edn. 87 pp. Orig qtr leather.
(Fye) **$250 [≃ £140]**

Barrera, M.
- Gems and Jewels. Their History, Geography,
Chemistry, and Ana. London: Bentley, 1860.
8vo. xxxii,382 pp. Orig dec cloth, spine
faded.   *(Gemmary)* **$150 [≃ £84]**

Barrett, C.G.
- The Lepidoptera of the British Islands.
London: 1892-1907. Large Paper. 11 vols.
Roy 8vo. 504 hand cold plates of num figs.
Lib stamps on titles & back of plates. Half
mor, not quite uniform, 2 vols reprd.
(Wheldon & Wesley) **£1,000 [≃ $1,780]**

Barrett, Florence E.
- Conception Control and its Effects on the
Individual and the Nation. London: 1922.
8vo. 48 pp. Orig cloth. Dw.
(Weiner) **£25 [≃ $45]**

Barrett, Sir William & Besterman, Theodore
- The Divining Rod. London: 1926. Lge 8vo. xxiii, 336,[8 advt] pp. 74 ills. Orig bndg, some rubbing & spotting. *(Hortulus)* **$60 [≈£34]**

Barron, Archibald F.
- Vines and Vine Culture. Fourth Edition, Revised and Enlarged. London: 1900. 8vo. xvi, 202, [8 advt] pp. 88 ills. Lib stamp on title verso. Cuttings on endpaper. Orig cloth gilt. *(Fenning)* **£32.50 [≈$59]**

Barry, D.
- Experimental Researches on the Influence Exercised by Atmospheric Pressure upon the Progression of the Blood in the Veins ... London: 1826. xvi,176 pp. Fldg frontis. Lib marks. Some foxing on plate. Contemp bds, rebacked, crnrs sl torn.
(Whitehart) **£200 [≈$356]**

Barry, Edward
- A Treatise on the Three Different Digestions and Discharges of the Human Body. And the Diseases of their Principal Organs. London: A. Millar, 1759. 1st edn. 8vo. xvi, 434 pp. 1 text ill. *(Spelman)* **£140 [≈$249]**

Barsky, Arthur
- Plastic Surgery. Phila: 1938. 1st edn. 355 pp. 432 ills. Ink notes on endpapers. Front endpaper torn. Orig bndg, spotted.
(Fye) **$100 [≈£56]**

Bartholomew, J.G., & others
- Atlas of Zoogeography, illustrating the Distribution of over Seven Hundred Families, Genera and Species of Existing Animals. Edinburgh: 1911. Folio. x,67,xi pp. 36 dble plates. New cloth.
(Wheldon & Wesley) **£100 [≈$178]**

Bartlett, John S.
- Maize or Indian Corn, its Advantages as a Cheap and Nutritious Article of Food, with Directions for its Use. London: 1846. 12mo. 24 pp. Stitched into later crude card wraps.
(Weiner) **£100 [≈$178]**

Barton, Benjamin Smith
- Collections for an Essay towards a Materia Medica of the United States ... Phila: for Edward Earle ..., 1810. 3rd edn. 4to. xvi,67, xv,53, [1],[2] pp. Half-title to Part 2. Orig calf backed bds. *(Hemlock)* **£350 [≈$197]**

Barton, Clara
- The Red Cross in Peace and War.

Washington: 1899. 1st edn. 703 pp. Num photo ills. Orig bndg. *(Fye)* **$100 [≈£56]**

Barwell, Richard
- A Treatise on Diseases of the Joints. New York: 1881. 2nd edn. 463 pp. 91 w'cuts. Orig bndg. *(Fye)* **$50 [≈£28]**

Bary, A.D.
- Comparative Anatomy of the Vegetative Organs of the Phanerogams and Ferns. Oxford: 1884. xvi,659 pp. 241 text figs. Binder's cloth. *(Whitehart)* **£35 [≈$62]**

Basset, A.B.
- A Treatise on Hydrodynamics with Numerous Examples. Cambridge: Deighton Bell, 1888. 1st edn. 2 vols. 8vo. Orig cloth, minor damp stain lower bd vol 2. Ptd pres slip from the author. *(Gaskell)* **£25 [≈$45]**
- A Treatise on Optical Physics. Cambridge: Deighton Bell, 1892. 1st edn. 8vo. xxiv, 412, 20 advt pp. Orig cloth, minor damp stain bd edges. *(Gaskell)* **£15 [≈$27]**

Bastholm, E.
- The History of Muscle Physiology. Copenhagen: 1950. 8vo. Ills. Orig bndg, uncut. *(Goodrich)* **$75 [≈£42]**

Bastin, Harold
- Insects. Their Life-Histories and Habits. London: 1913. 8vo. xii,349 pp. Ills. Orig dec cloth, t.e.g., a few spots.
(Hortulus) **$55 [≈£31]**

Bateman, Thomas
- A Practical Synopsis of Cutaneous Diseases, according to the Arrangement of Dr. Willan ... London: 1824. 6th edn. xxiv,346 pp. Cold frontis. Occas sl foxing. New endpapers. Half calf, rebacked in cloth.
(Whitehart) **£90 [≈$160]**
- A Practical Synopsis of Cutaneous Diseases, according to the arrangement of Dr. Willan ... Second American Edition. Phila: J. Crissy, 1824. 8vo. xxiii,320 pp. Browning. Contemp tree calf, upper hinge split, sm splits lower hinge. *(Hemlock)* **$250 [≈£140]**

Bates, G.L.
- Handbook of the Birds of West Africa. London: 1930. 8vo. xxiii,572 pp. Map, frontis, text figs. Orig cloth, spine sl darkened. *(Wheldon & Wesley)* **£60 [≈$107]**

Bates, K.F.
- Enameling: Principles and Practice. New York: The World Publ Co., 1951. 2nd edn.

8vo. 208 pp. 200 text figs. Orig cloth.
                    (Gemmary) **$45 [≈ £25]**

Bateson, Beatrice
- William Bateson, F.R.S., Naturalist: His
Essays & Addresses together with a Short
Account of his Life. Cambridge: 1928. 1st
edn. 469 pp. Orig bndg.   *(Fye)* **$75 [≈ £42]**

Bateson, William
- Materials for the Study of Variation treated
with especial regard to discontinuity in the
Origin of Species. London: 1894. 8vo. xvi,
598 pp. 209 text figs. Orig cloth, sl used.
              (Wheldon & Wesley) **£120 [≈ $214]**
- Mendel's Principles of Heredity. Cambridge:
1913. 3rd imp, with addtns. xiv, 413 pp. 3
ports, 6 cold plates, 38 text figs. Orig bndg,
spine v sl worn.   *(Whitehart)* **£38 [≈ $68]**

Battie, William
- A Treatise on Madness. Introduction by
James A. Brussel. New York: Brunner,
Mazel, 1969. vi,[2], vii,[1],99 pp. Orig cloth.
Dw.   *(Caius)* **$65 [≈ £37]**

Bauer, Louis
- Lectures on Orthopaedic Surgery. New York:
1868. 2nd edn, enlgd. 336 pp. Ills. Ex-lib.
Front bds detached, backstrip loose.
                    (Fye) **$250 [≈ £140]**

Bausch, E.
- Manipulation of the Microscope. New York:
Rochester, 1901. 4th edn. 8vo. 202,12 pp. 59
text figs. Inscrptn. Orig cloth.
                    (Savona) **£25 [≈ $45]**

Baxter, Evelyn V. & Rintoul, L.J.
- The Birds of Scotland. Edinburgh: Oliver &
Boyd, 1953. 2 vols. Roy 8vo. 2 cold frontises,
24 plates. Orig cloth. *(Egglishaw)* **£72 [≈ $128]**
- The Birds of Scotland. Their History,
Distribution and Migration. London: 1953. 2
vols. Roy 8vo. 2 cold & 24 photo plates.
Cloth, 1 crnr bumped.
              (Wheldon & Wesley) **£120 [≈ $214]**
- The Birds of Scotland ... Edinburgh: Oliver
& Boyd, 1953. 2 vols. 8vo. 2 cold frontis, fldg
map, 20 photos. Endpapers discold. Orig
cloth gilt. Dws (piece torn from one).
                    (Blackwell's) **£175 [≈ $312]**

Bayle, A.L.J. & Hollard, H.
- A Manual of General Anatomy ... Translated
from the French by Henry Storer. London: J.
Wilson, 1829. 12mo. xxii,318 pp. Orig bds,
uncut, edges worn. Inscrbd by Storer.
                    (Hemlock) **$275 [≈ £154]**

Bayliss, W.M.
- Principles of General Physiology. London:
1924. xxviii,882 pp. 258 figs. Orig bndg,
worn, scratched, front hinge loose.
                    (Whitehart) **£18 [≈ $32]**

Bazin, Giles Auguste
- The Natural History of Bees ... Translated
from the French. London: Knapton &
Vaillant, 1744. 8vo. [xvi], 452,[xvi] pp. 12
fldg plates. Contemp calf, crnrs worn,
rebacked.   *(Blackwell's)* **£175 [≈ $312]**

Beach, Wooster
- A Treatise on Anatomy, Physiology, and
Health. Designed for Students, Schools, and
Popular Use ... New York: the author, 1847.
1st edn. 8vo. 220,[2],[2 advt] pp. 26 hand cold
plates inc frontis, 2 colour ptd plates, text
figs. Orig calf, rebacked.
                    (Karmiole) **$150 [≈ £84]**

Beale, Lionel J.
- A Treatise on Deformities exhibiting a
Concise View of the Nature and Treatment of
the Principal Distortions and Contractions of
the Limbs, Joints, and Spine. London: 1830.
1st edn. 248 pp. 4 litho plates, text ills. Orig
bndg. Inscrbd by the author.
                    (Fye) **$1,000 [≈ £562]**

Beall, O. & Shryock, R.
- Cotton Mather: First Significant Figure in
American Medicine. Baltimore: 1954. 1st
edn. 71 pp. Orig bndg.   *(Fye)* **$50 [≈ £28]**

Beamish, Richard
- Memoir of the Life of Sir Marc Isambard
Brunel. Second Edition, Revised and
Corrected. London: Longman, Green, 1862.
8vo. xviii, [i], 357,[2 advt] pp. Port, 8 plates,
8 ills. Orig cloth gilt, inside jnts reprd.
                    (Fenning) **£85 [≈ $151]**

Beard, J.T.
- Mine Examination Questions and Answers.
New York: McGraw Hill, 1923. 1st edn. 3
vols. 8vo. Num text figs. Orig cloth.
                    (Gemmary) **$45 [≈ £25]**

Beasley, Henry
- The Druggist's General Receipt Book ...
London: John Churchill, 1857. 4th edn. Half-
title. Orig cloth, spine faded, jnts & ft of spine
rubbed.   *(Jarndyce)* **£25 [≈ $45]**
- The Druggist's Receipt Book. London: 1861.
5th edn. 494 pp. New cloth.
                    (Whitehart) **£18 [≈ $32]**

Beatty, R.T.
- Hearing in Man and Animals. London: 1932. xi, 227 pp. 98 figs. New cloth.
(Whitehart) **£15 [≈ $27]**

Beaufoy, Henry Benjamin Hanbury
- [Caption title] Journal kept by H.B.H.B. during an Aerial Voyage with Mr. James Sadler Sen. from Hackney, Middlesex, to East Thorpe, Essex ... August 29, 1811. London: G. Woodfall, printer, [1811]. 1st edn. 8vo. 39 pp. Margs sl spotted. Orig mrbld wraps. *(Burmester)* **£375 [≈ $668]**

Beaumont, John
- An Historical, Physiological and Theological Treatise of Spirits, Apparitions, Witchcrafts, and other Magical Practices ... London: D. Browne ..., 1705. 1st edn. Frontis. Some water stains & foxing. 10 pp browned. Contemp calf, sl rubbed, ft of spine missing.
(P and P Books) **£325 [≈ $579]**

Beaumont, R.
- Woollen and Worsted. The Theory and Technology of the Manufacture of Woollen, Worsted and Union Yarns and Fabrics. London: 1919. 3rd edn, rvsd. xxxix,716 pp. 42 plates, ca 500 text ills, 18 tables. Orig half rexine, edges worn, back stained.
(Whitehart) **£35 [≈ $62]**

Beaumont, William
- Beaumont's Formative Years: Two Early Notebooks. Edited by G. Miller. New York: 1947. 1st edn. 87 pp. Orig bndg.
(Fye) **$60 [≈ £34]**
- Experiments and Observations on the Gastric Juice and the Physiology of Digestion. Plattsburgh: Printed by F.P. Allen, 1833. 1st edn. 280 pp. Occas foxing. Orig muslin backed paper bds, paper label, some chipping & bumping. *(Reese)* **$1850 [≈ £1,039]**
- Experiments and Observations on the Gastric Juice and the Physiology of Digestion. Boston: Lilly, Wait & Co., 1834. 1st edn. 2nd issue, with Boston title-leaf. Narrow 4to. 280 pp. Occas sl foxing & staining. Orig muslin backed paper bds, spine sl cracked.
(Reese) **$850 [≈ £478]**
- Experiments and Observations on the Gastric Juice, and the Physiology of Digestion. Reprinted from the Plattsburgh Edition, with Notes by Andrew Combe, M.D. Edinburgh: 1838. 1st British edn. Half-title, xx, 319, advt pp. Orig cloth, uncut, some wear to headpiece. *(Goodrich)* **$775 [≈ £435]**

Beaupre, Moricheau
- A Treatise on the Effects and Properties of Cold, with a Sketch, Historical and Medical, of the Russian Campaign. Translated by John Clendinning with an Appendix ... Edinburgh: 1826. 375 pp. Name clipped from title. Orig bds, rebacked. Inscrbd by the translator.
(Fye) **$400 [≈ £225]**

Beavis, G.
- The Book of the Microscope. London: Sampson, Low & Marston, [ca 1931]. 8vo. x, 246, [16 ctlg] pp. Frontis, ills. Cloth. Inscrbd by the author. *(Savona)* **£25 [≈ $45]**

Bechstein, J.M.
- The Natural History of Cage Birds. Their Management, Habits, Food, Diseases ... London: 1888. 8vo. vi,311 pp. Cold frontis (sl foxed), num ills. Endpapers sl foxed. Orig pict cloth, sl soiled, spine soiled & chipped.
(Francis Edwards) **£25 [≈ $45]**

Beck, Carl
- The Crippled Hand and Arm. Phila: 1925. 1st edn. 243 pp. 302 ills. Orig bndg.
(Fye) **$200 [≈ £112]**

Beck, L.C.
- Mineralogy of New York. Albany: Natural History of New York Part III, 1842. 4to. xxiv, 536 pp. 8 plates, 533 ills. Sl foxing. Orig dec cloth, spine rubbed. *(Gemmary)* **$125 [≈ £70]**

Beckmann, John
- A History of Inventions and Discoveries. Translated from the German by William Johnston ... Third Edition. London: 1817. 4 vols. 8vo. Some marks. Tiny hole through 1 title & next few ff. Contemp half calf, some jnts cracking, others rubbed.
(Bow Windows) **£235 [≈ $418]**
- A History of Inventions, Discoveries, and Origins. Translated by W. Johnston. London: 1846-72. 4th edn. 2 vols. Frontis ports. Orig cloth, worn, hd of spines sl defective, vol 1 inner hinge sl cracked.
(Whitehart) **£40 [≈ $71]**
- A History of Inventions, Discoveries, and Origins. London: Bohn, 1846. 4th edn, enlgd. 2 vols. 8vo. Advts. Frontis ports. Orig cloth. *(Rostenberg & Stern)* **$125 [≈ £70]**

Beclard, P.A.
- Elements of General Anatomy: translated from the last edition of the French ... Notes and Corrections by Robert Knox ... Edinburgh: 1830. 8vo. xxvii,399 pp. Title damp stained. Orig bds, uncut, worn.

Translator's pres copy.
                    (Goodrich) **$195 [≈ £110]**

Beddard, F.E.
- A Book of Whales. London: Progressive Science Series, 1900. 1st edn. 8vo. xvi,320 pp. 40 ills. Lib stamp on half-title. Orig cloth, crnrs bumped.   *(Bow Windows)* **£55 [≈ $98]**

Bedford, Duke of
- Hortus Ericaeus Woburnensis, or a Catalogue of Heaths in the Collection of the Duke of Bedford at Woburn Abbey. Privately Printed: 1825. 4to. xiv,[ii],42 pp. 6 hand cold & 4 plain plates. Sl dust soiling. Mod half mor.
              (Wheldon & Wesley) **£500 [≈ $890]**

Bedford, Duke of & Forbes, J.
- Pinetum Woburnense, or a Catalogue of Coniferous Plants in the Collection of the Duke of Bedford at Woburn Abbey. Privately Printed: 1839. Imperial 8vo. xii,226 pp. Frontis, 68 hand cold plates. Mor.
          (Wheldon & Wesley) **£1,800 [≈ $3,204]**
- Salictum Woburnense, or a Catalogue of Willows, Indigenous and Foreign in the Collection of the Duke of Bedford at Woburn Abbey ... Privately Printed: 1829. Imperial 8vo. xvi,[i], [i],294 pp. Fldg frontis, 140 hand cold plates. Half mor.
          (Wheldon & Wesley) **£1,800 [≈ $3,204]**

Beebe, William
- A Monograph on the Pheasants. London: Witherby, 1918-22. One of 600. 4 vols. Folio. 20 maps, 91 cold plates, 87 gravures. B'plates removed. Orig cloth.
              (Bookpress) **$3,250 [≈ £1,826]**

Beers, Clifford W.
- A Mind that Found Itself: An Autobiography. Garden City: Doubleday, 1935. [8], 434 pp. Port frontis. Some foxing. Orig cloth.   *(Caius)* **$85 [≈ £48]**

Beeton, Isabella
- The Book of Household Management ... London: S.O. Beeton, 1861. 1st edn. One vol bound in 2. 8vo. Cold frontis & addtnl pict title in vol 1, duplicate frontis & ptd title in vol 2, 12 cold plates, num text ills. Contemp half calf, rebacked.
              (Burmester) **£500 [≈ $890]**
- The Book of Household Management. London: S.O. Beeton, 1888. 700th thousand. Thick sm 8vo. xlvi,[vi], 1644,[xxiv] pp. 13 cold plates, 68 w'cuts. Orig roan backed cloth gilt, recased, most of orig backstrip retained.
              (Hollett) **£75 [≈ $134]**

- Mrs. Beeton's Household Management. London: Ward, Lock, [1920s]. Demy 8vo. xvi, 1680, 8 pp. Plates (many cold). Orig cloth, few faint marks.   *(Ash)* **£50 [≈ $89]**
- Mrs. Beeton's Dictionary of Every-Day Cookery. London: S.O. Beeton, 1865. 1st edn. 8vo. viii,371,[i] pp. W'engvd ills. Orig maroon cloth gilt, elab gilt dec spine faded, hd of spine sl rubbed. *(Gough)* **£100 [≈ $178]**

Behrens, Charles (editor)
- Atomic Medicine. New York: 1949. 416 pp. Orig bndg.   *(Fye)* **$150 [≈ £84]**

Beirne, B.P.
- British Pyralid and Plume Moths, containing a Descriptive History of all the British Species ... London: Warne, Wayside & Woodland Series, 1952. 8vo. 208 pp. 16 cold plates, 189 text figs. Orig cloth. Dw.
              (Egglishaw) **£40 [≈ $71]**

Belcher, C.
- The Birds of Nyasaland, being a Classified List of the Species Recorded ... with Brief Descriptions and Field Notes. London: 1930. 8vo. xii,356 pp. Fldg map. Cloth, spine faded.   *(Wheldon & Wesley)* **£45 [≈ $80]**

Bell, A.N.
- Climatology and Mineral Waters of the United States. New York: 1885. 1st edn. 386 pp. Charts & maps. Orig bndg.
                    (Fye) **$100 [≈ £56]**

Bell, Sir Charles
- The Anatomy and Philosophy of Expression as connected with the Fine Arts. London: 1872. 6th edn. 4to. 275 pp. Num plates. Orig bndg.   *(Fye)* **$200 [≈ £112]**
- Essays on the Anatomy and Philosophy of Expression. London: 1824. 2nd edn. Large Paper. 4to. 218 pp. Plates. Orig bds, untrimmed, rebacked, preserving orig label.
                  (Fye) **$1,000 [≈ £562]**
- The Hand, Its Mechanism and Vital Endowments as Evincing Design. London: Pickering, 1833. 1st edn. 8vo. xv,288 pp. Ills. Leather, sl scuffed.
              (Key Books) **$400 [≈ £225]**
- The Hand. Its Mechanism and Vital Endowments as Evincing Design. London: 1834. 3rd edn. xvi,342 pp. Sl foxing. Book label. Contemp cloth, paper label.
              (Whitehart) **£90 [≈ $160]**
- The Hand. Its Mechanism and Vital Endowments as Evincing Design. London: William Pickering, 1837. 8vo. Contemp prize mor, lacks top panel of backstrip.

(Waterfield's) **£45£90 [≈ $80]**
- The Hand Its Mechanism and Vital Endowments as Evincing Design. London: Pickering, 1837. 8vo. xvi,368 pp. Num text engvs. Sl foxing. Early half roan.
(Goodrich) **$125 [≈ £70]**
- Idea of a New Anatomy of the Brain. A Facsimile of the Privately Printed Edition of 1811 with a Bio-Bibliographical Introduction. London: Dawson, 1966. 8vo. xi,36 pp. Half calf. *(Goodrich)* **$75 [≈ £42]**
- The Nervous System of the Human Body. Washington: The Register and Library of Medical and Chirurgical Science, 1833. 1st Amer edn. 8vo. 230 pp. 10 plates. Contemp half calf. *(Bookpress)* **$450 [≈ £253]**

Bell, Eric Temple
- The Development of Mathematics. New York: McGraw-Hill, 1945. 2nd edn. 8vo. xiii,637 pp. Lib pocket. Orig red cloth.
(Schoen) **$45 [≈ £25]**
- The Magic of Numbers. New York: McGraw Hill, 1946. 1st edn. 12mo. 418 pp. Lib b'plate & pocket. Orig cloth, upper jnt loose.
(Schoen) **$24 [≈ £13]**
- Men of Mathematics. New York: Simon & Schuster, 1937. 1st edn. 8vo. 492 pp. Num ills. Orig red cloth, jnt weak, sl marked.
(Schoen) **$50 [≈ £28]**

Bell, G.H. & E.F.
- Old English Barometers. Winchester: Warren & Son, 1952. 1st edn. 4to. ix,42 pp. 40 plates. Orig blue cloth. Dw.
(Frew Mackenzie) **£25 [≈ $45]**

Bell, R.C.
- The Use of Skin Grafts. London: 1973. 1st edn. 4to. 157 pp. Num ills. Stamp on title. Orig bndg. *(Fye)* **$75 [≈ £42]**

Bell, Robert Bruce, & others
- Report on a General Scheme of Improvements for the Harbour of Montreal by the Commission of Engineers. Glasgow: 1877. 8vo. 31,195 pp. 8 cold fldg plans. Orig cloth, sm tear spine. *(Weiner)* **£50 [≈ $89]**

Bell, T.
- A History of British Quadrupeds. London: 1874. 2nd edn. 8vo. xviii,474 pp. 160 w'cuts. Orig cloth, somewhat worn.
(Wheldon & Wesley) **£25 [≈ $45]**
- A History of the British Stalk-Eyed Crustacea. London: 1853. 8vo. lxv,386 pp. 174 w'engvs. Calf.
(Wheldon & Wesley) **£40 [≈ $71]**
- A History of British Reptiles. London: Van

Voorst, 1849. 2nd edn. 8vo. xxiv,[ii],159 pp. 50 w'engvs. Cloth. *(Egglishaw)* **£30 [≈ $53]**

Bell, Walter George
- The Great Plague in London in 1665. London: John Lowe, 1924. 1st edn. 8vo. xii, 374 pp. Num plates, text figs. Orig cloth, sm marks front cvr. *(David White)* **£40 [≈ $71]**
- The Great Plague in London in 1665. London: 1924. 1st edn. 374 pp. Ills. Orig bndg. *(Fye)* **$90 [≈ £51]**

Bellamy, J.C.
- The Natural History of South Devon. Plymouth: 1839. Cr 8vo. xxvi,[ii], viii,455 pp. 5 maps, 19 plates, 5 text figs. Some foxing. Mod qtr mor.
(Wheldon & Wesley) **£75 [≈ $134]**

Belluzzo, G.
- Steam Turbines. Translated by A.G. Bremner. London: 1926. xiv,746 pp. 36 plates, 716 ills. Orig bndg.
(Whitehart) **£18 [≈ $32]**

Bennett, A.W.
- The Flora of the Alps ... London: Nimmo, 1896. 1st edn. 2 vols. 8vo. 120 cold plates. Orig cloth gilt, t.e.g.
(Egglishaw) **£85 [≈ $151]**

Bennett, E.T. (editor)
- The Gardens and Menagerie of the Zoological Society delineated ... Chiswick: 1830-31. 2 vols. 8vo. Num engvs by W. Harvey & others. Half mor gilt.
(Egglishaw) **£95 [≈ $169]**

Bennett, John
- The Artificer's Complete Lexicon, for Terms and Prices ... London: John Bennett, 1833. 1st edn. 8vo. 476,[4 advt] pp. Text ills. Contemp tree calf gilt, flat gilt spine.
(Gaskell) **£300 [≈ $534]**

Bennett, N.
- The Science and Practice of Dental Surgery. London: 1931. 2nd edn. 2 vols. 1230 figs. Orig bndg. *(Whitehart)* **£35 [≈ $62]**

Bennett, S.
- A New Explanation of the Ebbing and Flowing of the Sea, upon the Principles of Gravitation. New York: 1816. 79 pp. Fldg plate. Occas sl foxing. Later bds.
(Whitehart) **£35 [≈ $62]**

Bennion, E.
- Antique Dental Instruments. London: 1986.

192 pp. 21 cold plates, 162 ills. Orig bndg.
(Whitehart) **£35 [≈ $62]**

Benson, William
- Principles of the Science of Colour concisely stated to aid and promote their useful application in the Decorative Arts. London: 1868 [1867]. 4to. x,48 pp. 6 plates with cold onlays, 6 other plates, ills (2 cold). Half calf, soiled, inner hinge reglued.
(Weiner) **£100 [≈ $178]**

Bentham, George
- Handbook of the British Flora, together with Illustrations of the British Flora and Further Illustrations of the British Flora. London: 1946-49. 3 vols. Cr 8vo. Orig cloth.
(Henly) **£30 [≈ $53]**
- Labiatarum Genera et Species: or, a Description of the Genera and Species of Plants in the Order Labiatae with their General History, Characters, Affinities and Geographical Distribution. London: 1832-36. Roy 8vo. lxviii,783 pp. Fldg table. Half mor.
(Wheldon & Wesley) **£130 [≈ $231]**

Berg, B.
- Birds of the North. Stockholm: 1925. Folio. 60 gravure plates. Orig cloth backed bds, faded. Author's pres copy.
(Wheldon & Wesley) **£40 [≈ $71]**

Berkeley, Edmund
- Computers - their Operation and Applications. New York: Reinhold, 1956. 1st edn. 8vo. 366 pp. Ills. Lib pocket. Orig green cloth. *(Schoen)* **$45 [≈ £25]**
- Giant Brains; or, Machines that Think. New York: Wiley, 1949. 1st edn. 8vo. xvi,270 pp. Lib pocket. Orig cloth. *(Schoen)* **$75 [≈ £42]**

Berkeley, M.J.
- Handbook of British Mosses ... London: Reeve, 1863. 8vo. xxxvi,324 pp. 1 plain & 23 hand cold plates. Marg notes. Orig cloth.
(Egglishaw) **£45 [≈ $80]**
- Handbook of British Mosses ... London: Reeve, 1895. 2nd edn. 8vo. 324 pp. 1 plain & 23 hand cold plates. Orig cloth.
(Egglishaw) **£35 [≈ $62]**
- Outlines of British Fungology ... London: Lovell Reeve, 1860. 1st edn. 8vo. xvii,442 pp. 1 plain & 23 hand cold litho plates. Orig cloth. *(Egglishaw)* **£70 [≈ $125]**

Berkenhout, J.
- Clavis Anglica Linguae Botanicae; or, a Botanical Lexicon; in which the Terms of Botany, particularly those of ... Linnaeus ...

are explained. London: 1764. Sm 8vo. xii, [215] pp. Lib b'plate. Contemp sheep.
(Wheldon & Wesley) **£35 [≈ $62]**
- Outlines of the Natural History of Great Britain and Ireland. London: 1769-72. 1st edn. 3 vols in 2. Contemp calf, sl worn, jnts cracked but not broken.
(Wheldon & Wesley) **£200 [≈ $356]**

Berkley, Henry J.
- A Treatise on Mental Diseases. New York: Appleton, 1900. 1st edn. xiv,[2], 601,[1],[6 advt] pp. 15 plates, text ills. Orig half mor, faded & rubbed. *(Caius)* **$85 [≈ £48]**

Berkley, M.J.
- Handbook of British Mosses ... London: 1863. 8vo. xxxvi,324,[24 advt] pp. 1 plain & 23 hand cold plates. Lib stamp removed from title. Cloth. *(Henly)* **£72 [≈ $128]**

Bernard, Claude
- An Introduction to the Study of Experimental Medicine. New York: 1927. 226 pp. Ex-lib.
(Fye) **$60 [≈ £34]**

Berrill, N.J.
- The Tunicata. With an Account of the British Species. London: Ray Society, 1950. 8vo. iii,354 pp. 120 text figs. Cloth.
(Wheldon & Wesley) **£30 [≈ $53]**

Berry, Theodore
- The Hand as a Mirror of Systemic Medicine. Phila: 1963. 1st edn. 4to. 216 pp. 132 ills. Dw. *(Fye)* **$75 [≈ £42]**

Bettany, G.T.
- Eminent Doctors: their Lives and their Work (1885). New York: 1972. 2 vols. ix,311; vi,318 pp. Orig bndg.
(Whitehart) **£18 [≈ $32]**

Bettesworth, John
- The New Universal Ready Reckoner; or Every Trader's Infallible Guide. London: [ca 1785]. 1st edn. 12mo. Frontis. Later cloth, roughly rebacked. *(Robertshaw)* **£25 [≈ $45]**

Bewick, Thomas
- A General History of Quadrupeds. Newcastle upon Tyne: 1807. 5th edn. Large Paper (145 x 233 mm). Roy 8vo. x,525 pp. Num ills. Contemp half calf, trifle rubbed.
(Egglishaw) **£110 [≈ $196]**
- A General History of Quadrupeds. Newcastle upon Tyne: 1824. 8th edn. 8vo. x,526 pp. Num w'engvs. Calf gilt, a.e.g., rebacked.
(Egglishaw) **£75 [≈ $134]**

- A History of British Birds ... Newcastle upon Tyne, 1809. 3rd edn. 2 vols in one. 8vo. Num w'engvs. Mod half calf antique style.
(Wheldon & Wesley) £150 [≈ $267]
- A History of British Birds. Newcastle: 1816. 2 vols. 8vo. 261 figs of birds, 262 vignettes. 1 page reprd. Contemp half calf, rubbed, jnts beginning to crack.
(Egglishaw) £130 [≈ $231]
- A History of British Birds. Newcastle: Edw. Walker for T. Bewick, 1826. 6th edn. 2 vols in one. 8vo. xliv,382; xxii,432 pp. Ills. 19th c green half calf gilt, a.e.g., crnrs sl scraped.
(Hollett) £220 [≈ $392]
- Figures of British Land Birds ... Volume I [all published]. Newcastle upon Tyne: 1800. [One of 500]. Lge 8vo. Title-page, 1 page of text. 133 (of 134) pp of plates. Lacks last page with indelicate vignette. Marg foxing. Contemp calf, rubbed, jnts & spine ends reprd.
(Spelman) £140 [≈ $249]
- A General History of Quadrupeds. Newcastle: S. Hodgson, 1791. 2nd edn. x,483 pp. Contemp diced russia gilt, backstrip relaid.
(Gough) £165 [≈ $294]
- A General History of Quadrupeds. Fourth Edition. Newcastle: S. Hodgson ..., 1800. x, 525 pp. W'engvd vignettes. Contemp half calf, gilt dec spine, hd of 1 jnt reprd.
(Gough) £195 [≈ $347]
- A General History of Quadrupeds. Newcastle: Bewick & Hodgson, 1807. 5th edn. 526 pp. Num w'engvs. Some foxing. Tree calf, wearing thin on jnts.
(Carol Howard) £118 [≈ $210]
- A General History of the Quadrupeds. London: 1970. Reprint of 5th edn. 8vo. 225 figs, 111 vignettes & tailpieces. Orig Dw.
(Henly) £28 [≈ $50]
- Works. Memorial Edition. Newcastle: 1885. 3 vols (Land Birds; Water Birds; Quadrupeds) of 5. Roy 8vo. Ills. Red qtr mor, t.e.g.
(Egglishaw) £110 [≈ $196]

Beyschlag, F., & others
- The Deposits of the Useful Minerals & Rocks: Their Origin, Form, and Content. London: Macmillan, 1914. Vols 1 & 2. 2 vols. 8vo. 467 ills. Orig cloth, hinges cracking.
(Gemmary) £125 [≈ $70]

Bick, Edgar
- Source Book of Orthopaedics. Baltimore: 1937. 1st edn. 376 pp. Orig bndg. Signed by the author and inscribed. *(Fye)* £175 [≈ $98]

Bickerton, W.
- The Home Life of the Terns or Sea Swallows. London: Witherby, 1912. 1st edn. Sm folio.

88 pp. 32 plates. Occas sl foxing. Bds, sl rubbed.
(Carol Howard) £20 [≈ $36]

Bicknell, C.
- Flowering Plants and Ferns of the Riviera and Neighbouring Mountains. London: 1885. Roy 8vo. viii,[166],iv pp. 82 cold plates. Some foxing.
(Wheldon & Wesley) £240 [≈ $427]

Bidwell, S.
- Curiosities of Light and Sight. London: 1899. xii,226 pp. 50 ills. Sm lib stamp on endpaper. Orig cloth, spine faded, sl marked.
(Whitehart) £35 [≈ $62]

Bigelow, Henry J.
- Ether and Chloroform. A Compendium of their History, Surgical Uses, Dangers and Discovery ... with ... Anaesthetic Agents, their Mode of Exhibition and Physiological Effect. Boston: 1848. Offprint. 18 pp. Wraps.
(Fye) $700 [≈ £393]
- Litholapaxy or Rapid Lithotrity with Evacuation. Boston: Williams, 1878. 8vo. 42 pp. 14 text ills. Orig cloth.
(Goodrich) $125 [≈ £70]

Bigelow, Horatio
- An International System of Electro-Therapeutics. Phila: 1895. 1st edn. Over 200 ills. Orig bndg. *(Fye)* $150 [≈ £84]

Bigelow, Jacob
- Elements of Technology. Boston: Hilliard Gray ..., 1829. 1st edn. 8vo. xii,507 pp. 22 plates (8 fldg). Foxed. Orig cloth, paper label, cvrs worn, hinges reinforced.
(Bookpress) $225 [≈ £126]
- Florula Bostoniensis. A Collection of Plants of Boston and its Vicinity ... Third Edition, enlarged ... Boston: Little & Brown, 1840. 8vo. vi,[2],468 pp. 2 ff loose. Some foxing. Orig cloth, spine chipped, edges worn.
(Hemlock) $150 [≈ £84]
- Nature in Disease, Illustrated in Various Discourses and Essays. Boston: 1854. 391 pp. Orig bndg, fine. *(Fye)* $200 [≈ £112]

Bigg, R. Heather
- Spinal Curvature comprising a Description of the Various Types of Curvature of the Spine with the Mechanical Appliances best suited for their Treatment. London: 1882. 1st edn. 128 pp. Ills. Orig bndg. *(Fye)* $75 [≈ £42]

Biggart, J.H.
- Pathology of the Nervous System. Edinburgh: 1936. xvi,335 pp. 204 text figs.

Cloth sl marked.　*(Whitehart)* £18 [≈ $32]

Bijl, H.J. Van der
- The Thermionic Vacuum Tube and its Applications. New York: McGraw Hill, 1920. 1st edn, 9th imp. 8vo. 391 pp. Lib b'plate. Orig cloth.　*(Schoen)* $110 [≈ £62]

Billings, John Shaw
- Selected Papers. Compiled, with a Life of Billings, by F.B. Rogers. London: Medical Lib Assoc, 1965. vi,300 pp. Port frontis. Orig bndg, sl dust stained & marked.
　(Whitehart) £25 [≈ $45]

Billroth, Theodor
- The Medical Sciences in the German Universities. New York: 1924. 292 pp. Ex-lib. Orig bndg.　*(Fye)* $75 [≈ £42]

Binet, Alfred
- Alterations of Personality. Translated by Helen Green Baldwin. With Notes and a Preface by J. Mark Baldwin. London: Chapman & Hall, 1896. 1st edn in English. [2],[v]-vi, [ix]-xii, 356 pp. Possibly lacks a leaf of prelims. Orig cloth, gilt spine.
　(Caius) $100 [≈ £56]

Bingley, W.
- Animal Biography, or, Popular Zoology ... London: 1829. Sm 8vo. 20 plates (browned, sl stained). Calf, sl worn.
　(Wheldon & Wesley) £60 [≈ $107]

Binney, W.G.
- Bibliography of North American Conchology previous to 1860. Washington: Smithsonian, 1864-64. 2 parts in one vol. 8vo. 650; 306 pp. New cloth. *(Wheldon & Wesley)* £75 [≈ $134]

Birch, Thomas
- The Life of the Honourable Robert Boyle. London: Millar, 1744. 1st sep edn. 8vo. Advts. 2 lib stamps. Lib b'plate. Cloth.
　(Rostenberg & Stern) $150 [≈ £84]

Bird, D.T.
- A Catalogue of Sixteenth-Century Medical Books in Edinburgh Libraries. Edinburgh: 1982. Lge 4to. xxxii,298 pp. 89 ills. Dw.
　(Goodrich) $125 [≈ £70]

Birkett, John
- The Diseases of the Breast, and their Treatment. London: 1850. 1st edn. 264 pp. 11 partly hand cold plates. Orig bndg.
　(Fye) $450 [≈ £253]

Bischof, G.
- Elements of Chemical and Physical Geology. Translated by Benjamin H. Paul and J. Drummond. London: Cavendish Society, 1854-55-59. 3 vols. 8vo. Tables. Orig dec cloth, worn.　*(Gemmary)* $500 [≈ £281]

Bisset, J.J.
- Sport and War, or Recollections of Fighting and Hunting in South Africa from 1834 to 1867. London: 1875. 8vo. xix,268 pp. Map, 8 plates. Orig cloth.
　(Wheldon & Wesley) £125 [≈ $223]

Blackburn, Mrs H.
- Birds from Moidart and Elsewhere. Edinburgh: Douglas, 1895. 8vo. viii,191 pp. 88 plates. Orig cloth gilt, t.e.g. Author's pres copy.　*(Egglishaw)* £65 [≈ $116]

Blackburn, I.W.
- Illustrations of the Gross Morbid Anatomy of the Brain in the Insane ... Washington: 1908. 1st edn. Lge 4to. vii,154 pp. 75 plates. Orig cloth.　*(Fenning)* £65 [≈ $116]
- Illustrations of the Gross Morbid Anatomy of the Brain in the Insane. A Selection of Seventy-Five Plates showing the Pathological Conditions found in Post-Mortem Examinations ... Washington: GPO, 1908. Lge 4to. 154 pp. 75 plates. Orig cloth, edges shelf worn.　*(Goodrich)* $120 [≈ £67]

Blacker, C.P. (editor)
- The Chances of Morbid Inheritance. London: 1934. 8vo. xi,449 pp. Diags (few fldg). Orig cloth. Inscrbd by the author.
　(Weiner) £25 [≈ $45]

Blackfan, K.D. & Diamond, L.K.
- Atlas of the Blood in Children. New York: 1944. 320 pp. 70 cold plates. Orig bndg.
　(Goodrich) $40 [≈ £22]

Blackwall, J.
- A History of the Spiders of Great Britain and Ireland. London: Ray Society, 1861-64. Folio. vi,384 pp. 29 hand cold plates. Few plates trifle foxed. Orig bds, 1 label sl defective. *(Wheldon & Wesley)* £300 [≈ $534]
- A History of the Spiders of Great Britain and Ireland. London: Ray Society, 1861-64. 2 vols in one. Folio. vi,384 pp. 29 hand cold plates. Old stamp on title & back of plates. Title creased. Sl used. Mod cloth.
　(Wheldon & Wesley) £300 [≈ $534]
- A History of the Spiders of Great Britain and Ireland. London: Ray Society, 1861-64. 2 vols in one. Folio. vi,384 pp. 28 cold plates, with

descriptive plates facing. Binder's blue buckram gilt, sl rubbed.
(Blackwell's) **£425 [≈ $757]**

- Researches in Zoology, illustrative of the Manners and Economy of Animals. London: 1834. 1st edn. 8vo. 434 pp. 3 cold plates. Some browning. Plates sl foxed. Mod cloth, orig backstrip preserved.
(Wheldon & Wesley) **£40 [≈ $71]**

Blades, William
- The Enemies of Books. London: 1880. 2nd edn. xiii,114 pp. Port frontis, 6 plates inc dble page woodburytype. Rebound in gilt dec mor, orig wraps bound in.
(Francis Edwards) **£60 [≈ $107]**

Blaikie, William
- How to Get Strong and How to Stay So. London: Sampson Low, 1880. 1st English edn. 32 pp ctlg. Ills. Orig pict cloth.
(Jarndyce) **£24 [≈ $43]**

Blaine, Delabere Pritchett
- Canine Pathology; or, a Description of the Diseases of Dogs ... Fourth Edition. Revised, Corrected and Enlarged. London: 1841. 8vo. [2], iv, 324, [16 advt] pp. Frontis. Lacks a blank flyleaf. Orig cloth.
(Fenning) **£85 [≈ $151]**
- A Concise Description of the Distemper in Dogs ... Fourth Edition, with great additions. London: T. Boosey, 1806. 12mo. [iv], 73, [3 advt] pp. Half-title. Frontis. Rec bds.
(Burmester) **£250 [≈ $445]**

Blair, David
- An Easy Grammar of Natural and Experimental Philosophy for the Use of Schools. With Ten Engravings. A New Edition, Corrected. London: for Richard Phillips, 1811. 12mo. [ii],vi,164 pp, inc 12 advt pp. 10 plates. Orig tree sheep, spine ends chipped. *(Rankin)* **£25 [≈ $45]**

Blair, P.
- Botanick Essays ... The Structure of the Flowers and the Fructification of Plants ... The Generation of Plants with their Sexes ... London: 1720. 8vo. xxxvi,414,[2 advt] pp. Imprimatur before title. 5 plates. Contemp calf, rebacked. *(Wheldon & Wesley)* **£360 [≈ $641]**

Blair, Robert
- Scientific Aphorisms, being the Outline of an Attempt to Establish Fixed Principles of Science ... Edinburgh: 1827. 8vo. xxxv, [v], 251 pp. 5 fldg plates. Orig bds, uncut, unopened, rebacked, dusty.
(Weiner) **£150 [≈ $267]**

Blair, V.P.
- Surgery and Diseases of the Mouth and Jaws. St. Louis, 1914. 1st edn. 638 pp. Orig bndg.
(Fye) **£450 [≈ £253]**
- Surgery and Diseases of the Mouth and Jaws. St. Louis, 1914. 2nd edn. 638 pp. Orig bndg.
(Fye) **$200 [≈ £112]**

Blake, E.
- Constipation and some Associated Disorders. London: 1900. 2nd edn. xv,286 pp. 29 text figs. Orig cloth, dust stained, sl worn.
(Whitehart) **£18 [≈ $32]**

Blake, J.L.
- Conversations on Natural Philosophy ... Eighth American Edition. Boston: Lincoln & Edmands, 1828. 252 pp. 23 plates inc frontis. Occas sl browning & spotting. Contemp calf, sm defect ft of spine. *(Hemlock)* **$150 [≈ £84]**

Blancard, Stephen (Steven Blankaart)
- The Physical Dictionary. London: Sam Crouch & John Sprint, 1720. 4th edn. Sm 8vo. [viii], 334,2 pp. Later mor.
(Bookpress) **$375 [≈ £211]**
- The Physical Dictionary ... London: 1726. 7th edn. [iv],370 pp. Marg damp stain in prelims. Orig leather, v worn but bndg firm.
(Whitehart) **£120 [≈ $214]**
- The Physical Dictionary wherein the Terms of Anatomy, the Names and Causes of Diseases, Chirurgical Instruments and their Use, are accurately described ... Medicinal Plants ... London: 1726. 7th edn in English. 8vo. viii, 370 pp. Old sheep, rubbed.
(Goodrich) **$195 [≈ £110]**

Blanton, Wyndham B.
- Medicine in Virginia in the Seventeenth Century. Richmond: William Byrd Press, (1930). 1st edn. 8vo. xix,337 pp. 40 plates. Cloth, dulled. *(Bookpress)* **$325 [≈ £183]**

Blizard, William
- A Lecture, on the Situation of the Large Blood-Vessels of the Extremities ... Third Edition ... added, a Brief Explanation of the Nature of Wounds ... London: Dilly, 1798. 8vo. 84 pp. 2 plates. Orig bds, uncut, recvrd.
(Gaskell) **£180 [≈ $320]**

Blundel, Walter
- Painless Tooth-Extraction without Chloroform. With Observations on Local Anaesthesia ... London: John Churchill, 1856. 2nd edn. Advt leaf. Cold frontis, ills. Orig cloth, faded, spine sl rubbed.
(Jarndyce) **£120 [≈ $214]**

Blunt, Wilfred
- Tulips and Tulipomania. London: 1977. Roy 8vo. 64 pp. 16 cold & 15 plain plates. Orig qtr calf. [With] McEwen, R. Atlas of 8 cold plates of Tulips. Folio. Portfolio. Together 2 vols. Orig pict box.
(Wheldon & Wesley) **£380 [≈ $676]**

Blunt, Wilfred & Raphael, Sandra
- The Illustrated Herbal. London: [ca 1979]. 4to. 191 pp. 64 cold plates, num ills. Orig cloth. Dw. *(Francis Edwards)* **£30 [≈ $53]**

Boas, J.E.V.
- Textbook of Zoology. London: Sampson Low, Marston, 1896. 1st English edn. 8vo. 558 pp. 427 figs. Prelims spotted. Orig dec cloth, sl rubbed, new endpapers.
(Savona) **£20 [≈ $36]**

Bock, Carl Ernst
- Atlas of the Human Anatomy, with Explanatory Text ... New York: William Wood, 1881. Lge folio. 38 cold plates. Orig cloth, fine. *(Wreden)* **$85 [≈ £48]**

Bode, Hendrik W.
- Network Analysis and Feedback Amplifier Design. New York: Van Nostrand, 1945. 1st edn. 8vo. xii,551 pp. Lib pocket. Orig bndg, rubbed. *(Schoen)* **$65 [≈ £37]**

Boerhaave, Hermann
- Boerhaave's Aphorisms: Concerning the Knowledge and Cure of Diseases. Translated from the last Edition printed in Latin at Leyden, 1728. With Useful Observations and Explanations. London: 1742. xvi,444,4 pp. Contemp calf, reprs to upper jnt & hd of spine. *(Whitehart)* **£250 [≈ $445]**
- Elements of Chemistry: being the Annual Lectures ... Translated from the Original Latin by Timothy Dallowe. London: 1735. 2 vols in one. 4to. xii,528,[8]; viii,376,[16] pp. 17 plates. Stain on crnr of many ff. Contemp calf, worn, ft of spine defective.
(Weiner) **£275 [≈ $490]**
- A New Method of Chemistry ... London: Osborn & Longman, 1727. 1st edn in English. 4to. 2 plates. Some soiling rear endpapers. Contemp calf gilt, rebacked, crnrs reprd. *(P and P Books)* **£450 [≈ $801]**

Boericke, William
- A Compend of the Principles of Homoeopathy as taught by Hahnemann, and verified by a Century of Clinical Application. San Francisco: 1896. 1st edn. 160 pp. Orig bndg. *(Fye)* **£125 [≈ £70]**

Bohler, Lorenz
- Medullary Nailing of Kuntscher. Baltimore: 1948. 1st edn in English. 185 pp. 1261 figs. Dw. *(Fye)* **$125 [≈ £70]**
- The Treatment of Fractures. Vienna: 1930. 2nd edn. 185 pp. Orig bndg, cvrs torn.
(Fye) **$45 [≈ £25]**
- The Treatment of Fractures. Baltimore: 1935. 4th edn, enlgd. 578 pp. Orig bndg.
(Fye) **$40 [≈ £22]**

Bohr, Harald
- Collected Mathematical Works. Copenhagen: 1952. 3 vols. Lge 8vo. Frontis ports. Few lib marks. Orig cloth, sl faded.
(Weiner) **£75 [≈ $134]**

Bohr, Niels
- Atomic Physics and Human Knowledge. New York: 1958. 1st edn. 101 pp. Dw.
(Fye) **$35 [≈ £20]**
- On the Application of the Quantum Theory to Atomic Structure Part I. The Fundamental Postulates. Cambridge: Proceedings of the Cambridge Philosophical Society (Supplement), 1924. Apparently all published. 8vo. 42 pp. *(Weiner)* **£25 [≈ $45]**
- On the Quantum Theory of Line-Spectra, Parts I-III. Copenhagen, 1928. 4to. 118 pp. Orig ptd wraps, unopened.
(Weiner) **£85 [≈ $151]**
- The Penetration of Atomic Particles through Matter. Copenhagen: E. Munksgaard, 1948. 1st edn. 8vo. 144 pp. Diags. Orig wraps, sm tear to spine. *(Schoen)* **$225 [≈ £126]**
- The Theory of Spectra and Atomic Constitution. Three Essays. Cambridge: 1922. 8vo. x,126 pp. Orig cloth, sl faded.
(Weiner) **£35 [≈ $62]**

Bois, E. & Trechslin, A.M.
- Roses. London: Nelson, 1962. Sm folio. 127 pp. 60 mtd cold plates. Dw (sl chipped).
(Carol Howard) **£40 [≈ $71]**

Bolam, G.
- The Birds of Northumberland and the Eastern Borders. Alnwick: 1912. 8vo. xvii,726 pp. Illust title, 27 plates. Foxed at ends. Orig cloth.
(Wheldon & Wesley) **£100 [≈ $178]**

Bolton, James
- Filices Britannicae; an History of the British Ferns. Leeds: [1785-] 1790. 4to. xvi, 59, [5], xvii-xxii, 60-81,[1] pp. 46 hand cold plates on 45 ff. Calf, rebacked.
(Wheldon & Wesley) **£800 [≈ $1,424]**

Bolton, John

- Geological Fragments collected principally from Rambles among the Rocks of Furness and Cartmel. Ulverston: 1869. 1st edn. 8vo. 264 pp. 5 plates. Orig cloth gilt.
(Hollett) **£95 [≈ $169]**

Bonhote, J. Lewis

- Birds of Britain. London: 1907. 1st edn. 8vo. x,405 pp. 100 cold plates by Dresser. Orig dec brown cloth, sl used, recased.
(Wheldon & Wesley) **£35 [≈ $62]**
- Birds of Britain. London: A. & C. Black, 1907. 1st edn. x,405 pp. 100 cold ills by Dresser. Foredge sl foxed. Orig dec red cloth, t.e.g. *(Argonaut)* **£250 [≈ $140]**
- Birds of Britain. London: A. & C. Black, 1907. 1st edn. 100 cold plates. Orig pict cloth gilt. *(Carol Howard)* **£28 [≈ $50]**

Boni, N., Russ, M. & Laurence, D.H.

- A Bibliographical Checklist and Index to the Published Writings of Albert Einstein. New Jersey: 1960. [2],84 pp. 4 ports, 2 text ills. Orig bndg. *(Whitehart)* **£21 [≈ $37]**

Bonney, T.G.

- The Story of Our Planet. London: 1898. 3rd edn. 8vo. xvi,592,18 pp. 6 cold plates, 170 text figs. Sm lib stamp title verso. Cloth.
(Henly) **£18 [≈ $32]**

Bonningshausen, C. von

- Therapeutic Pocket-Book for Homeopathic Physicians ... New York: 1847. 8vo. 504 pp. Marks, sl foxing. Half calf, worn, front inner jnt loose. *(Weiner)* **£40 [≈ $71]**

Bonnycastle, John

- An Introduction to Astronomy. In a Series of Letters from a Preceptor to a Pupil ... London: for J. Johnson, 1786. 1st edn. 8vo. vi,[ii], 431,[i] pp. Frontis, 20 plates (10 fldg, 1 misfolded). Contemp polished calf, flat back gilt, jnts starting, hd of spine chipped.
(Blackwell's) **£250 [≈ $445]**
- An Introduction to Astronomy ... The Fourth Edition, Corrected and Improved. London: 1803. 8vo. viii,443, [1,2 advt] pp. Frontis, 19 plates. Some stains & foxing. Contemp tree calf, rebacked, crnr tips rubbed.
(Bow Windows) **£125 [≈ $223]**
- An Introduction to Mensuration and Practical Geometry: Eleventh Edition Corrected and Improved. London: for J. Johnson, 1812. 8vo. xii,276 pp. Lacks half-title. Orig sheep, jnts cracked.
(Claude Cox) **£20 [≈ $36]**

Boole, George

- An Investigation of the Laws of Thought on which are founded the Mathematical Theories of Logic and Probabilities. New York: Dover, 1956. 12mo. 424 pp. Orig wraps. *(Schoen)* **£65 [≈ $37]**

Booth, Andrew Donald & Kathleen H.V.

- Automatic Digital Calculators. London: Butterworth, 1953. 1st edn. 12mo. 231 pp. Ills. Lib pocket. Orig bndg. *(Schoen)* **£75 [≈ $42]**

Borg, J.

- Descriptive Flora of the Maltese Islands including the Ferns and Flowering Plants. Malta: 1927. 8vo. 846 pp. Half mor.
(Wheldon & Wesley) **£65 [≈ $116]**

Born, M.

- Natural Philosophy of Causes and Chance. Oxford: 1949. 1st edn. viii,215 pp. Orig bndg. *(Whitehart)* **£25 [≈ $45]**

Bottomley, Sarah

- An Essay on Early Rising, as it is Favourable to Health, Business, and Devotion. Third Edition. Scarborough: 1822. 8vo. 16 pp. Disbound. *(Weiner)* **£21 [≈ $37]**

Boulenger, G.A.

- Catalogue of the Chelonians, Rhynchocephalians, and Crocodiles in the British Museum. London: (1889) 1966. 2nd edn. x, 311 pp. 6 plates.
(Wheldon & Wesley) **£30 [≈ $53]**
- Catalogue of the Lizards in the British Museum. London: 1885-87. 2nd edn. 3 vols. 8vo. 96 litho plates. Lib stamp on titles. Orig cloth, unopened. *(Egglishaw)* **£190 [≈ $338]**
- Catalogue of the Lizards in the British Museum (1885-87). London: 1965. 3 vols in 2. 1545 pp. 96 plates.
(Wheldon & Wesley) **£175 [≈ $312]**
- Catalogue of the Perciform Fishes in the British Museum. Volume 1. Second Edition. London: BM, 1895. All published. 8vo. xix,394 pp. 15 litho plates. Orig cloth, unopened. *(Egglishaw)* **£36 [≈ $64]**

Bourne, John

- A Treatise on the Steam Engine ... London: 1846. 1st edn. 4to. vii,259 pp. 38 plates (8 more than called for), ills, diags. Lib stamps on plate crnrs. Contemp half calf, v worn, backstrip relaid. *(Weiner)* **£150 [≈ $267]**
- Handbook of the Steam Engine ... London: 1879. 14th edn. Sm 8vo. xix,685 pp. 67 w'cuts. Lib stamp on title. Spine sl faded, lib mark on spine. *(Whitehart)* **£45 [≈ $80]**

Bousfield, Paul
- The Omnipotent Self: A Study in Self-Deception and Self-Cure. London: Kegan Paul, 1923. 1st edn. vii,[1],171 pp. Sl foxing. Name. Orig blue cloth, somewhat worn.
(Caius) **$50 [≈£28]**

Boutcher, William
- A Treatise on Forest Trees ... New and Useful Discoveries. Edinburgh: 1775. 1st edn. 4to. 4,xlviii,259,4 pp. Contemp mrbld bds, uncut, rebacked, new endpapers. Not signed by the author on title verso.
(Henly) **£125 [≈$223]**
- A Treatise on Forest-Trees ... Dublin: for William Wilson, 1784. 3rd edn. 8vo. xxviii, [4], 307 pp. Old calf, rebacked.
(Young's) **£90 [≈$160]**

Bowdich, S.
- Taxidermy: or the Art of Collecting, Preparing and Mounting Objects of Natural History. London: 1835. 5th edn. Post 8vo. 182 pp. 5 plates. Orig cloth. Anon.
(Wheldon & Wesley) **£25 [≈$45]**

Bowditch, Nathaniel
- The Improved Practical Navigator; Containing All Necessary Instruction for Determining the Latitude by Various Methods ... Revised ... by Thomas Kirby. Second Edition. London: Hardy, 1806. 22,[2],304, (252),4 advt pp. 12 plates, text figs. Rebound in calf.
(Karmiole) **$175 [≈£98]**

Bowen, Thomas
- An Historical Account of the Origin, Progress and Present State of Bethlem Hospital ... London: 1783. 1st edn. 4to. [iv], 16 pp. Calf backed bds, worn. Anon.
(Bookpress) **$275 [≈£154]**

Bower, F.O.
- The Ferns (Filicales). Cambridge: 1923-28. 3 vols. Roy 8vo. 762 ills. Cloth, trifle worn.
(Wheldon & Wesley) **£50 [≈$89]**
- The Origin of a Land Flora. London: 1908. 1st edn. xi,727 pp. Frontis, 361 text figs. Endpapers sl browned. Orig cloth, hd of spine chipped.
(Francis Edwards) **£25 [≈$45]**

Bowles, E.A.
- My Garden in Spring, Summer, Autumn and Winter. London: 1914-15. 3 vols. 8vo. 48 cold & 72 plain plates. Orig dec cloth.
(Wheldon & Wesley) **£180 [≈$320]**

Bowman, A.K.
- The Life and Teachings of Sir William MacEwen. London: 1942. 1st edn. 425 pp. Orig bndg.
(Fye) **$75 [≈£42]**

Boyer, Alexis, Baron
- A Treatise on Surgical Diseases, and the Operations suited to them. New York: 1815-16. 1st edn in English. 2 vols. 415; 395 pp. Leather.
(Fye) **$800 [≈£449]**
- A Treatise on Surgical Diseases, and the Operations Suited to Them. Translated from the French by Alexander H. Stevens, M.D. New York: Swords, 1815-16. 1st (abridged) edn in English. 2 vols in one. 8 plates. Browning. Orig calf, sl worn.
(Goodrich) **$145 [≈£81]**

Boyes, Joseph
- Bunnell's Surgery of the Hand. Phila: 1970. 5th edn. 727 pp. Orig bndg.
(Fye) **$50 [≈£28]**

Boyle, James Parkinson
- Compendium of Dr. Brown's Philosophy of the Human Mind ... New Edition ... Dublin: 1849. 12mo. iv,352 pp. Some underlining. Orig cloth.
(Weiner) **£25 [≈$45]**

Boyle, Robert
- Medicinal Experiments: or, a Collection of Choice and Safe Remedies ... In Three Parts ... The Sixth Edition ... London: Innys, 1718. 8vo. [24],168, (22),61 pp. Contemp calf.
(Hemlock) **$325 [≈£183]**
- New Experiments and Observations touching Cold ... With an Appendix ... London: 1683. [xlii], 325, 20,29 pp. 2 plates in facs. Contemp leather, rubbed, hinges cracked, sl shaken.
(Whitehart) **£400 [≈$712]**
- The Origin of Formes and Qualities ... Second Edition, augmented ... Oxford: H. Hall for Ric. Davis, 1667. 8vo. [xxxii],262, 265-289, [1], 291-362 pp. F8 present, lacks a4. Title sl creased. Contemp calf, shaken, jnts cracked. Wing B.4015.
(Gaskell) **£600 [≈$1,068]**

Boys, John
- General View of the Agriculture of the County of Kent ... Second Edition. London: 1805. 8vo. xxiv, 293, [1 blank, 4 advt] pp. Half-title. Fldg map, fldg table, 2 plates. Occas spotting. Orig bds, uncut, sl worn.
(Bow Windows) **£250 [≈$445]**

Braasch, W.F. & Emmett, J.L.
- Clinical Urography - an Atlas and Textbook of Roentgenologic Diagnosis. Phila: W.B.

Saunders, 1951. 1st edn. 8vo. v,736 pp. 1361 figs. Orig cloth. *(David White)* **£32 [≈ $57]**

Bracken, Henry
- The Gentleman's Pocket-Farrier, with Large Additions and Remarks. London: J. Clarke ..., 1735. 3rd edn. 8vo. Some staining to lower marg. Wraps, worn.
(Francis Edwards) **£60 [≈ $107]**

Brackett, Cyrus F., & others
- Electricity in Daily Life. London: 1891. 8vo. xvii,288 pp. Ills. Orig cloth.
(Weiner) **£20 [≈ $36]**

Bradbury, S. & Turner, G. L'E.
- Historical Aspects of Microscopy. Cambridge: Heffer for R.M.S., 1967. 8vo. 227 pp. Frontis, text ills. Orig cloth. Dw (sl torn). *(Savona)* **£30 [≈ $53]**

Bradford, Edward & Lovett, Robert
- Orthopedic Surgery. New York: 1911. 1st edn. 410 pp. Num ills. Orig bndg. Publisher's pres copy. *(Fye)* **$250 [≈ £140]**
- A Treatise on Orthopedic Surgery. New York: 1890. 1st edn. 783 pp. 789 ills. Orig bndg. *(Fye)* **$300 [≈ £169]**
- Treatise on Orthopedic Surgery. New York: 1905. 3rd edn. 669 pp. 592 ills. Orig bndg, rear inner hinge cracked. *(Fye)* **$100 [≈ £56]**

Bradley, Richard
- New Improvements of Planting and Gardening, Both Philosophical and Practical. In Three Parts ... Fourth Edition ... added ... Herefordshire-Orchards. London: W. Mears, 1724. 3 parts in one vol. 8vo. 11 plates. Contemp calf, rebacked, sl worn.
(Heritage) **$450 [≈ £253]**
- New Improvements of Planting and Gardening, both Philosophical and Practical. In Three Parts. To which is added Herefordshire Orchards, A Pattern for all England. London: [1730-] 1731. 6th edn. 8vo. [xiv], 608, [23] pp. Frontis, 18 plates (on 13 ff). Mod calf antique.
(Wheldon & Wesley) **£100 [≈ $178]**
- New Improvements of Planting and Gardening, both Philosophical and Practical, In Three Parts ... To which is added ... Herefordshire Orchards ... London: 1739. 7th edn. 8vo. [xvi],608,[xxiv] pp. Frontis, 13 plates (10 fldg). Contemp calf gilt, rubbed, backstrip relaid. *(Henly)* **£175 [≈ $312]**
- A Survey of the Ancient Husbandry and Gardening collected from Cato, Varro, Columella, Virgil, and others. London: 1725. 8vo. [xvi],373,[10] pp. 4 plates on 2 ff.

Contemp calf, rebacked with mor.
(Wheldon & Wesley) **£130 [≈ $231]**

Brady, G.S.
- A Monograph of the Free and Semi-Parasitic Copepoda of the British Islands. London: Ray Society, 1878-80. 3 vols. 8vo. 96 litho plates (some partially hand cold). Orig cloth, sm splits in backstrip. *(Egglishaw)* **£44 [≈ $78]**

Bragg, W.H.
- Atomic Structure of Minerals. Ithaca: Cornell UP, 1937. 8vo. xiii,292 pp. Port frontis, 144 text figs. Orig cloth. *(Gemmary)* **$75 [≈ £42]**
- An Introduction to Crystal Analysis. New York: Van Nostrand, 1929. 8vo. vii,168 pp. 105 text figs. Good ex-lib. Orig cloth.
(Gemmary) **$50 [≈ £28]**

Bragg, W.H. & W.L.
- X Rays and Crystal Structure. London: G. Bell & Sons, 1916. 2nd edn. 8vo. viii,229 pp. 4 plates, 75 text figs. Orig cloth.
(Gemmary) **$75 [≈ £42]**
- X Rays and Crystal Structure. London: G. Bell & Sons, 1924. 4th edn. 8vo. xi,322 pp. 8 plates, 106 text figs. Orig cloth.
(Gemmary) **$75 [≈ £42]**

Bragg, Sir William
- An Introduction to Crystal Analysis. London: 1928. vii,168 pp. 105 ills. Dw (worn).
(Francis Edwards) **£25 [≈ $45]**

Braid, James
- Braid on Hypnotism. Neurypnology, or the Rationale of Nervous Sleep considered in relation to Animal Magnetism or Mesmerism ... London: Redway, 1899. xii,380 pp. Orig cloth, gilt spine, sl worn.
(Caius) **$150 [≈ £84]**

Braisted, William
- Report on the Japanese Naval Medical and Sanitary Features of the Russo-Japanese War to the Surgeon-General, U.S. Navy. Washington: 1906. 1st edn. 82 pp. Photo ills. Ex-lib. Orig bndg. *(Fye)* **$150 [≈ £84]**

Braithwaite, Robert
- The British Moss-Flora. London: Reeve, 1887-1905. 3 vols. Lge 8vo. 128 plates (plate iii* is synonymous with xliv). Orig green cloth gilt. *(Blackwell's)* **£200 [≈ $356]**
- The Sphagnaceae or Peat-Mosses of Europe and North America. London: 1880. Imperial 8vo. 91 pp. 29 plain plates. Cloth, spine sl faded. *(Henly)* **£42 [≈ $75]**

Bramwell, Byrom
- The Diseases of the Spinal Cord. Edinburgh: Machalan, Stewart, 1882. 1st edn. 8vo. 300 pp. 151 ills (some cold). Orig green cloth. Inscrbd "With the author's compliments".
(*Goodrich*) **$795 [≈ £447]**
- Diseases of the Spinal Cord. New York: 1886. 2nd edn. xiv,298 pp. 53 cold plates, 102 ills. Sl foxing. New cloth.
(*Whitehart*) **£30 [≈ $53]**
- Diseases of the Spinal Cord. Edinburgh: 1884. 2nd edn. 359 pp. Num chromolitho ills. Orig bndg.   (*Fye*) **$100 [≈ £56]**

Bramwell, J. Milne
- Hypnotism and Treatment by Suggestion. London: Cassell, 1909. 1st edn. xii,216 pp. Orig green cloth, gilt spine.
(*Caius*) **$65 [≈ £37]**

Brande, William Thomas
- A Manual of Chemistry. London: 1830. 3rd edn. 2 vols. cliii,493; 744 pp. 3 plates (water stains), text figs. Sl foxing. Cloth backed bds, rebacked.   (*Whitehart*) **£100 [≈ $178]**
- Outlines of Geology; being the Substance of a Course of Lectures delivered in ... the Royal Institution ... London: Murray, 1817. 1st edn. 8vo. viii,144,[2 advt] pp. Hand cold fldg frontis. Orig bds, rubbed, label worn.
(*Burmester*) **£125 [≈ $223]**

Brandis, Dietrich
- Indian Trees. London: Constable, 1906. Lge 8vo. xxxiv,767 pp. 201 text ills. Orig cloth gilt, sl sunned.   (*Blackwell's*) **£165 [≈ $294]**

Brazier, Mary A.B.
- The Electrical Activity of the Nervous System. New York: Macmillan, [1958]. 2nd edn. xiv, 273 pp. 9 ports, text ills. Few ink underlinings. Orig cloth. (*Caius*) **$50 [≈ £28]**

Brecher, Ruth & Edward
- The Rays: A History of Radiology in the United States and Canada. New York: 1969. 1st edn. 484 pp. Orig bndg. (*Fye*) **$50 [≈ £28]**

Bremner, M.D.K.
- The Story of Dentistry: Dentistry from the Dawn of Civilization to the Present. New York: 1946. 2nd edn. 335 pp. Ills. Orig bndg.
(*Fye*) **$75 [≈ £42]**

Bretschneider, E.
- History of European Botanical Discoveries in China. London (St. Petersburg): 1898. 2 vols in one. Roy 8vo. Half calf, trifle rubbed.
(*Wheldon & Wesley*) **£240 [≈ $427]**

Breuer, J. & Freud, S.
- Studies in Hysteria. New York: 1936. 241 pp. Orig bndg, bds worn. (*Goodrich*) **$45 [≈ £25]**

Brewer, J.
- A New Flora of the Neighbourhood of Reigate, Surrey, with Lists of the Fauna. London: 1856. Post 8vo. ix,194 pp. Fldg map (reprd). Cloth, trifle soiled & faded.
(*Wheldon & Wesley*) **£30 [≈ $53]**

Brewster, Sir David
- The Life of Sir Isaac Newton. New York: Harper's Family Library, 1831. Sm 8vo. 323 pp. Frontis port, text figs. Occas foxing. Orig bndg, ft of spine split, occas foxing.
(*Whitehart*) **£25 [≈ $45]**
- The Life of Sir Isaac Newton. London: Murray, 1831. 1st edn. 12mo. xvi,366 pp. Port. Margs of few ff sl soiled. Contemp half calf, gilt spine.   (*Burmester*) **£75 [≈ $134]**
- The Life of Sir Isaac Newton. London: Murray, Family Library, 1831. 1st edn. 12mo. xvi, 366 pp. Engvd port & title. Orig ptd linen, sl rubbed & dark.
(*Burmester*) **£50 [≈ $89]**
- Memoirs of the Life, Writings, and Discoveries of Sir Isaac Newton. Volume II [only]. Edinburgh: 1855. xi,564 pp. Frontis. Occas foxing. Orig cloth, sl dull & worn.
(*Whitehart*) **£30 [≈ $53]**
- Memoirs of the Life, Writings, and Discoveries of Sir Isaac Newton. Edinburgh: 1855. 1st edn. 2 vols. 478; 564 pp. Half leather, split in 1 jnt.   (*Fye*) **£150 [≈ £84]**
- Memoirs of the Life, Writings, and Discoveries of Sir Isaac Newton. New York: The Sources of Science Series, 1965. Reprint of 1855 edn. 2 vols. Orig bndgs.
(*Whitehart*) **£45 [≈ $80]**
- A Treatise on Magnetism, forming the Article under that head in the Seventh Edition of the Encyclopaedia Britannica. Edinburgh: 1838. 8vo. (viii),363 pp. Fldg frontis map, ills. Orig cloth, spine ends worn.
(*Weiner*) **£85 [≈ $151]**
- A Treatise on New Philosophical Instruments, for Various Purposes in the Arts and Sciences ... Edinburgh: for Murray & Blackwood, 1813. 1st edn. 2 vols. 8vo. xx, 223; [2], 225-427 pp. 12 plates (foxed). Lib stamps. Mod qtr calf.
(*Heritage*) **$750 [≈ £421]**
- A Treatise on Optics. A New Edition. London: Lardner's Cabinet Cyclopaedia, 1833. 2nd edn. Sm 8vo. Orig cloth, paper label.   (*Fenning*) **£32.50 [≈ $59]**
- See also The Edinburgh Encyclopaedia

Bridgeman, Percy Williams
- The Physics of High Pressure. London: Bell, 1949. 12mo. 445 pp. Num ills. Lib pocket. Orig bndg.   *(Schoen)* **$85 [≈ £48]**

Bridgman, George
- The Book of a Hundred Hands. New York: Pellham, 1929. 3rd edn. 160 pp. Num ills. Orig bndg.   *(Fye)* **$100 [≈ £56]**

Brierre de Boismont, Alexandre
- Hallucinations, or, the Rational History of Apparitions, Visions, Dreams, Ecstasy, Magnetism, and Somnambulism. Phila: Lindsay & Blakiston, 1853. 1st edn in English. xx, [17]-557 pp. Poor ex-lib. Orig dec cloth.   *(Caius)* **$85 [≈ £48]**

Brigham, Amariah
- Remarks on the Influence of Mental Cultivation and Mental Excitement upon Health. Boston: Capen & Lyon, 1833. 2nd edn. 130 pp. Orig cloth, damp stained & wrinkled.   *(Caius)* **$175 [≈ £98]**

Bright, P.M. & Leeds, H.A.
- A Monograph of the British Aberrations of the Chalk-Hill Blue Butterfly Lysandra Coridon. Bournemouth: 1938. 1st edn. 4to. ix, 138, [4] pp. 6 pp errata (1941) inserted. Mor, rubbed.
            (Wheldon & Wesley) **£60 [≈ $107]**

Brindley, G.S.
- Physiology of the Retina and the Visual Pathway. London: 1960. x,298 pp. 63 figs. Some marg pencil marks. Dw (sl marked).
            (Whitehart) **£15 [≈ $27]**

Brisbin, James S.
- Trees and Tree-Planting. New York: Harper, 1888. 1st edn. 8vo. xxxii,258,[4 advt] pp. Port. Orig cloth.   *(Fenning)* **£24.50 [≈ $45]**

Bristow, H.W., & others
- The Geology of the Isle of Wight. London: 1889. 2nd edn. 8vo. xiv,349 pp. Cold geological map, 3 cold & 1 plain sections. Crnr cut from title. Cloth gilt, spine sl faded.
            (Henly) **£60 [≈ $107]**

Bristowe, J.S.
- A Treatise on the Theory and Practice of Medicine. London: 1887. 6th edn. xliv,1269 pp. 113 text figs. New cloth.
            (Whitehart) **£25 [≈ $45]**

Bristowe, J.S., & others
- Diseases of the Intestines and Peritoneum.

New York: Wood, 1879. Wood Library edn. 8vo. 243 pp. Orig bndg.
            (Goodrich) **$35 [≈ £20]**

Bristowe, William Syer
- The Comity of Spiders. London: Ray Society, 1939-41. 2 vols. 8vo. 22 plates, 96 text figs. Orig blue cloth, spines faded.
            (Blackwell's) **£110 [≈ $196]**
- The World of Spiders. London: 1958. 1st edn. xiii,301 pp. 4 cold & 32 other plates, 116 text ills. Dw (worn).
            (Francis Edwards) **£45 [≈ $80]**

British Pharmacopoeia
- British Pharmacopoeia 1858. London: 1867. xxiv, 434 pp. Spine sl torn, worn cvr.
            (Whitehart) **£35 [≈ $62]**
- British Pharmacopoeia. 1898. Issued 1911. 8vo. xxxii,535 pp. Corrigenda slip to 1902. Sl spotting half-title. Orig cloth, spine ends sl bumped.   *(David White)* **£28 [≈ $50]**

British Zoology Illustrated ...
- See Pennant, Thomas

Britten, James
- European Ferns. Illustrated by David Blair. London: Cassell, [ca 1870]. 4to. 196 pp. 30 cold litho plates, num w'cut ills. Orig pict gilt green cloth, a.e.g.
            (Carol Howard) **£52 [≈ $93]**
- European Ferns. London: Cassell, [ca 1880]. 4to. vii,xliv,196 pp. 30 cold plates, num w'cuts. Half mor gilt.
            (Egglishaw) **£55 [≈ $98]**

Britton, N.L.
- Flora of Bermuda. New York: 1918. 8vo. xii, 585 pp. Cold frontis, text figs. Cloth.
            (Wheldon & Wesley) **£35 [≈ $62]**

Britton, N.L. & Brown, A.
- An Illustrated Flora of the Northern United States, Canada ... New York: 1896-98. 3 vols. Roy 8vo. 4162 text figs. Sound ex-lib. Cloth, trifle loose. *(Wheldon & Wesley)* **£45 [≈ $80]**

Britton, N.L. & Millspaugh, C.F.
- The Bahama Flora. New York: the authors, 1920. 8vo. viii,695 pp. Cloth, sl affected by damp.   *(Wheldon & Wesley)* **£50 [≈ $89]**

Britton, N.L. & Rose, J.N.
- The Cactaceae. Descriptions and Illustrations of Plants of the Cactus Family. Washington: 1919-23. 1st edn. 4 vols. Lge 8vo. 137 plates, 1120 text figs. Orig bds, some staining.
            (Hortulus) **$525 [≈ £295]**

- The Cactaceae. Descriptions and Illustrations of Plants of the Cactus Family. Washington: Carnegie Institute, 1919-23. 4 vols. 4to. 107 cold & 30 plain plates, 1120 text ills. Half mor, vol 2 front cvr v sl spotted.
(Wheldon & Wesley) **£1,000 [≈ $1,780]**
- The Cactaceae. Descriptions and Illustrations of Plants of the Cactus Family. [Washington: 1919-23] Reprint 1964. 4 vols in 2. 4to. 1068 pp. 137 plain plates, 1120 ills.
(Wheldon & Wesley) **£52 [≈ $93]**

Broadbent, Sir William
- Selections from the Writings Medical and Neurological ... London: 1908. 1st edn. 444 pp. Orig bndg.   *(Fye)* **$100 [≈ £56]**

Brock, Arthur
- Greek Medicine, being Extracts Illustrative of Medical Writers from Hippocrates to Galen. London: 1929. 1st edn. 256 pp. Orig bndg.   *(Fye)* **$60 [≈ £34]**

Brockbank, William
- Ancient Therapeutics. The Fitzpatrick Lectures ... London: 1955. 1st reprint. 8vo. 162 pp. Ills. Dw.   *(Goodrich)* **$45 [≈ £25]**

Brockett, L.P.
- Battle-Field and Hospital; or, Lights and Shadows of the Great Rebellion. Phila: 1888. 512 pp. Orig bndg.   *(Fye)* **$150 [≈ £84]**
- Epidemic and Contagious Diseases: their History, Symptoms, and Treatment ... A Book for the Family and Home. New York: 1873. 1st edn. 507 pp. Cold plates. Leather, rubbed.   *(Fye)* **$200 [≈ £112]**

Broderip, W.J.
- Leaves from the Note Book of a Naturalist. London: 1852. Cr 8vo. xvi,413 pp. Frontis. Orig cloth, trifle worn.
(Wheldon & Wesley) **£25 [≈ $45]**
- Zoological Recreations. New Edition. London: 1849. 8vo. ix,384 pp. Sl foxing & soiling. Orig cloth, trifle used.
(Wheldon & Wesley) **£25 [≈ $45]**

Brons, J.
- The Blind Spot of Mariotte - Its Ordinary Imperceptibility or Filling-In and its Facultative Visibility. Copenhagen: Nordisk Verlag, 1939. 1st edn. 8vo. 348 pp. Ills. Orig wraps.   *(Schoen)* **$135 [≈ £76]**
- The Blind Spot of Mariotte ... Copenhagen & London: 1939. [xiii],348 pp. 30 figs. Orig ptd wraps. Author's pres copy.
(Whitehart) **£18 [≈ $32]**

Brook, Abraham
- Miscellaneous Experiments and Remarks on Electricity, the Air-Pump, and the Barometer ... Norwich: Crouse & Stevenson, for J. Johnson, London, 1789. 1st edn. 4to. 3 plates. Old lib stamp. Contemp calf gilt, crudely rebacked in cloth.
(Ximenes) **$500 [≈ £281]**

Brookes, R.
- The General Dispensatory. Containing a Translation of the Pharmacopoeias of the Royal Colleges of Physicians of London and Edinburgh. London: 1765. 2nd edn. x,390 pp. Endpapers & title sl torn. Foxing. Old leather, hinges sl cracked but firm.
(Whitehart) **£90 [≈ $160]**
- The General Practice of Physic ... London: 1754. 2nd edn. 332 pp. Occas sl foxing. Old calf, rebacked.   *(Whitehart)* **£180 [≈ $320]**

Brooks, Catharine
- The Complete English Cook; or Prudent Housewife ... Fourth Edition. London: for the authoress, & sold by J. Cooke, [ca 1765]. 8vo. 132 pp. 'To the Ladies' advt between A1 & A2. Frontis, 3 w'engvd ills. Early 19th c limp vellum.   *(Gough)* **£295 [≈ $525]**

Broom, R.
- The Origin of the Human Skeleton. London: 1930. 8vo. Ills. Cloth.
(Wheldon & Wesley) **£28 [≈ $50]**

Broomell, I.N. (editor)
- Practical Dentistry by Practical Dentists. Phila: 1908. vii,496 pp. Cloth sl discold, front inner hinge weak.   *(Whitehart)* **£18 [≈ $32]**

Brophy, Truman
- Cleft Lip and Palate. Phila: 1923. 1st edn. 340 pp. 463 ills. Orig bndg, spine ends rubbed.   *(Fye)* **$450 [≈ £253]**
- Oral Surgery: A Treatise on the Diseases, Injuries, and Malformations of the Mouth and Associated Parts. Phila: 1915. 1st edn. 1090 pp. Num cold plates. Orig bndg.
(Fye) **$250 [≈ £140]**

Broste, K. & Jorgensen, B.
- Prehistoric Man in Denmark. A Study in Physical Anthropology. Copenhagen, 1956. 2 vols (all published?). Folio. 159; 439 pp. 310 ills. Orig wraps.   *(Whitehart)* **£25 [≈ $45]**

Brougham, Henry Lord & Routh, E.J.
- Analytical View of Sir Isaac Newton's Principia. London: 1855. 1st edn. 8vo. xxxii, 442, 24 advt pp. Few ff carelessly opened.

Old pencil notes. Orig cloth, spine ends v sl worn. Inscrbd 'From Lord Brougham'.
(Bow Windows) **£115 [≃ $205]**

Broun, T.
- Manual of the New Zealand Coleoptera. Welllington: 1880-93. 7 parts in 2 vols. 8vo. New cloth.
(Wheldon & Wesley) **£130 [≃ $231]**

Brown, Alfred
- Old Masterpieces in Surgery. Omaha: 1928. 1st edn. 263 pp. 57 plates. Orig bndg.
(Fye) **$225 [≃ £126]**

Brown, B.
- Astronomical Atlases, Maps & Charts. An Historical & General Guide. London: 1932. 200 pp. Frontis, 19 plates. Bds gilt, sl warped.
(Whitehart) **£40 [≃ $71]**

Brown, F. Martin & Heineman, Bernard
- Jamaica and its Butterflies. London: 1972. Sm 4to. xv,478 pp. 11 cold plates. Endpaper maps. Dw (soiled & sl worn).
(Francis Edwards) **£35 [≃ $62]**

Brown, George
- The Surgery of Oral Diseases and Malformations. Phila: 1912. 1st edn. 740 pp. Num ills. Orig bndg. *(Fye)* **$250 [≃ £140]**
- The Surgery of Oral and Facial Diseases and Malformations: their Diagnosis and Treatment including Plastic Surgical Reconstruction. Phila: 1938. 4th edn. 778 pp. Orig bndg. *(Fye)* **$75 [≃ £42]**

Brown, Harold
- Rubber. Its Sources, Cultivation, and Preparation. London: Murray, Imperial Institute Handbooks, 1914. 1st edn. 8vo. xiii, 245 pp. 12 plates. Orig cloth, sl stained.
(Fenning) **£24.50 [≃ $45]**

Brown, Henry T.
- Five Hundred and Seven Mechanical Movements. Embracing all those which are most important in Dynamics, Hydraulics, Hydrostatics, Pneumatics, Steam Engines ... New York: Brown, Coombs, 1868. 1st edn. Sq 8vo. 122,[10 advt] pp. 507 ills. Orig cloth, sl frayed. *(Karmiole)* **$50 [≃ £28]**

Brown, J.B. & Brown, Buckminster
- Club-Foot, Spinal Curvatures, and Analagous Affections. Boston: 1860. 1st edn. 33 pp. 15 w'cut ills. Orig wraps. *(Fye)* **$125 [≃ £70]**

Brown, J.B. & McDowell, F.
- Neck Dissections. Springfield: 1954. 1st edn. 163 pp. Ills. Dw. *(Fye)* **$50 [≃ £28]**
- Plastic Surgery of the Nose. St. Louis: 1951. 1st edn. 427 pp. Orig bndg. *(Fye)* **$75 [≃ £42]**
- Skin Grafting. Phila: 1949. 2nd edn. 339 pp. 239 ills. Orig bndg. *(Fye)* **$50 [≃ £28]**
- Skin Grafting. Phila: 1949. 3rd edn. 411 pp. Num ills. Orig bndg. *(Fye)* **$60 [≃ £34]**

Brown, J.E.
- A Practical Treatise on Tree Culture in South Australia. Adelaide: 1886. 3rd edn. 8vo. ix,116 pp. 10 plates. Wraps, ex-lib.
(Wheldon & Wesley) **£25 [≃ $45]**

Brown, J.W.
- Congenital Heart Disease. London: 1950. 2nd edn. xiii,344 pp. 128 ills. Orig bndg.
(Whitehart) **£15 [≃ $27]**

Brown, James
- The Forester, a Practical Treatise on the Planting, Rearing and General Management of Forest Trees. London: 1851. 2nd edn. 8vo. xiv, 526 pp. 16 text figs. Orig cloth.
(Henly) **£32 [≃ $57]**
- The Forester, or, a Practical Treatise on the Planting, Rearing, and General Management of Forest-Trees. Fifth Edition - Enlarged and Improved. Edinburgh: 1882. Roy 8vo. xiv, 898, [1] pp. Fldg plate, 4 fldg tables, 185 ills. Lacks a blank flyleaf. Orig cloth.
(Fenning) **£48.50 [≃ $87]**

Brown, Leslie
- British Birds of Prey. A Study of Britain's 24 Diurnal Raptors. London: New Naturalist, 1976. 1st edn. 8vo. xiii,400 pp. 16 plates. Dw.
(Francis Edwards) **£35 [≃ $62]**

Brown, Leslie & Amadon, Dean
- Eagles, Hawks and Falcons of the World. London: Country Life, 1968. 1st edn. 2 vols. Num ills. Pict box. *(Gough)* **£145 [≃ $258]**

Brown, Percy
- American Martyrs to Science through the Roentgen Rays. Springfield: 1936. 1st edn. 276 pp. Ills. Orig bndg. *(Fye)* **$100 [≃ £56]**

Brown, Robert, of the British Museum
- Miscellaneous Botanical Works. Edited by J.J. Bennett. London: Ray Society, 1866-68. 2 vols. 8vo. Orig cloth. With folio Atlas of 38 plates. Perf stamp on plate margs. New cloth.
(Wheldon & Wesley) **£180 [≃ $320]**

Brown, Robert, M.A., Ph.D.
- Our Earth and its Story. A Popular Treatise
on Physical Geography ... London: Cassell,
[after 1886]. Lge 8vo. viii,376 pp. 12 cold
plates, 200 w'cut ills. Few sl marks. Free
endpapers replaced, frontis reinserted. Orig
gilt illust cloth.   *(Bow Windows)* **£40 [≈ $71]**

Brown, Thomas, 1778-1820
- Lectures on the Philosophy of the Human
Mind. With a Memoir of the Author by the
Rev. David Welsh. Edinburgh: 1830. 8vo.
692 pp. Port. Contemp half calf.
    (Robertshaw) **£36 [≈ $64]**

Brown, Thomas, Captain
- The Book of Butterflies, Sphinxes and
Moths. London & Edinburgh: Whittaker,
Constable's Miscellany, 1832-34. 1st edn. 3
vols. 12mo. 3 vignettes, 144 hand cold plates.
Orig cloth, paper labels, vol 3 sl rubbed.
    (Egglishaw) **£140 [≈ $249]**
- The Book of Butterflies, Sphinxes and
Moths. Vol 1 [only, of 3]. London: 1832. Sm
8vo. x, 216 pp. Title vignette (foxed), plate of
larvae, 59 hand cold plates of butterflies. 1
text leaf soiled. Cloth, rather soiled, recased,
new endpapers.
    (Wheldon & Wesley) **£70 [≈ $125]**
- Illustrations of the Land and Freshwater
Conchology of Great Britain and Ireland ...
London: Smith, Elder, 1845. Roy 8vo. xi,144
pp. 27 hand cold plates. Orig cloth (spine
ends worn).   *(Egglishaw)* **£160 [≈ $285]**
- Illustrations of the Recent Conchology of
Great Britain and Ireland. London: [1844].
2nd edn. 4to. xiii,144 pp. 62 plain plates.
Water stain on crnr of 3 plates & 2 ff of text.
New cloth.
    (Wheldon & Wesley) **£150 [≈ $267]**
- Illustrations of the Recent Conchology of
Great Britain and Ireland ... London: Smith,
Elder, 1844. Roy 4to. xv,144 pp. 62 hand
cold plates (1-59, 18*, 28*, 30*). New qtr
calf.   *(Egglishaw)* **£1,100 [≈ $1,958]**

Brown, W.R.
- The Horse of the Desert. An Authoritative
Book on the Arabian Horse. New York:
Derrydale Press, 1929. One of 750. Lge 4to.
218 pp. Ills. Orig bndg.
    (Trophy Room Books) **$1,100 [≈ £618]**

Browne, D.J.
- The Trees of America ... Pictorially and
Botanically Delineated. New York: (1846)
1851. Roy 8vo. xii,520 pp. Num ills. 2 pp sl
soiled. Trifle foxed. Mod half mor.
    (Wheldon & Wesley) **£60 [≈ $107]**

Browne, Edward
- Arabian Medicine. Cambridge: 1921. 1st edn.
138 pp. Orig bndg.   *(Fye)* **$100 [≈ £56]**

Browne, M.
- Practical Taxidermy. London: Upcott Gill,
(1884). 2nd edn, rvsd & enlgd. 8vo. Plates,
text figs. Orig dec cloth.
    (Egglishaw) **£22 [≈ $39]**

Browne, Sir Thomas
- Posthumous Works ... Printed from his
Original Manuscripts ... To which is prefix'd
his Life. London: E. Curll & R. Gosling,
1712. 8vo. [iv],xl,[ii], 74,[iv],8, 16,56,64 pp.
Port, 22 plates. Some plates damp stained.
Contemp panelled calf, rebacked, crnrs rprd.
    (Clark) **£225 [≈ $401]**
- Pseudodoxia Epidemica: or, Enquiries into
very many received Truths. London: T.H. for Edward
Dod, 1646. 1st edn. Sm folio. [xx],386 pp.
Licence leaf. Sm worm hole. Contemp sheep,
rebacked. Crack in upper jnt. Wing B.5159.
    (Burmester) **£350 [≈ $623]**
- Pseudodoxia Epidemica: or, Enquiries into
very many Received Tenents, and commonly
presumed Truths ... London: Harper for
Dod, 1646. 1st edn. Sm folio. [20],386 pp.
Final blank. Text within double rules. Orig
(?) panelled calf, v sl worn.
    (Goodrich) **$1,250 [≈ £702]**
- Pseudodoxia Epidemica: or Enquiries into
very many received Tenents, and commonly
presumed Truths. London: T.H. for Edward
Dod, 1646. 1st edn. Folio. A1 blank present.
Title laid down & reprd. Minor marg fraying
few ff. Mod qtr calf. Wing B.5159.
    (Waterfield's) **£375 [≈ $668]**
- Pseudodoxia Epidemica ... The Second
Edition, Corrected and much Enlarged by the
Author ... London: Miller ..., 1650. Sm folio.
[8],329,[5] pp. Sl browning. Later calf, gilt
inner dentelles.   *(Goodrich)* **$795 [≈ £447]**
- Pseudodoxia Epidemica: or, Enquiries into
Very many Received Tenents ... Second
Edition ... enlarged ... London: 1650. Folio.
8 ff, 329,[11] pp. Title dusty. Mod mor. Wing
B.5160.   *(Hemlock)* **$375 [≈ £211]**
- Religio Medici. The Seventh Edition,
Corrected and Amended. With Annotations
... also Observations By Sir Kenelm Digby ...
London: 1678. 8vo. [xvi],181, [ix], 185-371,
[3] pp. Frontis (edges sl chipped). Contemp
calf, rebacked, crnrs sl worn. Wing B.5177.
    (Clark) **£110 [≈ $196]**
- The Works ... London: Bassett, Chiswell ...,
1686. 1st coll edn. Folio. [xviii], 316, [xii],
[xiv],102,[viii], 52,[vi], "103" [ie 73], [v] pp.

Port frontis, 2 engvd ills. Final index leaf sl frayed, no loss. Contemp calf, rebacked, extrs sl worn. Wing B.5150. *(Clark)* **£450 [≈ $801]**

- The Works. Edited by Simon Wilkin. London: Bohn, 1852. 3 vols. 8vo. Frontis port (sl browned). Orig blue cloth, spines sl faded. *(David White)* **£65 [≈ $116]**

Browne, W.A.F.
- Morbid Appetite of the Insane. Reprinted from the Journal of Psychological Medicine for October 1875. London: Smith, Elder, 1875. 8vo. 15 pp. Orig wraps, sl dusty. *(Jarndyce)* **£15 [≈ $27]**

Bruce, John
- Description of a Pocket-Dial made for Robert Devereux, Earl of Essex, in 1593. London: 1867. 1st sep edn. 4to. [ii],18 pp. Plate. Orig wraps, frayed. *(Bow Windows)* **£25 [≈ $45]**

Bruel, Walter
- Praxis Medicinae, or, the Physician's Practice. London: William Sheares, 1632. 1st edn. Sm 4to. [iv],407,[4] pp. Contemp calf, rebacked, later endpapers. *(Bookpress)* **$1,250 [≈ £702]**

Brugis, Thomas
- Vade Mecum: or, a Companion for a Chirurgion ... The Third Edition, corrected ... London: J.S. for Tho. Williams, 1657. 8vo. 16 ff, 242 pp. Engvd frontis (margs restored). Lacks C3 (dedic) & last leaf of index. Contemp calf, rebacked. *(Hemlock)* **$550 [≈ £309]**

Brunings, W.
- Direct Laryngoscopy, Bronchoscopy, and Oesophagoscopy. Translated by W.G. Howarth. London: 1912. xiv,370 pp. 114 text ills. Orig bndg, lib label on cvr. *(Whitehart)* **£25 [≈ $45]**

Brunschwig, A.
- The Surgery of Pancreatic Tumours. London: 1942. 421 pp. 1 plate, 123 text ills. Orig bndg. *(Whitehart)* **£15 [≈ $27]**

Brunton, T. Lauder
- Collected Papers on Circulation and Respiration. First Series, chiefly containing Laboratory Researches. London: 1906. 1st edn. 696 pp. Orig bndg. *(Fye)* **$200 [≈ £112]**
- Pharmacology and Therapeutics; or, Medicine Past and Present. London: 1880. 1st edn. 212 pp. Orig bndg. *(Fye)* **$125 [≈ £70]**

Brunton, Sir Thomas L.
- The Bible and Science. London: Macmillan, 1881. Only edn. 8vo. 2 plates, 180 ills. Orig cloth. *(Fenning)* **£45 [≈ $80]**

Bruwer, Andre
- Classic Descriptions in Diagnostic Roentgenology. Springfield: 1964. 2 vols. 2059 pp. 1405 ills. Ex-lib. Orig bndgs. *(Fye)* **$200 [≈ £112]**

Bryan, Margaret
- A Compendious System of Astronomy ... London: ptd by C. & W. Galabin ..., 1805. 3rd edn, rvsd. xxii,[ii], 398,[2 advt] pp. Port frontis, 17 plates. Sev lib stamps. Contemp qtr calf, rebacked. *(Francis Edwards)* **£150 [≈ $267]**

Bryant, Joseph
- Manual of Operative Surgery. New York: 1884. 1st edn. 2 vols. 593 pp. 705 w'cut ills. Orig bndg. *(Fye)* **$125 [≈ £70]**

Bryant, W.W.
- A History of Astronomy. London: 1907. 1st edn. xiv,355 pp. 35 plates. Occas sl foxing. Cloth sl marked. *(Whitehart)* **£15 [≈ $27]**

Bryden, H.A. (editor)
- Great and Small Game of Africa ... London: Rowland Ward, 1899. One of 500, sgnd by the publisher. 4to. xx,612 pp. 15 hand cold plates (rather foxed). Half mor gilt, trifle faded. *(Wheldon & Wesley)* **£1,000 [≈ $1,780]**

Buch'hoz, Pierre Joseph
- The Toilet of Flora; or, a Collection of the most simple and approved Methods of Preparing Baths, Essences, Pomatums, Powders, Perfumes and Sweet-Scented Waters ... New Edition, improved. London: 1779. 12mo. Half-title. Frontis. Mod mor. Anon. *(Robertshaw)* **£165 [≈ $294]**

Buchan, A.
- A Handy Book of Meteorology. Edinburgh & London: 1867. [vi],204 pp. 5 plates, 53 text diags. Orig bndg, spine faded, sl worn. *(Whitehart)* **£25 [≈ $45]**

Buchan, William
- Advice to Mothers, on the Subject of their own Health; and on the Means for Promoting the Health, Strength and Beauty of their Offspring. London: Cadell & Davies, 1802. 1st edn. 8vo. 419 pp. New half calf. *(Goodrich)* **$395 [≈ £222]**

- Advice to Mothers, on the Subject of their own Health; and on the Means for Promoting the Health, Strength and Beauty of their Offspring. Phila: John Bioren, 1804. 1st Amer edn. 8vo. Orig mottled calf, bowed, new endpapers. *(Goodrich)* **$325 [≈ £183]**
- Domestic Medicine; or, The Family Physician. Edinburgh: Balfour, Auld, & Smellie, 1769. 1st edn. 8vo. xv,[i],624 pp. Browned. Later bds.
(Bookpress) **$400 [≈ £225]**
- Domestic Medicine. or, a Treatise on the Prevention and Cure of Diseases ... The Second Edition, with considerable additions ... London: 1772. 8vo. xxxvi,758 pp. Contemp half calf, worn.
(Goodrich) **$250 [≈ £140]**
- Domestic Medicine ... Carefully Corrected from the latest (8th) London Edition ... Phila: Joseph Cruikshank, 1784. 8vo. 540 pp. Some foxing & browning. Contemp calf, worn, jnts weak, sm piece missing from spine.
(Goodrich) **$150 [≈ £84]**
- Domestic Medicine ... Eighth Edition, Corrected and Enlarged. London: Strahan ..., 1784. xxxvi, 767, index pp. Lower marg last 4 index ff wormed. Few margs sl thumbed. Calf. *(Francis Edwards)* **£85 [≈ $151]**
- Domestic Medicine ... Fifteenth Edition: To which is added Observations concerning the Diet of the Common People ... London: Strahan & Cadell, 1797. 8vo. xl,746,(36) pp. Orig tree calf, sl rubbed.
(Goodrich) **$145 [≈ £81]**
- Domestic Medicine ... With Observations on Sea-bathing ... added A Dispensatory. From the Twenty-second English Edition with considerable additions. Exeter: Williams, 1828. 8vo. 496,xlviii pp. Foxed, early damp stain. New cloth. *(Goodrich)* **$95 [≈ £53]**

Buchanan, H.
- Nature into Art. A Treasury of Great Natural History Books. London: Weidenfeld & Nicolson, 1979. 4to. 220 pp. 124 ills (60 cold). Orig cloth. Dw.
(Egglishaw) **£35 [≈ $62]**

Buchanan, Joseph
- The Philosophy of Human Nature. Richmond: John A. Grimes, 1812. 1st edn. [viii],336 pp. Some foxing. Contemp calf, sl rubbed & scraped. *(Gach)* **$285 [≈ £160]**

Bucher, Elmer E.
- Vacuum Tubes in Wireless Communication. New York: Wireless Press, 1918. 1st edn. 8vo. viii, 174 pp. Ills. Orig bndg, spine faded.
(Schoen) **$85 [≈ £48]**

Buchwald, V.F.
- Handbook of Iron Meteorites. Their History, Distribution, Composition and Structure. Los Angeles: California UP, 1975. 3 vols. 4to. 2124 text figs. Orig cloth. Slipcase.
(Gemmary) **$175 [≈ £98]**

Buck, Albert
- A Treatise on Hygiene and Public Health. New York: 1879. 1st edn. 2 vols. 792; 657 pp. Some sections loose. Ex-lib. Shaken, inner hinges cracked. *(Fye)* **$100 [≈ £56]**

Buck, George Watson
- A Practical and Theoretical Essay on Oblique Bridges. Second Edition, Corrected ... London: John Weale, 1857. Roy 8vo. v, [2], 56 pp. 13 fldg plates. Bds.
(Fenning) **£85 [≈ $151]**
- A Practical and Theoretical Essay on Oblique Bridges. Second Edition ... London: 1857. Imperial 8vo. vii,56 pp. 13 fldg plates. Orig dec cloth, paper label. *(Weiner)* **£50 [≈ $89]**
- A Practical and Theoretical Essay on Oblique Bridges. Third Edition, revised by his son, J.H. Watson Buck ... London: 1880. 8vo. vii,76 pp. 13 fldg plates. Orig cloth, worn.
(Weiner) **£40 [≈ $71]**

Buckland, William
- Geology and Mineralogy considered with reference to Natural Theology. London: 1836. 1st edn. 2 vols. Cold map, fldg plates. Few lib marks. Leather, scuffed.
(Key Books) **£135 [≈ £76]**
- Geology and Mineralogy considered with reference to Natural Theology. London: William Pickering, 1836. 2 vols. 8vo. xv,468; vii,131 pp. Hand cold fldg plate, 87 b/w plates. Orig cloth, vol 1 unopened, vol 2 1 crnr water stained. *(Gemmary)* **$200 [≈ £112]**
- Geology and Mineralogy. London: Pickering, 1837. 2nd edn. 2 vols. 8vo. xvi,619; vii,129 pp. Ctlg. 87 plates. Orig cloth.
(Egglishaw) **£160 [≈ $285]**
- Geology and Mineralogy Considered with reference to Natural Theology. London: 1837. 2nd edn. 2 vols. 8vo. xvi,619; 4,ix,129 pp. Hand cold fldg section, 87 plain plates. Orig cloth. *(Henly)* **£85 [≈ $151]**
- Reliquiae Diluvianae; or, Observations on the Organic Remains contained in Caves ... London: 1823. 4to. viii,303 pp. 27 plates inc 2 cold maps & cold fldg sections, fldg table. Lib stamps on back of plates. Few plates sl foxed. Half calf, rebacked.
(Weiner) **£185 [≈ $329]**
- Reliquiae Diluvianae ... London: 1824. 2nd edn. 4to. viii,303 pp. 27 plates & maps (3

cold), fldg table. Cuttings on endpapers. Title
v sl foxed. Half calf. *(Weiner)* **£180 [≈ $320]**

Buckler, W.
- The Larvae of the British Butterflies and
Moths. Edited by H.T. Stainton and G.T.
Porritt. London: Ray Society, 1886-1901. 9
vols. 8vo. 164 cold plates. Cloth, 3 vols faded.
(Wheldon & Wesley) **£450 [≈ $801]**
- The Larvae of the British Butterflies and
Moths. Edited by H.T. Stainton and G.T.
Porritt. London: Ray Society, 1886-1901. 9
vols in 5. 8vo. 164 cold plates. Half mor.
(Wheldon & Wesley) **£500 [≈ $890]**
- The Larvae of the British Butterflies and
Moths. London: Ray Society, 1886-1901. 9
vols. 8vo. 164 hand cold plates. Orig cloth
gilt, t.e.g. [With] Haggett, G.M. Larvae of
the British Lepidoptera not figured by
Buckler. London: Brit Ent & Nat Hist Soc,
1981. 35 cold plates.
(Egglishaw) **£660 [≈ $1,175]**

Bucknall, Thomas Skip Dyot
- The Orchardist: or, A System of Close
Pruning and Medication, for establishing the
Science of Orcharding ... London: ptd by
William Bulmer, 1805. 2nd edn. Disbound.
(Jarndyce) **£85 [≈ $151]**

Bucknill, John
- The Psychology of Shakespeare. London:
1859. 1st edn. 264 pp. Backstrip chipped &
defective. *(Fye)* **$150 [≈ £84]**

Bucknill, John Charles & Tuke, Daniel H.
- A Manual of Psychological Medicine ...
Phila: Blanchard & Lea, 1858. 1st Amer edn.
[iii]-536, [30 advt] pp. Litho frontis. Lib
stamps. Rec buckram. *(Caius)* **$300 [≈ £169]**
- A Manual of Psychological Medicine ...
Phila: Lindsay & Blakiston, 1879. xx,815 pp.
12 litho plates (4 cold). Ex-lib. Orig black
cloth, strengthened with tape.
(Caius) **$150 [≈ £84]**

Buckton, G.B.
- Monograph of the British Aphides. London:
Ray Society, 1876. 4 vols. 8vo. 141 hand cold
& 9 plain plates. Cloth, vols 1 & 2 faded, vol
1 sl worn. *(Wheldon & Wesley)* **£140 [≈ $249]**

Budge, Sir E.A. Wallis
- Amulets and Talismans. New York:
University Books, 1961. Roy 8vo. xxxix,543
pp. 22 plates, 300 text figs. Orig bndg
(chipped). *(Gemmary)* **$40 [≈ £22]**
- The Divine Origin of the Craft of the
Herbalist. London: Society of Herbalists,

1928. 1st edn. 8vo. xii,96 pp. 13 plates & ills.
Orig cloth, v faded. *(Gough)* **£45 [≈ $80]**

Budgen, M.L.
- Episodes of Insect Life by Acheta Domestica
M.E.S. London: Reeve & Benham, 1849-51.
1st edn. 3 vols. 8vo. 3 frontis, engvd
vignettes. Orig dec cloth gilt, hd of 2 spines
sl frayed. *(Egglishaw)* **£95 [≈ $169]**
- Episodes of Insect Life. Edited and Revised
by the Rev. J.G. Wood. London: George Bell,
1879. Roy 8vo. xv,430 pp. Title vignette, 50
hand cold chapter headings, tail-pieces. Orig
dec cloth gilt, spine ends trifle worn.
(Egglishaw) **£60 [≈ $107]**

Bueren, H.G. van
- Imperfections in Crystals. Amsterdam: North
Holland Pub., 1961. 2nd edn. 8vo. xviii, 676
pp. Num ills. Cloth. *(Savona)* **£25 [≈ $45]**

Buffon, Georges Louis Leclerc, Comte de
- The System of Natural History ... Carefully
Abridged: and the Natural History of Insects
... Edinburgh: J. Ruthven & Sons, 1800. 2
vols. 8vo. viii,296; [iv],287 pp. 2 frontis, 64
plates. Period half russia, gilt spines.
(Rankin) **£100 [≈ $178]**

Buller, W.L.
- Birds of New Zealand. Edited and brought up
to date by E.G. Turbott. London: 1967.
Folio. xviii,261,[1] pp. 48 cold plates. Cloth.
(Wheldon & Wesley) **£55 [≈ $98]**

Bullinger, E.W.
- The Witness of the Stars. London: 1911. 3rd
edn. viii,204 pp. Fldg map, 41 plates, 5
engvs. 2 pp loose. Orig cloth gilt.
(Whitehart) **£25 [≈ $45]**

Bulloch, William
- The History of Bacteriology. Oxford: 1938.
8vo. 422 pp. Ex-lib. Orig cloth, rebacked. Lib
slipcase. *(Goodrich)* **$75 [≈ £42]**

Bumbury, C.J.F.
- Arboretum Notes. Notes on the Trees and
Shrubs cultivated at Barton - List of
Cultivated Ferns - Notes on Wild Plants ...
Mildenhall: Privately Printed, 1889. 8vo. 301
pp. Cloth, sl rubbed.
(Wheldon & Wesley) **£60 [≈ $107]**

Bunnell, Sterling
- Surgery of the Hand. Phila: 1944. 1st edn,
2nd printing. 734 pp. Orig bndg. Signed by
the author. *(Fye)* **$350 [≈ £197]**
- Surgery of the Hand. Phila: 1944. 1st edn,

3rd printing. 734 pp. Orig bndg.
(Fye) **$150 [≈£84]**
- Surgery of the Hand. Phila: 1956. 3rd edn.
1079 pp. Orig bndg,   *(Fye)* **$100 [≈£56]**

Bunyard, Edward A.
- Old Garden Roses. London: 1936. Roy 8vo.
xii, 163 pp. Cold frontis, 32 plates. Cloth.
(Wheldon & Wesley) **£45 [≈$80]**
- Old Garden Roses. London: Country Life,
1936. Lge 8vo. xii,163 pp. Cold frontis, 32
plates, ills. Orig cloth gilt.
(Hortulus) **$65 [≈£37]**

Burbridge, F.W.
- The Narcissus: Its History and Culture, with
Coloured Plates and Descriptions of all
Known Species ... London: 1875. Roy 8vo.
xvi, 95 pp. 48 hand cold plates. Occas sl
foxing. Half pigskin, sl rubbed.
(Wheldon & Wesley) **£500 [≈$890]**

Burbury, Samuel Hawksley
- A Treatise on the Kinetic Theory of Gases.
Cambridge: UP, 1899. 1st edn. 8vo. viii,158
pp. Orig cloth. Author's pres copy.
(Gaskell) **£20 [≈$36]**

Burch, G.E. & Winsor, T.
- A Primer of Electrocardiography. London:
1949. 2nd edn. 245 pp. Frontis, 265 ills.
B'plate. Spine faded. *(Whitehart)* **£15 [≈$27]**

Burgess, C.M.
- Cowries of the World. Cape Town: 1985. 4to.
xiv,289 pp. Cold ills. Bds.
(Wheldon & Wesley) **£76 [≈$135]**

Burgess, Renate
- Portraits of Doctors & Scientists in the
Wellcome Institute of the History of
Medicine. London: 1973. xxiv,459 pp. Ports.
Dw. *(Whitehart)* **£25 [≈$45]**
- Portraits of Doctors and Scientists in the
Wellcome Institute of the History of
Medicine. London: 1973. 1st edn. Sm folio.
459 pp. Ills. Dw. *(Robertshaw)* **£20 [≈$36]**

Burgh, N.P.
- A Treatise on Sugar Machinery: including
the Process of producing Sugar from the Cane
... London: 1863. Lge 4to. ii,64 pp. 16 plates.
Orig cloth, crnrs worn, rebacked with leather.
(Weiner) **£200 [≈$356]**

Burkill, Isaac H.
- A Dictionary of the Economic Products of the
Malay Peninsula ... London: 1935. 2 vols.
Roy 8vo. Orig buckram gilt, sl marked.

(Fenning) **£85 [≈$151]**

Burmeister, H.
- A Manual of Entomology. Translated by
W.E. Shuckard. London: 1836. 8vo. xii,654
pp. 33 plates (8 cold). Half calf, trifle used.
(Wheldon & Wesley) **£50 [≈$89]**

Burnet, E.
- Microbes & Toxins. London: 1912. xvi,304
pp. Frontis port, ills. Prelims sl foxed. Orig
bndg. *(Whitehart)* **£25 [≈$45]**

Burnet, Thomas
- The Sacred Theory of the Earth ... Sixth
Edition, to which is added the Author's
Defence of the Work ... London: 1726. 2 vols.
8vo. Frontis port, addtnl engvd title, fldg
plate, text ills. Ex-lib. Contemp calf, v worn,
1 bd detached. *(Weiner)* **£100 [≈$178]**

Burnett, G.T.
- An Encyclopaedia of Useful and Ornamental
Plants ... used in the Arts, in Medicine, and
for Ornament. New Edition by M.A. Burnett.
London: 1852. 2 vols. 4to. 260 hand cold
plates. Few marg reprs. Vol 1 title in facs.
Half mor.
(Wheldon & Wesley) **£2,800 [≈$4,984]**

Burns, Allen
- Observations on the Surgical Anatomy of the
Head and Neck, illustrated by Cases and
Engravings. First American Edition. With a
Life of the Author ... by Granville Sharp
Pattison. Baltimore: Toy, 1823. 8vo. xxix,
31-512, [1] pp. 10 plates. Lib stamps.
Contemp sheep. *(Hemlock)* **$300 [≈£169]**

Burr, Anna R.
- Weir Mitchell, his Life and Letters. New
York: 1929. 1st edn. 424 pp. Orig bndg.
(Fye) **$60 [≈£34]**

Burr, W.H.
- Ancient and Modern Engineering and the
Isthmian Canal. New York: 1902. xv,473 pp.
2 fldg plates, text ills. Orig cloth.
(Whitehart) **£25 [≈$45]**

Burrell, H.
- The Platypus: its Discovery, Zoological
Position, Form and Characteristics, etc.
Sydney: 1927. 8vo. viii,227 pp. 35 plates (1
cold). Good ex-lib. Cloth.
(Wheldon & Wesley) **£50 [≈$89]**

Burridge, John
- The Naval Dry Rot. An Address to the

British Navy, Ship-Builders, Owners, and Merchants ... Remedies, by Native Substitutes for Oak Bark ... London: 1824. 8vo. xxvi, 136, [3 advt] pp. Title sl chipped & soiled. Disbound.
(Francis Edwards) **£100 [≈ $178]**

Burrow, Edward John
- Elements of Conchology, according to the Linnaean System. London: James Duncan, 1825. 8vo. xix,245,[2] pp. 25 hand cold & 3 plain plates. Contemp half calf.
(Egglishaw) **£140 [≈ $249]**
- Elements of Conchology, according to the Linnaean System ... New Edition. London: 1825. 8vo. (iii)-(xxii), 245,[3] pp. 28 uncold plates. Few sl marks. Orig cloth, spine ends sl fingered.   *(Bow Windows)* **£50 [≈ $89]**

Burt, T. Seymour
- Miscellaneous Papers on Scientific Subjects, written chiefly in India. London: for the author, 1837. 8vo. [xii],190,[4 insert] pp. 3 fldg plates, text ills. Orig cloth, cvrs sl stained & bubbled.   *(Rankin)* **£75 [≈ $134]**

Burton, John
- A Treatise on the Non-Naturals ... subjoin'd, A Short Essay on the Chin-Cough ... York: ptd by A. Staples ..., 1738. 1st edn. 8vo. [ii],xxiii, [i],367 pp. Contemp calf, rebacked to style, new endpapers.
(Finch) **£400 [≈ $712]**

Burton, W.K.
- Practical Guide to Photographic & Photo-Mechanical Printing. Second Edition Revised and Enlarged. London: Marion & Co., 1892. xvii,415,46 advt pp. Half-title. Orig red cloth.
(Jermy & Westerman) **£50 [≈ $89]**

Burton, W.K. & Dumbleton, J.E.
- The Water Supply of Towns and the Construction of Waterworks, a Practical Treatise ... Fourth Edition. London: 1928. 2 vols. Lge 8vo. Frontis, 40 fldg plates, ca 250 text figs. Orig cloth.
(Bow Windows) **£125 [≈ $223]**

Burtt, Philip
- Control on the Railways. A Study in Methods. London: 1926. 1st edn. 8vo. 255 pp. 43 plates. Endpapers sl spotted. Dw (worn).   *(Francis Edwards)* **£25 [≈ $45]**

Bushnan, John Stevenson
- Hints on Certifying in Cases of Insanity. Salisbury: Frederick A. Blake, [1862]. 16 pp. Ptd wraps.   *(C.R. Johnson)* **£60 [≈ $107]**

Butler, A.G.
- Foreign Birds for Cage and Aviary. London: [1908-10]. 2 vols. Cr 4to. Num ills. Cloth, vol 2 trifle worn.
(Wheldon & Wesley) **£40 [≈ $71]**
- Foreign Finches in Captivity. London: 1899. 2nd edn. Roy 8vo. viii,317 pp. 60 cold plates. New cloth.
(Wheldon & Wesley) **£130 [≈ $231]**

Butler, Colin G.
- The World of the Honeybee. London: 1954. 1st edn. xiv,226 pp. Ills. Dw (sm tear).
(Francis Edwards) **£35 [≈ $62]**

Butler, Sir E.J. & Jones, S.G.
- Plant Pathology. London: Macmillan, 1955. 8vo. 979 pp. 435 text figs. Name, b'plate. Edges sl spotted. Buckram.
(Savona) **£25 [≈ $45]**

Butschli, Otto
- Investigation on Microscopic Foams and on Protoplasm. London: Black, 1894. 1st English edn. 8vo. xvi,379,[4 advt] pp. 12 litho plates, 23 text figs. Cloth, spine faded with some wear.   *(Savona)* **£30 [≈ $53]**

Buxton, J.
- The Redstart. London: Collins New Naturalist, 1950. 8vo. xii,180 pp. Ills. Orig cloth, faded. Dw (torn).
(Wheldon & Wesley) **£25 [≈ $45]**

Buxton, P.A.
- The Natural History of Tsetse Flies. London: 1955. Cr 4to. xviii,816 pp. 47 plates, text figs. Cloth.   *(Wheldon & Wesley)* **£35 [≈ $62]**

Byrne, Oliver
- Dual Arithmetic, a New Art. London: 1863. 1st edn. 8vo. xl,244 pp. Diags, tables. Orig cloth, spine faded & torn. A further vol was published in 1867.   *(Weiner)* **£38 [≈ $68]**

Bywater, John
- An Essay on the History, Practice, and Theory, of Electricity. London: for the author ..., 1810. Only edn. 8vo. [2],iii, [2], 127 pp. 2 fldg plates. Orig bds, uncut, rebacked.
(Fenning) **£110 [≈ $196]**
- An Essay on the History, Practice, and Theory, of Electricity. London: for the author ..., 1810. Only edn. 8vo. [2],iii, [2], 127 pp. 2 fldg plates. Early half calf.
(Fenning) **£85 [≈ $151]**

Cabot, Richard
- Training and Rewards of the Physician.

Phila: 1918. 1st edn. 153 pp. Orig bndg.
(Fye) **$75 [≃ £42]**

Cadogan, William
- A Dissertation on the Gout, and all Chronic Diseases ... Seventh Edition. London: Dodsley, 1771. 8vo. 100 pp. half-title. Contemp calf backed bds, some worming to hd of spine extending to last gathering, extrs rubbed.   *(Frew Mackenzie)* **£110 [≃ $196]**
- A Dissertation on the Gout, and all Chronic Diseases ... Addressed to all Invalids. The Third Edition. London: Dodsley, 1771. 8vo. x,[1],12-99 pp. Lacks half-title. Later wraps.
(Spelman) **£45 [≃ $80]**

Caelius Aurelianus
- On Acute Diseases and on Chronic Diseases. Chicago: 1950. 1019 pp. Dw.
(Fye) **$125 [≃ £70]**

Cajal, S.R.
- The Structure of Ammon's Horn. Springfield: 1968. xxii,78 pp. Few figs. Orig bndg.   *(Whitehart)* **£25 [≃ $45]**

Cajori, F.
- Sir Isaac Newton's Mathematical Principles of Natural Philosophy and his System of the World. Berkeley: 1960. 2nd English edn. xxxvi, 680 pp. Frontis port, plate, ills. Dw (sl torn & stained).   *(Whitehart)* **£40 [≃ $71]**

Calderwood, Henry
- The Relations of Mind and Brain. London: Macmillan, 1892. 3rd edn. xxii,551 pp. Text ills. Orig cloth, somewhat worn.
(Caius) **$65 [≃ £37]**

Callcott, M.
- A Scripture Herbal. London: 1842. 8vo. xxiii, 544 pp. W'cuts. Calf gilt.
(Wheldon & Wesley) **£50 [≃ $89]**

Calmann, G.
- Ehret Flower Painter Extraordinary. An Illustrated Biography. Oxford: 1977. 1st edn. Lge 4to. 160 pp. 40 cold & num other ills. Orig cloth. Dw. *(Bow Windows)* **£50 [≃ $89]**

Calot, F.
- Indispensable Orthopaedics. London: 1914. 1st edn in English. 1175 pp. 1252 ills. Orig bndg.   *(Fye)* **£200 [≃ £112]**

Calvert, J.
- The Gold Rocks of Great Britain and Ireland. London: Chapman & Hall, 1853. 8vo. xx, 324,x pp. Rec leather.

(Gemmary) **$325 [≃ £183]**
- The Gold Rocks of Great Britain and Ireland, with a Treatise on the Geology of Gold. London: 1853. 8vo. xx,324,2,x pp. Rec calf.
(Henly) **£150 [≃ $267]**

Camac, C.N.B.
- Epoch-Making Contributions to Medicine, Surgery and the Allied Sciences. Phila: 1909. 1st edn. 435 pp. Ex-lib. Orig bndg.
(Fye) **$60 [≃ £34]**

Cameron, G.R.
- Pathology of the Cell. Edinburgh: Oliver & Boyd, 1952. 1st edn. 8vo. xv,840 pp. 64 plates, 41 text figs. Cloth, some wear & marks.   *(Savona)* **£30 [≃ $53]**
- Pathology of the Cell. London: 1952. 1st edn. xv,840 pp. 64 plates, 41 text figs. Orig bndg.
(Whitehart) **£35 [≃ $62]**

Cameron, James Ross
- Motion Pictures with Sound. Manhattan Beach: Cameron, 1929. 1st edn. 12mo. 303 pp. Ills. Orig bndg, sm tear hd of spine.
(Schoen) **$45 [≃ £25]**

Cameron, P.
- A Monograph of the British Phytophagous Hymenoptera. London: Ray Society, 1882-93. 4 vols. 8vo. 84 plates (55 hand cold). Orig cloth gilt.   *(Egglishaw)* **£160 [≃ $285]**

Campbell, Edwin
- Zeppelins. The Past and Future. St. Albans: Campfield Press, 1918. 8vo. 43,[1] pp. 8 ills. Orig pict wraps, back wrapper dusty.
(Georges) **£50 [≃ $89]**

Campbell, F.R.
- The Language of Medicine: a Manual giving the Origin, Etymology, Pronunciation and Meaning of the Technical Terms found in Medical Literature. New York: 1888. 1st edn. 318 pp. Ex-lib. Orig bndg.
(Fye) **$125 [≃ £70]**

Campbell, Meredith
- Clinical Pediatric Urology ... Phila: W.B. Saunders, 1951. 1st edn. 8vo. xiii,1113 pp. 543 figs. Orig cloth.
(David White) **£20 [≃ $36]**

Campbell, Norman Robert
- Modern Electrical Theory. Cambridge: UP, 1913. 2nd edn. 8vo. xii,400 pp. Orig cloth.
(Gaskell) **£15 [≃ $27]**

Campbell, R.
- The London Tradesman. Being a Compendious View of all the Trades, Professions, Arts, both Liberal and Mechanic, now practised ... London: T. Gardner, 1747. 1st edn. 8vo. xii, 340 pp. Sl soiling, sl wear. Contemp calf, spine ends worn. *(Burmester)* **£450 [≈ $801]**

Canavan, Myrtelle
- Elmer Ernest Southard and his Parents. A Brain Study. Cambridge: 1925. Lge 4to. 29 pp. 6 plates. Ex-lib. Orig bndg.
(Goodrich) **$75 [≈ £42]**

Carey, George C.
- 500 Useful and Amusing Experiments in the Arts and Manufactures; with Observations on the Properties of the Substances employed ... London: 1822. 8vo. v,[xix],306 pp. 39 ills on 4 plates (1 fldg). Some marks. Old bds, worn, new leather spine. *(Weiner)* **£200 [≈ $356]**

Carey, Matthew
- A Short Account of the Malignant Fever, lately prevalent in Philadelphia ... Second Edition. Phila: the author, 1793. 8vo. viii, (9)-103, (10) pp. Disbound.
(Hemlock) **$200 [≈ £112]**

Carmichael, Richard
- An Essay on Venereal Diseases, and the Uses and Abuses of Mercury in their Treatment. Illustrated by Drawings of the Different Forms of Venereal Eruptions. London: 1825. 2nd edn. xvi,376 pp. 5 fldg cold plates. Occas sm lib stamp. Bds, uncut, rebacked.
(Francis Edwards) **£150 [≈ $267]**

Carmichael, Robert
- A Treatise on the Calculus of Operations ... London: Longman, 1855. 1st edn. 8vo.. xii, 110, 24 advt pp. Errata leaf. Orig cloth, spine & stitching worn. *(Gaskell)* **£20 [≈ $36]**

Carnot, N.-L.-S.
- Reflections on the Motive Power of Heat and on Machines fitted to develop that Power, from the Original French ... Edited by R.H. Thurston. London: 1890. 1st English edn. 8vo. xiii,260 pp. Port. Flyleaf cut away. Orig cloth. *(Weiner)* **£50 [≈ $89]**

Carpenter, William B.
- Animal Physiology ... New Edition, carefully revised. London: W.S. Orr, 1848. 8vo. [2],xii,579 pp. 287 ills. Orig cloth, sm tear 1 jnt. *(Fenning)* **£32.50 [≈ $59]**
- Introduction to the Study of the

Foraminifera. London: Ray Society, 1862. Folio. xxii,319 pp. 22 litho plates. Stamp on title. Orig bds. *(Egglishaw)* **£46 [≈ $82]**
- Is Man an Automaton? A Lecture delivered in the City Hall, Glasgow, on 23rd February 1875 ... London: William Collins, 1875. 32 pp. Ills. Disbound. *(Jarndyce)* **£20 [≈ $36]**
- Mesmerism, Spiritualism etc. Historically & Scientifically Considered. London: 1877. 1st edn. Orig bds. *(Deja Vu)* **£45 [≈ $80]**
- The Microscope and its Revelations. London: Churchill, 1862. 3rd edn. 8vo. xxiv, 792 pp. 10 plates (margs of 1 plate reprd), 395 text figs. Rebound in cloth. *(Savona)* **£45 [≈ $80]**
- The Microscope and its Revelations. London: Churchill, 1875. 5th edn. 8vo. xxxii, 848 pp. 25 plates, 449 text figs. Prelims sl foxed. Rebound in buckram. *(Savona)* **£40 [≈ $71]**
- The Microscope and its Revelations. Seventh Edition, by W.H. Dallinger. London: 1891. 8vo. xviii,1099 pp. 21 plates (7 cold), num text figs. Orig cloth, trifle worn.
(Wheldon & Wesley) **£50 [≈ $89]**
- The Microscope and its Revelations. Sixth Edition ... New York: Wood, 1883. 2 vols. 8vo. 388; 354 pp. Plates, ills. Orig bndgs.
(Goodrich) **$85 [≈ £48]**
- Vegetable Physiology and Botany ... Second, revised edition. London: W.S. Orr, 1847. 8vo. viii,[4], [v]-viii, 576 pp. 202 ills. Orig cloth, inner hinges cracked but firm.
(Fenning) **£28.50 [≈ $52]**
- Zoology: a Systematic Account of the General Structure, Habits, Instincts, and Uses of the Principal Families of the Animal Kingdom. London: W.S. Orr, 1848-45. 2 vols. 8vo. [2],viii, 576; [2],vii, 587 pp. 632 ills. Orig cloth. *(Fenning)* **£35 [≈ $62]**

Carrington, Charles (editor)
- Untrodden Fields of Anthropology ... By a French Army-Surgeon. Paris: Librairie de Medicine, Folklore et Anthropologie, 1898. 2nd ltd edn. One of 1000. 2 vols. Lge 8vo. Orig cloth, gilt lettering faded.
(Hollett) **£75 [≈ $134]**

Carrington, Richard Christopher
- Observations of the Spots on the Sun from November 9, 1853, to March 24, 1861, made at Redhill. London: 1863. Roy 4to. 248 pp. 166 plates. Orig cloth, spine worn, front inner hinge shaken. Inscrbd by the author.
(Weiner) **£150 [≈ $267]**

Carter, J.M.G.
- Catarrhal Diseases of the Respiratory Passages. Chicago: 1895. 135 pp. Orig bndg.
(Whitehart) **£18 [≈ $32]**

Cartwright, Frederick
- The Development of Modern Surgery. New York: 1968. 1st edn. 323 pp. Dw.
(Fye) **$50 [≈ £28]**

Casey, Robert S. & Perry, James (editors)
- Punched Cards; Their Application to Science and Industry. New York: Reinhold, 1951. 1st edn. 8vo. 506 pp. Ills. Lib pocket. Orig dec bndg, sl rubbed.   *(Schoen)* **$65 [≈ £37]**

Caspar, M.
- Kepler. Translated by C.D. Hellman. London: 1959. 401 pp. Orig bndg.
(Whitehart) **£28 [≈ $50]**

Casper, Johann
- A Handbook of the Practice of Forensic Medicine, based upon Personal Experience. London: 1861-65. 4 vols. Orig bndgs.
(Fye) **$300 [≈ £169]**

Cassell (publishers)
- Cassell's Cyclopaedia of Mechanics. Containing Receipts, Processes, and Memoranda for Workshop Use ... Edited by P.N. Hasluck. Special Edition. London: n.d. 8 vols. Lge 8vo. 32 cold & 8 plain plates. Orig dec cloth gilt, some sl mottling.
(Bow Windows) **£80 [≈ $142]**
- Cassell's Popular Gardening ... see Fish, D.T. (ed.)

Castiglioni, Arturo
- A History of Medicine. New York: 1941. 1st edn. 1013 pp. Orig bndg. *(Fye)* **$150 [≈ £84]**

Catesby, Mark
- Select Essays on Husbandry. Extracted from the Museum Rusticum, and Foreign Essays in Agriculture ... Edinburgh: for John Balfour ..., 1767. viii,408 pp. 2 plates, fldg table. Sl foxing & creasing. Speckled calf gilt, rubbed, lacks labels. Anon.
(Francis Edwards) **£160 [≈ $285]**

Catlow, Agnes
- Drops of Water: their Marvellous and Beautiful Inhabitants displayed by the Microscope. London: Reeve & Benham, 1851. Sq 12mo. xviii,194 pp. 4 hand cold plates. Orig cloth, a.e.g., hd of spine worn.
(Egglishaw) **£30 [≈ $53]**

Catlow, Maria E.
- Popular British Entomology. New Edition. London: Routledge, 1860. Sm 8vo. x,280 pp. 16 cold plates. Orig cloth gilt, sl loose.
(Egglishaw) **£22 [≈ $39]**

Cattelle, W.R.
- The Diamond. New York: John Lane, 1911. 8vo. 433 pp. 24 plates. Orig cloth, sl shaken.
(Gemmary) **$75 [≈ £42]**

Cave, F.O. & MacDonald, J.D.
- Birds of the Sudan. Their Identification and Distribution. London: 1955. 8vo. xxvii, 444 pp. 12 cold plates, 2 maps, photo ills. Orig cloth, sl wear hd of spine.
(Wheldon & Wesley) **£185 [≈ $329]**

Cayley, Arthur
- The Collected Mathematical Papers. Cambridge: UP, 1889-1898. 14 vols inc index. 4to. Plates. Sm lib stamps on endpapers. Orig parchment backed bds, spines sl dusty, 2 spines sl scuffed.
(Gaskell) **£300 [≈ $534]**

Cayley, N.W.
- Australian Parrots. Their Habits in the Field and Aviary. Sydney: 1938. 8vo. xxviii, 332 pp. 11 cold plates, 19 ills. Cloth, trifle worn.
(Wheldon & Wesley) **£50 [≈ $89]**
- The Fairy Wrens of Australia. Blue Birds of Happiness. Sydney: 1949. Roy 8vo. vi,88 pp. 4 cold maps, 8 + 1 cold plates, 20 ills. Sl foxing. Cloth.
(Wheldon & Wesley) **£40 [≈ $71]**

Celsus
- A. Cornelius Celsus Of Medicine. Translated by J. Greive. Revised by G. Futvoye. London: 1838. 3rd edn. xxviii, 468 pp. Lib stamp on title. Three qtr leather, gilt spine.
(Whitehart) **£55 [≈ $98]**

Certain Ancient Tracts ...
- Certain Ancient Tracts concerning the Management of Landed Property. London: for C. Bathurst ..., 1767. [vi],100 pp. Sl browning. Speckled calf gilt, jnts sl worn.
(Francis Edwards) **£150 [≈ $267]**

Chalkley, A.P.
- Diesel Engines for Land and Marine Work. With an Introductory Chapter by Dr. Rudolf Diesel. London: Constable, 1912. 1st edn. 8vo. xii,226 pp. 15 fldg & 67 other figs. Half-title pasted down. Orig cloth, sl soiled & worn.   *(Claude Cox)* **£35 [≈ $62]**

Chambers, G.F.
- A Handbook of Descriptive and Practical Astronomy. I. The Sun, Planets and Comets. Oxford: 1889. Vol I only. 4th edn. xxxii,676 pp. Cold frontis, 252 figs. Cloth, marked & worn.   *(Whitehart)* **£35 [≈ $62]**

- The Story of the Comets Simply Told for General Readers. Oxford: 1909. xiii,[1],256 pp. 106 text figs (27 plates).
(Whitehart) **£25 [≈ $45]**
- The Story of the Comets. Oxford: 1909. xiii,256 pp. 106 ills. Dw (sl stained & torn).
(Whitehart) **£25 [≈ $45]**

Chambers, John
- A Pocket Herbal ... With some Remarks on Bathing, Electricity, &c. Bury: for the author by P. Gedge ..., 1800. 1st edn. 8vo. xx, [iv], 328 pp. Subscribers. Contemp calf, upper jnt tender.   *(Burmester)* **£125 [≈ $223]**

Chambers, Robert
- Vestiges of the Natural History of Creation. London: 1844. 2nd edn. 8vo. vi,394 pp. New qtr calf. Anon.   *(Weiner)* **£150 [≈ $267]**
- Vestiges of the Natural History of Creation, with a Sequel. New York: 1846. 12mo. 303 pp. Fldg table at p 116. Orig dec cloth, sl worn & soiled. Anon. *(Weiner)* **£75 [≈ $134]**
- Vestiges of the Natural History of Creation. London: 1847. 6th edn. 8vo. iv,512 pp. New cloth. Anon. *(Wheldon & Wesley)* **£60 [≈ $107]**
- Vestiges of the Natural History of Creation. London: 1860. 11th edn. 8vo. vi,286,64 pp. Ills. Occas soil. Orig dec green cloth, sl worn & shaken. Anon. *(Weiner)* **£75 [≈ $134]**
- Vestiges of the Natural History of Creation. With an Introduction relating to the Authorship of the Work by Alexander Ireland. London & Edinburgh: 1884. 12th edn. 8vo. xxxi, 418, lxxxiv pp. Port. Orig pict cloth gilt.   *(Weiner)* **£100 [≈ $178]**

Chandler, G.
- A Treatise on the Diseases of the Eye and their Remedies to which is prefixed the Anatomy of the Eye; the Theory of Vision; and the Several Species of Imperfect Sight. London: Cadell, 1780. Only edn. v,[v],191 pp. 3 plates. Occas sl marg water stain. New bds, uncut. *(David White)* **£65 [≈ $116]**

Chanter, Charlotte
- Ferny Combes; A Ramble after Ferns in the Glens and Valleys of Devonshire. Second Edition. London: Lovell, Reeve, 1856. 118,[24 advt] pp. Dble page map, 8 hand cold plates. Title faintly damp marked. Orig pict cloth gilt, sl creased.   *(Gough)* **£35 [≈ $62]**

Chapin, J.P.
- The Birds of the Belgian Congo. New York: 1932-54. 4 vols. Roy 8vo. 73 plates (3 cold), map, 328 text figs. Mod cloth.
(Wheldon & Wesley) **£500 [≈ $890]**

Chapman, Abel
- Memories of Fourscore Years less Two, 1851-1929 ... London: Gurney & Jackson, 1930. 8vo. xxviii,257 pp. 24 cold & 4 plain plates, text ills. Orig cloth, t.e.g.
(Egglishaw) **£30 [≈ $53]**
- Retrospect. Reminiscences and Impressions of a Hunter-Naturalist in Three Continents, 1851-1928. London: Gurney & Jackson, 1928. xx, 353 pp. 20 cold & 34 plain plates, text ills. Orig cloth, t.e.g.
(Egglishaw) **£40 [≈ $71]**

Chapman, John
- Cases of Neuralgia and of Other Diseases of the Nervous System ... London: J. & A. Churchill, 1873. 1st edn. viii,183,[7 advt] pp. Lib stamp on title. Lib b'plates. Tear without loss to pp 1-4. Orig green cloth, some wear.
(Caius) **$65 [≈ £37]**

Chapman, Nathaniel
- Discourses on the Elements of Therapeutics and Materia medica. Phila: James Webster, 1817-19. 1st edn. 2 vols. 8vo. xvi,337; iv, 494, [5] pp. Later calf (vol 1) & contemp calf (vol 2, spine chipped). *(Bookpress)* **$200 [≈ £112]**

Chaptal, M.I.A.
- Elements of Chemistry. Translated from the French. Phila: 1796. 3 vols in one. 8vo. 673 pp. Title mtd. Lib stamp on title. Old calf, rebacked.   *(Goodrich)* **$195 [≈ £110]**

Charcot, Jean
- Clinical Lectures on the Diseases of Old Age. Translated by Leigh H. Hunt. With Additional Lectures by Alfred L. Loomis. New York: W. Wood, 1881. 1st edn in English. xv, 280 pp. 3 chromolitho plates, 28 text figs. Occas foxing. Orig cloth.
(Caius) **$175 [≈ £98]**
- Lectures on Bright's Disease of the Kidneys ... Translated ... by Henry B. Millard. New York: W. Wood, 1878. 1st edn in English. x,100 pp. 2 cold plates. Offset to 4 pp. Orig green cloth, spine damaged with chemical spotting.   *(Caius)* **$150 [≈ £84]**
- Lectures on the Diseases of the Nervous System. Second Series. Delivered at La Salpetriere. Translated and edited by G. Sigerson. London: 1881. xvi,400 pp. 16 pp cold plates. Orig cloth, spine torn, hinges loose.   *(Whitehart)* **£90 [≈ $160]**

Charleton, A.G.
- Tin. London: Spon, 1884. 8vo. xi,83 pp. 15 plates, text figs. Orig cloth.
(Gemmary) **$75 [≈ £42]**

Charleton, W.
- Enquiries into Human Nature in VI. Anatomic Praelections in the New Theatre of the Royal College of Physicians in London. London: 1680. [xl],149, 369-544,[4] pp. Frontis, 6 text figs. Lacks port. Wear & tear. Contemp calf, new label, crnrs reprd. Wing C.3676.   *(Whitehart)* **£180 [≈ $320]**

Chase, Robert
- Atlas of Hand Surgery. Phila: 1973. 1st edn. 4to. 438 pp. Orig bndg. *(Fye)* **$150 [≈ £84]**

Chasis, Herbert & Goldring, William (editors)
- Homer William Smith. His Scientific & Literary Achievements. New York: 1965. One of 300 sgnd by the editors. 282 pp. 17 photo ills. Slipcase. *(Goodrich)* **$85 [≈ £48]**

Chatley, Herbert
- Commercial Aeronautics in China (read to the Engineering Society of China). [Shanghai?]: 1920. 8vo. 20 pp. Orig ptd wraps, chipped. *(Weiner)* **£40 [≈ $71]**
- The Force of the Wind. London: 1909. 8vo. viii,83 pp. Diags. Orig cloth. Inscrbd by the author. *(Weiner)* **£25 [≈ $45]**
- The Force of the Wind. Second Edition. London: 1919. 8vo. viii,83 pp. Diags. Orig cloth. *(Weiner)* **£15 [≈ $27]**
- Pioneer Railway Engineering ... in accordance with the requirements of the Chinese Government. London: 1916. 8vo. 138 pp. Diags. Orig cloth. *(Weiner)* **£15 [≈ $27]**
- Practical Gyrostatic Balancing. London: 1912. 8vo. 73 pp. Frontis, diags. Orig cloth. Author's copy with few pencil notes. *(Weiner)* **£20 [≈ $36]**
- A Text-Book of Aeronautical Engineering: the Problem of Flight. Third Edition. London: 1921. 8vo. xii,150 pp. Ills, diags. Orig cloth. *(Weiner)* **£25 [≈ $45]**

Chatto, William Andrew
- A Paper:- of Tobacco; treating of the Rise, Progress, Pleasures, and Advantages of Smoking ... By Joseph Fume. London: 1839. 2nd edn, enlgd. 8vo. iv,173 pp. 6 plates, ills. Cutting pasted to half-title. Sl foxing. Orig pict bds, roughly rebacked. *(Weiner)* **£50 [≈ $89]**

Chaumont, F.S.B. de
- Lectures on State Medicine delivered before the Society of Apothecaries. London: 1875. vi,196 pp. 20 fldg charts. Few sm lib stamps. Half roan, rubbed & worn. *(Whitehart)* **£38 [≈ $68]**

Chauvenet, W.
- A Manual of Spherical and Practical Astronomy ... London: [1891]. 5th edn, rvsd. 2 vols. 708; 632 pp. 15 fldg plates. Sm lib stamp on title. New endpapers. *(Whitehart)* **£25 [≈ $45]**

Chauvois, L.
- William Harvey. His Life and Times; his Discoveries; his Methods. London: 1957. 271 pp. 18 plates, 14 text figs. Orig bndg. *(Whitehart)* **£15 [≈ $27]**

Cheeseman, T.F. & Hemsley, W.B.
- Illustrations of the New Zealand Flora. Wellington, N.Z.: John Mackay, 1914. 2 vols. 4to. 250 plates by Matilda Smith. Cancelled lib label. Orig green cloth gilt. *(Blackwell's)* **£275 [≈ $490]**

The Chemist
- The Chemist. Vols 1-2. London: 13 March 1824 - 16 April, 1825. 2 vols in one, all published. 8vo. viii,448,[vii]; 480,[vii] pp. Lacks half-titles & leaf announcing cessation of publication. New cloth backed bds. *(Weiner)* **£250 [≈ $445]**

Cheselden, William
- The Anatomy of the Human Body. London: James & John Knapton, 1726. 3rd edn. 8vo. [xvi], 376 pp. 34 plates. Contemp calf, jnts reprd. *(Bookpress)* **$325 [≈ £183]**
- Anatomy of the Human Body. London: William Bowyer, 1740. 5th edn. 4to. 5 ff,336 pp. Frontis, 40 plates. Offsetting from frontis to engvd title. Contemp calf, sl worn. *(Hemlock)* **$425 [≈ £239]**

Cheshire, F.R.
- Bees and Bee-Keeping; Scientific and Practical. London: 1886-88. 2 vols. Cr 8vo. viii, 336, 16 advt; iv, 652, 20 advt pp. 1 plate, 197 text ills. Orig cloth gilt, sl faded & soiled. *(Henly)* **£45 [≈ $80]**

Cheshire, Frank R.
- Bees and Beekeeping: Scientific and Practical. A Complete Treatise ... London: Upcott Gill, [1886-88]. 2 vols. 8vo. 9 plates, 198 text figs. Binder's linen gilt. *(Blackwell's)* **£100 [≈ $178]**

Cheyne, George
- The English Malady: or, a Treatise of Nervous Disorders ... London: Strahan & Leake, 1733. 1st edn. 8vo. [vi],xxxii,[ii], 370,[6 advt] pp. Contemp calf, upper jnt cracked. *(Gaskell)* **£600 [≈ $1,068]**

- The English Malady: or, A Treatise of
Nervous Diseases of all Kinds; as Spleen,
Vapours, Lowness of Spirits, Hypochondriacal,
and Hysterical Distempers ... The Fourth
Edition. London: Strahan, 1734. 8vo. xxxi,
370, advt pp. Some foxing. Contemp calf, jnts
cracked.   (Goodrich) $195 [≈ £110]
- An Essay of the True Nature and Due
Method of Treating the Gout ... and Quality
of Bath-Waters ... London: Strahan, 1738.
9th edn, enlgd. Title reprd. Rec calf.
          (P and P Books) £115 [≈ $205]
- An Essay on Health and Long Life. London:
1724. 1st edn. 8vo. Contemp calf, jnts
cracked.   (Goodrich) $295 [≈ £166]
- The Natural Method of Cureing the Diseases
of the Body, and the Disorders of the Mind
depending on the Body. London: 1742. 1st
edn. 8vo. 316 pp. Lib stamp on title & at end.
Contemp calf, worn, upper cvr detached.
          (Robertshaw) £125 [≈ $223]
- A New Theory of Acute and Slow Continu'd
Fevers ... Second Edition, with many
Additions. London: Strahan, 1702. 8vo. [viii],
37, 166,[1 advt] pp. W'cut text diags. Minor
marg worm. Contemp sprinkled sheep, jnts
worn. Anon.   (Gaskell) £450 [≈ $801]
- Philosophical Principles of Religion: Natural
and Revealed: in Two Parts ... Elements of
Natural Philosophy ... Nature and Kind of
Infinites ... London: Strahan, 1715. 1st
complete edn. Large Paper. 8vo. Occas sl
browning. Contemp mor gilt, a.e.g., v sl
rubbed.   (Gaskell) £850 [≈ $1,513]

Cheyne, John
- Essays on Partial Derangement of the Mind
in supposed Connexion with Religion.
Dublin: W. Curry ..., 1843. 1st edn. 8vo.
[4],272 pp. Lacks port. Orig cloth.
          (Fenning) £55 [≈ $98]

Cheyne, W. Watson (editor)
- Recent Essays by Various Authors on
Bacteria in relation to Disease. London: 1886.
1st edn. 650 pp. 8 chromolithos. Orig bndg.
          (Fye) $200 [≈ £112]

Cheyne, William
- Lister and his Achievement. London: 1925.
1st edn. 136 pp. Port. Orig bndg.
          (Fye) $40 [≈ £22]

Cheyne, Sir William W.
- The Treatment of Wounds, Ulcers, and
Abscesses. Edinburgh & London: Young J.
Pentland, 1894. 1st edn. Cr 8vo. xii,197,[16
advt] pp. Orig cloth, sl dull.
          (Fenning) £35 [≈ $62]

Chilson, F.
- Modern Cosmetics. The Formulation and
Production of Cosmetics ... New York: 1938.
2nd edn. xvi,564 pp. Num ills. Spine sl faded.
          (Whitehart) £15 [≈ $27]

Chilton, C. (editor)
- The Subantarctic Islands of New Zealand.
Reports on the Geophysics, Zoology and
Botany ... Wellington: 1909. 2 vols. 4to. 25
plates (3 cold). Orig cloth.
          (Wheldon & Wesley) £120 [≈ $214]

Chopra, R.N.
- Indigenous Drugs of India, their Medical and
Economic Aspects. Calcutta: 1933. 8vo. xxii,
655 pp. Orig cloth.   (Weiner) £40 [≈ $71]

Christie, H. Kenrick
- Techniques and Results of Grafting Skin.
New York: 1932. 1st edn. 67 pp. 31 photo
ills. Orig bndg.   (Fye) $150 [≈ £84]

Christison, Sir Robert
- The Life ... edited by his Sons. Edinburgh:
William Blackwood, 1885. 1st edn. 2 vols. 4
advt pp vol 1. Half-titles. Frontises. Orig
cloth.   (Jarndyce) £65 [≈ $116]

Chubb, John
- On the Construction of Locks and Keys.
(Excerpt Minutes Proceedings ICE Vol.IX).
London: (1850). 8vo. 36 pp. Engvd title, ills.
Orig gilt dec cloth, sl soiled.
          (Weiner) £75 [≈ $134]

Churchill, Frederick
- Face and Foot Deformities. Phila: 1885. 1st
Amer edn. 195 pp. Litho plates (3 cold),
w'cuts. Orig bndg, spine ends torn.
          (Fye) $450 [≈ £253]

Clagett, M.
- The Science of Mechanics in the Middle
Ages. Madison: (1959) reprint 1961. xxix,711
pp. Figs. Orig bndg. (Whitehart) £35 [≈ $62]

Clancey, P.A.
- The Birds of Natal and Zululand. London:
1964. Roy 8vo. xxxiv,511 pp. Map, 30 cold
plates & ills. Cloth.
          (Wheldon & Wesley) £60 [≈ $107]

Clanny, W.R.
- New Researches on Flame. Sunderland:
1834. Sm 8vo. 8 pp. Plain wraps.
          (Weiner) £75 [≈ $134]

Clare, Peter
- An Essay on the Cure of Abscesses by Caustic, and on the Treatment of Wounds and Ulcers ... London: Cadell, 1779. 1st edn. 154 pp. Contemp calf, red label, rubbed, scuffed. *(Jermy & Westerman)* **£275 [≈ $490]**

Claremont, L.
- The Gem-Cutter's Craft. London: George Bell & Sons, 1906. Roy 8vo. xv,296 pp. Ills. Orig cloth, worn, sl shaken.
(Gemmary) **$90 [≈ £51]**

Clark, James
- The Influence of Climate in the Prevention and Cure of Chronic Diseases ... Principal Places resorted to by Invalids ... Second Edition, enlarged. London: Murray, 1830. 8vo. xl,400,[12] pp. Half-title. Orig bds, paper label, uncut, spine reprd.
(Spelman) **£120 [≈ $214]**
- A Treatise on the Prevention of Diseases incidental to Horses ... subjoined, Observations on some of the Surgical and Medical Branches of Farriery. Phila: William Spotswood, 1791. 1st Amer edn. 12mo. 2 advt ff. Contemp sheep, split in spine. Half mor slipcase. *(Ximenes)* **$600 [≈ £337]**

Clark, R.W.
- The Life of Bertrand Russell. New York: 1976. 1st US edn. 766 pp. 16 dble sided plates. Orig bndg. *(Whitehart)* **£28 [≈ $50]**

Clark, W.
- Mollusca Testacea Marium Britannicorum. A History of the British Marine Testaceous Mollusca. London: Van Voorst, 1855. 8vo. xii, 536 pp. Orig cloth, sm tears hd of spine.
(Egglishaw) **£35 [≈ $62]**

Clark-Kennedy, A.E.
- Stephen Hales, D.D., F.R.S., an Eighteenth Century Biography. Cambridge: 1929. 1st edn. 256 pp. Orig bndg. *(Fye)* **$65 [≈ £37]**

Clarke, Charles Cowden
- Adam, the Gardener; or Information for the Florist, Horticulturist, and Naturalist ... London: A.K. Newman, 1843. 2nd edn. Frontis. Orig cloth gilt.
(Jarndyce) **£20 [≈ $36]**

Clarke, Edwin & Dewhurst, Kenneth
- An Illustrated History of Brain Function. Oxford: 1972. Lge 4to. 154 pp. 157 figs. Dw. *(Goodrich)* **$115 [≈ £65]**

Clarke, Samuel, 1675-1729
- A Collection of Papers, which passed between the late learned Mr Leibnitz, and Dr Clarke ... relating to the Principles of Natural Philosophy and Religion ... London: Knapton, 1717. 8vo. xiii,[4], 416,46 pp, advt leaf. Sl dusty. Vellum over calf, sl soiled.
(Spelman) **£120 [≈ $214]**

Clarke, W.E.
- Studies in Bird Migration. London: Gurney & Jackson, 1912. 2 vols. 8vo. Maps, charts, ills. Orig buckram gilt. *(Egglishaw)* **£40 [≈ $71]**

Clarke, W.G.
- In Breckland Wilds. London: 1937. 2nd edn. 8vo. viii,200 pp. Map, ills. Orig cloth.
(Wheldon & Wesley) **£20 [≈ $36]**

Clarkson, A.
- A Text-Book of Histology. Bristol: Wright, 1896. 1st edn. 8vo. xx,554,[4 advt] pp. 174 cold ills. Occas spotting. Orig cloth, backstrip relaid. *(Savona)* **£25 [≈ $45]**

Clausius, Rudolf
- The Mechanical Theory of Heat. Translated by Walter R. Browne. London: 1879. 8vo. xvi, 376 pp. Orig cloth.
(Weiner) **£75 [≈ $134]**

Clay, Reginald & Court, Thomas
- The History of the Microscope. London: 1975. 1st edn, reprinted. 266 pp. 164 ills. Orig bndg. *(Fye)* **$65 [≈ £37]**

Cleland, E.D.
- West Australian Mining Practice. Kalgoorlie: The Chamber of Mines of Western Australia, 1911. 4to. xvi,268, xvii-xxxi advt pp. 14 plates, 110 text figs. Orig cloth, edges worn.
(Gemmary) **$150 [≈ £84]**

Clerc, L.P.
- Photography - Theory and Practice. London: Focal Press, 1972. 2 vols. 890 pp. Num text figs. Cloth. Dws. *(Savona)* **£30 [≈ $53]**

Clerk, D.
- The Gas Engine. London: 1887. 2nd edn. vi, 279 pp. 101 figs. Occas sl foxing. Orig bndg. *(Whitehart)* **£40 [≈ $71]**

Clinch, G.
- English Hops. A History of Cultivation and Preparation for the Market from the Earliest Times. London: (1919). 1st edn. 8vo. viii,120 pp. 30 ills. Orig cloth.
(Bow Windows) **£60 [≈ $107]**

Clodd, Edward

- Magic in Names and in Other Things. London: Chapman & Hall, 1920. 1st edn. 8vo. Orig cloth, sl dull. *(Georges)* £30 [≈ $53]

Cloud, P.

- Cosmos, Earth, and Man; a Short History of the Universe. New Haven: 1978. 1st edn. 8vo. xvi,372 pp. 46 text figs, illust endpapers. Orig cloth. Dw. *(Henly)* £18 [≈ $32]

Clouston, Sir Thomas S.

- Clinical Lectures on Mental Diseases. Fifth Edition. London: J. & A. Churchill, 1898. 8vo. xii,727,[32 advt] pp. 19 plates (10 cold). Orig cloth. *(Fenning)* £24.50 [≈ $45]

Clow, A. & N.L.

- The Chemical Revolution. A Contribution to Social Technology. London: 1952. xvi,680 pp. Ills. Orig bndg, front inner hinge cracked. *(Whitehart)* £25 [≈ $45]

Cobbett, Anne

- The English Housekeeper: Or Manual of Domestic Management ... London: Anne Cobbett, [ca 1837]. 1st edn. 8vo. xxiii,481,xii pp. Frontis. Contemp cloth, faded, orig ptd label, rubbed, hd of spine sl chipped. *(Gough)* £195 [≈ $347]

Cobbett, William

- The American Gardener ... London: 1821. Stereotype edn. Sm 8vo. [300] pp. 4 plates. Contemp calf, rebacked, reprd. *(Wheldon & Wesley)* £80 [≈ $142]
- Cottage Economy: containing Information relative to the Brewing of Beer, Making of Bread ... London: 1st edn. 1823. Lge 12mo. 4 pp ctlg at front. Frontis. Antique style bds, uncut. *(Weiner)* £100 [≈ $178]
- The English Gardener ... London: [William Cobbett], 11, Bolt-court, Fleet-Street, 1833. 2nd edn. 8vo. [iv],338 pp. text ills. Orig cloth backed bds, partly unopened, label darkened & sl chipped, crnrs sl worn. *(Clark)* £110 [≈ $196]
- The English Gardener; or A Treatise on the Situation, Soil, Enclosing and Laying-Out, of Kitchen Gardens ... concluding with a Kalendar. London: 1833. 8vo. iv,338 pp. Fldg plate (sl foxed), 12 text ills. Spotted. Orig bds, rebacked. *(Henly)* £85 [≈ $151]
- The English Gardener. London: 1833. 8vo. iv, 338 pp. Plan. Half calf. *(Wheldon & Wesley)* £70 [≈ $125]
- A Treatise on Cobbett's Corn, containing Instructions for Propagating and Cultivating the Plant ... London: 1828. Lge 12mo. 3

plates. 1 leaf torn without loss. Antique style bds, uncut. *(Weiner)* £100 [≈ $178]
- The Woodlands. London: the author, 1825. 8vo. [342,2 advt] pp. 2 text ills. Occas foxing. Half calf, rubbed. *(Hortulus)* $125 [≈ £70]
- The Woodlands: or, A Treatise on the Preparing of Ground for Planting; on the Planting ... and on the cutting down of Forest Trees and Underwood. London: 1825. 1st edn. 8vo. A-Y3 [358] pp. 2 text ills. Half calf. *(Henly)* £120 [≈ $214]

Cochran-Patrick, R.W.

- Early Records relating to Mining in Scotland. Edinburgh: David Douglas, 1878. One of 350. 4to. lxv,205 pp. Frontis, title vignette. Half leather, edges worn. *(Gemmary)* $475 [≈ £267]

Cockburn, W.

- The Nature and Cures of Fluxes ... London: for John Clarke, 1724. 3rd edn. xlii,[iv],344 pp. Lacks fldg table. Crnr of a few pp chipped, not affecting text. Sl marg spotting. Few margs thumbed. Contemp calf, rebacked, hinges reprd. *(Francis Edwards)* £65 [≈ $116]

Cockrell, William D.

- Industrial Electronic Control. New York: McGraw Hill, 1944. 1st edn. 8vo. 247 pp. Lib pocket. Orig bndg. *(Schoen)* $65 [≈ £37]

Coddington, Henry

- A Treatise on the Reflexion and Refraction of Light, being Part I. of a System of Optics. Cambridge: 1829. 1st edn. 8vo. [4], xx, 296 pp, 2 errata ff. Half-title. 10 fldg plates. Rec bds, uncut. *(Fenning)* £45 [≈ $80]

Codman, E.A.

- Bone Sarcoma. New York: 1925. 1st edn. 93 pp. Ills. Orig bndg. *(Fye)* $85 [≈ £48]
- The Shoulder. Boston: 1934. 1st edn, 2nd printing. 513,29 pp. Orig bndg. *(Fye)* $250 [≈ £140]

Coghan or Cogan, Thomas

- The Haven of Health. London: Anne Griffin, 1636. Sm 4to. [xvi],321,[1 blank],[22 index] pp. Later mor. *(Bookpress)* $475 [≈ £267]

Cohausen, Johann Heinrich

- Hermippus Redivivus; Or, the Sage's Triumph over Old Age and the Grave ... London: J. Nourse, 1744. 1st edn in English. 8vo. [8],168 pp. Orig bds, rebacked. Translated by J. Campbell. Anon. *(O'Neal)* $200 [≈ £112]

- Hermippus Redivivus; Or, the Sage's Triumph over Old Age and the Grave ... London: 1748. Sm 8vo. 124 pp. Contemp calf, lacks label. Translated by J. Campbell. Anon.   *(Robertshaw)* **£56 [≈ $100]**

Cohnheim, Julius
- Lectures on General Pathology ... Translated from the Second German Edition by Alexander B. McKee. With Memoir by the Translator. London: New Sydenham Society, 1889-90. 3 vols. Ex-lib, no external marks. Orig cloth, worn, jnts cracked.
          (Goodrich) **$175 [≈ £98]**

Cole, F.J.
- A History of Comparative Anatomy. From Aristotle to the Eighteenth Century. London: 1949. viii,524 pp. 200 ills. Dw (sl frayed).
          (Francis Edwards) **£35 [≈ $62]**

Cole, G.
- Aids in Practical Geology. London: 1891. 1st edn. Cr 8vo. xiv,402,40 pp. 135 text figs. Orig cloth.   *(Henly)* **£18 [≈ $32]**
- Aids in Practical Geology. London: 1909. 6th edn. Cr 8vo. xiv,431,86 pp. 2 plates, 136 text figs. Cloth.   *(Henly)* **£14 [≈ $25]**

Cole, Grenville A.J.
- Aids to Practical Geology. London: Charles Griffin, 1891. 1st edn. 8vo. xiv,402,[32 advt] pp. Num ills. Orig cloth.
          (Fenning) **£18.50 [≈ $34]**

Coleman, A.P.
- Ice Ages Recent and Ancient. London: Macmillan, 1926. 1st edn. 8vo. 296 pp. 8 maps, 51 plates. Orig blue cloth.
          (Schoen) **$85 [≈ £48]**

Colgan, N. & Scully, R.W.
- Contributions towards a Cybele Hibernica, being Outlines of the Geographical Distribution of Plants in Ireland ... Dublin: Ponsonby, 1898. 2nd edn. 8vo. xcvi,538 pp. Subscribers. Map. Orig cloth.
          (de Burca) **££65 [≈ $116]**

Colles, Abraham
- Practical Observations on the Venereal Disease, and on the Use of Mercury. London: 1837. xvii,351 pp. Title & prelims sl spotted. Rebound in half mor.
          (Francis Edwards) **£185 [≈ $329]**
- Selections from the Works ... Edited with Annotations by Robert McDowell. London: 1891. 1st edn. 431 pp. Orig bndg.
          (Fye) **$150 [≈ £84]**

- Treatise on Surgical Anatomy. Phila: 1831. 2nd Amer edn. 186 pp. Leather, bds detached, backstrip worn, lacks label.
          (Fye) **$50 [≈ £28]**

Collier, Elisha Haydon
- On the Superior Advantages of the Patent Improved Steam-Boilers, invented by ... London: (1836). 8vo. 18 pp. Fldg plate (reprd with sl loss). Tear in title reprd. New card bds.   *(Weiner)* **£35 [≈ $62]**

Collignon, Charles
- The Miscellaneous Works of Charles Collignon, M.D. ... Cambridge: Hodson, 1786. 4to. Half-title, subscribers, [5],345 pp, errata leaf. Calf, jnts weak.
          (Goodrich) **$175 [≈ £98]**

Collingwood, Francis & Woolams, John
- The Universal Cook, and City and Country Housekeeper ... Second Edition. London: Noble for Scatcherd, 1797. 8vo. [viii], [xx],451,[i advt] pp. 13 (of 14, lacks port) plates. Plates sl browned. Sl later diced russia, later reback.   *(Gough)* **£250 [≈ $445]**

Collingwood, W.G.
- Astrology in the Apocalypse: An Essay on Biblical Allusions to Chaldean Science. Orpington: G. Allen, 1886. 1st edn. Sm 8vo. Orig bndg, sl scuffed & marked.
          (Deja Vu) **£55 [≈ $98]**

Collins, E.T.
- The History and Traditions of the Moorfields Eye Hospital. One Hundred Years of Ophthalmic Discovery and Development. London: 1929. xi,226 pp. Frontis, 26 plates. Orig bndg.   *(Whitehart)* **£38 [≈ $68]**

Collis, Edgar & Greenwood, Major
- The Health of the Industrial Worker. Phila: 1921. 1st Amer edn. 450 pp. Orig bndg.
          (Fye) **$100 [≈ £56]**

Colyer, F.
- Variations and Diseases of the Teeth of Animals. London: 1936. viii,750 pp. 1007 text figs. Half cloth. Inscrbd by the author.
          (Whitehart) **£50 [≈ $89]**

Colyer, J.F.
- Dental Surgery and Pathology. London: 1910. xvi,1000 pp. 890 text figs. Cloth sl dust stained & worn, inner hinge cracked.
          (Whitehart) **£15 [≈ $27]**
- Dental Surgery and Pathology. London: 1923. 5th edn. xiv,931 pp. 6 plates, 951 ills.

Orig cloth, sl worn. *(Whitehart)* **£15 [≈ $27]**

Combe, Andrew

- The Physiology of Digestion considered with relation to the Principles of Dietetics. Fifth American Edition. Boston: 1840. x, 11-310 pp. Sl foxing at ends. Contemp publisher's cloth.   *(Hemlock)* **$75 [≈ £42]**

Combe, George

- Elements of Phrenology. Edinburgh: J. Anderson Jr., 1825. 2nd edn, enlgd. 12mo. [iii]-xi, [1],240, [6 advt dated May 1825] pp. 2 plates inc fldg frontis. Lacks half-title. Plates foxed. Orig cloth backed bds, worn.
                          (Caius) **$175 [≈ £98]**
- Lectures on Phrenology. New York: 1847. 3rd Amer edn. 391 pp. Orig bndg.
                          (Fye) **$60 [≈ £34]**

Commerell, Abbe de

- An Account of the Culture and Use of the Mangel Wurzel, or Root of Scarcity, Translated from the French. London: 1787. 3rd edn. 8vo. xxxix,51 pp. Cold plate. Half calf, somewhat worn.
             (Wheldon & Wesley) **£60 [≈ $107]**

Complete ...

- The Complete English Farmer ... see Henry, David
- The Complete Family-Piece: and, Country Gentleman, and Farmer's Best Guide ... Second Edition. London: Bettesworth, Hitch ..., 1737. Lge 12mo. xii,520,[lxi] pp. Generally cropped at hd. Sm worm hole at start. Contemp style panelled calf.
                       (Gough) **£450 [≈ $801]**
- The Complete Farmer: or, a General Dictionary of Husbandry, in all its Branches ... The Second Edition, Corrected and Improved. By a Society of Gentlemen. London: 1769.   4to.   (A)1-2,B1-4R4, 4S1-2,*A1-*O4, *P1-2. 29 plates. Sl worn. Contemp calf, sl worn. *(Clark)* **£220 [≈ $392]**
- The Complete Grazier ... see Horne, T.H.

Comroe, Bernard

- Arthritis and Allied Conditions. Phila: 1940. 1st edn. 752 pp. Orig bndg.
                          (Fye) **$100 [≈ £56]**

Comstock, J.L.

- An Introduction to Mineralogy. New York: Pratt, Woodford, 1851. 16th edn. Cr 8vo. 369 pp. W'cut ills. Foxed. Leather, v worn, cvrs loose.   *(Gemmary)* **$100 [≈ £56]**

Conard, H.S.

- The Waterlilies, a Monograph of the Genus Nymphaea. Washington: Carnegie Inst., 1905. 4to. xiii,279 pp. 12 cold & 18 plain plates, 82 text figs. Half vellum.
             (Wheldon & Wesley) **£240 [≈ $427]**

Consentius, Ernst

- Master Johann Dietz Surgeon in the Army of the Great Elector and Barber to the Royal Court. New York: 1923. 315 pp. Orig bndg.
                          (Fye) **$50 [≈ £28]**

Constantine, Joseph

- Sir Isaac Holden, Bart., and His Theory of Healthy Long Life. London: John Heywood, 1898. 1st edn. 137,[39 advt] pp. 2 ports. Orig gilt dec cloth.   *(Caius)* **$100 [≈ £56]**

Conversations on Botany ...

- See Fitton, E. & S.M.

The Cook's Oracle ...

- See Kitchiner, William

Cook, Edward

- The Life of Florence Nightingale. London: 1913. 2 vols. 2 frontis, 5 plates. Sl foxing, some underlining. Orig bndg, worn, spines al faded.   *(Whitehart)* **£18 [≈ $32]**
- The Life of Florence Nightingale. New York: 1942. 2 vols in one. 507; 510 pp. Orig bndg.
                          (Fye) **$40 [≈ £22]**

Cook, John, coach builder

- Cursory Remarks on the Subject of Wheel Carriages. Parts I & II. London: 1817-18. 8vo. 32,52 pp. 21 plates. Lib stamp on part 1 title & blank plate margs. Occas offsetting & sl foxing. Cloth.   *(Weiner)* **£200 [≈ $356]**

Cook, M.

- The Manner of Raising, Ordering, and Improving Forest-Trees. London: 1724. 3rd edn. 8vo. xx,273 pp. Frontis, fldg plate. Lacks half-title. Calf, reprd.
             (Wheldon & Wesley) **£120 [≈ $214]**

Cooke, M.C.

- British Desmids, a Supplement to British Freshwater Algae. London: Williams & Norgate, 1887. 8vo. xiv,205 pp. 66 cold plates. New cloth, t.e.g.
                     (Egglishaw) **£65 [≈ $116]**
- Freaks and Marvels of Plant Life; or, Curiosities of Vegetation. London: 1882. 4th thousand. Cr 8vo. viii,463 pp. 97 figs. Blue calf gilt, mrbld edges.
             (Wheldon & Wesley) **£20 [≈ $36]**

- Illustrations of British Fungi (Hymenomycetes) to serve as an Atlas to the 'Handbook of British Fungi'. London: 1881-91. 8 vols. 8vo. 1198 cold plates. Mor, 2 vols rebacked, trifle rubbed, few jnts beginning to crack.
(Wheldon & Wesley) **£2,500 [≃ $4,450]**
- Introduction to the Study of Fungi. London: Black, 1895. 1st edn. 8vo. vi,360 pp. 148 figs. Cloth.   *(Savona)* **£30 [≃ $53]**
- Introduction to the Study of Fungi. Their Organography, Classification and Distribution. For the Use of Collectors. London: 1895. 1st edn. x,360 pp. Text ills. Orig cloth, unopened, sl soiled.
(Francis Edwards) **£25 [≃ $45]**
- A Legend of a Quekett Soiree, chanted for the Delectation of the Recalcitrant Excursionists at Leatherhead ... London: by Ye Cooke, 1877. 8vo. 14 pp. Plate. Sewn as issued.
(Weiner) **£40 [≃ $71]**
- A Plain and Easy Account of the British Fungi. London: Robert Hardwicke, 1871. New edn, rvsd. Fcap 8vo. viii,166 pp. Addtnl title & 23 hand cold plates. Few sl marks. Orig pict cloth gilt.   *(Ash)* **£100 [≃ $178]**
- Rust, Smut, Mildew & Mould. An Introduction to the Study of Microscopic Fungi. London: Hardwicke & Bogue, 1878. 4th edn, rvsd & enlgd. 8vo. 262 pp. 16 cold plates. Orig cloth, faded, sl rubbed.
(Savona) **£25 [≃ $45]**
- Rust, Smut, Mildew & Mould. An Introduction to the Study of Microscopic Fungi. London: Allen, 1902. 6th edn, rvsd & enlgd. 8vo. 262,[2 advt] pp. 16 plates, figs. Some browning endpapers. Orig dec cloth.
(Savona) **£25 [≃ $45]**
- Songs Written for the Excursionists' Annual Dinners, Q.M.C. London: 1878. 8vo. 25 pp. 2 ills. Orig ptd wraps, sl soiled.
(Weiner) **£50 [≃ $89]**

Cooke, Thomas Fothergill
- Authorship of the Practical Electric Telegraph of Great Britain; or, the Brunel Award vindicated ... Bath: 1868. 8vo. xxxii, 131 pp. Reprint of letter from Cooke taped to last leaf. Lib b'plate. Buckram.
(Weiner) **£60 [≃ $107]**

Cooper, Sir Astley
- The Anatomy and Surgical Treatment of Inguinal and Congenital Hernia. London: T. Cox, 1804. Lge atlas portfolio. vi,60 pp. 11 engvd plates & legend ff. Extra outline leaf. 1 plate partly cold. Sl browning. Contemp qtr calf, sometime rebacked.
(Goodrich) **$1,250 [≃ £702]**

- Lectures on the Principles and Practice of Surgery. As Delivered in the Theatre of St. Thomas's Hospital ... London: Westley, 1829. Sm 8vo. viii,636 pp. Lib stamp on title (which is loose). Orig roan & mrbld bds.
(Goodrich) **$495 [≃ £278]**
- Lectures on the Principles and Practice of Surgery. As Delivered in the Theatre of St. Thomas's Hospital. London: 1830. 2nd edn. viii,638 pp. Occas foxing & marg pencil lines. Contemp bds, sl torn & stained, crnrs worn.
(Whitehart) **£75 [≃ $134]**
- A Treatise on Dislocations and on Fractures of the Joints. Fourth Edition. London: 1824. 4to. xxiv,518 pp. 34 litho plates. Some foxing & pencillings. Name on half-title. Old half calf, rebacked, spine ends sl rubbed, tear in spine.   *(Bow Windows)* **£425 [≃ $757]**
- A Treatise on Dislocations and Fractures of the Joints. A New Edition, much enlarged. Edited by Bransby B. Cooper. Phila: 1851. 496 pp. Leather.   *(Fye)* **$200 [≃ £112]**

Cooper, Bransby B.
- Surgical Essays: The Result of Clinical Observations made at Guy's Hospital. London: 1843. 8vo. 4 cold litho plates. Orig bds.   *(Goodrich)* **$300 [≃ £169]**

Cooper, C.S. & Westell, W.P.
- Trees and Shrubs of the British Isles, Native and Acclimatised. London: 1908. 2 vols. 4to. 16 cold & 70 plain plates. Sl foxing edges of cold plates. Orig cloth gilt.
(Henly) **£38 [≃ $68]**

Cooper, Samuel
- A Dictionary of Practical Surgery ... With Notes and an Appendix by William Anderson. New York: 1823. 2 vols. 704; 710 pp. Hinges cracked, 1 bd nearly detached, lacks 1 label.   *(Fye)* **$150 [≃ £84]**
- Dictionary of Practical Surgery ... London: 1825. 5th edn. viii,1264 pp. Lacks half-title. Ink names on title, occas underlining. Contemp leather, rebacked.
(Whitehart) **£40 [≃ $71]**
- The First Lines of the Practice of Surgery ... London: 1807. 1st edn. 8vo. 554,vi pp. 9 plates. Orig calf. *(Goodrich)* **$395 [≃ £222]**

Copeland, Morris
- Country Life: A Handbook of Agriculture, Horticulture, and Landscape Gardening. Boston: 1860. 2nd edn. 8vo. x,814 pp. Dble page frontis, engvd plates, text w'cuts. Orig bndg, spine worn & faded, bds worn.
(Hortulus) **$85 [≃ £48]**

Copeman, W.S.C.
- A Short History of the Gout and the Rheumatic Diseases. Berkeley: 1964. 1st edn. 236 pp. Dw. *(Fye)* **$75 [≈ £42]**

Copley, Esther
- The Housekeeper's Guide; or a Plain and Practical System of Domestic Cookery. Second Edition. London: Longman ..., 1838. 12mo. x, 480 pp. Engvd frontis & title, 5 plates. Contemp half calf, mrbld bds, lower jnt reprd. *(Gough)* **£95 [≈ $169]**

Corbet, G.B. & Hill, J.E.
- A World List of Mammalian Species. London: BM, 1980. 1st edn. 8vo. viii,226 pp. Orig buckram. *(Francis Edwards)* **£25 [≈ $45]**

Corbet, P.S.
- A Biology of Dragonflies. London: 1962. 1st edn. 8vo. xvi,247 pp. Cold frontis, 6 plain plates, 115 text figs. Cloth. *(Wheldon & Wesley)* **£30 [≈ $53]**

Cordasco, Francesco
- A Bibliography of Robert Watt, M.D. ... Detroit: Gale Research Co., 1968. 2nd edn. 8vo. Port. Cloth. *(Bookpress)* **$35 [≈ £20]**

Corfe, George
- Man and His Many Changes, or Seven Times Seven. London: Houlston & Wright, 1862. 2nd edn. vi,91 pp. Orig limp cloth, sl worn. *(Caius)* **$60 [≈ £34]**

Corkill, Norman L.
- Snakes and Snake Bite in Iraq: a Handbook for Medical Officers. London: Bailliere, Tindall & Cox, 1932. 8vo. ix,51 pp. Minor cvr wear. *(McBlain)* **$90 [≈ £51]**

Corlett, William Thomas
- A Treatise on the Acute, Infectious Exanthemata including Variola, Rubeola, Scarlatine, Rubella ... Phila: 1901. 392 pp. 12 cold & 28 halftone plates. Orig cloth, worn. *(Goodrich)* **$45 [≈ £25]**

Cornaro, Luigi
- Discourses on a Sober and Temperate Life. Translated from the Italian Original. London: for Benjamin White, 1768. 1st edn of this translation. With the Italian text. 2 parts. 8vo. Some water stains. Contemp calf, rebacked, crnrs worn. *(Hannas)* **£45 [≈ $80]**

Corner, G.W.
- Two Centuries of Medicine. A History of the School of Medicine University of Pennsylvania. Phila: 1965. ix,363 pp. 12 plates. 2 crnrs sl bumped. *(Whitehart)* **£15 [≈ $27]**

Cornish, J.
- A View of the Present State of the Salmon. London: Longman, Hurst ..., 1824. 1st edn. 8vo. xii,217,[1] pp. Contemp half calf, worn. *(Bookpress)* **$275 [≈ £154]**

Cory, Charles Barney
- The Birds of Haiti and San Domingo. Boston: Estes & Lauriat, 1884-85. 3 parts. 4to. 56,198 pp. 23 b/w plates. Orig wraps, vol 1 broken. *(McBlain)* **$400 [≈ £225]**

Cory, R.
- Lectures on the Theory and Practice of Vaccination. London: 1898. 122 pp. 10 cold & 6 b/w ills. Ink notes on half-title. Orig bndg, sl scratched & worn. *(Whitehart)* **£25 [≈ $45]**

Cott, H.B.
- Adaptive Coloration in Animals. London: 1940. 4to. xxxii,508 pp. Cold frontis, 48 plates, 84 text figs. Lib bndg. *(Whitehart)* **£25 [≈ $45]**

Cotter, C.H.
- A History of Nautical Astronomy. New York: 1968. 4 plates, 49 ills. *(Whitehart)* **£18 [≈ $32]**

Cotton, William Charles
- My Bee Book. London: Rivington, 1842. 8vo. 368 pp. 72 text ills. Orig cloth gilt, mottled & faded. *(Hollett)* **£95 [≈ $169]**

Couch, John
- Surgery of the Hand: Some Practical Aspects. Toronto: 1939. 1st edn. 147 pp. Orig bndg. *(Fye)* **$100 [≈ £56]**
- Surgery of the Hand: Some Practical Aspects. Toronto: 1944. 2nd edn. 159 pp. Ills. Orig bndg. *(Fye)* **$50 [≈ £28]**

Cowan, A.
- Refraction of the Eye. London: 1948. 3rd edn. 288 pp. 3 cold & 16 other plates, 170 ills. Review stamp on title. Cvrs sl marked. *(Whitehart)* **£20 [≈ $36]**

Cowan, Lester (editor)
- Recording Sound for Motion Pictures. New York: McGraw Hill, 1931. 1st edn, 3rd printing. 12mo. 404 pp. Plates, ills. Orig bndg. *(Schoen)* **$65 [≈ £37]**

Coward, T.A.
- The Birds of the British Isles and their Eggs. London: 1953. 3 vols. Sm 8vo. 523 cold ills. Orig bndgs.   *(Carol Howard)* £36 [≈ $64]

Coward, T.A. (editor)
- The Vertebrate Fauna of Cheshire, and Liverpool Bay. London: 1910. 1st edn. 2 vols. Num ills. Endpapers v sl foxed. Orig cloth, t.e.g., spines v sl discold.
        (Francis Edwards) £65 [≈ $116]

Coward, T.A. & Oldham, Charles
- The Birds of Cheshire. Manchester: 1900. 1st edn. 278 pp. Fldg map, 6 ills. Orig cloth, upper hinge tender.
        (Francis Edwards) £35 [≈ $62]

Cowell, John
- The Curious and the Profitable Gardener ... London: Weaver Bickerton, 1730. 1st edn. 8vo. iv,[iv],126, [11],67,[1] pp. Frontis, 1 fldg plate. Contemp sheep, worn.
        (Bookpress) $650 [≈ £365]

Cox, A.
- Plate Tectonics and Geomagnetic Reversals. San Francisco: 1973. 4to. ix,702 pp. Num text figs. Orig wrappers. *(Henly)* £18 [≈ $32]

Cox, Herbert E.
- A Handbook of the Coleoptera or Beetles of Great Britain and Ireland. London: Janson, 1874. 2 vols. 8vo. viii,527; 366 pp. Orig cloth.   *(Egglishaw)* £30 [≈ $53]
- A Handbook of the Coleoptera or Beetles of Great Britain and Ireland. London: 1874. 2 vols. 8vo. viii,527; 366 pp. Few text ills. 3 lib stamps. Lib cloth.
        (Francis Edwards) £40 [≈ $71]

Cox, I. (editor)
- The Scallop. Studies of a Shell and its Influences on Humankind. London: 1957. 4to. 135 pp. Num cold ills. Orig cloth gilt.
        (Wheldon & Wesley) £15 [≈ $27]

Coxe, John Redman
- The American Dispensatory ... 4th edition, much improved. Phila: Thomas Dobson ..., 1818. x-clv,735,[1] pp. Lib stamps on endpapers & title. Browning. Contemp calf, front hinge cracked.   *(Hemlock)* $75 [≈ £42]

Craig, Sir John
- Newton at the Mint. Cambridge: UP, 1946. Cr 8vo. 4 plates. Orig bndg.
        (Georges) £35 [≈ $62]

Crane, W.R.
- Ore Mining Methods. New York: John Wiley & Sons, 1917. 2nd edn. 8vo. xiii,277 pp. 83 text figs. Good ex-lib. rebound in buckram.
        (Gemmary) $35 [≈ £20]

Crawford, John
- Cursus Medicinae; or a Complete Theory of Physic; in Five Parts ... Done, principally, from those admirable Institutions of H. Boerhaave. London: 1724. 1st edn. 8vo. 382 pp. Lib stamp on title. Contemp panelled calf, sl worn.   *(Robertshaw)* £68 [≈ $121]

Crawley, Alfred Ernest
- Studies of Savages and Sex. Edited by Theodore Besterman. London: Methuen, John Wiley, [1929]. 1st edn. 8vo. [ii],[x], 300, [ctlg] pp. Name stamps on title. Orig cloth.
        (Gach) $50 [≈ £28]

Crawshay, Richard
- The Birds of Tierra del Fuego. London: Quaritch, 1907. One of 300. 4to. xl,158 pp. Cold map, 21 hand cold & 23 mtd photo plates, 1 w'cut. Endpapers sl spotted. Orig qtr mor, t.e.g.   *(Gough)* £850 [≈ $1,513]

Creed, R.S. & others
- Reflex Activity of the Spinal Cord. Oxford: 1932. viii,184 pp. 14 plates, 55 ills. Name. Prelims sl foxed. Cvr sl marked.
        (Whitehart) £28 [≈ $50]

Creighton, Charles
- Contributions to the Physiology and Pathology of the Breast and its Lymphatic Glands. London: Macmillan, 1878. 8vo. xii,200 pp. 36 w'cuts in text. Unabused ex-lib. Orig bndg.   *(Goodrich)* $115 [≈ £65]
- Illustrations of Unconscious Memory in Disease. Including a Theory of Alternatives. London: 1886. xvi,212,16 pp. Orig bndg, front inner hinge cracked but firm. Signed by the author.   *(Whitehart)* £20 [≈ $36]
- Illustrations of Unconscious Memory in Disease Including a Theory of Alteratives. London: H.K. Lewis, 1886. 1st edn. xvi,212 pp. Orig cloth, gilt spine. *(Caius)* $75 [≈ £42]

Cressy, Edward
- Discoveries and Inventions of the Twentieth Century. London: 1923. 2nd edn, rvsd. xxiii,458 pp. 342 ills. Orig illust cloth.
        (Francis Edwards) £25 [≈ $45]

Creswick, Wilfred, & others
- Essays on the Prevention of Explosions and Accidents in Coal Mines ... London: 1874.

8vo. iv,79 pp. Fldg plans. New cloth.
(Weiner) **£65 [≈ $116]**

Cresy, Edward
- A Practical Treatise on Bridge-Building, and on the Equilibrium of Vaults and Arches ... London: John Williams, 1839. Folio. [4],3 pp. 37 (of 68) plates. Orig cloth backed ptd bds, loose, rubbed & worn, ties defective.
(Fenning) **£150 [≈ $267]**

Crile, George W.
- An Experimental and Clinical Research into Certain Problems relating to Surgical Operations ... Phila: 1901. 8vo. 200 pp. Ex-lib. Orig bndg. *(Goodrich)* **$65 [≈ £37]**

Crile, George W. & Lower, William E.
- Anoci-Association. Phila: Saunders, 1914. 8vo. 259 pp. Unabused ex-lib. Orig bndg.
(Goodrich) **$75 [≈ £42]**

Cripps, Ernest C.
- Plough Court, The Story of a Notable Pharmacy 1715-1927. London: Allen & Hanbury, 1927. 1st edn. 8vo. xviii,227 pp. Frontis, photo ills. Orig cloth.
(David White) **£15 [≈ $27]**

Croll, J.
- Stellar Evolution and its relations to Geological Time. London: 1889. xi,118 pp. Inner hinge sl cracked, sm lib label on spine.
(Whitehart) **£30 [≈ $53]**

Cromwell, Oliver
- Finger-Print Photography. London & Bradford: 1907. 8vo. 72 pp. 11 plates. Orig cloth. *(Weiner)* **£25 [≈ $45]**

Crook, C.
- Campanulas, their Cultivation and Classification. London: 1951. 8vo. 256 pp. 149 ills. Cloth.
(Wheldon & Wesley) **£40 [≈ $71]**

Crook, Ronald E.
- A Bibliography of Joseph Priestley 1733-1804. London: Library Association, 1966. 4to. Orig cloth. *(Stewart)* **£35 [≈ $62]**

Crookes, W.
- Diamonds. London: Harper, 1909. Sm 8vo. xvi, 146 pp. 24 mtd photo ills. Orig cloth.
(Gemmary) **$100 [≈ £56]**

Crookes, Sir William
- Researches in the Phenomena of Spiritualism. Reprinted from the Quarterly Journal of

Science. London: J. Burns, 1874. 1st coll edn. 8vo. 112 pp. 18 ills. Orig cloth gilt.
(Fenning) **£45 [≈ $80]**

Crookshank, Edgar (editor)
- History and Pathology of Vaccination. Phila: 1889. 1st Amer edn. 2 vols. 466; 610 pp. Orig bndgs. *(Fye)* **$350 [≈ £197]**

Crouch, E.A.
- An Illustrated Introduction to Lamarck's Conchology; contained in his Histoire Naturelle des Animaux sans Vertebres. London: 1827. 4to. iv,47 pp. 22 plates. Cloth, signs of use.
(Wheldon & Wesley) **£60 [≈ $107]**

Crowe, Samuel
- Halsted of Johns Hopkins: The Man and his Men. Springfield: 1957. 1st edn. 247 pp. Orig bndg. *(Fye)* **$50 [≈ £28]**

Cruikshank, William Cumberland
- The Anatomy of the Absorbing Vessels of the Human Body. The Second Edition, considerably enlarged ... London: for G. Nicol, 1790. 4to. viii,208, 207*-214*, 209-414 pp. 5 plates (ptd in cold inks). 1 plate marg reprd. Contemp tree calf, gilt.
(Gaskell) **£550 [≈ $979]**

Crumpe, S.
- An Inquiry into the Nature and Properties of Opium ... London: 1793. x,304 pp. Title sl foxed & dusty. Three qtr leather antique.
(Whitehart) **£150 [≈ $267]**

Culbertson, Howard
- Excision of the Larger Joints of the Extremities. Phila: 1876. 1st edn. 672 pp. Orig bndg. *(Fye)* **$150 [≈ £84]**

Cullen, William
- First Lines of the Practice of Physic. New York: 1793. 2 vols. xxxiv,442; xxi,410 pp. Frontis port. Water stains on endpapers, foxing on endpapers and titles & occas in text. Contemp tree calf, rebacked.
(Whitehart) **£200 [≈ $356]**
- A Treatise on the Materia Medica. Dublin: Luke White, 1789. 1st Dublin edn. 2 vols. 8vo. Calf. *(Goodrich)* **$150 [≈ £84]**

Cullingford, C.H.D.
- British Caving. London: Routledge & Kegan Paul, 1953. Roy 8vo. xvi,468 pp. 48 plates, 87 text figs. Orig cloth. Dw.
(Gemmary) **$45 [≈ £25]**

Culpeper, Nicholas
- Culpeper's Complete Herbal ... English Physician Enlarged ... Key to Physic ... London: Thomas Kelly, 1824. 4to. vi,398 pp. Port frontis (laid down), 40 hand cold plates. Sl marks & edge tears. Mod qtr calf.
(Hollett) £150 [≈ $267]
- The Complete Herbal. London: Kelly, 1843. 398, index pp. Frontis (chipped), 20 hand cold plates. Some browning & foxing. New endpapers. Half leather, rebacked.
(Carol Howard) £155 [≈ $276]
- Culpepper's School of Physick ... A Work never before Publisht. London: N. Brook, 1659. 1st edn. 8vo. [lviii],'361" [ie 461], [xxv] pp. Port frontis (marg sl cropped). 8 secondary titles. 6 advt pp at end. Contemp sheep, sometime rebacked, sl used. Wing C.7544(4to).   *(Clark)* £550 [≈ $979]
- The English Physician. Taunton [US]: Samuel W. Mortimer, 1826. Lge 12mo. 259,[5] pp. Some staining. Contemp calf, front jnt reprd.   *(Bookpress)* $225 [≈ £126]

Cumming, J.D.
- Diamond Drill Handbook. Toronto: J.K. Smit, 1956. 1st edn. 8vo. xxx,655 pp. 177 text figs. Orig cloth, edges worn.
(Gemmary) $50 [≈ £28]

Cunningham, Bryson
- A Treatise on the Principles and Practice of Dock Engineering. London: Charles Griffin, 1904. 8vo. xviii,559,[86 advt] pp. 34 fldg plates, num ills. Orig cloth gilt.
(Fenning) £38.50 [≈ $69]
- A Treatise on the Principles and Practice of Harbour Engineering. London: 1928. 3rd edn. xvi,432 pp. 35 plates, 294 text ills. Orig bndg.   *(Whitehart)* £25 [≈ $45]

Cunningham, William
- The Growth of English Industry and Commerce. Cambridge: UP, 1890-1892. 2nd edn, enlgd. 2 vols. demy 8vo. Few sl lib marks & sm reprs. Sl later half mor, lib labels, sl worn.   *(Ash)* £125 [≈ $223]

Curiosities ...
- Curiosities of Entomology ... Curiosities of Ornithology ... see Wood, T.W.

Curran, J. Milne
- The Geology of Sydney and the Blue Mountains. A Popular Introduction to the Study of Geology. Sydney: 1899. 391,[32 advt] pp. Map frontis, fldg cold map, 84 ills. Orig cloth, sl soiled, upper bd sl water stained.   *(Francis Edwards)* £60 [≈ $107]

Curry, James
- A Brief Sketch of the Causes which first gave rise to the late High price of Grain in Great Britain; and the Consequent Necessity for the Corn Bill ... London: 1815. 8vo. Half-title, 35 pp. Rec wraps.   *(Goodrich)* $65 [≈ £37]

Curtis, H.
- The Beauties of the Rose containing Portraits of the Principal Varieties ... Bristol: 1850-53. 2 vols in one. 4to. 38 hand cold plates. Half mor. *(Wheldon & Wesley)* £1,600 [≈ $2,848]

Curtis, J.
- British Entomology ... Coleoptera. London: Lovell Reeve, 1862. 2 vols. Roy 8vo. 256 hand cold plates. Half leather.
(Egglishaw) £875 [≈ $1,558]
- British Entomology ... Diptera. London: Lovell Reeve, 1862. Roy 8vo. 103 hand cold plates. Half leather.
(Egglishaw) £420 [≈ $748]
- British Entomology ... Hymenoptera. London: Lovell Reeve, 1862. Roy 8vo. 125 hand cold plates. Later cloth.
(Egglishaw) £395 [≈ $703]
- British Entomology ... London: 1862. 8 vols. Roy 8vo. 770 hand cold plates. Mod buckram, uncut.
(Egglishaw) £2,950 [≈ $5,251]
- Farm Insects. London: 1883. Roy 8vo. 528 pp. 16 hand cold plates. Sl foxing. Orig cloth, crnrs sl bumped.
(Wheldon & Wesley) £75 [≈ $134]

Curtis, W. Hugh
- William Curtis 1749-1799. Botanist and Entomologist. Winchester: Warren, 1941. 1st edn. 8vo. xvii,142 pp. Ills. Orig bndg.
(Any Amount) £20 [≈ $36]

Curtis, William
- Practical Directions for Laying Down or Improving Meadow and Pasture Land, with an Enumeration of the British Grasses ... Seventh Edition ... Additions ... London: Sherwood ..., 1834. 8vo. [iv],165,advt pp. 8 hand cold plates. Orig cloth backed bds.
(Burmester) £75 [≈ $134]
- Practical Observations on the British Grasses ... The Fourth Edition with Additions ... added a Short Account of ... Blight ... by Sir Joseph Banks. London: for H.D. Symonds, 1805. 8vo. [2],58,14,[2] pp. Fldg plate, 6 plates. Some browning. Contemp half calf, worn.   *(Claude Cox)* £40 [≈ $71]

Curwen, J.C.
- Hints on the Economy of Feeding Stock, and

the Bettering of the Condition of the Poor. London: 1808. 1st edn. 8vo. xvi,364,2 pp. 5 plates. Half-title & title browned, spotting at ends. Contemp half calf.
(Henly) **£100 [≈ $178]**

Cushing, Harvey
- The Life of Sir William Osler. Oxford: Clarendon Press, 1925. 1st edn. 2 vols. 8vo. 2 port frontis, num plates. Orig cloth, sl shelf wear. *(Heritage)* **$300 [≈ £169]**
- The Life of Sir William Osler. Second Impression. Oxford: 1925. 2 vols. 8vo. Frontises, ills. Orig cloth, spine ends v sl fingered, sm mark on 1 cvr.
(Bow Windows) **£65 [≈ $116]**
- The Life of Sir William Osler. Oxford: Clarendon Press, 1925. 1st edn, 2nd imp. 2 vols. 8vo. Ills. Occas lib stamps. Orig cloth.
(David White) **£50 [≈ $89]**
- The Life of Sir William Osler. Oxford: 1925. 1st edn. 3rd printing. 2 vols. 685; 728 pp. Orig bndg. *(Fye)* **$125 [≈ £70]**
- The Life of Sir William Osler. Oxford: 1940. 1417 pp. Orig bndg. *(Fye)* **$45 [≈ £25]**
- The Pituitary Body and its Disorders. Clinical States Produced by Disorders of the Hypophysis Cerebri. Phila: 1912. 1st edn, 1st imp. 8vo. 341 pp. Lib marks. Orig cloth, shelf wear. *(Goodrich)* **$395 [≈ £222]**

Cuvier, G.L.C.F.D., Baron
- Essay on the Theory of the Earth. New York: Kirk & Mercein, 1818. 8vo. xxiii,431 pp. 8 plates. Many pp water stained, foxed. Cloth.
(Gemmary) **$200 [≈ £112]**
- Essay on the Theory of the Earth. New York: Kirk & Mercein, 1818. 8vo. xxiii,431 pp. 8 plates. Some foxing. Qtr leather.
(Gemmary) **$375 [≈ £211]**

Da Costa, Emmanuel Mendes
- Elements of Conchology: or, an Introduction to the Knowledge of Shells ... London: for Benjamin White, 1776. 1st edn. 8vo. viii,vi, 318,[2 errata & advt] pp. 7 fldg plates, 2 fldg charts. Contemp tree calf.
(Claude Cox) **£110 [≈ $196]**

Da Costa, J.M.
- Harvey and his Discovery. Phila: 1879. 1st edn. 57 pp. Orig bndg. *(Fye)* **$50 [≈ £28]**

Daglish, E. Fitch
- Woodcuts of British Birds. London: Benn, 1925. One of 500. Sm 4to. 165 pp. 20 w'cuts. Orig bndg, sl soiled, ft of spine sl rubbed.
(Carol Howard) **£62 [≈ $110]**
- Woodcuts of British Birds. With Descriptions

by the Artist. London: Benn, 1925. One of 500. 4to. 165 pp. 20 w'engvd plates. Orig holland backed mrbld bds, upper hinge sl darkened. *(Hollett)* **£160 [≈ $285]**
- Birds of the British Isles, described and engraved. London: Dent, 1948. One of 1500. Roy 8vo. xviii,222 pp. 48 w'engvs (25 hand cold). Orig buckram, t.e.g.. Dw (torn).
(Egglishaw) **£55 [≈ $98]**
- Birds of the British Isles. London: Dent, 1948. One of 1500. Imperial 8vo. xviii,[224] pp. 48 plates (25 hand cold). Orig pict buckram gilt. Hand cold dw (v sl worn).
(Ash) **£200 [≈ $356]**

Dainton, C.
- The Story of England's Hospitals. London: 1961. 184 pp. 23 plates. Dw (sl dust stained). *(Whitehart)* **£15 [≈ $27]**

d'Albe, E.E.F.
- The Life of Sir William Crookes, O.M., F.R.S. With a Foreword by Sir Oliver Lodge. London: 1923. xix,413 pp. Frontis port, 4 plates. Orig bndg. *(Whitehart)* **£35 [≈ $62]**

Dallas, W.S.
- List of the Specimens of Hemipterous Insects in the British Museum. London: 1851-52. 2 parts in one vol. 12mo. 590 pp. 15 litho plates. New cloth. *(Egglishaw)* **£36 [≈ $64]**

Dallimore, W.
- Holly, Yew and Box, with Notes on Other Evergreens. London: 1908. 1st edn. 8vo. xiv, 284 pp. Num ills. New endpapers. Cloth, water stained. *(Wheldon & Wesley)* **£35 [≈ $62]**

Dalrymple, George
- The Practice of Modern Cookery ... Edinburgh: for the author ..., 1781. Only edn. 8vo. vi,475,[i errata] pp. Half-title. Contemp calf, jnts reprd, later label, rear bd scratched.
(Gough) **£675 [≈ $1,202]**

Dalziel, Hugh
- The St. Bernard: its History, Points, Breeding and Rearing. London: n.d. 8vo. [iv], 132 pp. 1 cold & 2 plain plates. Some marks. Orig illust cloth. *(Bow Windows)* **£55 [≈ $98]**

Dana, Charles L.
- The Peaks of Medical History. An Outline of the Evolution of Medicine. New York: Hoeber, 1928. 8vo. 105 pp. 40 plates, 16 text ills. Cloth rubbed. *(Goodrich)* **$75 [≈ £42]**

Dana, E.S.
- Third Appendix to the Fifth Edition of

Dana's Mineralogy. New York: John Wiley & Sons, 1882. 8vo. xiii,134 pp. Orig cloth, stained. *(Gemmary)* **$50 [≈ £28]**

Dana, E.S. & Dana, J.D.
- A Textbook of Mineralogy. New York: John Wiley & Sons, 1902. New edn. 8vo. vii,593 pp. Cold plates, num figs. Orig cloth.
(Gemmary) **$50 [≈ £28]**

Dana, James Dwight
- Corals and Coral Islands. New York: Dodd & Mead, 1872. 8vo. 398 pp. Num w'cuts. Orig cloth, worn, sl loose.
(Gemmary) **$125 [≈ £70]**
- Corals and Coral islands. New York: Dodd, Mead, 1879. 2nd edn. 8vo. 406 pp. 2 fldg maps, 3 plates, w'cut ills. Rebound in cloth.
(Gemmary) **$150 [≈ £84]**
- Corals and Coral Islands. New York: 1890. 3rd edn, rvsd & enlgd. 8vo. 440 pp. 17 plates (4 cold), num text figs. Few lib blind stamps, sl used. Cloth.
(Wheldon & Wesley) **£45 [≈ $80]**
- Manual of Geology. Phila: Theodore Bliss, 1863. 1st edn. 8vo. xvi,798 pp. Chart, figs. Rebound in lib buckram.
(Gemmary) **$65 [≈ £37]**
- Manual of Geology. New York: Amer Book Co., 1880. 3rd edn. 8vo. xiv,911 pp. Chart, 12 plates, text figs. Orig cloth.
(Gemmary) **$45 [≈ £25]**
- Manual of Geology. New York: Amer Book Co., 1894. 4th edn. 8vo. 1088 pp. 2 maps, 1575 text figs. Orig cloth, edges worn.
(Gemmary) **$45 [≈ £25]**
- A System of Mineralogy. New Haven: Durrie & Peck ..., 1837. 1st edn. 8vo. xiv, 452, 120, iv pp. 4 plates, 250 w'cuts. New qtr leather.
(Gemmary) **$575 [≈ £323]**
- A System of Mineralogy. New York: John Wiley & Son, 1869. 5th edn, with 2 Appendixes to 1875. 8vo. xlviii,827, iv,19,x,64 pp. Num w'cut ills. Rec qtr leather. *(Gemmary)* **$350 [≈ £197]**
- A System of Mineralogy. New York: John Wiley & Son, 1882. 5th edn. 8vo. xlviii,827, iv,19, x,64 pp. Num w'cut ills. Rec buckram.
(Gemmary) **$350 [≈ £197]**
- A System of Mineralogy. New York: John Wiley & Son, 1869. 5th edn. 8vo. xlviii,827 pp. Num w'cut ills. Rec buckram.
(Gemmary) **$325 [≈ £183]**
- The System of Mineralogy of James Dwight Dana. New York: John Wiley & Sons, 1899. 6th edn. Roy 8vo. lxiii,1134, ix,75 pp. Over 1400 figs. Buckram, worn.
(Gemmary) **$325 [≈ £183]**

- The System of Mineralogy of James Dwight Dana. New York: John Wiley & Sons, 1900. 6th edn. Roy 8vo. lxiii,1134, ix,75 pp. Over 1400 figs. Rec buckram.
(Gemmary) **$325 [≈ £183]**
- The System of Mineralogy of James Dwight Dana. New York: John Wiley & Sons, 1900. 6th edn. Roy 8vo. lxiii,1134, ix,75 pp. Over 1400 figs. Orig half leather, worn.
(Gemmary) **$325 [≈ £183]**
- The System of Mineralogy of James Dwight Dana. New York: John Wiley & Sons, 1911. 6th edn. Roy 8vo. lxiii,1134, ix,75,xi,114 pp. Over 1400 figs. Good ex-lib. Orig half leather, rubbed. *(Gemmary)* **$125 [≈ £70]**

Dance, S.P.
- Rare Shells. London: 1969. Roy 8vo. 128 pp. 24 cold plates. Cloth.
(Wheldon & Wesley) **£25 [≈ $45]**

Dandolo, Count
- The Art of Rearing Silk Worms. London: Murray, 1825. 1st edn. 8vo. xxiv,365 pp. Frontis, 2 fldg plates, 2 tables. Occas spotting. Rebound in half calf.
(Frew Mackenzie) **£120 [≈ $214]**

Dandy, Walter
- Benign Tumors in the Third Ventricle of the Brain: Diagnosis and Treatment. Springfield: 1933. 8vo. 171 pp. Num ills. Orig bndg.
(Goodrich) **$225 [≈ £126]**
- Intracranial Arterial Aneurysms. Ithaca: 1945. 2nd printing. 8vo. viii,146 pp. 5 fldg charts, num text ills. Orig bndg.
(Goodrich) **$350 [≈ £197]**

Daniel, Gabriel
- A Voyage to the World of Cartesius. Written originally in French, and now translated into English. London: Thomas Bennet, 1692. 1st edn in English. 8vo. [xvi],298,[6] pp. Text diags. Contemp calf, jnts reprd. Wing D.201. Anon. *(Gaskell)* **£480 [≈ $854]**

Darling, F.F.
- Natural History in the Highlands and Islands. London: Collins New Naturalist, 1947. 1st edn. Ills. Orig cloth. Dw.
(Egglishaw) **£18 [≈ $32]**

Darnell, A.W.
- Hardy and Half-Hardy Plants. Illustrations and Descriptions of Beautiful and Interesting Plants for Outdoor Culture in the British Isles. London: Privately Printed, 1930-31. 2 vols. 4to. 504 ills (some cold). Cloth.
(Wheldon & Wesley) **£65 [≈ $116]**

- Orchids for the Outdoor Garden. Ashford: 1930. 4to. xx,467 pp. 22 ills (1 cold). Endpapers sl marked. Cloth. Dw (edges sl chipped). *(Wheldon & Wesley)* £45 [≈ $80]

Darrach, William
- Drawings of the Anatomy of the Groin with Anatomical Remarks. Phila: 1844. 2nd edn. 127 pp. 4 litho plates. Foxing. Orig cloth, worn. *(Goodrich)* $75 [≈ £42]

Darwin, Charles
- The Descent of Man, and Selection in Relation to Sex. London: Murray, 1871. 1st edn, 2nd issue. 2 vols. Ills. Lacks advts. Three qtr calf, t.e.g. *(Wreden)* $160 [≈ £90]
- The Descent of Man and Selection in relation to Sex. London: 1871. 7th thousand. 2 vols. 76 figs. Sm tear 1 endpaper. Orig cloth, v sl worn, front inner hinges sl cracked. *(Whitehart)* £40 [≈ $71]
- The Descent of Man, and Selection in Relation to Sex. Second Edition (Fourteenth Thousand, Revised and Corrected). London: Murray, 1881. 8vo. xvi,693,[32 advt] pp. Orig green cloth. Freeman 953. *(Frew Mackenzie)* £65 [≈ $116]
- The Descent of Man, and Selection in Relation to Sex. Second Edition (Fourteenth Thousand, Revised and Corrected). London: Murray, 1881. 8vo. xvi,693,[32 advt] pp. Inscrptns. Orig green cloth, some wear & soiling. Freeman 953. *(Frew Mackenzie)* £35 [≈ $62]
- The Descent of Man, and Selection in relation to Sex. London: 1885. 2nd edn, rvsd (19th thousand). 8vo. xvi,693 pp. Text figs. Cloth. Freeman 959. *(Wheldon & Wesley)* £35 [≈ $62]
- The Descent of Man, and Selection in Relation to Sex. London: 1890. 2nd edn, 27th thousand. 8vo. xvi,693,32 pp. 78 ills. Orig cloth. Freeman 970. *(Henly)* £30 [≈ $53]
- The Descent of Man, and Selection in Relation to Sex. London: 1894. 2nd edn, 31st thousand. xvi,693 pp. Ills. Endpapers spotted. Cloth. *(Francis Edwards)* £40 [≈ $71]
- The Different Forms of Flowers on Plants of the Same Species. London: Murray, 1875. 1st edn. 8vo. viii,352,[32 advt] pp. Orig green cloth, largely unopened (2 pp sl carelessly opened). *(Frew Mackenzie)* £200 [≈ $356]
- The Different Forms of Flowers on Plants of the Same Species. Third Thousand. London: Murray, 1888. 8vo. xxiv,352,[32 advt] pp. Orig green cloth. Freeman 128. *(Frew Mackenzie)* £65 [≈ $116]
- The Effects of Cross and Self-Fertilisation in

the Vegetable Kingdom. London: 1888. 2nd edn, 2nd issue. 8vo. viii, 487 pp. Orig green cloth, spelling 'Fertilization' on spine. Freeman 1254. *(Wheldon & Wesley)* £70 [≈ $125]
- The Expression of the Emotions in Man and Animals. London: 1872. 1st edn. 2nd issue, with misprint on p 208. vi,374 pp. 7 plates, 21 figs. Some pp sl dusty. Orig cloth, worn, new endpapers. *(Whitehart)* £95 [≈ $169]
- The Expression of the Emotions in Man and Animals. London: 1872. 1st edn, 2nd issue. 8vo. vi,374 pp. 7 heliotype figs, 312 text figs. Name & some foxing on title. Marg tears on 2 plates reprd. Orig green cloth. Freeman 1142. *(Wheldon & Wesley)* £150 [≈ $267]
- The Expression of Emotions in Man and Animals. London: Murray, 1872. 1st edn, 2nd issue. 8vo. vi,374,[4 advt] pp. 7 heliotype plates, 21 figs. Orig bndg, edges worn. *(Key Books)* $280 [≈ £157]
- The Expression of the Emotions in Man and Animals. London: 1872. 8vo. vi,374 pp. 7 fldg heliotype plates, few ills. New green cloth to style, orig spine laid on. *(Weiner)* £75 [≈ $134]
- The Expression of the Emotions in Man and Animals. Tenth Thousand. London: Murray, 1873. 8vo. vi,374,[32 advt] pp. 2C3-4 discarded as often. Orig green cloth. Freeman 1144. *(Frew Mackenzie)* £65 [≈ $116]
- The Expression of the Emotions in Man and Animals. London: 1873. 10th thousand. 8vo. vi, 374 pp. 7 plates. Used, sl foxing & soiling, some pencil marks. Orig cloth, trifle loose. Freeman 1144. *(Wheldon & Wesley)* £65 [≈ $116]
- The Expression of the Emotions in Man and Animals. Second Edition, edited by F. Darwin. London: 1890. 8vo. viii,394 pp. 7 plates, 21 text figs. Sl foxing. Orig cloth, inner hinges sl weak. Freeman 1146. *(Wheldon & Wesley)* £45 [≈ $80]
- The Formation of Vegetable Mould through the Action of Worms with Observations on their Habits. London: 1881. 5th thousand. Sm 8vo. vii,326,[1 advt] pp. 15 ills. Endpapers v sl browned. Orig cloth. *(Francis Edwards)* £40 [≈ $71]
- The Formation of Vegetable Mould, through the Action of Worms ... Third Thousand. London: 1881. 8vo. vii,326 pp. Ills. Sm stamp on title verso & 1 marg. Orig cloth. Freeman 1359. *(Weiner)* £40 [≈ $71]
- The Formation of Vegetable Mould, through the Action of Worms ... London: Murray, 1882. 8vo. vii,328,[i advt] pp. Orig green cloth, extrs sl rubbed. Freeman 1362. *(Frew Mackenzie)* £90 [≈ $160]

- Geological Observations on the Volcanic Islands and Parts of South America visited during the Voyage of H.M.S. Beagle. London: 1876. 2nd edn. Cr 8vo. xiv,647 pp. 2 maps, cold plate, 4 plates of shells, 40 text figs. Orig cloth. Freeman 276.
(Wheldon & Wesley) **£170 [≃ $303]**
- Geological Observations on the Volcanic Islands and Parts of South America visited during the Voyage of H.M.S. 'Beagle'. London: 1891. 3rd edn. Sm 8vo. xiii,648 pp. 2 fldg maps, 5 fldg plates in pocket, 38 ills. Orig cloth.   *(Francis Edwards)* **£75 [≃ $134]**
- Geological Observations on the Volcanic Islands and Parts of South America visited during the Voyage of H.M.S. Beagle. New York: Appleton, 1891. 3rd edn. 12mo. 647 pp. Maps, fldg chart, ills. Orig bndg.
(Schoen) **$75 [≃ £42]**
- Geological Observations on the Volcanic Islands and Parts of South America visited during the Voyage of H.M.S. Beagle. London: 1891. 3rd edn. 8vo. xiii,648 pp. 2 fldg maps, fldg cold section, 4 fldg plates. Cloth, sl worn, sm hole on hinge. Freeman 282.   *(Henly)* **£60 [≃ $107]**
- Insectivorous Plants. London: 1875. 3rd thousand. 8vo. x,462 pp. Without the errata slip. Orig cloth, trifle worn. Freeman 1219.
(Wheldon & Wesley) **£60 [≃ $107]**
- Journal of Researches into the Natural History and Geology of the Countries Visited during the Voyage of H.M.S. Beagle round the World ... New Edition. London: Murray, 1870. 8vo. x,519 pp. Orig green cloth. Freeman 22.   *(Frew Mackenzie)* **£65 [≃ $116]**
- The Life and Letters ... including an Autobiographical Chapter. Edited by his son, Francis Darwin. New York: Appleton, 1896. 2 vols. 8vo. Lib stamps on titles. Contemp red half mor, t.e.g., rebacked. Freeman 1465.
(Frew Mackenzie) **£35 [≃ $62]**
- The Movements and Habits of Climbing Plants. Second Edition, revised. London: Murray, 1875. 1st hardcover edn. 8vo. vi, 208, [32 advt] pp. Publishers pres blind stamp. Orig green cloth, extrs sl worn. Freeman 836.
(Frew Mackenzie) **£160 [≃ $285]**
- On the Origin of Species by means of Natural Selection. London: 1860. 2nd edn. 5th thousand. 8vo. x,502 pp. Ctlg dated Jan 1860. Fldg diag. 2 ff sl defective. Orig green cloth, recased.   *(Wheldon & Wesley)* **£225 [≃ $401]**
- On the Origin of Species ... London: Murray, 1860. 2nd edn, 2nd issue. 8vo. ix,592 pp. Lacks the advts. Occas sl spotting. Contemp green half calf, gilt spine sl rubbed. Freeman 376.   *(Frew Mackenzie)* **£220 [≃ $392]**

- On the Origin of Species ... London: Murray, 1860. 2nd edn, 5th thousand. x,502 pp. Half-title. Fldg diag at p 117. Lacks advts. Contemp green half calf.
(Jermy & Westerman) **£240 [≃ $427]**
- On the Origin of Species by Means of Natural Selection. Fifth Thousand. London: 1860. 8vo. x,502,[Jan 1860 ctlg] pp. Fldg diag. Bndg variant b. Orig green cloth, trifle used, recased, front cvr trifle stained, endpapers sl damaged. Freeman 376.
(Wheldon & Wesley) **£250 [≃ $445]**
- The Origin of Species. London: 1872. 6th edn, 12th thousand. Sm 8vo. Endpapers foxed. Orig cloth, extrs worn, upper hinge cracked, sm split hd of spine.
(Francis Edwards) **£35 [≃ $62]**
- The Origin of Species ... Sixth Edition, with Additions and Corrections to 1872. (Twenty-fourth Thousand). London: Murray, 1882. 8vo. xxi,458 pp. Orig green cloth. Freeman 408.   *(Frew Mackenzie)* **£65 [≃ $116]**
- The Origin of Species by Means of Natural Selection. London: 1886. 6th edn (30th thousand). Cr 8vo. xxi,458 pp. Diag. Cloth. Freeman 417.
(Wheldon & Wesley) **£40 [≃ $71]**
- The Origin of Species by means of Natural Selection ... London: 1889. 37th thousand. xxi, 458 pp. Fldg table. Title sl soiled. Few marg pencil notes. Orig cloth, worn, hd of spine torn.   *(Whitehart)* **£25 [≃ $45]**
- The Origin of Species ... Sixth Edition, with Additions and Corrections. (Forty-seventh Thousand). London: Murray, 1895. 8vo. xxi,432 pp. Orig green cloth. Freeman 446.
(Frew Mackenzie) **£65 [≃ $116]**
- The Origin of Species ... Sixth Edition (Forty-Seventh Thousand). London: 1895. 8vo. xxi,432 pp. Fldg diag. Endpapers browned. Orig cloth, trifle speckled.
(Bow Windows) **£36 [≃ $64]**
- The Origin of Species. London: 1900. Sm 8vo. xxxi, 703 pp. Port frontis, 1 fldg diag. Endpapers sl foxed. Orig cloth.
(Francis Edwards) **£25 [≃ $45]**
- The Power of Movement in Plants. London: 1880. 1st edn, 1st issue. 8vo. x,592,[32 advt dated May 1878] pp. 196 text figs. Upper outer crnr v sl stained. Endpapers v sl foxed. Orig cloth, inner jnts cracked.
(Wheldon & Wesley) **£150 [≃ $267]**
- The Variation of Animals and Plants under Domestication. London: 1868. 1st edn, 2nd issue. 2 vols. 8vo. 43 text figs. Orig green cloth, trifle used. Freeman 878.
(Wheldon & Wesley) **£120 [≃ $214]**
- The Variation of Animals and Plants under Domestication. London: Murray, 1868. 1st

edn. 2nd issue, with Freeman's points. 2 vols.
8vo. 43 text figs. Orig green cloth gilt, 2-line
imprints on spines, vol 2 bumped, sl water
stained, lib label removed. Freeman 878.
(Blackwell's) **£185 [≃ $329]**
- The Variation of Animals and Plants under
Domestication. Authorized Edition with
Preface by Asa Gray. New York: [1868]. 2
vols. 8vo. Vol 1 title sl defective. Sl browned.
Inscrptns. Cloth, spines trifle marked.
(Wheldon & Wesley) **£55 [≃ $98]**
- The Variation of Animals and Plants under
Domestication. New York: (1868). 1st Amer
edn. 2 vols. Ills. Orig cloth, hd of spines
frayed, some wear.   *(King)* **£125 [≃ £70]**
- The Variation of Animals and Plants under
Domestication. Second Edition, revised. Fifth
Thousand. London: Murray, 1885. 2 vols.
8vo. Orig green cloth. Freeman 886.
(Frew Mackenzie) **£95 [≃ $169]**
- The Variation of Animals and Plants under
Domestication. London: 1888. 6th thousand.
2 vols. xiv,473; x,495 pp. 43 figs. Orig cloth.
(Whitehart) **£35 [≃ $62]**
- On the Various Contrivances by which
British and Foreign Orchids are Fertilised by
Insects. London: 1862. 1st edn. 8vo. vi,365
pp. 33 ills (1 fldg). Lacks advts. Half mor.
Freeman 800.
(Wheldon & Wesley) **£250 [≃ $445]**
- The Various Contrivances by which Orchids
are Fertilised by Insects. London: 1890. 2nd
edn, 5th thousand. 8vo. xvi,300 pp. 38 ills.
Orig cloth, trifle used. Freeman 810.
(Wheldon & Wesley) **£50 [≃ $89]**

Darwin, Erasmus
- Phytologia, or the Philosophy of Agriculture
and Gardening, with the Theory of Draining
Morasses,   and   with   an   improved
Construction of the Drill Plough. London:
1800. Lge 4to. viii,612,12 pp. 12 plates.
Foxing at ends. New half leather.
(Hortulus) **$220 [≃ £124]**
- Phytologia; or the Philosophy of Agriculture
and Gardening. With the Theory of Draining
Morasses,   and   with   an   improved
Construction of the Drill Plough. London:
for J. Johnson, 1800. 4to. viii,612,[12] pp. 12
plates (sl spotted). Mod half calf.
(Francis Edwards) **£215 [≃ $383]**
- Phytologia; or the Philosophy of Agriculture
and Gardening ... London: J. Johnson, 1800.
4to. viii,612,[xii] pp. 12 plates (foxed &
stained). Contemp calf, leather label, mrbld
bds.   *(Blackwell's)* **£190 [≃ $338]**

Dattner, B.
- The Management of Neurosyphilis. London:

1944. 398 pp. Cloth sl worn.
(Whitehart) **£15 [≃ $27]**

Daubeny, Charles
- An Introduction to the Atomic Theory.
Oxford, 1850. 2nd edn, enlgd. Sm 8vo. xxii,
502 pp. Errata slip. Diags. Lib stamps on
endpapers. Orig cloth, sl stained. Inscrbd
"from the Author". *(Weiner)* **£100 [≃ $178]**

Daumas, M.
- Scientific Instruments of the 17th & 18th
Centuries and their Makers. London:
Portman, 1972. 1st English edn. 4to. 361 pp.
142 ills. Cloth. Dw.   *(Savona)* **£25 [≃ $45]**

Davenport, John
- Aphrodisiacs and Anti-Aphrodisiacs: Three
Essays on the Powers of Reproduction.
London: privately printed, 1869. Sm 4to.
154,[1 advt] pp. 8 plates. Few pp sl frayed.
Half mor, gilt dec spine, crnrs & jnts worn, ft
of spine chipped.
(D & D Galleries) **$125 [≃ £70]**

Davey, M.J.B.
- Interpretative History of Flight ... London:
HMSO, 1937. 205 pp. 31 plates. Linen
backed bds.   *(Whitehart)* **£18 [≃ $32]**

Davey, W.P.
- A Study of Crystal Structure & Its
Application. New York: McGraw Hill, 1934.
1st edn. 8vo. xi,695 pp. Text figs. Orig cloth.
(Gemmary) **$45 [≃ £25]**

Davidson, John
- An Address on Embalming generally
delivered at the Royal Institution, on the
Unrolling of a Mummy. London: James
Ridgway, 1833. 2 plates. Frontis sl marked.
Orig wraps, a.e.g., dusty, spine sl defective.
Author's pres copy. *(Jarndyce)* **£80 [≃ $142]**

Davidson, Nathan (editor)
- The Gyroscope and Its Application. London:
Hutchinson, 1947. 2nd edn rvsd. 12mo. 256
pp. Num ills. Lib pocket. Orig cloth.
(Schoen) **$40 [≃ £22]**

Davie, O.
- Methods in the Art of Taxidermy. Phila:
1894. Roy 8vo. xiv,359 pp. 90 plates. Orig
cloth, recased.
(Wheldon & Wesley) **£45 [≃ $80]**

Davies, A.
- Dictionary of British Portraiture. London:
1979. 4 vols. Orig bndg.
(Whitehart) **£100 [≃ $178]**

Davies, Charles
- Treatise on Shades and Shadows and Linear Perspective. Second Edition. Hartford &c.: 1839. 159 pp. 21 fldg plates. Foxed. Orig bds, rebacked in calf.
(*D & D Galleries*) **$120 [≈ £67]**

Davies, D.C.
- A Treatise on Metalliferous Minerals & Mining. London: Crosby Lockwood, 1886. 3rd edn. 8vo. xxii,438,[48 ctlg] pp. 148 w'cut text figs. Orig dec cloth, rebacked.
(*Gemmary*) **$125 [≈ £70]**

Davies, John
- The Inn Keeper and Butler's Guide; or, A Directory in the making and managing of British Wines ... Leeds: George Wilson, 1807. 3rd edn. 12mo. Few pencil notes. Rebacked in half calf.
(*Jarndyce*) **£120 [≈ $214]**
- The Innkeeper's and Butler's Guide; or, A Directory for making and managing British Wines ... Tenth Edition, Revised and Corrected. Leeds: W. Preston, 1809. 12mo. iv, 199 pp. Orig ptd bds, uncut, backstrip damaged, stain on front cvr.
(*D & D Galleries*) **$150 [≈ £84]**

Davies, Oliver
- The Quaternary in the Coastlands of Guinea. Glasgow: 1964. 1st edn. Lge 8vo. 8 plates, 120 text figs. Orig cloth. Dw.
(*Bow Windows*) **£40 [≈ $71]**

Davies, Walter
- General View of the Agriculture and Domestic Economy of North Wales ... London: Richard Phillips ..., 1810. 8vo. xvi,510,[2 advt],[2 ctlg] pp. Fldg map frontis, 2 plates (browned & offset). Half mor gilt, sl worn.
(*Francis Edwards*) **£175 [≈ $312]**

Davis, Alfred Horace
- Modern Acoustics. London: Bell, 1934. 1st edn. 8vo. xi,345 pp. Ills. Orig cloth.
(*Schoen*) **$65 [≈ £37]**

Davis, David D.
- Acute Hydrocephalus, or Water in the Head ... Phila: Waldie, 1840. 8vo. 126 pp. Sl foxing & paper crease. Mod mrbld bds.
(*Goodrich*) **$250 [≈ £140]**

Davis, G.E.
- Practical Microscopy. London: 1889. New edn. 8vo. viii,436 pp. Cold frontis, 310 text figs. Prize calf, sl rubbed.
(*Wheldon & Wesley*) **£30 [≈ $53]**

Davis, John S.
- Plastic Surgery: Its Principles and Practice. Phila: 1919. 1st edn. 770 pp. 864 ills. Orig bndg, fine.
(*Fye*) **$750 [≈ £421]**
- Plastic Surgery: Its Principles and Practice. Phila: 1919. 1st edn. 770 pp. 864 ills. Water stain affecting marg of 100 ff. Orig bndg, soiled.
(*Fye*) **$300 [≈ £169]**

Davis, P.H. (editor)
- The Flora of Turkey and the East Aegean Islands. Edinburgh: 1965-88. 10 vols. Roy 8vo. Cloth.
(*Wheldon & Wesley*) **£520 [≈ $926]**

Davison, Charles
- The Hereford Earthquake of December 17, 1896. Birmingham: 1899. 8vo. xiii,303 pp. 3 fldg maps, diags. Orig cloth.
(*Weiner*) **£70 [≈ $125]**

Davison, Charles & Smith, Franklin
- Autoplastic Bone Surgery. Phila: 1916. 1st edn. 369 pp. Ills. Orig bndg.
(*Fye*) **$100 [≈ £56]**

Davy, Humphry
- Consolations in Travel, or the Last Days of a Philosopher. London: Murray, 1830. 1st edn. 8vo. [viii],282 pp. Contemp half calf, worn.
(*Gaskell*) **£120 [≈ $214]**
- Elements of Agricultural Chemistry, in a Course of Lectures for the Board of Agriculture. London: Longman ..., 1813. 1st edn. 4to. viii,323,lxiii pp. Some foxing. Calf, backstrip relaid. (*Key Books*) **$400 [≈ £225]**
- Elements of Agricultural Chemistry in a Course of Lectures for the Board of Agriculture. London: 1813. 1st edn. 4to. viii, 323,[1 blank], lxiii,[i blank],[4] pp. 10 plates (some foxed & offset). Few sl spots. Contemp calf, rebacked. (*Bow Windows*) **£215 [≈ $383]**
- Elements of Agricultural Chemistry, in a Course of Lectures for the Board of Agriculture. London: Longman ..., 1813. 1st edn. 4to. 323,lxiii, [4] pp. 10 plates (1 dble-page). Sm ink stamp on title. Contemp green mor gilt. (*Chapel Hill*) **$275 [≈ £154]**
- Salmonia: or Days of Fly Fishing ... With Some Account of the Habits of Fishes belonging to the Genus Salmo. By "An Angler". Second Edition. London: Murray, 1829. Sm 8vo. xv, 335 pp. 6 plates (some foxing), num text engvs. 19th c half calf, sl rubbed. Anon. (*Karmiole*) **$125 [≈ £70]**

Davy, John
- Memoirs of the Life of Sir Humphry Davy, Bart. By his Brother. London: 1836. 2 vols.

xii,507; vii,420 pp. Frontis port. Occas sl
foxing. Half leather.
(Whitehart) **£125 [≈ $223]**
- Memoirs of the Life of Sir Humphry Davy.
By his Brother. London: Smith, Elder, 1839.
8vo. [8],475,[6],[24 advt] pp. Errata slip. Port,
fldg plate. Addtnl title & half-title indicating
vol 1 of collected works. Rec bds.
(Fenning) **£55 [≈ $98]**

Davy, Richard
- New Inventions in Surgical Mechanisms.
London: 1875. 8vo. 21 pp. Ills. Disbound.
(Weiner) **£20 [≈ $36]**

Dawkins, W. Boyd
- Early Man in Britain and his Place in the
Tertiary Period. London: 1880. 1st edn. 8vo.
xxiv, 537,[2 advt] pp. 167 text ills. Sl foxing.
Orig cloth gilt, backstrip relaid.
(Henly) **£36 [≈ $64]**
- Early Man in Britain and his Place in the
Tertiary Period. London: 1880. xxiii,537 pp.
168 text figs. New cloth.
(Whitehart) **£25 [≈ $45]**

Dawson, George Pearson
- A Nosological Practice of Physic, embracing
Physiology. London: [Bishopwearmouth ptd]
for Longman, 1824. 1st edn. 8vo. [8],380,[4]
pp. Orig bds, uncut, rebacked.
(Spelman) **£60 [≈ $107]**

Dawson, Philip
- Electric Railways and Tramways. Their
Construction and Operation ... Entirely
Revised, Enlarged and Brought up to Date
from "Engineering". London: 1897. 4to.
xxv,677,[41 advt] pp. 503 ills, 183 tables.
Half mor, t.e.g., extrs rubbed, ft of spine
chipped.   *(Francis Edwards)* **£150 [≈ $267]**

Day, F.
- British and Irish Salmonidae. London:
Williams & Norgate, 1887. Roy 8vo. viii,299
pp. 12 plates (9 chromolithos), num text figs.
Orig cloth.   *(Egglishaw)* **£90 [≈ $160]**
- The Fishes of Great Britain and Ireland.
London: 1880-84. 2 vols. Roy 8vo. 180 plates
(1-179, 172A). Some foxing. New cloth.
(Wheldon & Wesley) **£250 [≈ $445]**
- The Fishes of Great Britain and Ireland.
London: Williams & Norgate, 1880-84. 2
vols. Roy 8vo. 180 litho plates. Lib stamp on
title. Minor spotting. Mor (jnts & crnrs sl
rubbed).   *(Egglishaw)* **£260 [≈ $463]**

Deacon, Richard
- John Dee: Scientist, Geographer, Astrologer

& Secret Agent to Elizabeth I. London: 1968.
1st edn. Ills. Dw.   *(Deja Vu)* **£25 [≈ $45]**

Deane, J.
- Ichnographs from the Sandstone of
Connecticut River. Boston: 1861. 4to. 61 pp.
9 photos, 37 tinted plates. Ex-lib, plates
unstamped. Orig cloth, worn.
(Wheldon & Wesley) **£150 [≈ $267]**

Deane, William
- The Description of the Copernican System ...
London: 1738. Imprint without advt beneath.
8vo. vi,106 pp. Fldg frontis (sl water stained),
7 fldg plates. New qtr calf.
(Weiner) **£350 [≈ $623]**

De Brutelle, Charles-Louis l'Heritier
- Sertum Anglicum 1788. Facsimile with
Critical Studies and a Translation.
Pittsburgh: The Hunt Botanical Library,
1963. Sm folio. Frontis, 34 plates. Orig japon
backed bds.   *(Francis Edwards)* **£40 [≈ $71]**

Debye, P.J.W. (editor)
- The Interference of Electrons. London &
Glasgow: 1931. 8vo. ix,85 pp. Diags. Orig
cloth.   *(Weiner)* **£40 [≈ $71]**

De Kay, J.E.
- Zoology of New York. Part 4. Fishes. Albany:
1842. 4to. xiv,415 pp. 79 plates. Some foxing.
Inscrptn on title. Mod cloth.
(Wheldon & Wesley) **£100 [≈ $178]**

de la Beche, Sir H.T.
- The Geological Observer. London: 1853. 2nd
edn. 8vo. xxviii,740 pp. 306 text figs. Cloth.
(Henly) **£80 [≈ $142]**

Delacour, J.
- Birds of Malaysia. New York: 1947. 8vo. xii,
382 pp. 84 ills. Cloth.
(Wheldon & Wesley) **£38 [≈ $68]**
- The Pheasants of the World. London: (1951)
1965. 4th imp. Cr 4to. 347 pp. 16 cold & 16
plain plates, 21 maps & diags. Orig cloth. Dw
(sl worn). *(Wheldon & Wesley)* **£140 [≈ $249]**
- The Pheasants of the World. London: (1977).
2nd edn, rvsd. Cr 4to. 432 pp. 33 plates (17
cold). Cloth.
(Wheldon & Wesley) **£65 [≈ $116]**

de la Cruz, Martin
- The Badianus Manuscript (Codex Barberini,
Latin 241) Vatican Library; An Aztec Herbal
of 1552. Introduction, Translation and
Annotations by Emily Walcott Emmart.
Baltimore: 1940. Folio. xxiv,341 pp. 118

plates, ills. Dw (worn).
(McBlain) **$150** [≃ **£84**]

De Moivre, Abraham
- Annuities upon Lives. London: by W.P. &
sold by Francis Fayram, 1725. 1st edn. Post
8vo. [ii],4,viii, 108,[ii] pp. Errata slip. Lacks
intl blank. Sl marg stains. Contemp calf,
rebacked.   (Ash) **£1,250** [≃ **$2,225**]

De Morgan, Augustus
- The Differential and Integral Calculus.
London: 1842. Thick 8vo. xx,785,64 pp. 3 sm
lib stamps. Orig dec cloth, sl worn, front
inner hinge loose.   (Weiner) **£40** [≃ **$71**]
- The Differential and Integral Calculus ...
Published under the superintendence of the
Society for the Diffusion of Useful
Knowledge. London: Baldwin & Cradock,
1842. 1st edn. 8vo. xx,785,64 pp. Contemp
calf gilt by Maclehose.
(Frew Mackenzie) **£195** [≃ **$347**]
- An Essay on Probabilities, and on their
Application to Life Contingencies and
Insurance Offices. London: Longman ...,
Lardner's Cabinet Cyclopaedia, 1838. 1st
edn. Sm 8vo. Addtnl engvd title. Orig cloth,
uncut, paper label (rubbed), v sl wear hd 1 jnt.
(Fenning) **£225** [≃ **$401**]

Dendy, Walter Cooper
- On the Phenomena of Dreams, and Other
Transient Illusions. London: Whittaker,
Treacher, 1832. 1st edn. iv,154,[2] pp. Orig
cloth backed bds, worn.
(Caius) **$250** [≃ **£140**]

Denman, James
- The Vine and Its Fruit; More especially in
relation to the Production of Wine ... Second
Edition, revised and Enlarged. London:
Longmans, Green, 1875. 8vo. xvi,518 pp. 2
fldg maps, plate. Orig pict gilt brown cloth,
fine.   (Gough) **£150** [≃ **$267**]

Denman, Thomas
- An Introduction to the Practice of Midwifery
... Brattleborough: William Fessenden, 1807.
xxxii,441,[14] pp. Contemp calf, edges sl
rubbed.   (Hemlock) **$325** [≃ **£183**]

Dennis, Frederic S. & Billings, John S.
- System of Surgery. Phila: Lea, 1895. 3 vols.
8vo. New cloth.   (Goodrich) **$135** [≃ **£76**]

Denny, G.A.
- Diamond Drilling for Gold & Other
Minerals. London: Crosby, Lockwood, 1900.
8vo. x,158 pp. 37 text ills. Good ex-lib. Orig

cloth.   (Gemmary) **$125** [≃ **£70**]

Denny, H.
- Monographia   Pselaphidarum   et
Scydmaenidarum Britanniae: an Essay on the
British Species of the Genera Pselaphus of
Herbst, and Scydmaenus, of Latreille.
Norwich: S. Wilkin, 1825. 8vo. vii,74 pp. 14
hand cold plates. Cloth, rebacked.
(Egglishaw) **£60** [≃ **$107**]

DePalma, Anthony
- Diseases of the Knee: Management in
Medicine and Surgery. Phila: 1954. 840 pp.
455 ills. Orig bndg.   (Fye) **$75** [≃ **£42**]
- Surgery of the Shoulder. Phila: 1950. 1st edn.
438 pp. Orig bndg.   (Fye) **$75** [≃ **£42**]

Deraniyagala, P.E.P.
- A Coloured Atlas of some Vertebrates from
Ceylon. Colombo: 1952-55. 3 vols. Oblong
4to. Port, 83 cold & 18 plain plates. Sm stamp
on titles. Cloth.
(Wheldon & Wesley) **£80** [≃ **$142**]

Derham, William
- The Artificial Clock-Maker. A Treatise of
Watch, and Clock-Work ... By W.D. London:
for James Knapton, 1696. 1st edn. 8vo.
[xii],132 pp. Fldg table, few text ills. 1 sm
marg tear. Contemp speckled calf, later label.
Wing D.1099. (Vanbrugh) **£2,955** [≃ **$5,260**]
- The Artificial Clock-Maker; A Treatise of
Watch and Clock-Work ... Third Edition.
London: for James Knapton, 1714. Sm 8vo.
[xvi], 140 pp. W'engvd fldg plate, 4 fldg
tables, sev w'cut text ills. Outer margs 3 ff sl
frayed. Contemp tree calf, rebacked. Anon.
(Gough) **£350** [≃ **$623**]

Desaguliers, John T.
- A Course of Experimental Philosophy. The
Third Edition Corrected. London: A. Millar
..., 1763. 2 vols. 4to. 46 fldg plates. Contemp
calf, gilt spines, red & green mor labels, v sl
reprs. John Cator's copy.
(Frew Mackenzie) **£480** [≃ **$854**]

Desault, P.J.
- A Treatise on Fractures, Luxations, and
Other Affections of the Bones ... Edited by
Xavier Bichat. Phila: 1817. 3rd Amer edn.
398 pp. 3 plates. Leather.
(Fye) **$250** [≃ **£140**]

Desmond, R.
- Dictionary of British and Irish Botanists and
Horticulturists, including Plant Collectors
and Botanical Artists. London: 1977. Roy

8vo. xxvi,747 pp. Orig cloth.
(Wheldon & Wesley) **£77 [≈ $137]**

Desruelles, H.M.J.
- Memoir on the Treatment of Venereal Diseases without Mercury, employed at the Military Hospital of the Val-De-Grace ... added ... Observations ... by G.J. Guthrie. Phila: Carey & Lea, 1830. 8vo. 215 pp. Foxing. Antique style bndg, uncut.
(Goodrich) **$95 [≈ £53]**

De Tabley, Lord
- The Flora of Cheshire. London: Longmans, Green, 1899. 1st edn. cxiv,399 pp. Port, fldg map. Orig pict green cloth gilt.
(Gough) **£50 [≈ $89]**

Deutsch, Sid
- Models of the Nervous System. New York: J. Wiley & Sons, [1967]. 1st edn. vii,[3],266 pp. Frontis, text diags. Name. Orig cloth. Dw.
(Caius) **$50 [≈ £28]**

De Vries, Hugo
- Intercellular Pangenesis including a Paper on Fertilization and Hybridization. Chicago: 1910. 270 pp. Orig bndg. *(Fye)* **$100 [≈ £56]**
- The Mutation Theory ... Translated by J.B. Farmer and A.D. Darbishire. London: 1910-11. 2 vols. Roy 8vo. 12 cold plates. Sl foxing & soiling. New cloth.
(Wheldon & Wesley) **£160 [≈ $285]**

Dewar, D.
- The Common Birds of India. The Sportsman's Birds, Wild Fowls, Game Birds and Pigeons. Calcutta: 1923. 4to. viii,126 pp. 44 ills. Orig pict cloth gilt.
(Henly) **£24 [≈ $43]**

Dewees, William Potts
- A Compendious System of Midwifery ... London: J. Miller, 1825. 1st English edn. 8vo. xii,628 pp. Ills. Lib stamp title verso. Orig cloth. *(Hemlock)* **$300 [≈ £169]**

Dewell, T.
- The Philosophy of Physic, founded on one General and Immutable Law of Nature ... Marlborough: ptd by E. Harold ..., 1785. 2nd edn, "revised & corrected". Sm 8vo. vii, [iii], xliii,[i],84 pp. Half-title. Sl damp staining. Contemp calf, jnt cracked, lacks label.
(Burmester) **£125 [≈ $223]**

Dey, Kanny Lall
- The Indigenous Drugs of India: Short Descriptive Notices ... Second Edition.

Calcutta: 1896. 8vo. xl,387 pp. Frontis port. Sl browned. Occas marg stamps. Orig cloth.
(Weiner) **£40 [≈ $71]**

Dialogues on Entomology ...
- Dialogues on Entomology, in which the Forms and Habits of Insects are Familiarly Explained. London: 1819. 8vo. xii,408 pp. 25 hand cold plates. Orig cloth, reprd.
(Wheldon & Wesley) **£50 [≈ $89]**

Dibdin, J.C. & Ayling, John
- The Book of the Lifeboat, with a Complete History of the Lifeboat Saturday Movement ... Edinburgh & London: 1894. Sq 8vo. xvi,270 pp. Num plates, ports, ills. Few lib stamps. Orig cloth, lib marks on spine.
(Weiner) **£35 [≈ $62]**

Dickinson, H.W.
- Matthew Boulton. Cambridge: UP, 1937. 1st edn. 8vo. Fldg plan, 15 plates, figs. Some foxing. Orig cloth. Dw.
(Bow Windows) **£45 [≈ $80]**

Dickinson, Joseph
- The Flora of Liverpool. London: Van Voorst, 1851. 1st edn. 8vo. 166 pp. Occas sl browning. Mod half mor gilt.
(Hollett) **£75 [≈ $134]**

Dickinson, Robert
- Improvement in British Ship-Building, Naval and Commercial ... by Changing the Material of which Ships are built from Wood to iron. Southwark: 1825. 8vo. Title,[7]-38 pp. Lacks Contents ff (pp 3-6). Disbound.
(Francis Edwards) **£85 [≈ $151]**

Dickson, A.
- A Treatise of Agriculture. A New Edition. London: 1770. 2 vols. 8vo. [vii],lxv, 487; [vii], 564 pp. 2 fldg plates. Contemp calf, jnts & crnrs worn. *(Henly)* **£125 [≈ $223]**

Dickson, James H.
- The Fibre Plants of India, Africa, and Our Colonies ... London: William Macintosh, [1864]. 1st edn. 8vo. Orig brown cloth.
(Georges) **£125 [≈ $223]**

Dickson, R.W.
- The Farmer's Companion: being a Complete System of Modern Husbandry ... Second Edition. London: Sherwood, Neely & Jones, 1813. 2 vols. 8vo. [vi],947,[i advt] pp. 103 plates (2 cold, 41 fldg). Some foxing & browning. Contemp half calf, sl worn.
(Blackwell's) **£210 [≈ $374]**

- Practical Agriculture; or, a Complete System of Modern Husbandry. London: for Richard Phillips, 1805. 1st edn. 2 vols. 4to. 87 plates (27 hand cold). Contemp calf, red & green labels, some wear to crnrs, hinges cracked but sides held on cords.
(Claude Cox) **£250 [≈ $445]**

Dickson, Sarah A.
- Panacea or Precious Bane. Tobacco in Sixteenth century Literature. New York: 1954. One of 400. 227 pp. Ills. Orig bndg.
(Goodrich) **$75 [≈ £42]**

Dickson, Sarah A. & O'Neil, Perry Hugh
- Tobacco. Its History Illustrated by the Books, Manuscripts and Engravings in the Library of George Arents Jr. ... New York: Rosenbach Co. & New York Public Library, 1937-52-58-69. One of 300. 5 vols, plus supplements I-X. Ills. 4to. Orig buckram & wraps.   *(Georges)* **£3,500 [≈ $6,230]**

A Dictionary of Natural History ...
- A Dictionary of Natural History; or, Complete Summary of Geology ... London: for Scatcherd & Letterman ..., 1815. 16mo. xxxvii, [ca 400] pp. 47 plates, each with 3 figs. Contemp green half calf.
(Claude Cox) **£45 [≈ $80]**

Diday, P.
- A Treatise on Syphilis in New-Born Children and Infants at the Breast. Translated by G. Whitley. London: New Sydenham Society, 1859. xii,272 pp. Margs v sl yellowed. Orig cloth gilt, edges sl rubbed, spine ends bumped, sl chipped.
(Francis Edwards) **£40 [≈ $71]**

Diesel, Rudolf
- Theory and Construction of a Rational Heat Motor. Translated from the German by Bryan Donkin. London: 1894. 8vo. viii,85 pp. 3 fldg plates, diags. Ex-lib. Sm marg tear 2 plates. Front free endpaper detached. Orig cloth, spine sl worn & marked.
(Weiner) **£125 [≈ $223]**

Dieterich, Karl
- The Analysis of Resins, Balsams and Gum Resins with a Bibliography. London: 1920. 8vo. xvi,431 pp. Orig cloth.
(Weiner) **£24 [≈ $43]**

Dieulefait, L.
- Diamonds and Precious Stones. London: Blackie, 1874. 8vo. xii,292 pp. 126 w'engvs. Orig dec cloth.   *(Gemmary)* **$80 [≈ £45]**

Digby, Sir Kenelm
- The Closet of Sir Kenelm Digby Knight opened: newly edited ... by Anne MacDonell. London: Philip Lee Warner, 1910. 8vo. lv, [1], 291,[1] pp. Port. Orig dec cloth, t.e.g., sl worn.   *(Goodrich)* **$125 [≈ £70]**
- Of Bodies, and of Mans Soul ... With Two Discourses. Of the Powder of Sympathy, and of the Vegetation of Plants. London: for Hohn Williams, 1669. 4to in 8s. [56],439,[1], [10], 231,[1] pp. W'cut diags. Sl marks. Contemp calf, rebacked, some rubbing, endpaper renewed. *(Goodrich)* **$600 [≈ £337]**
- Private Memoirs of Sir Kenelm Digby, Gentleman of the Bedchamber to King Charles the First. London: 1827. lxxxviii,328,50 pp. Frontis port. Occas foxing. Half leather.
(Whitehart) **£180 [≈ $320]**
- Two Treatises: in the one of which, The Nature of Bodies; In the other The Nature of Mans Soul, Is Looked Into. London: Williams, 1658. 4to. Text diags. Panelled calf. Wing D.1450.
(Rostenberg & Stern) **$675 [≈ £379]**

Dighton, C.A.A.
- A Manual of Diseases of the Naso-Pharynx ... London: 1912. xiii,168 pp. 5 cold plates, 68 text diags. Orig bndg, lib label.
(Whitehart) **£18 [≈ $32]**

Dillwyn, J.W.
- A Descriptive Catalogue of Recent Shells arranged according to the Linnaean Method. London: 1817. 2 vols. 8vo. xii,1092,[29] pp. New cloth.
(Wheldon & Wesley) **£120 [≈ $214]**

Dines, H.G.
- The Metalliferous Mining Region of South-West England. London: 1956. 2 vols. 8vo. 19 maps in pockets, 15 plates. Cloth. Dws.
(Henly) **£35 [≈ $62]**

Dingwall, Eric J.
- Artificial Cranial Deformation. A Contribution to the Study of Ethnic Mutations. London: John Bale, 1931. Sm 4to. xvi,313 pp. 55 plates. Orig cloth.
(Goodrich) **$500 [≈ £281]**
- The Girdle of Chastity: a Medico-Historical Study. London: 1931. 1st edn. 8vo. x,171 pp. 10 plates. Some marks. Inscrptn. Orig cloth.
(Bow Windows) **£40 [≈ $71]**
- Racial Pride and Prejudice. London: Watts, 1946. 1st edn. 8vo. Dw (torn).
(Any Amount) **£18 [≈ $32]**

Dinsdale, A.
- First Principles of Television. London: 1932. 1st edn. 8vo. xv,241 pp. Plates, ills. Half calf.
(Weiner) **£60 [≈ $107]**
- Television. London: 1926. 8vo. 62 pp. Frontis port, plates. Title soiled. Orig card cvrs, sl soiled. *(Weiner)* **£200 [≈ $356]**
- Television. London: 1926. 8vo. 62 pp. Frontis port, plates. V sl soiled. Orig card cvrs. Dw (sl soiled & chipped).
(Weiner) **£325 [≈ $579]**

Dioscorides
- The Greek Herbal of Dioscorides, illustrated by a Byzantine A.D. 512. Englished by J. Goodyer A.D. 1655, edited and first printed A.D. 1933 by R.T. Gunther. Oxford: 1934. One of 350. Roy 8vo. x,701 pp. 396 ills. Orig white buckram.
(Wheldon & Wesley) **£95 [≈ $169]**

Diplock, Joseph Bramah
- A New System of Heavy Goods Transport on Common Roads. London: 1902. 8vo. 116 pp. 2 plates, diags. Orig cloth.
(Weiner) **£75 [≈ $134]**

Disney, A.N. (editor)
- Origin and Development of the Microscope, as illustrated by Catalogues in the Collections of the Royal Microscopical Society. London: 1928. 8vo. xii,303 pp. 30 plates. Orig cloth, faded. *(Wheldon & Wesley)* **£70 [≈ $125]**

Dissertation ...
- A Dissertation on the Nature of Soils and the Properties of Manure ... London: Sherwood, Gilbert & Piper, 1833. 8vo. xi, 141, Appendix 45 pp. V occas foxing. Contemp half calf gilt, sl rubbed, upper jnt cracked.
(Blackwell's) **£55 [≈ $98]**

Ditmars, Raymond L.
- Reptiles of the World ... New Revised Edition. London: 1933. £Lge 8vo. xx,321 pp. Frontis, photo ills. Endpapers v sl browned. Orig cloth, some fading, minor soiling.
(Francis Edwards) **£25 [≈ $45]**

Dixon, E.S.
- The Dovecote and the Aviary. London: 1851. Sm 8vo. 458 pp. Frontis, w'cuts. New cloth.
(Wheldon & Wesley) **£30 [≈ $53]**

Dixon, Edward H.
- Scenes in the Practice of a New York Surgeon. With Eight Engravings by Darley. New York: Dewitt, 1855. 407 pp. Frontis, engvs. Orig cloth, worn.

(Goodrich) **$50 [≈ £28]**

Dixon, Henry H.
- Transpiration and the Ascent of Sap in Plants. London: Macmillan's Science Monographs, 1914. 1st edn. 8vo. viii,216,[2 advt] pp. Orig cloth.
(Fenning) **£38.50 [≈ $69]**

Dobson, G.E.
- Catalogue of the Chiroptera in the Collection of the British Museum. London: (1878) 1966. xlii,567 pp. 30 plates.
(Wheldon & Wesley) **£40 [≈ $71]**

Dodd, James Solas
- An Essay towards a Natural History of the Herring. London: for T. Vincent, 1752. 1st edn. 8vo. [8],178 pp, 12 contents ff, inc half-title. Final Proposal page. Lacks fldg plate. Disbound. *(Hannas)* **£70 [≈ $125]**

Dodgson, R.W.
- Report on Mussel Purification ... and Suggestions regarding the Sewage Pollution of Shellfish in its Public Health Aspect. London: Ministry of Agriculture & Fisheries, 1928. Lge 8vo. xvi,498 pp. Frontis, 15 plates, fldg charts & maps. Orig cloth.
(Weiner) **£30 [≈ $53]**

Dodoens, Rembert
- A New Herball, or Historie of Plants ... Translated ... by Henrie Lyte. London: Ninian Newton, 1586. 2nd edn. 4to. [40],916,[48] pp, irregular pagination but sgntrs consecutive. Few sl marks. 17th c calf, gilt spine, sl worn.
(Spelman) **£1,400 [≈ $2,492]**

Doherty, Terence
- The Anatomical Works of George Stubbs. London: Secker & Warburg, (1974). 1st edn. Folio. x,346 pp. Cold frontis, port, 272 plates. Orig cloth. Dw.
(Karmiole) **$75 [≈ £42]**

Dolge, Alfred
- Pianos and their Makers: a Comprehensive History of the Development of the Piano from the Monochord to the Concert Grand Player Piano. Covina: 1911. Lge 8vo. 478 pp. Plates, ports, ills. Orig cloth, rubbed.
(Weiner) **£150 [≈ $267]**

Donisthorpe, H.St.J.K.
- British Ants. Their Life Histories and Classification. London: 1927. 2nd edn, rvsd & enlgd. 8vo. xv,436 pp. 18 plates, 93 diags. Cloth. *(Wheldon & Wesley)* **£35 [≈ $62]**

- The Guests of British Ants. Their Habits and Life-Histories. London: 1927. 8vo. xxiii, 244 pp. 16 plates, 55 text figs. Cloth.
(Wheldon & Wesley) **£35 [≈ $62]**

Donn, J.
- Hortus Cantabrigiensis, or a Catalogue of Plants, Indigenous and Exotic. Cambridge: 1809. 5th edn. 8vo. 266 pp. Orig bds, rebacked. *(Wheldon & Wesley)* **£45 [≈ $80]**
- Hortus Cantabrigiensis, or an Accented Catalogue of Plants, Indigenous and Exotic, cultivated in Cambridge Botanic Garden. London: 1819. 9th edn, ed. F. Pursh. 8vo. 355 pp. Orig bds, dust soiled.
(Wheldon & Wesley) **£35 [≈ $62]**
- Hortus Cantabrigiensis. Cambridge: 1845. 13th edn, ed. P.N. Don. 8vo. xii,772 pp. Half calf, trifle worn.
(Wheldon & Wesley) **£45 [≈ $80]**

Donovan, E.
- The Natural History of British Shells ... London: for the author & Rivington, (1799-) 1800-04. 5 vols. Roy 8vo. 180 hand cold plates. Calf, dec spines gilt, t.e.g., fine.
(Egglishaw) **£2,000 [≈ $3,560]**

Donovan, Michael
- A Treatise on Chemistry. London: Lardner's Cabinet Cyclopaedia, 1832. 1st edn. Sm 8vo. Orig cloth, paper label. *(Fenning)* **£45 [≈ $80]**

Dorson, Richard M. (editor)
- Customs and Savage Myths. Selections from the British Folklorists. London: Routledge, 1968. 2 vols. 8vo. Orig cloth.
(Georges) **£35 [≈ $62]**

Dossie, R.
- The Elaboratory Laid Open, or, the Secrets of Modern Chemistry and Pharmacy Revealed ... London: J. Nourse, 1758. 1st edn. Some soiling to edges of endpapers. Calf gilt, gilt dec spine, crnrs sl bumped. Anon.
(P and P Books) **£275 [≈ $490]**

Douglas, A.V.
- The Life of Arthur Stanley Eddington. London: 1956. xiv,208 pp. Frontis, 7 dble sided plates. Dw (torn).
(Whitehart) **£25 [≈ $45]**

Dovar, Thomas
- The Ancient Physician's Legacy to his Country. London: R. Bradly, 1733. Pirated edn. 12mo. 216,[4] pp. Some foxing, tear in title reprd. Later mor.
(Bookpress) **$300 [≈ £169]**

Dove, H.W.
- The Distribution of Heat over the Surface of the Globe, illustrated by Isothermal, Thermic Isabnormal, and other Curves of Temperature. London: 1853. 1st edn. 4to. [iv], 27,[1] pp. 9 plates. Orig cloth, spine ends sl worn. *(Bow Windows)* **£85 [≈ $151]**
- The Law of Storms. Considered in Connection with the Ordinary Movements of the Atmosphere. London: 1862. x,324 pp. 4 charts, fldg map. Lib stamp on title & front cvr. *(Whitehart)* **£45 [≈ $80]**

Dover, Thomas
- The Ancient Physician's Legacy to his Country ... London: C. Hitch, 1742. 6th edn. 8vo. viii,245,[2] pp. Half-title marg reprd. Contemp calf, rebacked.
(Hemlock) **$275 [≈ £154]**

Dowsett, H.M.
- Wireless Telephony and Broadcasting. London: 1923-24. 1st edn. 2 vols. 5 + 2 plates, num figs. Occas sl foxing. Orig bndgs.
(Whitehart) **£45 [≈ $80]**

Doyen, Eugene
- Surgical Therapeutics and Operative Technique. London: 1917-20. 1st edn in English. 3 vols. 746; 680; 811 pp. 1975 ills. Orig bndgs, fine. *(Fye)* **$250 [≈ £140]**

Draper, John William
- A Treatise on the Forces which produce the Organization of Plants. With an Appendix ... New York: Harper, 1844. 1st edn. Sm folio. 216 pp. Hand cold frontis, 3 plates (1 dble-page). Orig cloth, spine tips worn, cvrs sl soiled & bubbled.
(Chapel Hill) **$350 [≈ £197]**

Dresser, H.E.
- A Monograph of the Coraciidae, or Family of the Rollers. London: 1893. One of 250. Imperial 4to. xx,111 pp. 27 hand cold plates by Keulemans. Green levant mor.
(Wheldon & Wesley) **£3,600 [≈ $6,408]**

Dreyer, J.L.E.
- History of the Planetary Systems. From Thales to Kepler. Cambridge: 1906. xii,432 pp. Cloth, sl faded. *(Whitehart)* **£40 [≈ $71]**
- Tycho Brahe. A Picture of Scientific Life and Work in the Sixteenth Century. Edinburgh: 1890. xvi,405 pp. 5 plates. Orig cloth, sl worn & marked. *(Whitehart)* **£38 [≈ $68]**

Driesch, Hans A.E.
- The Science and Philosophy of the Organism.

The Gifford Lectures ... London: A. & C. Black, 1908. 1st edn. 2 vols. 8vo. xiii, 329; xvi, 381 pp. Orig cloth.
(Fenning) **£75 [≈ $134]**

Druce, G.C.
- The Comital Flora of the British Isles. Arbroath: T. Buncle, 1932. 1st edn. xxxii,407 pp. Fldg map in pocket, frontis. Orig cloth.
(Gough) **£30 [≈ $53]**
- The Comital Flora of the British Isles. Arbroath: 1932. 8vo. xxxii,407 pp. Lge cold map, 2 ports. Cloth.
(Wheldon & Wesley) **£20 [≈ $36]**
- The Flora of Oxfordshire. London: 1886. 1st edn. Cr 8vo. lii,452 pp. Cold map in pocket. Rebound in cloth. *(Henly)* **£48 [≈ $85]**

Druitt, Robert
- The Principles and Practice of Modern Surgery. Edited by Joshua Flint. Phila: 1844. 568 pp. 153 w'cuts. Leather, scuffed.
(Fye) **$100 [≈ £56]**

Drury, Heber
- The Useful Plants of India; with Notices of their Chief Value in Commerce, Medicine and the Arts. Madras: 1873. 8vo. xvi,512 pp. Paper browned & brittle. Half-title detached. Cloth. *(Weiner)* **£35 [≈ $62]**

Du Toit, A.L.
- Our Wandering Continents. An Hypothesis of Continental Drifting. London: 1937. 8vo. xiii, 366 pp. 48 diags. Cloth, trifle used.
(Wheldon & Wesley) **£30 [≈ $53]**

The Dublin Dissector ...
- See Harrison, Robert

Duchene, Emile Auguste
- The Mechanics of the Aeroplane, a Study of the Principles of Flight. Translated from the French ... London: 1912. 1st edn in English. 8vo. x,231 pp. Diags. Lib stamps on pastedowns. Orig cloth. *(Weiner)* **£30 [≈ $53]**

Duchenne, G.B.
- Physiology of Motion demonstrated by means of Electrical Stimulation and Clinical Observation and Applied to the Study of Paralysis and Deformities. Phila: 1949. Ltd edn. 612 pp. Qtr leather. Slipcase.
(Fye) **$250 [≈ £140]**

Duclaux, E.
- Pasteur: The History of a Mind. Phila: 1920. 1st edn. 363 pp. Ills. Orig bndg.
(Fye) **$50 [≈ £28]**

Dufrenoy, Pierre Armand
- On the Use of Hot Air in the Iron Works of England and Scotland. Translated from a Report, made to the Director General of Mines in France, in 1834. London: 1836. 8vo. 103 pp. 10 plates (sl foxed). Inscrptn on title. Cloth. *(Weiner)* **£100 [≈ $178]**

Duggar, Benjamin M. (editor)
- Biological Effects of Radiation ... Washington: McGraw-Hill, for National Research Council, 1936. 1st edn, 2nd imp. 2 vols. 8vo. Orig cloth.
(Fenning) **£24.50 [≈ $45]**

Dugmore, A. Radclyffe
- The Romance of the Beaver. Being the History of the Beaver in the Western Hemisphere. Philadelphia & London: [ca 1921]. 8vo. xiv,225 pp. Num ills. Orig bndg.
(Northern Books) **$80 [≈ £45]**

Duhamel du Monceau, M.
- A Practical Treatise of Husbandry: wherein are contained, many Useful and Valuable Experiments and Observations in the New Husbandry ... Translated by John Mills. London: 1759. Sm 4to. xxiv,492,[7],[1 advt] pp. Fldg table, 6 plates. Later half leather.
(Hortulus) **$380 [≈ £213]**

Duhring, Louis A.
- Atlas of Skin Diseases. Phila: Lippincott, 1876. Folio. 36 cold plates. Lib stamp on title. Orig bds, rebacked.
(Goodrich) **$250 [≈ £140]**

Dujardin-Beaumetz, Prof.
- Diseases of the Stomach and Intestines. A Manual of Clinical Therapeutics ... Translated from the Fourth French Edition by E.P. Hurd, M.D. New York: Wood, 1886. xvi,389 pp. Fldg frontis (torn along folds), ills. Orig bndg. *(Goodrich)* **$45 [≈ £25]**

Duke-Elder, S.
- The Practice of Refraction. London: 1969. 8th edn. x,329 pp. 244 figs. Dw.
(Whitehart) **£15 [≈ $27]**

Duncan, A.
- Heads of Lectures on the Theory and Practice of Medicine. Edinburgh: 1790. 4th edn. xvi,300 pp. Lib marks on title & endpapers. Some discoloration of page edges. Contemp bds, crnrs sl worn. *(Whitehart)* **£180 [≈ $320]**

Duncan, J.
- British Moths, Sphinxes etc. London: Bohn,

Jardine's Naturalist's Library, n.d. Sm 8vo. 268 pp. Port, vignette, 30 cold plates. Cloth. *(Wheldon & Wesley)* **£40 [≈ $71]**

- The Natural History of Beetles. Edinburgh: Lizars, Jardine's Naturalist's Library, 1835. 1st edn. Sm 8vo. 269 pp. Port, cold title vignette, 30 hand cold plates. Binder's cloth. *(Egglishaw)* **£34 [≈ $61]**

- The Natural History of British Butterflies ... Edinburgh: Lizars, Jardine's Naturalist's Library, 1840. Sm 8vo. 246 pp. Port, cold title vignette, 32 hand cold plates. Occas spotting. Contemp mor, gilt spine, a.e.g. *(Egglishaw)* **£48 [≈ $85]**

- The Natural History of British Moths, Sphinxes etc. Edinburgh: Lizars, Jardine's Naturalist's Library, 1836. 1st edn. Sm 8vo. 268 pp. Vignette title, 30 hand cold plates. Orig cloth. *(Egglishaw)* **£45 [≈ $80]**

- The Natural History of British Moths, Sphinxes etc. Edinburgh: Lizars, Jardine's Naturalist's Library, 1841. Sm 8vo. 268 pp. Vignette title, 30 hand cold plates. Contemp mor, gilt spine, a.e.g. *(Egglishaw)* **£50 [≈ $89]**

Duncan, P.M.
- The Transformations of Insects. London: Cassell, 1882. 8vo. xii,531 pp. 40 plates, text ills. Orig dec cloth. *(Egglishaw)* **£28 [≈ $50]**

Duncumb, John
- A General View of the Agriculture of the County of Hereford. London: Richard Phillips, 1805. 8vo. viii,173,[3] pp. 2 fldg maps (1 hand cold), 3 plates. Orig bds, paper label (sm repr), crnrs bumped. *(Spelman)* **£95 [≈ $169]**

Dundonald, Archibald Cochrane, 9th Earl of
- A Treatise, shewing the intimate connection that subsists between Agriculture and Chemistry ... London: Murray & Highley, 1795. 1st edn. 4to. vii,[i],252 pp. Few sm lib marks. Orig bds, untrimmed, rebacked, marked, crnrs sl worn. *(Clark)* **£170 [≈ $303]**

Dunell, H.
- British Wire-Drawing and Wire-Working Machinery. London: 1925. Lge 4to. xv,188 pp. 181 text ills. Orig bndg. *(Whitehart)* **£25 [≈ $45]**

Dunglison, Robley
- History of Medicine from the Earliest Ages to the Commencement of the Nineteenth Century. Phila: 1872. 1st edn. 287 pp. Orig bndg. *(Fye)* **$150 [≈ £84]**

Dunkin, E.
- The Midnight Sky. Familiar Notes on the Stars and Planets. London: 1891. 2nd edn. xii, 428 pp. 32 maps, ills. Lib stamps. Orig dec cloth. *(Whitehart)* **£35 [≈ $62]**

Dunlap, Roy F.
- Gunsmithing. A Manual of Firearms Design, Construction, Alteration and Remodelling. For Amateur and Professional Gunsmiths ... South Carolina: 1950. 8vo. ix,714,[14 advt] pp. Num ills. Orig cloth, sl worn. *(Francis Edwards)* **£30 [≈ $53]**

Dunraven, Earl of
- Self-Instruction in the Practice and Theory of Navigation. London: 1900. 2 vols. 8vo. Num text figs. Endpapers v sl browned. Orig cloth, v sl marked. *(Francis Edwards)* **£85 [≈ $151]**

Duns, J.
- Memoir of Sir James Y. Simpson, Bart. Edinburgh: 1873. 1st edn. 544 pp. Port frontis. Orig bndg, front inner hinge cracked. *(Fye)* **$175 [≈ £98]**

Dunsterville, G.C.K. & Garay, L.
- Venezuelan Orchids Illustrated. Vol. 1. London: 1959. Demy 4to. 452 pp. 216 ills (16 cold). Buckram. *(Wheldon & Wesley)* **£60 [≈ $107]**

Du Pont, J.
- Philippine Birds. Delaware: 1971. 4to. 480 pp. 84 cold plates. Cloth. *(Wheldon & Wesley)* **£45 [≈ $80]**

Dupont, J.E.
- South Pacific Birds. Greenville: 1975. 8vo. xii,217 pp. 31 cold plates. Cloth. *(Wheldon & Wesley)* **£35 [≈ $62]**

Durham, Robert
- Encyclopedia of Medical Syndromes. New York: 1960. 1st edn. 628 pp. Orig bndg. *(Fye)* **$75 [≈ £42]**

Dutt, Uday Chand
- The Materia Medica of the Hindus ... With a Glossary of Indian Plants by George King. Revised Edition. Calcutta: 1900. 8vo. xx,355 pp. Title tissued, crnrs brittle, few sm worm holes. Cloth. *(Weiner)* **£35 [≈ $62]**

- The Materia Medica of the Hindus With a Glossary of Indian Plants by George King. Revised Edition. Calcutta: 1922. 8vo. xx,356 pp. Wraps. *(Weiner)* **£30 [≈ $53]**

Dyckman, Jacob
- An Inaugural Dissertation on the Pathology of the Human Fluids. New York: Van Winkle & Wiley, 1814. 8vo. Half-title,243 pp. Lib stamps on title. Later linen.
(Goodrich) **$250 [≈ £140]**

Dyer, B.
- The Society of Public Analysts and other Analytical Chemists. Some Reminiscences of its first Fifty Years ... Cambridge: The Society, 1932. 1st edn. Lge 8vo. 4 ports. Orig cloth, dull & marked.
(Bow Windows) **£30 [≈ $53]**

Dykes, W.R.
- The Genus Iris. Cambridge: 1913. Folio. 48 cold plates, 30 ills. Sl foxing. Orig half mor, sl marks on front cvr.
(Wheldon & Wesley) **£600 [≈ $1,068]**
- The Genus Iris. Cambridge: 1913. Folio. 48 cold plates. Sl foxing. Orig half mor, marks on front cvr.
(Wheldon & Wesley) **£600 [≈ $1,068]**
- Notes on the Tulip Species. London: 1930. Folio. 109 pp. 54 ills. Orig cloth, rubbed.
(Hortulus) **$180 [≈ £107]**
- Notes on Tulip Species. Edited and Illustrated by E.K. Dykes. London: 1930. Folio. 108 pp. 54 cold plates. Buckram, uncut, crnrs sl bumped.
(Wheldon & Wesley) **£100 [≈ $178]**

Dymock, William
- The Vegetable Materia Medica of Western India. Second Edition. Bombay: 1885. 8vo. xx, 1012 pp. Few sm wormholes. Sl browned. Occas sm stamps & reprs. Cloth.
(Weiner) **£50 [≈ $89]**

Dymock, William, & others
- Pharmacographia Indica; a History of the Principal Drugs of Vegetable Origin met with in British India. London, Bombay & Calcutta: (1889)-93. 7 parts in 3 vols, inc Index & Appendix. 8vo. Few marks. Occas browning. Half calf. *(Weiner)* **£250 [≈ $445]**

Eadon, John
- The Arithmetician's Guide: being a New, Improved, and Compendious System of Practical Arithmetic ... Sheffield: for W. Ward ..., 1766. 1st edn. 8vo. [iv],iv,[ii], v,333 pp. Few diags. Tear in last leaf (no loss). Contemp sheep. *(Burmester)* **£150 [≈ $267]**

Eales, N.B.
- The Cole Library of Early Medicine and Zoology. Catalogue of Books and Pamphlets.

Part 1. 1472 to 1800. Oxford: 1969. xiv,425 pp. Frontis. Orig bndg.
(Whitehart) **£30 [≈ $53]**

Eastman, Mary
- The Biography of Dio Lewis. New York: 1891. 1st edn. 398 pp. Orig bndg.
(Fye) **$70 [≈ £39]**

Easton, James
- Human Longevity: Recording the Name, Age, Place of Residence, and Year, of the Decease of 1712 Persons, who attained a Century and Upwards, from A.D. 66 to 1799 ... Salisbury: James Easton, 1799. 1st edn. 8vo. xxxii, [lx], 292 pp. Half-title. 19th c qtr calf. *(Young's)* **£190 [≈ $338]**

Eaton, Robert
- An Account of Dr. Eaton's Styptick Balsam. The Second Edition, with a Letter to the Royal Society, and other Additions. London: J. Peele, 1726. 8vo. xiv,[2],80 pp. Orig wraps.
(Hemlock) **$175 [≈ £98]**

Eccles, W.M.
- Hernia. Its Etiology, Symptoms and Treatment. London: 1902. 2nd edn. xvi,233 pp. 118 ills. Orig bndg, lib label on front cvr.
(Whitehart) **£18 [≈ $32]**

Eckhardt, George H.
- Electronic Television. Chicago: Eckhardt, 1936. 1st edn. 8vo. xx,162 pp. Frontis, ills. Lib pocket. Orig bndg. *(Schoen)* **$65 [≈ £37]**

Eddington, A.S.
- Fundamental Theory. Cambridge: UP, 1946. 1st edn. 4to. 292 pp. Orig bndg.
(Key Books) **$100 [≈ £56]**
- Report on the Relativity Theory of Gravitation. London: Fleetway Press, 1920. 2nd edn. Orig wraps bound in.
(Key Books) **$225 [≈ £126]**

Eddington, Sir Arthur
- The Expanding Universe; Presidential Address. Cambridge: 1932. Lge 8vo. 16 pp. Port. Orig ptd wraps. Inscrbd by the author.
(Weiner) **£40 [≈ $71]**
- The Expanding Universe. Cambridge: UP, 1933. 1st edn. 16mo. 127 pp. 2 photo plates. Orig green cloth bds, spine faded.
(Schoen) **$60 [≈ £34]**
- Report on the Relativity Theory of Gravitation. London: Physical Society of London, 1918. 1st edn. 8vo. viii,91 pp. Title sl dusty. New bds. MS notes by Sir Joseph Larmor. *(Gaskell)* **£145 [≈ $258]**

Eddy, William Crawford
- Television, The Eyes of Tomorrow. New York: Prentice Hall, 1945. 1st edn. 330 pp. Lib pocket. Orig bndg. *(Schoen)* **$40 [≈ £22]**

Eder, Josef Maria
- History of Photography. Translated by Edward Epstean. New York: Columbia UP, 1945. 1st Amer edn. Thick 8vo. xx,860 pp. Frontis. Orig cloth. *(Karmiole)* **$100 [≈ £56]**

Edgeworth, Richard Lovell
- An Essay on the Construction of Roads and Carriages. London: 1813. 1st edn. 8vo. x, iii, 202, [ii],194 pp. 4 fldg plates. Sl water staining. Occas marg lib stamp. Cloth backed mrbld bds. *(Weiner)* **£350 [≈ $623]**
- An Essay on the Construction of Roads and Carriages. The Second Edition: with a Report of Experiments ... London: 1817. 8vo. iv,2, [ii], 171 pp. 4 fldg plates. Occas marg lib stamps. Orig cloth backed mrbld bds. *(Weiner)* **£185 [≈ $329]**

The Edinburgh Encyclopaedia ...
- The Edinburgh Encyclopaedia ... in Eighteen Volumes. Edinburgh: William Blackwood, 1830. 21 vols, inc plates in 3 vols. 4to. 532 plates. Contemp diced calf gilt, red & green labels, spines sl rubbed. By David Brewster & others. *(Frew Mackenzie)* **£2,000 [≈ $3,560]**

Edridge-Green, F.W.
- Colour-Blindness and Colour Perception. London: International Scientific Series, 1891. 1st edn. 8vo. viii,312, [89,6] advt] pp. 3 cold plates, text ills. Orig cloth. *(Bookpress)* **$175 [≈ £98]**

Edwards's Botanical Register
- Edwards's Botanical Register, consisting of Coloured Figures of Exotic Plants cultivated in British Gardens. London: 1815-47. 33 vols. Complete set inc Appendix. 8vo. 2717 hand cold & 4 plain plates. Half mor. *(Wheldon & Wesley)* **£15,000 [≈ $26,700]**

Edwards, James
- The Hemiptera-Homoptera (Cicadina and Psyllina) of the British Islands. London: 1896. Large Paper. Roy 8vo. xii,271 pp. 28 cold & 2 plain plates. Occas foxing. Half mor, v rubbed but sound. *(Wheldon & Wesley)* **£100 [≈ $178]**
- The Hemiptera-Homoptera (Cicadina and Psyllina) of the British Islands ... London: L. Reeve (with Ashford over-slip), 1896. Lge 8vo. xii,271 pp. 28 cold & 2 plain plates. Orig green cloth gilt. *(Blackwell's)* **£250 [≈ $445]**

Edwards, Sydenham
- The Botanical Register ... Volume III. London: James Ridgway, 1817. 8vo. 86 hand cold plates. Contemp green mor gilt, a.e.g. *(Frew Mackenzie)* **£850 [≈ $1,513]**

Edwards, W.S.
- Alexis Carrell, Visionary Surgeon. Springfield: 1974. 1st edn. 143 pp. Orig bndg. Dw. *(Fye)* **$50 [≈ £28]**

Eigenmann, C.H.
- The American Characidae. Cambridge, Mass.: 1917-29. 5 parts. 4to. 558 pp. 101 plates. Wraps. *(Wheldon & Wesley)* **£80 [≈ $142]**

Einstein, Albert
- Relativity, the Special and the General Theory. London: 1920. 8vo. xiii,138 pp. Frontis port. Orig cloth. *(Weiner)* **£20 [≈ $36]**
- Relativity: The Special & The General Theory. A Popular Exposition. Authorized Translation by Robert W. Lawson. London: Methuen, (1920). 1st edn in English. 12mo. xii,138,[8 advt] pp. Offset endpapers, minor foxing. Orig red cloth, sl worn & soiled. *(D & D Galleries)* **$190 [≈ £107]**

Eissler, M.
- The Hydro-Metallurgy of Copper. London: Crosby Lockwood, 1902. 1st edn. 8vo. xii, 228, [64 ctlg] pp. 120 text figs. Orig cloth, spotted. *(Gemmary)* **$75 [≈ £42]**
- The Metallurgy of Gold. London: Crosby Lockwood, 1888. 1st edn. 8vo. xii,188,[56 ctlg] pp. 90 text figs.. Orig cloth, stained. *(Gemmary)* **$125 [≈ £70]**
- The Metallurgy of Gold. London: Crosby Lockwood, 1900. 5th edn. 8vo. xxvi,638 pp. Fldg plates, text figs. Orig cloth, spine worn, jnt torn. *(Gemmary)* **$150 [≈ £84]**
- The Metallurgy of Silver. London: Crosby Lockwood, 1891. 2nd edn. 8vo. xiv,362,[65 advt] pp. 124 ills. Orig dec cloth, shaken. *(Gemmary)* **$100 [≈ £56]**
- The Modern High Explosives. New York: John Wiley & Sons, 1909. 3rd edn. 8vo. xi,395 pp. 129 text figs. Orig cloth, worn. *(Gemmary)* **$60 [≈ £34]**

The Elaboratory Laid Open ...
- The Elaboratory Laid Open, or the Secrets of Modern Chemistry and Pharmacy Revealed ... London: J. Nourse, 1758. xiv,375,index pp. Trifle soiled. Lacks endpapers. Contemp calf, red label, front bd almost detached, worn. *(Jermy & Westerman)* **£75 [≈ $134]**

- See also Dossie, R.

Elam, Charles
- On Cerebria and Other Diseases of the Brain.
London: Churchill, 1872. 8vo. clviii, 142 pp.
Orig bndg. Author's pres copy.
(Goodrich) **$125 [≃ £70]**

The Elements of Optics ...
- See Emerson, William

Ellerman, J.R.
- The Families and Genera of Living Rodents,
with a List of Named Forms by R.W.
Hayman and G.W. Holt. London: 1940-41.
1st edn. 2 vols. Cr 4to. 249 text figs. Cloth.
(Henly) **£125 [≃ $223]**

Elliot, D.G.
- A Monograph of the Paradiseidae or Birds of
Paradise. New York & Amsterdam: 1977.
One of 250 (of 500) leather bound. Lge folio.
xxxii, [90] pp. 1 plain & 36 cold plates. Dark
blue half mor by Zaehnsdorf.
(Wheldon & Wesley) **£620 [≃ $1,104]**

Elliot, John
- An Account of the Nature and Medicinal
Virtues of the Principal Mineral Waters of
Great Britain and Ireland, and Those Most in
repute on the Continent. London: 1781. 236
pp. Fldg frontis, ills. Contemp polished calf,
gilt spine, sl stained & worn.
(Whitehart) **£200 [≃ $356]**
- An Account of the Nature and Medicinal
Virtues of the Principal Mineral Waters of
Great Britain and Ireland ... Second Edition,
Corrected and Enlarged. London: for J.
Johnson, 1789. 8vo. Fldg plate. Contemp half
calf, gilt spine. *(Waterfield's)* **£200 [≃ $356]**
- The Medical Pocket-Book. Containing a
Short but Plain Account of the Symptoms,
Causes, and Methods of Cure of the Diseases
incident to the Human Body ... Fourth
Edition ... London: for J. Johnson, 1794.
12mo. 183, [1 blank].[4] pp. Browning.
Contemp calf, spine & crnrs reprd.
(Spelman) **£40 [≃ $71]**

Elliott, A. & Dickson, J.H.
- Laboratory Instruments. Their Design and
Application. London: Chapman & Hall,
1951. 1st edn. 8vo. Num text figs. Cloth.
(Savona) **£20 [≃ $36]**

Elliott, Daniel Giraud
- The Birds of Daniel Giraud Elliott, a
Selection of Pheasants and Peacocks painted
by Joseph Wolf and taken from the Original

Monograph published in New York, 1872 ...
London: Ariel Press, 1979. One of 1000.
Folio. 12 cold plates. Orig cloth. Dw.
(Henly) **£75 [≃ $134]**

Elliott, F.A., & others
- Clinical Neurology. London: 1952. xxii,752
pp. 8 plates. Orig bndg.
(Whitehart) **£15 [≃ $27]**

Ellis, A.E.
- British Snails. London: 1926. Cr 8vo. 275 pp.
14 plates, text figs. Few pencil notes on
plates. Sm stain crnr of frontis. Cloth, trifle
used. *(Wheldon & Wesley)* **£20 [≃ $36]**

Ellis, D.
- An Inquiry into the Changes induced on
Atmospheric Air by the Germination of Seeds
... and the Respiration of Animals [with]
Farther Inquiries ... Edinburgh: 1807-11. 2
vols in one. 8vo. xv,246; x,375 pp. Some
foxing Contemp cloth, worn. Author's pres
copy. *(Wheldon & Wesley)* **£240 [≃ $427]**

Ellis, Edward
- A Practical Manual of the Diseases of
Children with a Formulary. Third Edition.
New York: Wood Library, 1879. 8vo. xii,213
pp. Orig bndg, hd of spine split.
(Goodrich) **$45 [≃ £25]**

Ellis, G.
- Modern Practical Carpentry. London: 1906.
xvi, 390 pp. Over 1000 ills. Orig bndg.
(Whitehart) **£40 [≃ $71]**

Ellis, George
- Memoir of Jacob Bigelow, M.D. LL.D.
Cambridge: 1880. 1st edn. 105 pp. Orig
bndg. *(Fye)* **$75 [≃ £42]**

Ellis, George Viner & Ford, G.H.
- Illustrations of Dissections in a Series of
Original Coloured Plates ... The Drawings
are from Nature and on Stone by Mr. Ford
from Dissections by Professor Ellis. London:
Walton, 1867. Folio. 58 cold plates. Some
reprs. Contemp qtr calf, rebacked. Text vol
recased. *(Goodrich)* **$950 [≃ £534]**

Ellis, J. & Solander, D.
- The Natural History of many curious and
uncommon Zoophytes, collected from
Various Parts of the Globe. London:
Benjamin White, 1786. 4to. xii,208 pp. 63
plates, orig tissue guards. Half calf, fine.
(Egglishaw) **£360 [≃ $641]**

Ellis, William
- Chiltern and Vale Farming Explained, according to the latest Improvements ... London: for Weaver Bickerton, [1733]. 1st edn. 8vo. Frontis. Contemp calf, gilt spine, minor rubbing.   *(Ximenes)* **$650 [≈£365]**
- The London and Country Brewer. Containing the Whole Art of Brewing all Sorts of Malt-Liquors ... Fifth Edition. London: Thomas Astley, 1744. 8vo. [2],[6],332,[4] pp. General title & 4 sectional title-pages. Contemp calf, jnts cracked.
(Spelman) **£180 [≈$320]**
- The Practical Farmer. London: for Weaver Bickerton ..., 1732. 1st edn. 8vo. iv, [164], [ii] pp. Contemp calf, rebacked.
(Ash) **£250 [≈$445]**

Eltringham, H.
- African Mimetic Butterflies. Oxford: 1910. 4to. 136 pp. Map, 10 cold plates. Title in facs. New cloth.
(Wheldon & Wesley) **£80 [≈$142]**

Emanuel, H.
- Diamonds and Precious Stones. London: John Camden Hotten, 1865. 1st edn. 8vo. xvii,266 pp. 5 plates, 27 text figs. Orig gilt dec cloth, shaken.   *(Gemmary)* **$65 [≈£37]**
- Diamonds and Precious Stones. London: John Camden Hotten, 1867. 2nd edn. 8vo. xvii,266 pp. 5 plates, 27 text figs. Orig gilt dec cloth.   *(Gemmary)* **$80 [≈£45]**

Emerson, William
- The Elements of Optics. In Four Books ... London: J. Nourse, 1768. 1st edn. 2 parts in one vol. 8vo. [ii],xii,244; vi,111 pp. 28 fldg plates. Contemp reversed calf, mor label, fine. Anon.   *(Finch)* **£350 [≈$623]**
- The Mathematical Principles of Geography ... London: J. Nourse, 1770. 1st edn. 2 parts in one. 8vo. [2],viii,172; iv,164 pp. 22 fldg engvd plates. Contemp diced calf gilt, backstrip laid down. Anon.   *(O'Neal)* **$300 [≈£169]**
- A System of Astronomy ... London: 1769. 8vo. x,ii,368,[4] pp. 16 fldg plates. Old calf, v worn, front bd & title detached.
(Weiner) **£40 [≈$71]**

Emmons, S.F.
- Ore Deposits. New York: A.I.M.E., 1913. 8vo. xlvii,954 pp. Text ills. Orig qtr leather, rubbed.   *(Gemmary)* **$60 [≈£34]**

Enfield, William
- Institutes of Natural Philosophy, Theoretical and Experimental ... added an Introduction to the first Principles of Chemistry. London: J.

Johnson, 1799. 2nd edn. 4to. xvi,428 pp. 13 plates. Minor spotting. Orig bds, rebacked, crnrs sl worn.   *(Clark)* **£160 [≈$285]**

Engel, C.E. (editor)
- Photography for the Scientist. London: Academic Press, 1969. 3rd printing. 8vo. xviii, 632 pp. Num text figs. Cloth. Dw.
(Savona) **£25 [≈$45]**

Epler, Percy
- The Life of Clara Barton. New York: 1915. 1st edn. 438 pp. Orig bndg. *(Fye)* **$50 [≈£28]**

Epps, Richard
- Epitome of the Homeopathic Family Instructor. London: James Epps, [ca 1865]. 16mo. Orig brown cloth.
(Jarndyce) **£32 [≈$57]**

Epstein, Ervin
- Skin Surgery. Phila: 1956. 1st edn. 228 pp. 101 plates. Orig bndg.   *(Fye)* **$75 [≈£42]**

Erb, Wilhelm
- Handbook of Electro-Therapeutics. Translated by L. Putzel. New York: Wood, 1883. 8vo. 366 pp. 39 w'cuts. Orig cloth.
(Goodrich) **$75 [≈£42]**

Ercker, Lazarus
- Treatise on Ores and Assaying. Translated from the German Edition of 1580 by Sisco & Smith. Chicago: UP, 1951. Cr 4to. xxxiii,360 pp. Ills. Orig cloth. *(Gemmary)* **$100 [≈£56]**

Erichsen, John
- Observations on Aneurism selected from the Works of the Principal Writers on that Disease from the Earliest Periods to the Close of the Last Century. London: 1844. 1st edn. 524 pp. Orig bndg.   *(Fye)* **$200 [≈£112]**

Esau, K.
- Plant Anatomy. New York: Wiley, 1953. 1st edn. 8vo. xii,735 pp. 84 plates, num text figs. Cloth.   *(Savona)* **£20 [≈$36]**

Esdaile, James
- Mesmerism in India, and its Practical Application in Surgery and Medicine. Hartford: Silus Andrus & Son, 1847. 1st Amer edn. Sm 8vo. 259 pp. Sl foxing. Orig brown cloth.   *(Chapel Hill)* **$200 [≈£112]**
- Mesmerism in India and its Practical Application in Surgery and Medicine. London: [1902]. 165 pp. Name on half-title. Orig cloth, worn, marked & stained.
(Whitehart) **£40 [≈$71]**

Essay(s) ...
- An Essay for the Construction of Roads on Mechanical and Physical principles. London: T. Davies, 1774. Half-title, iv,48 pp. Fldg plate. 2 sm old lib stamps. Rebound in cloth bds. *(C.R. Johnson)* **£225 [≈ $401]**
- An Essay for the Construction of Roads on Mechanical and Physical principles. London: T. Davies, 1774. Half-title, iv,48 pp. Fldg plate. Few sm old lib stamps. Rebound in cloth bds. *(C.R. Johnson)* **£225 [≈ $401]**
- Essays on Husbandry ... see Harte, Walter

Esser, J.F.S.
- Biological or Artery Flaps of the Face. Monaco: [1934]. 1st edn. Folio. 179 pp. 420 plates. Leather. *(Fye)* **$2,250 [≈ £1,264]**

Essig, Charles J. (editor)
- The American Text-Book of Prosthetic Dentistry, in Contributions by Eminent Authorities. London: 1901. Lge thick 8vo. 817 pp. 1089 ills & diags. Orig cloth, rebacked. *(Weiner)* **£50 [≈ $89]**

Evans, A.H.
- A Fauna of the Tweed Area. Edinburgh: Douglas, 1911. 8vo. xxviii,262 pp. Dec title, linen backed map, 21 plates, 7 text figs. Orig cloth, sl nick hd of spine. *(Egglishaw)* **£46 [≈ $82]**

Evans, A.H. & Buckey, T.E.
- A Vertebrate Fauna of the Shetland Islands. Edinburgh: 1899. 8vo. xxix,248 pp. Map, 15 plates. Half-title reprd. Orig cloth. *(Egglishaw)* **£38 [≈ $68]**

Evans, U.R.
- Metals and Metallic Compounds. London: 1923. 4 vols. Text figs. Orig bndgs. *(Whitehart)* **£38 [≈ $68]**

Eve, A.S.
- Rutherford. Being the Life and Letters of the Rt. Hon. Lord Rutherford, O.M. Cambridge: 1939. xvi,451 pp. Port frontis, 17 plates, 6 text figs. Ink splash on page edges. Orig cloth, sl worn, mark on spine. *(Whitehart)* **£28 [≈ $50]**

Eve, A.S. & Creasey, C.H.
- The Life and Work of John Tyndall. London: 1945. xxxii,404 pp. Frontis port, 24 plates. Dw (sl torn). *(Whitehart)* **£30 [≈ $53]**

Evelyn, Charles
- The Lady's Recreation: or, The Third and Last Part of the Art of Gardening Improv'd.

London: 1717. 8vo. iv,[viii],200 pp. Frontis. Half mor. *(Wheldon & Wesley)* **£100 [≈ $178]**

Evelyn, John
- Kalendarium Hortense: or, the Gardener's Almanac ... London: for R. Chiswell, 1691. 8th edn. 8vo. [xx],175,[15] pp. red & black title. Frontis, 1 plate. Contemp speckled sheep, sl rubbed. Wing E.3498. *(Young's)* **£165 [≈ $294]**
- Sylva, or a Discourse of Forest-Trees ... Pomono ... Kalendarium Hortense ... London: Martyn & Allestry, 1664. 1st edn. Folio. Errata leaf. Some browning. Contemp calf, backstrip relaid, new label, crnrs reprd. Wing E.3516. *(Spelman)* **£550 [≈ $979]**
- Sylva, Or A Discourse of Forest-Trees ... Pomona ... Kalendarium Hortense ... London: 1664. 1st edn. Folio. [xiv],120,[ii], 20, animadversion leaf, 21-83,[i errata] pp. Contemp calf, rebacked, new endpapers, sl surface damage to lower bd. Wing E.3516, *(Finch)* **£750 [≈ $1,335]**

Everest, Thomas R.
- A Popular View of Homoeopathy ... Second Edition, much enlarged and amended. London: Bailliere, 1836. 8vo. xxv,[ii],151 pp. Mor gilt, a.e.g., outer edges sl rubbed. Author's pres inscrptn. *(Rankin)* **£85 [≈ $151]**

Ewell, James
- The Planter's and Mariner's Medical Companion. Phila: John Bioren, 1807. 1st edn. 8vo. xvi,328,[1] pp. Contemp calf, some staining & pitting in leather. *(Bookpress)* **$600 [≈ £337]**

Exley, Thomas
- Physical Optics; or, The Phenomena of Optics explained according to Mechanical Science ... London: 1834. 1st edn. 8vo. xix, [1],4, 206,[2] pp. Errata slip. Litho port, 2 engvd plates. Orig cloth, unopened. Author's pres copy. *(Hemlock)* **$275 [≈ £154]**

Eyton, T.C.
- A History of the Rare British Birds. Illustrated with Woodcuts. [With] A Catalogue of British Birds. London: 1836. 1st edns. 8vo. Ills. Rec cloth. *(Bow Windows)* **£80 [≈ $142]**

Fabre, J.H.
- Fabre's Book of Insects. Retold from A.T. de Matto's Translation by Mrs Satwell. New York: 1936. 4to. x,271 pp. 12 cold plates. Orig green cloth gilt. *(Henly)* **£50 [≈ $89]**

Fage, A.
- The Aeroplane. A Concise Scientific Study. Second Edition, revised and enlarged. London: 1916. 8vo. viii,160,[6 advt] pp. Frontis, 63 text ills. Orig cloth, dull.
(Bow Windows) **£35 [≈ $62]**

Fairley, B.
- The Colliery Manager's Calculator ... Second Edition, Revised and Enlarged. London: 1866. 8vo. viii,82,[2],[3 advt] pp. Fldg cold plate (torn, dusty), 4 cold & 5 plain plates. Some marks. Orig cloth, marked.
(Bow Windows) **£40 [≈ $71]**

Faithorn, John
- Facts and Observations on Liver Complaints, and Bilious Disorders in General ... London: Longman, Hurst, 1823. 5th edn. 8vo. xii,164 pp. Orig bds, uncut, minor rubbing. Inscrbd by "the author".
(Caius) **$100 [≈ £56]**

Falconer, William
- A Dissertation on the Influence of the Passions upon Disorders of the Body; being the Essay to which the Fothergillian Medal was adjudged. London: 1788. 1st edn. 8vo. xix, 105,[3] pp. New calf.
(Weiner) **£200 [≈ $356]**
- Observations on Dr. Cadogan's Dissertation on the Gout and all Chronic Diseases. Second Edition with Corrections and Additions. Bath: R. Cruttwell, 1772. 8vo. 115 pp. Title browned. Last leaf cut no loss of text. Mod qtr mor.
(Robertshaw) **£48 [≈ $85]**
- Observations respecting the Pulse ... London: Cadell & Davies, 1796. 1st edn. Sm 8vo. [ii],158 pp. Lacks half-title. 2 sm marg tears. Rec bds.
(Burmester) **£175 [≈ $312]**

The Family Guide to Health ...
- The Family Guide to Health; or, a General Practice of Physic ... Methods ... from the Writings and Practice of the most Eminent Physicians ... London: for J. Fletcher; & B. Collins, Salisbury, 1767. 1st edn. 8vo. xvi, v-xix, [i], 331,[1] pp. Errata leaf. Contemp calf, rebacked.
(Burmester) **£240 [≈ $427]**

The Family Oracle of Health ...
- The Family Oracle of Health; Economy, Medicine, and Good Living ... Edited by A.F. Crell and W.A. Wallace. London: J. Walker, 1824-25. 6th edn. 2 vols. 8vo. iv,490; 484, [4] pp. Aquatint plate by Cruikshank. Some foxing. Contemp half calf, sm reprs to jnts.
(Spelman) **£30 [≈ $53]**

Faraday, Michael
- A Course of Six Lectures on the Chemical Composition of a Candle: To which is added a Lecture on Platinum. Edited by William Crookes. London: 1861. 1st edn. Sm 8vo. viii, 208, [8 advt] pp. 38 figs. Occas marks. Stamp on half-title. Rec half calf.
(Bow Windows) **£105 [≈ $187]**
- Experimental Researches in Electricity. London: 1849, 1844, 1855. Vol 1 2nd edn, vols 2 & 3 1st edns. 3 vols. 8vo. Half-titles vols 2 & 3. 17 plates. Orig green cloth, 2 vols sl faded, 2 hinges sl cracked.
(Frew Mackenzie) **£450 [≈ $801]**
- Experimental Researches in Electricity. London: 1839-44-45 [but facs reprint London: Quaritch, 1878]. 3 vols. 8vo. 17 plates. Lib stamps. Orig green cloth.
(Frew Mackenzie) **£360 [≈ $641]**
- Experimental Researches in Chemistry and Physics. London: Taylor & Francis, 1859. 1st edn. 8vo. viii,496 pp. 3 plates. Few lib marks. Orig cloth, worn & soiled, jnts reprd.
(Key Books) **$425 [≈ £239]**

Farley, John
- The London Art of Cookery and Housekeeper's Complete Assistant ... Ninth Edition. London: John Baker for James Scatcherd ..., 1800. 8vo. xxiv,448 pp. Frontis, 12 plates. Later half calf, gilt spine, mrbld bds.
(Frew Mackenzie) **£320 [≈ $570]**
- The London Art of Cookery, and Housekeeper's Complete Assistant ... London: for Scatcherd & Letterman ..., 1804. 10th edn. 8vo. xxiv,366,[2 advt] pp. Port, 12 plates. Farley's printed signature at end of preface. Some use. Contemp calf, later reback.
(Gough) **£195 [≈ $347]**

Farman, D.
- Auto-cars: Cars, Tramcars, and Small Cars. Translated from the French ... London: 1896. Sm 8vo. [x],249,[49 advt] pp. 12 figs. Marks. Orig cloth, dull & rubbed.
(Bow Windows) **£150 [≈ $267]**

Farmer ...
- The Farmer's Guide in Hiring and Stocking Farms ... see Young, Arthur
- The Farmer's Letters to the People of England ... see Young, Arthur
- The Farmer's Tour through the East of England ... see Young, Arthur

Farrer, Reginald
- Alpines and Bog Plants. London: 1908. Only edn. 8vo. xii,288 pp. 16 plates. 2 pencil notes. Cloth, t.e.g. *(Wheldon & Wesley)* **£50 [≈ $89]**

- In a Yorkshire Garden. London: 1909. Only edn. 8vo. xi,316 pp. 16 photo ills. Orig cloth. *(Wheldon & Wesley)* **£60 [≈ $107]**

Farrington, O.C.
- Catalogue of the Meteorites of North America to January 1, 1909. Washington: 1915. 4to. 513 pp. 36 map plates. Orig cloth, edges worn. *(Gemmary)* **$175 [≈ £98]**

Fawcett, Benjamin
- Observations on the Nature, Causes and Cure of Melancholy; especially of that which is called Religious Melancholy. Shrewsbury: J. Eddowes, 1780. [80] pp. Contemp qtr sheep, mrbld bds, rebacked.
(C.R. Johnson) **£225 [≈ $401]**

Fearing, F.
- Reflex Action: A Study in the History of Physiological Psychology. Baltimore: 1930. 1st edn. 350 pp. Spine spotted, dull. Inscribed by the author. *(Fye)* **$125 [≈ £70]**

Fennessy, R. & Brown, L.
- Birds of the African Bush. London: 1975. Folio. [xvi],[48] pp. 24 cold plates, 24 ills. Cloth. *(Wheldon & Wesley)* **£30 [≈ $53]**

Fenning, Daniel
- The Young Measurer's Complete Guide ... London: S. Crowder, 1772. 1st edn. 12mo. xii, liv,322 pp. Text diags. Contemp sheep, extrs sl worn, jnts cracked but firm.
(Clark) **£75 [≈ $134]**

Ferguson, Albert
- Orthopedic Surgery in Infancy and Childhood. Baltimore: 1957. 1st edn. 508 pp. 504 ills. Orig bndg. *(Fye)* **$100 [≈ £56]**

Ferguson, James
- The Art of Drawing in Perspective made easy to those who have no previous knowledge of the Mathematics. London: for W. Strahan, 1775. 1st edn. 8vo. xii,123,[1 advt] pp. 9 fldg plates. Lacks half-title. Sl browning. 1 sm repr. Rec bds. *(Fenning)* **£125 [≈ $223]**
- Astronomy Explained upon Sir Isaac Newton's Principles ... The Sixth Edition, Corrected. London: Strahan ..., 1778. 8vo. [viii], 501,[15] pp. Fldg frontis, 17 fldg plates. Contemp tree calf. *(Hartfield)* **$295 [≈ £166]**
- Astronomy explained upon Sir Isaac's Principles. Eighth Edition. London: 1790. 8vo. 503,index pp. 17 fldg plates. Mod cloth. *(Robertshaw)* **£50 [≈ $89]**
- Astronomy Explained upon Sir Isaac Newton's Principles. London: Rivington ...,

1790. 8th edn. 8vo. [8],503,[16] pp. 18 plates. Some tears. Occas stains & foxing. Contemp calf, sl worn. *(D & D Galleries)* **$150 [≈ £84]**
- An Introduction to Electricity. In Six Sections. London: Strahan & Cadell, 1770. 1st edn. 8vo. iv,140 pp. 3 fldg plates. Contemp calf, crnrs & spine ends worn, lacks free endpapers. *(Gaskell)* **£450 [≈ $801]**
- Lectures on Select Subjects in Mechanics, Hydrostatics, Pneumatics and Optics, with the Use of the Globes, the Art of Dialling ... London: 1764. 4to. viii,252,[4] pp. 23 fldg plates. Sm lib stamp title. Contemp calf, sl worn & marked. *(Weiner)* **£250 [≈ $445]**
- Lectures on Select Subjects in Mechanics, Hydrostatics, Pneumatics and Optics, with the Use of the Globes, the Art of Dialing ... Ninth Edition. London: 1799. 8vo. [xiv],396, [6],48 pp. 36 fldg plates. Contemp tree sheep, mor label. *(Weiner)* **£150 [≈ $267]**

Ferguson, John
- Bibliographical Notes on Histories of Inventions and Secrets. London: Holland Press, 1959. One of 350. 2 vols. 8vo. Orig cloth. *(Frew Mackenzie)* **£80 [≈ $142]**
- Bibliotheca Chemica. A Bibliography of Books on Alchemy, Chemistry and Pharmaceutics. London: Derek Verschoyle ..., 1954. 2 vols. Lge 8vo. Orig buckram.
(Frew Mackenzie) **£160 [≈ $285]**

Ferguson, Mungo
- Printed Books in the Library of the Hunterian Museum in the University of Glasgow: a Catalogue. Glasgow: 1930. 1st edn. Folio. 396 pp. Orig bndg.
(Fye) **$150 [≈ £84]**

Ferguson, William
- The Introductory Lecture delivered at King's College, London on the Opening of the Medical Session 1848-49. London: 1848. 32 pp. Calf gilt. *(Goodrich)* **$45 [≈ £25]**

Feris, Samuel
- A Dissertation on Milk ... Use ... Nature and Properties ... Effects ... London & Abraham: [1785]. 1st edn. 8vo. [viii], viii, 206, [i errata] pp. Title vignette. Orig wraps, uncut, largely unopened, spine defective. Cloth case.
(Finch) **£300 [≈ $534]**

Ferrel, W.
- A Popular Treatise on the Winds ... London: 1893. 1st edn. vii,505 pp. Frontis, 7 tables, 36 figs. Sm lib stamp on title. Orig cloth, sl marked & worn. *(Whitehart)* **£35 [≈ $62]**

Ferrier, David
- The Functions of the Brain. Second Edition, rewritten and enlarged. London: 1886. 8vo. xxiii,498 pp. Ills. Sl foxing. Sm blind stamps. Orig cloth, sl worn & shaken.
(Weiner) **£75 [≈ $134]**

Fessenden, Thomas Green
- The Register of Arts, or a Compendious View of some of the most useful modern Discoveries and Inventions ... Phila: C. & A. Conrad, 1808. 1st edn. 8vo. xi,404 pp. 2 plates. Some sl browning. Lib stamps. Contemp calf, reprd.   *(D & D Galleries)* **$140 [≈ £79]**

Festschriften
- Anniversary Volume dedicated to Professor Hantaro Nagaoka by his Friends and Pupils ... Tokyo: 1925. 1st edn. 4to. [ii],xvi,422,[2] pp. 4 pp errata inserted. 19 plates. Orig cloth.
(Gaskell) **£40 [≈ $71]**
- Science Medicine and History. Essays on the Evolution of Scientific Thought and Medical Practice written in honour of Charles Singer. Collected and edited by E. Ashworth Underwood. London: 1953. 2 vols. Roy 8vo. Dws.   *(Goodrich)* **$395 [≈ £222]**

Feuchtersleben, Ernst
- The Principles of Medical Psychology. London: 1847. 392 pp. Backstrip chipped & torn, hinges cracked.   *(Fye)* **$100 [≈ £56]**

Feuchtwanger, L.
- A Treatise on Gems, in reference to their Practical and Scientific Value ... New York: 1838. 8vo. 178 pp. 1st few ff trifle foxed. Lib b'plate. Lib blind stamp on title. Cloth, spine worn. Author's pres inscrptn.
(Wheldon & Wesley) **£350 [≈ $623]**

Ffoulkes, Charles
- The Gun-Founders of England. With List of English and Continental Gun-Founders from the XIV to the XIX Centuries ... Cambridge: UP, 1937. 1st edn. 4to. xvi,134 pp. 15 plates, 38 text ills. Occas v sl foxing. Cloth spotted & faded.   *(Francis Edwards)* **£100 [≈ $178]**

Fick, A. Eugen
- Diseases of the Eye and Ophthalmoscopy ... Authorized Translation by Albert B. Hale ... Phila: Blakiston, 1900. Later printing. 8vo. xvi-488,[32 advt] pp. 158 ills (many cold). Orig cloth.   *(Goodrich)* **$65 [≈ £37]**

Fielding, H.B. & Gardner, G.
- Sertum Plantarum; or Drawings and Descriptions from the Author's Herbarium.

London: 1844. 8vo. 75 plates (on 70 ff). Occas v sl foxing. Half calf, rubbed.
(Wheldon & Wesley) **£200 [≈ $356]**

Fifield, Lionel
- Infections of the Hand. London: 1926. 1st edn. 192 pp. Ex-lib. Orig bndg.
(Fye) **$100 [≈ £56]**

Finch-Davies, C.G.
- The Bird Paintings of C.G. Finch-Davies. Johannesburg: Winchester Press, 1984. One of 5000. Folio. 312 pp. 100 cold plates. Orig cloth slipcase.   *(Parmer)* **$150 [≈ £84]**
- The Birds of Southern Africa. With Text by A. Kemp. Johannesburg: 1982. Subscribers' Edition. 4to. 488 pp. Port, 177 cold plates. Orig buckram. Slipcase.
(Wheldon & Wesley) **£140 [≈ $249]**

Findlay, George
- The Working and Management of an English Railway. London: 1889. 1st edn. 8vo. vi, 270, [32 advt] pp. Num ills, some fldg. Orig pict gilt cloth, spine sl faded, sm split upper jnt.
(Francis Edwards) **£30 [≈ $53]**
- The Working and Management of an English Railway. London: Whitaker, 1890. 3rd edn, rvsd & enlgd. Advt leaf, 32 pp ctlg. Half-title. Plates. Orig cloth, spine sl faded.
(Jarndyce) **£48 [≈ $85]**

Findley, Palmer
- The Story of Childbirth. Garden City, New York: 1934. 1st edn. 376 pp. Orig bndg.
(Fye) **$100 [≈ £56]**

Finn, F. & Robinson, E.K.
- Birds of our Country. London: Hutchinson, (1923). 2 vols. 4to. 30 cold plates, num ills. Orig half leather gilt. *(Egglishaw)* **£25 [≈ $45]**

Firminger, Thomas
- A Manual of Gardening for Bengal and Upper India. Calcutta: Thacker, Spink, 1874. 3rd edn. Half-title, 16 ctlg pp. Ills. Orig pict cloth, sl marked, sm nick ft of spine.
(Jarndyce) **£85 [≈ $151]**

Fish, D.T. (editor)
- Cassell's Popular Gardening, with Numerous Illustrations. London: n.d. 4 vols in 2. Roy 8vo. Half calf.   *(Egglishaw)* **£24 [≈ $43]**

Fishbein, Morris
- Morris Fishbein, M.D. An Autobiography. Garden City: 1969. 1st edn. 505 pp. Orig bndg. Dw. Signed by the author.
(Fye) **$40 [≈ £22]**

Fisher, A.K.
- Hawks and Owls of the United States in their relation to Agriculture. Washington: 1893. 8vo. 210 pp. 26 cold plates. Cloth.
(Wheldon & Wesley) **£80 [≈ $142]**

Fisher, James & Lockley, R.M.
- Sea-Birds. London: Collins New Naturalist, 1954. 1st edn. 8vo. xvi,320 pp. Num ills. Orig cloth. Dw.
(Wheldon & Wesley) **£60 [≈ $107]**
- Sea-Birds. London: Collins New Naturalist, 1954. 1st edn. 8vo. xvi,320 pp. Num ills. Orig cloth, trifle used.
(Wheldon & Wesley) **£35 [≈ $62]**

Fitton, E. & S.M.
- Conversations on Botany. London: Longman, 1834. 8th edn. Sm 8vo. xvi,284 pp. 22 hand cold plates (one on 2 ff). Half calf. Anon.
(Egglishaw) **£75 [≈ $134]**

Fitzgibbon, A.
- Canadian Wild Flowers, Painted and Lithographed. With Botanical Descriptions by C.P. Traill. Montreal: 1869. 1st edn. Roy 4to. 86 pp. Cold title, 10 hand cold plates. Sl browned. Orig cloth gilt, reprd, sl used.
(Wheldon & Wesley) **£360 [≈ $641]**

Fitzroy, Robert
- The Weather Book: a Manual of Practical Meteorology. Second Edition. London: Longmans, Green ..., 1863. 8vo. xiv,[1],480 pp. 16 plates. Orig cloth, inner hinges sl weak. *(Fenning)* **£110 [≈ $196]**

Fitzsimons, Vivian F.W.
- The Natural History of South Africa: Birds. London: 1923. 2 vols. 8vo. 10 cold plates, ills. Cloth, trifle stained.
(Wheldon & Wesley) **£45 [≈ $80]**
- The Snakes of South Africa, their Venom and the Treatment of Snake Bite. Port Elizabeth: 1910. 1st edn. 8vo. xvi,160,[3] pp. Lge fldg cold plate, num ills. Orig cloth backed pict bds. *(Wheldon & Wesley)* **£80 [≈ $142]**
- The Snakes of South Africa. Their Venom and the Treatment of Snake Bite. Cape Town: [ca 1919]. 1st edn. 8vo. xvi,550 pp. Fldg cold plates, num ills. Orig cloth.
(Francis Edwards) **£45 [≈ $80]**
- The Snakes of Southern Africa. Cape Town: 1962. 4to. 423 pp. Cold frontis, 74 cold & 43 b/w ills, num text figs. Dw (sl chipped).
(Francis Edwards) **£35 [≈ $62]**

Fitzwilliams, Duncan
- On the Breast. London: 1924. 1st edn. 440

pp. Ills. Orig bndg, backstrip faded. Inscrbd & initialled by the author. *(Fye)* **$175 [≈ £98]**

Flammarion, Camille
- The Atmosphere. Translated from the French by C.B. Pitman. Edited by James Glaisher. New York: Harper, 1873. 4to. 453,7 advt pp. 10 chromolithographs, 86 w'cuts. Orig dec cloth, spine ends worn.
(Key Books) **$90 [≈ £51]**

Flatt, Adrian
- The Care of the Rheumatoid Hand. St. Louis, 1963. 1st edn. 222 pp. Ills. Orig bndg.
(Fye) **$50 [≈ £28]**

Fleetwood, John
- History of Medicine in Ireland. Dublin: 1951. 1st edn. 8vo. xvi,420 pp. 19 plates. Orig cloth. Dw. *(Fenning)* **£30 [≈ $53]**

Fleming, Alexander (editor)
- Penicillin. Its Practical Application. London: 1950. 2nd edn. xiii,491 pp. 63 ills. Orig bndg.
(Whitehart) **£15 [≈ $27]**

Fleming, D.
- William H. Welch and the Rise of Modern Medicine. Edited by O. Handlin. Boston: 1954. viii, 216 pp. 3 lib stamps. Lib label. Orig bndg, lib mark on spine. Dw (torn & stained). *(Whitehart)* **£15 [≈ $27]**

Fleming, J.A. (editor)
- The Electrical Educator. A Comprehensive, Practical and Authoritative Guide for all engaged in the Electrical Industry. London: 1927. 3 vols. xiv,[xii],[xi],1556 pp. Frontis ports, num ills. Orig cloth, rubbed, spine faded. *(Whitehart)* **£35 [≈ $62]**
- The Wireless Telegraphist's Pocket Book of Notes, Formulae, and Calculations. London: 1915. xii,347 pp. Frontis, 39 figs. Orig cloth, sl worn. *(Whitehart)* **£15 [≈ $27]**

Fletcher, L.
- The Optical Indicatrix and the Transmission of Light in Crystals. London: Henry Frowde, 1892. 8vo. xii,112 pp. 19 text figs. Orig cloth.
(Gemmary) **$65 [≈ £37]**

Fletcher, R.A.
- Steam-Ships. The Story of their Development to the Present Day. London: 1910. 1st edn. Roy 8vo. xx,422,[2] pp. 150 ills inc cold frontis. Minor marg foxing. Orig pict cloth, extrs rubbed, signs of wear.
(Francis Edwards) **£32 [≈ $57]**

Flett, Sir J.S.
- The First Hundred Years of the Geological Survey of Great Britain. London: 1937. 8vo. 280 pp. 13 plates. Crnr clipped from f.e.p. Cloth, sl worn.   *(Henly)* £24 [≈ $43]

Fleure, H.J.
- A Natural History of Man in Britain. London: Collins New Naturalist, 1951. 1st edn. Ills. Orig cloth. Dw.   *(Egglishaw)* £20 [≈ $36]

Flint, Austin
- A Treatise on the Principles and Practice of medicine ... Fifth Edition ... with an Appendix on the Researches of Koch ... Pulmonary Phthisis. Phila: 1884. 8vo. 1160, [32 advt] pp. Sl browned. Sheep, rubbed.   *(Goodrich)* $35 [≈ £20]

Flintoft, J.J.
- British Mosses in the English Lake District. Keswick: [ca 1830]. 8vo. Ptd title-page. 60 natural specimens mtd on 50 ff. MS names & localities. Trifle foxed. Orig cloth, trifle worn.   *(Wheldon & Wesley)* £60 [≈ $107]

Flora Domestica ...
- Flora Domestica ... with Directions for the Treatment of Plants in Pots ... New Edition, with Additions. London: Whittaker, Treacher, 1831. xliii,464,[16 advt] pp. Hand cold litho frontis. Orig green cloth, uncut, rebacked.   *(Gough)* £60 [≈ $107]

Flora Europaea ...
- See Tutin, T.G., & others (editors)

The Floral World ...
- The Floral World and Garden Guide for 1878. London: Groombridge, 1878. 8vo. vi,378 pp. 14 cold plates. w'engvs. Orig cloth gilt, rubbed.   *(Egglishaw)* £24 [≈ $43]

The Flower Garden ...
- See M'Intosh, Charles

Flower, W.H.
- Fashion in Deformity. As Illustrated in the Customs of Barbarous & Civilised Races. London: 1881. xii,86 pp. 23 figs. Occas sl foxing. Orig bndg, spine sl torn.   *(Whitehart)* £25 [≈ $45]

Flower, William Henry
- Diagrams of the Nerves of the Human Body ... London: Churchill, 1861. Lge folio. Title, 8 pp. 6 fldg plates. Unabused ex-lib. Orig half sheep, new cloth spine.   *(Goodrich)* $135 [≈ £76]

Floyer, Sir John
- The History of Cold Bathing. Both Ancient and Modern. London: 1706. 2nd edn. xxxii,264 pp. Sl foxing page edges. Contemp Cambridge panelled calf, rear hinge cracked but firm.   *(Whitehart)* £130 [≈ $231]
- [Title in greek, Psychrolousia] ... or, the History of Cold-Bathing ... in Two Parts ... The Second ... by Dr Edward Baynard. London: for Benj. Walford, 1709. 3rd edn. 8vo. [xxii],426,[32] pp. 2 advt pp. Contemp panelled calf, sl worn. *(Clark)* £185 [≈ $329]
- [Title in Greek] ... or, the History of Cold-Bathing, both Ancient and Modern. To which is added, an Appendix, by Dr Edward Baynard. The Fifth Edition. London: Innys, 1722. 8vo. [22],491, [30],[1 advt] pp. Contemp panelled calf, gilt spine reprd at ends, new label.   *(Spelman)* £160 [≈ $285]

Fomon, Samuel
- The Surgery of Injury and Plastic Repair. Baltimore: 1939. 1st (student) edn. 1409 pp. Orig bndg.   *(Fye)* $75 [≈ £42]

Forbes, A.C.
- English Estate Forestry. London: Edward Arnold, 1904. 8vo. ix,[3],332 pp. 13 plates. Frontis marg sl marked. Dark blue prize calf gilt.   *(Spelman)* £65 [≈ $116]

Forbes, E.
- A History of British Starfishes, and Other Animals of the Class Echinodermata. London: 1841. 8vo. xx,270 pp. Num w'cuts. Orig cloth. *(Wheldon & Wesley)* £30 [≈ $53]
- A History of British Starfishes and other Animals of the Class Echinodermata. London: Van Voorst, 1841. 8vo. xx,270 pp. Text ills. Half mor, lib stamp on spine.   *(Egglishaw)* £38 [≈ $68]
- A Monograph of the British Naked-Eyed Medusea, with Figures of all the Species. London: Ray Society, 1848. Folio. [viii],104 pp. 13 cold plates. Orig cloth backed bds.   *(Egglishaw)* £55 [≈ $98]

Forbes, H.O.
- A Hand-Book to the Primates. London: Allen's Naturalist's Library, 1894. 2 vols. 8vo. 8 maps, 29 cold plates. Few sm lib stamps. Half cloth.   *(Wheldon & Wesley)* £35 [≈ $62]

Forbes, J.
- Hortus Woburniensis, a Descriptive Catalogue of Upwards of 6,000 Ornamental Plants, cultivated at Woburn Abbey. London: 1833. Roy 8vo. xxiv,[iii], 440,[16] pp. Cold

frontis (margs stained), cold engvd title, 24 plates (14 cold). Straight grain half mor.
(Wheldon & Wesley) **£375 [≃ $668]**

- Occasional Papers on the Theory of Glaciers ... Edinburgh: 1859. 1st edn. 8vo. xxix, 278 pp. Cold frontis, 9 plates, 29 text figs. Some browning & marking. Rec qtr calf.
(Bow Windows) **£95 [≃ $169]**

Forbes, Sir John
- Of Nature and Art in the Cure of Disease. From the 2nd London Edition. New York: Wood, 1858. vi,7-261 pp. Orig cloth.
(Hemlock) **$100 [≃ £56]**

Forbes, R.J.
- Metallurgy in Antiquity. A Notebook for Archaeologists and Technologists ... Leiden: Brill, 1950. 8vo. [viii],489 pp. Fldg chart, 98 ills (5 fldg). Orig cloth. Dw.
(Blackwell's) **£70 [≃ $125]**

Ford, Frank R.
- Diseases of the Nervous System in Infancy, Childhood and Adolescence. Springfield: C.C. Thomas, 1944. 2nd edn. xviii,1143,[3] pp. Text ills. Orig cloth. *(Caius)* **$50 [≃ £28]**

Fordyce, W.
- A New Enquiry into the Causes, Symptoms and Cure of Putrid and Inflammatory Fevers. With an Appendix on the Hectic Fever, and on the Ulcerated and Malignant Sore Throat. London: 1777. 4th edn. xvi,228 pp. Contemp tree calf, rebacked.
(Whitehart) **£120 [≃ $214]**

Forel, Auguste Henri
- Hypnotism, or Suggestion and Psychotherapy. A Study of ... Hypnotism. Translated from the Fifth German Edition by H.W. Armit. London: Rebman, 1906. 1st edn in English. xii,370 pp. Sl foxing. Orig cloth.
(Caius) **$100 [≃ £56]**
- The Social World of the Ants compared with that of Man. Translated by C.K. Ogden. New York: Boni, 1929. 1st edn in English, 1st printing. 2 vols. Thick 8vo. Orig cloth (sl shelf worn). *(Gach)* **$225 [≃ £126]**

Forrest, H.E.
- The Fauna of Shropshire: the Mammals, Birds, Reptiles and Fishes found in the County. Shrewsbury: 1899. 8vo. 248,vi pp. 25 ills. Endpapers foxed. Orig cloth.
(Wheldon & Wesley) **£25 [≃ $45]**
- The Vertebrate Fauna of North Wales. London: Witherby, 1907. 1st edn. lxxiv,537 pp. Fldg map, 28 photo plates. Orig green

cloth, t.e.g., spine sl worn.
(Gough) **£38 [≃ $68]**
- The Vertebrate Fauna of North Wales. London: 1907. 8vo. lxxii,537 pp. 28 plates. rebound. *(Henly)* **£65 [≃ $116]**

Forrest, William Hutton
- Report, Chemical and Medical, of the Airthrey Mineral Springs: and a List of Phaenogamous Plants collected in their Vicinity. Stirling: John Hewit ..., 1831. 1st edn. 8vo. [ii],137 pp. Fldg frontis. Some pencil notes, sl stain at end. 19th c binder's cloth. *(Burmester)* **£60 [≃ $107]**

Forshaw, J.M.
- Parrots of the World. Melbourne: 1973. Imperial 4to. 584 pp. 158 cold plates by W. Cooper. Orig cloth. Dw.
(Wheldon & Wesley) **£375 [≃ $668]**
- Parrots of the World. New York: 1973. Imperial 4to. 584 pp. 158 cold plates by W.T. Cooper. Orig cloth. Dw.
(Wheldon & Wesley) **£360 [≃ $641]**

Forshaw, J.M. & Cooper, W.T.
- Birds of Paradise and Bower Birds. Sydney: 1977. 1st edn. Folio. 304 pp. 60 cold plates, maps, text figs. Orig cloth. Dw. Slipcase.
(Bow Windows) **£165 [≃ $294]**
- Birds of Paradise and Bower Birds. Sydney: 1977. Folio. 304 pp. 60 cold plates, maps, text figs. Orig cloth. Dw. Slipcase.
(Wheldon & Wesley) **£265 [≃ $472]**

Forster, T.
- Observations on the Brumal Retreat of the Swallow, to which is annexed a Copious Index to many Passages relating to this Bird. London: 1813. 3rd edn, crrctd & enlgd. 8vo. xiv, 46 pp. Leather backed bds.
(Wheldon & Wesley) **£30 [≃ $53]**

Forsyth, William
- A Treatise on the Culture and Management of Fruit Trees. London: 1803. 2nd edn. 8vo. xxvii, 523 pp. 13 fldg plates. Tree calf, rebacked. *(Henly)* **£76 [≃ $135]**
- A Treatise on the Culture and Management of Fruit Trees. London: 1803. 3rd edn. 8vo. xxvii, 523 pp. 13 plates. Calf, rebacked.
(Wheldon & Wesley) **£55 [≃ $98]**
- A Treatise on the Culture and Management of Fruit-Trees. London: 1806. 4th edn. 8vo. xxvii, 523,[16 advt] pp. 13 plates (foxed). Bds, disbound. *(Hortulus)* **$65 [≃ £37]**

Foster, Sir Michael
- Claude Bernard. London: 1899. 1st edn.

245 pp. Orig bndg.   *(Fye)* **$50 [≈£28]**
- Lectures on the History of Physiology during the Sixteenth, Seventeenth and Eighteenth Centuries. Cambridge: UP, 1901. 1st edn. 8vo. 310 pp. Frontis. Orig cloth gilt, spine ends sl bumped.   *(David White)* **£35 [≈$62]**
- Lectures on the History of Physiology during the Sixteenth, Seventeenth and Eighteenth Centuries. Cambridge: 1901. 1st edn. 310 pp. Orig bndg, backstrip torn, front inner hinge cracked.   *(Fye)* **$60 [≈£34]**
- Lectures on the History of Physiology. During the Sixteenth, Seventeenth and Eighteenth Centuries. Cambridge: 1924. 1st edn, 2nd imp. iv,304 pp. Frontis. Cloth sl worn at crnrs.   *(Whitehart)* **£35 [≈$62]**
- A Text Book of Physiology. New York: Macmillan, 1893. 5th & 6th edns. 4 vols. 8vo. Ills. Orig green cloth, worn, some vols shaken.   *(Goodrich)* **$250 [≈£140]**

Foster, W.D.
- A History of Medical Bacteriology and Immunology. London: 1970. 1st edn. 232 pp. Ills. Dw.   *(Fye)* **$75 [≈£42]**
- A History of Parasitology. Edinburgh: 1965. 1st edn. 202 pp. Ex-lib. Orig bndg.
          (Fye) **$50 [≈£28]**
- A Short History of Clinical Pathology. Edinburgh: 1961. 1st edn. 154 pp. Orig bndg.
          (Fye) **$75 [≈£42]**

Fourier, Joseph
- The Analytical Theory of Heat. Translated, with Notes, by Alexander Freeman. Cambridge: 1878. 1st English edn. 8vo. xxiii,466 pp. Orig cloth.
        (Weiner) **£150 [≈$267]**

Fournier d'Albe, Edmund Edward
- The Moon-Element; an Introduction to the Wonders of Selenium. London: Unwin, 1924. 1st edn. 8vo. 166 pp. Frontis, plates, ills. Orig bndg.   *(Schoen)* **$110 [≈£62]**

Foveau de Courmelles, Francois V.
- Hypnotism. Translated by Laura Ensor. London: Routledge, 1891. 1st English edn. xii, 321,[3] pp. 42 ills. Orig cloth, recased.   *(Caius)* **$150 [≈£84]**

Fowler, H.W.
- The Marine Fishes of West Africa. New York: Bull. Amer. Mus. N.H. Vol. 70, 1936. 2 vols. 8vo. 1493 pp. Cold plate, 567 figs. Binder's cloth.
    (Wheldon & Wesley) **£100 [≈$178]**

Fowler, Ralph Howard
- Statistical Mechanics. The Theory of the Properties of Matter in Equilibrium. Cambridge: UP, 1929. 1st edn. Roy 8vo. viii, 570 pp. Orig cloth.   *(Gaskell)* **£60 [≈$107]**

Fowler, W.W.
- The Coleoptera of the British Islands. London: 1887-91. 5 vols. Roy 8vo. 180 hand cold & 2 plain plates. Trifle used, ink notes. 1 fig on plate 33 defective. Rebound in orig style cloth.
    (Wheldon & Wesley) **£850 [≈$1,513]**
- The Coleoptera of the British Islands. London: 1887-1913. 6 vols. 8vo. 5 plain plates. Cloth.
    (Wheldon & Wesley) **£120 [≈$214]**
- The Coleoptera of the British Islands. London: 1887-91. 5 vols. Roy 8vo. 180 hand cold & 2 plain plates. Trifle used, ink annotations. 1 fig on plate 33 defective. Rebound in buckram to style.
    (Wheldon & Wesley) **£850 [≈$1,513]**

Fownes, G.
- A Manual of Elementary Chemistry, Theoretical and Practical. London: 1858. 7th edn. Sm 8vo. xvi,726 pp. Some foxing. Leather gilt.   *(Whitehart)* **£45 [≈$80]**

Fox, Charles
- An Introduction to the Calculus of Variations. London: OUP, 1950. 1st edn. 8vo. viii, 271 pp. Lib pocket. Orig bndg.
          (Schoen) **$45 [≈£25]**

Foxe, Arthur
- Plague: Laennec (1782-1826) Inventor of the Stethoscope and Father of Modern medicine. New York: 1947. 1st edn. 122 pp. Orig bndg. Inscrbd by the author.   *(Fye)* **$50 [≈£28]**

Fracastor (Fracastorius), Girolamo
- Contagion, Contagious Diseases and their Treatment. Translated by W. Wright. New York: 1930. 356 pp. Orig bndg.
          (Fye) **$100 [≈£56]**
- Fracastor. Syphilis or the French Disease. With a Translation, Notes, and Appendix by Heneage Wynne-Finch. London: 1935. 1st edn. 253 pp. Orig bndg. *(Fye)* **$100 [≈£56]**

Francis, F.
- Fish-Culture, a Practical Guide to the Modern System of Breeding and Rearing Fish. London: Routledge, 1863. 8vo. xviii,267 pp. Ills. Half mor.
        (Egglishaw) **£34 [≈$61]**

Francis, G.
- The Dictionary of the Arts, Sciences, and Manufactures. London: W. Brittain, 1842. 1st edn. 8vo. Engvd title, 1100 text engvs. Contemp half calf, some rubbing & wear.
(Bookpress) **$175 [≈ £98]**
- The Grammar of Botany. London: Simpkin, Marshall, 1840. 2 advt pp. Hand cold engvd title, w'cuts in text. Orig cloth, sl faded.
(Jarndyce) **£30 [≈ $53]**

Francis, G.W.
- An Analysis of the British Ferns and their Allies. Fourth Edition. London: Simpkin, Marshall, 1851. 8vo. viii,88,[8 advt] pp. Pict title & 9 plates, w'engvd vignettes in text. Orig cloth.
(Claude Cox) **£25 [≈ $45]**

Francis, William
- The Gentleman's, Farmer's, and Husbandman's most useful Assistant, in Measuring ... Land ... Second Edition ... London: for Wetton & Jarvis; Wetton, printer, Maidenhead, 1818. 8vo. v,[ii],118,[2] pp. Diags & tables. Orig dec ptd bds, minor rubbing.
(Burmester) **£45 [≈ $80]**

Frank, Philip
- Einstein - His Life and Times. New York: Knopf, 1947. 1st edn. 8vo. 298 pp. Ills. Endpapers yellowed. Orig bndg. Dw (torn).
(Schoen) **$65 [≈ £37]**

Franke, Georg
- Physical Optics in Photography. London: Focal Press, 1966. 8vo. 218 pp. Lib pocket. Orig bndg.
(Schoen) **$95 [≈ £53]**

Frankland, Edward
- Experimental Researches in Pure, Applied, and Physical Chemistry. London: 1877. 1st edn. Thick 8vo. xliv,1032 pp. Fldg charts, ills. Few marg lib stamps. Orig pict cloth, worn & soiled.
(Weiner) **£85 [≈ $151]**

Franklin, Benjamin
- Experiments and Observations on Electricity, made at Philadelphia in America ... Fifth Edition. London: for F. Newbery, 1774. 4th. [viii],514,[16] pp. Half-title. 7 plates. Sl browning & foxing. Contemp tree calf, rebacked, crnrs worn.
(Gaskell) **£1,500 [≈ $2,670]**

Franklin, Fabian
- The Life of Daniel Coit Gilman. New York: 1910. 1st edn. 446 pp. Orig bndg.
(Fye) **$45 [≈ £25]**

Franklin, K.J.
- A Short History of Physiology. London: 1949. 2nd edn. [16],147 pp. Frontis, 16 plates. Orig bndg. *(Whitehart)* **£18 [≈ $32]**
- William Harvey, Englishman, 1578-1657. London: 1961. 1st edn. 151 pp. Dw.
(Fye) **$50 [≈ £28]**

Franklin, R.H.
- Surgery of the Oesophagus. London: 1952. xi, 222 pp. 4 cold plates, 22 diags. Orig bndg.
(Whitehart) **£18 [≈ $32]**

Fraprie, Frank R. & O'Connor, Florence C.
- Photographic Amusements. Including Tricks and Unusual or Novel Effects Obtainable with the Camera. Eleventh Edition, Revised and Enlarged. Boston: Amer Photo Publ Co., 1937. 4to. viii,248 pp. 247 ills. Orig cloth. Dw (rubbed). *(Karmiole)* **$50 [≈ £28]**

Fraser, Sir James George
- The Fear of the Dead in Primitive Religion ... London: 1933-36. 3 vols. Occas sl spotting. Orig cloth, t.e.g.
(Francis Edwards) **£115 [≈ $205]**

Fraser, John
- Tuberculosis of the Bones and the Joints in Children. New York: 1914. 1st edn. 352 pp. 51 plates, 164 ills. Orig bndg.
(Fye) **$75 [≈ £42]**

Frazer, Mrs.
- The Practice of Cookery, Pastry, and Confectionary ... Fourth Edition, with Large Additions and Improvements. Edinburgh: for Peter Hill ..., 1804. [iii],304 pp. 2 plates. Occas sl spotting. Contemp sheep, upper jnt sl split, crnrs sl rubbed.
(Gough) **£250 [≈ $445]**

Frazer, J.G.
- The Golden Bough: A Study in Magic & Religion. London: 1922. 1st abridged edn. 750 pp. Frontis. Orig gilt dec cloth.
(Deja Vu) **£25 [≈ $45]**
- Man, God & Immortality: Thoughts on Human Progress. London: 1927. 1st edn. Orig bndg, t.e.g., hd of spine chipped.
(Deja Vu) **£18 [≈ $32]**
- Totemism and Exogamy. A Treatise on Certain Early Forms of Superstition and Society. London: Macmillan, 1910. 1st edn. 4 vols. 8 fldg maps. Orig cloth, rubbed.
(Claude Cox) **£75 [≈ $134]**

Frazier, Charles
- Surgery of the Spine and Spinal Cord. New

York: 1918. 1st edn. 971 pp. Orig bndg, inner hinges cracked, shaken. *(Fye)* **$200 [≈ £112]**

Fream, William
- The Rothamsted Experiments on the Growing Wheat, Barley, and the Mixed Herbage of Grass Land. London: Horace Cox, 1888. 32 advt pp. Orig cloth.
(Jarndyce) **£20 [≈ $36]**

Freese, Stanley
- Windmills and Millwrighting. Cambridge: 1957. 1st edn. 8vo. xvii,168 pp. Num plates, ills. Orig cloth. Dw. *(Fenning)* **£35 [≈ $62]**

Freind, John
- Emmenologia. London: T. Cox, 1729. 1st edn in English. 8vo. [xvi],222, [2],[16] pp. Contemp calf, rebacked.
(Bookpress) **$275 [≈ £154]**

French, Charles
- A Handbook of the Destructive Insects of Victoria ... Melbourne: Robert S. Brain, Govt Printer, 1891-93. 2 vols. 8vo. 153; 193 pp. 36 chromolitho & 23 w'engvd plates. Vol 1 orig purple cloth, spine faded, vol 2 orig green cloth. Further vols were published.
(Karmiole) **$175 [≈ £98]**

French, James Weir
- Modern Power Generators. Steam, Electric and Internal-Combustion and their Applications to Present-Day Requirements. London: 1908. 2 vols. Lge 4to. xix,201; xiv,203 pp. 11 composite sectional models, 500 text ills. Orig bndg.
(Whitehart) **£95 [≈ $169]**
- Modern Power Generators ... London: Gresham, 1908. 2 vols. Folio. xix,201; xiv,203 pp. 11 cold plates with 210 overlays, 1 fldg plate, num text ills. Orig cloth by Talwin Morris. *(Sotheran's)* **£175 [≈ $312]**

Frere, B.H.T.
- A Guide to the Flora of Gibraltar and the Neighbourhood. Gibraltar: 1910. 8vo. 159,vi pp. Orig cloth, sl marked.
(Wheldon & Wesley) **£40 [≈ $71]**

Fretter, V. & Graham, A.
- British Prosobranch Molluscs, their Functional Anatomy and Ecology. London: Ray Society, 1962. Roy 8vo. xvi,755 pp. 317 ills. Orig cloth. Dw. *(Egglishaw)* **£34 [≈ $61]**

Freud, Sigmund
- Beyond the Pleasure Principle. New York: Boni & Liveright, [1922]. 1st Amer edn (from the sheets ptd in Vienna, with cancel title). Orig grey cloth. Dw (spine perished).
(Mac Donnell) **$150 [≈ £84]**
- Collected Papers. Authorized Translation under the Supervision of Joan Riviere. New York: Basic Books, 1959. 1st Amer edn. 5 vols. Orig bndg. Slipcase (worn).
(Goodrich) **$100 [≈ £56]**
- The Ego and the Id. London: Hogarth Press, 1927. 1st English edn. Orig green cloth gilt, uncut. *(Mac Donnell)* **$250 [≈ £140]**
- The Future of an Illusion. New York: Liveright, Institute of Psycho-Analysis, 1928. 1st Amer edn. 8vo. Orig bndg. Dw.
(Hermitage) **$45 [≈ £25]**
- A General Introduction to Psychoanalysis. New York: Boni & Liveright, [1920]. 1st Amer edn. Orig blue cloth gilt. Dw (slightly nicked). *(Mac Donnell)* **$600 [≈ £337]**
- Group Psychology and the Analysis of the Ego. Translated by James Strachey. London: Intl Psycho-Analytic Press, 1922. 1st edn in English, 1st printing, 1st issue. Thin 8vo. Orig ptd cloth, sl chipping hd of spine. 1st state of bndg, without Hogarth imprint.
(Gach) **$150 [≈ £84]**
- The Interpretation of Dreams. New York: Macmillan, 1913. 1st edn in English. Orig blue-grey striped cloth gilt, few spots of rubbing. *(Mac Donnell)* **$850 [≈ £478]**
- The Problem of Anxiety. Translated from the German by Henry Alden Bunker, M.D. New York: Psychoanalytic Quarterly, [1936]. 1st Authorized translation into English. 127,[1] pp. 1 sentence underlined in ink. Orig bds. Dw (1 crnr clipped). *(Caius)* **$115 [≈ £65]**
- Totem and Taboo. London: Routledge, 1919. 1st British edn. Demy 8vo. xii,268 pp. Orig cloth, edges faintly spotted, v sl bump hd of spine. *(Ash)* **£125 [≈ $223]**

Frey, H.
- The Histology and Histochemistry of Man. London: Churchill, 1874. 8vo. ix,683,[23 ctlg] pp. 608 text figs. Orig cloth, backstrip laid down. *(Savona)* **£25 [≈ $45]**

Freyer, P.J.
- Clinical Lectures on Stricture of the Urethra and Enlargement of the Prostrate. Second Edition. London: Bailliere, 1902. 132 pp. Orig cloth, rebacked. *(Goodrich)* **$75 [≈ £42]**

Friedman, Joseph
- History of Color Photography. Boston: Amer Photo Publ Co., 1944. 1st edn. 8vo. x,514 pp. Orig cloth. *(Schoen)* **$40 [≈ £22]**

Friedman, William F. (editor)
- Articles on Cryptography and Cryptanalysis. Reprinted from The Signal Corps Bulletin. Washington: War Dept, 1942. 8vo. v,316 pp. Fldg maps, diags. Ex-lib. Orig cloth.
(Weiner) £40 [≈ $71]

Friedmann, H.
- The Cowbirds, a Study in the Biology of Social Parasitism. Springfield: 1929. Roy 8vo. xvii,421 pp. 28 plates, 13 text figs. Cloth. *(Wheldon & Wesley)* £40 [≈ $71]

Fries, T.M.
- Linnaeus. The Story of his Life. Adapted from the Swedish by B.D. Jackson. London: 1923. 8vo. Map, 7 plates, 4 figs. Cloth.
(Wheldon & Wesley) £60 [≈ $107]

Frink, H.W.
- Morbid Fears and Compulsions. Their Psychology and Psychoanalytical Treatment. London: 1921. xxiii,344 pp. 4 ills. Spine faded. *(Whitehart)* £15 [≈ $27]

Fritsch, Ernst & Schubart, Martin
- Introduction to Short-Wave Therapy: Technique and Indications. Berlin & Vienna: 1936. 8vo. viii,131 pp. Ills. Orig cloth.
(Weiner) £25 [≈ $45]

Froggatt, W.W.
- Australian Insects. Sydney: 1907. 8vo. xiv, 449 pp. 37 plates, 180 text figs. Rec cloth.
(Wheldon & Wesley) £50 [≈ $89]

Frohawk, F.W.
- Natural History of British Butterflies. A Complete Original Descriptive Account of the Life-History of Every Species occurring in the British Islands. London: [1924]. 2 vols. Folio. 60 cold & 5 plain plates. Sl foxing. Orig cloth, trifle used.
(Wheldon & Wesley) £200 [≈ $356]
- Varieties of British Butterflies. London: 1938 (1946). Roy 8vo. 200 pp. 48 cold plates. Orig cloth. *(Egglishaw)* £48 [≈ $85]

Frohlich, E.D. (editor)
- Pathophysiology. Altered Regulatory Mechanisms in Disease. Phila: 1972. xxvii,795 pp. Num diags. Orig bndg.
(Whitehart) £18 [≈ $32]

Fry, Joseph Storrs
- An Essay on the Construction of Wheel-Carriages as they affect both the Roads and the Horses ... London: for J. & A. Arch ... & T.J. Manchee, Bristol, 1820. 1st edn. 8vo. Sm

ptd slip before Appendix. W'cuts in text. Orig bds, sl worn. *(Georges)* £225 [≈ $401]
- An Essay on the Construction of Wheel-Carriages as they affect both the Roads and the Horses ... London: 1820. 8vo. vii,137 pp. Occas marg lib stamps. Cloth.
(Weiner) £180 [≈ $320]

Fry, W.H. (editor)
- A Complete Treatise on Artificial Fish-Breeding ... New York: Appleton, 1854. 1st edn. 8vo. x,188,[6 advt] pp. 3 plates. Lacks front free endpaper. Orig cloth.
(Karmiole) $75 [≈ £42]

Fryer, A., Bennett, A. & Morgan, R.
- Potamogetons (Pond Weeds) of the British Isles, with Descriptions of all the Species, Varieties, and Hybrids. London: Reeve, 1915. 4to. xi,94 pp. 60 hand cold litho plates. Orig cloth, t.e.g. *(Egglishaw)* £140 [≈ $249]

Fuller, Andrew
- The Grape Culturist: a Treatise on the Cultivation of the Native Grape. New York: Grange Judd, 1886. New edn, enlgd. Sm 8vo. vi,7-286,[2 advt] pp. Orig brown cloth gilt, sl worn. *(Hortulus)* $40 [≈ £22]

Fuller, Henry
- On Rheumatism, Rheumatic Gout, and Sciatica. New York: 1854. 1st Amer edn. 322 pp. Orig bndg. *(Fye)* $125 [≈ £70]

Fuller, Thomas
- Pharmacopoeia Extemporanea: or, A Body of Medicines, containing a Thousand Select Prescripts ... Fourth Edition. London: 1730. 8vo. Port. Blind stamp on title. Contemp calf, rebacked. *(Robertshaw)* £75 [≈ $134]

Fulton, John F.
- Harvey Cushing: A Biography. Springfield: 1946. 1st edn. 754 pp. Orig bndg.
(Fye) $40 [≈ £22]
- Harvey Cushing. A Biography. Illinois: 1946. xii,754 pp. Frontis port, 60 plates, num ills. Endpapers foxed. Orig bndg.
(Whitehart) £35 [≈ $62]
- Michael Servetus, Humanist and Martyr. New York: 1953. 1st edn. 98 pp. Orig bndg.
(Fye) $75 [≈ £42]
- Physiology of the Nervous System. New York: OUP, 1943. 2nd edn, rvsd. vii,[3],614 pp. Frontis, text ills. Orig cloth, somewhat worn. *(Caius)* $100 [≈ £56]
- Selected Readings in the History of Physiology. Springfield: 1966. 2nd edn. 492 pp. Ex-lib. Orig bndg. *(Fye)* $100 [≈ £56]

Furber, J.
- A Short Introduction to Gardening: or, a Guide to Gentlemen and Ladies, in furnishing their Gardens. Being several useful Catalogues of Fruits and Flowers. London: 1733. 8vo. [xviii],68,[1] pp. 2 plates. Half calf, trifle rubbed.
(Wheldon & Wesley) **£500 [≈ $890]**

Fyson, P.F.
- The Flora of the South Indian Hill Station. Madras: 1932. 2 vols. 8vo. Atlas of 611 plates. Vol 1 contents sl stained. Orig cloth, trifle used, 2-inch split in 1 jnt.
(Wheldon & Wesley) **£85 [≈ $151]**

Gale, Thomas
- An Antidotarie conteyning Hidde and Secrete Medicines Simple and Compounde: as also all suche as are required in Chirurgerie. London: Thomas Gale, 1563. 1st edn. Sm 8vo. [3],90 ff. 19th c calf, rebacked.
(Bookpress) **$750 [≈ £421]**

Galen of Pergamon
- Galen's Method of Physick ... Commentary ... by its translator, Peter English. Edinburgh: A.A. for Svintoun & Glen, 1656. 12mo. [4],344 pp. Some gatherings loose. Calf, rebacked. *(Goodrich)* **$1,750 [≈ £983]**
- On the Natural Faculties. London: 1916. Translated by Brock. 339 pp. Orig bndg.
(Fye) **$75 [≈ £42]**
- See also Siegel, R.E.

Gallup, Joseph Adams
- Sketches of Epidemic Diseases in the State of Vermont ... Boston: T.B. Wait & Sons ..., 1815. 1st edn. 8vo. 419 pp. 1 lib stamp. Mod bds. *(Hemlock)* **$225 [≈ £126]**

Galton, Douglas
- Observations on the Construction of Healthy Dwellings namely Houses, Hospitals, Barracks, Asylums, etc. Oxford: Clarendon Press, 1880. 1st edn. 8vo. Text figs. Orig cloth. *(Georges)* **£125 [≈ $223]**

Galton, Sir Francis
- Finger Prints. London: 1892. 8vo. xvi,216 pp. Half-title. 16 plates, tables. Few ink spots. Orig cloth. *(Weiner)* **£165 [≈ $294]**
- Fingerprints. London: Macmillan, 1892. 1st edn. 8vo. xvi,216 pp. 16 plates (15 listed). Orig mauve cloth, spine sl faded.
(Key Books) **$425 [≈ £239]**
- Hereditary Genius: an Inquiry into its Laws and Consequences. New and Revised Edition with an American Preface. New York:

Appleton, 1871. 8vo. xii,390,6 advt pp. Orig bndg, spine darkened, new endpapers.
(Key Books) **$60 [≈ £34]**
- Hereditary Genius ... New and Revised Edition. New York: 1871. xii,390 pp. 2 fldg plates, few text figs. Front endpaper reprd. Orig cloth, sl worn. *(Whitehart)* **£75 [≈ $134]**
- Hereditary Genius: An Inquiry into its Laws and Consequences. London: 1892. 2nd edn. 379 pp. Orig bndg. *(Fye)* **$100 [≈ £56]**

Gamble, J.S. & Fischer, C.E.C.
- Flora of the Presidency of Madras. London: 1915-36. 11 parts forming 3 vols. 8vo. Fldg map. Good ex-lib. Orig wraps, part 11 worn.
(Wheldon & Wesley) **£40 [≈ $71]**

Gamow, George
- Atomic Energy in Cosmic and Human Life - Fifty Years of Radioactivity. Cambridge: UP, 1946. 1st edn, 2nd printing. 12mo. 161 pp. Plates, ills. Orig bndg. Dw.
(Schoen) **$45 [≈ £25]**
- The Creation of the Universe. New York: Viking Press, 1952. 1st edn. 8vo. 147 pp. Cold frontis, 11 plates, 40 figs. Orig bndg. Dw (torn). *(Schoen)* **$45 [≈ £25]**

Gardiner, W.
- Twenty Lessons on British Mosses. London: 1852. 4th edn. Cr 8vo. 50 pp. 24 natural specimens. Title calls for 25, but none is apparently missing. Cloth, faded.
(Wheldon & Wesley) **£25 [≈ $45]**

Gardiner-Hill, H.
- Clinical Involvements or The Old Firm. Being Running Commentaries on the Round. London: 1958. vii,200 pp. Ills. Orig bndg.
(Whitehart) **£15 [≈ $27]**

Gardner, Augustus K.
- A History of the Art of Midwifery: A Lecture delivered at the College of Physicians and Surgeons, November 11th, 1851 ... New York: 1852. 8vo. Half-title,32 pp. New wraps. *(Goodrich)* **$95 [≈ £53]**

Gardner, Gerald
- Witchcraft Today. London: Rider, 1954. 1st edn. Ills. Orig bndg. Dw.
(Deja Vu) **£45 [≈ $80]**

Garnett, Frank W.
- Westmorland Agriculture 1800-1900. Kendal: Titus Wilson, 1912. Only edn. 302 pp. Ills. Qtr vellum, rear cvr strengthened internally. *(Carol Howard)* **£220 [≈ $392]**

Garnett, T.
- Popular Lectures on Zoonomia or the Laws of Animal Life in Health and Disease. London: 1804. 4to. xxii,325 pp. Port. Half calf, rebacked. *(Henly)* **£45 [≈ $80]**

Garretson, James E.
- A System of Oral Surgery. Phila: 1881. 3rd edn. 916 pp. 9 plates, over 500 w'cuts. Leather. *(Fye)* **$275 [≈ £154]**

Garrison, Fielding
- An Introduction to the History of Medicine. Phila: 1914. 1st edn, 2nd printing. 763 pp. Orig bndg. *(Fye)* **$100 [≈ £56]**
- An Introduction to the History of Medicine. Phila: 1929. 4th edn. 996 pp. Ills. Orig bndg. *(Fye)* **$90 [≈ £51]**
- The Principles of Anatomic Illustration before Vesalius. An Inquiry into the Rationale of Artistic Anatomy. New York: 1926. 1st edn. 58 pp. Ex-lib. Orig bndg. *(Fye)* **$80 [≈ £45]**

Garvey, Gideon
- The Vanities of Philosophy and Physick: Together with Directions and Medicines easily prepared ... London: 1700. 2nd edn, enlgd. 143 pp. Old calf, rebacked, new endpapers, hd of spine chipped. *(King)* **$250 [≈ £140]**

Gasquet, F.A.
- The Black Death of 1348 and 1349. London: Bell, 1908. 2nd edn. 8vo. xxv,272 pp. Occas sl spotting. Orig cloth. *(David White)* **£20 [≈ $36]**

Gatke, H.
- Heligoland as an Ornithological Observatory, the Result of Fifty Years' Experience. Translated by R. Rosenstock. Edinburgh: 1895. 8vo. xi,599 pp. Port. Cloth, trifle used & spotted. *(Wheldon & Wesley)* **£50 [≈ $89]**

Gatty, Mrs A.
- British Sea-Weeds, drawn from Professor Harvey's "Phycologia Britannica" ... London: Bell & Daldy, 1872. 2 vols. Roy 8vo. 80 chromolitho plates. Orig cloth gilt. *(Egglishaw)* **£115 [≈ $205]**

Gauger, Nicholas
- Fires Improv'd; being a New Method of Building Chimneys, so as to prevent their smoaking ... made English and improved by J.T. Desaguliers ... London: 1715. 1st edn. Sm 8vo. [vi],161, [9],[2 ctlg] pp. 9 fldg plates. Contemp polished calf. *(Weiner)* **£300 [≈ $534]**

Gaumann, E.
- Principles of Plant Infection. London: Lockwood, 1950. 8vo. 543 pp. 311 text figs. Buckram, backstrip relaid. *(Savona)* **£20 [≈ $36]**

Gazley, John G.
- The Life of Arthur Young 1741-1820. Phila: Amer Philosophical Society, 1973. 8vo. 3 maps, 23 ills. Dw. *(Georges)* **£45 [≈ $80]**

Gedde, John
- The English Apiary: or, the Compleat Bee-Master ... London: Curll, Mears, Corbet, 1721-22. 12mo. xxii,82,87-108 pp. Frontis (outer marg sl trimmed). Lacks the blank leaf between the 2 parts. Contemp sheep, rebacked. *(Blackwell's)* **£210 [≈ $374]**

Gee, George E.
- Gold Alloys. London: Crosby Lockwood, 1929. 8vo. viii,336 pp. 21 text figs. Lib marks. Buckram, worn. *(Gemmary)* **$45 [≈ £25]**
- The Goldsmith's Handbook ... Second Edition, considerably enlarged. London: Crosby Lockwood, 1881. Sm 8vo. xxii, 259, [1], [16,32 advt] pp. Orig cloth gilt, spine & label worn. *(Fenning)* **£35 [≈ $62]**
- The Goldsmith's Handbook. London: Crosby Lockwood, 1918. 2nd edn. Cr 8vo. xxii,259 pp. Orig cloth, worn. *(Gemmary)* **$60 [≈ £34]**
- The Goldsmith's Handbook. New York: Chemical Publ Co., 1937. 1st Amer edn. Cr 8vo. xxiv,263 pp. Orig cloth. *(Gemmary)* **$75 [≈ £42]**
- Recovering Precious Metals from Liquid Waste Residues. New York: Spon & Chamberlain, 1920. 8vo. viii,380 pp. 29 text figs. Orig cloth. *(Gemmary)* **$75 [≈ £42]**
- Silversmith's Handbook. London: Crosby Lockwood, 1921. 5th edn. Cr 8vo. xxx,222 pp. 40 text figs. Orig cloth. *(Gemmary)* **$60 [≈ £34]**

Geert, A. van
- Iconography of Indian Azaleas. Translated by T. Moore. Ghent: 1882. 4to. 81 pp. 36 cold plates. Half mor, trifle rubbed. *(Wheldon & Wesley)* **£550 [≈ $979]**

Gegenbaur, C.
- Elements of Comparative Anatomy. Translated by F.J. Bell. Revised by E.R. Lankester. London: 1878. xxvi,646 pp. 356 figs. Sl foxed throughout. Lib stamps at start. Orig bndg, worn & marked. *(Whitehart)* **£40 [≈ $71]**

Geikie, Sir Archibald
- The Founders of Geology. London: 1905. 2nd edn. 8vo. xi,486 pp. Cloth, faint stain on spine.   *(Wheldon & Wesley)* **£35 [≈ $62]**
- The Founders of Geology. London: 1905. 2nd edn. xi,486,[2 advt] pp. Ink stamp on pastedown. Orig cloth, partly unopened.
(Francis Edwards) **£30 [≈ $53]**
- The Scenery of Scotland Viewed in Connection with its Physical Geology. London: Macmillan, 1887. 2nd edn. 8vo. xx,481 pp. 2 maps, 85 text figs. Orig cloth, unopened.   *(Gemmary)* **$50 [≈ £28]**
- Text-Book of Geology. London: Macmillan, 1882. 1st edn. 8vo. xi,971 pp. Orig green cloth, inner hinges cracked.
(Frew Mackenzie) **£35 [≈ $62]**
- Text-Book of Geology. Second Edition. London: Macmillan, 1885. xvi,992,2 advt pp. Half-title. Fldg frontis, ills. Orig green cloth, cvrs stained & worn, hd of spine frayed.
(Jermy & Westerman) **£30 [≈ $53]**
- Text-Book of Geology. London: 1903. 4th edn. 2 vols. 1472,advt pp. Fldg frontis, text ills. Occas sl foxing. Endpapers sl browned. Orig cloth, unopened.
(Francis Edwards) **£40 [≈ $71]**
- Text Book of Geology. London: 1903. 4th edn. 2 vols. 8vo. xxi,702,2; ix,705-1472 pp. Frontis, 508 text ills. Orig cloth gilt.
(Henly) **£25 [≈ $45]**

Geikie, James
- Earth Sculpture, or, The Origin of Land-Forms. London: 1904. xvi,320 pp. 2 plates, 89 text figs. Endpapers sl foxed. Orig cloth, spine sl faded. *(Francis Edwards)* **£25 [≈ $45]**
- Fragments of Earth Lore, Sketches and Addresses Geological and Geographical. London: 1893. 8vo. 5 cold maps & a section. Cloth.   *(Henly)* **£16 [≈ $28]**
- The Great Ice Age and its relation to the Antiquity of Man. London: 1874. 8vo. xxiii, 575 pp. 17 maps etc. Orig cloth.
(Wheldon & Wesley) **£40 [≈ $71]**
- Structural and Field Geology. For Students of Pure and Applied Science. Edinburgh: 1905. 1st edn. xx,435 pp. 56 plates, 142 text ills. Orig cloth, sl faded.
(Francis Edwards) **£30 [≈ $53]**
- Structural and Field Geology. London: 1908. 2nd edn, rvsd. 8vo. xx,443 pp. 56 plates, 144 text figs. Cloth.   *(Henly)* **£18 [≈ $32]**

Gellert, C.E.
- Metallurgic Chymistry. Being a System of Mineralogy in General, and of all the Arts arising from this Science ... London: T.

Becket, 1776. Half-title. 4 fldg plates. Fldg table supplied in facsimile. Later sheep, gilt spine.   *(P and P Books)* **£325 [≈ $579]**

General ...
- General View of the Agriculture of the County of Suffolk. Third Edition. London: Richard Phillips, 1804. 8vo. xv,432,[16 advt] pp. Fldg hand cold map, 2 fldg plates. Orig bds, uncut, label reprd.
(Spelman) **£140 [≈ $249]**
- See also Young, Arthur.

Gentleman ...
- The Gentleman Farmer's Pocket Companion. London: the author, 1788. 1st edn. 12mo. 51, [1] pp. Disbound. *(Bookpress)* **$525 [≈ £295]**

Gerard, John
- A Catalogue of Plants cultivated in the Garden of John Gerard 1596-1599. Edited ... by B.D. Jackson. London: Privately Printed, 1876. One of 100 signed by the author. 4to. Orig bds. *(Wheldon & Wesley)* **£80 [≈ $142]**
- Gerard's Herball. The Essence thereof distilled by Marcus Woodward from the edition of Th. Johnson, 1636. London: Gerald Howe, 1927. One of 150. 4to. Ills. Vellum, t.e.g.   *(Egglishaw)* **£115 [≈ $205]**

Geschickter, Charles F.
- Diseases of the Breast. Diagnosis, Pathology, Treatment ... Phila: Lippincott, 1943. 8vo. 829,593 pp. Cold plate. Orig cloth, worn.
(Goodrich) **$65 [≈ £37]**

Gesner, Abraham
- A Practical Treatise on Coal, Petroleum, and other Distilled Oils. New York: Bailliere, 1861. 1st edn. 8vo. 134,[24 advt] pp. Frontis. Orig cloth, rear cvr sl spotted.
(Chapel Hill) **$450 [≈ £253]**

Ghalioungui, Paul
- Magic and Medical Science in Ancient Egypt. London: 1963. 1st edn. 189 pp. Orig bndg.
(Fye) **$50 [≈ £28]**

Gibbs-Smith, C.H.
- The Aeroplane. An Historical Survey of its Origins and Development. London: HMSO, 1960. 4to. x,375 pp. Frontis, 48 figs. Lacks 1st free endpaper. Orig bndg,
(Whitehart) **£18 [≈ $32]**
- A Directory and Nomenclature of the First Aeroplanes 1809 to 1909. London: Science Museum, 1966. xii,120 pp. Dw (sl soiled).
(Whitehart) **£18 [≈ $32]**
- The Rebirth of European Aviation

1902-1908. A Study of the Wright Brothers' Influence. London: HMSO, 1974. xx,387 pp. Frontis, 78 ills. Orig bndg.
(Whitehart) £18 [≈ $32]

Gibney, John
- Practical Observations on the Use and Abuse of Cold and Warm Sea-Bathing, in Various Diseases ... Second Edition. London: B. Mcmillan ... for Underwood, 1814. 8vo. [2], 144 pp. Orig bds, uncut, paper label sl chipped, crnrs bumped.
(Spelman) £80 [≈ $142]

Gibson, Edmund
- The Causes of the Discontents in relation to the Plague, and the Provisions against it fairly stated and consider'd. London: for J. Roberts, 1721. 4to. 14 pp. Rebound in bds, uncut. Anon. *(C.R. Johnson)* £165 [≈ $294]

Gibson, F.M.
- The Amateur Telescopist's Handbook. London: 1894. xiii,163 pp. 1 plate, 11 figs.
(Whitehart) £18 [≈ $32]

Gibson, G.A.
- Life of Sir William Tennant Gairdner with a Selection of Papers on General and Medical Subjects. Glasgow: 1912. 1st edn. 817 pp. Orig bndg. *(Fye)* £45 [≈ $25]
- The Nervous Affections of the Heart. Being the Morison Lectures delivered before the Royal College of Physicians of Edinburgh in 1902 and 1903. London: 1904. [ix],99 pp. 35 text figs. Edge of cloth sl nicked.
(Whitehart) £18 [≈ $32]
- The Physician's Art: an Attempt to expand John Locke's Fragment De Arte Medica. Oxford: 1933. 1st edn. 237 pp. Orig bndg.
(Fye) £50 [≈ $28]

Gibson, R.W.
- Francis Bacon. A Bibliography of His Works and of Baconiana to the Year 1750. Oxford: Scrivener Press, 1950. 4to. xvii,369 pp. Frontis, facss. Orig linen backed bds, uncut, sl soiled. *(Lamb)* £95 [≈ $169]

Gibson, William
- The Institutes and Practice of Surgery: being the Outline of a Course of Lectures. Phila: Lea & Blanchard, 1835. 4th edn. 2 vols. xxvi,17-468; 409,[1],[12] pp. 19 + 12 plates. Occas water stains. Contemp calf, rubbed.
(Bookpress) $225 [≈ £126]

Giedion, Siegfried
- Mechanization Takes Command. A Contribution to Anonymous History. New

York: OUP, 1948. 1st edn. 8vo. Num ills. Orig red linen, spine faded.
(Georges) £50 [≈ $89]

Gifford, Isabella
- The Marine Botanist; an Introduction to the Study of Algology ... London: Darton & Co., [ca 1840]. 1st edn. 12mo. 141,[12 advt] pp. Hand cold title vignette, 5 hand cold & 5 plain plates. Orig pict red cloth gilt.
(Gough) £35 [≈ $62]
- The Marine Botanist ... containing Descriptions of the commonest British Sea-Weeds. London: Darton; Bath: Binns & Goodwin, [1848]. 1st edn. Sm 8vo. xiv, xiv, 15-144 pp. 6 cold & 6 plain plates (inc cold title vignette). Sm marg water stain. Orig cloth gilt, sl worn & reprd.
(Wheldon & Wesley) £35 [≈ $62]
- The Marine Botanist: An Introduction to the Study of the British Sea-Weeds ... Brighton: 1853. 3rd edn. Sm 8vo. xl, 357, errata pp. 6 cold & 6 b/w plates. Sl marg browning. Orig cloth, gilt dec spine, sl soiled, extrs sl worn.
(Francis Edwards) £30 [≈ $53]

Gihon, A.L.
- Practical Suggestions in Naval Hygiene. Washington: 1871. [8],151 pp. Sm lib stamp on title & endpaper. Orig linen bds.
(Whitehart) £20 [≈ $36]

Gilbert, S.
- The Florist's Vade-Mecum, being a Choice Compendium ... the Rarest Flowers and Plants that our Climate and Skill ... will perswade to live with us. London: 1682. 12mo. [xxii], 1-120, 131-252, [22], [almanack 36] pp, correct. Port. Contemp calf, rebacked, edges reprd.
(Wheldon & Wesley) £120 [≈ $214]

Gilbert, William
- On the Loadstone and Magnetic Bodies, and on the Great Magnet the Earth ... A Translation by P. Fleury Mottelay. London: Quaritch, 1893. 8vo. Port, ills. Orig cloth, leather label, v sl bumped.
(Georges) £75 [≈ $134]

Gilbreth, Frank B.
- Motion Study. A Method for Increasing the Efficiency of the Workman ... New York: Van Nostrand, 1911. 1st edn. 8vo. xxiv,116,32 advt pp. Photo ills. Orig cloth, sl soiled.
(Karmiole) $100 [≈ £56]

Gilchrist, Ebenezer
- The Use of Sea Voyages in Medicine; and particularly in a Consumption: with

Observations on that Disease. London: for T. Cadell, 1771. 3rd edn, enlgd. 8vo. xiii, [iii], 308, [12] pp. Half-title. Sl marg stain few ff. Single worm hole. Contemp calf, sl worn.
(Burmester) **£150 [≈ $267]**

Giles, George M.
- A Handbook of the Gnats or Mosquitoes. Giving the Anatomy and Life History of the Culicidae. London: 1900. 1st edn. viii,374 pp. Fldg frontis, 7 plates, ills. Orig cloth, partly unopened, crnrs bumped, spine v sl faded & rubbed. *(Francis Edwards)* **£25 [≈ $45]**

Gill, J.B.
- Indigestion. What It Is; What It Leads To; and A New Method of Treating It. London: 1880. viii,250 pp. Some foxing prelims. Orig cloth, sl worn.   *(Whitehart)* **£18 [≈ $32]**

Gillespie, C.C.
- Lazare Carnot Savant. Princeton: 1971. Sm 4to. x,359 pp. Plates. Orig bndg.
(Whitehart) **£25 [≈ $45]**

Gillies, Harold D.
- Plastic Surgery of the Face based on selected Cases of War Injuries of the Face including Burns. London: Frowde, 1920. 1st edn. 4to. 844 figs. Lib stamps on title. Orig cloth, backstrip relaid. *(David White)* **£95 [≈ $169]**
- Plastic Surgery of the Face based on Selected Cases of War Injuries of the Face including Burns, with Original Illustrations. London: 1920. 1st edn. 4to. 408 pp. Photo ills. Orig bndg, fine.   *(Fye)* **$1,000 [≈ £562]**

Gillies, Harold & Millard, R.
- The Principles and Art of Plastic Surgery. Boston: 1957. 1st edn. 2 vols. 652 pp. Orig bndg.   *(Fye)* **$200 [≈ £112]**

Gillispie, Charles (editor)
- Dictionary of Scientific Biography. New York: 1970-80. 1st edn. 16 vols. Orig bndg.
(Fye) **$1,000 [≈ £562]**

Gillkrest, James
- Notes worth noticing relative to the Cholera which has for some time past, occupied the Public Attention. London: W.J. Colbourn, 1852. 8vo. Title & half-title detached. Disbound.   *(Waterfield's)* **£45 [≈ $80]**

Glaister, J.
- Medical Jurisprudence and Toxicology. Edinburgh: 1950. 9th edn. xii,756 pp. 88 cold & 146 other plates. Dw.
(Whitehart) **£25 [≈ $45]**

Glanvil, Joseph
- Saducismus Triumphatus: or, Full and Plaine Evidence concerning Witches and Apparitions. London: Newcomb, 1682; Lownds, 1681-2. 2nd edn. 5 parts in one. 8vo. [16], 52, [10],162, [4],78, [9],273,67, 45,[14], 24,[1] pp. Sl creased & soiled. Mod period style calf. Wing G.823
(D & D Galleries) **$475 [≈ £267]**
- Scepsis Scientifica: or, Confest Ignorance, the way to Science; In an Essay of The Vanity of Dogmatizing ... London: 1665. Sm 4to. [32],92,[4] pp. Imprimatur & errata ff. Longitudinal title. Sep title to Reply. Few sl marks. Contemp calf, rebacked, sl wear. Wing G.827/828. *(D & D Galleries)* **$500 [≈ £281]**

Glass, Samuel
- An Essay on Magnesia Alba. Wherein its History is attempted, its Virtues Pointed Out, and the Use of it Recommended ... Oxford: Davis & Fletcher, 1764. 1st edn. 8vo. 6,38 pp. Rec wraps.   *(Fenning)* **£245 [≈ $436]**

Glass, Thomas
- Twelve Commentaries on Fevers. Explaining the Method of Curing these Disorders, upon the Principles of Hippocrates. Translated by N. Peters. London: for S. Birt, & A. Tozer, 1752. 1st edn in English. 8vo. [ii],xvi,302 pp. Sl browning & foxing. Contemp calf.
(Burmester) **£150 [≈ $267]**

Glasscheib, H.S.
- The March of Medicine. Aberrations and Triumphs of the Healing Art. Translated by M. Savill. London: 1963. 360 pp. 41 plates. Edges sl foxed. Dw (torn).
(Whitehart) **£15 [≈ $27]**

Glasse, Hannah
- The Art of Cookery, Made Plain and Easy ... Eighth Edition. London: for A. Millar ..., 1763. 8vo. vi,[xxiv], 384,[24] pp. Hannah Glasse's printed signature at Chapter One. Contemp calf gilt, sm reprs.
(Gough) **£295 [≈ $525]**
- The Art of Cookery, made Plain and Easy ... By a Lady. New Edition. London: 1767. 8vo. vi,xxiv, 384,[xxiv] pp. MS notes on endpapers. Contemp calf, jnts sometime reprd, upper jnt cracked, sl worn. Anon.
(Frew Mackenzie) **£200 [≈ $356]**
- The Art of Cookery, Made Plain and Easy ... Edinburgh: for Alexander Donaldson ..., 1774. vi,[xviii], 440,[24] pp. Few sm stains. Lacks final blanks. Contemp calf, lower bd v sl split at hd.   *(Gough)* **£275 [≈ $490]**
- The Art of Cookery, made Plain and Easy ...

By a Lady. A New Edition, with all the Modern Improvements ... London: for Strahan, Rivington ..., 1778. 8vo. [ii],vi,[xx], 397, [25] pp. Lge fldg table (clean tear at fold). Contemp sheep, rebacked. Anon.
(Burmester) **£225 [≈ $401]**

Glasser, Otto
- Wilhelm Conrad Roentgen and the Early History of the Roentgen Rays ... Springfield: 1943. 1st edn. 494 pp. Ills. Ex-lib. Orig bndg.
(Fye) **$150 [≈ £84]**

Gleanings ...
- Gleanings from Books, on Agriculture and Gardening. Enlarged and Improved. London: W. Smith for Samuel Bagster ..., 1802. 2nd edn. 8vo. 4,vii, [i],432 pp. Errata. 2 plates (foxed). Later half calf, gilt spine.
(Vanbrugh) **£165 [≈ $294]**

Godfery, Masters John
- Monograph & Iconograph of Native British Orchidaceae. Cambridge: UP, 1933. Imperial 4to. xvi,259 pp. Errata leaf tucked in. 58 cold & 9 other plates, 11 text figs. Orig blue cloth gilt, spine dulled, crnrs sl bumped.
(Blackwell's) **£225 [≈ $401]**
- Monograph and Iconograph of Native British Orchidaceae. Cambridge: 1933. 4to. xvi,259 pp. Port, 67 plates (57 cold). Orig cloth. Dw.
(Egglishaw) **£195 [≈ $347]**

Godlee, Rickman John
- An Atlas of Human Anatomy Illustrating Most of the Ordinary Dissections and Many not usually Practised by the Student ... Plates Volume [only]. London: Churchill, 1880. Folio. 47 litho plates. Cvrs sl scuffed, backstrip laid down, new endpapers.
(Goodrich) **$375 [≈ £211]**
- Lord Lister. Oxford: 1917. 1st edn. 676 pp. Orig bndg.
(Fye) **$85 [≈ £48]**
- Lord Lister. Oxford: 1924. 3rd edn. 686 pp. Orig bndg.
(Fye) **$75 [≈ £42]**

Godman, John Davidson
- Addresses delivered on Various Public Occasions ... A Brief Explanation of the Injurious Effects of Tight Lacing ... Phila: 1829. 194 pp. Orig bds, uncut, rebacked.
(Goodrich) **$95 [≈ £53]**
- American Natural History. Part I. Mastology. Phila: 1831. All published. 2nd edn. 3 vols. 8vo. 3 engvd titles, 49 plates. Lib stamps on titles & back of a few plates. New bds.
(Wheldon & Wesley) **£100 [≈ $178]**

Godwin, Sir Harry
- The History of the British Flora. A Factual Basis for Phytogeography. Second Edition. Cambridge: 1975. 4to. x,541 pp. 28 plates, 175 figs, 48 tables. Orig cloth. Dw.
(Claude Cox) **£28 [≈ $50]**

Goldberg, Leo
- Atoms, Stars, and Nebulae. Phila: The Blakiston Co., 1943. 1st edn. 12mo. 323 pp. Num ills. Lib pocket. Orig bndg.
(Schoen) **$45 [≈ £25]**

Goldsmith, Oliver
- An History of the Earth and Animated Nature. Phila: for Mathew Carey, May 12, 1795. 4 vols. 8vo. 55 plates. Some offsetting. Rebound in cloth. *(Key Books)* **$150 [≈ £84]**
- A History of the Earth and Animated Nature, with an Introductory Note by Baron Cuvier and a Life of the Author by Washington Irving. London: Fullarton & Co., [?1855]. 2 vols. Roy 8vo. 2 hand cold title vignettes, 72 hand cold plates. Dec calf.
(Egglishaw) **£170 [≈ $303]**

Good, J.M.
- The Study of Medicine. Improved from the Author's Manuscripts and by reference to the latest Advances ... By S. Cooper. London: 1840. 4 vols. Vol 3 new endpapers. Orig cloth. *(Whitehart)* **£40 [≈ $71]**

Goode, J.M.
- The Book of Nature. London: 1826. 3 vols. 8vo. Calf. *(Wheldon & Wesley)* **£18 [≈ $32]**

Goodhart, Sir James F.
- The Student's Guide to Diseases of Children. London: J. & A. Churchill, 1885. 1st edn. Lge 12mo. xii,648, [16 advt] pp. Errata slip. Name & stamp on title. Orig cloth gilt.
(Fenning) **£35 [≈ $62]**

Goodhugh, Thomas
- The Art of Prosthetic Dentistry. London: 1924. 1st edn. 8vo. viii,448 pp. 218 ills. Occas marks. Orig cloth, trifle rubbed.
(Bow Windows) **£40 [≈ $71]**

Goodwin, D.
- Estrildid Finches of the World. London: BM, 1982. 4to. 328 pp. 8 cold plates, 1 plate of outlines, num figs & maps. Cloth.
(Wheldon & Wesley) **£45 [≈ $80]**

Gordon, A.
- Days with the Golden Eagle. London: 1927. Roy 8vo. xx,176 pp. Frontis, 2 cold & 16

plain plates, text figs. Minor foxing. Cloth, trifle marked.
(Wheldon & Wesley) **£28 [≈ $50]**

Gordon, Benjamin
- Medicine throughout Antiquity. Phila: 1949. 1st edn. 818 pp. 157 ills. Orig bndg.
(Fye) **$100 [≈ £56]**

Gordon, Seton
- Edward Grey of Fallodon, and his Birds. London: Country Life, 1937. One of 750 sgnd. 8vo. 20 pp. Frontis, 15 plates. Orig qtr cloth, gilt spine.   *(Gough)* **£30 [≈ $53]**

Gordon-Taylor, G. & Walls, E.W.
- Sir Charles Bell. His Life and Times. Edinburgh & London: 1958. xii,288 pp. 47 figs. Orig ptd wraps. *(Whitehart)* **£38 [≈ $68]**

Goring, C.R. & Pritchard, A.
- Microscopic Illustrations of a few New, Popular and Diverting Living Objects; with their Natural History ... London: 1833. 8vo. iv, 96 pp. 4 plates (foxed). Half mor, rubbed.
(Henly) **£48 [≈ $85]**

Gortvay, G. & Zoltan, I.
- Semmelweis: His Life and Work. Budapest: 1968. 288 pp. Ills. Orig bndg. Dw.
(Fye) **$75 [≈ £42]**

Gosse, Edmund
- The Naturalist of the Sea Shore. The Life of Philip Henry Gosse. London: 1896. 2nd edn. 8vo. ix,387 pp. Port. Orig cloth.
(Wheldon & Wesley) **£25 [≈ $45]**

Gosse, Philip Henry
- Actinologia britannica. A History of the British Sea-Anemones and Corals. London: Van Voorst, 1860. 8vo. xl,362 pp. 1 plain & 11 cold plates. Prize label. Orig cloth gilt.
(Egglishaw) **£60 [≈ $107]**
- Actinologia Britannica. A History of the British Sea Anemones and Corals. London: 1860. 8vo. xl,362 pp. 12 plates (11 cold). Orig dec cloth, sm split in rear jnt.
(Wheldon & Wesley) **£70 [≈ $125]**
- Actinologia Britannica. A History of the British Sea-Anemones and Corals. London: 1860. 8vo. xl,362,2 pp. 1 plain & 11 cold plates. Orig cloth gilt, fine.
(Henly) **£85 [≈ $151]**
- The Aquarium: an Unveiling of the Wonders of the Deep. London: 1854. 1st edn. 8vo. xiii, [i],278 pp. 6 cold & 6 plain plates. Orig blue cloth, a.e.g., used.
(Wheldon & Wesley) **£40 [≈ $71]**

- The Birds of Jamaica. London: 1847. Cr 8vo. x,447 pp. Errata slip. Orig cloth.
(Wheldon & Wesley) **£85 [≈ $151]**
- Evenings at the Microscope ... New York: 1860. xii,480 pp. Num ills. Sm perf lib stamp on title, inner margs of title & half-title reprd. New cloth retaining orig spine & front cvr.
(Whitehart) **£35 [≈ $62]**
- Evenings at the Microscope; or, Researches among the Minuter Organs and Forms of Animal Life. New Edition, Revised and Annotated. London: 1877. 8vo. xii,422 pp. Num text figs. Half leather, used.
(Wheldon & Wesley) **£30 [≈ $53]**
- A History of the British Sea-Anemones and Corals. London: Van Voorst, 1860. 1st edn. xl, 362 pp. 11 chromolitho plates, 1 plain plate. Contemp green panelled calf gilt, a.e.g., orig wraps bound in.
(Gough) **£120 [≈ $214]**
- An Introduction to Zoology. London: [1844]. 2 vols. Cr 8vo. Ills. Binder's cloth, sl used.
(Wheldon & Wesley) **£40 [≈ $71]**
- An Introduction to Zoology. London: SPCK, (1844). 2 vols. 8vo. xxi,383; iv,436 pp. Num w'engvs. Orig cloth. *(Egglishaw)* **£45 [≈ $80]**
- Life in its Lower, Intermediate and Higher Forms. London: 1870. 3rd edn. Sm 8vo. viii, 363 pp. 6 plates, text figs. Orig red cloth, worn, lower jnt split.
(Wheldon & Wesley) **£25 [≈ $45]**
- A Manual of Marine Zoology for the British Isles. London: 1855-56. 1st edn. 2 vols. Post 8vo. 674 figs. Ex-lib. Orig cloth, trifle used.
(Wheldon & Wesley) **£30 [≈ $53]**
- Natural History. Mollusca. London: SPCK, 1854. 8vo. viii,328,[4 advt] pp. Text figs. Orig cloth.   *(Egglishaw)* **£30 [≈ $53]**
- A Naturalist's Rambles on the Devonshire Coast. London: 1853. 8vo. xvi,451 pp. Inserted advts dated Dec 1858. 28 plates (12 cold). Cream endpapers (front free endpaper removed). Orig green cloth, lower jnt split at hd. *(Wheldon & Wesley)* **£50 [≈ $89]**
- A Naturalist's Rambles on the Devonshire Coast. London: Van Voorst, 1853. 1st edn. xvi, 451 pp. 12 chromolithographs & 16 plain lithos. Orig blue cloth, gilt spine.
(Gough) **£50 [≈ $89]**
- A Naturalist's Rambles on the Devonshire Coast. London: 1853. 8vo. xvi,451 pp. 12 cold & 16 plain plates (plates sl water stained). Orig green cloth, used, faded, reprd).
(Wheldon & Wesley) **£50 [≈ $89]**
- A Naturalist's Rambles on the Devonshire Coast. London: 1853. Cr 8vo. xvi,451 pp. 12 cold & 16 plain plates. Sl foxing. Half calf gilt, rebacked.   *(Henly)* **£72 [≈ $128]**

- A Naturalist's Rambles on the Devonshire Coast. London: 1853. 1st edn. xvi,451 pp. Advt leaf. 28 plates (some cold). Orig cloth, faded, sl worn.   *(Whitehart)* **£50 [≈ $89]**
- A Naturalist's Sojourn in Jamaica. London: 1851. 8vo. xxiv,508 pp. 4 cold & 4 tinted plates. Title & some plates foxed. Ex-lib. Orig cloth, rebacked, spine faded.
        (Wheldon & Wesley) **£85 [≈ $151]**
- The Ocean. London: 1845. 1st edn. Cr 8vo. xii, 360 pp. Num ills. Orig red cloth, reprd.
        (Wheldon & Wesley) **£35 [≈ $62]**
- The Ocean. London: [1854]. xii,360 pp. 52 ills. Page edges sl foxed. Orig cloth, sl worn, new front endpaper. *(Whitehart)* **£40 [≈ $71]**
- The Ocean. London: [1860]. 9th edn. Cr 8vo. xii,360 pp. Num ills. Half calf gilt, a.e.g.
        (Wheldon & Wesley) **£20 [≈ $36]**
- The Ocean. London: SPCK, (1860). 8vo. xii, 360 pp. Frontis, ills. Orig cloth.
        (Bow Windows) **£55 [≈ $98]**
- Omphalos: an Attempt to Untie the Geological Knot. London: 1857. 8vo. xii,384 pp. 56 w'engvs. Orig cloth, front cvr marked.
        (Wheldon & Wesley) **£50 [≈ $89]**
- The Romance of Natural History. London: 1861. 1st series 4th edn, 2nd series 1st edn. 2 vols. 21 plates. Orig green cloth gilt, trifle used.   *(Wheldon & Wesley)* **£40 [≈ $71]**
- Tenby: A Sea-Side Holiday. London: 1856. 12mo. xix,400 pp. 20 cold & 4 plain plates. Occas sl foxing inc margs of some plates. Half calf gilt.   *(Henly)* **£85 [≈ $151]**
- Tenby: a Sea-Side Holiday. London: 1856. 1st edn. 8vo. xix,[ii],400 pp. 24 plates (mostly cold, some margs foxed). Orig cloth, used & faded.   *(Wheldon & Wesley)* **£40 [≈ $71]**
- A Year at the Shore. London: 1865. 1st edn. Cr 8vo. xii,330,2 pp. 36 cold plates. Sl foxing at ends. Orig cloth gilt. *(Henly)* **£80 [≈ $142]**
- A Year at the Shore. London: 1865. 1st edn. 8vo. xii,330 pp. 36 colour-printed plates. Orig green cloth, spine marked.
        (Wheldon & Wesley) **£60 [≈ $107]**
- A Year at the Shore. London: Strahan, 1865. 1st edn. xii,330 pp. 36 chromolitho plates. Occas sl foxing. Orig pict green cloth gilt, t.e.g., hd of spine v sl split.
        (Gough) **£50 [≈ $89]**

Goulard, Thomas
- A Treatise on the Effects and Various Preparation of Lead ... for different Chirurgical Disorders. Third Edition. London: 1772. 8vo. Damp marks on last few ff. Contemp sheep, hd of spine worn.
        (Robertshaw) **£45 [≈ $80]**
- A Treatise on the Effects and Various

Preparations of Lead ... for different Chirurgical Disorders. Translated from the French. New Edition, with Remarks by G. Arnaud. London: Elmsly, 1773. Lge 12mo. [8], 232 pp. Contemp calf, rebacked.
        (Spelman) **£85 [≈ $151]**
- A Treatise on the Effects and Various Preparations of Lead ... for different Chirurgical Disorders. Translated from the French. The Sixth Edition, with Remarks by G. Arnaud. Dublin: 1777. Lge 12mo. [8],231,[1] pp. Contemp calf, new label.
        (Spelman) **£90 [≈ $160]**

Gould, John
- The Birds of Great Britain. London: Eric Maylin, 1980. One of 1100, sgnd by Peter Scott. 5 vols. Sm 8vo. 367 cold plates. Orig cloth gilt. Pict slipcase (sl rubbed).
        (Hollett) **£85 [≈ $151]**

Gould, William
- An Account of English Ants ... London: for A. Millar ..., 1747. Sm 8vo. Advt leaf at end. Progressive worming & browning affecting marg from p 19, text from p 91. Wraps, worn.
        (Francis Edwards) **£75 [≈ $134]**

Gower, Charles Foote
- The Scientific Phenomena of Domestic Life. Familiarly Explained. London: 1847. 2nd edn. 32 pp ctlg. Moveable frontis, ills. Few pencil notes. Orig cloth, sl spotted.
        (Jarndyce) **£30 [≈ $53]**

Gowers, William R.
- A Manual of Diseases of the Nervous System. Volume I. Diseases of the Spinal Cord and Nerves. London: 1886. 1st edn. 463 pp. Orig bndg, backstrip worn.   *(Fye)* **£150 [≈ £84]**
- A Manual of Diseases of the Nervous System. Third Edition revised and enlarged. Edited by W.R. Gowers and James Taylor. Phila: Blakiston, 1900. 2 vols. Some pp sl brittle & chipped at edges. Ex-lib. Orig cloth, recased.
        (Goodrich) **$95 [≈ £53]**
- Subjective Sensations of Sight and Sound, Abiotrophy, and other Lectures. Phila: Blakiston, 1904. 8vo. 250,[6],[31 advt] pp. Lib marks. Orig cloth, worn & rubbed.
        (Goodrich) **$95 [≈ £53]**

Gowland, W.
- The Metallurgy of Non-Ferrous Metals. London: Charles Griffin, 1914. 8vo. xxvii,496 pp. 4 plates, 191 text figs. Orig cloth.   *(Gemmary)* **$75 [≈ £42]**

Graham, Douglas
- A Practical Treatise on Massage: its History, Mode of Application, and Effects, Indications and Contra-Indications ... New York: 1884. 1st edn. 286 pp. Orig bndg.
(Fye) **$100 [≈ £56]**

Graham, Thomas
- Chemical and Physical Researches. Collected and Printed for Presentation Only. Preface and Analytical Contents. Edinburgh: 1876. 1st edn. 8vo. lvi,660 pp. Frontis, 3 plates. Orig cloth, worn, spine sl frayed.
(Gaskell) **£50 [≈ $89]**

Grainge, William
- Yorkshire Longevity: or, Records and Biographical Anecdotes of Persons who have attained to Extreme Old Age within that County. Pateley Bridge: Thomas Thorpe ..., 1864. 1st edn. Sm 8vo. 114,[2] pp. Half-title. Orig cloth gilt, faded.
(Burmester) **£38 [≈ $68]**

Grainger, R.D.
- Elements of General Anatomy, containing an Outline of the Organization of the Human Body. London: 1829. xxvi,526 pp. Occas foxing. Half cloth & mrbld bds, sl rubbed & worn.
(Whitehart) **£25 [≈ $45]**

Grainger, Thomas
- A Guide to the History of Bacteriology. New York: 1958. 1st edn. 210 pp. Orig bndg.
(Fye) **$50 [≈ £28]**

Grant, Archibald, attributed author
- A Dissertation on the Chief Obstacles to the Improvement of Land, and introducing better Methods of Agriculture throughout Scotland. Aberdeen: Francis Douglas ..., 1760. 1st edn. 8vo. [ii],94 pp. Disbound. Anon.
(Burmester) **£225 [≈ $401]**

Grant, H. Horace
- A Text-Book of Surgical Principles and Surgical Diseases of the Face, Mouth, and Jaws. Phila: 1902. 1st edn. 231 pp. 68 ills. Orig bndg.
(Fye) **$125 [≈ £70]**

Grant, William
- An Enquiry into the Nature, Rise and Progress of the the Fevers most common in London ... for the last twenty years ... London: 1771. 1st edn. 8vo. 463 pp. V sl marg worm at end. Lib stamp on title & at end. Contemp calf.
(Robertshaw) **£125 [≈ $223]**

Gratacap, L.P.
- A Popular Guide to Minerals. New York: Van Nostrand, 1912. 8vo. ii,330 pp. 74 photo plates, 400 text ills. Orig cloth, rear hinge loose.
(Gemmary) **$325 [≈ £183]**

Graves, R.J.
- Clinical Lectures on the Practice of Medicine. Edited by J.M. Neligan. Dublin: 1848. 2nd edn. 2 vols. Some marg pencil notes. Orig cloth, backstrips relaid.
(Whitehart) **£80 [≈ $142]**

Gravesande, William Jakob van 's
- An Explanation of the Newtonian Philosophy, in Lectures read to the Youth of the University of Leyden ... Translated into English by a Fellow of the Royal Society. London: Innys & Manby, 1735. 8vo. [xvi], 435, [13] pp. 17 plates. Sl used. Contemp calf, jnts reprd.
(Burmester) **£225 [≈ $401]**

Gray, Alexander
- The Theory and Practice of Absolute Measurements in Electricity and Magnetism. London: 1888-93. 3 vols. 302 figs. Lib marks. Orig cloth, sl marked, lib numbers on spines, inner hinges sl cracked.
(Whitehart) **£40 [≈ $71]**

Gray, Andrew
- The Experienced Millwright, or a Treatise on the Construction of some of the most useful Machines with the latest Improvements ... General Principles of Mechanics ... Edinburgh: 1806. Sm oblong folio. vi,73p 44 plates (some foxing). Half leather, sl rubbed.
(Hortulus) **$850 [≈ £478]**

Gray, Asa
- Darwiniana: Essays and Reviews pertaining to Darwinism. New York: 1876. 1st edn. 396 pp. Orig bndg. *(Fye)* **$150 [≈ £84]**

Gray, Henry
- Anatomy. Descriptive and Surgical. With T. Holmes. London: 1864. 3rd edn. xxxii,788 pp. 394 figs. Orig three qtr mor, v worn.
(Whitehart) **£40 [≈ $71]**
- Anatomy, Descriptive and Surgical. Edited by T. Pickering Pick. London: Longmans, 1897. 14th edn. 8vo. xl,1184, 16 advt pp. Title v sl spotted. Orig cloth, rebacked, new endpapers. *(David White)* **£15 [≈ $27]**

Gray, J.E.
- Catalogue of Carnivorous, Pachydermatous and Edentate Mammals in the British Museum. London: 1869. 8vo. vii,398 pp. 47

w'cuts. Lib stamp on title. Cloth, unopened.
(Egglishaw) **£28 [≈ $50]**
- Catalogue of Monkeys, Lemurs and Fruit-eating Bats in the British Museum. London: 1870. 8vo. viii,137 pp. 21 w'cuts. Lib stamp on title. Cloth, unopened.
(Egglishaw) **£26 [≈ $46]**
- Catalogue of Seals and Whales in the British Museum. London: 1866. 2nd edn. 8vo. vii, 402 pp. 101 text figs. Lib stamps. Orig cloth, rebacked.   *(Wheldon & Wesley)* **£40 [≈ $71]**
- Hand-List of Seals, Morses, Sea-Lions and Sea-Bears in the British Museum. London: 1874. 8vo. 44 pp. 30 litho plates. Lib stamp on title. Cloth, unopened.
(Egglishaw) **£28 [≈ $50]**
- Hand-list of the Edentate, Thick-skinned and Ruminant Mammals in the British Museum. London: 1873. 8vo. vii,176 pp. 42 plates. Lib stamp on title. Cloth, unopened.
(Egglishaw) **£25 [≈ $45]**

Gray, Robert
- The Birds of the West of Scotland, including the Outer Hebrides ... Glasgow: 1871. 1st edn. x,520 pp. 15 litho plates. Edges foxed. Orig pict gilt cloth, sl worn, spine chipped.
(Francis Edwards) **£75 [≈ $134]**

Gray, Thomas
- Observations on a General Iron Rail-Way; shewing its great superiority over all the Present Methods of Conveyance ... London: 1820. 1st edn. 8vo. 22 pp. Final blank leaf. Stamp on title. Qtr calf. Anon.
(Weiner) **£850 [≈ $1,513]**
- Observations on a General Iron Rail-Way ... Third Edition, Revised and Considerably Enlarged. London: 1822. 8vo. xii,131 pp. Frontis, 2 plans (sl foxed). Perf stamps through 1 leaf. Frontis sl foxed & offset to title. Qtr calf. Anon. *(Weiner)* **£350 [≈ $623]**

Green, C. Theodore
- The Flora of the Liverpool District. Liverpool: D. Marples, 1902. 1st edn. xii,207 pp. 20 photo ills, 804 text ills. Orig pict brown cloth gilt, spine ends sl worn.
(Gough) **£30 [≈ $53]**

Green, C.E. & Young, D.
- Encyclopaedia of Agriculture. London: William Green & Sons, 1908-09. 1st edn vols 3 & 4. 4 vols. Lge 8vo. Plates. Orig mor backed cloth.   *(Claude Cox)* **£45 [≈ $80]**

Green, T. (editor)
- The Flora of the Liverpool District. Liverpool: Marples, 1902. Map, num ills. Sl

foxing. Orig gilt dec bds, sl marked.
(Carol Howard) **£38 [≈ $68]**

Greenberg, L.A. & Lester, D.
- Handbook of Cosmetic Materials ... New York: 1954. xii,456 pp. Dw.
(Whitehart) **£15 [≈ $27]**

Greene, E.L.
- Illustrations of West American Oaks. San Francisco: 1889-90. 4to. xii,84 pp. 37 plates. Buckram. *(Wheldon & Wesley)* **£80 [≈ $142]**

Greenewalt, C.H.
- Humming Birds. New York: 1960. 1st printing. 4to. xxi,250 pp. Num ills. Orig buckram. *(Wheldon & Wesley)* **£160 [≈ $285]**
- Humming Birds. New York: 1960. One of 500 signed by the author. 4to. xxi,250 pp. 70 cold photos, num ills. Levant mor, pict onlay. Slipcase. *(Wheldon & Wesley)* **£350 [≈ $623]**

Greenhouse Favourites ...
- See Hibberd, Shirley

Greenwell, Dora
- On the Education of the Imbecile ... Edited for the Royal Albert Idiot Asylum, Lancaster. London: Strahan, 1869. 1st book edn. 8vo. 51,[3] pp. Disbound.
(Burmester) **£120 [≈ $214]**

Greenwell, G.C.
- A Practical Treatise on Mine Engineering. London: 1855. Lge 4to. [iv],204 pp. 63 plates inc frontis. Sl spotting. Good ex-lib. Later cloth.   *(Weiner)* **£100 [≈ $178]**
- A Practical Treatise on Mine Engineering. Newcastle upon Tyne: M. & M.W. Lambert, 1855. 1st edn. Roy 4to. 204 pp. Frontis, 61 cold plates. Lib marks. Some foxing. Buckram.   *(Gemmary)* **$550 [≈ £309]**
- A Practical Treatise on Mine Engineering. Second Edition. London: 1869. 4to. [viii], 255, [1 blank] pp. 64 cold plates. Occas spots & marks. Contemp half mor, t.e.g., cloth sides sl cockled.   *(Bow Windows)* **£495 [≈ $881]**

Greenwood, Major
- Some British Pioneers of Social Medicine. London: 1948. 118 pp. Occas sl foxing. Orig bndg, sl marked.   *(Whitehart)* **£15 [≈ $27]**

Greg, R.P. & Lettsom, W.G.
- Manual of the Mineralogy of Great Britain and Ireland. London: Van Voorst, 1858. 8vo. xvi, 483 pp. Num text ills. Orig cloth, edges worn, spine reprd. *(Gemmary)* **$175 [≈ £98]**
- Manual of the Mineralogy of Great Britain

and Ireland. London: Van Voorst, 1858. 8vo.
xvi, 483 pp. Num text ills. Rec qtr leather.
(Gemmary) **$250 [≈ £140]**

Gregory, G.
- A Dictionary of Arts and Sciences. London:
Richard Phillips, 1806. 1st edn. 2 vols. 4to.
[4],960; vi,[2],928 pp. 138 plates (some
foxed). Contemp half calf, rubbed, rebacked.
(Claude Cox) **£120 [≈ $214]**

Gregory, R.L.
- Mind in Science. A History of Explanations
in Psychology and Physics. London: 1981.
xiv, 642 pp. 47 ills. Dw (sl marked).
(Whitehart) **£18 [≈ $32]**

Gregory, William
- Letters to a Candid Inquirer on Animal
Magnetism. London: Taylor, Walton &
Maberly; Edinburgh: MacLachlan & Stewart,
1851. 1st edn. 8vo. xxii,[2],528 pp. Orig
cloth, dust soiled & sl rubbed.
(Claude Cox) **£40 [≈ $71]**

Grew, Nehemiah
- The Anatomy of Plants ... London: W.
Rawlins, 1682. 1st edn. Sm folio. 304,[19] pp.
83 plates. Unobtrusive blind stamps on title &
plates, plates sl damp stained. Mod half mor.
(Chapel Hill) **$1,200 [≈ £674]**
- Musaeum Regalis Societatis. or a Catalogue
of the Natural and Artificial Rarities
belonging to the Royal Society ... London: W.
Rawlins, 1681. 1st edn. Folio. [xii],386, [vi],
43,[i] pp. Port frontis, 31 plates. Few lib
marks. Rec calf. Wing G.1952.
(Clark) **£350 [≈ $623]**
- Museum Regalis Societatis. Or a Catalogue
and Description of the Natural and Artificial
Rarities belonging to the Royal Society ...
London: 1694. Folio. [xii],386,[ii], [iv],43 pp.
31 plates. Sl stain & v sl marg worm.
Contemp calf, rebacked & recrnrd.
(Frew Mackenzie) **£225 [≈ $401]**

Griesinger, Wilhelm
- Mental Pathology and Therapeutics.
Translated from the German (Second
Edition) by C. Lockhart Robertson ... New
York: Wood Library, 1882. viii,375 pp. Orig
bndg. *(Goodrich)* **$85 [≈ £48]**
- Mental Pathology and Therapeutics.
Translated from the German ... New York:
W. Wood, 1882. 1st Amer edn. viii,375,[1]
pp. Lib b'plate. 2 pp carelessly opened. Orig
cloth, spine ends sl chipped.
(Caius) **$175 [≈ £98]**

Grieve, S.
- The Great Auk, or Garefowl (Alca impennis,
Linn.) its History, Archaeology, and
Remains. London: 1885. 4to. xi,141,58 pp.
Cold map, 4 plates (2 cold), 6 ills. Foxed at
ends. Orig cloth, trifle used, front inner jnt
loose.   *(Wheldon & Wesley)* **£140 [≈ $249]**

Griffin, William
- A Treatise on Optics ... Second Edition.
Cambridge: University Press, 1842. 8vo. Orig
cloth backed bds, worn.
(Waterfield's) **£40 [≈ $71]**

Griffith, E.F.
- Doctors by Themselves. An Anthology.
London: 1951. xxii,614 pp. 16 plates. Sl
foxing. Orig bndg, sl marked.
(Whitehart) **£15 [≈ $27]**

Griffith, J.W. & Henfrey, A.
- The Micrographic Dictionary: a Guide to the
Examination and Investigation of the
Structure and Nature of Microscopic Objects.
London: 1875. 3rd edn. 2 vols. 48 plates, 812
text figs. Half roan, rubbed & worn.
(Whitehart) **£40 [≈ $71]**
- The Micrographic Dictionary; a Guide to the
Examination and Investigation of the
Structure and Nature of Microscopic Objects.
London: 1883. 2 vols in one. Thick 8vo. xlvi,
829 pp. 53 plates (inc hand cold). Occas sl
marg marks. Orig cloth, sl worn.
(Francis Edwards) **£40 [≈ $71]**

Griffith, John E.
- The Flora of Anglesey & Carnarvonshire.
Bangor: Nixon & Jarvis, [1895]. 1st edn. xx,
288 pp. Fldg map. Orig green cloth, gilt
spine.   *(Gough)* **£50 [≈ $89]**

Griffiths, J.C.
- Scientific Method in Analysis of Sediments.
New York: 1967. 8vo. xiii,508 pp. Text figs.
Orig cloth. Dw.   *(Henly)* **£22 [≈ $39]**

Grimwade, R.
- An Anthology of the Eucalypts. Sydney:
1930. 2nd rvsd edn. 4to. 103 plates (some
cold). Cloth.
(Wheldon & Wesley) **£60 [≈ $107]**

Grindon, Leo Hartley
- The Manchester Flora ... London: William
White, 1857. 1st edn. x,575 pp. 232 text ills.
Orig dec cloth gilt.   *(Gough)* **£40 [≈ $71]**

Grinstein, Alexander
- The Index of Psychoanalytic Writings. New

York: 1956. 1st edn. 5 vols. 2802 pp. Orig
bndg. Inscrbd by the author.
(Fye) **$150 [≈ £84]**

Grisebach, A.H.R.
- Flora of the West Indian Islands. London:
[1859-] 1864. Roy 8vo. xvi,789 pp. Half mor.
(Wheldon & Wesley) **£95 [≈ $169]**

Grodzinski, P.
- Diamond Technology. London: N.A.G.
Press, 1953. 2nd edn. 8vo. xxiv,784 pp. 486
ills, 93 tables. Orig cloth.
(Gemmary) **$75 [≈ £42]**
- Diamond Tools. New York: Anton Smit,
1944. Cr 8vo. vii,379 pp. Text ills. Orig
cloth.   *(Gemmary)* **$50 [≈ £28]**

Gross, Samuel D.
- Autobiography ... with Sketches of his
Contemporaries. Edited by his Sons. Phila:
1887. 2 vols. 2 frontis. Orig bndgs, uncut.
(Goodrich) **$125 [≈ £70]**
- Autobiography of Samuel D. Gross, M.D.
With Sketches of his Contemporaries. Phila:
1887. 1st edn. 2 vols. 407; 438 pp. Ills. Ex-
lib. Orig bndgs (1 green, 1 red).
(Fye) **$150 [≈ £84]**
- Elements of Pathological Anatomy ... Second
Edition, thoroughly revised, and greatly
enlarged. Phila: 1845. 822,[2 advt] pp. Cold
& other ills. Contemp calf, jnts rubbed.
(Hemlock) **$350 [≈ £197]**
- A System of Surgery: Pathological,
Diagnostic, Therapeutic and Operative.
Phila: 1862. 2nd edn. 2 vols. 1062; 1134 pp.
1227 w'cut ills. Leather. *(Fye)* **$450 [≈ £253]**

Gross, Samuel W.
- A Practical Treatise on Tumors of the
Mammary Gland: Embracing their
Histology, Pathology, Diagnosis and
Treatment. New York: 1880. 8vo. 246 pp.
Ills. Orig cloth, fine.
(Goodrich) **$495 [≈ £278]**

Grosvenor, Benjamin
- Health: an Essay on its Nature, Value,
Uncertainty, Preservation and Best
Improvement ... Second Edition. London: for
H. Piers, sold by R. Hett, 1748. 12mo. Minor
damage to half-title. Contemp sheep, worn
but sound, front jnt cracked.
(Waterfield's) **£40 [≈ $71]**

Groth, P.
- The Optical Properties of Crystals. New
York: John Wiley & Sons, 1910. 1st edn. 8vo.
xiv,309 pp. 2 cold plates, 121 text figs. Orig

cloth.   *(Gemmary)* **$75 [≈ £42]**

Grove, William Robert
- The Correlation of Physical Forces with other
Contributions to Science. London: 1874. 6th
edn. xx,466 pp. Ills. Occas sl foxing. Cloth,
worn, sl marked.   *(Whitehart)* **£25 [≈ $45]**
- On the Correlation of Physical Forces; being
the Substance of a Course of Lectures
delivered in the London Institution, in the
year 1843. London: Samuel Highley, 1846.
1st edn. 8vo. iv,52 pp. New cloth.
(Weiner) **£250 [≈ $445]**

Grunwald, L.
- Atlas and Epitome of Diseases of the Mouth,
Pharynx, and Nose. Phila: 1903. 2nd edn.
219 pp. 104 ills. Orig bndg. *(Fye)* **$75 [≈ £42]**

Guenther, A.
- Catalogue of the Fishes in the British
Museum. London: BM, 1859-70. 8 vols. 8vo.
4268 pp. Sound ex-lib. Orig cloth.
(Wheldon & Wesley) **£240 [≈ $427]**

Guillain, Georges
- J.-M. Charcot 1825-1893. His Life - his
Work. New York: 1959. 202 pp. Orig bndg.
(Fye) **$60 [≈ £34]**

Guillemin, A.
- The Applications of Physical Forces.
Translated from the French, and edited ... by
J. Norman Lockyer. London: 1877. 1st edn.
Lge 8vo. 4 cold & 21 engvd plates, over 460
figs. Few sl marks. Contemp prize calf, sl
rubbed, spine ends chipped.
(Bow Windows) **£50 [≈ $89]**

Guillet de Saint Georges, Georges
- The Gentleman's Dictionary. In Three Parts
... The Art of Riding the Great Horse ... The
Military Art ... The Art of Navigation ...
London: 1705. 1st edn in English. 8vo. [370]
pp. 3 fldg plates. Contemp calf, spine sl worn,
crnrs rubbed, hd of front jnt cracking.
(Finch) **£300 [≈ $534]**

Gunn, John C.
- Gunn's Domestic Medicine, or Poor Man's
Friend ... Second Edition. Madisonville, TN:
J.F. Grant, 1834. 8vo. 604 pp. Foxing. Orig
calf, mor label, rubbed.
(Chapel Hill) **$550 [≈ £309]**
- Gunn's Domestic Medicine, or Poor Man's
Friend, in the Hours of Affliction, Pain, and
Sickness ... Medicinal Roots and Herbs ...
New York: 1842. 893 pp. Port. Leather.
(Fye) **$200 [≈ £112]**

Gurney, E., & others
- Phantasms of the Living. London: 1918. 1st abridged edn. Lge 8vo. 570 pp. Ills. Orig bndg.   *(Deja Vu)* **£45 [≈ $80]**

Gurney, J.H.
- Early Annals of Ornithology. London: 1921. 1st edn. 8vo. viii,240 pp. 36 ills. Orig cloth.   *(Henly)* **£35 [≈ $62]**

Guthrie, D.M. & Tindall, A.R.
- The Biology of the Cockroach. London: 1968. 8vo. 416 pp. Ills. Cloth.
(Wheldon & Wesley) **£25 [≈ $45]**

Guthrie, Douglas
- A History of Medicine. London: 1945. 1st edn. 448 pp. Orig bndg.   *(Fye)* **$50 [≈ £28]**
- A History of Medicine. Revised Edition, with Supplement. London: 1960. 8vo. 72 plates. Dw.   *(Robertshaw)* **£16 [≈ $28]**
- Lord Lister, his Life and Doctrine. Baltimore: 1949. 1st Amer edn. 128 pp. Orig bndg.   *(Fye)* **£40 [≈ $22]**

Guttmann, Paul
- A Handbook of Physical Diagnosis. Comprising the Throat, Thorax and Abdomen. Translated by A. Napier. London: New Sydenham Society, 1879. xii,441 pp. Orig cloth.   *(Whitehart)* **£15 [≈ $27]**
- A Handbook of Physical Diagnosis comprising the Throat, Thorax, and Abdomen. Translated from the Third German Edition by Alex Napier. New York: Wood Library, 1880. 8vo. x,344 pp. Ills. Orig bndg.   *(Goodrich)* **$75 [≈ £42]**

Guy, William
- Principles of Forensic Medicine. London: Renshaw, 1844. 1st edn. 8vo. vii,[ix],568 pp. Name on title. Some water stain prelims. Orig cloth, recased.   *(David White)* **£55 [≈ $98]**

Haab, O.
- Atlas and Epitome of Ophthalmoscopy and Ophthalmic Diagnosis ... Phila: Saunders, 1901. 1st edn in English. 8vo. 85 pp. 152 cold litho ills. Orig cloth, sl marked.
(David White) **£30 [≈ $53]**

Haagensen, C.D.
- Diseases of the Breast. Phila: 1956. 1st edn. 751 pp. Num ills. Orig bndg.
(Fye) **$100 [≈ £56]**

Hachisuka, M.
- The Dodo and Kindred Birds, or the Extinct Birds of the Mascarene Islands. London:

1953. One of 485. 4to. 264 pp. 11 cold & 11 plain plates. Orig buckram, trifle spotted.
(Wheldon & Wesley) **£280 [≈ $498]**

Hadfield, Sir Robert A.
- Metallurgy. And its Influence on Modern Progress ... London: 1925. 1st edn. Lge 8vo. xvi,388 pp. Frontis, 70 plates. Endpapers sl browned. Orig cloth gilt, sl worn. Author's pres copy.   *(Francis Edwards)* **£30 [≈ $53]**

Haggard, Horward W.
- Devils, Drugs, and Doctors. The Story of the Science of Healing from Medicine-Man to Doctor. New York: 1929. 8vo. 405 pp. Ills. Orig cloth, spine sl faded.
(Hortulus) **$70 [≈ £39]**

Hahnemann, Samuel
- The Chronic Diseases. Their Peculiar Nature and their Homeopathic Cure ... Vol. 1 [only]. Calcutta: [1845-46]. 824 pp. Cold frontis. Name, ink notes. Stamp on title. Bndg worn.
(Whitehart) **£25 [≈ $45]**
- The Chronic Diseases: their Specific Nature and Homoeopathic Treatment ... New York: 1845-46. Vols 1-3 (of 5). 3 vols. 8vo. Orig dec cloth, hd of 1 spine defective.
(Weiner) **£75 [≈ $134]**
- The Lesser Writings of Samuel Hahnemann. New York: 1852. 1184 pp. Ex-lib. Half leather.   *(Fye)* **$300 [≈ £169]**
- Materia Medica Pura. Translated and Edited by Charles Julius Hempel. New York: 1846. 4 vols in one. 8vo. Qtr calf, worn, front inner jnt defective.   *(Weiner)* **£75 [≈ $134]**
- Organon of Homeopathic Medicine. Third American Edition ... New York: 1849. 8vo. 230 pp. Inscrptn on title. Orig cloth, spine torn.   *(Weiner)* **£35 [≈ $62]**

Haig, A.
- Uric Acid as a Factor in the Causation of Disease ... London: 1894. 2nd edn. xi,400 pp. 36 figs. Orig cloth, t.e.g., sl stained.
(Whitehart) **£15 [≈ $27]**
- Uric Acid as a Factor in the Causation of Disease. London: 1908. 7th edn. xii,888,51 pp. 75 text figs. 2 sm lib stamps. Orig cloth.
(Whitehart) **£15 [≈ $27]**

Haigh, James
- The Dyer's Assistant in the Art of Dying Wool and Woollen Goods ... With Additions and Practical Experiments. York: Crask & Lund ..., 1787. 3rd edn. 12mo. xvi,[iv], 17-256 pp. Some soil & use. Contemp calf backed bds, worn but sound.
(Burmester) **£300 [≈ $534]**

Haldane, J.B.S.

- Heredity and Politics. London: Allen & Unwin, 1938. 1st edn. 8vo. 185,advt pp. Orig cloth. *(David White)* £18 [≈ $32]

Hale-White, Sir William

- Great Doctors of the Nineteenth century. London: Edward Arnold, 1935. 1st edn. 8vo. viii, 325 pp. Orig cloth. Dw (sl soiled). *(David White)* £25 [≈ $45]

Half-Hours Underground ...

- Half-Hours Underground. London: James Nisbet, 1905. Cr 8vo. xii,369 pp. Num text figs. Orig dec cloth. *(Gemmary)* $50 [≈ £28]

Hall, A.L.

- The Bushveld Igneous Complex of the Central Transvaal. Pretoris: 1932. 8vo. 560 pp. 40 plates, 65 tables. Lacks map. Buckram. *(Henly)* £36 [≈ $64]

Hall, Marshall

- A Descriptive, Diagnostic, and Practical Essay on Disorders of the Digestive Organs and General Health ... Second Edition. Keene, NH: 1823. 8vo. 142 pp. Some damp stains inner margs of prelims. Orig bds, uncut, spine worn. *(Goodrich)* $110 [≈ £62]

Hall, Mrs Marshall

- Memoirs of Marshall Hall, M.D., F.R.S. ... By his Widow. London: bentley, 1861. 8vo. xiv, 518 pp. Port frontis. Orig cloth, unopened. *(Goodrich)* $295 [≈ £166]

Hall, T.S.

- History of General Physiology. 600 BC to AD 1900. Chicago: (1969) 1975. 2 vols. Orig wraps. *(Whitehart)* £18 [≈ $32]

Hall, T.Y.

- On the Safety Lamp, for the Use of Coal Mines. London: 1853. 8vo. 16 pp. Fldg plate. Orig ptd wraps bound into later plain wraps. *(Weiner)* £65 [≈ $116]

Hallimond, A.F.

- Manual of the Polarizing Microscope. York: Cooke, Troughton & Sims, 1953. 2nd edn. 8vo. 204 pp. 92 figs. Cloth, new endpapers. *(Savona)* £25 [≈ $45]

Halliwell-Phillipps, James Orchard (editor)

- A Collection from the Reign of Queen Elizabeth to that of Charles the Second. London: The Historical Society of Science, 1841. 8vo. xx,124,12 pp. Orig cloth, faded & soiled, rebacked. *(Karmiole)* $100 [≈ £56]

Halsted, William

- The Employment of Fine Silk in preference to Cat-Gut: The Advantages of Transfixing Tissues and Vessels in controlling Hemorrhage ... Boston: 1939. 1st book edn. 34 pp. Vellum. *(Fye)* $100 [≈ £56]
- Surgical Papers by William Stewart Halsted. Baltimore: 1924. 1st edn. 2 vols. 586; 603 pp. Ills. Orig bndg. *(Fye)* $375 [≈ £211]
- Surgical Papers. Baltimore: Hopkins, 1952. 2nd printing. 2 vols. Roy 8vo. Orig bndgs. *(Goodrich)* $175 [≈ £98]

Hamilton, Frank

- A Practical Treatise on Fractures and Dislocations. Phila: 1875. 5th edn. 831 pp. 344 w'cut ills. Leather. *(Fye)* $75 [≈ £42]

Hamilton, M.

- Incubation. The Cure of Disease in Pagan Temples and Christian Churches. London: 1906. vi, 224, index pp. Foxing. Name. Occas marg pencil notes. Orig bndg. *(Whitehart)* £18 [≈ $32]

Hamilton, R.

- Observations on Scrophulous Affections. With Remarks on Schirrus, Cancer and Rachitis. London: 1791. xii,236 pp. Fldg ills (lib stamp). Lib inscrptns on endpapers & title. Old leather, rebacked. *(Whitehart)* £60 [≈ $107]

Hamilton, William

- Observations on Mount Vesuvius, Mount Etna, and Other Volcanos: in a Series of Letters to the Royal Society ... Second Edition. London: 1773. 8vo. iv,179 pp. Fldg map, 5 plates. Sm lib stamp title verso. Half calf. *(Weiner)* £160 [≈ $285]
- Observations on Mount Vesuvius, Mount Etna, and Other Volcanos: in a Series of Letters, addressed to the Royal Society ... Second Edition. London: Cadell, 1773. 8vo. iv, 179, [1 advt] pp. 5 plates inc fldg map. Sm marg water stain. Contemp sheep, mor label. *(Gaskell)* £250 [≈ $445]

Hammer, William J.

- Radium, and other Radio-Active Substances; Polonium, Actinium, and Thorium ... New York: 1903. 8vo. viii,72 pp. Frontis, ills. Orig cloth. *(Weiner)* £100 [≈ $178]

Hammond, William A.

- Spiritualism and Allied Causes and Conditions of Nervous Derangement. London: Lewis, 1876. 8vo. xii,366 pp. 9 text engvs. Orig cloth, some wear. *(Goodrich)* $125 [≈ £70]

Hancock, James & Elliott, Hugh
- The Herons of the World. Paintings by Robert Gillmor and Peter Hayman. L; [ca 1978]. 4to. 304 pp. 61 cold plates, num ills. Dw (hd of spine torn).
(Francis Edwards) £45 [≈ $80]

Hancock, Thomas
- Essay on Instinct, and its Physical and Moral Relations. London: W. Phillips, 1824. xi, [5], 551 pp. Contemp half calf, gilt spine, mor label. *(Caius)* $95 [≈ £53]

Hancocke, John
- Febrifugium Magnum; or, Common Water the Best Cure for Fevers, and probably for the Plague. Third Edition. London: 1723. 8vo. 108 pp. One leaf torn without loss. Disbound, stained. *(Weiner)* £40 [≈ $71]

Hanley, S.
- The Conchologist's Book of Species: containing Descriptions of 600 Species of Univalves. London: 1842. 2nd edn, enlgd. 8vo. xii,154 pp. Cold frontis, 37 figs. Orig cloth, reprd.
(Wheldon & Wesley) £50 [≈ $89]
- Ipsa Linnaei Conchylia. The Shells of Linnaeus, determined from his Manuscripts and Collection ... London: 1855. 8vo. 556 pp. 5 cold plates. Sm stamp on title. Cloth.
(Wheldon & Wesley) £160 [≈ $285]

Hannay, N.B. (editor)
- Semiconductors. New York: Reinhold, 1959. 1st edn. 8vo. 767 pp. Lib pocket. Orig bndg.
(Schoen) $65 [≈ £37]

Hapgood, Richard
- History of the Harvard Dental School. Boston: 1930. One of 1000. 343 pp.
(Goodrich) $75 [≈ £42]

Hardaway, W.A.
- Essentials of Vaccination; a Compilation of Facts relating to Vaccine Inoculation and its Influence in the Prevention of Small-Pox. St. Louis: 1886. 1st edn. 46 pp. Orig bndg.
(Fye) $75 [≈ £42]

Hardie, James
- An Account of the Yellow Fever which occurred in the City of New-York in the Year 1822 ... New York: Samuel Marks, 1822. 1st edn. iv,120 pp. Orig ptd wraps, uncut.
(Hemlock) $300 [≈ £169]

Hardwich, T. Frederick
- A Manual of Photographic Chemistry, Including the Practice of the Collodion Process. Fifth Edition. London: John Churchill, 1859. xvi,516 pp. Half-title. Text ills. Orig brown cloth.
(Jermy & Westerman) £75 [≈ $134]

Hardy, G.H.
- Collected Papers ... Including Joint Papers with J.E. Littlewood and Others. Oxford: 1966-69. Vols 1-4 (of 7). 4 vols. Lge thick 8vo. 4 frontis ports. Unabused ex-lib. Dws.
(Weiner) £100 [≈ $178]

Harker, A.
- The Tertiary Igneous Rocks of Skye. London: 1904. 8vo. xi,481 pp. Fldg cold geological map, 27 plates, 84 text figs. Cloth gilt. *(Henly)* £65 [≈ $116]

Harker, Janet E.
- The Physiology of Diurnal Rhythms. Cambridge: 1964. 8vo. 114 pp. Diags. Orig cloth. Dw. *(Weiner)* £20 [≈ $36]

Harkins, Henry
- The Treatment of Burns. London: 1942. 1st edn. 457 pp. 120 ills. Orig bndg.
(Fye) $150 [≈ £84]

Harlan, R.
- Fauna Americana: being a Description of the Mammiferous Animals inhabiting North America. Phila: 1825. 8vo. 318,[2] pp. Ptd slip pasted to title. Lib stamp on title. New half calf. *(Wheldon & Wesley)* £120 [≈ $214]

Harmsworth, Alfred C. (editor)
- Motors and Motor-Driving. London: Longmans, Green, Badminton Library, 1902. 1st edn. Post 8vo. xx,456,[iv] pp. Plates, ills. Mod half mor, a.e.g. *(Ash)* £200 [≈ $356]

Harris, J.R.
- An Angler's Entomology. London: New Naturalist, 1952. 1st edn. 8vo. Ills. Orig cloth, trifle marked & dull.
(Bow Windows) £30 [≈ $53]

Harris, James E. & Weeks, Kent R.
- X-Raying the Pharaohs. London: Macdonald, 1973. 8vo. 11 cold & num other ills. Dw.
(Georges) £35 [≈ $62]

Harris, John
- Lexicon Technicum: or an Universal English Dictionary of Arts and Sciences ... London: 1704-10. 1st edn. 2 vols. folio. [xx,906; xxiv, 758] pp. Port, 7 + 7 plates. Occas sl browning. Contemp panelled calf, sl worn.

(Gaskell) **£6,000 [≃ $10,680]**
- Lexicon Technicum: or, an Universal English Dictionary of Arts and Sciences [Volume I] ... London: 1704. 1st edn. Folio. [xii], [vi],[894] pp. Port frontis, 7 plates (2 in facs). 1 sm repr, sm marg water stain at front. Contemp leather, rebacked & recrnrd.
(Whitehart) **£350 [≃ $623]**

Harris, Joseph
- The Description and Use of the Globes and the Orrery. To which is prefixed by way of Introduction a brief Account of the Solar System. London: 1745. 6th edn. viii,190 pp. 6 plates (1 v sl cropped). Few sl stains. Contemp leather, rebacked.
(Whitehart) **£60 [≃ $107]**

Harris, M.
- An Exposition of English Insects, including the several Classes of Neuroptera, Hymenoptera and Diptera, or Bees, Flies and Libellulae. London: 1786. 2nd edn, 2nd issue. 4to. viii,9-166,[4] pp. Engvd title, cold chart, plain plate, 50 hand cold plates. Minor browning. Contemp calf, rebacked.
(Wheldon & Wesley) **£600 [≃ $1,068]**

Harris, Wilfred
- The Morphology of the Brachial Plexus ... London: OUP, 1939. 1st edn. xviii,117 pp. Num ills. Orig cloth.   *(Caius)* **£75 [≃ £42]**

Harrison, Charles
- A Treatise on the Culture and Management of Fruit Trees. London: 1852. 2nd edn. 8vo. xii, 365 pp. Text ills. Endpapers marked. Orig bds, some bubbling & tear hd of spine.
(Hortulus) **£85 [≃ £48]**

Harrison, D.L.
- The Mammals of Arabia. Vols 1 and 2 [of 3]. London: 1964-68. 2 vols. 4to. 2 frontis, fldg map, 128 plates, 169 figs, 174 tables. Good ex-lib. Buckram.
(Wheldon & Wesley) **£120 [≃ $214]**

Harrison, James M.
- The Birds of Kent. London: Witherby, (1953). 1st edn. 2 vols. Lge imperial 8vo. Cold plates, photo ills. Orig bndgs.
(Ash) **£100 [≃ $178]**

Harrison, R.
- Lectures on the Surgical Disorders of the Urinary Organs. London: 1887. 3rd edn. xi,583 pp. 117 ills. Name on title. Orig cloth, sl water stained.   *(Whitehart)* **£25 [≃ $45]**

Harrison, Robert
- The Dublin Dissector. Washington: Duff Green, 1835. 1st Amer edn. 8vo. [vi],314 pp. Minor water staining, browning & foxing. Contemp calf. Anon.
(Bookpress) **$150 [≃ £84]**

Harrison, Sarah
- The House-Keeper's Pocket-Book, and Compleat Family Cook ... Seventh Edition, Revised and Corrected ... by Mary Morris. London: for C. & R. Ware, 1760. [iv], 216, [xxiv], 36,[viii] pp. 20 w'engvd plates. Later half calf.   *(Gough)* **£295 [≃ $525]**

Hart, Bernard
- The Psychology of Insanity. Cambridge: UP, 1912. 1st edn. ix,[1],176,[4 advt] pp. Orig cloth, faded.   *(Caius)* **£65 [≃ £37]**

Hart, I.B.
- The Mechanical Investigations of Leonardo da Vinci. London: 1925. vi,240 pp. 7 plates, 136 text figs. Occas sl foxing. Cloth, sl dusty.
(Whitehart) **£38 [≃ $68]**

Harte, Walter
- Essays on Husbandry ... London: for W. Frederick in Bath, & sold by J. Hinton ..., 1764. 1st edn. 8vo. 5 plates, w'cuts in text. Contemp calf, gilt spine. Anon.
(Georges) **£200 [≃ $356]**
- Essays on Husbandry. Essay I. A General Introduction ... London: for W. Frederick in Bath ..., 1764. 1st edn. 8vo. xviii,[i errata], 232 pp. 5 plates (numbered 2,4,5, 4,5), num text diags. Sone ink notes. 1 plate reprd. Speckled calf, sl rubbed, lacks label. Anon.
(Francis Edwards) **£250 [≃ $445]**

Harting, James Edmund
- The Birds of Cornwall ... see Rodd, Edward Hearle
- Rambles in Search of Shells, Land and Fresh-Water. London: 1875. 8vo. viii,110,2 pp. 10 hand cold plates. Orig cloth gilt.
(Henly) **£32 [≃ $57]**

Hartland, Edwin Sidney
- Primitive Paternity: The Myth of Supernatural Birth in relation to the History of the Family. London: David Nutt for the Folk-Lore Society, 1909-10. 1st edn. 2 vols. 8vo. Orig cloth.   *(Gach)* **$100 [≃ £56]**

Hartley, H.
- Studies in the History of Chemistry. Oxford: 1971. xii,243 pp. 15 plates. Lib label. Orig bndg.   *(Whitehart)* **£15 [≃ $27]**

Hartlib, Samuel
- Samuel Hartlib; His Legacy of Husbandry ... London: J.M. for Richard Wodnothe, 1655. 3rd edn. 8vo. 303 pp. Some old MS notes. Mod calf, mor label.
(Chapel Hill) **$450** [≈ £253]

Hartmann, Franz
- Diseases of Children and their Homoeopathic Treatment. Translated, with Notes ... by C.J. Hempel. New York: 1853. 8vo. xii,516 pp. Qtr cloth, soiled.   *(Weiner)* **£30** [≈ $53]
- The Life of Philippus Theophrastus Bombast of Hohenheim known by the name of Paracelsus ... London: 1896. 2nd edn. 311 pp. Orig bndg.   *(Fye)* **$100** [≈ £56]

Hartmann, Karl Robert Eduard von
- Philosophy of the Unconscious ... Authorized Translation ... by William Chatterton Coupland. London: Kegan Paul ..., 1884. 1st edn in English. 3 vols. 8vo. Tips sl chipped, spines & edges somewhat darkened.
(Gach) **$200** [≈ £112]

Hartree, Douglas R.
- Calculating Instruments and Machines. Urbana: Univ of Illinois Press, 1949. 1st edn. 4to. 138 pp. Lib pocket. Orig bndg.
(Schoen) **$135** [≈ £76]

Hartridge, G.
- The Ophthalmoscope. A Manual for Students. London: 1897. 3rd edn. xiii,154,28 pp. 68 figs. Spine sl stained & chipped.
(Whitehart) **£40** [≈ $71]

Harvey, Gideon
- The Family Physician, and the House Apothecary ... London: for T.R[ooks]., 1676. 1st edn. 12mo. [24],165,[1] pp, errata leaf. 18th c half calf, 19th c endpapers, jnts & crnrs reprd, new label. Wing H.1064.
(Spelman) **£680** [≈ $1,210]

Harvey, James
- Praesagium Medicum, or, the Prognostick Sings of Acute Diseases; Established by Ancient Observations, and Explain'd by the Best Modern Discoveries. London: Strahan, 1706. 1st edn. 8vo. xxix,216 pp. Panelled calf.   *(Goodrich)* **$395** [≈ £222]

Harvey, W.H.
- A Manual of the British Marine Algae ... London: 1841. 1st edn. 8vo. lvii,229 pp. Some pencil notes. Orig cloth, trifle used.
(Wheldon & Wesley) **£25** [≈ $45]
- A Manual of the British Marine Algae.

London: 1849. 2nd edn. 8vo. lii,252 pp. Port (foxed), 27 plates. Num ink notes. New cloth.
(Wheldon & Wesley) **£80** [≈ $142]
- Phycologia Britannica: or a History of British Sea-Weeds ... London: Reeve & Benham, 1846-51. 1st edn. 4 vols. Roy 8vo. 360 cold plates. Contemp green half calf, gilt spines, red labels.   *(Egglishaw)* **£700** [≈ $1,246]
- Phycologia Britannica; or, a History of British Sea-Weeds. London: 1846-51. 4 vols. Roy 8vo. 360 cold plates. Cloth, refixed, new endpapers, sm defect 1 jnt.
(Wheldon & Wesley) **£450** [≈ $801]

Harvey, William
- The Anatomical Exercises ... De Motu Cordis 1628: De Circulatione Sanguinis 1649 ... Edited by Geoffrey Keynes. London: Nonesuch Press, (1928). 8vo. Browning on some prelims. Niger mor, t.e.g.
(Appelfeld) **$225** [≈ £126]
- Prelectiones Anatomiae Universalis. Edited ... by a Committee of the Royal College of Physicians of London. London: 1886. 1st edn. 4to. 98 pp. Facss. Orig bndg.
(Fye) **$350** [≈ £197]
- The Works ... Translated from the Latin with a Life of the Author by Robert Willis. London: 1847. 1st edn. 624 pp. Orig bndg.
(Fye) **$300** [≈ £169]
- The Works ... Translated from the Latin with a Life of the Author by Robert Willis (London 1847). New York: 1965. 624 pp. Orig bndg.   *(Fye)* **$50** [≈ £28]

Harvie-Brown, J.A. & Buckley, T.E.
- A Fauna of the Moray Basin. Edinburgh: Douglas, 1895. 2 vols. 8vo. Linen backed map, 23 plates. Orig cloth.
(Egglishaw) **£70** [≈ $125]
- A Vertebrate Fauna of Argyll and the Inner Hebrides. London: 1892. 1st edn. Sq 8vo. lxxxiv, 262,[xx] pp. Addtnl illust title, 7 maps, 8 plates. Orig cloth, sl worn.
(Francis Edwards) **£40** [≈ $71]
- A Vertebrate Fauna of Sutherland, Caithness and West Cromarty. Edinburgh: Douglas, 1887. 8vo. xi,344 pp. Map, plates, ills. Orig cloth, spine faded & sl worn at hd.
(Egglishaw) **£55** [≈ $98]

Harvie-Brown, J.A. & Macpherson, H.A.
- A Fauna of the North-West Highlands and Skye. Edinburgh: David Douglas, 1904. 1st edn. civ,378,[15 advt] pp. 3 maps (1 fldg), 19 plates, num text ills. Orig green cloth, spine trifle faded.   *(Gough)* **£90** [≈ $160]

Haselden, R.B.
- Scientific Aids for the Study of Manuscripts. Oxford: 1935. xiv,108 pp. 16 plates. Orig wraps, edges sl worn.
(Whitehart) **£25 [≈ $45]**

Hasluck, Paul N.
- Cyclopaedia of Mechanics ... see under Cassell (publisher)

Hassall, A.H.
- A History of the British Freshwater Algae, including Descriptions of the Desmideae and Diatomaceae. London: Longman, (1845) 1857. 2 vols. 8vo. viii,462; 24 pp. 103 cold plates (some foxed). Orig cloth.
(Egglishaw) **£90 [≈ $160]**

Hassall, Arthur Hill
- Food and its Adulterations: Comprising the Reports of the Analytical Sanitary Commission of "The Lancet" for the Years 1851 to 1854 ... London: Longman ..., 1855. xlviii,659,60 advt pp. 159 ills. Orig cloth, sl rubbed.   *(Jermy & Westerman)* **£50 [≈ $89]**
- The Microscopic Anatomy of the Human Body, in Health and Disease. London: 1849. 1st edn. 2 vols in one. Thick 8vo. xxiv,570 pp. 69 plates (some tinted or partly cold). Occas minor marg soil. Half mor, gilt spine, some wear to extrs.
(Francis Edwards) **£280 [≈ $498]**

Hasse, C.E.
- An Anatomical Description of the Diseases of the Organs of Circulation and Respiration. Translated by W.E. Swaine. London: Sydenham Society, 1846. xiv,400 pp. Orig cloth, sl worn & dust stained.
(Whitehart) **£40 [≈ $71]**

Hastings, Cecil, Jr.
- Approximations for Digital Computers. Princeton: UP, 1955. 1st edn. 8vo. 204 pp. Lib pocket. Orig bndg. *(Schoen)* **$65 [≈ £37]**

Hastings, Frank H.
- A Treatise of Military Surgery and Hygiene. New York: Bailliere, 1865. 2nd edn, enlgd. 648 pp. 127 text engvs. Lib stamp on title. Lib buckram.   *(Goodrich)* **$595 [≈ £334]**

Hatch, F.H. & Corstorphine, G.S.
- The Geology of South Africa. London: 1905. 8vo. xiv,348 pp. Fldg cold map, plates, ills. Orig cloth, front jnt shaken.
(Weiner) **£40 [≈ $71]**

Hatton, Edward
- Comes Commercii, or, the Trader's-Companion. The Ninth Edition, with large Additions. Accurately revised ... by W. Hume. [With] A Supplement to Comes Commercii ... London: Innys, Richardson, 1754. Tall narrow 8vo. [8],318,[2], 90,[2] pp. Contemp calf, spine ends reprd.
(Spelman) **£85 [≈ $151]**
- A Mathematical Manual: or, Delightful Associate ... The whole very useful and pleasant ... London: for S. Illidge, 1728. 1st edn. 8vo. viii,246,[10 advt] pp. Contemp calf, jnts trifle cracked but firm.
(Burmester) **£150 [≈ $267]**

Haughton, S.
- Manual of Geology. London: 1876. 4th edn. Cr 8vo. xvi,415 pp. Plates, tables, diags, text figs. Cloth, hd of spine chipped.
(Henly) **£22 [≈ $39]**

Haven, Joseph
- Mental Philosophy: Including the Intellect, Sensibilities, and Will. Boston: Gould & Lincoln, 1872. 590,[10 advt] pp. Orig cloth, somewhat worn.   *(Caius)* **$75 [≈ £42]**

Hawkins, G.
- On the Oak. An Inquiry into the Origin and Constitution of Dry Rot, and its Increase of Late Years ... London: 1826. 8vo. 27 pp. Text fig. Disbound. *(Francis Edwards)* **£55 [≈ $98]**

Hawkins, N.
- New Catechism of the Steam Engine. With Chapters on Gas, Oil and Hot Air Engines ... New York: Theo. Andel & Co., 1902. 8vo. 438, [14 advt] pp. Num ills. Orig cloth gilt.
(Karmiole) **$40 [≈ £22]**

Hayek, Friedrich A.
- Individualism and Economic Order. London: Routledge & Kegan Paul, (1949). 1st British edn. Demy 8vo. Sl dusty. Orig bndg. Dw.
(Ash) **£50 [≈ $89]**

Hayes, Richard
- Interest at One View, calculated to a Farthing ... The Eighteenth Edition, corrected. London: for Johnson & Robinson, 1789. 12mo. 384 pp. Orig sheep, jnts broken but cords holding.   *(Claude Cox)* **£25 [≈ $45]**
- The Negociator's Magazine: or the most Authentic Account of the Monies, Weights, and Measures, of the Principal Places of Trade in the Known World ... Eleventh Edition, revised ... by Benjamin Webb ... London: 1777. [xvi], 466 pp. Tables (2 fldg).

Contemp roan, rebacked.
                    (C.R. Johnson) **£250 [≈ $445]**

Haynes, Thomas
- A Treatise on the Improved Culture of the
Strawberry, Raspberry, and Gooseberry.
London: for B. & R. Crosby, (1812). 2nd edn.
3 advt pp. Date cropped from ft of title.
Disbound.   *(Jarndyce)* **£85 [≈ $151]**

Hayward, George
- Surgical reports, and Miscellaneous Papers
on Medical Subjects. Boston: 1855. 1st edn.
452 pp. Orig bndg.   *(Fye)* **$225 [≈ £126]**

Haywood, Mrs.
- A New Present for a Servant-Maid:
Containing Rules for the Moral Conduct ...
The Whole Art of Cookery ... London: for G.
Pearch, 1771. 1st edn. Lge 12mo. xiv,272 pp.
Frontis. Few marks. Contemp mottled sheep,
rebacked, crnrs reprd. *(Gough)* **£395 [≈ $703]**

Head, Sir Francis Bond
- Stokers and Pokers; or, The London and
North-Western Railway, the Electric
Telegraph and Railway Clearing-House ...
London: Murray, Hone & Colonial Library,
1850. 2nd edn. Orig ptd wraps, dusty, rear
wrappers sl creased. Anon.
                         (Jarndyce) **£45 [≈ $80]**

Headley, F.W.
- Life and Evolution. London: 1906. 1st edn.
xvi,272 pp. Frontis, 98 ills. Some browning.
Endpapers sl marked. Orig cloth, sl marked &
faded.   *(Francis Edwards)* **£28 [≈ $50]**

Heagerty, J.J.
- Four Centuries of Medical History in
Canada. And a Sketch of the Medical History
of Newfoundland. Volume II. Bristol: 1928.
vii, 374 pp. 20 plates. Cloth dull.
                       (Whitehart) **£25 [≈ $45]**

Healde, Thomas
- The New Pharmacopoeia of the Royal
College of Physicians of London. Translated
into English. With Notes ... Third Edition,
Corrected. London: Galabin for Longman,
1788. 8vo. xvi,368 pp. Intl approbation leaf.
Contemp calf, green edges.
                          (Finch) **£120 [≈ $214]**
- The Pharmacopoeia of the Royal College of
Physicians of London. Translated into
English with Notes ... Translated by Thomas
Healde. London: 1801. 8th edn. xx,390 pp.
Page edges discold. Contemp bds, crnrs worn,
cloth spine, paper label, front hinge sl loose.
                     (Whitehart) **£120 [≈ $214]**

The Healing Art ...
- The Healing Art; or, Chapters upon
Medicine, Diseases, Remedies, and
Physicians, Historical, Biographical, and
Descriptive. London: 1887. 1st edn. 2 vols.
316; 377 pp. Orig bndg. *(Fye)* **$175 [≈ £98]**

Heathcote, E.D.
- Flowers of the Engadine, Drawn from
Nature. Winchester: 1891. 32 pp. 224 uncold
plates.   *(Wheldon & Wesley)* **£55 [≈ $98]**

Heaton, J.M.
- The Eye, Phenomenology and Psychology of
Function and Disorder. London: 1968.
xii,336 pp. 10 plates, text figs. Orig bndg.
                        (Whitehart) **£15 [≈ $27]**

Heberden, William
- Commentaries on the History and Cure of
Diseases. London: T. Payne, 1803. 3rd edn.
8vo. xii,516 pp. Lib stamp on title. Qtr calf,
later reback.   *(Goodrich)* **$195 [≈ £110]**
- Commentaries on the History and Cure of
Diseases. London: 1816. 4th edn. xii,432 pp.
Occas sl foxing & dusting. Old leather,
rebacked.   *(Whitehart)* **£220 [≈ $392]**

Hecker, J.F.C.
- The Black Death, and the Dancing Mania of
the Middle Ages. New York: 1883. 1st Amer
edn. 109 pp. Orig bndg.   *(Fye)* **$65 [≈ £37]**
- The Epidemics of the Middle Ages. London:
Sydenham Society, 1844. 8vo. xx,418 pp. Lib
stamps on endpapers. Orig cloth, minor nicks
spine ends.   *(Frew Mackenzie)* **£48 [≈ $85]**

Hehn, V.
- The Wanderings of Plants and Animals from
their First Home. Edited by J.S. Stallybrass.
London: 1888. 8vo. 523 pp. Orig cloth, trifle
used, spine stained.
                   (Wheldon & Wesley) **£35 [≈ $62]**

Heisler, J.C.
- A Text-Book of Embryology. Phila:
Saunders, 1899. 1st edn. 8vo. 405,[30 ctlg]
pp. 7 cold plates, 170 text figs. Cloth, lib label
on front cvr.   *(Savona)* **£25 [≈ $45]**

Helferich, H.
- Fractures and Dislocations. Translated by J.
Hutchinson. London: Sydenham Society,
1899. 162 pp. 68 plates, 126 text figs. Orig
cloth, spine sl faded. *(Whitehart)* **£40 [≈ $71]**

Helmuth, William Tod
- "Scratches" of a Surgeon. Chicago: 1879.
12mo. 120 pp. Orig cloth, extrs rubbed. Pres

copy. *(Hemlock)* **$75 [≈ £42]**

Helsham, Richard
- A Course of Lectures in Natural Philosophy ... Published by Bryan Robinson, M.D. London: 1739. 1st edn. 8vo. viii,404,[3] pp. 11 fldg plates. Title sl soiled, name cut from blank crnr. New qtr calf.
(Weiner) **£150 [≈ $267]**
- A Course of Lectures in Natural Philosophy. Published by Bryan Robinson, M.D. The Second Edition. London: J. Nourse, 1743. 404 pp. Advt leaf. Fldg plates. Contemp calf, rebacked. *(C.R. Johnson)* **£95 [≈ $169]**
- A Course of Lectures in Natural Philosophy. London: 1743. 2nd edn. 8vo. x, 402, 2 advt pp. 11 fldg plates. Contemp calf, worn, lacks label. *(Henly)* **£78 [≈ $139]**
- A Course of Lectures in Natural Philosophy. London: 1855. 3rd edn. x,404 pp. 11 fldg plates. Contemp calf, rebacked.
(Whitehart) **£80 [≈ $142]**

Henderson, Robert
- A Treatise on the Breeding of Swine, and Curing of Bacon; with Hints on Agricultural Subjects. Leith: Archibald Allardyce ..., 1811. 1st edn. 8vo. viii,118 pp. Frontis (sl offset onto title), engvd plan. Orig bds, jnts cracked, spine sl worn.
(Burmester) **£350 [≈ $623]**

Henderson, William Augustus
- The Housekeeper's Instructor; or, Universal Family Cook ... Seventh Edition. London: W. & J. Stratford ..., [ca 1798]. 8vo. 440, [xvi index], [4 subscribers] pp. Frontis, 11 plates (2 fldg). Contemp sheep, sl worn.
(Gough) **£500 [≈ $890]**

Henisch, H.K. (editor)
- Semi-Conducting Materials. London: Butterworth, 1951. 1st edn. 8vo. xv,281 pp. Ills. Lib pocket. Orig cloth.
(Schoen) **$100 [≈ £56]**

Hennen, John
- Principles of Military Surgery ... London: 1829. 3rd edn. 583 pp. Rec rebound, new endpapers. *(Fye)* **$250 [≈ £140]**

Henrey, Blanche
- British Botanical and Horticultural Literature before 1800. London: 1975. 3 vols. Roy 8vo. 1128 pp. 32 cold & num other ills. Cloth. *(Wheldon & Wesley)* **£180 [≈ $320]**

Henry, C.R.
- Classification and Use of Fingerprints.

London: 1900. 1st edn. lv,112 pp. 3 fldg & 6 other plates. Lib stamp on title. Rebound in cloth. *(Whitehart)* **£45 [≈ $80]**

Henry, David
- The Complete English Farmer. London: for F. Newbery, 1771. 1st edn. Demy 8vo. [xxviii], 432, 2 pp. 2 plates. Occas sl foxing. Mod half calf gilt. Anon. *(Ash)* **£200 [≈ $356]**

Henry, E.R.
- Classification and Uses of Finger Prints. London: 1900. 8vo. iv,112 pp. 11 plates, ills, tables. 1 sheet loose. Orig cloth.
(Weiner) **£75 [≈ $134]**
- Classification and Uses of Fingerprints. London: Routledge, 1900. 1st edn. 8vo. iv,112 pp. 5 plates, 164 ills. Orig cloth, rubbed. *(Spelman)* **£50 [≈ $89]**
- Classification and Uses of Finger prints. London: 1900. 1st edn. 112 pp. 11 plates (3 fldg), 42 figs. Lib stamp on title. Lib bndg.
(Whitehart) **£40 [≈ $71]**

Henry, J.D.
- Oil Fields of the Empire. A Survey of British Imperial Petroleum Questions ... London: 1910. 1st edn. 4to. xxix,278,[28 advt] pp. Num maps, ills, diags. Orig cloth, t.e.g., lib marks, sl worn.
(Francis Edwards) **£85 [≈ $151]**

Henwood, G.
- Four Lectures on Geology and Mining ... London: 1855. 1st edn. 8vo. viii,23, [i],27, [i],23, [i],21 pp. Fldg frontis (torn). Some dust marks. Orig cloth, sl marked.
(Bow Windows) **£85 [≈ $151]**

Herman, R.A.
- A Treatise on Geometrical Optics. Cambridge: UP, 1900. 1st edn. 8vo. vi,344 pp. Orig cloth. *(Gaskell)* **£15 [≈ $27]**

Hermippus Redivivus ...
- See Cohausen, Johann Heinrich

Hero, of Alexandria
- The Pneumatics of Hero of Alexandria from the Original Greek. London: Walton & Maberly, 1851. 8vo. xix,117 pp. Ills. Some cvr wear. *(McBlain)* **$150 [≈ £84]**

Herrlinger, Robert
- History of Medical Illustration from Antiquity to 1600. New York: 1970. 4to. 178 pp. Ills. Orig bndg. Slipcase.
(Fye) **$150 [≈ £84]**
- History of Medical Illustration from

Antiquity to 1600. Translated by Graham
Fulton-Smith. Medicina Rara: 1970. 4to. Ills,
inc cold. Boxed.   *(Goodrich)* **$95 [≈ £53]**
- History of Medical Illustration from
Antiquity to 1600. New York: Editions
Medicina Rara, (1970). 1st edn in English.
Sm 4to. [iv],178 pp. Num ills. Orig cloth.
Slipcase.   *(Oak Knoll)* **$85 [≈ £48]**

Herschel, Sir John F.W.
- An Essay, entitled the Yard, the Pendulum, &
the Metre, considered in reference to the
Choice of a Standard of Length. London:
1863. 8vo. 24 pp. Half calf.
        (Weiner) **£40 [≈ $71]**
- Essays from the Edinburgh and Quarterly
Reviews, with Addresses and Other Pieces.
London: Longman, Brown ..., 1857. 8vo.
iv,750 pp. Contemp half calf, elab gilt spine,
green label.   *(Rankin)* **£45 [≈ $80]**
- Essays from the Edinburgh and Quarterly
Reviews, with Addresses and Other Pieces.
London: Longman, 1857. 1st edn. 8vo. iv,750
pp. Title spotted. Contemp mor, gilt spine,
a.e.g., jnts sl rubbed.
        (Burmester) **£110 [≈ $196]**
- Essays from the Edinburgh and Quarterly
Reviews, with Addresses and Other Pieces.
London: 1857. 1st edn. 8vo. iv,750 pp. Occas
spots & marks. Orig cloth, faded & dull.
        (Bow Windows) **£75 [≈ $134]**
- Familiar Lectures on Scientific Subjects.
London: 1867. 1st edn. 8vo. xii,507 pp. Orig
cloth, inner hinges strained.
        (Bow Windows) **£50 [≈ $89]**
- A Manual of Scientific Enquiry; Prepared for
the Use of Officers in Her Majesty's Navy;
and Travellers in general ... London: 1851.
2nd edn. Sm thick 8vo. xi,503,[32 advt] pp. 2
charts. Mod cloth.
        (Francis Edwards) **£35 [≈ $62]**
- Outlines of Astronomy. Ninth Edition.
London: 1867. 8vo. xxiv,741,[1,2 advt] pp. 9
plates. Occas spotting. Orig cloth, sl fingered
at hd, extreme crnr tips trifle rubbed, spine
faded.   *(Bow Windows)* **£55 [≈ $98]**

Hertzler, A.E.
- Clinical Surgery by Case Histories. London:
1921. 2 vols. xvi,546; xii,547-1106 pp. 284 +
199 ills. Orig cloth, sl worn & dusty, hd vol
2 spine reprd.   *(Whitehart)* **£40 [≈ $71]**

Hervey, A.B.
- Sea Mosses. A Collector's Guide and an
Introduction to the Study of Marine Algae.
Boston: 1881. 8vo. xv,281 pp. 20 cold plates.
Inscrptn on title. Cloth.
        (Wheldon & Wesley) **£40 [≈ $71]**

Hervey, Christopher
- Letters from Portugal, Spain, Italy and
Germany, in the Years 1759, 1760 and 1761.
London: J. Davis ... for R. Faulder, 1785. 1st
edn. 3 vols. 8vo. Contemp tree calf, gilt spines
(worn, new labels).
        (Frew Mackenzie) **£250 [≈ $445]**

Hervieux de Chanteloup, J.C.
- A New Treatise of Canary-Birds. Containing
the Manner of Breeding and Coupling Them
... Translated into English. London: for
Bernard Lintot ..., 1718. 1st edn in English.
12mo. [viii], 163,[5 blank & advt] pp. 2 w'cut
plates. Lacks half-title. Contemp sheep, worn.
        (Burmester) **£350 [≈ $623]**

Hess, Alfred Fabian
- Rickets, including Osteomalacia and Tetany.
Phila: Lea & Febiger, 1929. 485 pp. 52 engvs.
Orig cloth.   *(Goodrich)* **$95 [≈ £53]**

Hetley, Mrs C.
- The Native Flowers of New Zealand
illustrated in Colours ... from Drawings
Coloured to Nature. London: [1887-] 1888.
Imperial 4to. 36 chromolithos & 3 plain
plates. Orig cloth.
        (Wheldon & Wesley) **£375 [≈ $668]**

Heton, Thomas
- Some Account of Mines, and the Advantages
of them to this Kingdom. With an Appendix
relating to the Mine-Adventures in Wales.
London: W.B. for John Wyat, 1707. 1st edn.
Sl marg worming at end. Contemp calf,
sometime rebacked, split in front jnt. Anon.
        (P and P Books) **£650 [≈ $1,157]**

Heurch, H. Van
- A Treatise on the Diatomaceae. London:
Wesley, 1962. 8vo. xx,558 pp. 35 plates.
Name. Cloth.   *(Savona)* **£40 [≈ $71]**

Hevesy, George
- Radioactive Indicators. Their Application in
Biochemistry, Animal Physiology, and
Pathology. New York: Interscience
Publishers, 1948. 1st edn. Table in rear
pocket, ills. Orig bndg.
        (Key Books) **$45 [≈ £25]**

Hewsholme, H.P.
- Health, Disease & Integration ... London:
1929. 328 pp. Lib stamp on endpaper. Orig
bndg, lib mark on spine.
        (Whitehart) **£15 [≈ $27]**

Hewson, J.B.
- A History of the Practice of Navigation. Glasgow: (1951) 1963. viii,270 pp. Figs. Orig bndg. *(Whitehart)* £30 [≈ $53]

Hewson, William
- The Works ... Edited with an Introduction and Notes by George Gulliver ... London: Sydenham Society, 1846. 1st edn. 8vo. lvi,360 pp. Orig cloth, t.e.g., sl worn. *(Hemlock)* $375 [≈ £211]
- The Works of William Hewson, F.R.S., edited with an Introduction and Notes by George Gulliver. London: 1846. 1st edn. 360 pp. Orig bndg. *(Fye)* $250 [≈ £140]

Hey, M.H.
- Catalogue of Meteorites. London: BM, 1966. 3rd edn. 8vo. lxviii,637 pp. Orig cloth. Dw. *(Gemmary)* $50 [≈ £28]

Hibbard, David R.
- A Treatise on Cow-Pox. In which the Existence of Small-Pox, or Varioloid in any Form, subsequent to Vaccination, is show to arise from some Imperfection in its Performance ... New York: Harper, 1835. 1st edn. 12mo. 70,[28 advt] pp. Orig cloth gilt, soiled, sl frayed. *(Karmiole)* $100 [≈ £56]

Hibberd, Shirley
- The Amateur's Flower Garden ... London: Groombridge, 1871. 1st edn. iv,284,[14 advt] pp. 6 chromolitho plates. Orig cloth, backstrip relaid. *(Gough)* £48 [≈ $85]
- The Amateur's Greenhouse and Conservatory ... London: Groombridge, 1873. 1st edn. 272 pp. 4 fldg cold plates, num ills. Orig pict green cloth gilt. *(Gough)* £50 [≈ $89]
- The Amateur's Rose Book ... New Edition, Revised and Enlarged. London: Groombridge, 1874. viii,258,[6 advt] pp. 6 fldg cold plates. Orig dec green cloth gilt. *(Gough)* £75 [≈ $134]
- The Fern Garden. London: Groombridge, 1877. 7th edn. 8vo. 148,advt pp. 8 cold plates, 40 w'engvs. Occas sl foxing. Orig green cloth gilt, a.e.g. *(Carol Howard)* £20 [≈ $36]
- Greenhouse Favourites; A Description of Choice Greenhouse Plants ... London: Groombridge, [ca 1870]. 1st edn. 4to. viii, 310 pp. 35 chromolitho plates. Contemp green half calf, gilt spine, fine. Anon. *(Gough)* £265 [≈ $472]
- The Ivy; A Monograph. Its History, Uses and Characteristics ... London: Groombridge, 1862. 1st edn. Sm 4to. xii,115 pp. 4 cold plates. Orig elab pict green cloth gilt, a.e.g.,

fine. *(Gough)* £135 [≈ $240]
- New and Rare Beautiful-Leaved Plants ... London: Bell & Daldy, 1870. 1st edn. Lge 8vo. viii, 144 pp. 54 cold plates. Sl used, plates unfoxed. Orig green cloth, soiled & cockled, sm split upper jnt.
(Claude Cox) £65 [≈ $116]
- The Sea-Weed Collector ... London: Groombridge, [1872]. 8vo. vii,152 pp. 8 cold plates by Lydon, num w'engvs. Orig dec cloth gilt, a.e.g. *(Egglishaw)* £18 [≈ $32]
- Wild Flowers. A Handy-Book for the Rambling Botanist ... London: 1878. 2nd edn. Cr 8vo. iv,156 pp. 8 cold plates, text ills. Ends browned. Orig cloth gilt, rebacked.
(Henly) £28 [≈ $50]

Higgins, Bryan
- Experiments and Observations made with a View of improving the Art of composing and applying Calcareous Cements and of preparing Quick-lime ... London: Cadell, 1780. Sm 8vo. xi, 233 pp. Half-title. Rec half calf. *(Blackwell's)* £550 [≈ $979]

Higgins, William
- Experiments and Observations on the Atomic Theory, and Electrical Phenomena. London: 1814. 8vo. 180 pp. Diags. Few crnrs creased. Old cloth, crnr of lower bd cracked.
(Weiner) £300 [≈ $534]

Highley, S.
- Reade's Prism for Microscope Illumination, by which the true Form of Diatom Markings is made clear. London: 1867. 8vo. 4,24 pp. 19 ills. Wraps (sl foxed). *(Henly)* £18 [≈ $32]

Hill, A.V.
- First and Last Experiments in Muscle Mechanics. Cambridge: 1970. xv,141 pp. Diags. Orig bndg. *(Whitehart)* £18 [≈ $32]

Hill, Claude W.
- Electric Crane Construction. London: 1911. xx, 313 pp. Num fldg diags. Sl dusty & foxed. Orig bndg. *(Whitehart)* £25 [≈ $45]

Hill, J.
- The Exact Dealer Refined: Being a Useful Companion for all Traders. In Three Parts ... Fourth Edition, enlarged. London: 1698. 12mo. 164, index, advt pp. Lacks F12. Contemp calf, some wear. Wing H.1991A. Anon. *(Robertshaw)* £40 [≈ $71]

Hill, J.B. & MacAlister, D.A.
- The Geology of Falmouth and of the Mining District of Cambrone and Redruth. London:

1906. 8vo. x,335 pp. 24 plates, 65 text figs. Some foxing. Cloth gilt, rebacked.
(Henly) **£75 [≈ $134]**

Hill, "Sir" John
- The British Herbal ... London: Osborne, Shipton ..., 1756. 1st edn. Lge folio. [iii], 533, [3] pp. Frontis, title vignette, 75 plates. Sm marg repr. Contemp calf, rebacked.
(Vanbrugh) **£475 [≈ $846]**
- The Construction of Timber, from its Early Growth; explained by the Microscope ... London: for the author ..., 1770. 1st edn. 8vo. 170,[8],[2] pp. 43 plates (inc plate 14 in 2 states, plain & cold). Contemp calf, sm reprs.
(Gaskell) **£550 [≈ $979]**
- Essays in Natural History and Philosophy containing a Series of Discoveries by the Assistance of Microscopes. London: 1752. 8vo. [viii], 415 pp. Title foxed. Mod bds.
(Wheldon & Wesley) **£125 [≈ $223]**
- The Family Herbal, or An Account of all those English Plants which are remarkable for their Virtues and of the Drugs which are produced by Vegetables of Other Countries. London: [ca 1835]. 8vo. xi,376 pp. 54 hand cold plates. Contemp calf, backstrip relaid.
(Henly) **£175 [≈ $312]**
- A General Natural History or New and Accurate Descriptions of the Animals, Vegetables, and Minerals of the Different Parts of the World ... Vol. 1 The History of Fossils. London: for Thomas Osborne, 1748. 1st edn. Folio. 12 plates, fldg table. Some foxing. Cloth   *(Key Books)* **$325 [≈ £183]**
- A History of Fossils. London: for Thomas Osborne, 1748. Folio. [2],vi,654,vi pp. Fldg table, 12 plates. Leather, rebacked. Vol 1 of "A General Natural History".
(Gemmary) **$1,000 [≈ £562]**
- Theophrastus's History of Stones. London: for C. Davis, 1746. 1st edn. 8vo. xxiii, 211, [1], 21 pp. Subscribers. Calf, rebacked.
(Gemmary) **$1,350 [≈ £758]**
- [Greek title, then] Theophrastus's History of Stones, with an English Version, and Critical and Philosophical Notes ... London: for C. Davis, 1746. 1st edn. 8vo. xxiii,[i], 211, [1] pp. Subscribers. Contemp speckled calf, jnts sl cracked.   *(Burmester)* **£500 [≈ $890]**

Hillary, William
- Observations on the Changes of the Air, and Concomitant Epidemical Diseases in the Island of Barbadoes ... Yellow Fever ... With Notes by Benjamin Rush, M.D. Phila: Kite, 1811. xii,260,[4] pp. Foxing. Sheep, rebacked.   *(Goodrich)* **$175 [≈ £98]**

Hiller, L.
- Surgery through the Ages: A Pictorial Chronicle. New York: 1944. 1st edn. 177 pp. Ills. Orig bndg.   *(Fye)* **$75 [≈ £42]**

Hilton, John
- On Rest and Pain. New York: 1879. 2nd Amer edn. 299 pp. Orig bndg.
(Fye) **$50 [≈ £28]**
- On Rest and Pain: A Course of Lectures on the Influence of Mechanical and Physiological Rest in the Treatment of Accidents and Surgical Disease ... New York: W. Wood, 1879. 2nd edn. xii,299 pp. Text ills. Orig cloth, somewhat worn.
(Caius) **$150 [≈ £84]**

Hinshelwood, C.N.
- The Structure of Physical Chemistry. Oxford: 1951. 1st edn. viii,476 pp. Figs. Orig bndg.   *(Whitehart)* **£20 [≈ $36]**

Hipkins, W.E.
- The Wire Rope and its Applications. Birmingham: 1896. Lge 8vo. 92,[12] pp. 86 cold & b/w ills. Orig cloth.
(Spelman) **£180 [≈ $320]**

Hippocrates
- The Genuine Works. Translated by F. Adams. London: Sydenham Society, 1849. 2 vols. 8 plates. Sm piece cut from titles. Mod cloth, orig labels. *(David White)* **£55 [≈ $98]**
- The Genuine Works of Hippocrates. Translated from the Greek with a Preliminary Discourse and Annotations by Francis Adams. New York: Wood Library, 1886. 2 vols. 8vo. 8 plates. Orig cloth, worn.
(Goodrich) **$125 [≈ £70]**
- The Genuine Works. Translated from the Greek by Francis Adams. With an Introduction by E.C. Kelly. Baltimore: Williams & Wilkins, 1939. 8vo. viii,[ii],384 pp. 8 plates. Orig cloth.   *(David White)* **£33 [≈ $59]**
- The Genuine Works of Hippocrates. Translated by F. Adams. London: 1849. 2 vols. x, 872 pp. 51 figs. Some foxing. Endpaper creased. Orig cloth gilt.
(Whitehart) **£130 [≈ $231]**

Hirsch, August
- Handbook of Geographical and Historical Pathology. London: 1883-86. 3 vols. Orig bndg.   *(Fye)* **$300 [≈ £169]**

Historical ...
- An Historical Account of the Origin, Progress and Present State of Bethlem Hospital ... see Bowen, Thomas

Hitt, Thomas
- The Modern Gardener. London: for Hawes, Clarke & Collins ..., 1771. 1st edn. Post 12mo. 8, "530" [i.e. 532] pp. Plates. Sl discolouration. 1 leaf torn with sl loss. Contemp sheep, rebacked.
(Ash) **£200 [≈ $356]**

Hobson, Ernest William
- The Theory of Functions of a Real Variable and the Theory of Fourier's Series. Cambridge: UP, 1907. 1st edn. Roy 8vo. xvi, 772 pp. Orig cloth. *(Gaskell)* **£60 [≈ $107]**

Hochberg, Lew
- Thoracic Surgery before the 20th Century. New York: 1960. 1st edn. 858 pp. Orig bndg.
(Fye) **£175 [≈ £98]**

Hochstetter, Ferdinand von & Petermann, A.
- The Geology of New Zealand: in Explanation of the Geographical and Topographical Atlas of New Zealand ... Auckland: 1864. 8vo. 113 pp. Ex-lib. Orig limp cloth, worn, sl soiled.
(Weiner) **£40 [≈ $71]**

Hodder, James
- Hodder's Arithmetick. Or that necessary Art made easie ... The Twelfth Edition, revised ... by Henry Mose ... London: T.H. for Ric. Chiswell, 1678. [10], 216 pp. Frontis port. Contemp sheep, crnrs sl worn. Wing H.2286A. *(C.R. Johnson)* **£225 [≈ $401]**

Hodges, Nathaniel
- Loimologia: or, An Historical Account of the Plague in London in 1665 ... added, An Essay ... by John Quincy. London: 1720. vi, 288 pp. Fldg table. Contemp calf, fine.
(Hemlock) **$600 [≈ £337]**

Hoe, Robert
- A Short History of the Printing Press ... New York: Robert Hoe, 1902. 1st edn. 4to. Num ills. Orig stiff paper wraps, worn.
(Oak Knoll) **$85 [≈ £48]**

Hoff, E.C. & Fulton, J.F.
- A Bibliography of Aviation Medicine. Springfield: 1942. xv, 237 pp. Orig cloth, sl marked. *(Whitehart)* **£35 [≈ $62]**

Hoffman, F. & Ramazzini, B.
- A Dissertation on Endemial Diseases ... with a Treatise on the Diseases of Tradesmen ... Translated by Dr. James. London: 1746. xv, 432,4 advt pp. Sl foxing & discoloration of page edges. Leather, sl worn, rebacked.
(Whitehart) **£180 [≈ $320]**

Hogan, John Vincent Lawless
- The Outline of Radio. Boston: Brown, 1923. 1st edn. 12mo. xviii, 256 pp. Frontis, plates, ills. Orig bndg. Inscrbd by the author.
(Schoen) **$85 [≈ £48]**

Hogg, Jabez
- The Microscope ... London: 1854. 1st edn. 8vo. xvi, 440 pp. Engvd title, 15 plates, 169 text figs. Sl foxing. Orig cloth, trifle used.
(Wheldon & Wesley) **£50 [≈ $89]**
- The Microscope ... London: The Illustrated London Library, 1854. 1st edn. 8vo. xvi, 440, [8 advt] pp. Addtnl vignette title, 16 plates, 169 text figs. Orig gilt illust cloth.
(Bow Windows) **£110 [≈ $196]**
- The Microscope ... London: 1858. 3rd edn. 8vo. xiv, 607 pp. Frontis, text figs. Signs of use. Cloth, rebacked.
(Wheldon & Wesley) **£30 [≈ $53]**
- The Microscope ... London: 1861. 5th edn. Post 8vo. xiv, 621 pp. Frontis, num text figs. Orig cloth, recased.
(Wheldon & Wesley) **£30 [≈ $53]**
- The Microscope: its History, Construction and Application. London: 1867. 6th edn. Cr 8vo. xx, 752 pp. 8 cold plates, 355 text figs. Cloth gilt, sm repr hd of spine.
(Henly) **£42 [≈ $75]**
- The Microscope ... London: 1883. 10th edn. Cr 8vo. xx, 764 pp. 9 plates (8 cold), 354 text figs. Orig cloth, used.
(Wheldon & Wesley) **£30 [≈ $53]**
- The Microscope: its History, Construction, and Application ... London: Routledge, 1886. 11th edn. 8vo. xx, 764 pp. 8 cold plates, 500 engvs. Prize calf gilt. *(Egglishaw)* **£45 [≈ $80]**
- The Microscope ... London: 1887. 12th edn. 8vo. 764 pp. 8 cold plates, over 500 engvs. Orig cloth, trifle used.
(Wheldon & Wesley) **£25 [≈ $45]**

Hogg, Robert
- The Apple and its Varieties: being a History and Description of the Varieties of Apples cultivated in the Gardens and Orchards of Great Britain. London: Groombridge, 1859. Cheap edn. Ills. Orig cloth, sm mark front bd.
(Jarndyce) **£40 [≈ $71]**
- The Dahlia: its History and Cultivation, with Descriptions of all the best Show Flowers. London: 1853. Roy 8vo. viii, 40 pp. 9 hand cold plates by James Andrews. Cloth, orig wraps bound in.
(Wheldon & Wesley) **£200 [≈ $356]**

Hoke, C.M.
- Refining Precious Metal Wastes. New York: Metallurgical Publishing Co., 1940. 8vo.

362 pp. Num text figs. Orig cloth.
(Gemmary) **$75 [≈ £42]**

Holdsworth, W.G.
- Cleft Lip and Palate. London: 1951. 1st edn, 2nd printing. 126 pp. Orig bndg.
(Fye) **$100 [≈ £56]**
- Cleft Lip and Palate. New York: 1957. 2nd edn. 187 pp. Orig bndg.   *(Fye)* **$50 [≈ £28]**

Holland, G. Calvert
- The Philosophy of Animated Nature; or the Laws and Action of the Nervous System. London: Churchill, 1848. 512 pp. Spotted. Cloth, worn.   *(Goodrich)* **$125 [≈ £70]**

Holland, Henry
- Essays on Scientific and Other Subjects. London: 1862. 1st edn. 499 pp. Orig bndg.
(Fye) **$60 [≈ £34]**
- Essays on Scientific and other Subjects contributed to the Edinburgh and Quarterly Reviews. London: 1862. v,499 pp. Orig cloth.
(Whitehart) **£25 [≈ $45]**
- General View of the Agriculture of Cheshire; with Observations drawn up for the consideration of the Board of Agriculture. London: Richard Phillips, 1808. 8vo. viii, 375, [5 advt] pp. 2 fldg maps (1 hand cold), fldg plate, 5 plates (3 hand cold). Orig bds, paper label.   *(Spelman)* **£180 [≈ $320]**
- Medical Notes and Reflections. Phila: 1839. 1st Amer edn. 383 pp. Half leather.
(Fye) **$100 [≈ £56]**

Hollander, Bernard
- The First Signs of Insanity: Their Prevention and Treatment. London: S. Paul, [1912]. 1st edn. 347,[1],[48 advt] pp. Orig cloth, some wear, spine ends fraying. *(Caius)* **$85 [≈ £48]**
- The Mental Functions of the Brain. An Investigation into their Localisation and their Manifestation in Health and Disease. London: 1901. xviii,512 pp. Frontis, 37 ills. Edges foxed. Cloth sl worn.
(Whitehart) **£25 [≈ $45]**

Hollom, P.A.D.
- The Popular Handbook of British Birds. London: 1952. 8vo. xxiii,424 pp. 132 cold & 22 plain plates. Orig cloth. Dw.
(Henly) **£22 [≈ $39]**

Holmboe, J.
- Studies on the Vegetation of Cyprus, based upon Researches during the Spring and Summer of 1905. Bergen: 1914. 4to. 344 pp. 144 ills. Half mor.
(Wheldon & Wesley) **£50 [≈ $89]**

Holmes, E.M.
- Catalogue of the Hanbury Herbarium in the Museum of the Pharmaceutical Society of Great Britain ... London: 1892. 1st edn. 4to. [viii], 136, xiv pp. Endpapers browned. Orig cloth, t.e.g.   *(Bow Windows)* **£484 [≈ $85]**

Holmes, J.H.H.
- A Treatise on the Coal Mines of Durham and Northumberland ... containing Accounts of the Explosions from Fire-Damp ... London: Baldwin, Cradock, & Joy, 1816. 1st edn. 8vo. xxii, [ii], 259, [5] pp. 5 advt pp at end. 7 plates (sl spotting). Orig bds, worn.
(Clark) **£110 [≈ $196]**

Holmes, Oliver Wendell
- Border Lines of Knowledge in Some Provinces of Medical Science. Boston: 1862. 1st edn. 80 pp. Ex-lib. Orig bndg.
(Fye) **$150 [≈ £84]**
- Currents and Counter-Currents in Medical Science with Other Addresses and Essays. Boston: 1861. 1st edn. 406 pp. Orig bndg, hd of backstrip chipped.   *(Fye)* **$125 [≈ £70]**
- A Dissertation on Acute Pericarditis. Boston: 1937. 1st edn. 12mo. 39 pp. Vellum.
(Fye) **$60 [≈ £34]**
- Mechanism in Thought and Morals ... Boston: Osgood, 1871. 1st edn. 12mo. [iv], 101, [5] pp. Orig cloth. *(Gach)* **$125 [≈ £70]**
- Mechanism in Thought and Morals. Boston: 1882. 6th edn. 101 pp. Orig bndg.
(Fye) **$75 [≈ £42]**
- Puerperal Fever, as a Private Pestilence. Boston: Ticknor & Fields, 1855. 1st edn. 60 pp. Orig ptd wraps, faint crease, v sl chips crnrs.   *(Hemlock)* **$2,500 [≈ £1,404]**

Holmes, T.V. & Sherborn, C.D. (editors)
- A Record of Excursions made between 1860 and 1890. London: 1891. vii,571 pp. 2 fldg plates, 213 text figs. Orig bndg, spine dull, jnts sl weak.   *(Whitehart)* **£25 [≈ $45]**

Holmes, Timothy (editor)
- A System of Surgery, Theoretical and Practical, in Treatises by Various Authors. Phila: 1882. 1st Amer edn. 3 vols. 1007; 1063; 1059 pp. Ills. Leather.
(Fye) **$300 [≈ £169]**

Holt, E. Emmett
- The Diseases of Infancy and Childhood. New York: Appleton, 1897. 1st edn. 8vo. 1117 pp. Ills. Orig green cloth.
(Goodrich) **$250 [≈ £140]**

Holt, Richard
- A Short Treatise of Artificial Stone, as 'tis now made, and converted into all manner of Curious Embellishments, and Proper Ornaments ... London: for Stephen Austin, & John Brindley, 1730. 1st edn. 8vo. viii,55 pp. Sl soiled. Qtr mor, sl marked.
(Burmester) **£450 [≈ $801]**

Holzer, Wolfgang & Weisenberg, Eugen
- Foundations of Short-Wave Therapy ... London: 1935. 8vo. 228 pp. Ills. Orig cloth, sl worn.
(Weiner) **£25 [≈ $45]**

Home, Francis
- Clinical Experiments, Histories, and Dissections. Edinburgh: 1780. 1st edn. 8vo. xvi,458 pp, errata leaf. Lib stamp on dedic leaf. Contemp calf, rebacked, orig label, crnrs reprd.
(Spelman) **£180 [≈ $320]**
- Principia Medicinae. Third Edition. Edinburgh: 1770. 8vo. xii,340,16 advt pp. Contemp calf, jnts & spine ends reprd.
(Spelman) **£85 [≈ $151]**

Hood, P.
- The Successful Treatment of Scarlet Fever: also Observations on the Pathology and Treatment of Crowing Inspiration. London: 1857. iv,200 pp. Orig cloth.
(Whitehart) **£40 [≈ $71]**

Hooke, Robert
- An Attempt to Prove the Motion of the Earth from Observations ... London: for John Martyn, 1674. 1st edn. 4to. [viii],28 pp. Fldg plate. 1st word of title & sev headlines shaved, title sl dusty, fold marks at ft. Contemp style mor. Wing H.2613.
(Gaskell) **£2,250 [≈ $4,005]**
- A Description of Helioscopes, and some other Instruments made by Robert Hooke. London: for John Martyn, 1676. 1st edn. 4to. [ii], 32 pp. 3 fldg plates on 2 ff. Rec mor. Wing H.2614.
(Gaskell) **£1,250 [≈ $2,225]**

Hooker, Joseph D.
- Flora of British India. London: 1875-97. 1st edn. 7 vols. 8vo. Some titlepages sl foxed. Half mor. *(Wheldon & Wesley)* **£300 [≈ $534]**
- Handbook of the New Zealand Flora: a Systematic Description of the Native Plants of New Zealand. London: 1864-67. 1st edn. 8vo. 15, lxviii, 798 pp. Orig cloth.
(Wheldon & Wesley) **£100 [≈ $178]**

Hooker, Joseph D. & Thomson, T.
- Flora Indica, being a Systematic Account of the Plants of British India. Vol. 1 [all

published]. London: 1855. 8vo. xvi,280,285 pp. 2 maps. Sm tears in map, leaf of text reprd. Half mor.
(Wheldon & Wesley) **£75 [≈ $134]**

Hooker, W.J.
- Companion to the Botanical Magazine ... London: 1835-36. 2 vols (all published). Roy 8vo. 2 (of 3) ports, 27 hand cold & 5 plain plates. Some browning & offsetting. Calf gilt, trifle rubbed.
(Wheldon & Wesley) **£400 [≈ $712]**
- The Journal of Botany, being a Second Series of the Botanical Miscellany. London: 1834-42. 4 vols (all published). 8vo. 71 (on 65) plates, 5 ports. Orig cloth.
(Wheldon & Wesley) **£250 [≈ $445]**

Hooker, W.J. & Baker, J.G.
- Synopsis Filicum: or a Synopsis of all Known Ferns. London: 1883. 2nd edn. 8vo. xiv, 9-559 pp. 9 hand cold plates. Cloth.
(Wheldon & Wesley) **£75 [≈ $134]**

Hooker, W.J. & Taylor, T.
- Muscologia Britannica: containing the Mosses of Great Britain and Ireland. London: 1818. 1st edn. 8vo. xxxvi,152 pp. 31 plain plates. Sound ex-lib. Half mor.
(Wheldon & Wesley) **£70 [≈ $125]**

Hooker, William & Salisbury, R.A.
- The Paradisus Londinensis: containing Plants cultivated in the Vicinity of the Metropolis. London: 1805-08. 2 vols in one. 4to. 119 hand cold plates (inc 14 & 67 bis). Contemp calf, rebacked.
(Wheldon & Wesley) **£2,000 [≈ $3,560]**

Hooson, William
- The Miners Dictionary ... Wrexham: the author & T. Payne, 1747. 8vo. [vi,224] pp. Subscribers. Browned. Marg worm in 1st 10 gatherings. Rec calf gilt. The Kenny copy.
(Blackwell's) **£500 [≈ $890]**

Hope, Mrs James
- Memoir of the late James Hope, M.D. London: 1848. 4th edn. 367 pp. Orig bndg.
(Fye) **$100 [≈ £56]**

Hopewell-Smith, A.
- An Introduction to Dental Anatomy and Physiology. Descriptive and Applied. Philadelphia & New York: 1913. 372 pp. Frontis, 5 plates, 334 diags. Spine sl worn. Author's pres copy. *(Whitehart)* **£35 [≈ $62]**

Hopkins, Evan
- On the Connexion of Geology with Terrestrial Magnetism ... London: 1844. 1st edn. 8vo. viii,129 pp. 24 plates. Some marks & stains. Name. Orig cloth, sl dull & marked, spine ends worn. *(Bow Windows)* **£55 [≈ $98]**

Hoppus, Edward
- Practical Measuring made easy to the meanest Capacity, by a New Set of Tables ... A New Edition, greatly improved ... York: Wilson & Spence, 1800. Narrow 8vo. [v], xiv-lxxvi, 207 pp. Half-title. Fldg frontis. Contemp sheep, sl worn.   *(Burmester)* **£60 [≈ $107]**

Horblit, Harrison
- One Hundred Books Famous in Science, based on an Exhibition held at the Grolier Club. New York: 1964. 1st edn. 4to. 464 pp. 220 ills. Orig bndg.   *(Fye)* **$450 [≈ £253]**

Horine, Emmet
- Daniel Drake (1785-1852), Pioneer Physician of the Midwest. Phila: 1961. 1st edn. 425 pp. Orig bndg.   *(Fye)* **$45 [≈ £25]**

Horne, Henry
- Essays concerning Iron and Steel. London: T. Cadell, 1773. 1st edn. 12mo. iii,223 pp. Later polished calf, backstrip relaid.
          (Bookpress) **$2,500 [≈ £1,404]**

Horne, T.H.
- The Complete Grazier; Or Farmer's and Cattle-Breeder and Dealer's Assistant ... By a Lincolnshire Grazier. London: for Baldwin, Cradock & Joy ..., 1816. 4th edn, rvsd & enlgd. Lge 8vo. [xvi],592 pp. Frontis (stained), 4 plates, text ills. Orig bds, sl worn. Anon.   *(Francis Edwards)* **£150 [≈ $267]**

Horney, Karen
- Self-Analysis. London: Kegan Paul, [1942]. 1st English edn. 309 pp. Pencil underlining. Orig cloth.   *(Caius)* **$65 [≈ £37]**

Hornor, S.S.
- The Medical Student's Guide in Extracting Teeth: with Numerous Cases in the Surgical Branch of Dentistry. Phila: 1851. 76 pp. 1 plate (only, of 2). Lib marks. Orig bndg.
          (Whitehart) **£30 [≈ $53]**

Horrax, Gilbert
- Neurosurgery. An Historical Sketch. Springfield: 1952. 135 pp. Dw.
          (Goodrich) **$95 [≈ £53]**

Horsley, John
- A Short and General Account of the most necessary and fundamental Principles of Natural Philosophy ... Revised, corrected and adapted ... by John Booth. Glasgow: Andrew Stanton, 1743. Sm 8vo. iv,100 pp. 4 fldg plates. Sl affected by damp. Contemp calf, sl worn.   *(Burmester)* **£120 [≈ $214]**

Horsley, Samuel
- Elementary Treatises on the Fundamental Principles of Practical Mathematics for the use of Students, by Samuel Lord Bishop of Rochester. Oxford: Clarendon Press, 1801. 8vo. 11 fldg plates. Contemp qtr vellum. John Cator's b'plate.   *(Waterfield's)* **£75 [≈ $134]**

Horwood, A.R.
- A New British Flora. British Wild Flowers in their Natural Haunts. London: 1919. 6 vols. 4to. 3 maps, 64 cold plates, num photo ills. A few lib stamps. Cloth.
          (Wheldon & Wesley) **£35 [≈ $62]**

Hosack, Alexander
- A Memoir upon Staphyloraphy ... New York: 1833. 1st edn. 21 pp. Fldg plate. Orig wraps, soiled. Inscrbd by the author.
          (Fye) **$325 [≈ £183]**

Hoskins, George Gordon
- An Hour with a Sewer Rat; or A Few Plain Hints on House Drainage and Sewer Gas. London: Simpkin Marshall, 1879. Half-title. Frontis, ills. Orig cloth, rear foredge sl damp stained.   *(Jarndyce)* **£42 [≈ $75]**

Houghton, John
- Husbandry and Trade Improv'd ... Revised, Corrected, and Published ... by Richard Bradley ... London: Woodman & Lyon, 1727. 1st edn in book form. 3 vols. 8vo. Contemp mottled calf gilt, spine ends sl chipped, crnrs bumped. A 4th vol was published in 1728.
          (Frew Mackenzie) **£150 [≈ $267]**

Houghton, W.
- British Fresh-Water Fishes. London: [1879]. 2 vols. Folio. xxvi,204 pp. 41 cold plates of 64 figs by A.F. Lydon, num text figs. Sl marg stain 1 plate. Orig dec cloth gilt, recased, new endpapers.
          (Wheldon & Wesley) **£750 [≈ $1,335]**
- British Fresh-Water Fishes. London: William Mackenzie, [1879]. 2 vols in one. Folio. xxvi,204 pp. 41 chromolitho plates. Occas sl spotting. Contemp qtr russia, spine worn.
          (Frew Mackenzie) **£780 [≈ $1,388]**
- Country Walks of a Naturalist with his

Children. London: Groombridge, 1869. 1st edn. Sm 8vo. 6 cold plates, num w'engvs. Orig pict gilt cloth (hd of spine frayed).
(Egglishaw) **£25 [≈ $45]**

House, H.D.
- Wild Flowers of New York. Albany: New York State Museum Memoir 15, (1918) 1923. 2 vols. 4to. 264 cold plates. Orig cloth, vol 1 back cvr sl loose.
(Wheldon & Wesley) **£60 [≈ $107]**

Howard, H.E.
- Territory in Bird Life. London: Murray, 1920. 1st edn. 8vo. xiii,308 pp. 11 plates. Orig cloth. *(Egglishaw)* **£26 [≈ $46]**

Howard, Thomas
- On the Loss of Teeth; and on the Best Means of Restoring Them ... London: Simpkin & Marshall, 1856. 26th edn. 60 pp. Final advt leaf. Frontis with flap. Orig brown cloth, a.e.g. *(Jarndyce)* **£65 [≈ $116]**

Howell, A.H.
- Florida Bird Life. New York: 1932. 4to. xxiv, 579 pp. 58 cold plates, 72 maps in text. Endpapers & half-title sl stained. Orig rexine.
(Wheldon & Wesley) **£40 [≈ $71]**

Howland, Arthur (editor)
- Materials towards a History of Witchcraft collected by Henry Charles Lea. Phila: 1939. 1st edn. 3 vols. 1548 pp. Orig bndg.
(Fye) **$200 [≈ £112]**

Huber, P.
- The Natural History of Ants. Translated from the French, with Additional Notes, by J.R. Johnson. London: 1820. Post 8vo. xiv,398 pp. 2 plates (1 cold). Sl foxing. Half calf, trifle worn. Translator's pres copy.
(Wheldon & Wesley) **£60 [≈ $107]**

Hudson, C.T.
- The Rotifera: or Wheel-Animalcules ... assisted by P.H. Gosse. London: 1868. 2 vols. Roy 8vo. vii,128; 144 pp. 34 plates (most cold fldg). Lib stamps on text & plate margs. Half mor, v rubbed. *(Weiner)* **£75 [≈ $134]**

Hudson, G.V.
- New Zealand Moths and Butterflies (Macrolepidoptera). London: 1898. 4to. xix, 144 pp. 11 cold & 2 plain plates. New cloth.
(Wheldon & Wesley) **£125 [≈ $223]**

Hudson, J.
- The Florist's Companion, containing the

Culture and Properties of the Auricula, Polyanthus, Hyacinth, etc. Newcastle upon Tyne, [1794]. 12mo. xii,84 pp. Tailpieces by T. Bewick. Contemp calf, rebacked.
(Wheldon & Wesley) **£75 [≈ $134]**

Hudson, N. (editor)
- An Early English Version of Hortus Sanitatis. A Recent Bibliographical Discovery ... London: 1954. One of 550. xvi,164, xvii-xxxi pp. Num ills. Orig cloth, sl marked.
(Whitehart) **£25 [≈ $45]**

Hudson, W.H.
- Birds of La Plata. London: Dent, 1920. One of 1500. 2 vols. Sm 4to. xvii,244; ix,240 pp. 22 cold plates. Outer margs sl browned. Orig qtr linen & green cloth gilt.
(Carol Howard) **£80 [≈ $142]**

Huggins, Sir William
- The Royal Society or, Science in the State and in the Schools. New York: 1906. 4to. 131 pp. 25 ills. Orig bndg, uncut & unopened.
(Goodrich) **$65 [≈ £37]**

Hughes, A.
- A History of Cytology. London: Abelard-Schumann, 1959. 1st edn. 8vo. x,158 pp. 12 plates. Orig cloth. Dw. *(Savona)* **£30 [≈ $53]**

Hughes, Samuel
- A Treatise on Gas-Works and the Practice of Manufacturing and Distributing Coal-Gas ... London: John Weale, 1853. 1st edn. 6 advt pp dated 1857. Orig green cloth, ptd label, spine faded. *(Jarndyce)* **£20 [≈ $36]**

Hughes, Wendell
- Reconstructive Surgery of the Eyelids. St. Louis: 1943. 1st edn. 160 pp. Ills. Orig bndg.
(Fye) **$125 [≈ £70]**

Huish, R.
- A Treatise on the Nature, Economy, and Practical Management of Bees ... London: 1815. 1st edn. 8vo. xxiii,414 pp. 6 plates (trifle foxed). Mod half calf.
(Wheldon & Wesley) **£100 [≈ $178]**

Hull, E.
- Monograph of the Sub-Oceanic Physiography of the North Atlantic Ocean. London: 1912. Folio. viii,40 pp. 11 maps. Cloth.
(Wheldon & Wesley) **£40 [≈ $71]**

Hulme, F.E.
- Familiar Wild Flowers. London: (1877-85). 1st edn. 4 vols. 160 cold plates on thick paper,

tissue guards. Half calf, red labels, crnrs sl rubbed.   *(Egglishaw)* **£64 [≈ $114]**
- Familiar Wild Flowers. London: Cassell, 1902. 7 vols. Cold plates. Orig dec cloth, fine.
                          (Egglishaw) **£60 [≈ $107]**
- Familiar Wild Flowers. Series 1-7. London: Cassell, 1902. 3 vols. 8vo. 120; 160; 160; 160; 160; 160; 160, index, advt pp. Num cold plates. Orig green cloth, sl rubbed.
                      (Carol Howard) **£55 [≈ $98]**

Humboldt, Alexander von
- A Geognostical Essay on the Superposition of Rocks in both Hemispheres, translated from the Original French ... London: 1823. 8vo. viii, 482 pp. Later bds, uncut.
                        (Weiner) **£125 [≈ $223]**
- Letters of Alexander von Humboldt, written between the years 1827 and 1858 to Varnhagen von Ense ... London: 1860. xxvi,334 pp. Orig cloth, sm tear side of spine.
                       (Whitehart) **£25 [≈ $45]**

Hume, A.O. & Marshall, C.H.T.
- The Game Birds of India, Burmah and Ceylon. Calcutta: 1879-81. 3 vols. Roy 8vo. 144 cold plates. Sl foxing. Stamps on title versos. Orig green cloth gilt, vol 1 recased.
              (Wheldon & Wesley) **£275 [≈ $490]**

Hume, Edgar E.
- Medical Work of the Knights Hospitallers of Saint John of Jerusalem ... Baltimore: 1940. 371 pp. Frontis. Orig bndg.
                        (Goodrich) **$65 [≈ £37]**

Humphreys, Henry Noel
- The Genera of British Moths. London: [1858]. Imperial 8vo. 206 pp. 62 hand cold plates. Name on title. V sl foxing. Half calf, t.e.g.   *(Wheldon & Wesley)* **£300 [≈ $534]**
- The Genera of British Moths ... London: Allmann, (1860). Roy 8vo. 206 pp. 62 hand cold plates. Later cloth.
                       (Egglishaw) **£210 [≈ $374]**
- Ocean and River Gardens: a History of the Marine and Freshwater Aquaria. London: Sampson Low, 1857. 8vo. viii,117, vii,108 pp. 20 hand cold plates. Some ff frayed. Orig cloth gilt, a.e.g., rubbed.
                        (Egglishaw) **£75 [≈ $134]**

Humphreys, Henry Noel & Westwood, J.O.
- British Butterflies and their Transformations. New Edition, revised and Corrected by the Author. London: 1857. 4to. xii, 140 pp. Illuminated title, 42 hand cold plates. Sgntr on title. Contemp half mor, worn.
              (Wheldon & Wesley) **£350 [≈ $623]**

Humphreys, W.J.
- Physics of the Air. Phila: Lippincott, 1920. 1st edn. 8vo. 665 pp. Ills. Lib stamps on endpapers. Orig bndg.   *(Schoen)* **$95 [≈ £53]**

Hun, Henry
- An Atlas of the Differential Diagnosis of the Diseases of the Nervous System ... Troy: Southworth, 1922. 3rd edn, rvsd. Fldg charts & plates. Orig cloth.   *(Caius)* **$95 [≈ £53]**

Hunt, H. Ernest
- A Manual of Hypnotism. London: Wm. Rider, 1915. Cr 8vo. Orig dec cloth.
                        (Georges) **£25 [≈ $45]**

Hunt, H. Lyons
- Plastic Surgery of the Head, Face and Neck. Phila: 1926. 1st edn. 404 pp. Extensive ink underlining. Orig bndg.   *(Fye)* **$150 [≈ £84]**

Hunt, Thomas
- A Defence of the Charter, and Municipal Rights of the City of London. And the Rights of other Municipal Cities and Towns of England. Directed to the Citizens of London. London: Baldwin, [1682]. 1st edn. Sm 4to. [ii], 46 pp. Cloth backed bds. Wing H.3750.
                (Frew Mackenzie) **£60 [≈ $107]**

Hunter, Alexander
- Culina Famulatrix Medicinae; or, Receipts in Modern Cookery; with a Medical Commentary. New Edition. York: Wilson & Son ..., 1810. 310, 22 pp. Frontis. Contemp polished calf gilt, elab gilt spine, fine.
                        (Gough) **£250 [≈ $445]**

Hunter, Charles
- Mechanical Dentistry, a Practical Treatment on the Construction of the Various Kinds of Artificial Dentures ... Fourth Edition. London: 1895. 8vo. xv,268 pp. 101 ills. Occas soiling. Orig cloth, soiled.
                        (Weiner) **£18 [≈ $32]**

Hunter, John
- A Treatise on the Blood, Inflammation, and Gun-Shot Wounds. To which is prefixed a Short Account of the Author's Life ... London: Nicol, 1794. 1st edn. 4to. lxvii,575 pp. Port, 9 plates. Orig bds, uncut, sm tear in headband.   *(Gaskell)* **£1,850 [≈ $3,293]**
- A Treatise on the Blood, Inflammation, and Gun-Shot Wounds. Phila: 1817. 2nd Amer edn. 514 pp. 8 plates. Name marked through on title. Leather, lacks label.
                        (Fye) **$50 [≈ £28]**
- A Treatise on the Blood, Inflammation and

Gun-Shot Wounds ... prefixed a Short Account of the Author's Life by Everard Home (1794). Classics of Medicine Library: 1982. 4to. lxviii, 565 pp. Frontis port, 8 plates. Leather gilt, a.e.g.
(Whitehart) £80 [≈ $142]

- A Treatise on the Venereal Disease. London: 1788. 2nd edn. 4to. [xii],398,index pp. 7 plates. Lib stamps on pastedowns & title. Lacks free endpapers. Some spotting. Bds, rebacked, crnrs sl worn, hinges reprd.
(Francis Edwards) £300 [≈ $534]

- A Treatise on the Venereal Disease. With an Introduction and Commentary, by Joseph Adams. The Second Edition with Additions ... London: Sherwood ..., 1818. 8vo. Half-title, xx, 568 pp. 6 plates. Orig bds, partly unopened, rebacked.
(Goodrich) $350 [≈ £197]

- Works of John Hunter. Four Volumes. Phila: 1839. 1st Amer edn. 4 vols. Foxed. Half leather, rubbed, bds detached.
(Fye) $250 [≈ £140]

Hunter, R. & MacAlpine, I.
- Three Hundred Years of Psychiatry, 1535-1850. London: OUP, 1963. 1st edn. Orig bndg. Dw. *(Goodrich)* $125 [≈ £70]

Hurst, A.F. & Stewart, M.J.
- Gastric and Duodenal Ulcer. Oxford: 1929. 4to. xvii,544 pp. 159 text ills. Orig bndg, hd of spine v sl worn. *(Whitehart)* £25 [≈ $45]

Hurst, C.C.
- Experiments in Genetics. Cambridge: 1925. xxiv, 578 pp. Fldg maps, 2 fldg plates, 174 ills. Cloth, rubbed, spine faded & worn.
(Whitehart) £35 [≈ $62]

Hussey, E.L.
- Miscellanea Medico-Chirurgica. Cases in Practice, Reports, Letters, and Occasional Papers. Oxford: 1882. vii,418 pp. Lib stamp on title. Few page edges sl torn. Orig cloth, spine sl worn. *(Whitehart)* £25 [≈ $45]

Hutchinson's Animals of all Countries ...
- Hutchinson's Animals of all Countries. The Living Animals of the World in Picture and Story. London: [1923-25]. 4 vols. 4to. 50 cold plates, ca 2000 ills. Orig half mor.
(Wheldon & Wesley) £25 [≈ $45]

Hutchinson, H.N.
- Marriage Customs in Many Lands. London: Seeley, 1897. 1st edn. 8vo. xii,348 pp. 24 plates. Orig pict cloth. *(Gach)* $75 [≈ £42]

Hutchinson, Herbert
- Jonathan Hutchinson: Life and Letters. London: 1946. 1st edn. 257 pp. Orig bndg.
(Fye) $40 [≈ £22]

Hutchinson, J.
- The Families of Flowering Plants. London: 1959. 2nd edn. 2 vols. Roy 8vo. Cloth. Dws. *(Wheldon & Wesley)* £38 [≈ $68]

Hutchinson, R.W.
- Television Up-to-Date. London: 1935. xii, 184 pp. Frontis, 125 text figs. Dw.
(Whitehart) £25 [≈ $45]

Hutchison, C.S.
- Laboratory Handbook of Petrographic Techniques. New York: John Wiley & Sons, 1974. Roy 8vo. xxvii,527 pp. Text figs. Few lib marks. Orig cloth.
(Gemmary) $50 [≈ £28]

Hutton, J.
- Theory of the Earth, with Proofs and Illustrations (Edinburgh 1795). London: 1972. 2 vols. 8vo. Cloth..
(Wheldon & Wesley) £60 [≈ $107]

Huxham, John
- An Essay on Fevers. To which is now added, a Dissertation on the Malignant, Ulcerous Sore-Throat. Third Edition. London: 1757. 8vo. 356 pp. Contemp calf, sl worn.
(Robertshaw) £90 [≈ $160]

- Medical and Chemical Observations upon Antimony. London: 1756. 1st edn. 78 pp. Half-title. Disbound.
(Robertshaw) £65 [≈ $116]

- Observations on the Air and Epidemic Diseases from the Year 1728 to 1737 inclusive ... Translated from the Latin ... London: 1759-67. 1st English edn. 2 vols. 8vo. Lib stamps on titles. Contemp calf, worn.
(Hemlock) $225 [≈ £126]

Huxley, Leonard
- Evolution, the Modern Synthesis. London: 1942. 1st edn. 8vo. 645 pp. Orig cloth. Dw (sl worn). *(Wheldon & Wesley)* £25 [≈ $45]
- Life and Letters of Thomas Henry Huxley. New York: 1901. 1st Amer edn. 2 vols. 539; 541 pp. Orig bndgs. *(Fye)* $50 [≈ £28]

Huxley, Thomas Henry
- The Crayfish. An Introduction to the Study of Zoology. London: 1881. 3rd edn. 8vo. xiv, 371 pp. 82 figs. Half mor.
(Wheldon & Wesley) £20 [≈ $36]

- An Elementary Atlas of Comparative

Osteology in Twelve Plates ... Drawn on Stone by B. Waterhouse Hawkins. London: Williams & Norgate, 1864. Only edn. Folio. 12 plates (few sl spots). Title sl browned. Orig cloth, damage to spine ends.
(David White) **£75 [≈ $134]**

- Essays upon some Controverted Questions. London: 1892. 1st edn. viii,625 pp. Inscrptn on half-title. Cloth, worn, sl marked.
(Whitehart) **£25 [≈ $45]**

- A Manual of the Anatomy of Invertebrated Animals. London: J. & A. Churchill, 1877. 1st edn. 8vo in 12s. 596,[16 advt Feb 1884] pp. 158 figs. Orig cloth.
(Bow Windows) **£60 [≈ $107]**

- The Oceanic Hydrozoa ... observed during the Voyage of H.M.S. 'Rattlesnake'. London: Ray Society, 1859. 4to. x,143 pp. 12 plates. Half mor, worn.
(Wheldon & Wesley) **£70 [≈ $125]**

- Physiography: an Introduction to the Study of Nature. London: 1877. 1st edn. sm 8vo. xx, 384 pp. 5 cold maps & diags, ills. Orig cloth, sl worn & shaken. *(Weiner)* **£50 [≈ $89]**

- The Scientific Memoirs of Thomas Henry Huxley. Edited by Michael Foster and E. Ray Lankester. London: 1898-1902. 1st edn. 2529 pp. 4 ports, over 100 plates. Ex-lib. Orig bndg. *(Fye)* **$400 [≈ £225]**

Hyams, Edward
- Great Botanical Gardens of the World. London: Nelson, (1969). 1st edn. Folio. 288 pp. Num ills. Orig gilt dec cloth. Dw.
(Wreden) **$50 [≈ £28]**

Hyams, E. & Jackson, A.A.
- The Orchard and Fruit Garden. London: 1961. Roy 4to. xv,208 pp. 80 cold plates. Dec buckram. Slipcase.
(Wheldon & Wesley) **£45 [≈ $80]**

Hyman, L.
- The Invertebrates. London: 1940-67. 6 vols (all published). 8vo. 1422 text figs. Cloth.
(Wheldon & Wesley) **£200 [≈ $356]**

Hyslop, James
- Enigmas of Psychical Research. Boston: 1906. 1st edn. 427 pp. Orig bndg.
(Fye) **$75 [≈ £42]**

I.C.S., Reference Library
- Incandescent Lighting, Arc Lighting, Electric Signs, Electric Heating, Electric Wiring. London: [1907?]. Thick 8vo. Num ills. Orig half mor. *(Weiner)* **£40 [≈ $71]**

Iddings, J.P.
- Igneous Rocks. New York: John Wiley & Sons, 1909-13. 2 vols. Text figs, tables. Few lib marks. Orig cloth, worn.
(Gemmary) **$75 [≈ £42]**

Ihde, A.J.
- The Development of Modern Chemistry. New York: 1964. xii,851 pp. Ports, text ills. Orig bndg. Dw. *(Whitehart)* **£25 [≈ $45]**

Illustrations of Natural History ...
- Illustrations of Natural History ... Engravings and Descriptive Accounts of the most interesting and popular Genera and Species of the Animal World ... London: (1829-30). 4to. [ii],248 pp. Title vignette. Some marks. Orig pict gilt cloth, a.e.g., rebacked.
(Bow Windows) **£105 [≈ $187]**

Imison, John
- A Treatise of the Mechanical Powers. I. Of the Lever ... VI. The Inclined Plane ... London: for the author, sold by J. Murray, [1787]. 1st edn. 8vo. [iv],39 pp. 2 fldg plates inc frontis. Sm tear in 2nd plate without loss. Mod qtr calf. *(Finch)* **£225 [≈ $401]**

Immergut, M.A.
- Classical Articles in Urology. London: 1967. xv,329 pp. Text ills. Traces of label removal. Orig cloth, crnrs sl bumped.
(Whitehart) **£18 [≈ $32]**

Imperial Journal ...
- The Imperial Journal of Art, Science, Mechanics and Engineering ... Vols I-III. Manchester: [1840]. 3 vols, all published. 4to. Frontis vols 1 & 2, num fldg plates, ills. Half calf, rubbed. *(Weiner)* **£100 [≈ $178]**

Ingen-Housz, John
- Experiments upon Vegetables, discovering their great Power of Purifying the Common Air in the Sun-shine ... London: for P. Elmsly, 1779. 1st edn. 8vo. lxviii,302,[18] pp. Title sl dusty & sm marg tear. Contemp tree calf, rebacked, crnrs worn.
(Gaskell) **£1,800 [≈ $3,204]**

Ingle, R.W.
- British Crabs. London: BM, 1980. 8vo. vi, 222 pp. 34 plates, 108 figs. Cloth.
(Wheldon & Wesley) **£44 [≈ $78]**

Inglis, Brian
- A History of Medicine. London: 1965. xv, 196 pp. 8 cold & 44 b/w ills. Ptd wraps sl torn. *(Whitehart)* **£18 [≈ $32]**

Innes, J.R.M. & Saunders, L.Z.
- Comparative Neuropathology. London: 1962. xx, 839 pp. Num text ills. Traces of label removal. Lib stamp title verso. Orig bndg. *(Whitehart)* £25 [≈ $45]

Inskip, R.M.
- Navigation and Nautical Astronomy ... Portsea: 1865. 1st edn. viii,170 pp. Num figs. Orig cloth, sl worn, sm ink stains.
(Whitehart) £18 [≈ $32]

The Instructive Picture Book ...
- See Yonge, C.M.

The Intellectual Observer ...
- The Intellectual Observer: Review of Natural History, Microscopic Research, and Recreative Science. London: Groombridge, 1862-68. 12 vols complete. 8vo. 84 chromolithos, num tinted plates, w'cuts. Mod half mor gilt. *(Hollett)* £480 [≈ $854]

Iredale, T.
- Birds of Paradise and Humming Birds. Melbourne: 1950. 4to. xii,239 pp. 33 cold plates by Lilian Medland. Orig half mor.
(Wheldon & Wesley) £160 [≈ $285]

Iselin, Marc
- Surgery of the Hand: Wounds, Infections, and Closed Traumata. London: 1940. 1st edn in English. 353 pp. Orig bndg.
(Fye) £300 [≈ £169]

Jackson, F.J.
- Notes on the Game-Birds of Kenya and Uganda ... London: 1926. 8vo. xvi,258 pp. 13 cold plates. Cloth.
(Wheldon & Wesley) £70 [≈ $125]

Jackson, James
- Letters to a Young Physician just entering upon Practice. Boston: 1855. 1st edn. 344 pp. Orig bndg. *(Fye)* £60 [≈ £34]
- A Memoir of James Jackson, Jr. M.D. With Extracts from his Letters to his Father; and Medical Cases Collected by Him. Boston: 1835. 444 pp. Some foxing of endpapers. Contemp cloth, paper label. Author's pres copy. *(Whitehart)* £180 [≈ $320]

Jackson, Miss M.A.
- The Pictorial Flora, or British Botany delineated in 1500 Lithographic Drawings of all the Species of Flowering Plants. London: 1840. iv,42 pp. 130 plates of figs. Polished calf. *(Wheldon & Wesley)* £35 [≈ $62]

Jackson, Robert
- A Systematic View of the Formation, Discipline, and Economy of Armies. London: for the author, 1804. 4to. xxxi,347 pp. Contemp bds, uncut, rebacked.
(Goodrich) $325 [≈ £183]

Jacob, J.
- Observations on the Structure and Draught of Wheel-Carriages. London: E. & C. Dilly, 1773. 1st edn. 4to. 14 fldg plates. Contemp calf, rebacked, orig label.
(Spelman) £550 [≈ $979]

Jacob, W.
- An Historical Inquiry into the Production and Consumption of the Precious Metals. London: Murray, 1831. 2 vols. 8vo. xvi,380; xi,415 pp. Leather & mrbld bds, rubbed.
(Gemmary) $250 [≈ £140]

Jacobi, Abraham
- Therapeutics of Infancy and Childhood. Phila: Lippincott, 1896. 8vo. 518 pp. Orig cloth, sl worn. Author's pres inscrptn.
(Goodrich) $250 [≈ £140]
- A Treatise on Diphtheria. New York: Wood, 1880. x,252 pp. Orig bndg.
(Goodrich) $85 [≈ £48]

Jaeger, F.M.
- Lectures on the Principle of Symmetry & Its Application in all Natural Sciences. Amsterdam: Elsevier, 1917. 8vo. xii,333 pp. 170 text figs. Cloth. *(Gemmary)* $75 [≈ £42]

James, Sir Henry
- Instructions for Taking Meteorological Observations; with Tables for their Corrections and Notes on Meteorological Phenomena. London: HMSO, 1861. 1st edn. 52,34 pp. 20 cold plates, fldg charts. Orig bndg. *(Schoen)* $65 [≈ £37]

James, Prosser
- The Therapeutics of the Respiratory Passages. New York: Wood Library, 1884. 8vo. 316 pp. 23 text w'cuts. Orig bndg.
(Goodrich) $35 [≈ £20]

James, William
- A Pluralistic Universe: Hibbert Lectures ... New York: Longmans, Green, 1909. 1st edn. 8vo. Orig cloth backed bds, paper label chipped. Author's compliments slip laid in. *(Gach)* $100 [≈ £56]
- The Principles of Psychology. New York: Henry Holt, 1890. 1st ed. 1st issue, with Psychology in advts hyphenated, & with sans

serif type in spine imprints. 2 vols. 8vo. Title edges sl chipped. Orig cloth, vol 1 hinges cracked, jnts sl rubbed.
(Gach) **$1,750 [≈ £983]**
- The Principles of Psychology. New York: Henry Holt, 1890. 1st ed. 3rd printing, without Psy-chology in advts, "notice, and" at page 307 line 19, & with Holt imprint in serif type. 2 vols. 8vo. Sound ex-lib. Orig cloth, hinges cracked (reprd vol 1).
(Gach) **$175 [≈ £98]**
- The Principles of Psychology. New York: Henry Holt, 1890. 1st ed. 3rd printing, without Psy-chology in advts, "notice, and" at page 307 line 19, & with Holt imprint in serif type. 2 vols. 8vo. Orig cloth, sl shelf wear to extrs.
(Gach) **$375 [≈ £211]**
- The Principles of Psychology. New York: 1890. 1st edn. 2 vols. Names. Orig bndgs, v sl rubbed.
(Polyanthos) **$300 [≈ £169]**
- The Varieties of Religious Experience. New York: Longmans, Green, 1902. 1st edn, 2nd printing, rvsd. 8vo. Inscrptn. Orig cloth, paper label (chipped), rubbed, hinges cracked.
(Gach) **$125 [≈ £70]**

Jameson, E.
- The Natural History of Quackery. London: 1961. 224 pp. Frontis, 7 dble-sided plates. Orig bndg.
(Whitehart) **£15 [≈ $27]**

Jameson, R.
- System of Mineralogy. Edinburgh: for Archibald Constable, 1816. 2nd edn. 3 vols. 8vo. xix,537; xiii,489; xii,599,4 pp. Sl water stain 1 crnr of text & plates vol 3. New qtr leather.
(Gemmary) **$1,100 [≈ £618]**
- A Treatise on the External, Chemical and Physical Characters of Minerals. Edinburgh: Constable, 1817. 3rd edn. 8vo. xi,304 pp. Foxed. Polished calf.
(Gemmary) **$550 [≈ £309]**

Jameson, Thomas
- Essays on the Changes of the Human Body, at its Different Ages; the Diseases to which it is predisposed ... London: Longman ..., 1811. 8vo. xxxiii,360 pp. Ex-lib. Orig qtr calf, front jnt split.
(Goodrich) **$165 [≈ £93]**

Jamieson, Robert
- Mind and Body: a Discourse on the Physiology of the Phrenical Action of the Cerebrum. Aberdeen: 1858. 8vo. 24 pp. Diags. pencillings. Title soiled. Disbound.
(Weiner) **£30 [≈ $53]**

Janson, E.W.
- British Beetles, transferred from Curtis's

British Entomology. London: 1863. Roy 8vo. [62] pp. 29 cold plates of 259 figs. Half mor.
(Wheldon & Wesley) **£100 [≈ $178]**

Jaramillo-Arango, Jaime
- The Conquest of Malaria. London: 1950. 1st edn. 125 pp. Dw.
(Fye) **$65 [≈ £37]**

Jarcho, S.
- Essays on the History of Medicine. Selected from the Bulletin of the New York Academy of Medicine. New York: 1976. xii,446 pp. 36 plates. Cloth sl dust marked.
(Whitehart) **£25 [≈ $45]**

Jardine, Sir William
- The Natural History of Humming-Birds. Volume I. Edinburgh: 1833. 8vo. iv,166 pp. Port, cold vignette, 30 cold plates. Orig cloth, spine faded.
(Wheldon & Wesley) **£80 [≈ $142]**
- Humming-Birds. Edinburgh: Jardine's Naturalist's Library, 1833-34. 2 vols. Cr 8vo. 2 ports, 2 cold vignettes, 64 cold plates. Orig cloth, trifle loose.
(Wheldon & Wesley) **£180 [≈ $320]**
- Illustrations of the Duck Tribe. Lockerby: the author, [ca 1839]. 4to. [iii] pp. 9 engvd plates. Rec buckram.
(Blackwell's) **£275 [≈ $490]**
- The Natural History of Monkeys. Edinburgh: Lizars, Jardine's Naturalist's Library, 1833. 1st edn. Sm 8vo. 230 pp. Port, cold title vignette, 30 hand cold plates. Contemp mor, gilt spine, a.e.g., jnts sl rubbed.
(Egglishaw) **£60 [≈ $107]**
- The Natural History of the Felinae. Edinburgh: Lizars, Jardine's Naturalist's Library, 1834. 1st edn. Sm 8vo. 276 pp. Port, vignette title, 36 hand cold plates. New qtr calf.
(Egglishaw) **£60 [≈ $107]**
- The Natural History of the Felinae. Edinburgh: Jardine's Naturalist's Library, 1834. Sm 8vo. 272 pp. Port, vignette, 36 cold plates. Orig cloth, trifle faded.
(Wheldon & Wesley) **£45 [≈ $80]**

Jeaffreson, John Cordy
- A Book about Doctors. London: Hurst & Blackett, 1860. 1st edn. 2 vols. 8vo. 2 frontis. Orig brown cloth, upper hinge vol 1 cracked but firm.
(Frew Mackenzie) **£50 [≈ $89]**

Jeans, J.S.
- Railway Problems: an Inquiry into the Economic Conditions of Railway Working in Different Countries. London: 1887. 8vo. xxviii, 560 pp. Occas perf lib stamp. Orig pict cloth gilt, sl soiled.
(Weiner) **£50 [≈ $89]**

Jeans, Sir James Hopwood

- Atomicity and Quanta being the Rouse Ball Lecture delivered on May 11, 1925. Cambridge: UP, 1926. 1st edn. 8vo. 64 pp. Orig ptd bds, sl dust soiled.
(Claude Cox) £25 [≈ $45]
- The Dynamical Theory of Gases. Cambridge: UP, 1904. 1st edn. Roy 8vo. viii,352 pp. Orig cloth. *(Gaskell)* £40 [≈ $71]
- The Mathematical Theory of Electricity and Magnetism. Cambridge: UP, 1933. 5th edn. 4to. vii, 652 pp. Orig bndg.
(Key Books) $50 [≈ £28]
- Report on Radiation and the Quantum-Theory. London: Physical Society of London, 1914. 1st edn. 8vo. iv,90 pp. Sl dusty. Orig ptd wraps. *(Gaskell)* £45 [≈ $80]
- Report on Radiation and the Quantum-Theory. London: Physical Society of London, 1924. 2nd edn. 8vo. iv,86 pp. Orig ptd wraps.
(Gaskell) £25 [≈ $45]
- Through Space and Time. New York: Macmillan, 1934. 1st edn. 8vo. 224 pp. 53 plates, 106 figs. Sm stain lower foredge. Orig blue cloth gilt. *(Schoen)* $50 [≈ £28]

Jeffreys, John Gwyn

- British Conchology ... London: Van Voorst, 1862-69. 5 vols. 8vo. 5 hand cold frontis, 142 plain plates. Sm ink stamp on titles. Half mor, gilt dec spines. ALS (1870) by author bound in. *(Egglishaw)* £340 [≈ $605]
- Land and Freshwater Shells of Great Britain. London: Van Voorst, 1904. 8vo. cxiv, 341 pp. Cold frontis, 8 plain plates. Cloth.
(Egglishaw) £24 [≈ $43]

Jeffreys, Julius

- Views upon the Statics of the Human Chest, Animal Heat, and Determinations of Blood to the Head. London: Longman ..., 1843. 233 pp. Lacks front flyleaf. Some browning. Orig cloth, uncut & unopened, worn.
(Goodrich) $75 [≈ £42]

Jeffries, David

- A Treatise on Diamonds and Pearls. London: W.L. Molyneux, 1871. 4th edn. Cr 8vo. xv, 96, 30 pp. Orig cloth, faded.
(Gemmary) $225 [≈ £126]
- A Treatise on Diamonds and Pearls ... London: W.L. Molyneux, 1871. 4th edn, crrctd. 8vo. xxiv,96 pp. 30 litho plates & tables. Orig cloth, faded.
(Burmester) £70 [≈ $125]
- A Treatise on Diamonds and Pearls. London: E. Lumley, n.d. 4th edn. Cr 8vo. xvi,3,30,116 pp. Orig cloth. *(Gemmary)* $250 [≈ £140]

Jehl, Francis

- The Manufacture of Carbons for Electric Lighting and other Purposes. London: [1899]. 8vo. ix,232 pp. Fldg plate, ills. Orig cloth. *(Weiner)* £40 [≈ $71]

Jekyll, F.

- Gertrude Jekyll, a Memoir. London: Cape, 1934. 8vo. 248 pp. Plates, text figs. Orig cloth. *(Egglishaw)* £28 [≈ $50]

Jekyll, Gertrude

- A Gardener's Testament. London: Country Life, 1937. 8vo. xiv,258 pp. Num ills. Orig cloth. *(Egglishaw)* £30 [≈ $53]
- Lilies for English Gardens. London: Country Life, 1901. 1st edn. 8vo. xii,72 pp. 62 plates, text figs. Orig buckram, sl soiled.
(Egglishaw) £34 [≈ $61]
- Wall, Water and Woodland Gardens, including the Rock Garden and the Heath Garden. London: Country Life, 1933. 8th edn, rvsd. 8vo. xvi,246 pp. Ills. Orig cloth, rear cvr edge sl discold.
(Egglishaw) £34 [≈ $61]
- Wood and Garden. London: Longmans, 1899. 8vo. xvi,286 pp. Photo ills. Orig blue buckram gilt, spine faded, front cvr marked.
(Egglishaw) £26 [≈ $46]

Jekyll, Gertrude & Mawley, E.

- Roses for English Gardens. London: Country Life, 1902. 1st edn. 8vo. xvi,166 pp. Num ills. Orig cloth, some fading, sl wear hd of spine. *(Egglishaw)* £35 [≈ $62]

Jennings, C.

- The Eggs of British Birds ... Copied and Coloured from Nature, with Descriptions of British Birds. Bath: [1853]. Sm 8vo. xxx, [ii], 200 pp. Cold title, 7 cold plates. Orig cloth gilt. *(Wheldon & Wesley)* £45 [≈ $80]

Jennings, James

- The Family Cyclopaedia, or Manual of Useful and Necessary Information ... Inventions, Discoveries ... Domestic Economy, Agriculture, and Chemistry ... Second Edition ... London: Sherwood ..., (1822). 8vo. 1376 pp. Frontis, 1 plate. Early half mor. *(Fenning)* £85 [≈ $151]
- A Practical Treatise on the History, Medical Properties, and Cultivation of Tobacco. London: Sherwood, Gilbert, & Piper, 1830. [8],159,[13] pp. Advts. Orig bds, cloth spine, paper label. *(C.R. Johnson)* £150 [≈ $267]

Jennings, O.

- On the Cure of the Morphia Habit without

Suffering ... New York: 1901. 2nd edn. xii, 212 pp. 6 figs. Orig cloth, sl stained.
(Whitehart) **£40 [≈ $71]**

Jenyns (later Blomefield), Leonard
- Observations in Meteorology ... London: Van Voorst, 1858. 1st edn. 8vo. ix,[3],415 pp, advt leaf. Orig cloth. *(Fenning)* **£38.50 [≈ $69]**

Jenyns, L.
- A Manual of British Vertebrate Animals. Cambridge: 1835. 8vo. xxxii,559 pp. Few lib marks. Contemp cloth backed bds, reprd.
(Wheldon & Wesley) **£40 [≈ $71]**

Jerdon, T.C.
- The Birds of India ... to which is added his Supplementary Notes published in Ibis 1871-72, reprinted by H.H. Godwin-Austen. Calcutta: 1877. 3 vols. 8vo. Marg worm throughout. New bds.
(Wheldon & Wesley) **£75 [≈ $134]**
- The Mammals of India. London: 1874. Roy 8vo. xxxi,335 pp. 2 names on title. New cloth.
(Wheldon & Wesley) **£40 [≈ $71]**

Jervis, Thomas Best
- Records of Ancient Science, exemplified and authenticated in the Primitive Universal Standard of Weights and Measures ... Calcutta: Baptist Mission Press, 1835. 1st edn. 8vo. xiv,97 pp. Lacks front flyleaf. Orig cloth, sl discold. *(Burmester)* **£150 [≈ $267]**

Jervis, W.P.
- The Mineral Resources of Central Italy ... London: Edward Stanford, 1868. 8vo. [viii], 132 pp. Frontis, map, 2 plates, text ills, 12 fldg tables. Orig cloth. *(Rankin)* **£65 [≈ $116]**

Jesse, Edward
- Anecdotes of Dogs. London: Bohn, 1858. 8vo. xvi,491 pp. 34 steel engvs, 40 w'engvs. Orig cloth, a.e.g., backstrip relaid.
(Bookline) **£45 [≈ $80]**

Jesse, George R.
- Researches into the History of the British Dog, from Ancient Laws, Charters, and Historical Records. London: 1866. 2 vols. Lge 8vo. 20 plates. Sl damp stain bottom crnr of 1 vol. Mod half calf gilt, t.e.g.
(D & D Galleries) **$500 [≈ £281]**

Jevons, W.S.
- The Principles of Science. A Treatise on Logic and Scientific Method. Second Edition, revised. London: 1877. 8vo. xliv,786,[2] pp. Frontis. Name, few sm tears & folded crnrs.

Pencil & ink notes, occas marks. Orig cloth, dull, spine ends & crnrs sl worn.
(Bow Windows) **£105 [≈ $187]**

John, E.R.
- Mechanisms of Memory. New York: 1967. xii, 468 pp. 64 figs. Orig bndg, sl marked.
(Whitehart) **£18 [≈ $32]**

Johnes, Arthur James
- Philological Proofs of the Original Unity and Recent Origin of the Human Race. London: Samuel Clarke, 1843. 1st edn. Demy 8vo. lx, (104), 20 pp. Endpapers sl split, few ff carelessly opened. Orig late Victorian cloth, v sl rubbed. *(Ash)* **£100 [≈ $178]**

Johnson, C. Pierpoint & Sowerby, J.E.
- British Wild Flowers ... see Sowerby, J.E. & Johnson, C.P.

Johnson, C.W.
- The Farmer's Encyclopaedia and Dictionary of Rural Affairs ... London: 1842. [xvi], iv, 1320, [16] pp. Figs, tables. Sl dusty. Orig cloth, worn, sl stained, spine marked & worn.
(Whitehart) **£40 [≈ $71]**

Johnson, G.W.
- A History of English Gardening, Chronological, Biographical, Literary and Critical. London: 1829. 8vo. iv,444 pp. Half calf, trifle rubbed.
(Wheldon & Wesley) **£140 [≈ $249]**

Johnson, Howard F.
- The Treatment of Incurable Diseases. London: Longman, Brown ..., 1851. 1st edn. 8vo. Advt leaf at end. Frontis. Orig mauve cloth, rebacked, partly unopened.
(Georges) **£65 [≈ $116]**

Johnson, Laurence
- A Medical Formulary based on the United States and British Pharmacopoeias ... New York: Wood Library, 1881. 8vo. vii,402 pp. Orig cloth. *(Goodrich)* **$75 [≈ £42]**
- A Medical Formulary based on the United States and British Pharmacopoeias ... New York: Wood Library, 1881. vii,402 pp. Orig cloth. *(Goodrich)* **$50 [≈ £28]**

Johnson, Louisa
- Every Lady Her Own Flower Gardener. London: Wm. S. Orr, 1839. 96 pp. Half-title. Hand cold engvd title. Orig cloth, a.e.g.
(Jarndyce) **£30 [≈ $53]**

Johnson, Robert Wallace
- Friendly Cautions to the Heads of Families and Others ... with ample Directions to Nurses who attend the Sick, Women in Child-Bed, etc. ... Third Edition, with Additions. Phila: James Humphreys, 1804. 1st Amer edn. 8vo. xii,155,[4] pp. Foxed. Orig calf, rebacked. *(Goodrich)* **$175 [≈ £98]**

Johnson, S.J.
- Historical and Future Eclipses, with Notes on Planets, Double Stars, and other Celestial Matters. London: 1896. New edn. Sm 8vo. viii, 178 pp. 12 pp of diags. Cloth over bds. *(Whitehart)* **£18 [≈ $32]**

Johnson, Stephen
- The History of Cardiac Surgery 1896-1955. Baltimore: 1970. 1st edn. 201 pp. Dw. *(Fye)* **$90 [≈ £51]**

Johnston, G.
- A History of the British Zoophytes. London: 1838. 8vo. xii,341 pp. 45 plates, text figs. Some foxing. Orig cloth gilt, sl worn. *(Wheldon & Wesley)* **£40 [≈ $71]**
- A History of British Zoophytes. London: 1847. 2nd edn. 2 vols. 8vo. 73 plates (1-34, 34*, 35-63, 66-74, as issued). Sl foxing at ends. Some offsetting of plates. Cloth. *(Henly)* **£55 [≈ $98]**
- A History of British Sponges and Lithophytes. Edinburgh: 1842. 1st edn. 8vo. xii, 264 pp. 25 tinted plates, 23 text figs. Orig cloth, spine faded. *(Bow Windows)* **£105 [≈ $187]**
- An Introduction to Conchology; or, Elements of the Natural History of Molluscous Animals. London: 1850. 8vo. xvi,614 pp. 102 text figs. New cloth. *(Wheldon & Wesley)* **£50 [≈ $89]**

Johnston, James Finlay Weir
- The Chemistry of Common Life. London: William Blackwood, 1855. 1st edn. 2 vols. Map, text ills. Half calf, gilt spines. *(Jermy & Westerman)* **£50 [≈ $89]**
- Experimental Agriculture being the Results of Past, and Suggestions for Future Experiments in Scientific and Practical Agriculture. Edinburgh & London: Blackwood, 1849. 1st edn. 8vo. xv,265 pp, advt leaf. Orig cloth, uncut, paper label, spine faded. *(Claude Cox)* **£30 [≈ $53]**
- Experimental Agriculture being the Results of Past, and Suggestions for Future Experiments in Scientific and Practical Agriculture. Edinburgh: Blackwood, 1849. 1st edn. 8vo. xvi,266 pp, advt leaf. Lacks free

endpapers. Orig cloth, sl soiled.
(Karmiole) **$100 [≈ £56]**
- Lectures on Agricultural Chemistry and Geology with an Appendix containing Suggestions for Experiments in Practical Agriculture. London: 1844. 1st edn. 911, 116, xx pp. Contemp three qtr roan, gilt spine, edges sl worn, spine sl rubbed. *(Whitehart)* **£45 [≈ $80]**

Johnston, Thomas
- General View of the Agriculture of the County of Tweedale with Observations ... London: Bulmer, 1794. 1st edn. 4to. 42,[2 blank] pp. Half-title. Disbound. *(Claude Cox)* **£30 [≈ $53]**
- General View of the Agriculture of the County of Selkirk, with Observations ... London: Bulmer, 1794. 1st edn. 4to. 50,[2 blank] pp. Half-title. Disbound. *(Claude Cox)* **£30 [≈ $53]**

Johnstone, John
- An Account of the Mode of Draining Land, according to the System Practised by Mr Joseph Elkington ... London: for Richard Phillips ..., 1801. 2nd edn, crrctd & enlgd. xvi, 164 pp. 18 fldg plans (of 19). Minor browning. Orig bds, sl worn. *(Francis Edwards)* **£85 [≈ $151]**

Joll, Cecil A.
- Diseases of the Thyroid Gland with Special reference to Thyrotoxis. London: 1932. Lge 8vo. xviii,682 pp. Frontis port, 24 cold plates, num ills. Orig cloth. *(Weiner)* **£50 [≈ $89]**
- Joll's Diseases of the Thyroid Gland. Revised by F.F. Rundle. London: 1951. 2nd edn. x,520 pp. Frontis port, 165 figs. Orig bndg. Dw. *(Whitehart)* **£25 [≈ $45]**

Jolley, Leonard, & others
- Theory and Design of Illuminating Engineering Equipment. London: Chapman & Hall, 1930. 1st edn. 8vo. 709 pp. Plates, ills, fldg diags. Lib pocket. Orig green cloth. *(Schoen)* **$50 [≈ £28]**
- The Theory and Design of Illuminating Engineering Equipment. London: [1930]. xxxi, 709 pp. 555 figs (some on plates). Orig bndg. *(Whitehart)* **£18 [≈ $32]**

Joly, Charles Jasper
- A Manual of Quaternions. London: Macmillan, 1905. 1st edn. 8vo. xxvii,320 pp. Orig cloth. *(Fenning)* **£28.50 [≈ $52]**

Joly, John
- Radioactivity and Geology. An Account of

the Influence of Radioactive Energy on Terrestrial History. New York: Van Nostrand, 1909. 1st edn. Few lib marks. Orig bndg, spine darkened, label removed.
(Key Books) **$40 [≈ £22]**
- Radioactivity and Geology. An Account of the Influence of Radioactive Energy on Terrestrial History. London: 1909. 1st edn. 8vo. xv,287 pp. Frontis, 5 plates, text ills. Orig cloth, sl soiled, extrs sl worn.
(Francis Edwards) **£28 [≈ $50]**

Jones, B.E. (editor)
- The Amateur Mechanic. A Practical Guide for the Handyman. London: [1922]. 2nd edn, enlgd. 4 vols. Num ills & diags. Orig cloth, sl dusty & worn.   *(Whitehart)* **£20 [≈ $36]**

Jones, Bence
- The Life and Letters of Michael Faraday ... Second Edition, revised. London: Longmans, 1870. 2 vols. 8vo. Sm lib stamps on titles. Orig cloth, backstrips worn, vol 1 recased, vol 2 backstrip relaid. *(Waterfield's)* **£50 [≈ $89]**

Jones, C.H. & Sieveking, E.H.
- A Manual of Pathological Anatomy. London: 1854. xii,788 pp. 167 text figs. Orig cloth, rebacked.   *(Whitehart)* **£30 [≈ $53]**

Jones, Charles
- Refuse Destructors, with Results up to the Present Time. Second and Revised Edition. London: 1894. 8vo. Frontis, 2 plates, fldg table, 22 extending plans. Orig cloth.
(Bow Windows) **£48 [≈ $85]**

Jones, Ernest
- On the Nightmare. London: Hogarth Press, 1931. 1st edn. 374 pp. Frontis. Sm lib marks removed. Orig cloth.   *(Caius)* **$65 [≈ £37]**

Jones, Frederic Wood
- Coral and Atolls. Their History, Description, Theories of their Origin ... London: 1910. xxiii,392 pp. Frontis port, map, 27 plates, 79 text figs. Orig bndg. *(Whitehart)* **£38 [≈ $68]**
- The Principles of Anatomy as seen in the Hand. London: 1920. 1st edn. 325 pp. 123 ills. Orig bndg.   *(Fye)* **$250 [≈ £140]**
- The Principles of Anatomy as seen in the Hand. London: 1946. 2nd edn, enlgd. 418 pp. 144 figs. Orig bndg. *(Fye)* **$125 [≈ £70]**

Jones, H.E.
- Illustrations of the Nests and Eggs of the Birds of Ohio. Circleville, Ohio: 1879-86. 2 vols. Folio. 68 plates (3 cold). Mod half mor.
(Wheldon & Wesley) **£2,200 [≈ $3,916]**

Jones, John Frederick Drake
- A Treatise on the Process Employed by Nature in Suppressing the Hemorrhage from Divided and Punctured Arteries. and on the Use of the Ligature ... London: 1805. xvi,270 pp. 15 engvs. Lib stamps on title & plates. Occas water stains & foxing. Contemp calf backed bds, worn. *(Whitehart)* **£180 [≈ $320]**
- A Treatise on the Process Employed by Nature in Suppressing the Hemorrhage from Divided and Punctured Arteries ... Phila: Thomas Dobson ..., 1811. 1st Amer edn. xv,237 pp. 15 plates. Contemp tree calf, jnts cracked.   *(Hemlock)* **$175 [≈ £98]**

Jones, Joseph
- Man, Moral and Physical: or the Influence of Health and Disease on Religious Experiences. Phila: 1861. 324 pp. Orig bndg.
(Fye) **$75 [≈ £42]**

Jones, Paul
- Flora Magnifica. Selected and Painted by the Artist, text by Wilfred Blunt. London: 1976. One of 506 sgnd by the artist. Imperial folio. 45 pp. 16 cold ills. Orig half vellum gilt. Slipcase.   *(Henly)* **£240 [≈ $427]**

Jones, R.
- An Inquiry into the State of Medicine, on the Principles of Inductive Philosophy. With an Appendix ... Edinburgh: 1781. xvi,376 pp. Some discoloration page edges. Contemp tree calf, backstrip relaid on cloth reback.
(Whitehart) **£140 [≈ $249]**

Jones, Robert (editor)
- Orthopaedic Surgery of Injuries. By Various Authors. London: 1921. 1st edn. 2 vols. 540; 692 pp. Orig bndgs.   *(Fye)* **$150 [≈ £84]**

Jones, Robert & Lovett, Robert
- Orthopedic Surgery. New York: 1924. 1st Amer edn. 699 pp. Orig bndg, fine.
(Fye) **$250 [≈ £140]**
- Orthopedic Surgery. Baltimore: 1933. 2nd edn, enlgd. 807 pp. Orig bndg.
(Fye) **$75 [≈ £42]**

Jones, Stephen
- Rudiments of Reason; or, The Young Experimental Philosopher ... London: E. Newbery, 1793. 1st edn. 3 vols in one. xv, 163; 186; 204, 20 pp. Lacks front f.e.p. Reversed calf, rubbed.
(Jermy & Westerman) **£150 [≈ $267]**

Jones, T.R.
- General Outlines of the Organisation of the

Animal Kingdom. London: 1871. 4th edn. 8vo. xliii,886 pp. 571 text figs. Qtr calf, rebacked. *(Henly)* **£22 [≈$39]**
- A Monograph of the Entomostraca of the Cretaceous Formation of England. London: Palaeontographical Soc., 1849. 4to. 40 pp. 7 litho plates. Occas sl foxing. Later cloth backed bds, ptd label. *(Savona)* **£35 [≈$62]**

Jones, W.H.S.
- Malaria and Greek History to which is added the History of Greek Therapeutics and the Malaria Theory. Manchester: 1909. 1st edn. 175 pp. Ex-lib. Orig bndg, hd of spine torn. *(Fye)* **$75 [≈£42]**

Jones, William
- The Gardener's Receipt Book: containing Methods for destroying all kinds of Vermin and Insects ... Diseases of Plants ... London: Groombridge, 1849. 2nd edn. 12mo. Half-title. 8 advt pp. Orig cloth. *(Jarndyce)* **£30 [≈$53]**

Jordan, D.S.
- A Guide to the Study of Fishes. New York: 1905. 2 vols. 4to. 2 cold frontis, 934 text figs. Some lib marks & use. Orig buckram, vol 2 reprd. *(Wheldon & Wesley)* **£120 [≈$214]**

Jordan, R.J.
- Skin Diseases and their Remedies. London: 1860. xi,283 pp. Lacks endpapers. Orig cloth, spine ends sl defective.
(Whitehart) **£35 [≈$62]**

Joule, James Prescott
- Scientific Papers ... and the Joint Papers. London: Physical Soc., 1884-87. 1st edn. 2 vols. Plates, ills. Lib pockets. Orig bndg, vol 1 hd of spine torn. *(Schoen)* **$150 [≈£84]**

The Journal of a Naturalist ...
- See Knapp, J.L.

Joyce, Jeremiah
- Scientific Dialogues ... New Edition, Complete in One Volume ... London: Darton & Co., [ca 1836]. 12mo. viii,492 pp. Frontis, 200 w'cuts. Orig cloth.
(Fenning) **£28.50 [≈$52]**

Judd, John W.
- The Geology of Rutland ... London: Longmans, Stanford, 1875. Tall 8vo. xv,320 pp. 3 fldg diags, 8 tinted lithos, 19 text w'cuts. 4 ff sl creased & soiled at edges. Lib stamp title verso. Orig cloth gilt, faded.
(Hollett) **£120 [≈$214]**

- Volcanoes What They Are and What They Teach. Fifth Edition. London: International Scientific Series, 1893. 8vo. xvi,381 pp. 96 ills. Few minor spots. Orig cloth, spine ends sl dull & rubbed. *(Bow Windows)* **£25 [≈$45]**

Judson, Adoniram Brown
- The Influence of Growth on Congenital and Acquired Deformities. New York: 1905. 1st edn. 275 pp. 134 ills. Orig bndg.
(Fye) **$250 [≈£140]**

Jukes, J., Playfair, Lyon, & others
- Lectures on Gold for the Instruction of Emigrants about to proceed to Australia. Delivered at the Museum of Practical Geology. London: David Bogue, 1852. 1st edn. 8vo. [viii],215 pp. Rec bds, orig back stiff wrapper bound in.
(Burmester) **£110 [≈$196]**

Jukes, J.B.
- The Student's Manual of Geology. London: 1857. 1st edn. Cr 8vo. xiii,610 pp. Text figs. Cloth, faded, new endpapers.
(Henly) **£25 [≈$45]**
- The Student's Manual of Geology. Edinburgh: 1872. 3rd edn. xx,778 pp. Frontis, 167 text figs. Half roan, rubbed, jnts cracked but firm. *(Whitehart)* **£25 [≈$45]**

Jung, C.G.
- The Psychology of Dementia Praecox. Authorized Translation by A.A. Brill. New York: 1936. 150 pp. Orig wraps, uncut, spine worn. *(Goodrich)* **$45 [≈£25]**
- The Collected Works. Translated from the German by R.F.C. Hull. London: Routledge, 1981-86. 20 vols. Orig cloth. Dws.
(Frew Mackenzie) **£500 [≈$890]**

Kanavel, Allen
- Infections of the Hand ... Second Edition ... Illustrated with 147 Engravings. Phila: 1914. 463 pp. Orig bndg. *(Goodrich)* **$65 [≈£37]**

Kane, Robert
- Elements of Chemistry including the most Recent Discoveries and Applications of the Science to Medicine and Pharmacy, and to the Arts. Dublin: 1842. Thick 8vo. xx,1204 pp. W'cuts. Orig cloth, backstrip relaid.
(Weiner) **£45 [≈$80]**

Kaplan, Emanuel
- Functional and Surgical Anatomy of the Hand. Phila: 1953. 1st edn. 288 pp. Dw.
(Fye) **$100 [≈£56]**
- Functional and Surgical Anatomy of the

Hand. Phila: 1965. 2nd edn. 337 pp. Dw.
(Fye) **$50 [≈ £28]**

Kappel, A.W. & Kirby, W.E.
- Beetles, Butterflies, Moths and Other Insects.
London: Cassell, 1893. Sm 4to. 182, advt pp.
12 cold plates, b/w ills. Orig dec bds, sl soiled.
(Carol Howard) **£42 [≈ $75]**

Kater, H. & Lardner, D.
- A Treatise on Mechanics. London: 1830. ix,
342 pp. 224 figs on plates. Sl marg water stain
on title. Half leather, worn.
(Whitehart) **£35 [≈ $62]**

Kaup, J.J.
- Catalogue of Apodal Fish in the Collection of
the British Museum. London: 1856. 8vo. viii,
163 pp. Lib stamp on title. Cloth, unopened.
(Egglishaw) **£30 [≈ $53]**

Kayser, E.
- Textbook of Comparative Geology. London:
1893. 8vo. xii,426 pp. 73 plates, 68 text figs.
Orig cloth, spine worn. *(Henly)* **£15 [≈ $27]**
- Text Book of Comparative Geology.
Translated and Edited by P. Lake. Second
Edition. London: 1895. 8vo. xii,426 pp. Num
ills. Few sl marks & spots. Orig cloth, tiny
nick in spine, 1 crnr bumped.
(Bow Windows) **£30 [≈ $53]**

Keay, Isaac
- The Practical Measurer his Pocket
Companion ... The Third Edition ... With an
Appendix ... London: T. Wood, for J.
Knapton ..., 1724. Narrow 8vo. [iv],3,[xiii],
143, [1], 15, [3],10 pp. Tables. Contemp
sheep, fine. *(Burmester)* **£150 [≈ $267]**

Keen, W.W. (editor)
- Surgery. Its Principles and Practice. Phila:
1910-26. 8 vols. 8vo. Orig red cloth.
(Goodrich) **$150 [≈ £84]**

Keilin, David
- The History of Cell Respiration and
Cytochrome. Cambridge: 1966. 1st edn. 416
pp. Ex-lib. Orig bndg. *(Fye)* **$75 [≈ £42]**

Keill, John
- An Introduction to the True Astronomy ...
London: 1760. 5th edn. 8vo. xvii,396 pp. 25
plates. Calf, spine worn.
(Key Books) **$600 [≈ £337]**

Keith, A.
- The Antiquity of Man. London: 1925. 2nd
edn. 2 vols. 8vo. Cloth.

(Wheldon & Wesley) **£25 [≈ $45]**

Kelley, S.W.
- Surgical Diseases of Children. A Modern
Treatise on Pediatric Surgery. New York:
1909. 765 pp. 293 ills. Few rough edges to
pp. Orig cloth, sl dust stained.
(Whitehart) **£25 [≈ $45]**

Kellogg, J.H.
- Ladies' Guide in Health and Disease.
Girlhood,   Maidenhood,   Wifehood,
Motherhood. International Tract Society:
1900. Roy 8vo. 673 pp. Port frontis, 1 cold &
35 tinted plates. Hinges tender, lower edge of
bds sl damp stained.
(Francis Edwards) **£30 [≈ $53]**
- Rational Hydrotherapy ... Second Edition.
Phila: 1903. Thick 8vo. xxxi,(21)-1193 pp.
277 ills on num plates. Lacks front free
endpaper. Orig cloth, shaken.
(Weiner) **£25 [≈ $45]**
- Rational Hydrotherapy ... Third Edition.
Phila: 1906. Thick 8vo. xxxi,(21)-1217 pp.
293 ills on num plates. Blank crnr of few ff
stained. Orig cloth, worn.
(Weiner) **£25 [≈ $45]**

Kelly, Emerson
- Encyclopedia of Medical Sources. Baltimore:
1948. 1st edn. 476 pp. Ex-lib. Orig bndg.
(Fye) **$60 [≈ £34]**

Kelly, Howard A.
- Medical Gynecology. New York: Appleton,
1908. 1st edn. 8vo. 662 pp. 163 ills. Orig qtr
sheep, rubbed, hd of spine chipped.
(Goodrich) **$125 [≈ £70]**

Kelly, Howard A. & Noble, Charles
- Gynecology and Abdominal Surgery ... Phila:
Saunders, 1908. 2 vols. 8vo. Ills. Ex-lib. Orig
cloth, rubbed, some soiling of bds.
(Goodrich) **$65 [≈ £37]**

Kelsey, Charles B.
- Diseases of the Rectum and Anus. New York:
Wood, 1882. 8vo. xii,299 pp. 52 w'cuts. Orig
bndg. *(Goodrich)* **$55 [≈ £31]**

Keltie, Sir John Scott (editor)
- Adventures in the Air. Being Memorable
Experiences of Great Aeronauts. London:
Edward Stanford, 1877. 1st edn. Cr 8vo. xvi,
304,[32] pp. Num plates & ills. Few faint
marks. Orig pict cloth, v sl shaken.
(Ash) **£125 [≈ $223]**

Kelvin, Sir William Thomson, Baron
- Baltimore Lectures on Molecular Dynamics and the Wave Theory of Light. London: C.J. Clay, 1904. 1st printed edn. 8vo. xxii,703 pp. Pp 695-703 index loosely inserted. Orig (?) blue buckram.   *(Gaskell)* £85 [≈ $151]
- Elasticity and Heat, being Articles contributed to the Encyclopaedia Britannica. Edinburgh: (1878)-1880. 4to. 66 pp. Errata leaf. Diags. Orig bds.   *(Weiner)* £40 [≈ $71]

Kelvin, Sir William Thomson, Baron & Tait, P.G.
- Treatise on Natural Philosophy. Cambridge: UP, 1912. 2 vols. 8vo. Orig cloth.
          (Bow Windows) £70 [≈ $125]

Kemp, D.A.
- Astronomy and Astrophysics. A Bibliographical Guide. London: 1970. 584 pp. Orig bndg.   *(Whitehart)* £25 [≈ $45]

Kendall, P.F. & Wroot, H.E.
- Geology of Yorkshire. Privately Printed: 1924. 8vo. xxii,995 pp. Num ills. Cloth.
             (Henly) £50 [≈ $89]

Kennedy, John, gardener
- A Treatise upon Planting, Gardening, and the Management of the Hot-House ... Dublin: for W. Wilson, 1784. 1st Dublin edn. 8vo. xiii, [iii], 462,[2 advt] pp. Tiny marg worm, occas sl spot. Contemp tree calf, smooth spine, mor label, spine worn, sides rubbed.
             (Finch) £75 [≈ $134]
- A Treatise upon Planting, Gardening, and the Management of the Hot-House ... Dublin: W. Wilson, 1784. 1st Irish edn. 462,2 advt pp. Contemp calf, red label.
          (C.R. Johnson) £175 [≈ $312]

Kennedy, John
- The History of Steam Navigation. Liverpool: 1903. 8vo. xvii,359,[16 advt] pp. Num ills. Orig cloth, sl shaken, sl soiled, extrs sl worn.
          (Francis Edwards) £45 [≈ $80]

Kennedy, R.
- The Book of the Motor Car ... London: [1913]. 3 vols. ix,216; ix,213; ix,222 pp. 23 plates, 782 figs. Model on front endpaper of each vol. Orig bndgs, spines faded.
             (Whitehart) £45 [≈ $80]
- Modern Engines and Power Generators ... London: [1905]. 6 vols. Num plates, ills. Orig cloth.   *(Whitehart)* £35 [≈ $62]

Kensley, Brian
- Sea Shells of Southern African Gastropods.

Cape Town: 1973. 1st (ltd) edn. Sm 4to. 225, [xi] pp. 910 ills, some cold. Illust endpapers. Full mod leather.
          (Francis Edwards) £28 [≈ $50]

Kent, Nathaniel
- General View of the Agriculture of the County of Norfolk ... Norwich: the Norfolk Press ..., 1794. 2nd edn. 8vo. Errata leaf. Fldg map, 3 plates (1 fldg). Contemp red half mor, grey bds sides sl marked.
             (Georges) £200 [≈ $356]
- General View of the Agriculture of the County of Norfolk. London: Richard Phillips, 1796. 8vo. xvi,236,[2] pp. Fldg hand cold map, 3 plates. Orig bds, paper label.
             (Spelman) £170 [≈ $303]
- Hints to Gentlemen of Landed Property ... London: Dodsley, 1775. 1st edn. 8vo. vii, [i], 268 pp. 10 fldg plates, tables in text. Contemp calf, mor label, gilt spine, hd of spine chipped, crnrs worn, jnts cracked.
             (Finch) £165 [≈ $294]
- Hints to Gentlemen of Landed Property ... London: Dodsley, 1776. 2nd edn. 8vo. vii,282 pp. 9 fldg plates. Sm worm hole occas touching a letter. Rec half calf.
             (Young's) £120 [≈ $214]
- Hints to Gentlemen of Landed Property. To which are now first added, Supplementary Hints. London: Dodsley, 1793. New edn. 8vo. vii, 286 pp. 10 plates (6 fldg). Rebound in half calf. *(Francis Edwards)* £140 [≈ $249]

Kent, W.S.
- A Manual of the Infusoria ... London: 1880-82. 2 vols & atlas. Roy 8vo. 1 cold & 52 plain plates. Orig cloth, vol 1 & atlas recased.
             (Henly) £160 [≈ $285]

Kenyon, G.H.
- The Glass Industry of the Weald. Leicester: UP; New York: A.M. Kelley, 1968. Lge 8vo. Map, 22 plates, 20 figs. Orig cloth. Dw.
          (Bow Windows) £40 [≈ $71]

Kerr, Richard
- Nature through Microscope and Camera. London: 1905. 1st edn. 197,[6 advt] pp. 65 ills. Ink stamp on endpaper. Orig illust cloth, spine faded.   *(Francis Edwards)* £30 [≈ $53]
- Nature through Microscope and Camera. London: RTS, 1909. 2nd imp. 8vo. 197 pp. 65 ills. Orig pict cloth. *(Savona)* £25 [≈ $45]

Kersey, John
- The Elements of that Mathematical Art commonly called Algebra ... London: Godbin for Passenger & Hurlock, 1673-74. 1st edn.

2 vols in one. Folio. [x],323,[i]; [iv],416 pp. 2 errata pp. Occas sl foxing. Contemp calf, gilt spine, hinges cracked but firm. Wing K.352.
(Vanbrugh) **£495 [≃ $881]**
- The Elements of that Mathematical Art commonly called Algebra, expounded in Four Books. London: William Godbid for Thomas Passinger and Benjamin Hurlock, 1673-74. 1st edn. 2 vols in one. [x],323; [iv],323 pp. Intl blank. Port. Contemp calf, sl worn. Wing K.352.   *(Gaskell)* **£850 [≃ $1,513]**

Keynes, Sir Geoffrey
- A Bibliography of Sir Thomas Browne, Kt. Cambridge: UP, 1924. 1st edn. 4to. Frontis. Note on p 137. Orig buckram, t.e.g., hd of spine torn.   *(Stewart)* **£75 [≃ $134]**
- A Bibliography of Sir Thomas Browne, Kt. M.D. Cambridge: 1924. 1st edn. One of 500. 4to. 255 pp. Ills. Orig bndg, jnts cracked.
(Fye) **$150 [≃ £84]**
- Dr. Timothie Bright, 1550-1615. A Survey of his Life with a Bibliography of his Writings. London: Wellcome, 1962. Thin 8vo. v,47 pp. 17 plates. Orig bndg.
(Francis Edwards) **£30 [≃ $53]**
- Dr. Timothie Bright, 1550-1615. A Survey of his Life with a Bibliography of his Writings. London: 1962. 1st edn. 47 pp. Orig bndg.
(Fye) **$50 [≃ £28]**
- The Life of William Harvey. Oxford: 1966. 1st edn. 483 pp. Ex-lib. Orig bndg. Dw.
(Fye) **$125 [≃ £70]**

Keys, J.
- The Antient Bee-Master's Farewell; or, Full and Plain Directions for the Management of Bees. London: 1796. 1st edn. 8vo. xvi,273 pp. 2 plates. trifle foxed. Calf, reprd.
(Wheldon & Wesley) **£175 [≃ $312]**

Keys, Thomas E.
- The History of Surgical Anaesthesia. New York: 1945. 1st edn. 191 pp. Ex-lib. Orig bndg.   *(Fye)* **$75 [≃ £42]**
- The History of Surgical Anesthesia. New York: Schuman, 1945. 191 pp. Orig bndg, sl worn.   *(Goodrich)* **$75 [≃ £42]**

Khory, R.N.
- The Bombay Materia Medica and their Therapeutics. Bombay: 1887. 8vo. 600,xxxix pp. Browned. Sm marg worm holes. Cloth.
(Weiner) **£40 [≃ $71]**

Kidd, John
- On the Adaptation of External Nature to the Physical Condition of Man ... London: William Pickering, 1833. 1st edn. 8vo. [8

inserted advt], xvi,375,[1] pp. Prize calf, front bd detached.   *(Gach)* **$85 [≃ £48]**
- On the Adaptation of External Nature to the Physical Condition of Man ... London: 1834. 3rd edn. 8vo. 8,2, xvi,375 pp. Orig cloth, rebacked.   *(Henly)* **£24 [≃ $43]**

Kidd, John (compiler)
- Catalogue of the Works in Medicine and Natural History contained in the Radcliffe Library. Oxford: S. Collingwood, 1835. 1st edn. 8vo. viii,330 pp. Endpapers & intl ff foxed. Orig cloth, mor label. Anon. Compiler's pres inscrptn.
(Finch) **£250 [≃ $445]**

Killian, J.
- Crystals. Secrets of the Inorganic. London: The Scientific Book Club, 1940. 8vo. 263 pp. 7 plates, 67 text figs. Orig cloth. Dw.
(Gemmary) **$45 [≃ £25]**

Killington, F.J.
- A Monograph of the British Neuroptera. London: Ray Society, 1936-37. 1st edn. 2 vols. 8vo. 30 plates (8 cold). Orig cloth.
(Wheldon & Wesley) **£60 [≃ $107]**

King, Charles William
- The Natural History of Gems or Decorative Stones. London: bell & Daldy, 1867. 8vo. xii, 377 pp. W'cut frontis. Orig cloth, worn, sl shaken.   *(Gemmary)* **$75 [≃ £42]**
- The Natural History of Precious Stones and of the Precious Metals. London: Bell & Daldy; Cambridge: Deighton, Bell, 1867. 2nd edn, enlgd. 8vo. xii,364 pp. Frontis, plates. Orig cloth.   *(Burmester)* **£78 [≃ $139]**
- The Natural History, Ancient and Modern, of Precious Stones and Gems, and of the Precious Metals. London: bell & Daldy, 1865. 1st edn. Roy 8vo. xii,442 pp. 6 plates. Orig cloth, worn, hinges loose.
(Gemmary) **$125 [≃ £70]**

King, H.C.
- The History of the Telescope. London: 1955. xvi,456 pp. 194 ills. Lib stamp on title. Cloth, sl rubbed.   *(Whitehart)* **£40 [≃ $71]**

Kingsley, Charles
- Glaucus; or, The Wonders of the Shore. Cambridge: Macmillan, 1855. 1st edn. 16 pp ctlg dated May 1855. Frontis (water stain in bottom margin). Orig drab cloth, blocked in black & gilt, spine sl rubbed.
(Jarndyce) **£45 [≃ $80]**
- Glaucus; or, The Wonders of the Shore. Cambridge: Macmillan, 1855. 2nd edn. Half-

title, 16 advt pp. Frontis (sl water stained). Orig dec brown cloth. *(Jarndyce)* **£20 [≈ $36]**
- Glaucus; or, The Wonders of the Shore. Cambridge: Macmillan, 1856. 3rd edn, crrctd & enlgd. Half-title. 16 ctlg pp dated August 1856. frontis (foxed). Orig buff cloth, blocked in black & gilt, a.e.g. *(Jarndyce)* **£20 [≈ $36]**
- Glaucus; or, the Wonders of the Shore. Cambridge: 1859. 4th edn, enlgd. Post 8vo. [viii], 230 pp. 12 chromolitho plates by G.B. Sowerby. Orig cloth gilt, a.e.g.
  (Wheldon & Wesley) **£40 [≈ $71]**
- Glaucus; or, the Wonders of the Shore. Cambridge: 1859. 4th edn, crrctd & enlgd. Post 8vo. [viii],230 pp. 12 chromolitho plates. Orig cloth gilt, a.e.g.
  (Wheldon & Wesley) **£40 [≈ $71]**

Kirby, William
- On the Power, Wisdom, and Goodness of God, as manifested in the Creation of Animals ... New Edition with Notes by Thomas Rymer Jones. London: Bohn, 1853. 2 vols. 12mo. Ills. Rebound in cloth.
  (Key Books) **$60 [≈ £34]**

Kirby, William & Spence, William
- An Introduction to Entomology ... London: Longman, 1815. 2 vols. 8vo. xxiv,512; 529,[2] pp. 5 hand cold plates (sl offsetting). Old speckled calf gilt, contrasting labels, rubbed.
  (Hollett) **£150 [≈ $267]**
- An Introduction to Entomology. London: 1822-26. Vol 1 4th edn, vol 2 3rd edn, vols 3 & 4 1st edn. 4 vols. 8vo. 2 ports, 6 hand cold & 24 plain plates. Some foxing. Calf.
  (Wheldon & Wesley) **£95 [≈ $169]**
- An Introduction to Entomology. London: Longman, 1828. 5th edn. 4 vols. 8vo. 2 ports, 6 hand cold & 24 plain plates. Rec half mor, red labels, t.e.g. *(Egglishaw)* **£125 [≈ $223]**
- An Introduction to Entomology. London: Longman, Brown ..., 1843 [advts dated 1856]. 6th edn, enlgd. 2 vols. Roy 8vo. 5 hand cold plates. Some foxing. Orig green cloth gilt, spines sl browned & rubbed.
  (Ash) **£75 [≈ $134]**

Kirby, William Forsell
- The Butterflies and Moths of Europe. London: Cassell, 1903. 4to. lxxii,432 pp. 1 plain & 54 cold plates, text ills. Orig cloth, a.e.g. *(Egglishaw)* **£145 [≈ $258]**
- The Butterflies and Moths of Europe. London: Cassell, 1903. Lge 8vo. lxxii,432 pp. 54 cold & 1 plain plate. Some marks. Lacks front fly leaf. Orig pict cloth, sl shaken, inner hinges torn, extrs sl rubbed.
  (Bow Windows) **£90 [≈ $160]**

- The Butterflies and Moths of Europe. London: Cassell, 1907. 4to. lxxii,432 pp. 1 plain & 54 cold plates, text ills. Rebound in cloth. *(Egglishaw)* **£95 [≈ $169]**
- The Butterflies and Moths of Europe. London: 1907. 4to. lxxii,432 pp. 1 plain & 54 cold plates. Sl foxing & soiling. Few margs sl frayed. Orig cloth, trifle worn, recased.
  (Wheldon & Wesley) **£90 [≈ $160]**
- Elementary Text-Book of Entomology. Second Edition Revised and Augmented. London: 1892. 8vo. [iv],viii,281 pp. 87 plates. Occas dust marks. Orig cloth, ink lines on lower cvr. *(Bow Windows)* **£70 [≈ $125]**
- A Hand-Book to the Order Lepidoptera. London: Lloyd's Natural History, 1896-97. 5 vols. Cr 8vo. 156 cold & 2 plain plates. Sl foxing. Orig cloth, 3 vols faded.
  (Wheldon & Wesley) **£60 [≈ $107]**

Kirk, T.
- The Forest Flora of New Zealand. Wellington: 1889. Sm folio. xv,345 pp. 159 plates. Inscrptns on title. Orig cloth, trifle used. *(Wheldon & Wesley)* **£150 [≈ $267]**
- The Forest Flora of New Zealand. London: 1889. Folio. xv,345 pp. 159 plates. Title sl spotted. Orig cloth gilt.
  (Henly) **£220 [≈ $392]**

Kirkby, W.
- The Evolution of Artificial Mineral Waters. Manchester: 1902. x,155 pp. 21 plates, 50 ills. Orig cloth, sl worn.
  (Whitehart) **£18 [≈ $32]**

Kirkland, James
- An Appendix to an Inquiry into the Present State of Medical Surgery ... Cure of Ulcers ... London: Underwood & Black, 1813. 1st edn. xi-144 pp. Errata slip. Occas foxing. Half calf, rubbed, spine worn, lacks label.
  (Jermy & Westerman) **£95 [≈ $169]**

Kirkland, Thomas
- A Commentary on Apoplectic and Paralytic Affections and on Diseases connected with the Subject. London: Wm. Dawson, 1797. 8vo. vii,191, index,[1 advt] pp. Contemp calf, later gilt spine.
  (Bates & Hindmarch) **£325 [≈ $579]**

Kirkman, F.B. & Hutchinson, H.G.
- British Sporting Birds. London: Jack, 1936. 1st edn. 4to. xii,428 pp. 43 cold plates. Orig bndg. *(Carol Howard)* **£22 [≈ $39]**

Kirkman, F.B. & Jourdain, F.C.R.
- British Birds ... London: Nelson & Jack,

1938. Sm 4to. xvi,209 pp. 200 cold plates. Orig bndg. *(Carol Howard)* **£20 [≈ $36]**

Kitchiner, William
- The Art of Invigorating and Prolonging Life, by Food, Clothes, Air, Exercise, Wine, Sleep etc., and Peptic Precepts ... Second Edition. London: 1821. 12mo. 276 pp. Lacks free endpaper. Orig cloth backed bds, worn. Anon.   *(Robertshaw)* **£28 [≈ $50]**
- The Cook's Oracle: Containing Receipts for Plain Cookery ... Third Edition ... Edinburgh: Constable; London: Hurst Robinson, 1821. Lge 12mo. xvi,464 pp. W'engvd text ills. Sl foxing. Contemp calf, backstrip laid down. Anon.
 (Gough) **£135 [≈ $240]**
- The Cook's Oracle. Containing Receipts for Plain Cookery ... New Edition. London: for Cadell & Co, 1829. 12mo. xix,512,[1],[6 advt] pp. Orig bds, uncut, backstrip chipped.
 (Karmiole) **$125 [≈ £70]**

Klein, D.B.
- A History of Scientific Psychology. New York: Basic Books, [1970]. 1st edn. 8vo. Orig cloth. Dw.   *(Gach)* **$50 [≈ £28]**

Klein, Felix
- Famous Problems of Elementary Geometry: the Duplication of the Cube, the Trisection of an Angle ... Translated by W.W. Beman and David Eugene Smith. Boston: 1897. 8vo. ix,80 pp. Orig cloth.   *(Weiner)* **£25 [≈ $45]**

Knaggs, R.L.
- The Inflammatory and Toxic Diseases of Bone. London: 1926. xii,416 pp. 197 text figs. Orig bndg.   *(Whitehart)* **£15 [≈ $27]**

Knapp, John L.
- Gramina Britannica: or Representations of the British Grasses, with Remarks and Occasional Descriptions. London: 1804. 1st edn. 4to. 119 hand cold plates. Some browning, sl foxing, sl offset from text on some plates. Russia gilt, rebacked.
 (Wheldon & Wesley) **£400 [≈ $712]**
- The Journal of a Naturalist. London: 1829. 1st edn. 8vo. xii,403 pp. 7 plates. Half calf. Anon.   *(Wheldon & Wesley)* **£45 [≈ $80]**
- The Journal of a Naturalist. London: 1830. 3rd edn. 8vo. xvi,440 pp. 7 plates (1 cold). Orig cloth, trifle used.
 (Wheldon & Wesley) **£25 [≈ $45]**
- The Journal of a Naturalist. London: Murray, 1830. 3rd edn. 8vo. xvi,432 pp. 7 plates, 8 w'cuts. Navy calf gilt, wear at hd & hinges of spine. *(Carol Howard)* **£45 [≈ $80]**

Knight, Charles
- The Pictorial Museum of Animated Nature. London: [1856-58]. 2 vols. Cr folio. 2 cold frontis, 3906 engvd ills of ca 5000 figs. Frontis & title vol 2 waterstained. Half leather, trifle used.
 (Wheldon & Wesley) **£75 [≈ $134]**
- Pictorial Museum of Animated Nature: and Companion for the Zoological Gardens. London: (1856-58). 2 vols. Folio. 4000 w'engvs. Half mor gilt.
 (Egglishaw) **£45 [≈ $80]**

Knight, Charles W.R.
- The Book of the Golden Eagle. London: [1927]. 1st edn. 4to. xii,295 pp. 40 plates. Lib stamp on title verso. Orig cloth.
 (Fenning) **£28.50 [≈ $52]**

Knight, T.A.
- A Treatise on the Culture of the Apple and Pear, and on the Manufacture of Cider and Perry. Ludlow: H. Procter, 1809. 3rd edn, enlgd. Disbound.   *(Jarndyce)* **£85 [≈ $151]**

Knocker, D.
- Accidents in their Medico-Legal Aspect. London: 1912. xxviii,1254 pp. 4 plates, 202 text figs. Traces of label removal. Orig bndg.
 (Whitehart) **£18 [≈ $32]**

Knott, Cargill Gilston
- Life and Scientific Work of Peter Guthrie Tait. Supplementing the Two Volumes of Scientific Papers published in 1898 and 1900. Cambridge: 1911. x,379 pp. Port frontis. Orig bndg.   *(Whitehart)* **£45 [≈ $80]**
- Life and Scientific Work of Peter Guthrie Tait. Cambridge: UP, 1911. 1st edn. 4to. x, 379 pp. 5 ports. Orig cloth.
 (Gaskell) **£85 [≈ $151]**

Knox, Arthur Edward
- Game Birds and Wild Fowl: their Friends and their Foes. London: 1850. Post 8vo. x,264 pp. 4 plates by Joseph Wolf. Orig cloth gilt, trifle faded & worn.
 (Wheldon & Wesley) **£30 [≈ $53]**
- Ornithological Rambles in Sussex. London: Van Voorst, 1849. 1st edn. Roy 12mo. [viii], 250, [iv],[4] pp. Litho plates. Sl foxing. Orig green pict cloth, sl browned.
 (Ash) **£75 [≈ $134]**
- Ornithological Rambles in Sussex. London: 1850. 2nd edn. 8vo. x,254 pp. 4 plates. Sl foxing. Half calf gilt, trifle rubbed.
 (Wheldon & Wesley) **£25 [≈ $45]**

Kobler, J.
- The Reluctant Surgeon. The Life of John Hunter. London: 1960. 360 pp. Page edges sl foxed. Dw (worn). *(Whitehart)* £15 [≈ $27]

Kocher, Theodor
- Text-Book of Operative Surgery. Third English Authorised Translation from the Fifth German Edition by Harold J. Stiles and C. Balfour Paul. New York: Macmillan, 1911. 8vo. 723 pp. 415 ills. Ex-lib. Orig cloth, rubbed. *(Goodrich)* $125 [≈ £70]

Koehler, Wolfgang
- The Mentality of Apes. Translated ... by Ella Winter. London: 1925. 1st English edn. 8vo. viii,342 pp. Plates. Orig cloth.
  (Weiner) £35 [≈ $62]

Kolle, Fredrik
- Plastic and Cosmetic Surgery. New York: 1911. 1st edn. 511 pp. Num ills. Orig bndg, fine. *(Fye)* $500 [≈ £281]

Kolliker, A.
- A Manual of Human Microscopic Anatomy. London: Parker, 1860. 8vo. xvi,633,[16 ctlg] pp. 249 text figs. Orig cloth, backstrip relaid. *(Savona)* £50 [≈ $89]

Kopal, Z.
- Close Binary Systems. New York: International Astrophysics Series Vol 5, 1959. xiv,558 pp. Text diags. Orig cloth, backstrip relaid. *(Whitehart)* £18 [≈ $32]

Korn, Granino A. & Korn, Theresa M.
- Electronic Analog Computers. New York: McGraw Hill, 1952. 1st edn. 8vo. 378 pp. Ills. Lib pocket. Orig bndg.
  (Schoen) $75 [≈ £42]

Koster, J.T.
- Description of a New Improved Method of Constructing Wheel Carriages ... Liverpool: 1819. 8vo. 41 pp. Errata slip. Fldg plate. Lib stamp on title, plate crnr, & marg of 2 pp. Cloth. *(Weiner)* £125 [≈ $223]

Kraepelin, Emil
- Lectures on Clinical Psychiatry. London: Bailliere, Tindall & Cox, 1906. 2nd English edn. xvii,[2],352 pp. Orig cloth gilt.
  (Caius) $135 [≈ £76]

Krause, Fedor
- Surgery of the Brain and Spinal Cord based on Personal Experiences. Translated by Hermann A. Haubold ... New York: Rebman,

[ca 1911]. 2 vols (vols 1 & 2 only, of 3). 4to. Cold plates. Unabused ex-lib. Orig cloth.
  (Goodrich) $195 [≈ £110]

Kremers, E. & Urdang, G.
- History of Pharmacy. A Guide and a Survey. Phila: 1951. 2nd edn. xiv,622 pp. 16 plates. Lib labels, perf lib stamp on title. Orig bndg, lib marks, back cvr stained.
  (Whitehart) £18 [≈ $32]

Krogh, A.
- The Anatomy and Physiology of Capillaries. New York: 1930. 2nd edn. xli,422 pp. Frontis, 101 figs. Lib label & stamp. Orig bndg. *(Whitehart)* £18 [≈ $32]

Kuiper, G.P. (editor)
- The Earth as a Planet. Chicago: (1954) 1969. xvii,751 pp. Num figs. Orig bndg.
  (Whitehart) £25 [≈ $45]

Kuntz, A.
- The Neuroanatomic Basis of Surgery of the Autonomic Nervous System. Oxford: 1949. 83 pp. 11 figs. Limp cloth, dust stained. *(Whitehart)* £18 [≈ $32]

Kunz, George Frederick
- Gems and Precious Stones of North America. New York: The Scientific Publishing Co., 1890. 1st edn. Cr 4to. 336 pp. 8 cold litho plates, 16 ills. Few lib marks. Cloth, worn.
  (Gemmary) $200 [≈ £112]
- Gems and Precious Stones of North America. New York: The Scientific Publishing Co., 1892. 2nd edn. Cr 4to. vi,367 pp. 8 cold litho & 16 b/w plates. Rebound in cloth.
  (Gemmary) $250 [≈ £140]

Kunz, George Frederick & Stevenson, C.H.
- The Book of the Pearl. New York: century, 1908. 1st edn. 4to. xix,548 pp. Over 100 plates, text maps & figs. Orig elab gilt cloth. *(Gemmary)* $850 [≈ £478]

Kuroda, N.
- A Bibliography of the Duck Tribe: Anatidae ... Tokyo: 1942. 8vo. 852 pp. Orig cloth bds. *(Wheldon & Wesley)* £48 [≈ $85]
- A Contribution to the Knowledge of the Avifauna of the Riu Kiu islands and the Vicinity. Tokyo: 1925. Folio. vi,293 pp. Map, 8 cold plates. New cloth.
  (Wheldon & Wesley) £450 [≈ $801]

Kurr, J.G.
- The Mineral Kingdom. Edinburgh:

Edmonston & Douglas, 1859. Sm folio. 70,48 pp. 1 b/w & 23 hand cold plates. Half leather, rebacked.   *(Gemmary)* **$1,250 [≈ £702]**

Kustel, G.
- A Treatise on Concentration of all Kinds of Ores. San Francisco: Mining & Scientific Press, 1868. 8vo. 259 pp. 7 plates, 120 text figs. Few lib marks. Orig cloth, spotted.
          (Gemmary) **$175 [≈ £98]**

Kuurten, B. & Anderson, E.
- Pleistocene Mammals of North America. New York: 1980. 8vo. 442 pp. Cloth.
          (Wheldon & Wesley) **£48 [≈ $85]**

Lack, D.
- Darwin's Finches. Cambridge: 1947. 1st edn. 8vo. x,208 pp. 9 plates (4 cold), text figs. Cloth, crnr sl bumped. Dw.
          (Wheldon & Wesley) **£30 [≈ $53]**

The Lady's Own Cookery Book ...
- The Lady's Own Cookery Book, and New Dinner-Table Directory ... London: Colburn & Bentley, 1832. 1st edn. 8vo. xx,390 pp. Contemp half calf, gilt dec spine.
          (Gough) **£125 [≈ $223]**

Laennec, R.T.H.
- A Treatise on the Diseases of the Chest and on Mediate Auscultation. Translated from the latest French edition with copious Notes and a Sketch of the Author's Life, by J. Forbes. London: 1834. 4th edn, enlgd. xliv, 675 pp. 2 plates (sl foxed). Contemp calf, rebacked.   *(Whitehart)* **£190 [≈ $338]**

Lamb, Horace
- The Dynamical Theory of Sound. London: Edward Arnold, 1910. 1st edn. 8vo. viii,303,8 advt pp. Orig cloth. Author's pres copy.
          (Gaskell) **£25 [≈ $45]**
- Hydrodynamics. Cambridge: UP, 1906. 3rd edn. 4to. xvi,634 pp. Orig cloth.
          (Gaskell) **£25 [≈ $45]**
- A Treatise on the Mathematical Theory of the Motion of Fluids. Cambridge: UP, 1879. 1st edn. 8vo. x,258,[2],24 advt pp. Orig cloth.
          (Gaskell) **£25 [≈ $45]**

Lamb, Patrick
- Royal Cookery: or, The Compleat Court Cook ... Second Edition ... London: for Nutt & Roper ..., 1716. 2nd edn, enlgd. viii, 302, [iii], [v],[i] pp. 40 plates. V occas sl damp stains. Some plates sl torn at hinges. Contemp calf, sometime rebacked.
          (Gough) **£600 [≈ $1,068]**

Lambert, A.B.
- An Illustration of the Genus Cinchona ... London: 1821. 4to. x,181 pp. 5 plates (sl foxed). New bds.
          (Wheldon & Wesley) **£375 [≈ $668]**

Lamond, H.
- The Sea Trout. A Study in Natural History. London: 1916. Imperial 8vo. x,219 pp. 9 cold & 38 plain plates. Lib blind stamps on title & plates. Cloth, t.e.g.
          (Wheldon & Wesley) **£40 [≈ $71]**

Lancereaux, E.
- A Treatise on Syphilis. Historical and Practical. Translated by G. Whitley. London: New Sydenham Society, 1868. 2 vols. Margs v sl yellowed. Orig cloth, sl worn, vol 2 backstrip relaid.
          (Francis Edwards) **£60 [≈ $107]**

Lancisi, G.M.
- Aneurysms: The Latin Text of Rome, 1745, translated and edited by W.C. Wright. New York: 1952. 362 pp. Orig bndg.
          (Fye) **$50 [≈ £28]**

Landolt, H.
- Handbook of the Polariscope and its Practical Applications. London: 1882. 1st edn. xvi,262 pp. 57 ills. Endpaper & half-title sl holed. Orig cloth.   *(Whitehart)* **£38 [≈ $68]**

Landsborough, D.A.
- A Popular History of British Seaweeds. London: 1849. 1st edn. 8vo. xx,368,4 pp. 20 hand cold & 2 plain plates. Half calf, sl rubbed.   *(Henly)* **£40 [≈ $71]**
- A Popular History of British Seaweeds ... London: 1857. 3rd edn. Sm 8vo. 400 pp. 20 cold & 2 b/w plates. New cloth.
          (Whitehart) **£25 [≈ $45]**
- A Popular History of British Seaweeds. London: Lovell Reeve, 1857. 3rd edn. 8vo. xvi,400 pp. 20 cold & 2 plain plates. Orig cloth.   *(Egglishaw)* **£25 [≈ $45]**

Lane, Levi
- The Surgery of the Hand and Neck. Phila: 1898. 2nd edn. 1180 pp. Orig bndg.
          (Fye) **$200 [≈ £112]**

Lane, Richard J.
- Life at the Water Cure or A Month at Malvern: a Diary. London: Longman, Brown ..., 1846. 1st edn. 32 advt pp. Fldg frontis, num ills. Orig cloth. *(Jarndyce)* **£40 [≈ $71]**

Lane, W. Arbuthnot
- Cleft Palate; Treatment of Simple Fractures by Operation; Diseases of Joints ... London: 1897. 1st edn. 278 pp. Ills. Orig bndg.
(Fye) **$200 [≈ £112]**

Langdon, W.E.
- The Application of Electricity in Railway Working. London: 1897. 2nd edn. xvi,331 pp. Frontis, 4 full page ills, 142 text ills. Orig cloth. *(Whitehart)* **£25 [≈ $45]**

Langley, S.P.
- The 1900 Solar Eclipse Expedition of the Astrophysical Observatory of the Smithsonian Institution. Washington: GPO, 1904. Num plates. Rebound.
(Key Books) **$50 [≈ £28]**
- Researches on Solar Heat and its Absorption by the Earth's Atmosphere. A Report of the Mount Whitney Expedition. Washington: GPO, 1884. 242 pp. Fldg plates, lithos. Few lib marks. Orig bndg, spine worn, jnts cracked. *(Key Books)* **$95 [≈ £53]**

Lankester, E. Roy
- The Advancement of Science: Occasional Essays & Addresses. London: 1890. 1st edn. 387 pp. Orig bndg. *(Fye)* **$50 [≈ £28]**
- Extinct Animals. London: 1906. 2nd imp. xxiii, 331 pp. Frontis port, 218 ills. Spine faded, back hinge sl cracked.
(Whitehart) **£25 [≈ $45]**

Lankester, E. Roy & Ridewood, W.G.
- Monograph of the Okapi. Atlas. London: BM, 1910. All published. 4to. 48 plates. Lib b'plate. Orig cloth, spine trifle worn.
(Wheldon & Wesley) **£75 [≈ $134]**
- Monograph of the Okapi. London: BM, 1910. Atlas vol (all published). 4to. 48 plates (2 cold) with explanations. Lib number on title verso. Cloth (sl wear to spine ends).
(Egglishaw) **£55 [≈ $98]**

Laplace, Pierre Simon
- The System of the World. Translated from the French and Elucidated with Explanatory Notes by H.H. Harte. Dublin: 1830. 2 vols. viii,513; iv,539 pp. Lib stamps on titles. Orig bds, rebacked. *(Whitehart)* **£150 [≈ $267]**
- See also Young, Thomas

Lardner, Dionysus
- Hand-Book of Natural Philosophy. Hydrostatics, Pneumatics, and Heat. London: 1855. xv,408 pp. Frontis, 292 ills. Name on title. Orig cloth.
(Whitehart) **£18 [≈ $32]**
- Lectures on the Steam Engine ... London: 1832. 4th edn. xiv,268 pp. Frontis, 36 figs. Prelims foxed. Orig bndg, jnts sl weak.
(Whitehart) **£25 [≈ $45]**
- A Treatise on Hydrostatics and Pneumatics. London: Lardner's Cabinet Cyclopaedia, 1831. Lge 12mo. viii,353 pp. Engvd title, 130 figs. Some foxing of outer ff. Contemp half mor, rubbed. *(Bow Windows)* **£20 [≈ $36]**

Larmor, Joseph
- Mathematical and Physical Papers. Cambridge: UP, 1928-29. 1st edn. 2 vols. Roy 8vo. Corrigenda slip vol 2. Orig cloth, sl dusty. 2 slips with MS notes by the author laid in. *(Gaskell)* **£200 [≈ $356]**
- Mathematical and Physical Papers. Cambridge: 1929. 2 vols. Lge 8vo. xii,679; xxxii,831 pp. Lib stamp on titles & front pastedowns. Orig cloth.
(Weiner) **£195 [≈ $347]**

Laslett, Peter (editor)
- The Physical Basis of Mind: A Series of Broadcast Talks ... Oxford: Blackwell, 1950. 1st edn. viii,79 pp. Name. Orig cloth. Price-clipped dw. *(Caius)* **$75 [≈ £42]**

Latham, Peter M.
- The Collected Works ... With Memoir by Sir Thomas Watson. London: 1876-78. 1st edn. 2 vols. 480; 575 pp. Orig bndg.
(Fye) **$225 [≈ £126]**

Laurence, John
- The Fruit-Garden Kalendar: or, A Summary of the Art of Managing the Fruit-Garden. London: 1718. 1st edn. 8vo. [ii],vi,v, [i], 149,[3] pp. Fldg plate, text ills. Lacks half-title. Later sprinkled calf, jnt weak.
(Henly) **£100 [≈ $178]**
- A New System of Agriculture. Being a Complete Body of Husbandry and Gardening ... London: for Tho. Woodward, 1726. 1st edn. Folio. [xxiv],456 pp. Frontis, 2 plates, w'cut ornaments. Contemp calf, few scrapes. Earl of Hadington b'plate.
(Sotheran's) **£598 [≈ $1,064]**

Lavater, Jean-Caspar
- Essays on Physiognomy ... Translated from the last Paris Edition by the Rev. C. Moore ... London: 1797. 4 vols. 243; 186; 288; 334 pp. Num engvd plates (inc 3 by William Blake). Later leather. *(Fye)* **$500 [≈ £281]**
- Essays on Physiognomy ... also One Hundred Physiognomical Rules ... and a Memoir of the Author. Translated by T. Holcroft. London: [ca 1886]. 19th edn. cxxviii,507,]4] pp. Port,

num ills. Orig cloth, v sl worn & dust stained.
(*Whitehart*) £35 [≈ $62]

Laveran, A.
- Paludism. Translated by J.W. Martin.
London: New Sydenham Society, 1893. 8vo.
xii, 197 pp. 6 plates. Endpapers sl browned.
Orig cloth.   (*David White*) £32 [≈ $57]

LaWall, Charles
- The Curious Lore of Drugs and Medicines
(Four Thousand Years of Pharmacy). Garden
City, New York: 1927. 1st edn. 665 pp. Orig
bndg.   (*Fye*) $60 [≈ £34]

Lawrence, John
- The New Farmer's Calendar; or, Monthly
Remembrancer, for all kinds of Country
Business ... By a Farmer and Breeder.
London: C. Whittingham, for H.D. Symonds
..., 1800. 1st edn. 8vo. vi,[ii],616 pp. Fldg
frontis. Orig bds, jnts reprd. Anon.
(*Burmester*) £150 [≈ $267]

Lawrence, R.M.
- Primitive Psycho-Therapy & Quackery.
London: 1910. 1st edn. 8vo. Orig bndg.
(*Deja Vu*) £60 [≈ $107]

Lawrence, Sir William
- Lectures on Physiology, Zoology, and the
Natural History of Man. Delivered at the
Royal College of Surgeons. London: 1823.
3rd edn. 8vo. xix,496 pp. 13 plates. Sl foxing
& soiling. Sm tear in fldg plate without loss.
Contemp half calf, sl rubbed.
(*Wheldon & Wesley*) £40 [≈ $71]
- A Treatise on the Diseases of the Eye. Third
Edition, revised ... London: Bohn, 1844. 8vo.
xv,820 pp. Minor foxing. Name cut from
title. Rec bds.   (*Fenning*) £45 [≈ $80]

Lawson, William
- A New Orchard and Garden ... with The
Country Housewife's Garden, etc., reprinted
from the 3rd edition with a Preface by E.S.
Rohde. London: Cresset Press, 1927. One of
650. Sm 4to. xxvi,116 pp. W'cuts. Half
parchment. Dw (trifle frayed).
(*Wheldon & Wesley*) £45 [≈ $80]

Lawson, William & Hunter, Charles D.
- Ten Years of Gentleman Farming at
Blennerhasset, with Co-operative Objects.
London: Longmans, Green, 1874. 408 pp.
Name cut from title. Orig brown cloth, sl
damp stain.   (*Carol Howard*) £43 [≈ $77]
- Ten Years of Gentleman Farming in
Blennerhasset, with Co-operative Objects.

London: Longmans, Green, 1874. 1st edn. Cr
8vo. 2 cold plans. Orig cloth.
(*Georges*) £125 [≈ $223]

Lawson, William & Markham, Gervase
- A New Orchard and Garden ... With
[Gervase Markham's] The Country
Housewifes Garden ... London: Okes for
Harrison, 1631. 4th edn. Sm 4to. [viii],74,
[ii],77-134 pp. Colophon at end. Num w'cuts.
Sm worm in gutter. 19th c bds, rebacked.
STC 17396.   (*Vanbrugh*) £275 [≈ $490]

Lea, I.
- Contributions to Geology. Phila: 1833. Roy
8vo. 227 pp. 6 tinted plates. Blind stamp on
title. New bds.
(*Wheldon & Wesley*) £80 [≈ $142]

Le Clerc, Daniel
- The Compleat Surgeon. Second Part ...
Containing an Exact and Complete Treatise
of Osteology ... London: 1710. x,348 pp.
Contemp calf, rebacked.
(*Whitehart*) £120 [≈ $214]
- The Compleat Surgeon. or, The Whole Art of
Surgery explain'd in a most familiar Method.
London: 1727. 6th edn. Occas sl foxing. Tear
in last page. Contemp Cambridge calf, sl
worn, new label. (*Whitehart*) £350 [≈ $623]

Le Clerc, Sebastien
- Practical Geometry: Or, A New and Easy
Method of Treating that Art ... London: for
T. Bowles, Print and Map-Seller ..., 1727.
3rd edn. 8vo. 195,[6] pp. 80 engvd letterpress
plates. Occas sl soiling. Contemp panelled
calf, front jnt cracking.
(*Young's*) £260 [≈ $463]

Lee, A.B.
- The Microtomist's Vade-Mecum. A
Handbook of the Methods of Microscopic
Anatomy. London: Churchill, 1913. 7th edn.
8vo. x,526 pp. Orig cloth, rubbed, sm split hd
of spine.   (*David White*) £20 [≈ $36]

Lee, Henry
- Lectures on Syphilitic and Vaccino-Syphilitic
Inoculations: Their Prevention, Diagnosis,
and Treatment. London: 1863. 2nd edn.
[iii],335,[32 ctlg] pp. 5 cold plates. Prelims sl
spotted. Orig cloth, edges rubbed.
(*Francis Edwards*) £40 [≈ $71]

Lee, J.E.
- Note-Book of an Amateur Geologist. London:
1881. 1st edn. 8vo. v,90 pp. Woodburytype
frontis, 209 plates, 17 text figs. Title
browned. Cloth gilt.   (*Henly*) £48 [≈ $85]

Leech, J.H.

- British Pyralides, including the Pterophoridae. London: 1886. Cr 8vo. viii,122 pp. 18 hand cold plates. New cloth.
(Wheldon & Wesley) **£50 [≈ $89]**

Lees, F.A.

- The Flora of West Yorkshire. London: 1888. 8vo. xii,843 pp. Cold map. Orig cloth, spine faded, jnts loose.
(Wheldon & Wesley) **£40 [≈ $71]**

Le Fanu, William

- A Bio-Bibliography of Edward Jenner 1749-1823. London: 1951. 1st edn. One of 1000. 8vo. 176 pp. Ills. Orig bndg.
(Robertshaw) **£35 [≈ $62]**
- A Bio-Bibliography of Edward Jenner 1749-1823. London: 1951. 1st edn. 176 pp. Orig bndg.
(Fye) **$60 [≈ £34]**

Le Grand, Anthony

- Entire Body of Philosophy, according to the Principles of the Famous Renate Des Cartes, in Three Books ... Now Carefully Translated ... London: 1694. 1st edn in English. [xxviii],403, [2],[264] pp. 102 engvs (1 fldg). Contemp leather, bds loose.
(Gach) **$650 [≈ £365]**

Lehmann, K.B. & Neumann, R.

- Atlas and Essentials of Bacteriology. London: Bailliere, Tindall & Cox, 1897. 8vo. vii,204 pp. 63 chromolitho plates. Cloth.
(Savona) **£30 [≈ $53]**

Le Keux, J. & Sands, R.

- Illustrations of Natural History: embracing a Series of Engravings and Descriptive Accounts ... [Mammals]. London: [183-]. 8vo. vi,384 pp. 50 plates of 114 figs. Half calf, somewhat worn.
(Wheldon & Wesley) **£50 [≈ $89]**

Lemery, Louis

- A Treatise of all Sorts of Foods, Both Animal and Vegetable: also of Drinkables ... Translated by D. Hay, M.D. ... Third Edition ... London: for T. Osborne, 1745. Lge 12mo. xii,372,[xxiv] pp. Approbation leaf before title. V sl marg worm. Contemp calf, spine ends sl chipped.
(Gough) **£350 [≈ $623]**

Lemery, Nicholas

- A Course of Chymistry ... Second Edition, very much Inlarged, translated ... by Walter Harris ... London: for Walter Kettilby, 1686. 8vo. [27],548,[16] pp. Imprimatur leaf, advt

leaf. 3 plates. Contemp calf, rebacked.
(Hemlock) **$825 [≈ £463]**
- A Course of Chymistry, containing an easie Method of Preparing those Chymical Medicines which are used in Physick ... London: R.N. for Kettilby, 1698. 3rd edn. 7 plates & Explication. New calf, orig bds laid down. Wing L.1040.
(P and P Books) **£280 [≈ $498]**

Lendenfeld, R. von

- A Monograph of the Horny Sponges. London: 1889. 4to. 936 pp. 51 plates. Sl foxing. Cloth, inner jnts loose.
(Wheldon & Wesley) **£150 [≈ $267]**

Leno, John Bedford

- The Art of Boot and Shoemaking, a Practical Handbook ... London: 1905. 8vo. xvi, 237 pp. Frontis, ills. Orig cloth. *(Weiner)* **£25 [≈ $45]**

Leonardo, Richard

- History of Surgery. New York: 1943. 1st edn. 504 pp. 100 plates. Ex-lib. Orig bndg.
(Fye) **$200 [≈ £112]**

Lesley, J.P.

- Manual of Coal and its Topography ... Phila: Lippincott, 1856. 1st edn. 12mo. 224 pp. 66 text ills. Orig cloth, spine extrs & rear outer hinge frayed. ALS by author inserted.
(Karmiole) **$100 [≈ £56]**

Leslie, A.S. & Shipley, A.E.

- The Grouse in Health and Disease. Popular Edition. London: 1912. 8vo. xx,472 pp. Map, 21 plates (12 cold). Cloth, trifle used.
(Wheldon & Wesley) **£30 [≈ $53]**

Leslie, John

- The Philosophy of Arithmetic: exhibiting a Progressive View of the Theory and Practice of Calculation ... Edinburgh: 1817. 1st edn. 8vo. iv,240 pp. Fldg table, text diags. 1 gathering sl foxed. Polished calf, spine label defective. *(Weiner)* **£75 [≈ $134]**

Less, F.A.

- The Flora of West Yorkshire. London: 1888. 8vo. xii,843 pp. Cold map. Orig cloth, spine faded, jnts loose.
(Wheldon & Wesley) **£45 [≈ $80]**

Lester-Garland, L.V.

- A Flora of the Island of Jersey with a List of the Plants of the Channel Islands in general. London: 1903. Cr 8vo. xv,205 pp. Fldg map. Cloth. *(Wheldon & Wesley)* **£30 [≈ $53]**

Letter(s) ...
- Letters and Papers on Agriculture, Planting, &c. Selected from the Correspondence-Book of the Society instituted at Bath ... Bath: R. Cruttwell ..., 1780. xii, 264, 100 pp. Occas sl marg browning. Speckled calf gilt, sl worn.
(Francis Edwards) **£165 [≈ $294]**
- Letters on Entomology, intended for the Amusement and Instruction of Young Persons, and to facilitate their acquiring a Knowledge of the Natural History of Insects. London: 1825. 8vo. viii,160 pp. 3 hand cold plates. Trifle foxed. Bds, uncut, spine worn.
(Wheldon & Wesley) **£25 [≈ $45]**

Lettsom, J.C.
- Memoirs of John Fothergill, M.D. London: 1786. 4th edn. 8vo. viii,280,[8] pp. Engvd title, 5 ports. Mod buckram.
(Wheldon & Wesley) **£70 [≈ $125]**

Leutz, Charles Roland
- Modern Radio Reception. New York: Experimenters Information, 1925. 1st edn. 8vo. 337 pp. Num ills. Orig bndg. Author's pres inscrptn. *(Schoen)* **$135 [≈ £76]**

Leutz, Charles Roland & Gable, Robert B.
- Short Waves. Altona: Leutz, 1930. 1st edn. 8vo. 384 pp. Orig bndg.
(Schoen) **$125 [≈ £70]**

Levick, G. Murray
- Antarctic Penguins. A Study of their Social Habits. London: Heinemann, 1915. 3rd imp. x,140 pp. Num photo plates. Orig dec cloth.
(High Latitude) **$50 [≈ £28]**

Lewes, George Henry
- Aristotle: A Chapter from the History of Science, including Analysis of Aristotle's Scientific Writings. London: 1864. 1st edn. 8vo. [xii],404 pp. Lib stamp on title. Orig cloth, recased. *(Gach)* **$125 [≈ £70]**
- Problems of Life and Mind ... First Series: The Foundations of a Creed. Vol. 1. Boston: Houghton, osgood, 1879. 1st Amer edn. Sm 8vo. Orig cloth. *(Gach)* **$46.50 [≈ £26]**
- Sea-Side Studies at Ilfracombe, Tenby, The Scilly Isles and Jersey. Edinburgh: Blackwood, 1858. 1st edn. 8vo. ix,414,advt pp. 7 plates. Orig cloth gilt (rubbed).
(Egglishaw) **£20 [≈ $36]**
- Sea-Side Studies at Ilfracombe, Tenby, the Scilly Isles and Jersey. London: 1858. 8vo. ix, 414 pp. 7 plates. Half calf, front jnt cracking. *(Wheldon & Wesley)* **£30 [≈ $53]**

Lewin, Philip
- The Knee and Related Structures: Injuries, deformities, Diseases, Disabilities. Phila: 1952. 1st edn in English. 914 pp. Orig bndg.
(Fye) **$75 [≈ £42]**

Lewis, H.C.
- Papers and Notes on the Glacial Geology of Great Britain and Ireland. London: 1894. lxxxi, 469 pp. 10 maps, 82 text figs. New cloth. *(Whitehart)* **£28 [≈ $50]**

Lewis, T.
- Diseases of the Heart described for Practitioners and Students. London: 1933. Reprint. xx,297 pp. 45 figs. Orig bndg, inner hinge cracked. *(Whitehart)* **£15 [≈ $27]**

Lewis, T.R.
- Physiological and Pathological Researches: being a Reprint of the Principal Scientific Writings ... London: 1888. Lge 8vo. xxxvii, 732 pp. Mtd photo frontis, 43 plates (few cold), ills. Sm tear ft of title. Orig cloth, recased. *(Weiner)* **£100 [≈ $178]**

Lewis, Thomas
- The Soldier's Heart and the Effort Syndrome. London: Shaw & Sons, (1918). 1st edn. 8vo. xi,144 pp. Erratum slip. Orig cloth.
(David White) **£85 [≈ $151]**

Lewis, W.B.
- Electrical Counting. With Special Reference to Counting Alpha and Beta Particles. Cambridge: 1942. vii,144 pp. Text figs. Orig bndg. *(Whitehart)* **£18 [≈ $32]**

Lewis, William
- Commercium Philosopho-Technicum; or, the Philosophical Commerce of Arts ... London: 1763. 4to. xviii,x, 646,[14] pp. Dble-page frontis, 5 plates. Lacks licence & privilege leaf. Polished calf, worn, front jnt cracked. *(Weiner)* **£275 [≈ $490]**
- The New Dispensatory: containing I. The Theory and Practice of Pharmacy ... V. A Collection of Cheap Remedies for the Use of the Poor ... London: J. Nourse, 1753. 1st edn. 8vo. Contemp calf, trivial wear, jnts cracked but firm. Anon. *(Georges)* **£125 [≈ $223]**
- The New Dispensatory containing I. The Theory and Practice of Pharmacy ... V. A Collection of Cheap Remedies for the Use of the Poor ... London: Nourse, 1753. 1st edn. 8vo. xii,664 pp. Contemp calf, backstrip relaid. Anon. *(David White)* **£180 [≈ $320]**

Ley, W.
- Rockets, Missiles and Space Travel. London: 1951. 1st edn. xii,436 pp. 64 figs. Cloth, sl faded. *(Whitehart)* £18 [≈ $32]

Leybourn, William
- An Introduction to Astronomy and Geography ... London: for Morden & Berry, 1675. 1st edn. 8vo. [viii],234 pp. 5 plates. Running title trimmed close in parts. Contemp calf, rebacked. Wing L.1915.
(Vanbrugh) £275 [≈ $490]
- An Introduction to Astronomy and Geography: being a Plain and Easie Treatise of the Globes. In VII Parts. London: J.C. for Robert Morden & William Berry, 1675. 8vo. Fldg plate at end. Occas headline shaved. Contemp calf, rebacked. Wing L.1915.
(Waterfield's) £125 [≈ $223]
- Leybourn's Dialling, Improv'd. Or, the Whole Art Perform'd. I. Geometrically ... Concluding with Tables ... by Henry Wilson. London: Wilford & Jauncy, 1721. 12mo. [12], 276 pp. 12 fldg plates. Orig calf, rebacked, crnrs rubbed. *(Karmiole)* $200 [≈ £112]

Lichtenstein, Ben W.
- A Textbook of Neuropathology ... Phila: W.B. Saunders, 1949. 1st edn. xviii,474 pp. Ills. Name. Orig cloth. *(Caius)* $75 [≈ £42]

Lidell, John A.
- A Treatise on Apoplexy, Cerebral Hemorrhage, Cerebral Embolism, Cerebral Gout, Cerebral Rheumatism, and Epidemic Cerebro-Spinal Meningitis. New York: William Wood, 1873. 8vo. xix,395 pp. Orig cloth, rubbed, spine worn, stain on back bd. *(Goodrich)* £295 [≈ £166]

Liebig, Justus von, Baron
- Chemistry in its Application to Agriculture and Physiology. Edited from the Manuscript of the Author by Lyon Playfair. Second Edition, with very numerous additions. London: for Taylor & Walton, 1842. 8vo. xii, 409, [1,2,8 advt] pp. Rec bds.
(Fenning) £45 [≈ $80]
- Chemistry in its Application to Agriculture and Physiology ... Edited from the Manuscript of the Author by Lyon Playfair ... Third Edition. London: for Taylor & Walton, 1843. 8vo. Orig green cloth.
(Waterfield's) £40 [≈ $71]
- Letters on Modern Agriculture. Edited by John Blyth. London: 1859. 8 advt, 4 ctlg pp. Orig cloth, mottled. *(Jarndyce)* £50 [≈ $89]
- Letters on Modern Agriculture. Edited by J. Blyth. London: 1859. 1st English edn. xxviii,

284 pp. Occas foxing. Orig cloth, dusty, sl worn, front inner hinge sl cracked but firm.
(Whitehart) £40 [≈ $71]
- The Natural Laws of Husbandry. Edited by John Blyth. London: Walton & Maberly, 1863. 4 advt, 4 ctlg pp. Orig cloth, spine sl rubbed & v sl faded. *(Jarndyce)* £65 [≈ $116]
- The Natural Laws of Husbandry. New York: 1863. 8vo. 387,[8 advt] pp. Early cloth.
(Hortulus) $60 [≈ £34]

Lilford, Lord
- Coloured Figures of the Birds of the British Islands. London: 1885-97. 1st edn. 7 vols. Roy 8vo. Port, 421 cold plates. Somewhat foxed, mainly on text. red half mor, a.e.g., jnts tender. *(Wheldon & Wesley)* £1,650 [≈ $2,937]

Lind, James
- A Treatise on the Scurvy ... London: A. Millar, 1757. 8vo. xvi,[4],476 pp. Minimal foxing. Contemp half calf, gilt spine, sl wear front jnt. *(Hemlock)* $2,000 [≈ £1,124]
- A Treatise on the Scurvy in Three Parts ... London: 1772. 3rd edn. xvi,554 pp. Some foxing. Some marg worm, affecting text minimally. Contemp calf, some worm.
(Whitehart) £180 [≈ $320]

Lind, L.R.
- Studies in Pre-Vesalian Anatomy, Biography, Translations, Documents. Phila: 1975. Lge 4to. 344 pp. Ills. Orig bndg. Dw.
(Goodrich) $65 [≈ £37]

Lindeboom, G.A.
- Bibliographia Boerhaaviana. List of Publications written or provided by H. Boerhaave or based upon his Work and Teachings. Leiden: 1959. 1st edn. 8vo. 105 pp. 4 plates. Orig bndg.
(Robertshaw) £20 [≈ $36]
- Boerhaave and his Time. Leiden: 1970. 1st edn. 174 pp. Ex-lib. *(Fye)* $50 [≈ £28]
- Herman Boerhaave, the Man and his Work. London: 1968. 1st edn. 452 pp. Dw.
(Fye) $60 [≈ £34]

Linden, Diederick Wessel
- Three Letters on Mining ... added, a Fourth Letter; setting forth, a Discovery of an Easy Method to secure Ships Bottoms from Worms. London: George Keith, 1750. 96 pp. Rec wraps. *(C.R. Johnson)* £225 [≈ $401]
- A Treatise on the Three Medicinal Waters at Llandrindod ... London: Everingham & Reynolds, 1756. Half-title. Frontis. Occas sl spotting. Contemp calf, rebacked.
(P and P Books) £250 [≈ $445]

Lindley, John
- Elements of Botany, Structural, Physiological, Systematical, and Medical. London: 1841. 8vo. iv,292 pp. Text figs. Orig cloth, reprd.
(Wheldon & Wesley) £30 [≈ $53]
- An Introduction to Botany. London: 1832. 8vo. xvi,557 pp. 6 plates. Half-title trifle soiled, edges brittle. Half cloth.
(Wheldon & Wesley) £30 [≈ $53]
- An Introduction to the Natural System of Botany. London: 1830. 1st edn. 8vo. xlviii, 374, [1] pp. Good ex-lib. Sl foxed. Half calf, sl used.   *(Wheldon & Wesley)* £60 [≈ $107]
- Ladies' Botany, or a Familiar Introduction to the Study of the Natural System of Botany. London: Ridgway, [ca 1835]. 2nd edn. 8vo. xvi, 302 pp. 25 hand cold plates. Occas sl foxing. Cloth, backstrip relaid.
(Egglishaw) £50 [≈ $89]
- Ladies' Botany ... London: Ridgway, n.d. Vol 1 4th edn, vol 2 2nd edn. 2 vols. 8vo. 50 cold plates. New qtr calf.
(Blackwell's) £210 [≈ $374]
- A Natural System of Botany, or a Systematic View of the Organisation, Natural Affinities and Geographical Distribution of the Whole Vegetable Kingdom. London: 1836. 2nd edn. 8vo. xxvi,526 pp. Sl foxed at ends. Half mor.
(Wheldon & Wesley) £60 [≈ $107]
- The Theory of Horticulture; or an Attempt to Explain the Principal Operations of Gardening upon Physiological Principles. London: 1840. 1st edn. 8vo. xvi,387 pp. Figs. Orig cloth, jnts reprd.
(Bow Windows) £45 [≈ $80]
- The Theory of Horticulture; or, An Attempt to Explain the Principal Operations of Gardening upon Physiological Principles. London: Longmans, 1840. 1st edn. 32 ctlg pp. Orig cloth, spine faded & rubbed at hd.
(Jarndyce) £30 [≈ $53]
- The Theory of Horticulture. London: 1840. 8vo. xvi,387 pp. 37 text figs. Orig cloth, reprd.   *(Wheldon & Wesley)* £40 [≈ $71]
- The Theory and Practice of Horticulture; or an Attempt to Explain the Chief Operations of Gardening upon Physiological Grounds. London: 1855. 2nd edn of Theory of Horticulture. 8vo. xvi,606 pp. Orig cloth, sl faded, sm tear in jnt.
(Wheldon & Wesley) £35 [≈ $62]

Lindley, John & Moore, T.
- The Treasury of Botany. With Numerous Illustrations by Fitch, Branston and Adlard. London: 1866. 2 vols. Sm 8vo. Minor foxing. Calf gilt, mrbld edges.
(Wheldon & Wesley) £30 [≈ $53]

- The Treasury of Botany. New Edition, with Supplement. London: 1876. 2 vols. Cr 8vo. 20 plates. Calf, rubbed.
(Wheldon & Wesley) £30 [≈ $53]
- The Treasury of Botany: a Popular Dictionary of the Vegetable Kingdom and Glossary of Botanical Terms. London: 1884. 4th edn. 2 vols. Cr 8vo. 20 plates, num text figs. Orig cloth, backstrips relaid.
(Henly) £38 [≈ $68]

Lindsay, W.L.
- A Popular History of British Lichens. London: Reeve, 1856. 1st edn. Sm 8vo. xxxii, 352 pp. 22 hand cold litho plates. Orig dec cloth.   *(Egglishaw)* £35 [≈ $62]

Linssen, E.F. (editor)
- Medical Photography in Practice. London: 1961. 1st edn. 343 pp. Ills. Orig bndg.
(Fye) $100 [≈ £56]

Linton, E.F.
- Flora of Bournemouth, including the Island of Purbeck. London: [1900]. Cr 8vo. ix,290 pp. Map. Cloth.
(Wheldon & Wesley) £20 [≈ $36]

Linton, William Richardson
- Flora of Derbyshire ... London: Bemrose & Sons, 1903. 1st edn. vii,457 pp. 2 fldg maps. Contemp cloth.   *(Gough)* £45 [≈ $80]

Lisle, Edward
- Observations in Husbandry. London: J. Hughs, for C. Hitch & L. Hawes ..., 1757. 1st edn. Lge 4to. xvi,450,[4] pp. Port frontis. Contemp calf, rebacked.
(Karmiole) $450 [≈ £253]

Lisney, A.A.
- A Bibliography of British Lepidoptera 1608 to 1799. London: Chiswick Press, 1960. One of 500. Roy 8vo. 320 pp. Frontis, 39 ills. Buckram. *(Wheldon & Wesley)* £70 [≈ $125]

Lister, A.
- A Monograph of the Mycetozoa, being a Descriptive Catalogue of the Species in the Herbarium of the British Museum. London: 1894. 8vo. 224,18 advt pp. 78 plates, 51 text figs. Stamp on title. Orig cloth, unopened.
(Egglishaw) £45 [≈ $80]
- A Monograph of the Mycetozoa. A Descriptive Catalogue of the Species in the Herbarium of the British Museum. London: BM, 1925. 3rd edn, rvsd. 8vo. xxxii,296 pp. 223 cold plates, 56 text ills. Cloth.
(Savona) £50 [≈ $89]

Lister, Joseph
- The Third Huxley Lecture. London: 1907. 1st edn. 58 pp. Orig bndg. *(Fye)* **$80** [≈ £45]

Liston, Robert
- Elements of Surgery. Phila: 1837. 1st Amer edn. 540 pp. Half leather.
(Fye) **$200** [≈ £112]
- Practical Surgery. London: 1840. 3rd edn. vi,592 pp. 150 w'engvs. Foxing on page edges. Orig cloth, rebacked.
(Whitehart) **£50** [≈ $89]

Little, E.M.
- History of the British Medical Association 1832-1932. London: B.M.A., (1932). 8vo. [6], 342 pp. Num plates. Orig cloth.
(David White) **£30** [≈ $53]

Liverpool Medical Institution
- Catalogue of the Books in the Liverpool Medical Institution Library (to the End of the Nineteenth Century). Liverpool: 1968. [iv], 569 pp. Frontis. Orig bndg.
(Whitehart) **£28** [≈ $50]

Lives of British Physicians ...
- See MacMichael, William

Lloyd, F.J.
- The Science of Agriculture. London: 1884. 1st edn. 8vo. viii,365 pp. Occas foxing. Orig cloth, sl marked. *(Bow Windows)* **£30** [≈ $53]

Lloyd, W.
- Hay-Fever, Hay-Asthma. Its Causes, Diagnosis and Treatment. London: 1908. 2nd edn. vi,102 pp. Frontis, ills. Ink dedic by author on half-title. Prelims sl foxed. Orig bndg, spine faded. *(Whitehart)* **£18** [≈ $32]

Lobb, T.
- A Practical Treatise of Painful Distempers, with some Effectual Methods of Curing them, exemplified in a great Variety of suitable Histories. London: 1739. xxx,[2], 320,[14] pp. Contemp mottled calf, rebacked, edges & crnrs worn. *(Whitehart)* **£120** [≈ $214]

Lobstein, John Fred.
- A Treatise on the Structure, Function and Diseases of the Human Sympathetic Nerve, Illustrated with Plates. Translated from the Latin, with Notes. Phila: Auner, 1831. 1st edn in English. 158 pp. 6 plates. Some marking, plates clean. Orig linen, spotted.
(Goodrich) **$175** [≈ £98]

Locke, Richard Adams
- The Moon Hoax; or, a Discovery that the Moon has a Vast Population of Human Beings. New York: William Gowans, 1859. Frontis. Lib stamp on title. Rebound in leather. *(Key Books)* **$165** [≈ £93]

Locket, G.H., & others
- British Spiders. London: Ray Society, 1951-74. 3 vols. 8vo. 612 maps, 471 text figs. Cloth. *(Wheldon & Wesley)* **£35** [≈ $62]

Lockyer, J. Norman
- The Spectroscope and its Applications. London: Macmillan, 1873. 2nd edn. 126 pp, inc advt plate. Cold plate, ills. Orig cloth. *(Jermy & Westerman)* **£20** [≈ $36]

Lodge, Oliver J.
- Lightning Conductors and Lightning Guards. London: Whittaker, 1892. 1st edn. 12mo. xii, 544 pp. Num ills. Orig bndg, hd of spine sl defective. *(Key Books)* **$55** [≈ £31]
- Modern Views of Electricity. London: 1889. xvi, 422 pp. 55 figs. Sev lib stamps. Orig bndg, spine defective.
(Whitehart) **£18** [≈ $32]

Lomax, Montagu
- The Experiences of an Asylum Doctor. With Suggestions for Asylum and Lunacy Law Reform. London: Allen & Unwin, [1921]. 1st edn. 255, [1] pp. Pencil notes. Name. Orig cloth. *(Caius)* **$50** [≈ £28]

The London and Country Brewer ...
- The London and Country Brewer, containing the Whole Art of Brewing all sorts of Malt-Liquors ... Seventh Edition. London: (1758)-59. 4 parts in one vol. 8vo. 4 ff, 332, [4] pp. Sep title to each part. Old calf, worn, backstrip relaid. *(Weiner)* **£200** [≈ $356]

Long, Esmond
- A History of Pathology. Baltimore: 1928. 1st edn. 291 pp. Orig bndg. *(Fye)* **$125** [≈ £70]

Longfield, C.
- The Dragonflies of the British Isles. London: Warne, Wayside and Woodland Series, 1949. 2nd edn. Cr 8vo. 256 pp. 16 cold & 42 other plates, text figs. Orig cloth gilt. Dw. *(Egglishaw)* **£30** [≈ $53]
- The Dragonflies of the British Isles. London: (1949). 2nd edn, enlgd. Sm 8vo. 256 pp. 16 cold & num other ills. Orig cloth. *(Bow Windows)* **£40** [≈ $71]

Longmore, Thomas
- A Treatise on Gunshot Wounds. Phila: 1862. 1st edn. 132 pp. Orig bndg, fine.
  (Fye) **$400 [≈ £225]**

Longstreth, Morris
- Rheumatism, Gout and Some Allied Disorders. New York: Wood Library, 1882. 8vo. 280 pp. Orig bndg, hd of spine sl worn.
  (Goodrich) **$45 [≈ £25]**

Lonsdale, Henry
- A Sketch of the Life and Writings of Robert Knox, the Anatomist. London: 1870. xx, 420 pp. Frontis port. Orig cloth, backstrip crudely relaid. *(Whitehart)* **£35 [≈ $62]**
- A Sketch of the Life and Writings of Robert Knox The Anatomist. London: Macmillan, 1870. 420 pp. Frontis port. Orig bndg.
  (Goodrich) **$75 [≈ £42]**

Lord, W.B.
- Crab, Shrimp, and Lobster Lore ... London: 1867. 1st edn. Sm 8vo. xvi,122,[6 advt] pp. Frontis, text ills. Occas spots. Orig pict gilt cloth. *(Bow Windows)* **£45 [≈ $80]**

Lorentz, Hendrik Anton
- Clerk Maxwell's Electromagnetic Theory; the Rede Lecture for 1923. Cambridge: 1923. 8vo. 35 pp. Orig ptd card wraps.
  (Weiner) **£20 [≈ $36]**
- The Theory of Electrons and its Application to the Phenomena of Light and Radiant Heat ... Leipzig: Teubner, 1906. 2nd edn. 8vo. 343 pp. Edges worn, spine browned.
  (Key Books) **$55 [≈ £31]**

Loudon, Jane
- Instructions in Gardening for Ladies. London: Murray, 1840. 1st edn. 12mo. xii, 406, [8 advt] pp. Engvd title. Orig dec green cloth gilt, trifle faded. *(Gough)* **£40 [≈ $71]**
- The Ladies Companion to the Flower Garden ... Fourth Edition. London: William Smith, 1846. viii,351,[16 advt] pp. Hand cold frontis. Orig dec green cloth gilt, a.e.g., spine ends trifle rubbed. *(Gough)* **£48 [≈ $85]**
- The Ladies Companion to the Flower Garden ... Sixth Edition. London: Bradbury & Evans, 1853. 12mo. viii,355 pp. Hand cold frontis. Orig dec green cloth gilt, faded, ft of spine trifle rubbed. *(Gough)* **£40 [≈ $71]**
- The Ladies Country Companion; or, How to Enjoy a Country Life Rationally. Second Edition, Improved and Enlarged. London: Longman ..., 1846. 8vo. 436,[30 ctlg] pp. Frontis (spotted), 18 w'cut ills. Orig cloth.
  (Clark) **£100 [≈ $178]**

- The Ladies' Flower Garden of Ornamental Annuals. London: 1840. 1st edn. 4to. 48 hand cold plates. Contemp half mor.
  (Wheldon & Wesley) **£2,000 [≈ $3,560]**
- The Ladies' Flower Garden of Ornamental Bulbous Plants. London: 1841. 1st edn. 4to. 58 hand cold plates. Half mor.
  (Wheldon & Wesley) **£2,000 [≈ $3,560]**
- The Ladies' Flower Garden of Ornamental Perennials. London: 1843-44. 1st edn. 2 vols. 4to. 96 hand cold plates. Half calf, a.e.g., trifle rubbed.
  (Wheldon & Wesley) **£3,500 [≈ $6,230]**
- The Ladies' Flower Garden of Ornamental Greenhouse Plants. London: 1848. 1st edn. 4to. 42 hand cold plates. Sl foxing at beginning. Half mor, a.e.g., trifle rubbed.
  (Wheldon & Wesley) **£1,750 [≈ $3,115]**
- My Own Garden, or, The Young Gardener's Yearbook. London: Kerby & Son, 1855. 1st edn. 12mo. iv,98,[2 advt] pp. 4 hand cold plates. Text sl spotted. Orig pict green cloth gilt, sl marked & faded. *(Gough)* **£50 [≈ $89]**

Loudon, John Claudius
- Arboretum et Fruticetum Britannicum; or, the Trees and Shrubs of Britain ... London: for the author, 1838. 1st edn. 8 vols. 8vo. 412 plates. Contemp green half mor, gilt spines.
  (Spelman) **£320 [≈ $570]**
- Arboretum et Fruticetum Britannicum; or the Trees and Shrubs of Great Britain, Native and Foreign, Hardy and Half Hardy. London: 1854. 2nd edn. 8 vols. 8vo. ccxxx,2694 pp. 412 hand cold plates, 2546 text figs. Unfoxed. Pigskin gilt.
  (Wheldon & Wesley) **£800 [≈ $1,424]**
- Arboretum et Fruticetum Britannicum; or, the Trees and Shrubs of Britain ... London: 1844. 2nd edn. 8 vols (4 text, 4 plates). 412 plates, 2546 text figs. Occas foxing. Orig green cloth, partly unopened, few chips & sm splits. *(Francis Edwards)* **£210 [≈ $374]**
- An Encyclopaedia of Trees and Shrubs ... for the Use of Nurserymen, Gardeners, and Foresters. London: 1869. Thick 8vo. lxvi, 1162, [2 advt] pp. Ca 2100 text engvs. Title sl foxed. Rec cloth.
  (Bow Windows) **£60 [≈ $107]**
- The Green-House Companion. Principal Green-House Plants in Cultivation: with a Descriptive Catalogue ... London: 1832. 3rd edn. 8vo. xii,408 pp. Hand cold frontis, 7 text figs. Orig cloth, label worn.
  (Henly) **£60 [≈ $107]**
- Loudon's Encyclopaedia of Plants ... New Edition, Corrected to the Present Time ... Edited by Mrs. Loudon and Others. London: 1855. Thick 8vo. xxii,1574,24 advt pp. Num

text ills. Title dust marked. Rec half mor, t.e.g.   *(Bow Windows)* **£85 [≈ $151]**
- Trees and Shrubs: an Abridgment of the Arboretum et Fruticetum Britannicum. London: Warne, 1875. 8vo. lxxii,1162 pp. Over 2000 text figs. New cloth, old calf backstrip laid down. *(Egglishaw)* **£48 [≈ $85]**

Louis, Pierre C.A.
- Pathological Researches on Phthisis. London: 1835. li,388 pp. Orig cloth, crnrs sl worn, unlettered reback.   *(Whitehart)* **£40 [≈ $71]**
- Researches on Phthisis. Anatomical, Pathological and Therapeutical ... Second Edition Considerably Enlarged. Translated by Walter Hayle. London: Sydenham Society, 1846. 8vo. xxxv,[1],571,[1] pp. Orig cloth.
                              (Hemlock) **$225 [≈ £126]**

Lousley, J.E.
- Wild Flowers of Chalk & Limestone. London: New Naturalist, 1950. 1st edn. xvii,254 pp. Ills. Dw (sl soiled).
                        (Francis Edwards) **£30 [≈ $53]**

Love, Augustus Edward Hough
- Some Problems of Geodynamics. Cambridge: UP, 1911. 1st edn. Roy 8vo. xxvii,180 pp. Orig cloth.   *(Gaskell)* **£90 [≈ $160]**
- Theoretical Mechanics. An Introductory Treatise on the Principles of Dynamics. Cambridge: UP, 1906. 2nd edn. 8vo. xvi,367 pp. Orig cloth.   *(Gaskell)* **£35 [≈ $62]**

Love, J.K.
- Diseases of the Ear: for Practitioners and Students of Medicine. London: 1904. xvi,339 pp. 2 cold plates, 54 stereo ills, 63 text ills. Orig bndg.   *(Whitehart)* **£38 [≈ $68]**

Love, John
- Geodaesia: or The Art of Surveying and Measuring of Land Made Easy ... Also, How to Lay Out New Lands in America, or Elsewhere ... The Fourth Edition. London: Bettesworth & Hitch, 1731. 8vo. [20],196, [16],4,[26] pp. Diags & tables. Rec calf.
                          (Karmiole) **$150 [≈ £84]**

Lovett, Robert
- The Treatment of Infantile Paralysis. Phila: 1916. 1st edn. 163 pp. Orig bndg.
                              (Fye) **$125 [≈ £70]**
- The Treatment of Infantile Paralysis. Phila: 1917. 2nd edn. 175 pp. Num ills. Orig bndg.
                              (Fye) **$75 [≈ £42]**

Low, David
- Elements of Practical Agriculture ... London:

1838. 2nd edn. 8vo. xvi,719,[16 advt] pp. Text ills. Few pencil notes, v sl marg browning. Orig cloth, backstrip relaid, crnrs sl bumped & worn.
                      (Francis Edwards) **£45 [≈ $80]**

Low, R.
- Amazon Parrots. London: 1983. One of 475. Folio. 178 pp. 28 cold plates by Elizabeth Butterfield. Orig silk. Box.
              (Wheldon & Wesley) **£595 [≈ $1,059]**

Low, R.C. & Dodds, T.C.
- Atlas of Bacteriology. Edinburgh: Livingstone, 1947. 1st edn. Roy 8vo. 104 plates. Cloth. Dw.   *(Savona)* **£20 [≈ $36]**

Lowe, E.J.
- Fern Growing. Fifty Years' Experience in Crossing and Cultivation with a List of the most important Varieties ... New York: 1898. Sm 4to. xi,196 pp. Port frontis, 2 plates (1 cold), 59 text ills. Occas sl spotting. Orig gilt dec cloth, sl rubbed.
                        (Francis Edwards) **£45 [≈ $80]**
- A Natural History of British Grasses. London: 1858. 1st edn. Roy 8vo. vi,245 pp. 74 cold plates. Orig cloth, fine.
                              (Henly) **£85 [≈ $151]**
- A Natural History of British Grasses. London: 1862. Roy 8vo. 245 pp. 74 cold plates. Orig cloth, spine faded.
                    (Wheldon & Wesley) **£35 [≈ $62]**
- A Natural History of British Grasses. London: Groombridge, 1865. Roy 8vo. 245 pp. 74 cold plates. Orig green cloth, sl wear to edges of spine.
                      (Carol Howard) **£80 [≈ $142]**
- A Natural History of British Grasses. London: 1865. Roy 8vo. vi,245 pp. 74 cold plates. Orig cloth, sl worn & loose.
                    (Wheldon & Wesley) **£35 [≈ $62]**
- A Natural History of British Grasses. London: 1868. 8vo. vi,245 pp. 74 cold plates. Green half mor gilt, a.e.g., fine.
                    (Wheldon & Wesley) **£50 [≈ $89]**
- A Natural History of British Grasses. Third Edition. London: 1891. Lge 8vo. viii, 245 pp. 74 cold plates. Minor marks. Orig cloth, spine ends & crnr tips v sl rubbed.
                        (Bow Windows) **£60 [≈ $107]**
- A Natural History of New and Rare Ferns, none of which are included in "Ferns, British and Exotic". London: Groombridge, 1862. Roy 8vo. viii,192 pp. 72 cold plates, w'cuts in text. Half mor, jnts sl rubbed.
                          (Egglishaw) **£45 [≈ $80]**
- Our Native Ferns. London: Bell, 1874. 1st edn. 2 vols. 348,advt; 492,advt pp. 36 + 42

cold plates, w'engvs. Occas sl foxing. Orig
green cloth gilt, sl worn.
(Carol Howard) £60 [≈ $107]

Lowe, John
- A Treatise on the Solar Creation and
Universal Deluge of the Earth ... By a Native
of Manchester. London: for the author, [ca
1790]. 1st edn. 8vo. [2],viii,viii subscribers,
361 pp. Sl browned & foxed. Contemp calf,
worn.   (D & D Galleries) $150 [≈ £84]

Lowe, R.T.
- A Manual Flora of Madeira and the Adjacent
Islands of Porto Santo and the Desertas. Vol
1 and Vol 2 Part 1 [all published]. London:
[1857-] 1868 [-72]. 8vo. xii,618,113 pp. Sl
foxing. Orig cloth, trifle used, inner jnts
weak.   (Wheldon & Wesley) £75 [≈ $134]

Lowe, Robert
- General View of the Agriculture of the
County of Nottingham. London: Richard
Phillips, 1798. 8vo. xii,192,[16 advt] pp. Fldg
hand cold map. Orig bds, paper label, uncut,
crnrs sl bumped, spine ends reprd.
(Spelman) £80 [≈ $142]

Lowell, Percival
- Annals of the Lowell Observatory. Vols I-III.
Boston, New York & Cambridge: 1898-1905.
3 vols, all published. Lge 4to. 2 cold frontis,
fldg map, plates, ills. Vols 1 & 2 half mor
(rubbed), vol 3 orig ptd bds (backstrip relaid).
(Weiner) £500 [≈ $890]

Lower, Richard
- Richard Lower's Vindicatio. A Defence of the
Experimental Method. A Facsimile Edition
... Edited by K. Dewhurst. Oxford: 1983.
xxxiv, 314 pp. Orig bndg.
(Whitehart) £38 [≈ $68]

Lowis, L.
- Familiar Indian Flowers. London: 1878.
Imperial 8vo. 30 cold plates. Orig cloth.
(Wheldon & Wesley) £50 [≈ $89]

Lowne, B.T.
- The Anatomy, Physiology, Morphology, and
Development of the Blow-Fly ... London:
1890-95. 2 vols in one. 8vo. 52 plates. Few
blind stamps & pencil notes. Half mor, sl
rubbed.   (Wheldon & Wesley) £60 [≈ $107]

Lubbock, Sir John
- Ants, Bees, and Wasps: a Record of
Observations on the Habits of the Social
Hymenoptera. Seventh Edition. London: Intl
Scientific Series, 1885. 8vo. xix,450 pp. 5

cold plates. Orig cloth, spine dull & sl
fingered at ends, sm ink stain.
(Bow Windows) £25 [≈ $45]
- Scientific Lectures. London: 1879. 1st edn.
8vo. x,187,4,35 pp. Cold frontis, 148 text
figs. Sm lib stamp on title. Cloth, backstrip
relaid.   (Henly) £18 [≈ $32]

Lubbock, R.
- Observations on the Fauna of Norfolk.
Norwich: 1879. 2nd edn. 8vo. xxxvi,239 pp.
Map, 2 plates. Unstamped ex-lib. Half calf.
(Wheldon & Wesley) £50 [≈ $89]

Lucas, A.
- Ancient Egyptian Materials and Industries.
Third Edition, revised. London: Edward
Arnold, 1948. 8vo. [ii],570 pp. Orig cloth gilt.
Dw.   (Blackwell's) £50 [≈ $89]

Lucas, A.H.S. & Le Souef, W.H.D.
- The Birds of Australia. Melbourne: 1911. 1st
edn. 8vo. xii,489 pp. Cold frontis, num ills
(some cold). Orig cloth.
(Wheldon & Wesley) £35 [≈ $62]

Lucas, W.J.
- British Dragonflies (Odonata). London: 1900.
1st edn. xiv,356 pp. 27 cold plates, 57 ills.
Orig illust cloth, sl worn, hinges tender.
(Francis Edwards) £45 [≈ $80]
- British Dragonflies (Odonata). London:
Upcott Gill, 1900. 8vo. xiv,356 pp. 27 cold
plates, 57 text figs. Orig dec buckram, hinges
reprd.   (Egglishaw) £70 [≈ $125]

Ludovici, L.J.
- Cone of Oblivion. A Vendetta in Science.
[The ether controversy]. London: 1961. 224
pp. Orig bndg.   (Whitehart) £15 [≈ $27]

Ludwick, Maria Thompson
- Indium. New York: Indium Corp., 1950. 1st
edn. 8vo. 276 pp. Frontis, ills. Lib pocket.
Orig bndg.   (Schoen) $150 [≈ £84]

Lukin, J. (editor)
- Turning Lathes: a Manual for Technical
Schools and Apprentices ... London: 1889.
1st edn. vii,160,[34 advt] pp. 194 text ills.
Orig pict cloth, sl worn.
(Whitehart) £25 [≈ $45]

Lund, Edward
- Hunterian Lectures on some of the Injuries
and Diseases of the Neck and Head, the
Genito-Urinary Organs, and the Rectum.
London: 1886. 1st edn. 116 pp. 4 photo ills.
Orig bndg.   (Fye) $175 [≈ £98]

Lund, F.B.
- Greek Medicine. New York: Clio Medica, 1936. xiii,161 pp. 7 ills. Orig bndg.
(Whitehart) **£18 [≈ $32]**

Lydekker, R.
- Catalogue of the Fossil Birds in the British Museum ... London: 1891. 1st edn. 8vo. xxviii,368,[18] pp. 75 figs. Occas spotting. Lib stamp on title verso. Orig cloth.
(Bow Windows) **£65 [≈ $116]**
- The Game Animals of India Burma Malaya and Tibet. London: Rowland Ward, 1924. 412 pp. Ills. Orig green cloth.
(Trophy Room Books) **$325 [≈ £183]**
- A Geographical History of Mammals. Cambridge: 1896. 8vo. xii,400 pp. Map, text figs. Cloth, trifle used.
(Wheldon & Wesley) **£36 [≈ $64]**
- Guide to the Great Game Animals (Ungulata) in the British Museum (Nat. Hist.). London: 1907. 8vo. viii,93 pp. 50 ills on 20 plates & in text. Bds. Anon.
(Wheldon & Wesley) **£25 [≈ $45]**
- A Handbook to the Marsupialia and Monotremata. London: Lloyd's Natural History, 1896. Cr 8vo. xvi,320 pp. 38 cold plates. Good ex-lib. Cloth.
(Wheldon & Wesley) **£30 [≈ $53]**
- A Handbook to the Marsupialia and Monotremata. London: 1896. Cr 8vo. xvi,320 pp. 38 cold plates. Cloth.
(Wheldon & Wesley) **£35 [≈ $62]**
- Horns and Hoofs, or Chapters on Hoofed Animals. London: 1893. 8vo. xv,411 pp. 82 text figs. Cloth.
(Wheldon & Wesley) **£45 [≈ $80]**
- Wild Life of the World. London: [1916]. 3 vols. 4to. 120 cold plates, over 600 engvs. Orig cloth, trifle used.
(Wheldon & Wesley) **£120 [≈ $214]**

Lydekker, R. & Blaine, G.
- Catalogue of the Ungulate Mammals in the British Museum. London: 1913-16. 5 vols. 8vo. 225 text figs. Lib stamp on 3 titles. Orig cloth.
(Egglishaw) **£80 [≈ $142]**

Lyell, Sir Charles
- Elements of Geology. London: Murray, 1838. 1st edn. Lge 12mo. xix,543 pp. Hand cold frontis, 294 text ills. Orig qtr green cloth, paper label, bds trifle marked.
(Gough) **£200 [≈ $356]**
- Elements of Geology. London: 1838. 1st edn. 12mo. xix,[1],543,[1] pp. Cold frontis, num text figs. Some colour transfer from frontis to title. Orig bds, worn, jnts torn.
(Bow Windows) **£170 [≈ $303]**

- Elements of Geology. London: 1838. 1st edn. 12mo. Cold frontis, num text figs. Few sl marks. Orig cloth backed bds, marked, crnr tips worn.
(Bow Windows) **£200 [≈ $356]**
- Elements of Geology. London: 1841. 2nd edn. 2 vols. Post 8vo. 2 cold maps, 2 cold & 4 plain plates. Orig bds, cloth backs, vol 1 recased, sm stamp on cvrs.
(Wheldon & Wesley) **£95 [≈ $169]**
- The Geological Evidences of the Antiquity of Man ... London: Murray, 1863. 1st edn. 8vo. xii, 520,[32] advt dated Jan 1863] pp. Appendix 507-513, [1]. 2 plates, 58 ills. Sl pencil marks. Rec cloth.
(Fenning) **£85 [≈ $151]**
- The Geological Evidences of the Antiquity of Man. With Remarks on Theories of the Origin of Species by Variation. Phila: George W. Childs, 1863. 2nd Amer edn. 8vo. x,526 pp. W'cut ills. Orig dec bndg, tear in cloth of spine.
(Key Books) **$50 [≈ £28]**
- The Geological Evidences of the Antiquity of Man with Remarks on Theories of the Origin of Species by Variation. Third Edition, revised. London: 1863. 8vo. xvi,551 pp. Frontis, ills. Orig cloth, sl soiled, backstrip relaid.
(Weiner) **£75 [≈ $134]**
- The Geological Evidences of the Antiquity of Man ... Phila: George W. Childs, 1863. 1st Amer edn. Tall 8vo. x,518 pp. 2 plates, 58 text ills. Orig cloth, sm stain upper spine.
(Karmiole) **$85 [≈ £48]**
- The Geological Evidences of the Antiquity of Man. London: 1873. 4th edn. 8vo. xix,572 pp. 2 plates, 56 text figs. Cloth gilt, sl worn.
(Henly) **£48 [≈ $85]**
- The Geological Evidences of the Antiquity of Man. London: 1873. 4th edn. 8vo. xix,572 pp. 2 plates, 56 text figs. Orig cloth gilt, sl worn.
(Henly) **£48 [≈ $85]**
- A Manual of Elementary Geology ... Fifth Edition, greatly enlarged ... London: Murray, 1855. 8vo. xvi,655 pp. Frontis. Stain upper crnr 1st few ff. Rec bds.
(Fenning) **£38.50 [≈ $69]**
- Principles of Geology ... Second Edition. London: 1832-33. 3 vols. 8vo. 11 plates (4 cold), text figs. Marg of 1 leaf with with sl loss. Contemp half calf, rubbed, ft of 1 spine sl chipped. *(Bow Windows)* **£700 [≈ $1,246]**
- Principles of Geology. London: 1834. 3rd edn. 4 vols. Sm 8vo. Frontis, 13 plates & maps (some cold). Frontis foxed. Contemp half calf, trifle rubbed.
(Wheldon & Wesley) **£150 [≈ $267]**
- Principles of Geology ... Sixth Edition. London: 1840. 3 vols. Sm 8vo. Fldg maps, plates, ills. Lib stamps on titles. New cloth backed bds.
(Weiner) **£150 [≈ $267]**

- Principles of Geology ... London: 1847. 7th edn. 8vo. xvii,810,16 pp. 7 maps, 5 plates. Orig cloth gilt, backstrip relaid.
  (Henly) £85 [≈ $151]
- Principles of Geology. London: 1847. 7th edn, rvsd. 8vo. xvi,[i],810 pp. 7 maps, 4 plates, 98 text figs. Orig cloth, spine reprd.
  (Wheldon & Wesley) £85 [≈ $151]
- The Student's Elements of Geology. London: 1871. 1st edn. 8vo. xix,624 pp. Frontis, ills. Prize mor gilt, a.e.g., rubbed.
  (Weiner) £21 [≈ $37]
- The Student's Elements of Geology. London: 1874. 2nd edn. 12mo. xix,672 pp. Frontis, table, 645 text ills. Orig cloth gilt.
  (Henly) £25 [≈ $45]

Lyell, D.
- The African Elephant and its Hunters. London: 1924. 1st edn. 221 pp. Orig bndg.
  (Trophy Room Books) $750 [≈ £421]

Lyman, Henry
- Artificial Anaesthesia and Anaesthetics. New York: 1881. 1st edn. 338 pp. Orig bndg.
  (Fye) $100 [≈ £56]

Lyman, Henry M.
- Insomnia; and Other Disorders of Sleep. Chicago: W.T. Keener, 1885. 1st edn. x,239 pp. Orig cloth.
  (Caius) $75 [≈ £42]

Lyman, Henry M. (editor)
- Artificial Anesthesia and Anaesthetics. New York: Wood, 1881. Wood Library edn. 8vo. vii,338 pp. Orig bndg.
  (Goodrich) $85 [≈ £48]

Lynch, Bernard
- A Guide to Health ... London: for the author, & Mrs. Cooper ..., 1744. 1st edn. 8vo. xxxii,480 pp. Subscribers. Errata page. Contemp calf gilt, front hinge cracked but firm.
  (Vanbrugh) £375 [≈ $668]

Lynd, Robert S. & Lynd, Helen M.
- Middletown: A Study in American Culture. New York: Harcourt, Brace, 1929. x,[2],550 pp. Orig cloth.
  (Caius) $100 [≈ £56]

Lyon, John
- Experiments and Observations made with a View to Point Out the Errors of the Present Received Theory of Electricity ... London: 1780. 4to. xxiv,280,[8] pp. 2 fldg plates. Orig bds, uncut, unopened, worn, spine defective, front bd sl loose. *(Weiner)* £600 [≈ $1,068]

Lyon, P.
- Observations on the Barrenness of Fruit Trees, and the Means of Prevention and Cure. Edinburgh: C. Stewart for William Blackwood, 1813. 80 pp. Half-title. frontis. Disbound.   *(Jarndyce)* £85 [≈ $151]

Lysons, Daniel
- Practical Essays upon Intermitting Fevers, Dropsies, Diseases of the Liver ... Bath: 1772. 1st edn. 8vo. xxiv,214,[2] pp. Some browning at ends. Contemp calf, gilt spine.
  (Spelman) £180 [≈ $320]

M'Adam, John Loudon
- Remarks on the Present System of Road Making; with Observations ... Second Edition ... with Considerable Additions and an Appendix. Bristol: 1819. 8vo. 47 pp. Lib stamp on title. Cloth. *(Weiner)* £180 [≈ $320]

M'Alpine, D.
- The Botanical Atlas ... Edinburgh: 1883. 2 vols. Folio. Cold frontis, 26 cold plates. Orig dec cloth gilt.   *(Egglishaw)* £48 [≈ $85]

Macalpine, I. & Hunter, R.A.
- Schizophrenia 1677. A Psychiatric Study of an Illustrated Autobiographical Record of Demoniacal Possession. London: 1956. 1st edn. Lge 8vo. x,197 pp. Cold frontis, 8 mtd cold plates, ills. Orig buckram.
  (Bow Windows) £40 [≈ $71]

Macaulay, J. (editor)
- Modern Railway Working. A Practical Treatise by Engineering and Administrative Experts. London: 1912-14. 8 vols. [1739] pp. 87 plates, 723 text figs. Orig pict cloth gilt.
  (Whitehart) £50 [≈ $89]

Macaulay, James, & others
- Vivisection, Scientifically and Ethically Considered in Prize Essays. London: 1881. 8vo. xi,317,viii pp. Perf lib stamp through title & last leaf. Orig cloth.
  (Weiner) £38 [≈ $68]

MacBride, David
- Methodical Introduction to the Theory and Practice of Physic. London: Strahan, Cadell ..., 1772. 1st edn. 4to. [iv],xvi,660 pp. Orig bds, uncut, crnrs & spine worn.
  (Gaskell) £225 [≈ $401]

McBride, P.
- A Guide to the Study of Ear Disease. London: [1884]. [3],198 pp. 10 plates. Orig cloth, dull & faded.   *(Whitehart)* £15 [≈ $27]

McClung, C.E.
- Handbook of Microscopical Technique. New York: Hoeber, 1929. 495 pp. 1 leaf loose. Orig cloth, worn & shaken.
(Goodrich) **$65 [≈ £37]**

MacCulloch, John
- An Essay on the Remittent and Intermittent Diseases including generically Marsh Fever and Neurologia ... Phila: 1830. 8vo. xiv,474 pp. Sheep, worn.
(Goodrich) **$65 [≈ £37]**

MacDermot, V.
- The Cult of the Seer in the Ancient Middle East. A Contribution to Current Research on Hallucinations drawn from Coptic and Other Texts. London: Wellcome Institute, 1971. 2 vols. Dws.
(Whitehart) **£35 [≈ $62]**

McDonald, Donald
- Agricultural Writers from Sir Walter of Henley to Arthur Young, 1200-1800 ... London: 1908. Roy 8vo. Prelims,228 pp. Num ills. Cloth, paper label.
(Francis Edwards) **£25 [≈ $45]**

MacDonald, Hector Munro
- Electric Waves being an Adams Prize Essay in the University of Cambridge. Cambridge: UP, 1902. 1st edn. 8vo. xiv,200 pp. Orig cloth.
(Gaskell) **£40 [≈ $71]**

MacDonald, J.D.
- A Guide to the Microscopical Examination of Drinking Water. With an Appendix on ... Air. Second Edition. London: 1883. 8vo. [xiv], 83,[1 blank] pp. 25 litho plates. Orig cloth, loose.
(Bow Windows) **£30 [≈ $53]**

MacDonald, R.A.
- Hemochromatosis and Hemosiderosis. Illinois: 1964. xi,374 pp. 42 plates. Orig bndg.
(Whitehart) **£18 [≈ $32]**

Maceroni, Francis
- Expositions and Illustrations, interesting to all those concerned in Steam Power, whether as applied to Rail-Roads, Common Roads, or to Sea and Inland Navigation. London: 1835. 8vo. 126 pp. W'cut frontis. Lib stamp on half-title. New qtr calf.
(Weiner) **£500 [≈ $890]**

MacGillivray, W.
- A History of the Molluscous Animals of the Counties of Aberdeen, Kincardine, and Banff ... London: Cunningham & Mortimer, 1843. 1st edn. Sm 8vo. xxiv,372 pp. Orig cloth, crudely rebacked.
(Egglishaw) **£28 [≈ $50]**
- Manual of British Birds. London: 1846. 2nd edn. Cr 8vo. 248,300 pp. 31 text ills. Orig cloth, trifle used.
(Wheldon & Wesley) **£25 [≈ $45]**

Mach, Ernst
- Popular Scientific Lectures. Translated by Thomas J. McCormack. Chicago: Open Court, 1895. 1st edn in English. 12mo. Orig cloth, sl flecked.
(Gach) **$100 [≈ £56]**
- The Science of Mechanics: a Critical and Historical Account of its Development. Translated by J. McCormack. London: 1960. 6th edn. xxxi,634 pp. Diags. Orig bndg.
(Whitehart) **£25 [≈ $45]**
- Space and Geometry in the Light of Physiological, Psychological and Physical Inquiry. Translated from the German ... Chicago: Open Court, 1906. 1st Amer edn. 148 pp. B'plate, name. Cloth sl worn & soiled.
(Hermitage) **$75 [≈ £42]**

Macilwain, George
- Memoirs of John Abernethy, F.R.S. With a View of his Lectures, Writings, and Character. New York: 1853. 1st edn. 434 pp. Orig bndg.
(Fye) **$75 [≈ £42]**
- Memoirs of John Abernethy, with a View of his Lectures, his Writings and Character. London: 1856. 3rd edn. xiv,396 pp. Frontis port, 1 plate, facs letter. Orig cloth, backstrip relaid.
(Whitehart) **£45 [≈ $80]**

MacInnes, C.M.
- The Early English Tobacco Trade. London: Kegan Paul ..., 1926. 1st edn. Cr 8vo. 8 plates. Orig bndg.
(Georges) **£50 [≈ $89]**

McInnes, W., & others
- The Coal Resources of the World. Toronto: 1913. Folio. 48 maps & sections. Sm lib stamps on endpaper & title. Orig wraps, upper cvr soiled.
(Henly) **£48 [≈ $85]**

M'Intosh, Charles
- The Flower Garden ... London: Wm. Orr, 1838. 1st edn. 12mo. 515 pp. Hand cold vignette title, 10 hand cold plates. Orig dec green cloth gilt, fine. Anon.
(Gough) **£95 [≈ $169]**
- The Flower Garden ... A New Edition carefully revised. London: Wm. S. Orr, 1839. Sm 8vo. iv,515 pp. Hand cold title vignette, 10 hand cold plates. A few spots. Contemp half mor gilt. Anon. *(Hollett)* **£120 [≈ $214]**
- The Flower Garden. New Edition. London: Wm. Orr, 1847. 8vo. viii,515 pp. Hand cold title vignette, 10 hand cold plates. Orig dec green cloth, backstrip relaid.
(Gough) **£75 [≈ $134]**

- The Greenhouse, Hot House and Stove ... London: Wm. S. Orr, 1838. 8vo. vi,[ii],415 pp. Hand cold frontis, title, 15 plates, & 1 Baxter print. Frontis & title sl browned, foredge sl spotted. Orig cloth gilt, a.e.g., spine faded, recased. *(Hollett)* **£125 [≃ $223]**
- The Greenhouse, Hot House and Stove ... London: Orr & Co, 1838. Cr 8vo. vii,415 pp. Hand cold frontis, addtnl cold title, 16 cold plates (inc 1 by Baxter). Orig cloth gilt.
(Egglishaw) **£180 [≃ $320]**
- The New and Improved Practical Gardener, and Modern Horticulturist ... London: Thomas Kelly, 1851. 1st edn. 8vo. [15],[1],972 pp. Port frontis, 10 hand cold plates, num text ills. Rec period style half mor. *(Spelman)* **£110 [≃ $196]**
- The Practical Gardener and Modern Horticulturalist. London: for Thomas Kelly, 1828. 1st edn. 2 vols. viii,554; 555-1122 pp. Engvd title with vignette, frontis, 25 plates (12 hand cold). Some spotting or browning. Mod qtr mor gilt. *(Hollett)* **£140 [≃ $249]**
- The Practical Gardener, and Modern Horticulturist ... London: Thomas Kelly, (1828) 1833-34. 2 vols. 8vo. xxviii,1120, Supplement 142 pp. Title vignette, 16 hand cold & 15 plain plates. Some of the plain plates foxed. New half calf.
(Egglishaw) **£180 [≃ $320]**

McIntosh, W.C.
- The Resources of the Sea, as shown in the Scientific Experiments to test the effects of Trawling and of ... certain effects off the Scottish Shores. London: 1899. 1st edn. 8vo. Frontis, 17 plates, 32 tables. Orig pict gilt cloth. *(Bow Windows)* **£125 [≃ $223]**

Mackay, Andrew
- The Complete Navigator: or, an Easy and Familiar Guide to the Theory and Practice of Navigation ... London: 1810. 2nd edn. 8vo. xxiii,265 pp, (1-16, 57-258 tables), [2 advt] pp. 7 plates. Lacks free endpapers. Contemp calf, spine sl chipped, jnts sl cracked.
(Francis Edwards) **£90 [≃ $160]**

McKendrick, John
- Hermann Ludwig Ferdinand Von Helmholtz. London: 1899. 1st edn. 299 pp. Orig bndg.
(Fye) **$50 [≃ £28]**

Mackenzie, G.S.
- Illustrations of Phrenology. Edinburgh: 1820. xii,274 pp. Port frontis, 17 engvs. Occas sl foxing. Contemp calf gilt, sl scratched, backstrip relaid.
(Whitehart) **£120 [≃ $214]**

Mackenzie, James, M.D., of Edinburgh
- The History of Health and the Art of Preserving It ... Edinburgh: 1758. xii,464 pp. Lib stamp on title verso & front endpaper. Occas foxing. Half leather & mrbld bds.
(Whitehart) **£130 [≃ $231]**

Mackenzie, Sir James
- Diseases of the Heart. Oxford: 1913. 3rd edn. xxiii,502 pp. 264 text figs. Orig bndg.
(Whitehart) **£35 [≃ $62]**
- The Future of Medicine. London: 1919. 1st edn. [3],288 pp. Lacks front free endpaper. Orig cloth, spine faded.
(Whitehart) **£18 [≃ $32]**
- Principles of Diagnosis and Treatment in Heart Affections. London: 1918. 4th imp. viii, 264 pp. 26 figs. Orig bndg, spine sl faded. *(Whitehart)* **£15 [≃ $27]**

Mackenzie, Morell
- The Fatal Illness of Frederick the Noble. London: 1888. 1st edn. 246 pp. Orig bndg.
(Fye) **$75 [≃ £42]**

Mackenzie, P.
- Practical Observations on the Medical Powers of the most celebrated Mineral Waters and of the Various Modes of Bathing. Intended for the Use of Invalids. London: 1819. iii, 151 pp. Orig bds, rebacked.
(Whitehart) **£40 [≃ $71]**

Mackintosh, Donald J.
- Construction, Equipment, and Management of a General Hospital. Second Edition. London: William Hodge, 1916. Lge 8vo. xii,[2], 164, [xxviii advt] pp. 17 fldg plans, 52 text ills. Orig cloth. *(Spelman)* **£30 [≃ $53]**

Mackrell, G., & others
- On the Action upon the Galvanometer by Arrangements of Coloured Liquids in a U Tube ... London: 1850. 8vo. 50 pp. Lib stamp on title & 1m marg. Orig ptd wraps, dusty. *(Weiner)* **£35 [≃ $62]**

Mackworth-Praed, C.W. & Grant, C.H.B.
- Birds of Eastern and North Eastern Africa. London: Longmans, Green, 1957-60. 2nd edn, enlgd. 2 vols. 8vo.. 96 cold plates, 19 photos, text ills. Orig buckram. Dws (rubbed). *(Claude Cox)* **£45 [≃ $80]**
- Birds of the Southern Third of Africa. Series 2, Volumes 1 and 2. London: Longmans, 1969-63. Vol 1 2nd imp, vol 2 1st edn. 2 vols. 8vo. Num cold & other plates & ills. Dws.
(Gough) **£50 [≃ $89]**

McLachlan, Norman William
- The New Acoustics - A Survey of Modern Development in Acoustical Engineering. London: OUP, 1936. 1st edn. 16mo. 166 pp. Ills. Orig bndg.   *(Schoen)* **$75 [≈£42]**

MacLagan, T.J.
- Rheumatism. Its Nature, Its Pathology and Its Successful Treatment. New York: Wood Library, 1886. 8vo. viii,277 pp. Orig cloth.   *(Goodrich)* **$95 [≈£53]**

Maclaren, C.
- A Sketch of the Geology of Fife and the Lothians including detailed Descriptions of Arthur's Seat and Pentland Hills. London: 1866. 2nd edn. 8vo. xix,320 pp. 3 geological maps & 3 sections (all cold), text figs. Cloth, edges sl damp stained.   *(Henly)* **£36 [≈$64]**

McLaren, Samuel Bruce
- Scientific Papers mainly on Electrodynamics and Natural Radiation. Cambridge: UP, 1925. 1st edn. 8vo. viii,112 pp. Port. Orig cloth.   *(Gaskell)* **£35 [≈$62]**

McLaurin, John J.
- Sketches in Crude-Oil. Some Accidents and Incidents of the Petroleum Development in all Parts of the World. Harrisburg: 1896. 1st edn. x,406 pp. Port frontis, num ills. Orig illust cloth, sl worn.   *(Francis Edwards)* **£60 [≈$107]**

Maclean, Charles
- Results of an Investigation respecting Epidemic and Pestilential Diseases; including Researches in the Levant, concerning the Plague. London: Underwood, 1817-18. 1st edn. 2 vols. 8vo. xii,[16],492; xii,[12],524 pp. Half-title vol 1. Browned. Rebound in qtr cloth.   *(Spelman)* **£90 [≈$160]**

MacLennan, A.
- Surgical Materials and their Uses. London: 1915. viii,252 pp. 277 ills. Lib label on endpaper. Orig cloth, sl dust stained.   *(Whitehart)* **£18 [≈$32]**

MacLeod, George H.B.
- Notes on the Surgery of the War in the Crimea. With Remarks on the Treatment of Gunshot Wounds. Phila: Lippincott, 1862. 1st Amer edn. 12mo. 404 pp. Orig cloth, spine extrs sl frayed, lower cvr bumped.   *(Karmiole)* **$75 [≈£42]**

Maclise, Joseph
- Comparative Osteology: being Morphological Studies to demonstrate the Archetype

Skeleton of Vertebrated Animals. London: 1847. Lge folio. iv,15 pp. 54 litho plates. Occas foxing. New cloth.   *(Weiner)* **£350 [≈$623]**

MacMichael, William
- The Gold-Headed Cane. Second Edition. London: Murray, 1828. 8vo. 267 pp. Plates. Orig bds, uncut, rebacked preserving orig label.   *(Goodrich)* **$150 [≈£84]**
- Lives of British Physicians. London: Murray, 1830. Sm 8vo. ix,341 pp. Title vignette, 4 ports. Frontis & title browned. Polished calf gilt, recased. Anon.   *(Hollett)* **£50 [≈$89]**

McMinnies, W.G.
- Practical Flying. Complete Course of Flying Instructions. London: 1918. 1st edn. viii,237,advt pp. Frontis, fldg map, num ills. Endpapers sl discold. Orig cloth, dusty.   *(Whitehart)* **£25 [≈$45]**

McMullen, Thomas
- Hand-Book of Wines, Practical, Theoretical, and Historical: with a Description of Foreign Spirits and Liqueurs. New York: 1852. 8vo. xii,327 pp. Lib blind stamp on title. Sm marg tear to title. Lib cloth.   *(Weiner)* **£150 [≈$267]**

McMurrich, J. Playfair
- Leonardo Da Vinci: The Anatomist (1452-1519). Baltimore: 1930. 1st edn. 265 pp. Ills. Orig bndg.   *(Fye)* **$125 [≈£70]**

McNab, William
- Hints on the Planting and General Treatment of Hardy Evergreens, in the Climate of Scotland ... Edinburgh: Thomas Clark, 1830. 40 pp. Sl dusty. Rec wraps.   *(Jarndyce)* **£35 [≈$62]**

MacNish, Robert
- The Philosophy of Sleep. Glasgow: 1830. 1st edn. xi,268 pp. Half calf, mrbld bds, rubbed.   *(Weiner)* **£100 [≈$178]**
- The Philosophy of Sleep. Glasgow: W.R. M'Phun, 1834. 2nd edn. xii,336,[2 advt] pp. Rec cloth.   *(Caius)* **$85 [≈£48]**

Macoun, J. & J.M.
- Catalogue of Canadian Birds. Revised Edition. Ottawa: 1909. Roy 8vo. 761,xviii pp. Half leather.   *(Wheldon & Wesley)* **£35 [≈$62]**

Macpherson, H.
- Makers of Astronomy. Oxford: 1933. 244 pp. 9 plates. Orig bndg. *(Whitehart)* **£25 [≈$45]**

Macrobin, J.
- An Introduction to the Study of Practical Medicine ... Lectures delivered in the Marischal College of Aberdeen. London: 1835. viii,226 pp. Lib stamp on title & endpaper. Three qtr calf, rebacked.
(Whitehart) **£85 [≃ $151]**

McWatt, J.
- The Primulas of Europe. London: 1932. Cr 8vo. xvi,208 pp. 49 ills (8 cold). Front f.e.p. removed. Boards.
(Wheldon & Wesley) **£40 [≃ $71]**

McWilliam, J.M.
- The Birds of the Island of Bute. London: 1927. 8vo. 128 pp. Map, 9 plates. Lacks front free endpaper. Sl foxing. Cloth, spine faded.
(Wheldon & Wesley) **£30 [≃ $53]**

McWilliam, Robert
- An Essay on the Origin and Operation of the Dry Rot, with a View to its Prevention or Cure ... Cultivation of Forest Trees ... Forest Laws. London: J. Taylor, 1818. 4to. xx, 420 pp. Instructions to binder. 3 plates. Occas sl marks. Contemp sprinkled calf gilt.
(Spelman) **£280 [≃ $498]**
- An Essay on the Origin and Operation of the Dry Rot. London: J. Taylor, 1818. 1st edn. Lge 4to. xx,420 pp. Errata slip. 3 plates. Some foxing. Half calf.
(Bookpress) **$450 [≃ £253]**

Madden, Richard Robert
- Phantasmata or Illusions and Fanaticisms of Protean Forms Productive of Great Evils. London: T.C. Newby, 1857. 1st edn. 2 vols. 8vo. Frontis vol 1. Foxed. Orig cloth.
(Gach) **$285 [≃ £160]**

Maddock, James
- The Florist's Directory, a Treatise on the Culture of Flowers. New Edition, by S. Curtis. London: 1810. 8vo. viii,271,[9] pp. 8 hand cold plates. Contemp calf gilt, trifle rubbed, sl wear hd of spine.
(Wheldon & Wesley) **£85 [≃ $151]**
- The Florist's Directory; A Treatise on the Culture of Flowers ... New Edition, Improved by Samuel Curtis. London: for John Harding, 1810. 8vo. viii,271,[36 ctlg] pp. 8 hand cold plates. Contemp gilt panelled tree calf, gilt dec spine, fine.
(Gough) **£295 [≃ $525]**

Magill, E.M.
- Notes on Galvanism and Faradism. London: 1921. 2nd edn. xvi,224 pp. 67 ills. Orig cloth, sl rubbed.
(Whitehart) **£15 [≃ $27]**

Magnus, Hugo
- Superstition in Medicine. New York: 1905. 205 pp. Orig bndg.
(Fye) **$65 [≃ £37]**

Magoun, Horace W.
- The Waking Brain. Springfield: C.C. Thomas, [1958]. 1st edn. viii,138 pp. Num ills. Orig cloth. Dw (faded).
(Caius) **$65 [≃ £37]**

Maiden, J.H.
- A Manual of the Grasses of New South Wales. Sydney: 1898. 8vo. iv,199 pp. 24 plates. Trifle foxed. Cloth portfolio.
(Wheldon & Wesley) **£35 [≃ $62]**

Maiden, J.H. & Campbell, W.S.
- The Flowering Plants and Ferns of New South Wales. Sydney: Govt. printer, 1895-98. Parts 1-7 in one vol, all published. Sm 4to. 80 pp. 28 cold plates. No title-page or index were published. Qtr mor, wrappers bound in.
(Wheldon & Wesley) **£400 [≃ $712]**

Maillet, Benoit de
- Telliamed: or, Discourses between an Indian Philosopher and a French Missionary, on the Dimunition of the Sea, the Formation of the Earth, the Origin of Men and Animals ... London: 1750. 8vo. lii,284 pp. Contemp calf, worn, rebacked.
(Weiner) **£200 [≃ $356]**

Major, Ralph
- A History of Medicine. Springfield: 1954. 1st edn. 2 vols. 1155 pp. Orig bndg.
(Fye) **$175 [≃ £98]**

Makins, G.H.
- Surgical Experiences in South Africa 1899-1900. Being mainly a Clinical Study of the Nature and Effects of Injuries produced by Bullets of Small Calibre. London: 1913. 2nd edn. xvi,504 pp. 105 figs. Endpapers sl marked. Orig bndg. *(Whitehart)* **£40 [≃ $71]**

Makower, Walter
- The Radioactive Substances; their Properties and Behaviour. London: 1908. 8vo. xii, 301 pp. Diags. Orig cloth. *(Weiner)* **£25 [≃ $45]**

Malcolm, J.D.
- The Physiology of Death from Traumatic Fever. A Study in Abdominal Surgery. London: 1893. iv,129 pp. Orig bndg, inner hinge sl cracked. *(Whitehart)* **£25 [≃ $45]**

Malinowski, Bronislaw
- Coral Gardens and their Magic: A Study of the Methods of Tilling the Soil and of

Agricultural Rites in the Trobriand Islands. New York: Amer Book Co., [1935]. 1st Amer edn, British sheets. 2 vols. Maps, ills, figs. Orig cloth.   *(Gach)* **$125 [≈ £70]**

Malloch, P.D.
- Life History and Habits of the Salmon, Sea-Trout and other Freshwater Fish. London: Black, 1910. Roy 8vo. xvi,264 pp. 239 ills. Orig cloth, pict onlays.
             (Egglishaw) **£40 [≈ $71]**
- Life-History and Habits of the Salmon. London: Black, 1912. 2nd edn. Roy 8vo. xix,294 pp. 274 ills. Orig cloth, pict onlays.
             (Egglishaw) **£45 [≈ $80]**
- Life-History and Habits of the Salmon, Sea Trout, Trout and other Freshwater Fish. London: 1910. Roy 8vo. xvi,264 pp. 239 ills. Cloth.   *(Wheldon & Wesley)* **£35 [≈ $62]**

Malortie, Colonel De
- The Theory of Field Fortification. London: 1819. 2nd edn. 8vo. 227 pp. Half-title. 31 fldg plates. Contemp calf, jnts cracking, extrs worn, label chipped.
             (Francis Edwards) **£75 [≈ $134]**

Malthus, Thomas Robert
- An Essay on the Principle of Population ... Sixth Edition. London: Murray, 1826. 2 vols. 8vo. xviii,535; iv,528 pp. Red half mor by Zaehnsdorf.   *(O'Neal)* **$600 [≈ £337]**
- The Grounds of an Opinion on the Policy of Restricting the Importation of Foreign Corn; intended as an Appendix to 'Observations on the Corn Laws." London: for Murray, Johnson, 1815. 1st edn. 8vo. [ii],48 pp. Half-title not called for. Contemp style qtr calf.
             (Burmester) **£1,500 [≈ $2,670]**
- An Inquiry into the Nature and Progress of Rent, and the Principles by which it is regulated. London: for Murray, Johnson, 1815. 1st edn. 8vo. [iv],61,[1] pp. Contemp style qtr calf. *(Burmester)* **£1,650 [≈ $2,937]**
- Observations on the Effects of the Corn Laws, and of the Rise and Fall in the Price of Corn on the Agriculture and General Wealth of the Country. London: J. Johnson, 1814. 2nd edn. 44 pp. Sl spotted. Disbound.
             (Jarndyce) **£320 [≈ $570]**

Maltz, Maxwell
- Evolution of Plastic Surgery. New York: 1946. 1st edn. 368 pp. Ills. Orig bndg.
             (Fye) **£350 [≈ £197]**
- New Faces - New Futures: Rebuilding Character with Plastic Surgery. New York: 1936. 1st edn. 315 pp. Orig bndg.
             (Fye) **$100 [≈ £56]**

Manaceine, Marie de
- Sleep: Its Physiology, Pathology, Hygiene, and Psychology. London: W. Scott, Contemporary Science Series, 1897. [4],vii, [1], 341,[1],[18 advt] pp. Orig cloth, sl worn.
             (Caius) **$65 [≈ £37]**

Mann, J.D.
- Forensic Medicine and Toxicology. London: 1908. 4th edn. xii,710 pp. 28 ills. Stamp on half-title. Some foxing prelims. Spine worn.
             (Whitehart) **£15 [≈ $27]**

Manning, L.A.
- Bibliography of the Ionosphere. An Annotated Survey through 1960. Stanford: 1962. xiii,613 pp. Orig bndg.
             (Whitehart) **£25 [≈ $45]**

Mansell-Pleydell, J.C.
- The Mollusca of Dorsetshire and the Brachiopoda. Dorchester: 1898. 8vo. xxxxii, 110,errata pp. Fldg map. Orig cloth gilt. Author's pres copy. *(Egglishaw)* **£30 [≈ $53]**

Mantell, G.A.
- Geological Excursions round the Isle of Wight, and along the adjacent Coast of Dorsetshire. London: Bohn, 1854. 3rd edn. 8vo. xxxii,356,[32 Bohn ctlg] pp. Fldg cold map, table, 19 litho plates, num ills. Orig cloth.   *(Egglishaw)* **£50 [≈ $89]**
- The Journal of Gideon Mantell. Edited by E.C. Curwen. London: OUP, 1940. 1st edn. 8vo. xii,315 pp. 4 plates. Cloth.
             (Savona) **£25 [≈ $45]**
- Petrifactions and their Teachings; or, a Hand-Book to the Gallery of Organic Remains of the British Museum. London: 1851. Cr 8vo. xi,496 pp. 2 plates, text figs. Half calf, rubbed.   *(Wheldon & Wesley)* **£50 [≈ $89]**
- A Pictorial Atlas of Fossil Remains. London: Bohn, 1850. 4to. 207 pp. Cold frontis, 74 plain litho plates. New cloth gilt.
             (Egglishaw) **£165 [≈ $294]**
- Thoughts on Animalcules, or a Glimpse of the Invisible World revealed by the Microscope. London: 1846. xvi,144, 3,8 pp. 12 hand cold plates. 6 plates sl foxed. Sm lib stamp on title. Orig cloth, spine faded & worn.   *(Henly)* **£80 [≈ $142]**

Maplet, J.
- A Greene Forest or a Naturall Historie ... Reprinted from the Edition of 1567, with an Introduction by W.H. Davies. London: Hesperides Press, 1930. One of 500. Sm 4to. ix,184,[2] pp. Orig buckram.
             (Wheldon & Wesley) **£50 [≈ $89]**

Marcet, W.
- A Contribution to the History of the Respiration of Man. Being the Croonian Lectures ... 1895. London: 1897. 120 pp. 34 plates of charts. Lib b'plate. Some ff loose. Orig cloth, spine ends sl worn, hinges loose.
(Whitehart) **£120 [≈ $214]**

Mares, G.C.
- The History of the Typewriter ... London: Pitman, 1909. 8vo. 318 pp. 217 text ills. Sm lib marks on title verso. Orig cloth gilt, label removed from spine.   *(Hollett)* **£85 [≈ $151]**

Markham, Clements Robert
- Peruvian Bark: A Popular Account of the Introduction of Cinchona Cultivation into British India, 1860-1880. London: Murray, 1880. 1st edn. xxiii,550 pp. 3 fldg maps, 3 w'cut ills. Orig brown cloth gilt, sl rubbed.
(Gough) **£48 [≈ $85]**

Markham, Gervase
- Cheape and Good Husbandry ... The fift Edition. London: Okes for Harrison, 1631. Sm 4to. [xxvi],188 pp. Lacks A1 (blank). Sm worm hole through centre of text touching some letters. Lge w'cut of garden. Rec half calf. STC 17339. *(Vanbrugh)* **£275 [≈ $490]**
- The English House-Wife ... Now the Fourth Time much augmented ... By G.M. London: Nicholas Oakes for John Harrison, 1631. Sm 4to. [x],252 pp. Lacks blank A1. Rec half calf. STC 17353.   *(Vanbrugh)* **£455 [≈ $810]**
- Markhams Farewell to Husbandry ... London: E. Brewster & George Sawbridge, 1656. 6th edn. [vi],126,[4] pp. Later half calf. Wing M.650.   *(Bookpress)* **$285 [≈ £160]**

Marks, E.C.R.
- Notes on the Construction of Cranes and Lifting Machinery. Manchester: 1899. xi,183 pp. 155 text figs. Orig cloth, inner hinges cracked.   *(Whitehart)* **£25 [≈ $45]**

Marryat, H. (editor)
- Electrical Wiring and Contracting. A Practical and Authoritative Work dealing with all Branches of the Trade ... London: 1929-30. 28 weekly parts. Ills. Orig wraps, sl dust stained & worn. 7 cloth binding cases, sl marked.   *(Whitehart)* **£45 [≈ $80]**

Marshall, A.J.
- Bower Birds, their Displays and Breeding Cycles: a Preliminary Statement. London: 1954. Roy 8vo. 212 pp. 26 plates, 21 text figs. Good ex-lib. Cloth.
(Wheldon & Wesley) **£50 [≈ $89]**

Marshall, C.
- An Introduction to the Knowledge and Practice of Gardening. London: 1796. 1st edn. 12mo. xvi,432,x pp. Inscrptns on title. Tree calf gilt.   *(Henly)* **£60 [≈ $107]**

Marshall, C.F. Dendy
- Centenary History of the Liverpool and Manchester Railway ... London: 1930. 4to. ix, 192 pp. 28 plates inc map frontis. Orig 2-tone cloth, soiled, hinges tender.
(Francis Edwards) **£75 [≈ $134]**

Marshall, William
- Planting and Rural Ornament. Being a Second Edition with large additions of Planting and Ornamental Gardening, a Practical Treatise. London: 1796. 2 vols. 8vo. xxxii,408,[8]; xx,454,[6] pp. Contemp tree calf, part of 1 label missing.   *(Henly)* **£152 [≈ $271]**
- Planting and Rural Ornament: being a Second Edition, with large additions of Planting and Ornamental Gardening, a Practical Treatise. London: G. Nichol, 1796. 2 vols. 8vo. xxxii,408,[8]; xx,454,[4] pp. Contemp half calf, raised gilt bands, gilt spine & labels.   *(Spelman)* **£200 [≈ $356]**
- The Rural Economy of the West of England. London: for G. Nicol ..., 1796. 1st edn. 2 vols. 8vo. 2 advt ff vol 1. Fldg map. Vol 1 title sl spotted. Mod calf, uncut.
(Claude Cox) **£140 [≈ $249]**
- The Rural Economy of the West of England ... Dublin: for P. Wogan ..., 1797. 1st Dublin edn. 8vo. 9,[i],xxxviii, 489,[20] pp. Title dusty. Rebound in half mor, old mrbld bds.
(Claude Cox) **£85 [≈ $151]**

Martin, Benjamin
- The Philosophical Grammar; Being a View of the Present State of Experimented Physiology, or Natural Philosophy. In Four Parts ... London: John Noon, 1748. 3rd edn. 2 tables, 26 fldg plates. Occas foxing & sl browning. Contemp calf, rebacked.
(P and P Books) **£145 [≈ $258]**

Martin, E.G.
- Principles of the Cold Water Treatment of Diseases, and its Application. London: Whittaker, [1843]. 1st edn. 8vo. [ii],50 pp. Cloth backed bds, paper label.
(Bookpress) **$135 [≈ £76]**

Martin, H.T.
- Castorologia, or the History and Traditions of the Canadian Beaver. London: 1892. 8vo. xvi,238 pp. Frontis, num ills. Good ex lib. Cloth.   *(Wheldon & Wesley)* **£75 [≈ $134]**

Martin, J.H.
- A Manual of Microscopic Mounting with Notes on the Collection and Examination of Objects. London: 1872. 8vo. vii,200 pp. 10 plates (3 foxed). Repr to title & dedic. Half mor.   *(Henly)* **£42 [≈ $75]**

Martin, Marcus J.
- Wireless Transmission of Photographs. London: 1916. 8vo. xi,117 pp. 3 plates, diags. Orig cloth.   *(Weiner)* **£100 [≈ $178]**

Martin, T.
- Faraday's Discovery of Electro-Magnetic Induction. London: 1949. 160 pp. 55 figs. Sl foxing. Orig bndg.   *(Whitehart)* **£18 [≈ $32]**

Martin, Thomas
- The Circle of the Mechanical Arts ... London: Richard Rees ..., 1813. 1st edn. 4to. viii, 616 pp. Num plates. Occas sl foxing. Contemp tree calf, rebacked.
                    (Bookpress) **$625 [≈ £351]**

Martinier, P. & Lemerle, G.
- Injuries of the Face and Jaw and the Repair and Treatment of Fractured Jaws. New York: 1917. 1st edn in English. 345 pp. Ills. Orig bndg.   *(Fye)* **$100 [≈ £56]**

Martyn, Thomas
- The English Entomologist exhibiting all the Coleopterous Insects found in England. London: 1792. Roy 4to. [v],33,[vi], 41,[4] pp. 2 engvd titles, 2 plates of medals, 24 hand cold plates. Contemp half russia, rebacked, crnrs reprd.
              (Wheldon & Wesley) **£750 [≈ $1,335]**
- Thirty-Eight Plates, with Explanations; intended to Illustrate Linnaeus's System of Vegetables. London: B. White, 1788. 1st edn. 8vo. [vi],72,2 pp. 38 plates. Orig bds, uncut, sl worn, jnts weak. *(Bookpress)* **$275 [≈ £154]**

Mason, Charlotte
- The Ladies' Assistant for Regulating and Supplying the Table ... Sixth Edition, Enlarged, Corrected and Improved ... London: for J. Walter, 1787. 8vo. [xviii],484, [xix, [i advt] pp. Half-title. Contemp tree calf, sometime rebacked.   *(Gough)* **£275 [≈ $490]**

Mason, Thomas Monck
- Creation by the Immediate Agency of God, as opposed to Creation by Natural Law; being a refutation of the Work entitled Vestiges of the Natural History of Creation. London: John W. Parker, 1845. 8vo. viii,182,[2],4 advt pp. Orig cloth.   *(Spelman)* **£25 [≈ $45]**

Masselon, Roberts, & Cillard
- Celluloid. Its Manufacture, Applications and Substitutes. Translated from the French by H.H. Hodgson. London: 1912. 8vo. xix,352 pp. 7 plates, ills. Orig cloth.
                    (Weiner) **£35 [≈ $62]**

Masson, F.
- Robert Boyle. A Biography. London: 1914. ix,323 pp. Frontis port. Orig cloth.
                (Whitehart) **£20 [≈ $36]**

Masters, Maxwell Tylden
- Vegetable Teratology. An Account of the Principal Deviations from the Usual Construction of Plants ... London: Robt. Hardwicke for the Ray Society, 1869. 1st edn. 8vo. xxxviii,534 pp. Text ills. Orig cloth, uncut.   *(Claude Cox)* **£30 [≈ $53]**

The Mathematical Principles of Geography ...
- See Emerson, William

Mathews, G.M. & Iredale, T.
- Manual of the Birds of Australia. Volume I. Orders Casuarii to Columbae. London: 1921. All published. Cr 4to. xxiv,279 pp. 46 plates (10 cold). Trifle foxed. Cloth.
              (Wheldon & Wesley) **£65 [≈ $116]**

Matland, G.R. & T.C.
- The Teeth in Health and Disease. London: 1902. 1st edn. Sm 8vo. 174 pp. 90 figs. Some spotting. Orig cloth.
                (Bow Windows) **£35 [≈ $62]**

Matthews, D.N.
- The Surgery of Repair, Injuries and Burns. Springfield: 1943. 1st edn. 386 pp. 198 ills. Orig bndg.   *(Fye)* **$100 [≈ £56]**

Matthews, L.G.
- The Royal Apothecaries. London: 1967. 191 pp. Dw. Pres copy. *(Goodrich)* **$65 [≈ £37]**

Matthews, L.H.
- British Mammals. London: Collins New Naturalist, 1952. 1st edn. 8vo. Ills. Orig cloth. Dw.   *(Egglishaw)* **£25 [≈ $45]**

Maudsley, Henry
- Body and Will ... London: Kegan Paul, Trench, 1883. 1st edn. Inscrptn. Orig cloth, crnrs bumped.   *(Gach)* **$125 [≈ £70]**
- Life in Mind and Conduct ... London: Macmillan; New York: Macmillan, 1870. 1st edn. 8vo. Orig cloth. *(Gach)* **$125 [≈ £70]**
- The Physiology of Mind ... London:

Macmillan, 1876. xix,[1],547 pp. Stamp on title. Blank part of half-title renewed. Orig cloth, somewhat worn. *(Caius)* **$80 [≈ £45]**

Maupin, B.
- Blood Platelets in Man and Animals. London: 1969. 2 vols. Traces of label removal. Orig bndg, vol 1 inner hinge loose. *(Whitehart)* **£20 [≈ $36]**

Maury, M.F.
- Explanations and Sailing Directions to Accompany the Wind and Current Charts. Washington: 1852. 4th edn. 414 pp. 19 plates. Sl foxing. Cloth, spine wrinkled. *(Whitehart)* **£25 [≈ $45]**
- Explanations and Sailing Directions to Accompany the Wind and Current Charts. Washington: 1858. 2nd edn. 2 vols. 12 maps, 39 + 5 plates. Occas sl foxing. Cloth, spine faded. *(Whitehart)* **£50 [≈ $89]**
- The Physical Geography of the Sea. New York: Harper, 1855. 1st edn. 8vo. 274 pp. 12 ills inc 8 fldg maps & charts. Endpapers discold. Orig cloth, fine. *(Heritage)* **$500 [≈ £281]**
- The Physical Geography of the Sea. New York: Harper, 1855. 1st edn. 8vo. 274 pp. 8 fldg plates, 4 text ills. Orig cloth, chipped. *(Bookpress)* **$585 [≈ £329]**
- The Physical Geography of the Sea. New Edition with Addenda. London & New York: 1857. 8vo. 360 pp. 13 plates. Some foxing, heavy at beginning. Lib stamp on title. Orig cloth, trifle used. *(Wheldon & Wesley)* **£45 [≈ $80]**

Mavor, William
- The Catechism of Health ... Second Edition. London: Lackington, Allen, 1809. 72 pp. Mod wraps. *(Hemlock)* **$150 [≈ £84]**

Mawe, J.
- The Linnaean System of Conchology describing the Orders, Genera and Species of Shells ... London: for the author, 1823. xv,207 pp. 37 hand cold litho plates. Lib stamp title verso. New half calf, gilt dec spine. *(Egglishaw)* **£320 [≈ $570]**
- A Treatise on Diamonds and Precious Stones. London: John Mawe, 1823. 2nd edn. Cr 8vo. xx,148 pp. Hand cold frontis, 3 b/w plates (1 partly cold). New half leather. *(Gemmary)* **$575 [≈ £323]**
- The Voyager's Companion, or Shell Collector's Pilot, with Instructions and Directions where to find the Finest Shells. London: 1825. 4th edn. 12mo. [iv],vii,75 pp. 2 cold plates. Orig cloth.

(Wheldon & Wesley) **£35 [≈ $62]**

Mawe, Thomas (& Abercrombie, John)
- Every Man his own Gardener ... London: 1767. 1st edn. 12mo. [iv],1-72, 73*-84*, 73-422 pp. Lacks frontis. Red mor gilt. *(Wheldon & Wesley)* **£100 [≈ $178]**
- Every Man his own Gardener ... Dublin: for P. Byrne, 1798. 14th edn. 8vo. [iv],626,[19] pp. Old sheep, rubbed. *(Young's)* **£42 [≈ $75]**
- Every Man his own Gardener ... London: 1800. 16th edn. 12mo. vii,758,[96] pp. Engvd frontis. Tree calf, rebacked. *(Henly)* **£48 [≈ $85]**

Maxwell, James Clerk
- Matter and Motion. Reprinted, with Notes and Appendix, by Sir Joseph Larmor. London: 1920. 8vo. xv,163 pp. Port. Orig cloth. *(Weiner)* **£20 [≈ $36]**
- A Treatise on Electricity and Magnetism. Third Edition, edited by J.J. Thomson. London: 1904. 2 vols. 8vo. xxxii,506; xxiv,500 pp. 20 plates, diags. Unabused ex-lib. Orig cloth. *(Weiner)* **£60 [≈ $107]**

Maxwell, Robert
- The Practical Husbandman ... Edinburgh: 1757. 1st edn. 432, index pp. Sl staining. Signed by the author on title verso. Old calf, v worn & spotted. *(King)* **$95 [≈ £53]**
- The Practical Husbandman: being a Collection of Miscellaneous Papers on Husbandry. Edinburgh: C. Wright for the author, 1757. xii,432,[6] pp. Fldg plate. Contemp calf, red label. *(C.R. Johnson)* **£350 [≈ $623]**

May, Hans
- Reconstructive and Reparative Surgery. Phila: 1947. 1st edn. 964 pp. 967 ills. Orig bndg. *(Fye)* **$100 [≈ £56]**

May, J.B.
- The Hawks of North America ... New York: National Assoc of Audubon Societies, 1935. Roy 8vo. xxxii,140 pp. 37 cold & 4 plain plates. Orig cloth. *(Egglishaw)* **£45 [≈ $80]**
- The Hawks of North America. New York: 1935. Roy 8vo. xxxii,140 pp. 41 plates (37 cold). Cloth. *(Wheldon & Wesley)* **£55 [≈ $98]**

May, W.
- The Queen's Closet Opened. Incomparable Secrets in Physick, Chirurgery, Preserving and Candying, &c. ... Corrected ... London: Blagrave, 1683. 12mo. [10],190,[8]; 106,[4]; 123,[7] pp. 4 ff supplied in facs. Port frontis.

Mod calf antique. Wing M.104.
(Hemlock) **$700 [≈ £393]**

Mayhew, Henry
- London Labour and the London Poor ...
London: Griffin, Bohn, 1861. 1st edn. 4 vols
(inc the Extra Volume). 8vo. W'engvd ills.
Lacks 1 plate & 1 flyleaf. Orig cloth, front bds
sl marked by damp.   *(Gach)* **$350 [≈ £197]**

Mayo, Herbert
- Outlines of Human Physiology. London:
1827. xviii,406 pp. Contemp qtr roan & bds,
paper label. Inscrbd by the author.
(Whitehart) **£130 [≈ $231]**
- The Philosophy of Living. London: 1838.
2nd edn. Sm 8vo. xv,320 pp. Orig cloth, torn.
(Weiner) **£25 [≈ $45]**

Mayr, E.
- Systematics and the Origin of Species. New
York: 1942. 1st edn. 8vo. xiv,334 pp. 29 ills.
Minor foxing. Cloth, trifle used.
(Wheldon & Wesley) **£35 [≈ $62]**

Mead, Richard
- A Mechanical Account of Poisons in Several
Essays. London: J.R. for Ralph South, 1702.
1st edn. 8vo. [viii],175,[1] pp. Fldg plate.
Contemp calf, rebacked, ft of spine & 1 crnr
worn.   *(Burmester)* **£275 [≈ $490]**
- A Mechanical Account of Poisons in Several
Essays. Fourth Edition. Dublin: 1736. 8vo.
[8], 109, [3] pp. Fldg plate. Contemp calf,
spine reprd, new label.
(Spelman) **£120 [≈ $214]**
- The Medical Works ... London: Hitch,
Hawes ..., 1762. 4to. xxiv,xxvi-662, [48] pp.
Sl foxing. Contemp calf, backstrip relaid.
(Goodrich) **$895 [≈ £503]**
- A Treatise concerning the Influence of the
Sun and Moon upon Human Bodies and the
Diseases thereby produced. Translated from
the Latin by Thomas Stack. London:
Brindley, 1748. 2 vols in one. 8vo. 130,204
pp. Title dusty & chipped at foredge. New old
style bds.   *(Goodrich)* **$145 [≈ £81]**

Meager, L.
- The English Gardner: or a Sure Guide to
Young Planters. London: 1688. Sm 4to. viii,
144 pp. 24 plates. Half calf.
(Wheldon & Wesley) **£220 [≈ $392]**

Medical Directory
- Medical Directory 1945. London: 1945.
101st annual issue. xcii,2559 pp, inc advts.
Endpapers sl soiled. 3 ff loose. Orig cloth,
dust stained, sl marked.

(Whitehart) **£35 [≈ $62]**

The Medical Register
- The Medical Register 1874. London: 1874.
xxxvi,574 pp. Edges sl foxed. New bndg.
(Whitehart) **£50 [≈ $89]**

Meek, S.E. & Hildebrand, S.F.
- The Marine Fishes of Panama. Chicago:
1923-28. 3 vols. 8vo. 1045 pp. 102 plates.
Orig wraps.
(Wheldon & Wesley) **£75 [≈ $134]**

Meetham, A.R.
- Atmospheric Pollution - Its Origin and
Prevention. London: Pergamon Press, 1952.
1st edn. 12mo. 268 pp. Lib stamp. Orig
buckram, dw glued to pastedown.
(Schoen) **$75 [≈ £42]**

Meikle, Desmond
- Flora of Cyprus. London: 1977-85. 2 vols.
8vo. 1969 pp. 2 cold frontis, 105 plates.
Cloth.   *(Wheldon & Wesley)* **£60 [≈ $107]**
- Wild Flowers of Cyprus. Paintings by Elektra
Megaw. London: Phillimore, 1973. Folio. 40
cold plates. Orig bndg.
(Blackwell's) **£50 [≈ $89]**

Meinertzhagen, R.
- Birds of Arabia. London: 1954. Roy 8vo.
xiii,624 pp. Fldg map in pocket, 19 cold & 9
photo plates. Cloth, 1 crnr sl bumped, trifle
faded.   *(Wheldon & Wesley)* **£400 [≈ $712]**
- Pirates and Predators. The Piratical and
Predatory Habits of Birds. London: 1959. Cr
4to. ix,230 pp. 18 cold & 26 plain plates.
Cloth, spine faded.
(Wheldon & Wesley) **£160 [≈ $285]**

Memoirs of a Stomach ...
- See Whiting, Sydney

Menon, L.F.H. de, Marquis de Turbilly
- A Discourse on the Cultivation of Waste and
Barren Lands. Translated from the French ...
Part I [all published]. London: Dodsley,
1762. 1st edn in English. 8vo. [iv],xv, [i], 111
pp. W'cut frontis. Old wraps.
(Burmester) **£150 [≈ $267]**

Meredith, Louisa Anne, nee Twamley
- Our Wild Flowers; Familiarly Described and
Illustrated. London: Tilt, 1839. 1st edn.
vii,312,[4 advt] pp. 12 hand cold plates. Orig
elab pict mor gilt, a.e.g., backstrip relaid.
(Gough) **£150 [≈ $267]**
- Some of My Bush Friends in Tasmania ...
London: Day & Son, 1860. Folio. Cold title,

11 numbered cold plates, 1 unnumbered cold
endpiece plate, 2 cold border decs. Occas sl
spotting. 1 plate foredge reprd. Orig cloth gilt
extra, recased, rubbed, crnrs bumped.
(Hollett) **£475 [≈ $846]**

Merrifield, M.P.
- A Sketch of the Natural History of Brighton
and its Vicinity. Brighton: 1864. 2nd edn.
8vo. xi,227 pp. Fldg map. Orig cloth, sl worn.
(Henly) **£36 [≈ $64]**

Merriman, Samuel
- A Synopsis of the Various Kinds of Difficult
Parturition   ...   Third   Edition,   with
considerable additions ... London: 1820. 8vo.
viii,[2],329 pp. 5 plates. Contemp three qtr
calf, jnts cracked.   *(Hemlock)* **$250 [≈ £140]**

Metcalfe, C.R. & Chalk, L.
- Anatomy of the Dicotyledons: Leaves, Stem,
and Wood in relation to Taxonomy, with
Notes on Economic Uses. Oxford: 1950. 2
vols. Roy 8vo. Text figs. Cloth.
(Wheldon & Wesley) **£45 [≈ $80]**

Metchnikoff, Elie
- Immunity in Infective Diseases. Translated
from the French by Francis G. Binnie ...
Cambridge: UP, 1905. 8vo. xvi,591 pp. 45
text ills. Endpapers spotted. Orig cloth, v sl
rubbed, spine sl discold.
(Francis Edwards) **£150 [≈ $267]**
- Immunity in Infective Diseases. Cambridge:
1905. xvi,591 pp. 45 text figs, some cold.
Orig bds, rebacked. *(Goodrich)* **$125 [≈ £70]**
- The Nature of Man. Studies in Optimistic
Philosophy. London: 1903. 309 pp. Orig
bndg.   *(Fye)* **$100 [≈ £56]**
- The Prolongation of Life. Optimistic Studies.
The English Translation edited by P.
Chalmers Mitchell. London: 1907. xx,343
pp. Num ills. Endpapers v sl browned. Orig
cloth, spine v sl chipped.
(Francis Edwards) **£26 [≈ $46]**

Methuen, H.H.
- Life in the Wilderness, or Wanderings in
South Africa. London: 1846. 8vo. xiii,363 pp.
3 plates, text figs. Plates foxed. Orig cloth,
trifle faded.
(Wheldon & Wesley) **£160 [≈ $285]**

Meyer, Edouard
- A Practical Treatise on Diseases of the Eye.
Translated ... by Freeland Fergus. London:
1887. Lge thick 8vo. xi,637 pp. 3 cold plates,
ills. Orig cloth, unopened.
(Weiner) **£50 [≈ $89]**

Meyer, W. & Schmieden, V.
- Bier's Hyperemic Treatment in Surgery,
Medicine, and the Specialities. A Manual of
its Practical Application. Phila: 1908. 209 pp.
95 text ills. Occas sl foxing endpapers. Orig
bndg, spine ends sl worn.
(Whitehart) **£25 [≈ $45]**

Meyer de Schauensee, R.
- The Species of Birds of South America and
their Distribution. Phila: 1966. 8vo. xvii, 578
pp. 5 pp addenda loose. 2 endpaper maps.
Cloth, trifle used.
(Wheldon & Wesley) **£50 [≈ $89]**

**Meyer de Schauensee, R. & Phelps, W.H.
Jr.**
- A Guide to the Birds of Venezuela. Princeton:
1978. 8vo. 446 pp. 53 plates (40 cold). 41 text
figs. Cloth. *(Wheldon & Wesley)* **£50 [≈ $89]**

Meyrick, William
- The New Family Herbal; or, Domestic
Physician ... Birmingham: Thomas Pearson,
1790. 1st edn. 8vo. xxiv,498,[6 advt] pp,
errata leaf. Frontis, 14 plates. Occas sl marg
spotting. Contemp half calf, rubbed, sl worn.
(Claude Cox) **£165 [≈ $294]**

Michael, A.D.
- British Oribatidae. London: Ray Society,
1884-88. 2 vols. xi,336; 337-657 pp. 62 plates
(mostly cold). Orig cloth gilt, t.e.g., spines
faded.   *(Egglishaw)* **£145 [≈ $258]**
- British Tyroglyphidae. London: Ray Society,
1901-03. 2 vols. 8vo. 42 plates (28 cold).
Good ex-lib. Cloth.
(Wheldon & Wesley) **£45 [≈ $80]**

Michell, John
- A Treatise of Artificial Magnets ... Mariner's
Needle ... The Second Edition corrected and
improved. Cambridge: Joseph Bentham,
1751. 78 pp. Fldg plate. Cloth bds.
(C.R. Johnson) **£160 [≈ $285]**

Michell, William
- On Difficult Cases of Parturition: and the
Use of the Ergot of Rye. London:
Underwood, 1826. 1st edn. Tall 8vo. [2
ctlg],[2 blank], xv,[1],128 pp. Orig bds,
uncut, front bd detached, spine defective,
remains of label.   *(Hemlock)* **$275 [≈ £154]**

Michelson, Albert A.
- Light Waves and their Uses. Chicago: UP,
1907. 1st edn, 2nd printing. 12mo. xii,166
pp. 2 cold plates, 108 text figs. Orig cloth.
(Schoen) **$75 [≈ £42]**

Middleton, John
- View of the Agriculture of Middlesex. Second Edition. London: Richard Phillips, 1807. 8vo. xvi,704,[4 advt] pp. Fldg hand cold map. Orig bds, uncut, paper label, crnrs sl bumped.
(Spelman) **£140 [≈ $249]**

Middleton, W.E.K.
- A History of the Thermometer and its Use in Meteorology. Baltimore: 1966. xiii,249 pp. Frontis, plate, text diags. Orig bndg.
(Whitehart) **£35 [≈ $62]**

Miers, Sir H.
- Mineralogy. An Introduction to the Scientific Study of Minerals. London: 1929. 2nd edn. 8vo. xx,658 pp. 729 text figs. Cloth. Dw.
(Henly) **£25 [≈ $45]**

Miers, J.
- The Apocynaceae of South America, with Some Preliminary Remarks on the Whole Family. London: 1878. Roy 4to. 291 pp. 35 plates. Cloth.
(Wheldon & Wesley) **£60 [≈ $107]**
- Contributions to Botany, Iconographic and Descriptive, detailing the Characters of Plants that are either New or Imperfectly Described. London: 1851-71. 3 vols. 4to. 154 litho plates. Some foxing. Orig cloth (colour not uniform), vol 3 spine sl defective.
(Wheldon & Wesley) **£160 [≈ $285]**
- Illustrations of South American Plants. London: 1849-57. 2 vols. 4to. 87 plates (sl foxing). Binder's cloth.
(Wheldon & Wesley) **£100 [≈ $178]**

Miles, A.
- Surgical Ward Work and Nursing. A Handbook for Nurses and Others. London: [1921]. 4th edn. viii,418 pp. 392 figs. Orig bndg.
(Whitehart) **£25 [≈ $45]**

Miles, W.J.
- Modern Practical Farriery ... London: [ca 1899]. 4to. vi,vii,538,96 pp. Num litho plates (inc chromolithos), num b/w ills. Half calf gilt, sl worn, hinges reinforced.
(Francis Edwards) **£75 [≈ $134]**
- Modern Practical Farriery, a Complete System of the Veterinary Art. London: The Gresham Publishing Co., [ca 1900]. Lge 4to. [2],538,vi,96 pp. 20 cold & 28 b/w plates, num text ills. Contemp half calf, sl rubbed & marked.
(Claude Cox) **£70 [≈ $125]**

Mill, James
- Elements of Political Economy. London: for Baldwin, Cradock, & Joy, 1824. 2nd edn, rvsd & crrctd. 8vo. viii,299,300-304 advt pp. Occas sl foxing. Contemp calf, gilt spine, jnts sl cracked at hd. *(Burmester)* **£180 [≈ $320]**
- Elements of Political Economy. London: Baldwin, Cradock & Joy, 1824. 2nd edn, rvsd & crrctd. Contemp calf, rubbed & marked, rebacked.
(Jarndyce) **£360 [≈ $641]**

Mill, John Stuart
- Essays on Some Unsettled Questions of Political Economy. London: John W. Parker, 1844. 1st edn. 8vo. 164,[4 advt] pp. Orig bds, unopened, lacks label, wear to spine.
(Chapel Hill) **$950 [≈ £534]**
- An Examination of Sir William Hamilton's Philosophy and of the Principal Questions discussed in his Writings. London: Longmans, 1865. 2nd edn. Half-title, addendum leaf. Orig maroon cloth, spine faded, 2 sm holes in jnt.
(Jarndyce) **£110 [≈ $196]**
- Nature, The Utility of Religion, Theism. London: Longmans, Green ..., 1874. 1st edn. 8vo. [xiv],257,[3] pp. Orig green buckram, sl rubbed.
(Gach) **$100 [≈ £56]**
- On Liberty. London: John W. Parker, 1859. 1st edn. 8vo. 207 pp. Blank crnr of title renewed. Front f.e.p. renewed. Orig cloth, spine ends reprd. *(Burmester)* **£450 [≈ $801]**
- On Liberty. London: Longman, 1864. 3rd edn. Orig brown cloth, spine sl faded.
(Jarndyce) **£120 [≈ $214]**
- Principles of Political Economy with Some of their Applications to Social Philosophy. London: John W. Parker, 1848. 1st edn. 2 vols. 8vo. 593,[2]; 549,[1] pp. Orig green cloth, paper labels (darkened), spine ends & 2 crnrs sl rubbed.
(Chapel Hill) **$2,400 [≈ £1,348]**
- Principles of Political Economy with some of their Applications to Social Philosophy. People's Edition. London: Longmans, 1867. Half-title. 32 pp ctlg dated July 1867. Orig purple cloth, spine faded & sl rubbed.
(Jarndyce) **£15 [≈ $27]**
- The Subjection of Women. Second Edition. London: Longman ..., 1869. 8vo. [iv],188 pp. Name on title. Orig cloth, untrimmed, sl soiled & spotted. *(Blackwell's)* **£75 [≈ $134]**
- The Subjection of Women. London: Longmans, 1869. 2nd edn. Half-title. Few marg pencil marks. Orig mustard cloth, dulled. *(Jarndyce)* **£160 [≈ $285]**
- A System of Logic ... London: Longman, 1879. 10th edn. 2 vols. 8vo. Contemp half calf, gilt spines, contrasting labels, fine.
(Burmester) **£120 [≈ $214]**

Millais, J.G.
- British Deer and their Horns. London: Sotheran, 1897. Folio. xviii,224 pp. Cold frontis, gravures, ills. Front f.e.p. creased. Orig buckram. *(Egglishaw)* **£190 [≈ $338]**
- Game Birds and Shooting Sketches ... London: Sotheran, 1892. 1st edn. Lge 4to. xii,62 pp. Port, 15 chromolitho & 18 b/w plates, 31 w'engvs. Orig red half mor gilt. *(Gough)* **£375 [≈ $668]**
- The Mammals of Great Britain and Ireland. London: Longmans, Green, 1904-06. One of 1025. 3 vols. Thick roy 4to. 62 cold & 62 gravure plates, 149 other plates. Orig half buckram, t.e.g., spines sl frayed. *(Egglishaw)* **£315 [≈ $561]**
- The Natural History of British Surface-Feeding Ducks. London: Longmans, Green, 1902. One of 600. Roy 4to. 6 gravures, 41 cold plates, 25 ills. Orig cloth, t.e.g. *(Claude Cox)* **£485 [≈ $863]**
- The Natural History of British Surface-Feeding Ducks. London: Longmans, Green, 1902. One of 600. Roy 4to. Pict half-title, 6 gravures, 41 cold plates, 25 ills. Orig cloth, t.e.g. *(Egglishaw)* **£500 [≈ $890]**
- Rhododendrons: in which is set forth an Account of all Species of the Genus Rhododendron (including Azaleas) and the Various Hybrids. London: 1917-24. One of 550. 2 vols. Folio. 34 cold & 28 collotype plates, 30 photo ills. Orig cloth, trifle used. *(Wheldon & Wesley)* **£800 [≈ $1,424]**

Miller, Charles
- Cosmetic Surgery: The Correction of Featural Imperfections. Phila: 1924. 1st edn. 135 ills. Orig bndg, inner hinges cracked. *(Fye)* **$250 [≈ £140]**

Miller, Dayton Clarence
- Anecdotal History of the Science of Sound to the Beginning of the 20th Century. New York: Macmillan, 1935. 1st edn. 12mo. xii,114 pp. Frontis, plates, ills. Orig bndg. *(Schoen)* **$65 [≈ £37]**
- The Science of Musical Sounds. New York: Macmillan, 1916. 1st edn. 8vo. viii,286 pp. Fldg frontis, ills. Orig bndg. *(Schoen)* **$65 [≈ £37]**
- Sound Waves: their Shape and Speed; a Description of the Phonodeik and its Application ... New York: Macmillan, 1937. 1st edn, 1st printing. 12mo. xi,164 pp. Frontis, plates. Orig cloth. *(Schoen)* **$65 [≈ £37]**

Miller, E. & Whiting, M.C.
- Wild Flowers of the North-Eastern States.

New York: 1904. Roy 8vo. 633 pp. 308 ills. Buckram, used. *(Wheldon & Wesley)* **£30 [≈ $53]**

Miller, Edward
- The Medical Works of Edward Miller, M.D. Late Professor of the Practice of Physic in the University of New York ... New York: Collins, 1814. 1st edn. 2nd iss, with prelims reset & port added. 8vo. 392 pp. 2 ports. Ex-lib. Orig bds, cloth reback. *(Goodrich)* **$195 [≈ £110]**

Miller, G.S.
- The Families and Genera of Bats. London: (1907) 1967. xviii,282 pp. 14 plates. *(Wheldon & Wesley)* **£37 [≈ $66]**

Miller, H.A.
- Cold Cathode Fluorescent Lighting. London: 1949. viii,130 pp. 50 figs. Orig bndg. *(Whitehart)* **£18 [≈ $32]**

Miller, Hugh
- The Cruise of the Betsey: or A Summer Ramble among the Fossiliferous Deposits of the Hebrides. With Rambles of a Geologist. Edinburgh: Constable, 1858. 1st edn. iv,486,5 advt pp. Orig cloth. *(Jermy & Westerman)* **£45 [≈ $80]**

Miller, Philip
- Miller's Dictionary of Gardening, Botany and Agriculture. Parts 1 to 3 [all published]. London: Oct-Dec 1834. 3 parts in one vol. Roy 8vo. 4,192 pp. 2 cold & 3 plain plates. Mod buckram, orig wraps bound in. *(Wheldon & Wesley)* **£180 [≈ $320]**
- The Gardener's and Botanist's Dictionary. Ninth Edition, edited by T. Martyn. London: 1797-1807. 2 vols in 4. Folio. 18 (of 20) plates. Dedic mtd. Mod half leather. *(Wheldon & Wesley)* **£275 [≈ $490]**
- The Gardener's Dictionary ... London: for the author, & sold by C. Rivington, 1731. 1st edn. Folio. xvi,[iv] pp, B1-8D2, a1-zz2 in 2s. Frontis, 4 fldg plates. Occas stains, sm marg worm, sm hole 1 leaf. Contemp calf, rebacked, crnrs reprd. *(Clark)* **£280 [≈ $498]**
- The Gardeners Kalendar ... London: 1732. 1st edn. 8vo. xv,252 pp. Frontis. New half calf, antique style. *(Wheldon & Wesley)* **£120 [≈ $214]**
- The Gardeners Kalendar. London: for John Rivington ..., 1757. Post 8vo. 352, [xii] pp. Frontis. Some ff discold. Contemp (orig?) calf, sl worn. *(Ash)* **£125 [≈ $223]**
- The Gardener's Kalendar ... Thirteenth Edition, adapted to the New Style ... London:

for the author, 1762. 8vo. xv,47,369,[1] pp. Frontis, 5 fldg plates. Sl browning & soiling. Contemp calf, extrs worn, lower jnt cracked. *(Claude Cox)* **£75 [≈$134]**

- The Gardeners Kalendar ... The Fourteenth Edition. With a List of the Medicinal Plants ... London: for the author, 1765. 8vo. xvi, 50, 376,[22] pp. Frontis, 5 fldg plates. Contemp calf, sl rubbed, sm chip hd of spine. *(Karmiole)* **$150 [≈£84]**

- The Gardeners Kalendar ... The Fifteenth Edition. London: Rivington, 1769. 8vo. lxvi, [2 blank],282,[22] pp. Frontis, 5 fldg plates. Contemp calf, gilt backstrip relaid. *(Spelman)* **£90 [≈$160]**

Miller, W.H.

- A Treatise on Crystallography. Cambridge: for J. & J.J. Deighton, 1839. 1st edn. 8vo. viii,139,8 advt pp. 10 plates. Orig cloth backed bds. *(Gaskell)* **£45 [≈$80]**

Millikan, Robert Andrews

- The Electron, Its Isolation and Measurement and the Determination of Some of its Properties. Chicago: UP, 1917. 1st edn. 12mo. xii,268 pp. Ills. Orig bndg, sl shelf worn, spine faded. *(Schoen)* **$75 [≈£42]**

- Electrons (+ and -), Protons, Photons, Neutrons and Cosmic Rays. Chicago: UP, 1935. 16mo. 402 pp. Num ills. Orig bndg, upper hinge weak. *(Schoen)* **$75 [≈£42]**

Millingen, J.G.

- Curiosities of Medical Experience. London: 1839. xvi,566 pp. Foxed. Name. Three qtr calf, gilt spine. *(Whitehart)* **£40 [≈$71]**

Millington, John

- An Epitome of the Elementary Principles of Natural and Experimental Philosophy. Part the First ... Steam Engine. London: for the author, 1823. vii,358 pp. Hand cold frontis, 13 fldg plates. New leather. *(Key Books)* **$130 [≈£73]**

Mills, Edmund J.

- Destructive Distillation: a Manualette of the Paraffin, Coal Tar, Rosin Oil, Petroleum, and Kindred Industries. London: 1877. 8vo. 56 pp. Orig cloth, soiled. *(Weiner)* **£25 [≈$45]**

Milne, David

- Essay on Comets, which gained the first of Dr. Fellowes's Prizes ... Edinburgh: 1828. 4to. xii,189 pp, errata leaf. Orig bds, uncut, worn. Inscrbd by the author. *(Weiner)* **£50 [≈$89]**

Milne, J.

- Earthquakes and Other Earth Movements. New York: International Scientific Series, 1886. xiv, 363 pp. 38 text figs. Orig cloth, dull, sl dusty, spine sl marked. *(Whitehart)* **£15 [≈$27]**

Milne-Edwards, H. & Haime, J.

- A Monograph of the British Fossil Corals. London: Pal. Soc., 1850-54. lxxxv,322 pp. 72 litho plates. New cloth. *(Egglishaw)* **£130 [≈$231]**

Milner, H.B.

- Sedimentary Petrography. London: Murby, 1940. 3rd edn, rvsd & enlgd. 8vo. xxiii,666 pp. 52 plates, 100 text figs. Cloth. *(Savona)* **£25 [≈$45]**

Milton, John Laws

- On the Pathology and Treatment of Gonorrhoea. New York: Wood Library, 1884. 5th edn. 8vo. 306 pp. Orig dec bds. *(Goodrich)* **$45 [≈£25]**

Minerals and Metals ...

- Minerals and Metals. Their Natural History and Uses in the Arts; with Incidental Accounts of Mines and Mining. London: John W. Parker, 1847. 5th edn. 12mo. xii,255 pp. 9 plates. Qtr leather, v worn. *(Gemmary)* **$100 [≈£56]**

Mitchell, A.

- Dreaming, Laughing and Blushing. Edinburgh: 1905. [1],157 pp. 2 lib stamps. Orig cloth, spine sl marked, sm stain front cvr. *(Whitehart)* **£20 [≈$36]**

Mitchell, C. Ainsworth

- Documents and their Scientific Examination with especial reference to the Chemistry involved in cases of Suspected Forgery ... London: 1922. 8vo. xii,215 pp. Ills. Orig cloth. *(Weiner)* **£35 [≈$62]**

Mitchell, James

- The Portable Encyclopaedia: or a Dictionary of the Arts and Sciences, on the basis of Dr. Gregory's ... London: for Thomas Tegg ..., 1828. Roy 8vo. iv,710 pp. Frontis, 51 plates. Contemp half calf. *(Fenning)* **£85 [≈$151]**

Mitchell, John Kearsley

- Five Essays ... Edited by S. Weir Mitchell. Phila: 1859. 1st edn. 371 pp. 1 section starting. Orig bndg, spine rubbed, hinges reinforced. *(Fye)* **$200 [≈£112]**

Mitchell, S. Weir
- Researches upon the Venom of the Rattlesnake. Washington: 1861. Lge 4to. 145 pp. Ills. Orig ptd wraps, lacks rear wrapper, front wrapper detached.
(*Goodrich*) **$495 [≈ £278]**
- Some Recently Discovered Letters of William Harvey with Other Miscellanea with a Bibliography of Harvey's Works by Charles Perry Fisher. Phila: 1912. 1st edn. 59 pp. Wraps.
(*Fye*) **$100 [≈ £56]**

Mivart, G.
- The Cat. An Introduction to the Study of Backboned Animals especially Mammals. London: 1881. xxiii,557 pp. Frontis, 209 figs. Lib stamps on title. Lib bndg.
(*Whitehart*) **£40 [≈ $71]**

Modern ...
- The Modern Practice of the London Hospitals ... A New Edition. With an useful Index of Diseases, and their Remedies. London: for G. Lister, [1785]. 121 pp. Frontis. Rec bds.
(*C.R. Johnson*) **£180 [≈ $320]**

Moeller, F. Peckel
- Cod-Liver Oil and Chemistry. London: 1894. 1st edn. 4to. 508 pp. Frontis, map, text diags. Orig dec cloth, spine sl soiled. Pres copy.
(*Robertshaw*) **£20 [≈ $36]**

Moffet, Thomas
- Health's Improvement; or Rules Comprizing and Discovering the Nature, Method and Manner of Preparing all Sorts of Food ... Enlarged by Christopher Bennet ... London: 1746. 2nd edn. 8vo. xxxii,398 pp. Sl used. Contemp sheep, spine ends reprd, crnrs trifle rubbed.
(*Gough*) **£450 [≈ $801]**

Moll, Albert
- Hypnotism. London: W. Scott, Contemporary Science Series, 1890. 2nd edn. xii,410,[10 advt] pp. Orig cloth gilt, spine faded, front hinge tender.
(*Caius*) **$75 [≈ £42]**
- Hypnotism. London: W. Scott, Contemporary Science Series, [ca 1890]. 3rd edn. [4],xii, 410,[18 advt] pp. Orig cloth gilt, somewhat worn. (*Caius*) **$65 [≈ £37]**

Moller, F.P.
- Cod-Liver Oil and Chemistry. London: 1895. 4to. cxxiii,508 pp. 2 fldg tables, num text diags. Marg ink notes. New cloth.
(*Whitehart*) **£35 [≈ $62]**

Molloy, E. (editor)
- Practical Electrical Engineering. London: [1928]. 5 vols. viii,1928 pp. Num ills.
(*Whitehart*) **£25 [≈ $45]**

Monge, Gaspard
- An Elementary Treatise on Descriptive Geometry, with a Theory of Shadows and of Perspective ... London: John Weale, 1851. 1st edn in English (?). 12mo. vi,137,[2 advt dated 1857] pp. 14 litho plates. Orig green cloth, paper label, spine sl frayed.
(*Gaskell*) **£185 [≈ $329]**

Monro, Alexander, senior
- The Anatomy of the Human Bones and Nerves ... Edinburgh: Monro & Drummond, 1741. 3rd edn, crrctd & enlgd. Sm 8vo. ix,324 pp. Some margs sl thumbed, lacks rear free endpaper. Calf bds, sl worn, sl loss hd of spine. (*Francis Edwards*) **£150 [≈ $267]**

Monro, Alexander, junior
- Essays and Heads of Lectures on Anatomy, Physiology, Pathology and Surgery. With a Memoir of his Life, and Copious Notes ... by his Son and Successor. Edinburgh: 1840. clxx, 132 pp. Frontis port, 6 engvs. Sl foxing, trace of label removal. Orig cloth.
(*Whitehart*) **£160 [≈ $285]**
- The Structure and Physiology of Fishes explained, and compared with those of Man and Other Animals. Edinburgh: 1785. Large Paper. Folio (455 x 285 mm). 50 engvd plates on 44 ff. Occas minor foxing. 2 sm marg reprs. Contemp bds, rebacked in calf.
(*Wheldon & Wesley*) **£400 [≈ $712]**

Monro, D.
- A Treatise on Mineral Waters. London: 1770. 2 vols. xxiv,476; viii,420 pp. Old calf, v worn, water stains on rear cvr of vol 1.
(*Whitehart*) **£180 [≈ $320]**

Monro, T.K.
- The Physician as Man of Letters, Science and Action. Edinburgh & London: 1951. 2nd edn. vi,260 pp. Dw. (*Whitehart*) **£35 [≈ $62]**

Montagu, G.
- Ornithological Dictionary, or, an Alphabetical Synopsis of British Birds. London: 1802. 2 vols. Cold frontis. [With] Supplement. London: 1813. Together 3 vols. 8vo. Contemp half calf, sl worn, Supplement vol rebacked.
(*Wheldon & Wesley*) **£150 [≈ $267]**
- Testacea Britannica, or Natural History of British Shells. [With] Supplement. London:

1803-08. 3 vols. 4to. 2 engvd titles, 16 + 14 cold plates. Sm stamp on titles. Few ff foxed. New half mor.
(Wheldon & Wesley) **£325 [≈ $579]**
- Testacea Britannica, or Natural History of British Shells. London: 1803. 2 vols in one. 4to. 2 engvd titles each with cold vignette, 16 hand cold plates. Mod half calf antique style.
(Wheldon & Wesley) **£200 [≈ $356]**

Monteath, R.
- The Forester's Guide; or A Practical Treatise on the Training and Pruning of Forest Trees ... Stirling: 1820. 1st edn. 12mo. xxiv,212 pp. 2 fldg plates. New bds. and Profitable Planter. London: 1836. 3rd edn. 8vo. xii,500 pp. 16 plates. New cloth. *(Henly)* **£48 [≈ $85]**
- The Forester's Guide and Profitable Planter. London: 1836. 3rd edn. 8vo. xii,500 pp. 16 plates. New cloth.
(Wheldon & Wesley) **£70 [≈ $125]**

Monti, Achille
- Antonio Scarpa and Scientific History and his Role in the Fortunes of the University of Pavia. New York: 1957. 125 pp. Orig bndg.
(Fye) **$50 [≈ £28]**

Moore, George
- The Use of the Body in Relation to the Mind. London: 1847. 2nd edn. viii,433 pp. Orig cloth, faded & worn, crnrs worn, rear inner hinge cracked. *(Whitehart)* **£25 [≈ $45]**
- The Use of the Body in relation to the Mind. London: Longman, Brown, Green, 1847. 2nd edn. viii,433,[1] pp. Contemp calf, gilt spine, rubbed. *(Caius)* **$75 [≈ £42]**

Moore, Henry Charles
- Omnibuses and Cabs. Their Origin and History. London: 1902. 8vo. xiv,282 pp. 31 ills. Orig pict cloth, spine faded & stained by damp. *(Francis Edwards)* **£35 [≈ $62]**

Moore, James
- The History and Practice of Vaccination. London: Callow, 1817. 8vo. 300 pp. Contemp half calf, uncut, rebacked.
(Goodrich) **$395 [≈ £222]**

Moore, John
- Medical Sketches, in Two Parts. London: 1786. 1st edn. 8vo. xii,[2],537,[3] pp. Lib stamps on title. Disbound, sl marked.
(Hemlock) **$125 [≈ £70]**

Moore, N.
- The History of St. Bartholomew's Hospital. London: 1918. 2 vols. xii,614; xiv,992 pp. 2

frontis, 45 plates. Half mor, sl faded in places.
(Whitehart) **£80 [≈ $142]**
- The Physician in English History. Cambridge: 1913. 57 pp. Orig bndg.
(Whitehart) **£15 [≈ $27]**

Moore, P. (editor)
- Astronomical Telescopes and Observatories for Amateurs. Newton Abbot, 1973. 256 pp. 16 plates, 60 text ills. Remains of lib labels.
(Whitehart) **£15 [≈ $27]**

Moore, T.S. & Philip, J.C.
- The Chemical Society, 1841-1941. A Historical Review. London: 1947. 236 pp. 10 plates. Orig bndg. *(Whitehart)* **£15 [≈ $27]**

Moore, Thomas
- British Wild Flowers. Familiarly Described in the Four Seasons ... London: Reeve & Co., 1867. 8vo. xxviii,424,[16 advt] pp. 24 hand cold plates. B'plate partly removed. Orig green cloth gilt. *(Hollett)* **£95 [≈ $169]**

Moore, W.J.
- Health Resorts for Tropical Invalids. In India, at Home, and Abroad. London: 1881. vi,196 pp. Lib stamps on title. Orig bndg.
(Whitehart) **£18 [≈ $32]**

Moorhead, John
- Traumatic Surgery. Phila: 1918. 1st edn. 760 pp. Ills. Orig bndg. *(Fye)* **$60 [≈ £34]**

More, Alexander Goodman
- Life and Letters ... Edited by C.B. Moffat. With Selections from his Zoological and Botanical Writings ... Dublin: Figgis, 1898. 8vo. xii,642 pp. Orig cloth.
(de Burca) **£45 [≈ $80]**

More, L.T.
- Isaac Newton. A Biography. London: 1934. 1st edn. xii,675 pp. Frontis port. Orig bndg, sl worn. *(Whitehart)* **£25 [≈ $45]**

Moreau, R.E.
- The Bird Faunas of Africa and its Islands. London: 1966. Roy 8vo. ix,424 pp. Map, 105 ills. Cloth. *(Wheldon & Wesley)* **£60 [≈ $107]**

Morey, F.
- A Guide to the Natural History of the Isle of Wight. London: 1909. 8vo. xx,560 pp. Map, 31 plates. Cloth.
(Wheldon & Wesley) **£45 [≈ $80]**

Morgan, T.
- The Mechanical Practice of Physick: in

which the Specifick Method is Examin'd and Exploded ... London: 1735. 362 pp. New calf gilt.   *(Goodrich)* **$265 [≈ £149]**
- The Mechanical Practice of Physick. In which the Specifick method is Examin'd and Exploded; and the Bellinian Hypothesis of Animal Secretion and Muscular Motion, Consider'd and refuted. London: 1735. xvi,362 pp. Contemp calf, sl marked.
              (Whitehart) **£375 [≈ $668]**

Morgan, Thomas Hunt
- A Critique on the Theory of Evolution. Princeton: 1916. 1st edn. 197 pp. Orig bndg.
              (Fye) **$75 [≈ £42]**

Morley, Henry
- The Life of Girolamo Cardano of Milan, Physician. London: Chapman & Hall, 1854. 2 vols in one. Sm 4to. Half calf, rebacked.
              (David White) **£45 [≈ $80]**

Morley, J.
- Abdominal Pain. Edinburgh: 1931. xv,191 pp. 22 diags. 1 sm biro note. Orig bndg.
              (Whitehart) **£15 [≈ $27]**

Morrice, Alexander
- A Treatise on Brewing. London: Sherwood, Neely & Jones, 1915. 5th edn. 8vo. xxiv, 179, [1] pp. Bds, rebacked, sl worn.
              (Bookpress) **$185 [≈ £104]**

Morris, A.J.T.
- Treatise on Meteorology: The Barometer, Thermometer, Hygrometer, Rain-Gauge and Ozonometer ... Edinburgh: 1866. viii,98 pp. Orig bndg, spine defective.
              (Whitehart) **£25 [≈ $45]**

Morris, F. & Eames, E.A.
- Our Wild Orchids. New York: 1929. 8vo. xxxi,464 pp. 130 plates (4 cold). Flyleaf & rear endpaper removed. Sm stamp on half-title. Cloth. *(Wheldon & Wesley)* **£50 [≈ $89]**

Morris, F.T.
- Birds of Prey of Australia. Melbourne: 1973. One of 500 signed by the author. Lge folio. 171,4 pp. 24 cold plates & 24 ills by the author. Sheep.
              (Wheldon & Wesley) **£250 [≈ $445]**
- Folio of Finches. Melbourne: 1976. One of 350. Folio. 68 pp. 18 cold plates. Quarter calf.
              (Wheldon & Wesley) **£130 [≈ $231]**

Morris, Francis Orpen
- Book of Natural History, containing a Description of Animals and Birds. London:

1852. 8vo. ii,318 pp. Hand cold half-title, 159 hand cold plates. Sl browning. 1 plate marg torn. Sl dusty. Mod cloth.
              (Wheldon & Wesley) **£120 [≈ $214]**
- A History of British Birds. London: Groombridge, (1863-67). Cabinet edn. 8 vols. Cr 8vo. 358 hand cold plates. Orig red cloth gilt, t.e.g.   *(Egglishaw)* **£520 [≈ $926]**
- A History of British Birds. London: [1863-67]. Cabinet Edition. 8 vols. Cr 8vo. 358 hand cold plates. V sl foxing. Orig red cloth.   *(Wheldon & Wesley)* **£350 [≈ $623]**
- A History of British Birds. Third Edition newly revised, corrected and enlarged. London: Nimmo, 1891. 6 vols. Lge 8vo. 194 hand cold plates. Orig gilt dec green cloth, sl shelf wear.   *(Heritage)* **$1,250 [≈ £702]**
- A History of British Birds. London: Nimmo, 1891. 3rd edn, enlgd. 6 vols. 394 hand cold plates. Sl foxing. Orig dec green cloth gilt, some wear spine ends.
              (Carol Howard) **£550 [≈ $979]**
- A History of British Birds. London: Nimmo, 1895-97. 4tn edn, rvsd, crrctd & enlgd. 6 vols. Roy 8vo. 394 hand cold plates. Orig pict cloth gilt, t.e.g., uncut, partly unopened, fine.
              (Egglishaw) **£680 [≈ $1,210]**
- A History of British Butterflies. London: Groombridge, 1868. Roy 8vo. viii,235,29 pp. 71 hand cold & 2 other plates. Endpapers darkened. Orig cloth gilt, sl wear jnts & edges.   *(Egglishaw)* **£115 [≈ $205]**
- A History of British Butterflies. London: 1890. 6th edn. Roy 8vo. viii,184 pp. 72 hand cold & 2 plain plates. Orig cloth, spine reprd.
              (Wheldon & Wesley) **£90 [≈ $160]**
- A History of British Butterflies. London: 1891. 6th edn. 8vo. [ii],viii,184 pp. 72 hand cold & 2 plain plates. Few ink notes. Orig gilt cloth.   *(Bow Windows)* **£205 [≈ $365]**
- A History of British Butterflies. London: 1893. 7th edn. 4to. viii,234 pp. 79 hand cold & 2 plain plates. Sm blind stamps. Orig cloth gilt, recased.   *(Henly)* **£60 [≈ $107]**
- A Natural History of British Moths. London: Bell & Daldy, 1872. 4 vols. Roy 8vo. 132 hand cold litho plates. Orig cloth, sm tear hd of 1 spine, crnrs sl bumped.
              (Egglishaw) **£105 [≈ $187]**
- A Natural History of British Moths ... London: Bell, 1872. 3rd edn. 4 vols. Lge 8vo. 132 plates containing 1926 cold figs. V occas spotting, mostly to tissues. Orig green cloth gilt, fine.   *(Blackwell's)* **£200 [≈ $356]**
- A Natural History of British Moths ... London: 1891. 4 vols. 132 hand cold plates. Edges spotted. Orig cloth, sl rubbed.
              (King) **$150 [≈ £84]**

- A Natural History of British Moths. London: 1894. 4th edn. 4 vols. Imperial 8vo. 132 hand cold plates. Sm blind stamps. Orig cloth gilt, new endpapers. *(Henly)* £90 [≈ $160]
- A History of British Moths. With an Introduction by W.E. Kirby. London: 1903. 6th edn. 4 vols. Roy 8vo. 132 hand cold plates. Cloth.
  (Wheldon & Wesley) £100 [≈ $178]
- A Natural History of the Eggs and Nests of British Birds. London: Nimmo, 1893. 3rd edn, rvsd & enlgd. 3 vols. 250 hand cold plates. Orig dec green cloth gilt.
  (Carol Howard) £175 [≈ $312]

Morris, Henry
- The Origin and Progress of Renal Surgery. London: 1898. 1st edn. 288 pp. Orig bndg.
  (Fye) $200 [≈ £112]

Morris, Sir Malcolm
- Diseases of the Skin. An Outline of the Principles and Practice of Dermatology. London: Cassell, 1911. 5th edn. 8vo. xv,762 pp. 10 cold & 67 b/w plates. Orig cloth, recased. *(David White)* £18 [≈ $32]

Morris, R.
- Flora Conspicua; a Selection of the most Ornamental Flowering, Hardy, Exotic and Indigenous Trees, Shrubs and Herbaceous Plants ... London: 1830. 8vo. 60 hand cold plates. Half calf, rebacked.
  (Wheldon & Wesley) £750 [≈ $1,335]

Morrow, Prince A.
- Atlas of Skin and Venereal Diseases. New York: Wood, 1889. 2 vols. Lge folio. 75 cold plates. Marg damp stains. Orig bds, backstrips relaid. *(Goodrich)* $150 [≈ £84]

Morse, John T.
- Life and Letters of Oliver Wendell Holmes. Boston: 1896. 1st edn. 2 vols. 358; 335 pp. Orig bndg. *(Fye)* $50 [≈ £28]

Morselli, Enrico Agostino
- Suicide: An Essay on Comparative Moral Statistics. London: Kegan Paul, Trench, 1881. 1st edn in English. 12mo. [4],[xii],388 pp. 32 pp ctlg. 4 fldg maps. Orig dec cloth, edges darkened & shelfworn, hinges taped.
  (Gach) $85 [≈ £48]

Mortensen, T.
- Handbook of the Echinoderms of the British Isles. London: 1927. 8vo. viii,471 pp. 269 text figs. Cloth.
  (Wheldon & Wesley) £45 [≈ $80]

Mortimer, J.
- The Whole Art of Husbandry ... added, The Country-Man's Kalendar ... London: for D. Browne ..., 1761. 6th edn, enlgd. xvi,388, [iv],viii, 450,[vi] pp. Frontis, num text ills. Some browning prelims. Speckled calf gilt, minor wear extrs, lacks 2 labels.
  (Francis Edwards) £260 [≈ $463]

Morton, J.
- On the Nature and Property of Soils: their Connexion with the Geological Formations on which they rest ... Profits of Agriculture. London: 1838. 1st edn. Sm 8vo. xix,235 pp. Cloth, spine sl faded. *(Henly)* £25 [≈ $45]

Morton, Samuel George
- Illustrations of Pulmonary Consumption ... Second Edition. Phila: Edward C. Biddle, 1837. 4to. xiv,15-349,[1] pp. Half-title. 13 cold plates. Orig cloth.
  (Hemlock) $350 [≈ £197]

Morton, Thomas G.
- The History of the Pennsylvania Hospital 1751-1895. Phila: 1895. 1st edn. 573 pp. Orig bndg. *(Fye)* $175 [≈ £98]

Moseley, Benjamin
- A Treatise on Sugar. With Miscellaneous Medical Observations ... Second Edition, with considerable additions. London: Nichols for Robinson, 1800. 8vo. [1-2],iv,3-276 pp. Tiny marg worm few crnrs. V sl browned. Contemp tree calf, rebacked.
  (Finch) £175 [≈ $312]

Moseley, H.F.
- Shoulder Lesions. Springfield: 1945. 1st edn. 181 pp. Dw. *(Fye)* $75 [≈ £42]

Moseley, M.E.
- The British Caddis Flies (Trichoptera), a Collector's Handbook. London: 1939. Roy 8vo. xiv,320 pp. Port, 3 plates, text figs. Cloth. *(Wheldon & Wesley)* £30 [≈ $53]

Mosely, Ephraim
- Teeth, their Natural History: with the Physiology of the Human Mouth, in Regard to Artificial Teeth. London: Robert Hardwick, 1862. 1st edn. Sm 8vo. Orig purple cloth, faded, dusty.
  (Ximenes) $150 [≈ £84]

Moss, Thomas
- A Treatise of Gauging. Containing not only what is common ... but likewise a great variety of New and Interesting Improvements ...

London: for the author ..., also by W. Owen
..., 1765. 1st edn. 8vo. [xii],268 pp. Fldg
plate. Single marg worm hole. Contemp calf.
(Burmester) £250 [≈ $445]

Motte, Andrew
- A Treatise of the Mechanical Powers,
wherein the Laws of Motion, and the
Properties of those Powers are explained ...
London: for Benjamin Motte, 1727. 1st edn.
8vo. [viii],222,[1 errata],[1 advt] pp. 3 plates.
Contemp calf gilt, rubbed, jnts cracked but
sound.   (Gaskell) £650 [≈ $1,157]

Mottelay, Paul Fleury
- Bibliographical History of Electricity &
Magnetism   chronologically   arranged.
London: Charles Griffin, 1922. 8vo. Frontis,
13 plates. Orig blue cloth gilt.
(Clark) £180 [≈ $320]
- Bibliographical History of Electricity &
Magnetism   chronologically   arranged   ...
London: Charles Griffin, 1922. Lge 8vo. Orig
blue cloth gilt.
(Frew Mackenzie) £230 [≈ $409]

Moxon, Elizabeth
- English Housewifery. Exemplified in above
Four Hundred and Fifty Receipts ... with an
Appendix ... Introduction ... Leeds: Griffith
Wright ..., 1775. 11th edn. Lge 12mo. viii,
203, 33,[vii], [vii] pp. Fldg table, 8 plates on
5 ff. Sm reprs. Contemp sheep, rebacked.
(Gough) £275 [≈ $490]

Moxon, J.
- A Tutor to Astronomy ... New York: 1968.
Facs of 1674 edn. viii,272 pp. Orig bndg.
(Whitehart) £35 [≈ $62]

Moyer, James Ambrose
- Radio Receiving Tubes ... New York:
McGraw Hill, 1929. 1st edn, 3rd imp. 12mo.
ix,410 pp. Ills. Orig bndg.
(Schoen) $50 [≈ £28]

Mudie, R.
- The Feathered Tribes of the British Islands.
London: Whittaker, 1834. 1st edn. 2 vols.
8vo. Cold vignette titles, 19 hand cold engvd
plates. Half calf, green labels.
(Egglishaw) £135 [≈ $240]

Mueller, F. von
- The Vegetation of the Chatham Islands.
Melbourne: 1864. 8vo. 86 pp. 7 plates (sl
foxed). Qtr mor.
(Wheldon & Wesley) £80 [≈ $142]

Muffett, Thomas
- Healths Improvement: or, Rules comprizing
and discovering the Nature, Method, and
Manner of Preparing all Sorts of Food used in
this Nation ... Enlarged by Christopher
Bennet ... London: 1655. 4to. Imprimatur
leaf, 8,296 pp. Contemp sheep, sm splits in
jnts. Wing M.2382.
(C.R. Johnson) £2,200 [≈ $3,916]

Muirhead, George
- The Birds of Berwickshire ... Edinburgh:
David Douglas, 1889. One of 100 Large
Paper. 2 vols. Sm 4to. Orig etching, fldg map,
num text ills. Orig buckram gilt, spines
darkened.   (Hollett) £180 [≈ $320]

Mullens, W.H. & Swann, H.K.
- A Bibliography of British Ornithology from
the Earliest Times to the end of 1912.
London: [1916-] 1917. 1st edn. 8vo. xx,691
pp. Sm stain in lower outer crnr of ca 250 pp.
New cloth.
(Wheldon & Wesley) £180 [≈ $320]

Muller, J.
- Elements of Physiology. Translated from the
German, with Notes, by W. Baly. London:
1840-42-48. 1st English edn. 3 vols incl
Supplement. Num ills. Few lib stamps. Some
foxing. Contemp cloth, paper labels, rather
worn.   (Whitehart) £150 [≈ $267]

Muller, John
- The Attack and Defence of Fortified Places.
In Three Parts ... The Fourth Edition;
Corrected, and very much Enlarged, by Isaac
Landmann ... London: Egerton, 1791. 8vo.
xv,[i], 222,[2 blank], 32 pp, advt leaf. 29
plates (1-XXV, V bis, 1-3). Contemp calf, gilt
label.   (Spelman) £260 [≈ $463]
- A Treatise of Artillery ... London: 1780. 3rd
edn, enlgd. 8vo. [viii],xl,214,[2 advt] pp.
Frontis, 28 fldg plates. V sl marg browning at
ends. Contemp calf, jnts splitting, spine
chipped.   (Francis Edwards) £400 [≈ $712]

Munk, William
- Euthanasia: or, Medical Treatment in Aid of
an Easy Death. London: 1887. 1st edn. 105
pp. Orig bndg.   (Fye) $150 [≈ £84]

Murchison, C.
- Functional Derangements of the Liver. The
Croonian Lecture. London: 1874. xvi,182 pp.
6 text figs. Orig cloth, worn & stained.
(Whitehart) £30 [≈ $53]

Murchison, Roderick I.
- Siluria. The History of the Oldest Known Rocks containing Organic Remains. London: 1854. 8vo. xvi,523 pp. Fldg cold geological map, map, 37 plates, text figs. Sm blind stamps. Orig cloth, rebacked.
(Wheldon & Wesley) **£135 [≈ $240]**
- Siluria ... London: Murray, 1872. 5th edn. xvii,566 pp. Cold frontis, num text ills. 1 leaf refixed, occas sl spotting. Panelled calf gilt, few sl marks. *(Hollett)* **£75 [≈ $134]**

Murphy, R.C.
- Oceanic Birds of South America. New York: Amer Mus Nat Hist, 1936. 1st edn. 2 vols. 4to. 88 plates (16 cold), 80 text figs. Sl foxing. Orig buckram, trifle used.
(Wheldon & Wesley) **£200 [≈ $356]**
- Oceanic Birds of South America. New York: [1948]. 2 vols. 4to. 88 plates (16 cold). Buckram. *(Wheldon & Wesley)* **£130 [≈ $231]**

Murray, A.
- The Geographical Distribution of Mammals. London: 1866. 4to. xvi,420 pp. 2 cold plates, 103 cold maps on 61 ff. Blind stamps on title & plates. Orig cloth, reprd.
(Wheldon & Wesley) **£120 [≈ $214]**

Murray, Francis Joseph
- The Theory of Mathematical Machines. New York: King's Crown Press, 1947. 1st edn, 2nd printing. 4to. 116 pp. Ills. Lib pocket. Wrappers, spiral bound. *(Schoen)* **$100 [≈ £56]**

Murray, J.
- The Natural History of the Silk Worm, with the most approved Methods of Rearing Silk and Cultivating the Mulberry applied to our Colonies and Islands. London: 1838. 2nd edn. 8vo. viii,67 pp. Plate. Mod cloth.
(Wheldon & Wesley) **£25 [≈ $45]**

Murray, John
- A Memoir on the Diamond. London: 1831. 12mo. 61,[6] pp. Frontis (inner margin sl defective). Tear in title reprd with tape. Half-title remargined. Prelims soiled. Ex-lib. Qtr mor. *(Weiner)* **£75 [≈ $134]**
- Scepticism in Geology and the Reasons for It ... by Verifier. London: 1878. 2nd edn. 8vo. xiii,132 pp. Errata slip. Plates, ills. Orig cloth. *(Weiner)* **£25 [≈ $45]**

Murray, P.D.F.
- Bones: A Study of the Development and Structure of the Vertebrate Skeleton. Cambridge: 1936. 1st edn. 203 pp. Orig bndg. *(Fye)* **$50 [≈ £28]**

Muschler, R.
- A Manual Flora of Egypt. Berlin: 1912. 2 vols. 8vo. x,1312 pp. Orig cloth.
(Wheldon & Wesley) **£80 [≈ $142]**

Museum Rusticum et Commerciale ...
- Museum Rusticum et Commerciale: or, Select papers on Agriculture, Commerce, Arts, and Manufactures ... Volume the First. London: 1764. viii,488 pp. Frontis. Leather spine v worn, hinges cracked, spine ends defective. *(Whitehart)* **£40 [≈ $71]**

Mushet, David
- Papers on Iron and Steel, Practical and Experimental: a Series of Communications made to the Philosophical Magazine ... London: 1840. Lge thick 8vo. xxvi,952 pp. 6 fldg plates. Orig cloth, sl worn & dusty, backstrip relaid. *(Weiner)* **£100 [≈ $178]**

Myer, Jesse
- Life and Letters of Dr. William Beaumont. Introduction by William Osler. St. Louis: 1939. 327 pp. Orig bndg. *(Fye)* **$75 [≈ £42]**

Myers, L.M.
- Television Optics - An Introduction. London: Pitman, 1936. 1st edn. 12mo. 338 pp. Ills. Orig cloth. *(Schoen)* **$47 [≈ £26]**

Naegele, Franz Carl
- The Obliquely Contracted Pelvis containing also an Appendix of the most important Defects of the Female Pelvis ... Translated from the Original German Edition (1839). New York: 1939. One of 360. 8vo. [10],69,[1] pp. 16 plates. Qtr cloth, shelf worn.
(Goodrich) **$125 [≈ £70]**

Naismith, John
- General View of the Agriculture of the County of Clydesdale ... London: Richard Phillips, 1806. 8vo. xix,[i],252,[4 advt] pp. Fldg hand cold map. Orig bds, paper label, uncut. *(Spelman)* **£150 [≈ $267]**
- Thoughts on Various Objects of Industry pursued in Scotland, with a View to Enquire by what means the Labour of the People may be directed to promote the Public Prosperity. Edinburgh: for the author 1790. Thick 8vo. xii, 656,24 pp. 1 p soiled. Mod half calf.
(Weiner) **£350 [≈ $623]**

Nangle, E.J.
- Instruments and Apparatus in Orthopaedic Surgery. Oxford: 1951. 231 pp. Num ills. Orig bndg. *(Fye)* **$75 [≈ £42]**

Napier, James
- A Manual of the Art of Dyeing. Glasgow: 1853. 1st edn. xvi,405,[8 advt] pp. Text ills. Orig cloth, crnrs bumped, sm dent.
                    (Francis Edwards) **£25 [≈ $45]**

Napier, L.E.
- The Principles and Practice of Tropical Medicine. Calcutta: Thacker, Spink, 1943. 1st edn. 8vo. xii,522 pp. 5 cold & 13 b/w plates, 138 figs. New cloth.
                    (Savona) **£20 [≈ $36]**

Nasmyth, J. & Carpenter, J.
- The Moon: considered as a Planet, a World, and a Satellite. London: 1874. 2nd edn. 4to. xvi,189 pp. 24 plates inc woodburytypes, num w'cuts. Orig pict cloth, edges & spine worn, hinges sl loose.
                    (Whitehart) **£95 [≈ $169]**

Nassim, R. & Burrows, H.J. (editor)
- Modern Trends in Diseases of the Vertebral Column. London: 1959. ix,292,[11] pp. 172 figs. Orig bndg.   *(Whitehart)* **£18 [≈ $32]**

Nattrass, F.J.
- The Commoner Nervous Diseases. For General Practitioners and Students. London: 1931. [vii], 218 pp. 2 cold plates, 15 text ills. 2 names. Orig bndg. *(Whitehart)* **£18 [≈ $32]**

The Natural History of Quadrupeds ...
- The Natural History of Quadrupeds, and Cetaceous Animals, from the Works of the Best Authors, Ancient and Modern. Bungay: Brightly & Co, 1811. 2 vols. 8vo. 120 hand cold engvs. Sl browning. Rec qtr crimson mor, a.e.g.   *(Blackwell's)* **£350 [≈ $623]**

Navier, C.L.M.H.
- On the Means of Comparing the Respective Advantages of Different Lines of Railway ... and on the Use of Locomotive Engines, translated from the French ... by John Macneill. London: 1836. 8vo. xv,[i],(3)-97 pp. Table. 2 old marg reprs. New cloth.
                    (Weiner) **£100 [≈ $178]**

Needham, J.
- Biochemistry   and   Morphogenesis. Cambridge: 1942. 1st edn. Roy 8vo. xvi,785,[2] pp. 35 plates. Cloth, trifle used & loose.   *(Wheldon & Wesley)* **£30 [≈ $53]**

Neil, Samuel (editor)
- The Home Teacher. A Cyclopaedia of Self-Instruction ... London: William Mackenzie, [ca 1886]. 2 vols. 4to. [2],672; 673-1440 pp.

105 plates (many cold), num text figs. Half calf, spine extrs & crnrs scraped.
                    (Karmiole) **$85 [≈ £48]**

Nelson, E.
- The   Moon   and   the   Condition   and Configuration of its Surface. London: 1876. Roy 8vo. xviii,576 pp. 25 maps, 5 plates. Orig cloth, backstrip relaid.   *(Henly)* **£24 [≈ $43]**

Nelson, J. Bryan
- The Sulidae. Gannets and Boobies. OUP: 1978. 4to. xii,1012 pp. Num ills. Dw.
                    (Francis Edwards) **£65 [≈ $116]**

Nelson, Thomas H.
- The Birds of Yorkshire ... London: A. Brown, 1907. 2 vols. 8vo. 2 cold frontis, 206 ills. Orig cloth, gilt faded. *(Blackwell's)* **£150 [≈ $267]**
- The Birds of Yorkshire. A Historical Account of the Avifauna of the County. London: A. Brown & Sons, 1907. 1st edn. 2 vols. 8vo. Errata slip vol 1. 2 cold frontis, dec titles, 208 plates on 161 sheets. Orig cloth, sl rubbed, some fading ft of spines.
                    (Spelman) **£60 [≈ $107]**

Nernst, Walther
- Experimental and Theoretical Applications of Thermodynamics to Chemistry. London: 1907. 8vo. x,123 pp. Orig cloth, sl discold.
                    (Weiner) **£65 [≈ $116]**

Nethersole-Thompson, Desmond
- The Greenshank. London: Collins New Naturalist, 1951. 1st edn. 8vo. 244 pp. 12 maps & diags, 4 cold & 42 b/w plates. Orig cloth gilt. Dw (hd of spine internally strengthened).   *(Hollett)* **£65 [≈ $116]**

Neuberger, M.
- The Historical Development of Experimental Brain and Spinal Cord Physiology before Flourens.   Translated   by   E.   Clarke. Baltimore: 1981. xxv,391 pp. Frontis port. Orig bndg.   *(Whitehart)* **£35 [≈ $62]**

Neugebauer, D.
- The Exact Sciences in Antiquity. Providence: Brown UP, 1957. 2nd edn. 8vo. xvi, 240 pp. Frontis, 14 plates, text ills. Orig cloth. Dw (sl soiled).   *(Worldwide)* **$45 [≈ £25]**

Neumann, Erich
- The Great Mother: an Analysis of the Archetype. New York: Bollingen, 1955. 1st edn. Num ills. Orig bndg.
                    (Deja Vu) **£100 [≈ $178]**
- The Origins & History of Consciousness.

Foreword by C.G. Jung. London: Bollingen, 1954. 1st edn in English. Ills. Dw.
(Deja Vu) **£65 [≈ $116]**

New ...
- The New Dispensatory ... see Lewis, William
- The New Domestic Cookery, or the Housewife's Sure Guide ... By a Lady. Derby: Thomas Richardson; Simpkin, Marshall, London, [ca 1835]. 1st edn. 8vo. 24 pp. Hand cold fldg frontis (tear in 1 fold without loss). Disbound.   *(Burmester)* **£120 [≈ $214]**
- The New Farmer's Calendar ... see Lawrence, John.
- A New Theory of Acute and Slow Continu'd Fevers ... see Cheyne, George

Newberry, J.S.
- The Later Extinct Floras of North America. Washington: 1898. 4to. 295,x pp. 68 plates. Sl staining. New half calf.
(Wheldon & Wesley) **£45 [≈ $80]**

Newlands, John
- On the Discovery of the Periodic Law and on Relations among the Atomic Weights. London: 1884. 8vo. viii,39 pp. Fldg tables. Orig cloth, v sl shaken & soiled. Inscrbd by the author.   *(Weiner)* **£100 [≈ $178]**

Newman, Charles
- The Evolution of Medical Education in the Nineteenth Century. London: 1957. 1st edn. 340 pp. Orig bndg.   *(Fye)* **£100 [≈ £56]**

Newman, Edward
- A Familiar Introduction to the History of Insects, being a new and greatly improved edition of The Grammar of Entomology. London: Van Voorst, 1841. Roy 8vo. 288 pp. Num ills. Cloth on endpaper. Cloth.
(Egglishaw) **£28 [≈ $50]**
- A History of British Ferns. London: Van Voorst, 1844. 2nd edn, enlgd. 8vo. xxxii, 424, [8 advt] pp. Lacks a blank flyleaf. Orig cloth, v sl discold.   *(Fenning)* **£24.50 [≈ $45]**
- An Illustrated Natural History of British Moths. London: Tweedie, 1869. 1st edn. Roy 8vo. 486 pp. Interleaved. Ca 730 text figs. Half calf, jnts split.   *(Egglishaw)* **£21 [≈ $37]**
- An Illustrated Natural History of British Butterflies and Moths. The Figures Drawn by George Willis and Engraved by John Kirchner. London: Glaisher, [1870s]. Roy 8vo. xvi,176, viii,486 pp. Num text figs. Orig pict cloth gilt.   *(Egglishaw)* **£25 [≈ $45]**

Newman, L.H.
- Hawk-Moths of Great Britain and Europe.

London: Cassell, 1965. 8vo. [xvii],148 pp. Photo ills. Orig cloth. Dw.
(Egglishaw) **£25 [≈ $45]**

Newnham, W.
- Essay on Superstition; being an Inquiry into the Effects of Physical Influence on the Mind, in the Production of Dreams, Visions, Ghosts and other Supernatural Appearances. London: 1830. 8vo. xvi,430 pp. New cloth.
(Weiner) **£150 [≈ $267]**

Newsholme, A.
- The Elements of Vital Statistics. London: 1899. 3rd edn. xii,353 pp. 40 text figs. Orig cloth, dull & marked.
(Whitehart) **£15 [≈ $27]**
- Epidemic Diphtheria. A Research on the Origin and Spread of the Disease from an International Standpoint. London: 1898. iv,196 pp. 60 text figs. 2 lib stamps. Orig cloth.   *(Whitehart)* **£25 [≈ $45]**

Newton, A., & others
- A Dictionary of Birds. London: 1896. 8vo. xii,1088 pp. Fldg map, text figs. Orig cloth.
(Henly) **£22 [≈ $39]**

Newton, Sir Isaac
- The Correspondence (1661-1718). Edited by H.W. Turnbull and others. Volumes 1-6. Cambridge: UP, for the Royal Society, 1959-76. 6 vols. 4to. 5 frontis, diags, plates. Orig cloth gilt.   *(Hollett)* **£140 [≈ $249]**
- The Correspondence (1661-1727). Edited by H.W. Turnbull and others. Volumes 1-7. Cambridge: UP, for the Royal Society, 1959-77. 7 vols. 4to. Ills. Orig bndgs, 3 vols with dw.   *(Whitehart)* **£380 [≈ $676]**
- The Correspondence. London: 1959-77. 7 vols. Lge thick 8vo. Ports, few plates. Occas lib marks. Orig cloth. Dws.
(Weiner) **£500 [≈ $890]**
- The Mathematical Papers, 1664-1673. Cambridge, 1967-69. Vols 1-3 (of 8). 3 vols. Lge thick 8vo. Diags. Unabused ex-lib. Dws.
(Weiner) **£120 [≈ $214]**
- The Mathematical Principles of Natural Philosophy. Translated into English by Andrew Motte. To which is added Newton's System of the World. New York: Daniel Adee, 1848. 1st Amer edn. 8vo. vii,8-581 pp. Frontis. Some foxing. Cloth.
(Key Books) **$375 [≈ £211]**
- Opticks ... The Fourth Edition, Corrected. London: for William Innys ..., 1730. 8vo. [viii], 383,[2 advt] pp. 12 fldg plates. Occas sl marks. Old speckled calf, rebacked, sl rubbed.
(Bow Windows) **£800 [≈ $1,424]**

- The System of the World Demonstrated in an Easy and Popular Manner ... Second Edition, Corrected and Improved. London: for J. Robinson, 1740. Reissue of 1st edn of 1731, the title-page is a a cancel. 8vo. 2 plates. Contemp calf, front jnt cracked, lacks label. *(Waterfield's)* £400 [≈ $712]
- A Treatise of the Method of Fluxions and Infinite Series ... Translated from the Latin edition not yet published ... London: for Woodman & Millan, 1737. 1st edn. 2nd issue, with errata on 2B3v. 8vo. 4 fldg tables. Contemp calf, rubbed, jnts cracked but sound. *(Gaskell)* £850 [≈ $1,513]

Newton, J.
- A Complete Herbal, containing the Prints and the English Names of several Thousand Trees, Plants, Shrubs, Flowers, Exotics, etc. ... London: 1802. 6th edn. [xvi] pp. Port, 175 engvd plates of figs. Old calf, rebacked. *(Wheldon & Wesley)* £250 [≈ $445]

Newton, L.
- Handbook of the British Seaweeds. London: BM, 1931. 1st edn. 8vo. 478 pp. 270 figs. Cloth, trifle used. *(Wheldon & Wesley)* £28 [≈ $50]

Niccol, Robert
- Essay on Sugar, and General Treatise on Sugar refining, as practised in the Clyde Refineries ... Greenock: A. Mackenzie, 1864. 1st edn. 4to. [ii],iv,63 pp. Frontis, 26 plates. Orig cloth backed bds, crnrs bumped, ink stain upper cvr. *(Finch)* £110 [≈ $196]

Nichol, John P.
- The Planet Neptune: an Exposition and History. Edinburgh: 1848. Only edn. 8vo. 133 pp. 6 plates. Occas sl marg water stain. Orig cloth, sl wear hd of spine. *(Fenning)* £35 [≈ $62]

Nichols, H. Minor
- Manual of Hand Injuries. Chicago: 1955. 1st edn. 352 pp. 180 ills. Orig bndg. *(Fye)* $100 [≈ £56]

Nichols, T.
- Observations on the Propagation and Management of Oak Trees in general; but more immediately applying to His Majesty's New-Forest in Hampshire ... Southampton: [ca 1791]. 8vo. 42,[i table] pp. Minor browning. Disbound. *(Francis Edwards)* £75 [≈ $134]

Nicholson, G.W. de P.
- Studies on Tumour Formation. London:

1950. xii,637 pp. 183 text ills. Lib label on endpaper, few sm marg lib stamps. Orig cloth, sl worn & dull. *(Whitehart)* £15 [≈ $27]

Nicholson, George (editor)
- The Dictionary of Gardening. London: Upcott Gill, [ca 1900]. 12 vols. Chromolithos, engvs. Orig dec green cloth gilt, a.e.g., sl damp stain on 1 front cvr, trace of worm to cloth of 1 vol. *(Carol Howard)* £125 [≈ $223]
- The Illustrated Dictionary of Gardening. A Practical and Scientific Encyclopaedia of Horticulture ... London: Upcott Gill, 1881-88-1901. 12 vols. 4to. 36 cold lithos, num text w'cuts. Orig pict green cloth gilt, a.e.g., extrs worn. *(Hollett)* £95 [≈ $169]

Nicholson, H.A.
- Lives and Labours of Leading Naturalists. London: 1894. vi,312 pp. 17 ills. New cloth. *(Whitehart)* £18 [≈ $32]
- A Manual of Palaeontology for the Use of Students. With a General Introduction ... London: 1879. 2nd edn. 2 vols. 722 text figs. Orig pict cloth. *(Whitehart)* £35 [≈ $62]

Nicholson, John
- The Operative Mechanic, and British Machinist; being a Practical Display of the Manufactories and Mechanical Arts of the United Kingdom. London: 1825. 2nd edn. 8vo. xvi,796 pp. Fldg frontis, plates. Orig (?) parchment backed bds, uncut, sl worn. *(Weiner)* £175 [≈ $312]

Nicol, Walter
- The Gardener's Kalendar; or Monthly Directory of Operations in every Branch of Horticulture. Edinburgh: 1810. 8vo. xxiv,646 pp. Frontis (foxed). Sl foxing. Contemp half calf, trifle rubbed. *(Wheldon & Wesley)* £45 [≈ $80]
- The Planter's Kalendar; or the Nurseryman's & Forester's Guide. Edited and Completed by Edward Sang. Edinburgh: 1812. 8vo. xx,595,advt pp. 1 plain & 2 cold plates. Contemp calf, gilt label. *(Spelman)* £95 [≈ $169]

Niemeyer, Felix von
- A Textbook of Practical Medicine with particular reference to Physiology and Pathological Anatomy. Translated ... by George H. Humphreys and Charles E. Hackley. Revised Edition. New York: Appleton, 1878. 2 vols. 8vo. Sl foxing. Orig sheep, some wear. *(Goodrich)* $75 [≈ £42]

Nightingale, Florence
- Selected Writings. Edited by L.R. Seymer. New York: 1954. xvi,398 pp. 5 figs. Orig bndg. *(Whitehart)* £15 [≈ $27]

'Nimrod" (C.J. Apperley)
- The Horse and the Hound. Their Various Uses and Treatment including Practical Instructions on Horsemanship and a Treatise on Horse-Dealing. Edinburgh: A. & C. Black, 1842. 1st edn. 8vo. viii,524 pp. 8 plates, text engvs. Half leather, gilt spine (sl scuffed). *(Bookline)* £105 [≈ $187]
- Remarks on the Condition of Hunters, the Choice of Horses, and their Management ... Third Edition. London: 1837. 8vo. viii,503,[1 blank] pp. Few sm marks. Later red half calf. *(Bow Windows)* £75 [≈ $134]

Noad, H.M.
- A Manual of Electricity ... London: 1855-57. 2 vols. 2 frontis, 497 text figs. Orig cloth, rebacked, edges worn. *(Whitehart)* £70 [≈ $125]

Noble, Edward
- The Elements of Linear Perspective demonstrated by Geometrical Principles ... London: for T. Davies, 1771. 1st edn. 8vo. [iv], cxvi,298 pp. 52 plates. Contemp calf, gilt spine, jnts reprd. *(Burmester)* £180 [≈ $320]

Nordenskiold, Erik
- The History of Biology. A Survey. Translated from the Swedish ... New York: Tudor, 1946. 8vo. 32 ports. Orig cloth, sl soiled. *(David White)* £25 [≈ $45]

Norie, John William
- A Complete Epitome of Practical Navigation ... 16th (Stereotype) Edition. London: for the author, 1856. xii,336, xliv,360 pp. 9 plates, 57 tables. Occas sl spotting. Speckled calf gilt, crnrs rubbed. *(Francis Edwards)* £75 [≈ $134]

Norris, William
- The Hunterian Oration delivered before the Royal College of Surgeons on Friday, February 14, 1817 ... London: Cadell & Davies, 1817. Lge 4to. 68 pp. Contemp style bds. *(Goodrich)* $135 [≈ £76]

North, F.J.
- Limestones their Origins, Distribution, and Uses. London: 1930. 1st edn. 8vo. Frontis, 236 ills. Fly leaf marked. Orig cloth. *(Bow Windows)* £30 [≈ $53]

North, F.J., & others
- Snowdonia. The National Park of North Wales. London: Collins New Naturalist, 1949. 1st edn. 8vo. 6 maps, 40 cold & 32 plain plates, 25 diags. Cloth, sl faded. Dw (sl frayed). *(Wheldon & Wesley)* £28 [≈ $50]

North, R.
- The History of Esculent Fish, with Plates ... by E. Albin: and an Essay on the Breeding of Fish, and the Construction of Fish-Ponds. London: 1794. 4to. 80 pp. 18 hand cold plates (sl offset onto text). 1 fig sl trimmed. Contemp straight grain blue mor. *(Wheldon & Wesley)* £750 [≈ $1,335]

Norton, John
- Directions for Taking the Drops. London: [ca 1780]. Lge folio. Single sheet, ptd on both sides. Sm piece torn from crnr just touching text. *(Burmester)* £200 [≈ $356]

Nott, John
- The Cooks and Confectioners Dictionary: or, the Accomplish'd Housewives Companion ... Third Edition, Revised and Recommended. London: H.P. for Charles Rivington, 1726. 8vo. [viii],[620] pp. Frontis, w'engvd 'Model of a Desert'. Contemp calf gilt, sl worn. *(Gough)* £550 [≈ $979]

Novotny, A. & Smith, C. (editors)
- Images of Healing. A Portfolio of American Medical and Pharmaceutical Practice in the 18th, 19th and Early 20th Centuries. New York: 1980. 144 pp. Num ills. Orig bndg. *(Whitehart)* £15 [≈ $27]

Nuland, S.B.
- The Origins of Anaesthesia. London: Classics of Medicine Library, 1983. Sm 4to. Ills. Leather gilt, a.e.g. *(Whitehart)* £65 [≈ $116]

Numbers, R.L.
- The Education of American Physicians. Historical Essays. Berkeley: 1980. xiii,345 pp. Dw. *(Whitehart)* £15 [≈ $27]

Nutt, Frederick
- The Complete Confectioner; or, the Whole Art of Confectionary Made Easy: also Receipts for Home-Made Wines ... Second Edition, Enlarged and Improved by J.J. Machet ... London: 1815. Lge 12mo. xxiv,261, [4 advt] pp. Half-title. Frontis, 10 plates. Contemp half roan, upper hinge reprd. *(Gough)* £250 [≈ $445]

Nutt, T.
- Humanity to Honey Bees; or, Practical Directions for the Management of Honey Bees upon an Improved and Humane Plan. Wisbech: 1839. 5th edn. 8vo. xxx,281 pp. Frontis, text figs. Cloth, spine faded.
(Wheldon & Wesley) £50 [≈ $89]

O'Connell, F.W. & Henry, R.M. (editors)
- An Irish Corpus Astronomiae. Being Manus O'Donnell's Seventeenth Century Version of the Lunario of Geronymo Cortes ... London: 1915. xxxvii,252 pp. Frontis. Orig bndg.
(Whitehart) £25 [≈ $45]

O'Malley, A. & Walsh, J.J.
- Essays in Pastoral Medicine. London: (1906) 1917. x,363 pp. Occas foxing & pencil lines. Orig cloth, faded & worn.
(Whitehart) £25 [≈ $45]

O'Malley, C.D.
- Andreas Vesalius of Brussels. Berkeley: 1964. 1st edn. 480 pp. Orig bndg. *(Fye)* $90 [≈ £51]

Observations on a General Iron Rail-Way...
- See Gray, Thomas

Odling, William
- A Course of Six Lectures on the Chemical Changes of Carbon, reprinted from 'The Chemical News', with Notes by William Crookes. London: 1869. 8vo. xii,162 pp. Marg notes, few ff stained. Orig cloth, spine faded. *(Weiner)* £35 [≈ $62]

Oesterlen, F.
- Medical Logic. London: 1855. 1st English translation. 437 pp. Orig bndg.
(Fye) $75 [≈ £42]

Oesterreich, T.K.
- Possession - Demoniacal & Other among Primitive Races in Antiquity, the Middle Ages & Modern Times. London: Kegan Paul, 1930. 1st UK edn. 400 pp. Orig bndg.
(Deja Vu) £25 [≈ $45]

Ohwi, Jisaburo
- Flora of Japan ... Edited by Frederick G. Meyer and Egbert H. Walker. Washington: Smithsonian, 1965. 4to.x,1068 pp. Frontis, 16 plates, 17 text figs. Orig cloth gilt, ft of spine sl soiled. *(Karmiole)* $100 [≈ £56]

Oldroyd, H.
- The Horse-Flies of the Ethiopian Region. London: BM, 1952-57. 3 vols. Roy 8vo. Ills. Buckram. *(Wheldon & Wesley)* £45 [≈ $80]

Oliver, G.
- A Contribution to the Study of the Blood and Blood-Pressure. Founded on Portions of the Croonian Lectures delivered before the Royal College of Physicians, 1896. London: 1901. xii,276 pp. 54 figs. Lib inscrptn on half-title. Orig bndg, hinge cracked, spine faded.
(Whitehart) £30 [≈ $53]

Oliver, H.C.
- Annotated Index to some early New Zealand Bird Literature. Wellington: 1968. x,222 pp. Bds. *(Wheldon & Wesley)* £35 [≈ $62]

Oliver, W.R.B.
- The Moas of New Zealand and Australia. Wellington: Dominion Museum, 1949. Cr 4to. ix, 206 pp. 143 ills. Orig wraps.
(Wheldon & Wesley) £40 [≈ $71]
- New Zealand Birds. Wellington: 1930. 1st edn. Roy 8vo. 6 cold plates, num ills. Orig cloth, sl faded.
(Wheldon & Wesley) £60 [≈ $107]
- New Zealand Birds. Wellington: 1955. 2nd edn, rvsd & enlgd. 4to. 661 pp. 12 cold plates, num ills. Sm stain on title & frontis marg. Cloth. *(Wheldon & Wesley)* £55 [≈ $98]

Oliver, W.W.
- Stalkers of Pestilence. The Story of Man's Ideas of Infection. New York: 1930. xix,251 pp. 23 ills. Orig bndg.
(Whitehart) £18 [≈ $32]

Olmsted, Denison
- An Introduction to Natural Philosophy ... New Haven: Hezekiah Howl, 1831-32. 1st edn. 2 vols. xvi,346; x,352 pp. Fldg plate, 500 text figs. Foxed. Contemp calf, front hinge reinforced, leather pitted.
(Bookpress) $185 [≈ £104]

Olmsted, J.M.D.
- Claude Bernard, Physiologist. New York: 1938. 1st edn. 272 pp. Orig bndg.
(Fye) $45 [≈ £25]
- Francois Magendie: Pioneer in Experimental Physiology and Scientific Medicine in XIX Century France. New York: 1944. 1st edn. 290 pp. Orig bndg. *(Fye)* $60 [≈ £34]

Olson, Harry Ferdinand
- Dynamical Analogies. New York: Van Nostrand, (1943) 1944. 196 pp. Lib pocket. Orig bndg. *(Schoen)* $45 [≈ £25]

Oosten, H. van
- The Dutch Gardener: or, the Compleat Florist ... Written in Dutch. Translated into

English. London: 1711. 2nd edn. 8vo. [vi], 249, [i],11,[1] pp. Frontis, 2 plates. Contemp panelled calf, trifle used.
(Wheldon & Wesley) **£260 [≈ $463]**

Oppenheimer, Jane
- New Aspects of John and William Hunter ... New York: 1946. xviii,188 pp. Frontis, 4 plates. Orig bndg, unopened.
(Whitehart) **£18 [≈ $32]**
- New Aspects of John and William Hunter. New York: 1946. 1st edn. 188 pp. Orig bndg.
(Fye) **$50 [≈ £28]**

Orage, A.R.
- National Guilds. An Inquiry into the Wage System and the Way Out. London: G. Bell & Sons, 1914. 1st edn. 8vo. viii,370,[6 advt] pp. Orig cloth.
(Claude Cox) **£20 [≈ $36]**

Osler, Sir William
- An Alabama Student and Other Biographical Addresses. London: 1926. 334 pp.
(Fye) **$100 [≈ £56]**
- The Evolution of Modern Medicine. New Haven: 1921. 1st edn. 243 pp. Orig bndg, shaken, rubbed.
(Fye) **$125 [≈ £70]**
- Man's Redemption of Man. New York: 1913. 1st edn in book form. 63 pp. Orig bndg.
(Fye) **$100 [≈ £56]**
- The Old Humanities and the New Science. Boston: 1920. 64 pp. Port. Orig bndg.
(Fye) **$100 [≈ £56]**
- The Principles and Practice of Medicine. New York: 1892. 1st edn. 1079 pp. Orig leather, rubbed, front hinge tender.
(Fye) **$1,000 [≈ £562]**
- The Principles and Practice of Medicine. London: Appleton, 1909. 7th edn, rvsd. 8vo. xvii,1143 pp. Orig cloth, backstrip relaid.
(David White) **£40 [≈ $71]**
- The Principles and Practice of Medicine ... Ninth thoroughly revised edition. New York & London: 1921. Thick 8vo. xxiv,1168 pp. Endpapers marked. Orig cloth, sl dull.
(Bow Windows) **£35 [≈ $62]**
- Science and Immortality. Boston: 1904. 1st edn. 54 pp. Orig bndg. *(Fye)* **$125 [≈ £70]**
- Selected Writings ... with an Introduction by G.L. Keynes. London: 1951. 1st edn. 278 pp. Orig bndg.
(Fye) **$75 [≈ £42]**

Ostwald, Wilhelm
- Manual of Physico-Chemical Experiments. Translated, with Author's Sanction, by James Walker. London: 1894. 8vo. xii,255 pp. Tables in pocket, diags. Occas ink underlining. Orig cloth. *(Weiner)* **£25 [≈ $45]**

- The Scientific Foundations of Analytical Chemistry treated in an Elementary Manner. Translated by G. McGowan. London: 1895. 1st edn. xviii,207 pp. Orig bndg.
(Whitehart) **£25 [≈ $45]**

Oswald, Felix
- Vaccination a Crime, with Comments on Other Sanitary Superstitions. New York: 1901. 1st edn. 195 pp. Half leather.
(Fye) **$75 [≈ £42]**

Otis, George
- A Report on Excisions of the Head of the Femur for Gun-Shot Injury. Washington: 1869. 1st edn. 4to. 143 pp. Lithos ills. Rec cloth. *(Fye)* **$200 [≈ £112]**

Ottley, D. (editor)
- Observations on Surgical Diseases of the Head and Neck. Selected from the Memoirs of the Royal Academy of Surgery of France. London: Sydenham Society, 1848. x,293 pp. Occas foxing & dust staining. Orig cloth, dust stained & worn. *(Whitehart)* **£40 [≈ $71]**

Oudemans, A.C.
- The Great Sea-Serpent. An Historical and Critical Treatise ... London: 1892. Lge 8vo. xv,592 pp. 82 ills. Lib b'plate. Orig pict gilt cloth. *(Francis Edwards)* **£125 [≈ $223]**

Owen, Charles
- An Essay towards a Natural History of Serpents. London: 1742. 4to. xxiii,240,[12] pp. 7 plates. V sl marg staining. Mod half calf antique style.
(Wheldon & Wesley) **£300 [≈ $534]**
- An Essay towards a Natural History of Serpents ... London: John Gray, 1742. 1st edn. Sm 4to. xxiii,240,[12] pp. 7 plates. 1st 23 pp browned in outer marg. Later calf, sl rubbed. *(Bromer)* **$750 [≈ £421]**

Owen, Richard
- A History of British Fossil Mammals and Birds. London: 1846. 1st edn. Roy 8vo. xlvi, 560 pp. 237 w'cuts. Endpapers sl browned. Orig cloth, v sl faded, sm nick hd of spine.
(Francis Edwards) **£95 [≈ $169]**
- The Life of Richard Owen with the Scientific Portions revised by C. Davies Sherborn, also an Essay on Owen's Position in Anatomical Science by T.H. Huxley. London: 1894. 1st edn. 2 vols. 409; 393 pp. Ex-lib. Orig bndg.
(Fye) **$75 [≈ £42]**
- Memoir on the Megatherium, or Giant Ground-Sloth of America (Megatherium americanum Cuvier). London: Royal Society

of London, 1860. 84 pp. 27 litho plates (some sl spotted). New cloth, unopened.
(*Egglishaw*) **£85 [≈ $151]**
- On the Dental Characters of Genera and Species, chiefly of Fishes ... London: 1867. 8vo. 72 pp. 14 partly cold plates. Title & last leaf chipped & soiled. New cloth. Inscribed by the author.   (*Weiner*) **£75 [≈ $134]**

Padgett, Earl
- Plastic and Reconstructive Surgery. Springfield: 1948. 1st edn. 4to. 945 pp. Num ills. Orig bndg.   (*Fye*) **$150 [≈ £84]**
- Skin Grafting from a Personal and Experimental Viewpoint. Springfield: 1942. 1st edn. 149 pp. Ills. Orig bndg.
(*Fye*) **$100 [≈ £56]**

Page, I.
- Guide for Drawing the Acanthus, and every Description of Ornamental Foliage. London: 1840. Sm 8vo. 60 plates (4 cold), num ills. Half calf.   (*Wheldon & Wesley*) **£30 [≈ $53]**

Page, John
- Receipts for Preparing and Compounding the Principal Medicines Made Use of by the late Mr. Ward ... London: Henry Whitridge, 1763. 1st edn. 8vo. [2],33 pp. Disbound.
(*Young's*) **£200 [≈ $356]**

Pagel, Walter
- New Light on William Harvey. New York: 1976. 1st edn. 189 pp. Orig wraps.
(*Fye*) **$60 [≈ £34]**

Paget, Sir James
- On the Cause of the Rhythmic Motion of the Heart. London: 1857. 8vo. 16 pp. Orig wraps, sm defect.   (*Hemlock*) **$200 [≈ £112]**

Paget, Stephen
- Ambroise Pare and his Times, 1510-1590. New York: 1897. 1st edn. 309 pp. Orig bndg.
(*Fye*) **$50 [≈ £28]**

Palmer, Charles F.
- Inebriety: Its Source, Prevention, and Cure. Phila: Union Press, [ca 1900]. 8th edn. 109,[1] pp. Fldg diag. Orig blue cloth.
(*Caius*) **$50 [≈ £28]**

Palmer, Henry R.
- Description of a Railway on a New Principle ... London: 1823. 8vo. vii,60 pp. 2 fldg plates. Occas lib stamps. Cloth.
(*Weiner*) **£275 [≈ $490]**

Palmer, Ralph S.
- Handbook of North American Birds. New Haven: Yale UP, 1976-88. Mixed edns. Vols 1,2,3 & 5. 4 vols. Num ills. Dws.
(*Gough*) **£150 [≈ $267]**

Palmer, T.S.
- Index Generum Mammalium. A List of the Genera of Mammals. Washington: North American Fauna no. 23, 1904. 1st edn. 8vo. 984 pp. Qtr cloth.
(*Wheldon & Wesley*) **£65 [≈ $116]**

Papworth, John
- Essay on the Causes of Dry Rot in Buildings ... London: 1803. 1st edn. Thin 4to. 46 pp. Half-title. Sm lib stamp on title. Contemp half mor, sl worn & chipped.
(*Francis Edwards*) **£175 [≈ $312]**

Paracelsus
- Selected Writings. Edited with Introduction by Jolande Jacobi. Foreword by C.G. Jung. London: 1951. 1st edn in English. 148 ills. Inscrptn. Orig bndg. (*Deja Vu*) **£65 [≈ $116]**
- Selected Writings. Edited with an Introduction by Jolande Jacobi. New York: 1951. 1st English translation. 347 pp. Orig bndg.   (*Fye*) **$75 [≈ £42]**

Pare, Ambroise
- The Apologie and Treatise of Ambroise Pare, containing the Voyages made into Divers Places. Edited and with an Introduction by Geoffrey Keynes. London: Falcon, 1951. 8vo. [xiii],227 pp. 4 ports. Orig cloth. Dw.
(*David White*) **£24 [≈ $43]**
- An Explanation of the Fashion and Use of Three and Fifty Instruments of Chirurgery (1634) ... Edited by H. Crooke. Edinburgh: 1982. [12],118 pp. Orig bndg.
(*Whitehart*) **£15 [≈ $27]**
- The Workes of that famous Chirurgion Ambrose Parey. Translated out of Latine and compared with the French by Jh. Johnson. London: Th. Cotes, 1634, reprinted New York: Milford House, 1968. Folio. Ills. Slipcase.   (*Goodrich*) **$175 [≈ £98]**

Paris, John Ayrton
- The Life of Sir Humphry Davy, Bart. LL.D. Late President of the Royal Society ... London: 1831. 2 vols. xvi,416; viii,463 pp. Port frontis (foxed), fldg facs letter. Minor soil. Cloth backed bds, sl worn & chipped.
(*Francis Edwards*) **£75 [≈ $134]**
- The Life of Sir Humphry Davy. London: 1831. Large Paper. xv,547 pp. Frontis port. Occas sl foxing. Sm lib stamps on title verso.

Later half leather. *(Whitehart)* £125 [≈ $223]
- Pharmacologia. An Extended Inquiry into the Operations of Medicinal Bodies upon which are founded the Theory and Art of Prescribing. London: 1843. 9th edn. xvi,622 pp. Orig cloth, sl stained & worn.
(Whitehart) £40 [≈ $71]
- A Treatise on Diet: with a View to establish on Practical Grounds, a System of Rules for the Prevention and Cure of Diseases incident to a Disordered State of the Digestive Functions. Third Edition, Corrected and Enlarged. London: 1828. 439pp. Spotting. Mod cloth. *(Robertshaw)* £25 [≈ $45]
- A Treatise on Diet: with a View to Establish, on Practical grounds, a System of Rules for the Prevention and Cure of the Diseases incident to a Disordered State of the Digestive Functions. New York: Collins, 1828. 210 pp. V foxed. Orig cloth backed bds, uncut, worn.
(Goodrich) $75 [≈ £42]

Park, Roswell
- Selected Papers, Surgical and Scientific. Buffalo: 1914. 1st edn. 383 pp. Orig bndg.
(Fye) $100 [≈ £56]

Parker, George
- The Elementary Nervous System. Phila: 1919. 8vo. 229 pp. Ills. Orig bndg.
(Goodrich) $75 [≈ £42]

Parker, Harry L.
- Clinical Studies in Neurology. Springfield: C.C. Thomas, [1956]. xiii,[1], 364,[2] pp. Orig cloth. *(Caius)* $50 [≈ £28]

Parker, J.
- Elementary Thermodynamics. Cambridge: UP, 1891. 1st edn. 8vo. viii,408,24 advt pp. Orig cloth. *(Gaskell)* £15 [≈ $27]

Parker, W. Kitchen
- On Mammalian Descent: the Hunterian Lectures for 1884 ... London: 1885. 8vo. xii, 229 pp. Ills. Orig cloth. *(Weiner)* £25 [≈ $45]
- A Monograph on the Structure and Development of the Shoulder Girdle and Sternum in the Vertebrata. London: Ray Society, 1868. 4to. xii,237,[1] pp. 30 tinted litho plates. Lib stamp on title. Orig bds, unopened. *(Egglishaw)* £54 [≈ $96]

Parkes, Samuel
- The Chemical Catechism, with Tables, Notes, Illustrations, and Experiments. London: 1824. 11th edn. xxix,586 pp. Frontis, fldg plate, 1 other plate. Leather, hinges split but bndg firm.

(Whitehart) £60 [≈ $107]
- The Chemical Catechism. London: 1826. 12th edn. 8vo. xxxv,586 pp. Port, fldg plate, plate. Rec half leather, uncut.
(Weiner) £40 [≈ $71]
- An Elementary Treatise on Chemistry, upon the Basis of the Chemical Catechism ... A New Edition ... Adapted to the Present State of Chemical Science. London: [1852?]. 8vo. xii, 411 pp. W'cuts. Orig dec cloth.
(Weiner) £30 [≈ $53]

Parkinson, E.M.
- Catalogue of Medical Books in Manchester University Library 1480-1700. Manchester: 1972. [vii],399 pp. Frontis. Orig bndg.
(Whitehart) £35 [≈ $62]

Parkinson, James
- Organic Remains of a Former World, an Examination of the Mineralized Remains of the Vegetables and Animals of the Antediluvian World ... London: 1820-08-11 pp. 3 vols. 4to. 3 frontis (2 cold), 3 title vignettes, 51 cold plates. Text browned. Lacks vol 1 half-title. Half calf.
(Wheldon & Wesley) £750 [≈ $1,335]

Parkinson, James
- The Chemical Pocket-Book, or Memoranda Chemica ... London: H. Fry, 1800. 1st edn. Sm 8vo. xii,229,[3 errata & advt] pp. Contemp half sheep, label.
(Blackwell's) £300 [≈ $534]

Parkinson, John
- Paradisi in Sole Paradisus Terrestris. Faithfully Reprinted from the Edition of 1629. London: 1904. Folio. 8 ff, 612,16 pp. Num ills. Orig cloth backed bds, sl worn & soiled. *(Weiner)* £275 [≈ $490]
- Theatrum Botanicum ... An Herball of Large Extent ... London: Thos. Cotes, 1640. 1st edn. Folio. xviii,1738 pp, errata leaf. W'cuts. Ptd title, errata leaf & 1st 7 ff laid down with loss. Lacks engvd title & last 2 ff of Table at end. 19th c calf, upper jnts sl split.
(Gough) £495 [≈ $881]

Parnell, E.A. (editor)
- Applied Chemistry; in Manufactures, Arts, and Domestic Economy. Volume 1 [only, of 2]. London: 1844. xvi,453 pp. 23 fabric samples, 40 figs. Occas sl foxing. Inscrptn. Half leather, backstrip relaid.
(Whitehart) £60 [≈ $107]

Parr, Bartholomew
- The London Medical Dictionary ... Phila:

Mitchell, 1819. 1st Amer edn. Lge thick 4to. 57 plates. Browned. Orig calf, rebacked.
(Goodrich) **$395 [≈ £222]**

Parry, E.J.
- Parry's Encyclopaedia of Perfumery. London: 1925. 1st edn. 2 vols. 8vo. [vi],840 pp. Orig cloth.   *(Bow Windows)* **£75 [≈ $134]**

Parry, Thomas
- On Diet, with its Influence on Man; being an Address to Parents etc. ... London: 1844. 1st edn. 8vo. 119 pp. Mod bds, unopened.
(Robertshaw) **£25 [≈ $45]**

Parsons, Robert Percival
- History of Haitian Medicine. New York: Hoeber, 1930. 12mo. xxviii,196 pp. Fldg map frontis, photo ills. Orig bndg, soiled & spotted.   *(McBlain)* **$50 [≈ £28]**

Parsons, William, 3rd Earl of Rosse
- The Scientific Papers, collected and republished by the Hon. Sir Charles Parsons. London: 1926. Lge 4to. [iv],221 pp. Plates. 2 lib stamps. Orig cloth. *(Weiner)* **£75 [≈ $134]**

Partington, C.F.
- The Century of Inventions of the Marquis of Worcester. From the Original MS, with Historical and Explanatory Notes and a Biographical Memoir. London: 1825. Sm 8vo. lxxix, 138 pp. Text ills. Sl marg soiling. Mod bds.   *(Francis Edwards)* **£40 [≈ $71]**
- An Historical and Descriptive Account of the Steam Engine ... London: 1822. xvi,187,90 pp. 8 fldg plates inc frontis. Sl dust staining & browning. Orig bds, new cloth spine.
(Whitehart) **£80 [≈ $142]**

Partington, J.R.
- A History of Greek Fire and Gunpowder. Cambridge: 1960. xvi,382 pp. Frontis, 21 figs. Traces of label removal from endpaper. Orig bndg.   *(Whitehart)* **£40 [≈ $71]**

Pashley, H.N.
- Notes on the Birds of Cley, Norfolk. London: Witherby, 1925. 1st edn. 8vo. 138 pp. 2 photo plates. Prelims sl spotted. Orig green cloth, gilt spine.   *(Gough)* **£80 [≈ $142]**

Pass, Crispin de
- Hortus Floridus. Contayning a very lively and true description of the Flowers of the Springe, Summer, Autumn and Winter. Translated from the Latin by S. Savage ... London: Cresset Press, 1928-29. One of 500. 2 vols. Oblong 4to. Orig half leather. Worn

dw vol 2. *(Wheldon & Wesley)* **£160 [≈ $285]**

Pasteur, Louis
- Studies on Fermentation. London: Macmillan, 1879. 1st English edn. 8vo. xv,418 pp. 12 plates, 85 text figs. Lacks half-title. Occas sl foxing, blind stamp on title. Orig cloth, sl marked & worn.
(Savona) **£70 [≈ $125]**

Patoun, Archibald
- A Complete Treatise of Practical Navigation, demonstrated from its First Principles ... London: for W. Mount, 1770. 8th edn. xii,525 pp. Qtr mor, uncut.
(Young's) **£90 [≈ $160]**

Patten, C.J.
- The Aquatic Birds of Great Britain and Ireland. London: Porter, 1906. 8vo. xxx,590 pp. 56 plates, 68 text figs. New cloth.
(Egglishaw) **£28 [≈ $50]**

Pavlov, I.P.
- Conditioned Reflexes ... Translated and edited by G.V. Anrep. OUP: 1927. 1st English edn. 8vo. xv,430 pp. Orig cloth.
(David White) **£90 [≈ $160]**
- The Work of the Digestive Glands. Second English Edition. London: 1910. 266 pp. Perf lib stamp on title. New cloth.
(Goodrich) **$115 [≈ £65]**

Pavy, Frederick William
- A Treatise on Food and Dietetics, Physiologically and Therapeutically Considered. Second Edition. London: Churchill, 1875. 8vo. x,613,[4 advt] pp. Orig cloth, reprd. Author's inscrptn.
(Fenning) **£65 [≈ $116]**
- A Treatise on Food and Dietetics Physiologically and Therapeutically Considered. Second Edition. New York: Wood, 1881. 8vo. 402 pp. Orig bndg.
(Goodrich) **$65 [≈ £37]**

Paxton, Sir Joseph & Lindley, J.
- Paxton's Flower Garden. Second Edition. London: Cassell, Petter & Galpin, 1882-84. 3 vols. 4to. 108 chromolitho plates. Prelims sl spotted. Orig pict blue cloth gilt, t.e.g., fine.
(Gough) **£975 [≈ $1,736]**

Payne, J.F.
- Observations on some Rare Diseases of the Skin ... London: 1889. 51 pp. 4 plates (2 cold). Lib stamps on title & endpaper. Orig bndg, spine sl marked.
(Whitehart) **£18 [≈ $32]**

- Thomas Sydenham. Masters of Medicine. London: 1900. xvi,264 pp. Frontis port. Prelims sl foxed. Orig cloth, gilt spine sl faded. *(Whitehart)* £18 [≈ $32]

Paynter, H. (editor)
- A Palimpsest on the Electronic Analog Art. Boston: Philbrick, 1955. 4to. 270 pp. Num ills. Lib pocket. Orig dec wraps, sm tears. *(Schoen)* $75 [≈ £42]

Peacock, T.
- Life of Thomas Young, M.D., F.R.S. London: 1855. xiii,514 pp. Frontis port, 1 plate. Sm lib stamp on title. Orig cloth rebacked. Family inscrptn. *(Whitehart)* £50 [≈ $89]

Pearce, E.K.
- Typical Flies. A Photographic Atlas of Diptera, including Aphaniptera. Cambridge: 1915-28. 3 vols. Roy 8vo. 143 plates. Bds. *(Wheldon & Wesley)* £30 [≈ $53]

Pearsall, W.H.
- Mountain and Moorlands. London: Collins New Naturalist, 1950. 1st edn. Plates. Orig cloth. *(Egglishaw)* £25 [≈ $45]

Pearson, John
- The Life of William Hey, Esq. F.R.S. London: 1822. lxxii,356 pp. Frontis port, 2 engvs. Occas foxing, inscrptn on half-title. Three qtr mor. *(Whitehart)* £80 [≈ $142]
- The Life of William Hey. London: 1823. 2nd edn. 2 vols in one. 200; 296 pp. Orig bndg. *(Fye)* $100 [≈ £56]

Pearson, Karl
- The Grammar of Science. London: 1900. 2nd edn. 548 pp. Orig bndg. *(Fye)* $60 [≈ £34]
- The Life, Letters and Labours of Francis Galton. Cambridge: 1914. 1st edn. 3 vols in 4. Orig bndg, vol 1 rebound in buckram. *(Fye)* $200 [≈ £112]

Pearson, R.
- Thesaurus Medicaminum. A New Collection of Medical Prescriptions ... London: 1804. 3rd edn. xii,342 pp. Name on half-title. Top of title cut. Occas foxing. Contemp bds, crnrs v worn, rebacked in cloth. *(Whitehart)* £90 [≈ $160]

Peattie, D.C.
- Green Laurels. The Lives and Achievements of the Great Naturalists. London: 1937. 8vo. 383 pp. 29 plates. Orig cloth gilt. *(Henly)* £21 [≈ $37]

Pechey, John
- Collections of Acute Diseases, in Five Parts ... London: sold by Henry Bonwicke, 1691 [-88]. 2nd edn. Sm 8vo. [viii],101, [ix], [2 blank],8,[iii], 100,[vii],[ii],94, [iv],[iv], 107,[v] pp. Divisional titles, licence leaf. Some mostly marg worm. New calf. Wing P.1020. *(Blackwell's)* £600 [≈ $1,068]

Peck, T.W. & Wilkinson, K.D.
- William Withering of Birmingham. London: 1950. viii,240 pp. 52 plates. Orig bndg. *(Whitehart)* £15 [≈ $27]

Peckham, G.W. & E.G.
- Wasps Social and Solitary. London: 1905. Cr 8vo. xvi,311 pp. Num ills. Orig cloth, trifle used. *(Wheldon & Wesley)* £20 [≈ $36]

Peddie, W.
- Colour Vision. A Discussion of the Leading Phenomena and their Physical Laws. London: 1922. xii,208 pp. 30 text figs. Sev lib stamps. Orig bndg. *(Whitehart)* £18 [≈ $32]

Pederson, O.
- Early Physics and Astronomy. A Historical Introduction. London: History of Science Library, 1974. vi,414 pp. 119 ills. Orig bndg. *(Whitehart)* £18 [≈ $32]

Peek, B.M.
- The Planet Jupiter. London: 1958. 283 pp. 16 plates, 15 text figs. Orig bndg. *(Whitehart)* £18 [≈ $32]

Pegge, Samuel
- The Forme of Cury, A Roll of Ancient English Cookery, Compiled, about A.D. 1390 ... London: J. Nichols ..., 1780. 1st edn. iv,xxxvi,188 pp. Port of Pegge (dated 1785), 1 plate. Contemp mottled calf, gilt dec spine, jnts cracked but sound, hd of spine reprd. *(Gough)* £675 [≈ $1,202]

Peierls, Rudolf Ernst
- Quantum Theory of Solids. Oxford: Clarendon, 1955. 1st edn. 8vo. 229 pp. Lib pocket. Orig cloth. *(Schoen)* $35 [≈ £20]

Pemberton, Henry
- The Dispensatory of the Royal College of Physicians, London. Translated into English with Remarks ... London: 1746. x,420 pp. Contemp calf, early reback, crnrs reprd. *(Whitehart)* £180 [≈ $320]
- The Dispensatory of the Royal College of Physicians, London, Translated into English with remarks ... London: for Longman ...,

1746. 1st edn. 8vo. Contemp calf, gilt spine, fine.   *(Georges)* **£350 [≃$623]**
- The Dispensatory of the Royal College of Physicians, London. Translated into English with Remarks ... London: 1748. 2nd edn. x,414 pp. Contemp calf gilt, mor label, crnr edges worn.   *(Whitehart)* **£135 [≃$240]**
- The Dispensatory of the Royal College of Physicians, London. Translated into English with Remarks, &c. Fourth Edition. London: J. Nourse, 1760. 8vo. x,414 pp. Contemp calf, orig paper label, sm surface damage rear bd.   *(Spelman)* **£140 [≃$249]**
- A View of Sir Isaac Newton's Philosophy. London: S. Palmer, 1728. 1st edn. 4to. [50], 407 pp. 12 plates, engvd decs. Contemp calf, rebacked.   *(O'Neal)* **$325 [≃£183]**
- A View of Sir Isaac Newton's Philosophy. London: S. Palmer, 1728. 1st edn. 4to. Title, [xlviii], 407 pp. 12 fldg plates. Repr to title verso, tiny hole p 203. Contemp calf, sometime rebacked. Anon.
                    (Frew Mackenzie) **£350 [≃$623]**
- A View of Sir Isaac Newton's Philosophy. London: S. Palmer, 1728. 4to. Subscribers. 12 plates, num decs by Pine. Few sm marg worm holes. Contemp calf, rebacked. Anon.
                    (Waterfield's) **£450 [≃$801]**
- A View of Sir Isaac Newton's Philosophy. Dublin: re-printed by and for John Hyde, 1728. 44,333 pp. 12 fldg plates. Contemp calf, red label. *(C.R. Johnson)* **£350 [≃$623]**

Pendleton, John
- Our Railways, their Origin, Development, Incident and Romance. London: Cassell, 1896. 2 vols. 8vo. 18 plates, num ills. Occas foxing. Half calf, gilt spines faded.
                    (Bow Windows) **£85 [≃$151]**

Pengelly, Hester (editor)
- A Memoir of William Pengelly, of Torquay, F.R.S., Geologist, with a Selection from his Correspondence ... London: 1897. 1st edn. 8vo. xii,341 pp. Port, 10 plates. Orig cloth, trifle marked. *(Bow Windows)* **£60 [≃$107]**

Penhallow, Dunlap
- Military Surgery. London: 1916. 1st edn. 432 pp. 150 ills. Endpapers & few index ff v spotted. Orig bndg, faded & stained.
                    (Fye) **$80 [≃£45]**

Penn, Granville
- A Comparative Estimate of the Mineral and Mosaical Geologies. Second Edition Revised and Enlarged with relation to the latest Publications in Geology. London: 1825. 2 vols. 8vo. lxv,353; viii,426 pp. Orig bds,

uncut, spines worn. *(Weiner)* **£100 [≃$178]**
- Conversations on Geology ... London: 1840. 2nd edn. 12mo. [xviii],309,[3] pp. 2 cold & 8 other plates. Name on frontis recto. Orig cloth, recased. *(Bow Windows)* **£65 [≃$116]**

Pennant, Thomas
- British Zoology Illustrated by Plates and Brief Explanations. London: 1770. 8vo. iv, 96, [iv] pp. 103 plates. Contemp calf. Anon.
                    (Wheldon & Wesley) **£120 [≃$214]**
- British Zoology. New Edition. London: 1812. 4 vols. 8vo. 4 addtnl engvd titles, 293 engvs. Calf, rebacked. *(Henly)* **£220 [≃$392]**

Penning, William H.
- Field Geology. With a Section on Palaeontology. By A.J. Jukes-Brown. London: Bailliere, Tindall, & Cox, (1876). 1st edn. 8vo. Cold frontis, 25 ills. Orig cloth.
                    (Fenning) **£28.50 [≃$52]**

Pennington, A.S.
- British Zoophytes. London: 1885. 8vo. xvi, 363 pp. 24 plates. Cloth.
                    (Wheldon & Wesley) **£20 [≃$36]**

Penrose, Lionel S.
- The Biology of Mental Defect. London: Sidgwick & Jackson, [1949]. 1st edn. xiv,285 pp. Orig cloth.   *(Caius)* **$50 [≃£28]**

Penzer, N.M.
- Poison-Damsels and other Essays in Folklore and Anthropology. Privately Printed: 1952. 1st edn. Sm 4to. 319 pp. Dw (sl chipped).
                    (Francis Edwards) **£45 [≃$80]**

Pepper, William (editor)
- An American Text-Book of the Theory and Practice of Medicine. Phila: 1893. 2 vols. 8vo. Orig cloth.   *(Goodrich)* **$95 [≃£53]**

Percy, John
- Metallurgy ... Fuel, Fire-Clays, Copper, Zinc, Brass, Etc. London: 1861. 8vo. xiv,635 pp. Ills. Orig cloth. *(Weiner)* **£65 [≃$116]**
- The Metallurgy of Lead, including Desilverization and Cupellation. London: 1870. 8vo. xvi,567 pp. Plate, ills (3 cold by crayon). New cloth. *(Weiner)* **£75 [≃$134]**

Pereira, Jonathan
- The Elements of Materia Medica and Therapeutics. London: Longman, 1842. 2nd edn, enlgd. 4 vols. xlii,1926 pp. Interleaved. Text figs. Half mor, gilt spines.
                    (David White) **£95 [≃$169]**
- A Treatise on Food and Diet: with

Observations on the Dietetical Regimen
suited for Disordered States of the Digestive
Organs ... London: Longmans, 1843. 1st edn.
32 pp ctlg. Contemp cloth, sl rubbed &
marked.   *(Jarndyce)* **£95 [≈ $169]**

Pernetti, Jacques
- Philosophical Letters upon Physiognomies.
To which are added, Dissertations ...
London: for R. Griffiths ..., 1751. 1st edn in
English. 8vo. xxiv,259, [1 blank],[4 advt] pp.
Old wraps, uncut. Anon.
                   (Burmester) **£140 [≈ $249]**

Perrin, Mrs H. & Boulger, G.S.
- British Flowering Plants. London: 1914. One
of 1000. 4 vols. Roy 4to. 300 cold plates. Orig
buckram gilt.   *(Henly)* **£150 [≈ $267]**
- British Flowering Plants. New and Revised
Edition. Edited by A.K. Jackson. London:
Ward, Lock, 1939. Roy 4to. 667 pp. 260 cold
plates. Cloth.   *(Egglishaw)* **£28 [≈ $50]**

Perrot, C.L.E.
- A Selection of British Birds. Ilkley: 1979.
One of 250. Folio. [vi,5] pp. 5 cold plates.
Half mor. Half mor slipcase (sl water stained).
            (Wheldon & Wesley) **£75 [≈ $134]**

Perry, George
- Conchology, or the Natural History of Shells
... London: 1811. 1st edn. 1st issue, with no
later watermark. Folio. 61 hand cold plates.
Unfoxed. V sl offsetting. 2 v sm reprs. New
half mor.
     (Wheldon & Wesley) **£3,000 [≈ $5,340]**
- Conchology, or the Natural History of Shells
... London: W. Miller, 1811. 1st edn. Lge
folio. 61 hand cold plates. Occas sl foxing &
offsetting. 19th c half mor, gilt dec spine,
uncut.   *(Heritage)* **$5,000 [≈ £2,809]**

Person, David
- Varieties: or, a Surveigh of Rare and
Excellent Matters, necessary and delectable
for all sorts of Persons ... London: for
Thomas Alchorn, 1635. 1st edn. 4to. Sep title
to each part. 2 sm paper flaws. Contemp calf,
backstrip laid down, crnrs worn. STC 19781.
                (Gaskell) **£600 [≈ $1,068]**

Peterkin, A., & others
- Commissioned Officers in the Medical
Services of the British Army 1660-1960.
London: Wellcome Hist Med Lib, 1968. 2
vols. Lge 8vo. Orig buckram.
                 (Bow Windows) **£30 [≈ $53]**

Peters, H.
- Pictorial History of Ancient Pharmacy; with
Sketches of Early Medical Practice.
Translated by W. Netter. Chicago: 1902. 3rd
edn. xiv,212 pp. Ills. Orig half mor, rebacked,
edges worn.   *(Whitehart)* **£60 [≈ $107]**

Peterson, R.T.
- Sir Kenelm Digby. The Ornament of
England. Harvard: 1956. 8vo. 336 pp. Ills.
Dw.   *(Goodrich)* **$65 [≈ £37]**

Pettey, George
- The Narcotic Drug Diseases and Allied
Ailments: Pathology, Pathogenesis, and
Treatment. Phila: 1913. 1st edn. 516 pp. Orig
bndg.   *(Fye)* **$75 [≈ £42]**

Pettigrew, Thomas Joseph
- Memoirs of the Life and Writings of the late
John Coakley Lettsom. London: 1817. 3 vols.
Frontis. Occas sl foxing. Contemp roan &
bds, spines worn. *(Whitehart)* **£250 [≈ $445]**
- On Superstitions connected with the History
and Practice of Medicine and Surgery.
London: 1844. 1st edn. 167 pp. Orig bndg.
                   (Fye) **$200 [≈ £112]**

Pettus, Sir John
- Fleta Minor. The Laws of Art and Nature, in
... Metals. In Two Parts ... London: Stephen
Bateman, 1686. 1st edn. 3rd issue, with the
sep titled dictionary of terms dated 1683.
Folio. Errata. Port frontis. num text engvs.
Contemp calf, rebacked. Wing P.1907.
                 (Vanbrugh) **£1,855 [≈ $3,302]**
- Volatiles from the History of Adam and Eve:
containing, many unquestioned Truths, and
allowable Notions, of several Natures.
London: for T. Bassett, 1674. 1st edn. 8vo.
Errata leaf. Lacks final blank leaf. Contemp
sheep, rebacked. Wing P.1912.
                   (Hannas) **£160 [≈ $285]**

Pfaundler, M. Schlossmann
- The Diseases of Children. A Work for the
Practising Physician. English Translation by
Henry Shaw and Linnaeus L. Fetra ... Phila:
1908. 1st English edn. 4 vols. Lge 8vo. Orig
cloth.   *(Goodrich)* **$95 [≈ £53]**

Pharmacopoeia ...
- Pharmacopoeia of the United States of
America. By the Authority of the Medical
Societies and Colleges. Boston: Wells & Lilly
for Charles Ewer, 1820. 1st edn. 8vo. 272 pp.
Contemp calf, mor label, rubbed.
                  (Hemlock) **$475 [≈ £267]**

Phelps, William
- Calendarium Botanicum, or a Botanical Calendar. London: Lackington, Allen, 1810. 1st edn. Roy 8vo. [xvi],186,[ii] pp. 5 hand cold plates. Sl marking of text. Contemp red half mor, sl rubbed.   *(Ash)* **£100 [≈ $178]**

Philip, A.P.W.
- A Treatise on Indigestion and its Consequences called Nervous and Bilious Complaints ... London: 1828. 6th edn. xxviii, 416 pp. Marg foxing. Old bds, worn, rebacked.   *(Whitehart)* **£90 [≈ $160]**

Phillips, Charles D.F.
- Materia Medica and Therapeutics - Vegetable Kingdom. Edited and Adapted to the U.S. Pharmacopoeia by Henry G. Piffard. New York: Wood Library, 1879. 8vo. 323 pp. Orig bndg, some wear to spine ends.
    (Goodrich) **$45 [≈ £25]**

Phillips, Henry
- Pomarium Britannicum: an Historical and Botanical Account of Fruits, known in Great Britain. London: T. & J. Allman, 1820. 1st edn. Lge 8vo. [x],viii,378 pp. 3 hand cold plates. Diced calf, sl rubbed. *(Hortulus)* **$270 [≈ £152]**
- Pomarium Britannicum; an Historical and Botanical Account of the Fruits known in Great Britain. Third Edition, considerably enlarged and improved. London: Colburn, 1823. 8vo. xx,372 pp. 3 hand cold plates. Sl foxing. Contemp calf gilt, sl rubbed.
    (Blackwell's) **£100 [≈ $178]**
- Sylva Florifera: The Shrubbery, Historically & Botanically treated, with Observations on the Formation of Ornamental Plantations, and Picturesque Scenery. London: 1823. 1st edn. 2 vols. Sl browning. Orig cloth backed bds, worn.   *(Hortulus)* **$150 [≈ £84]**

Phillips, John
- On the Remains of Microscopic Animals in the Rocks of Yorkshire. Leeds: 1846. 8vo. 14 pp. Plate. Disbound, old front wrapper preserved. Author's pres inscrptn.
    (Weiner) **£30 [≈ $53]**

Phillips, Philip
- The Forth Bridge in its Various Stages of Construction ... Edinburgh: Grant, (1899). 1st edn. Oblong folio. [x],233 pp, inc 52 plates. Later qtr mor, orig pict cvr laid down.
    (Bookpress) **$2,500 [≈ £1,404]**

Phillips, Sarah
- The Ladies Handmaid: or, a Compleat System of Cookery ... London: for J. Coote,

1758. Only edn. 8vo. 472,[18] pp. Frontis incorporating a port of the author & 4 copperplates. Rec half calf over old mrbld bds.   *(Sotheran's)* **£995 [≈ $1,771]**

Phillips, T.E.R. & Steavenson, W.H. (editors)
- Hutchinson's Splendour of the Heavens. A Popular Authoritative Astronomy. London: [1923]. 2 vols in one. Lge 4to. 980 pp. 25 cold plates, 1104 b/w ills. Orig cloth, sl worn, spine sl weak.   *(Whitehart)* **£38 [≈ $68]**

Phillips, William
- An Outline of Mineralogy and Geology ... London: 1815. 1st edn. Sm 8vo. [xii],193,[1 blank] pp. 4 plates (2 hand cold). Stain at ft of frontis. Some foxing. Few pencil notes. Old half calf, jnts cracked, spine ends chipped.
    (Bow Windows) **£165 [≈ $294]**

Philosophical Letters upon Physiognomies...
- See Pernetti, Jacques.

A Physical Vade Mecum ...
- See Poole, Robert

Pidgeon, Edward
- The Fossil Remains of the Animal Kingdom. London: 1830. 1st edn. Lge 8vo. 544 pp. 49 plates. Occas browning. Amateur half mor.
    (Francis Edwards) **£48 [≈ $85]**

Piesse, G.W. Septimus
- The Art of Perfumery and the Methods of Obtaining the Odour of Plants ... Fourth Edition. London: 1879. 8vo. ills. Orig bndg.
    (Robertshaw) **£35 [≈ $62]**

Pike, Nicholas
- A New and Complete System of Arithmetic, composed for the Use of the Citizens of the United States. Newbury-port: John Mycall, 1788. 1st edn. 8vo. Some wear & tear. Lacks half-title & 2 advt ff. Contemp calf, rebacked, worn.   *(D & D Galleries)* **$250 [≈ £140]**

Pilcher, Lewis
- A List of Books by Some of the Old Masters of Medicine and Surgery together with Books on the History of Medicine ... in the possession of Lewis Stephen Pilcher ... Brooklyn: 1918. One of 250. 201 pp. Orig bndg.   *(Fye)* **$250 [≈ £140]**

Pindborg, J.J. & Marvitz, L.
- The Dentist in Art. London: George Proffer, 1961. 1st edn. 4to. 144 pp. Num ills. Dw.
    (Any Amount) **£35 [≈ $62]**

Pirquet, C.F. von
- Serum Sickness. Translated by B. Schick. Baltimore: Williams & Wilkins, 1951. 1st edn in English. 8vo. ix,130 pp. Dw (sm tear hd of spine).   *(David White)* £18 [≈$32]

Pitt, J.I.
- The Genus Penicillium. London: Academic Press, 1979. 1st edn. 8vo. 634 pp. 132 text figs. Cloth. Dw.   *(Savona)* £20 [≈$36]

Pittonia
- Pittonia. A Series of Papers relating to Botany and Botanists. Edited by E.L. Greene. Berkeley, Calif.: 1887-1905. 5 vols (complete). Roy 8vo. 14 plates. Half mor, vol 1 spine scuffed.
                    (Wheldon & Wesley) £75 [≈$134]

Platt, Sir Hugh
- The Garden of Eden. Or an accurate Description of all Flowers and Fruits now growing in England ... The fifth edition. London: William Leake, 1660. 1st edn of part 2. 2 parts in one vol. 12mo. 175,[i]; [16], 159, [i] pp. Some browning. Contemp calf, rebacked, crnrs rubbed. Wing 2387A.
                    (Spelman) £420 [≈$748]
- The Garden of Eden: or, an accurate Description of all Flowers and Fruits now growing in England ... London: 1675. 6th edn. 2 parts in one vol. Sm 8vo. [xxviii],148, [xiv], 159 pp. Mod calf.
                    (Wheldon & Wesley) £275 [≈$490]

Plattes, Gabriel
- A Discovery of Subterraneal Treasure: viz. Of all manner of Mines and Minerals, from Gold to the Coal ... London: for J.E., 1653. 60 pp. Sm marg tear title. Disbound. Wing P.2410. Anon.   *(C.R. Johnson)* £750 [≈$1,335]

Playfair, John
- The Works, with a Memoir of the Author (by James G. Playfair, the editor, and Lord Jeffrey). Edinburgh: 1822. 4 vols. 8vo. 8 fldg plates. Sm lib stamp on titles. Polished calf, worn, backstrips relaid.
                    (Weiner) £300 [≈$534]

Plesch Library
- The Magnificent Botanical Library of the Stiftung fur Botanik ... Collected by the late Arpad Plesch. London: Sotheby Parke Bernet, 1975-76. 3 vols. Tall 4to. Num plates. Orig ptd bds, sl worn. Price list.
                    (Terramedia) $180 [≈£101]

Plot, Robert
- The Natural History of Oxfordshire ... Second Edition, with large Additions and Corrections ... Oxford: Leon. Lichfield ..., 1705. Folio. [xii],366,[x] pp. Fldg map (linen backed), 16 plates. Contemp calf, sometime rebacked, crnrs reprd, edges sl rubbed.
                    (Blackwell's) £500 [≈$890]

Pluche, Noel-Antoine
- The History of the Heavens, considered according to the Notions of the Poets and Philosophers, compared with the Doctrines of Moses ... Second Edition. London: Osborn, 1743. 2nd English edn. 2 vols. 12mo. Frontis & 24 plates vol 1. Contemp calf, worn, jnts cracked but firm.   *(Gaskell)* £140 [≈$249]
- Spectacle de la Nature: or Nature Display'd ... Translated from the Original French, by Mr. Humphreys. London: 1740-49. Vols 1-3 5th edn, vol 4 3rd edn, 5-7 2nd edn. 7 vols. 12mo. 207 plates (of 208, lacks 2 plates but with 1 duplicate). Rec half calf. Anon.
                    (Frew Mackenzie) £295 [≈$525]

Plues, Margaret
- British Ferns ... London: Reeve, 1866. 8vo. x,281 pp. 16 hand cold plates. Orig cloth.
                    (Egglishaw) £30 [≈$53]
- British Ferns: an Introduction to the Study of the Ferns, Lycopods and Equiseta. London: 1866. 8vo. x,281 pp. 16 cold plates, 59 text figs. Sl foxing. Cloth, spine worn.
                    (Wheldon & Wesley) £20 [≈$36]
- Rambles in Search of Flowerless Plants. London: Journal of Horticulture, 1864. 1st edn. viii,317 pp. 8 hand cold & 12 colour-printed plates. Orig green cloth, crinkled, spine sl bumped.   *(Gough)* £35 [≈$62]

Plunket, E.M.
- Ancient Calendars and Constellations. London: 1903. xvi,255 pp. 24 plates, figs. Occas foxing prelims, sm marks half-title. Orig cloth, sl worn & marked.
                    (Whitehart) £25 [≈$45]

Plymley, Joseph
- General View of the Agriculture of Shropshire. London: Richard Phillips, 1803. 8vo. xxiv,366,[2 advt] pp. Map, 5 fldg plates. Orig bds, uncut, paper label, crnrs sl bumped, spine ends reprd. *(Spelman)* £160 [≈$285]

Pointer, John
- A Rational Account of the Weather, shewing Sings of its Several Changes and Alterations, together with the Philosophical Reasons of them. Oxford: L.L. for S. Wilmot ..., 1723.

76 pp. Rebound in panelled calf.
(*C.R. Johnson*) **£220 [≈ $392]**

Pole, Thomas
- The Anatomical Instructor; or, an Illustration of the Modern and most Approved Methods of preparing and preserving the different Parts of the Human Body and of Quadrupeds ... London: 1790. 8vo. lxxx,[6], 304,[7] pp. 10 plates. Calf, jnts split.
(*Goodrich*) **$275 [≈ £154]**

Polehampton, Edward & Good, J.M.
- The Gallery of Nature and Art; or, A Tour through Creation and Science ... London: sold by Baldwin, Craddock & Joy ..., 1818. 6 vols. 8vo. 100 engvs (2 hand cold). Occas spotting. Contemp polished calf, gilt spines, green labels. (*Frew Mackenzie*) **£350 [≈ $623]**

Pollard, H.B.C.
- Game Birds, Rearing, Preservation and Shooting. London: Eyre & Spottiswoode, 1929. 4to. xi,186 pp. 22 cold plates by Philip Rickman. Orig cloth, uncut.
(*Egglishaw*) **£65 [≈ $116]**

Polunin, O. & Smythies, B.E.
- Flowers of South-West Europe, a Field Guide. London: 1973. 8vo. xv,480 pp. 78 cold plates, num ills. Cloth.
(*Wheldon & Wesley*) **£35 [≈ $62]**

Pontey, William
- The Profitable Planter: a Treatise on the Theory and Practice of Planting Forest Trees ... London: for J. Harding, 1814. 4th edn, enlgd. Advt leaf inserted. Orig blue bds, brown spine & ptd label chipped.
(*Jarndyce*) **£48 [≈ $85]**

Ponton, Mungo
- The Great Architect, as Manifested in the Material Universe. London: Nelson, 1866. 2nd edn. vi,276 pp. 11 cold litho plates. Orig dec cloth gilt, spine faded, crnrs v sl worn.
(*Europa*) **£35 [≈ $62]**

Poole, Robert
- A Physical Vade Mecum or Fifth Gift of Theophilus Philanthropos. Wherein is Contain'd, the Dispensatory of St. Thomas's Hospital ... London: 1741. liv,324,[xii] pp. Frontis. Contemp leather, rebacked.
(*Whitehart*) **£375 [≈ $668]**
- A Physical Vade Mecum: or Fifth Gift of Theophilus Philanthropos. Contain'd, the Dispensatory of St. Thomas's Hospital ... London: E. Duncomb, 1741. 1st edn. 8vo. [ii],xviii, liv,324,[xii] pp. Contemp

calf, some wear, sl used. Anon.
(*Sotheran's*) **£350 [≈ $623]**

Pope, William
- The Triumphal Chariot of Friction, or a Familiar Elucidation of the Origin of Magnetic Attraction, &c. &c. London: for the author, 1829. 4to. vii,108 pp. Subscribers. Engvd title, 10 plates (sl foxed). Title remargd & sl stained. Orig bds, rebacked.
(*Weiner*) **£85 [≈ $151]**

Portal, Paul
- The Compleat Practice of Men and Woman Midwives, or, the True Manner of Assisting a Woman in Child-Bearing ... London: H. Clark, for S. Crouch, 1705. 1st English edn. 8vo. [xvi], 245,[3 advt] pp. 2 plates. Sl stain on title. Rec contemp style calf.
(*Young's*) **£450 [≈ $801]**

Portlock, J.E.
- Report on the Geology of the County of Londonderry and of Parts of Tyrone and Fermanagh. Dublin: Milliken, 1843. 8vo. xxxi,784 pp. Fldg map, plates. Orig cloth.
(*de Burca*) **£100 [≈ $178]**
- Report on the Geology of the County of Londonderry and of Parts of Tyrone and Fermanagh. Dublin: 1843. 8vo. xxxii,784 pp. Hand cold geological map, 5 fldg hand cold sections, 45 plates of fossils, 4 fldg plates. Cloth, backstrip relaid.
(*Henly*) **£150 [≈ $267]**

Postlethwayt, Malachy
- Universal Dictionary of Trade and Commerce, translated from the French of the celebrated Monsieur Savary ... with Large Additions and Improvements ... London: 1757. 2nd edn. 2 vols. Folio. xxii,xiv, 1917,[1]; [viii],856 pp. Frontis, fldg table. Lib cloth. (*Whitehart*) **£200 [≈ $356]**

Poucher, W.A.
- Perfumes and Cosmetics with especial reference to Synthetics. London: 1923. xi,462 pp. Plates, ills. Orig bndg.
(*Whitehart*) **£25 [≈ $45]**

Pouchet, F.A.
- The Universe: or, The Infinitely Great and the Infinitely Little. New Edition ... London: 1874. One vol in 4 divisions. Lge 8vo. 8 cold plates, 343 w'engvs. Some foxing & red crayoning. Sev sections loose. Orig dec cloth gilt, a.e.g. (*Bow Windows*) **£75 [≈ $134]**
- The Universe: The Infinitely Great & the Infinitely Small. London: Blackie, [inscrptn dated 1898]. Tall 8vo. 564 pp. 4

chromolithos, 270 w'engvs. Orig gilt dec red cloth, a.e.g. *(Carol Howard)* **£35 [≈$62]**

Powell, Sir Allan
- The Metropolitan Asylums Board and Its Work, 1867-1930. London: 1930. 1st edn. 106 pp. Cold frontis, photo plates. Name. Orig cloth, hd of spine sl bumped.
(Caius) **$65 [≈£37]**

Power, Sir D'Arcy
- Selected Writings 1877-1930. Oxford: 1931. x,368 pp. Frontis port, fldg map, 16 plates, 9 text figs. Orig bndg. *(Whitehart)* **£35 [≈$62]**
- William Harvey. Masters of Medicine. London: 1897. xii,284 pp. Frontis port. Prelims foxed. Orig cloth, gilt spine sl faded.
(Whitehart) **£18 [≈$32]**

Poynter, F.N.L. (editor)
- Chemistry in the Service of Medicine. London: 1963. viii,208 pp. 34 ills. Orig bndg. Dw. *(Whitehart)* **£18 [≈$32]**

Poynting, G.
- Eggs of British Birds, with an Account of their Breeding Habits. Limicolae. London: 1895-96. 4to. 54 cold plates. Contemp dark red half mor gilt, t.e.g., orig wraps bound in, fine. *(Egglishaw)* **£315 [≈$561]**

Poynting, John Henry
- Collected Scientific Papers. Cambridge: UP, 1920. 1st edn. Roy 8vo. xxxii,768 pp. Port. Orig cloth. *(Gaskell)* **£85 [≈$151]**

The Practical Housewife ...
- The Practical Housewife; A Complete Encyclopaedia of Domestic Economy ... New Edition, Revised and Greatly Enlarged. London: Houlston & Sons, [ca 1880]. 8vo. xvi, 336 pp. Frontis, w'engvd ills. Orig pict brown cloth gilt, fine. *(Gough)* **£50 [≈$89]**

Praeger, R.L.
- The Botanist in Ireland. Dublin: Figgis, 1934. 8vo. Fldg maps, ills. Orig cloth, rebacked. *(de Burca)* **£50 [≈$89]**
- Natural History of Ireland. A Sketch of Its Fauna and Flora. London: 1950. 8vo. 350 pp. 3 maps, diags, endpaper map. Cloth.
(Wheldon & Wesley) **£35 [≈$62]**
- A Tourist's Flora of the West of Ireland. Dublin: Figgis, 1909. 8vo. Fldg map, ills. Some pencil notes. Orig cloth.
(de Burca) **£60 [≈$107]**
- The Way that I went. An Irishman in Ireland. London: Methuen, 1947. 8vo. Ills. Orig cloth. Dw. *(de Burca)* **£30 [≈$53]**

Pratt, Anne
- Chapters on the Common Things of the Sea-Coast. London: SPCK, 1853. 1st edn. 12mo. x,345 pp. W'engvd frontis & vignette. Orig cloth. *(Claude Cox)* **£18 [≈$32]**
- The Ferns of Great Britain. London: SPCK, [ca 1850s]. 2nd edn. 8vo. 164 pp. 41 cold plates. Orig cloth, a.e.g., fine.
(Carol Howard) **£50 [≈$89]**
- The Ferns of Great Britain and their Allies ... London: SPCK, (1862). 2nd edn. 8vo. iv,164 pp. 41 cold plates. Orig cloth, sl wear spine ends. *(Egglishaw)* **£22 [≈$39]**
- The Ferns of Great Britain and their Allies the Club Mosses, Pepperworts and Horsetails. London: n.d. 8vo. 41 cold plates. Orig cloth, backstrip relaid.
(Henly) **£35 [≈$62]**
- The Flowering Plants of Great Britain [including the Grasses, Sedges and Ferns]. London: SPCK, [ca 1860]. 4 vols. 320 cold plates. Orig pict green cloth gilt, a.e.g.
(Gough) **£245 [≈$436]**
- Wild Flowers of the Year. London: 1929. Cr 8vo. xii,284,4 advt pp. Cold title vignette, 47 cold plates. Orig cloth, sl damp stain front cvr & top edge. *(Henly)* **£21 [≈$37]**

Prescott, H.P.
- Strong Drink and Tobacco Smoke. (The Structure, Growth, and Uses of Malt, Hops, Yeats, and Tobacco). London: Macmillan, 1869. 1st edn. 8vo. xii,71,[55 ctlg] pp. 10 plates. Orig cloth, backstrip relaid, crnrs worn. *(Savona)* **£45 [≈$80]**

Preston, Thomas
- The Theory of Light. Second Edition. London: 1895. 8vo. xvii,[1 blank],574,[2 advt] pp. Text figs. Lib stamp on title. Orig cloth, sl marked. *(Bow Windows)* **£35 [≈$62]**

Prestwich, G.
- Geology, Chemical, Physical, and Stratigraphical. London: 1886-88. 2 vols. Roy 8vo. 2 cold geol maps, 3 maps (2 cold), 3 plates of sections (2 cold), 16 plates, 474 text figs. Cloth. *(Wheldon & Wesley)* **£45 [≈$80]**

Price, Harry
- Fifty Years of Psychical Research. A Critical Survey. London: Longmans, Green, 1939. 1st edn. 8vo. Frontis, 14 plates, 3 text ills. Orig cloth, sl dust soiled.
(Claude Cox) **£25 [≈$45]**

Price, Sarah
- Illustrations of the Fungi of Our Fields and Woods. Drawn from Natural Specimens.

[First & Second Series]. London: for the
author by Lovell Reeve & Co, 1864-65. 1st
edn. 2 vols. 4to. 20 hand cold plates. Orig
green cloth gilt, near fine.
        (Chapel Hill) **$800 [≈ £449]**

Prichard, James Cowles
- The Natural History of Man ... Fourth
Edition, Edited and Enlarged by Edward
Norris. London: Bailliere, 1855. 2 vols. 8vo.
62 plates (all but 5 hand cold), 100 w'engvs in
text. Orig pict cloth, fine.
        (Gach) **$375 [≈ £211]**
- Researches into the Physical History of
Mankind. London: 1836-37. 3rd edn. 2 vols.
xx,376; xv,373 pp. Hand cold frontis, 14 figs
on plates, 5 plates. Occas sl foxing. Orig
cloth, worn & dull. *(Whitehart)* **£40 [≈ $71]**

Priest, C.D.
- The Birds of Southern Rhodesia. London:
1933-36. 4 vols, all published. Roy 8vo. Map,
40 cold plates, 521 text figs. Cloth, spines
faded, cloth lifting slightly.
        (Wheldon & Wesley) **£300 [≈ $534]**
- The Birds of Southern Rhodesia. London:
1933-36. 4 vols. 4to. Fldg map, 40 cold plates,
521 ills. Orig bndg.
        (Chalmers Hallam) **£270 [≈ $481]**

Priestley, Joseph
- Heads of Lectures on a Course of
Experimental Philosophy, particularly
including Chemistry, delivered at the New
College in Hackney. Dublin: 1794. 12mo.
208 pp. Contemp calf, lower cvr damaged.
        (Robertshaw) **£55 [≈ $98]**

Prince, Morton
- The Nature of Mind and Human
Automatism. Philadelphia & London:
Lippincott, 1885. 1st edn. 12mo. [ii],x,173,[5]
pp. Sm lib marks. Orig cloth.
        (Gach) **$250 [≈ £140]**

Pringle, J.
- Observations upon Diseases of the Army, in
Camp and Garrison. The Second Edition,
corrected with additions. London: 1753.
xxvii, 403,51 pp. Orig calf, jnts reprd.
        (Whitehart) **£280 [≈ $498]**

Pringle, J.H.
- Fractures and their Treatment. Oxford: 1910.
xii,384 pp. 142 text figs. Orig bndg.
        (Whitehart) **£18 [≈ $32]**

Prior, Thomas
- An Authentic Narrative of the Success of Tar-

Water in curing a Great Number and Variety
of Distempers ... Dublin: R. Gunne, 1746.
1st edn. 8vo. [iv],248 pp. Some browning.
Contemp calf, front hinge cracked.
        (Bookpress) **$300 [≈ £169]**

Pritchard, Andrew
- A History of Infusoria, including the
Desmidiaceae and Diatomaceae, British and
Foreign. London: 1861. 4th edn. 8vo. xii,968
pp. 40 plain plates. Trifle foxed. Orig cloth,
recased.   *(Wheldon & Wesley)* **£65 [≈ $116]**
- The Natural History of Animalcules:
containing Descriptions of all the Known
Species of Infusoria ... London: 1834. 1st
edn. 8vo. 196 pp. Fldg litho frontis, 6 engvd
plates (some foxing & spotting). Orig bds,
roughly rebacked in cloth.
        (Robertshaw) **£50 [≈ $89]**

Proctor, Richard Anthony
- Chance and Luck: a Discussion of the Laws
of Luck, Coincidences, Wagers, Lotteries,
and the Fallacies of Gambling ... New
Edition. London: 1889. 8vo. vi,263 pp. Orig
cloth, worn & soiled.   *(Weiner)* **£21 [≈ $37]**
- Myths and Marvels of Astronomy. London:
1878. vii,363 pp. Orig cloth, sl worn & dusty,
label removed from spine.
        (Whitehart) **£25 [≈ $45]**
- Science Byways: A Series of Familiar
Dissertations on Life in other Worlds;
Comets and the Sun ... Mental Feats ...
London: 1875. Cr 8vo. xv,422,3 pp. Frontis.
Orig cloth, unopened.   *(Henly)* **£35 [≈ $62]**

Prout, William
- Chemistry Meteorology and the Function of
Digestion. Considered with reference to
Natural Theology. London: 1834. xxiii, [iv],
564 pp. Fldg map. Half mor gilt, extrs sl
rubbed, minor staining.
        (Francis Edwards) **£60 [≈ $107]**
- Chemistry, Meteorology, and the Function of
Digestion, considered with reference to
Natural Theology ... Edited by J.W. Griffith.
London: Bohn, 1855. 4th edn. 12mo. xxviii,
419, [32 advt] pp. Fldg cold map, frontis.
Rebound in cloth. *(Key Books)* **$45 [≈ £25]**

Pufendorf, Samuel
- Of the Law of Nature and Nations. Oxford:
L. Lichfield for A. & J. Churchil ..., 1703. 1st
edn in English. Folio. [xxiv],400, 262,[2
errata] pp. Title foxed, few sm marg dust
marks. Contemp calf, gilt spine, edges sl
rubbed, spine varnished.
        (Gach) **$1,500 [≈ £843]**

Pulteney, Richard
- A General View of the Writings of Linnaeus. London: 1781. 1st edn. 8vo. iv, 425, [1] pp. Mod half vellum.
(Wheldon & Wesley) **£175 [≈ $312]**
- Historical and Biographical Sketches of the Progress of Botany in England ... London: Cadell, 1790. 1st edn. 2 vols. xx,360; viii, 352, index, 32,2 pp. Orig bds, untrimmed, vol 1 sl worn.
(Jermy & Westerman) **£240 [≈ $427]**

Purser, Paul E.
- Manned Spacecraft: Engineering Design and Operation. New York: Fairchild, 1964. 4to. 497 pp. Ills. Lib pocket. Orig bndg.
(Schoen) **$150 [≈ £84]**

Pusey, W.A.
- The Principles and Practice of Dermatology Designed for Students and Practitioners. London: 1907. xxiv,1021 pp. 1 cold plate, 367 text ills. Lib stamp on title verso. Orig cloth, lib stamp on spine.
(Whitehart) **£25 [≈ $45]**

Putnam, Ruth
- Life and Letters of Mary Putnam Jacobi. New York: 1925. 1st edn. 381 pp. Ex-lib. Orig bndg.
(Fye) **$75 [≈ £42]**

Putzel, L.
- A Treatise on Common Forms of Functional Nervous Diseases. New York: Wood Library, 1880. 8vo. 256,[45 ctlg] pp. Orig bndg.
(Goodrich) **$35 [≈ £20]**

Quarrington, C.A.
- Modern Practical Radio and Television. London: Caxton Publishing Co., 1955. 4 vols. Lge 8vo. x,250; viii,196; viii,208; vi,90 pp. 17 plates, 7 fldg diags, num text figs. Orig blue cloth. *(Claude Cox)* **£20 [≈ $36]**

Quincy, John
- The Dispensatory of the Royal College of Physicians in London ... London: for R. Knaplock ..., 1721. 1st edn. 8vo. [xvi], 362, [363-377] pp. Errata. Occas sl stains. Title marg sl worn. Contemp calf, crnrs bumped.
(Vanbrugh) **£255 [≈ $454]**
- Lexicon Physico-Medicum: or, a New Medical Dictionary ... The Fourth Edition, with new Improvements ... London: Osborn & Longman, 1730. 8vo. xvi,480 pp. Sm marg tear title. Contemp panelled calf.
(Spelman) **£140 [≈ $249]**
- Pharmacopoeia Officinalis & Extemporanea: or a Complete English Dispensatory in Four

Parts ... Fourth Edition, much enlarged ... London: E. Bell, 1722. 8vo. xvi,674,59 pp. Contemp panelled leather, worn but firm.
(Bates & Hindmarch) **£85 [≈ $151]**
- Pharmacopoeia Officinalis & Extemporanea: or, a Complete English Dispensatory, in Four Parts ... London: for J. Osborn ..., 1730. 8th edn, enlgd. Occas v sl browning. Panelled calf, jnts sl rubbed, spine rubbed & lacks label. *(Francis Edwards)* **£125 [≈ $223]**
- Pharmacopoeia Officinalis & Extemporanea: or, A Compleat English Dispensatory. The Twelfth Edition, much enlarged and corrected. London: for Thomas Longman, 1742. 8vo. xvi, 700, ix pp. Sm reprs to title. Occas sl browning. Old calf, rebacked.
(David White) **£38 [≈ $68]**
- Pharmacopoeia Officinalis & Extemporanea: or, A Complete English Dispensatory, in Two Parts, Theoretic and Practical. London: 1761. 13th edn. xxiv,704,index pp. Endpapers detached & torn. Old leather, sl worn, *(Whitehart)* **£120 [≈ $214]**

Race, R.R. & Sanger, R.
- Blood Groups in Man. London: 1975. 6th edn. ix,659 pp. Text figs. Traces of label removal. Orig bndg. *(Whitehart)* **£18 [≈ $32]**

Rackstrow, Benjamin
- An Explanation of the Figure of Anatomy, Wherein the Circulation of the Blood is made visible thro' Glass Veins and Arteries ... [London]: 1747. 2nd edn. 8vo. 15,[1] pp. Fldg plate. Unbound & uncut.
(Goodrich) **$395 [≈ £222]**

Radcliffe, J.N.
- Fiends, Ghosts & Sprites. London: 1854. 1st edn. Orig bndg. *(Deja Vu)* **£55 [≈ $98]**

Radcliffe-Crocker, H.
- Diseases of the Skin ... London: 1903. 3rd edn. 2 vols. 4 plates, 112 ills. Few sm lib stamps. Orig bndg, inner hinge vol 2 cracked.
(Whitehart) **£25 [≈ $45]**

Raffald, Elizabeth
- The Experienced English Housekeeper ... Ninth Edition ... London: for R. Baldwin, 1784. 8vo. viii,384,[13] pp. Port, 3 fldg plates. Raffald's signature printed across the heading of Chapter 1. Half mor, by Bayntun.
(Gough) **£375 [≈ $668]**
- The Experienced English Housekeeper, for the Use and Ease of Ladies, Housekeepers, Cooks, &c. ... New Edition ... together with the Complete Art of Carving and Marketing. Manchester: G. Bancks, [ca 1800?]. 12mo.

viii, 434 pp. Port, 4 plates. Contemp calf, rebacked.   *(D & D Galleries)* **$250 [≈£140]**

Rafter, W. & Baker, M.N.
- Sewage Disposal in the United States. Second Edition. New York: Van Nostrand, 1894. Lge 8vo. xxvii,598,[5 advt] pp. 7 fldg plates, 116 text figs, tables. Orig cloth gilt, extrs sl rubbed.   *(Karmiole)* **$60 [≈£34]**

Rajharhia, Chand Mull
- Mining, Processing, and Uses of Indian Mica. New York: McGraw Hill, 1951. 1st edn. 8vo. 388 pp. Maps, ills. Lib pocket. Orig cloth.   *(Schoen)* **$50 [≈£28]**

Rakkine, W.J. Macquorn
- Miscellaneous Scientific Papers ... with a Memoir of the Author by P.G. Tait. Edited by W.J. Millar. London: 1881. Thick 8vo. xxxvi, 567 pp. Fldg chart, diags. Prize calf gilt, sl worn.   *(Weiner)* **£75 [≈$134]**

Ralfs, J.
- The British Desmidieae. The Drawings by Edward Jenner. London: Reeve, 1848. 1st edn. xxiv,226,18 advt pp. 1 plain & 34 hand cold plates. New qtr calf.
    (Egglishaw) **£140 [≈$249]**

Ralph, T.S.
- Icones Carpologicae, or Figures and Descriptions of Fruits and Seeds - Leguminosae [all published]. London: 1849. 4to. [vi],48,[4] pp. 40 plates. Plate margs sl foxed. Mod bds.
    (Wheldon & Wesley) **£55 [≈$98]**

Ramadge, Francis Hopkins
- Asthma, its Species and Complications ... London: 1835. 1st edn. 4to. vii,[1],380 pp. 6 cold plates. Orig bds, uncut, fine.
    (Hemlock) **$400 [≈£225]**
- Consumption Curable ... added A Mode of Treatment ... London: 1836. 3rd edn. 8vo. 7 litho plates (6 cold). Half calf.
    (Hemlock) **$300 [≈£169]**

Ramazzini, B.
- De Morbis Artificium Diatriba. Diseases of the Workers. The Latin Text of 1713, revised with Translations and Notes by Wilmer Cave Wright. Chicago: Classics of Medicine Library, (1940) 1983. xliv,549 pp. Port, ills. Leather gilt, a.e.g. *(Whitehart)* **£80 [≈$142]**

Ramsay, Sir William
- Essays Biographical and Chemical. London: Constable, 1908. 1st edn. 247 pp. Orig bndg,

spine sl faded. Author's pres inscrptn.
    (Key Books) **$95 [≈£53]**
- The Life and Letters of Joseph Black. London: 1918. xix,148 pp. Frontis port, 6 plates. Prelims sl foxed. Cloth.
    (Whitehart) **£35 [≈$62]**
- The Life and Letters of Sir Joseph Black. With an Introduction dealing with the Life and Work of Sir William Ramsay. London: 1918. xix,148 pp. Port frontis, 6 plates. Page edges ragged. Orig bndg, spine faded.
    (Whitehart) **£35 [≈$62]**

Ramsbotham, Francis H.
- The Principles and Practice of Obstetric Medicine and Surgery, in reference to the Process of Parturition. Fifth Edition, revised. London: Churchill, 1868. 8vo. xxiii, 752, [2,40 advt] pp. 94 plates. Occas sl water stain. Rec bds.   *(Fenning)* **£48.50 [≈$87]**

Ramsbottom, J.
- Mushrooms and Toadstools. London: Collins New Naturalist, 1953. 1st edn. 8vo. 142 photos (84 cold). Orig cloth, trifle spotted. Dw.   *(Wheldon & Wesley)* **£20 [≈$36]**

Randall, John
- The Semi-Virgilian Husbandry, deduced from Various Experiments: or, an Essay towards a New Course of National Farming ... London: B. Law ..., 1764. 1st edn. 8vo. lxiii,[i], 356, 11, [i] pp. 3 plates. Contemp calf, gilt dec spine (ends chipped).
    (Clark) **£200 [≈$356]**

Rang, M.
- Anthology of Orthopaedics. London: 1966. xi,243 pp. Text ills. Orig cloth, sl marked.
    (Whitehart) **£15 [≈$27]**

Rank, B.K. & Wakefield, A.R.
- Surgery of Repair as applied to Hand Injuries. Edinburgh: 1960. 2nd edn. 282 pp. 219 ills. Dw.   *(Fye)* **$125 [≈£70]**
- Surgery of Repair as applied to Hand Injuries. Edinburgh: 1968. 3rd edn. Dw.
    (Fye) **$60 [≈£34]**

Rankine, W.J.M.
- A Manual of Applied Mechanics. London: 1872. 6th edn. 2 vols. xvi,648 pp. 265 figs. Binder's cloth.   *(Whitehart)* **£40 [≈$71]**

Raunkiaer, C.
- The Life Forms of Plants and Statistical Plant Geography being the Collected Papers ... Oxford: 1934. Roy 8vo. xvi,632 pp. 189 ills. Cloth, worn, trifle wormed.

(Wheldon & Wesley) **£45** [≈ $80]

Raven, Charles E.
- English Naturalists from Neckham to Ray. A Study of the Making of the Modern World. Cambridge: 1947. 1st edn. 8vo. x,379 pp. Cloth.   *(Wheldon & Wesley)* **£60** [≈ $107]
- English Naturalists from Neckham to Ray. A Study of the Making of the Modern World. Cambridge: UP, 1947. 1st edn. Lge 8vo. x,379 pp. Mark to endpaper. Price-clipped dustwrapper. *(Francis Edwards)* **£35** [≈ $62]
- John Ray, Naturalist; his Life and Works. Cambridge: 1942. 8vo. xix,502 pp. Port. Cloth, trifle used.
          (Wheldon & Wesley) **£60** [≈ $107]
- John Ray, Naturalist. His Life and Works. Cambridge: UP, 1950. 2nd edn. Lge 8vo. xix,506 pp. Endpapers v sl foxed. Price-clipped dustwrapper.
          (Francis Edwards) **£50** [≈ $89]

Ray, John
- Select Remains of the Learned John Ray. With his Life by William Derham. London: 1760. 8vo. vii,336 pp. Frontis port, 3 text engvs. Lacks errata slip. Contemp calf, rebacked, crnrs reprd.
          (Weiner) **£180** [≈ $320]

Rayleigh, John William Strutt, Lord
- Scientific Papers. Cambridge: UP, 1899-1920. 1st edn. 6 vols. Roy 8vo. Port. V sl dust soiling. Orig cloth.
          (Gaskell) **£300** [≈ $534]
- Scientific Papers (1899-1920). New York: 1964. 6 vols in 3. Lge thick 8vo. Plates, diags. Lib stamps on endpapers & title versos. Orig cloth. Dws.   *(Weiner)* **£110** [≈ $196]
- The Theory of Sound. London: Macmillan, 1926. 2nd edn, rvsd & enlgd, (reprint). 2 vols. 12mo. 480; 504 pp. Orig bndgs.
          (Schoen) **$85** [≈ £48]

Rayleigh, Hon. R.J. Strutt, Lord
- The Becquerel Rays and the Properties of Radium. London: Edward Arnold, 1906. 2nd edn. 8vo. vi,215,4 pp. Ills. Few lib marks. Orig bndg, spine ends worn, label removed.
          (Key Books) **$150** [≈ £84]

Rea [or Ray], John
- Flora: seu De Florum Cultura. Or a Complete Florilege ... With many Additions ... London: for George Marriott, 1676. 2nd edn. Folio. [xxiv],231, [232-239] pp. 'Mind of front leaf'. Frontis, 8 plates, 2 text engvs. Contemp calf, front hinge cracked, crnrs bumped. Wing R.422.   *(Vanbrugh)* **£655** [≈ $1,166]

- Flora: seu, de Florum Cultura. or, a Complete Florilege furnished with all Requisites belonging to a Florist. London: 1676. 2nd edn. Folio. [xxvi],231,[9] pp. 'Mind of the Front' leaf. Frontis, 3 engvd headpieces, 8 plates of 16 plans. Contemp calf, worn, rebacked.
          (Wheldon & Wesley) **£600** [≈ $1,068]

Read, Alexander
- The Workes of that famous Physitian [sic] Dr. Alexander Read ... Third Edition. London: E.T. for Richard Thrale, 1659. Sm 4to. [8], 524, [6] pp. Lacks Nn2-4. Lacks A1 (blank?). Title reprd. Some browning. Contemp calf, 19th c reback. Wing R.426.
          (Spelman) **£200** [≈ $356]

Read, J.
- Humour and Humanism in Chemistry. A Procession of Ideas & Personalities. London: (1957) 1961. xvii,206 pp. 49 figs. Orig bndg.
          (Whitehart) **£28** [≈ $50]

Reade, T.M.
- The Origin of Mountain Ranges considered experimentally, structurally, dynamically. London: 1886. 8vo. xviii,359 pp. 42 plates. Sm blind stamps. Cloth.
          (Wheldon & Wesley) **£30** [≈ $53]

Record, Robert
- Record's Arithmetick: or, The Ground of Arts ... London: James Flesher, 1654. 8vo. [xxiv], 629,[i] pp. Minor worming at end, affecting a few letters. Occas sl staining. Few headlines cropped. Contemp sheep, rubbed. Wing R.644.   *(Clark)* **£280** [≈ $498]
- The Urinall of Physicke. London: Thomas Dawson, 1599. 8vo. Black Letter. 3 w'cuts. Lacks last 2 ff (k7-8). Marg reprs to title. Some soiling & staining. 19th c calf, rebacked. STC 20819.   *(Goodrich)* **$1,650** [≈ £927]

Redgrove, H.S.
- Alchemy: Ancient and Modern. London: 1922. 2nd edn, rvsd. 8vo. xx,141 pp. 20 plates. Orig cloth.
          (Wheldon & Wesley) **£25** [≈ $45]

Redwood, Sir B.
- Petroleum: A Treatise on the Geographical Distribution and Geological Occurrence of Petroleum and Natural Gas; The Physical and Chemical Properties ... London: 1913. 3rd edn. 3 vols. 3 frontis, 29 plates, 345 text figs. Piece torn from 1 half-title. Orig cloth, dusty.   *(Whitehart)* **£35** [≈ $62]

Redwood, Boverton
- Petroleum: A Treatise on Geographical Distribution and Geological Occurrence on Petroleum and Natural Gas ... London: 1896. 1st edn. 2 vols. Cold frontis, maps, plates, ills. Some lib marks. Orig cloth, sl worn.
(Francis Edwards) £60 [≈ $107]

Reece, R.
- The Medical Guide. For the Use of the Clergy, Heads of Families and Practitioners in Medicine and Surgery ... London: 1817. 12th edn. xx,418 pp. Occas sl foxing. Cloth backed bds, marked, sl stained.
(Whitehart) £80 [≈ $142]

Reeve, L.
- Elements of Conchology, an Introduction to the Natural History of Shells and of the Animals which form them. London: 1860. 2 vols. Roy 8vo. 62 hand cold plates (1-46, A-I,K-Q). Orig cloth.
(Wheldon & Wesley) £475 [≈ $846]

Regnault, Noel
- Philosophical Conversations: or, a New System of Physics, by Way of Dialogue. Translated into English and illustrated with Notes by Thomas Dale, M.D. London: for W. Innys ..., 1731. 1st edn in English. 3 vols. 8vo. 89 plates. Contemp calf, spines rubbed, some wear to spine ends.
(Burmester) £450 [≈ $801]

Reid, E.P.
- Historical and Literary Botany ... to which is added Flowers: or, the Artists ... from the French of Madame de Genlis. Windsor: 1826. 3 vols. 12mo. Half calf, mrbld edges, trifle rubbed. *(Wheldon & Wesley)* £80 [≈ $142]

Reid, John
- Physiological, Anatomical, and Pathological Researches. Edinburgh: 1848. 1st edn. 659 pp. Orig bndg. *(Fye)* £225 [≈ £126]

Reid, T.W. (editor)
- A Memoir of John Deakin Heaton of Leeds. London: 1883. [v],315 pp. Frontis port. Lib labels. Few pencil notes. Cloth, sl worn, lib label on front cvr, jnts sl cracked.
(Whitehart) £25 [≈ $45]

Reid, Thomas
- Essays on the Intellectual Powers of Man. Edinburgh: for Bell & Robinson, London, 1785. 1st edn. 4to. xii,766 pp. Sl browning. Mod buckram. *(Gach)* $850 [≈ £478]
- An Inquiry into the Human Mind, on the

Principles of Common Sense. Glasgow: W. Falconer, 1817. 400 pp. Spotted. Orig bds, uncut, paper label, somewhat worn.
(Caius) $100 [≈ £56]

Remondino, P.C.
- History of Circumcision from the Earliest Times to the Present with a History of Eunuchism, Hermaphroditism, etc. Phila: 1891. 1st edn. 346 pp. Orig bndg, spotted. Author's pres copy. *(Fye)* $100 [≈ £56]

Rendle, A.B. & others
- Catalogue of the Plants Collected by Mr. & Mrs. P.A. Talbot in the Oban District of South Nigeria. London: BM, 1913. 1st edn. 8vo. x,157 pp. 17 plates. Lib b'plates. Endpapers browned. Orig cloth.
(Francis Edwards) £40 [≈ $71]

Rennie, J.
- Headaches, Colds, and Indigestion, Prevented or Cured; with Popular Directions, Prescriptions, and Cases. London: John Anderson, 1826. 3rd edn. 12mo. Disbound.
(Jarndyce) £32 [≈ $57]
- Insect Architecture. London: Library of Entertaining Knowledge, 1830. 2nd edn. xii, 420 pp. Text ills. Orig cloth, rebacked.
(Whitehart) £18 [≈ $32]

Renouard, Pierre Victor
- History of Medicine ... to the Nineteenth Century. Translated ... by C.G. Comegys. Cincinnati: 1856. 8vo. 719 pp. Sheep, worn. Translator's pres copy.
(Goodrich) $125 [≈ £70]
- History of Medicine from its Origin to the Nineteenth Century ... Translated from the French ... Cincinnati: Moore, Wilstach ..., 1856. 1st Amer edn. 8vo. xvi,ix-xxii, [2], (25)-719 pp. Contemp calf, sl rubbed, lacks label. *(Hemlock)* $175 [≈ £98]

Reulueaux, F.
- The Kinematics of Machinery. Outlines of a Theory of Machines. Translated by A.B.W. Kennedy. London: 1876. 1st edn. xvi,622 pp. 451 ills. Cloth, worn & marked.
(Whitehart) £40 [≈ $71]

Reynolds, Edward
- A Treatise of the Passions and Faculties of the Soul of Man ... London: for Robert Bostock, 1647. 2nd edn. 4to. xviii,324, 391-553 pp. 2 lib stamps. Date altered in ink. Contemp sheep, headcap reprd. Wing R.1294.
(Gaskell) £550 [≈ $979]

Reynolds, Gilbert Westacott
- The Aloes of South Africa ... Johannesburg: 1950. 1st edn. 4to. xxiv,520 pp. 4 pp subscribers. Num plates (many cold). Dec endpapers. Orig cloth, minor staining upper bd.   *(Francis Edwards)* **£38 [≈ $68]**

Reynolds, Philip Keep
- The Banana. Its History, Cultivation and Place among Staple Foods. Boston & New York: 1927. 8vo. xiii,181 pp. Num ills. V occas sl spotting. Cloth.
        (Francis Edwards) **£20 [≈ $36]**

Reynolds, Robert
- The New Professed Cook ... Second Edition, with Considerable Additions. London: for J. Booth, 1829. xxiv,374,[4 advt] pp. 6 illust pp. Contemp cloth, faded, backstrip with ptd label laid down.   *(Gough)* **£135 [≈ $240]**

Rham, W.L.
- The Dictionary of the Farm. Revised and re-edited with Supplementary Matter by William and Hugh Raynbird. London: Routledge, 1853. Half-title. Frontis. Orig pink cloth.   *(Jarndyce)* **£30 [≈ $53]**

Rhind, William
- A History of the Vegetable Kingdom. London: 1868. 2nd edn. Roy 8vo. xvi,744 pp. Port, addtnl engvd title with hand cold vignette, 22 hand cold & 23 plain plates, text figs. Occas foxing. Half mor.
        (Henly) **£78 [≈ $139]**
- Miscellany of Natural History. Edited by Sir Thomas Dick Lauder. Vol II. The Feline Species. By William Rhind. Edinburgh: Fraser; London: Smith, Elder ..., 1834. Sm 8vo. 161 pp. Engvd frontis & title, 35 hand cold plates. Orig bds.   *(Bookline)* **£45 [≈ $80]**

Rhine, J.B.
- Extra-Sensory Perception ... London: Faber, [1935]. 1st English edn. xxxii,243 pp. Frontis port. Some ink underlining. Orig cloth, gilt spine.   *(Caius)* **$100 [≈ £56]**

Riadore, J.E.
- On Local Treatment of the Mucous Membrane of the Throat, for Cough and Bronchitis. London: John Churchill, 1855. Fcap 8vo. xi,[1], 99,[1 advt] pp. Half-title. Orig cloth, spine faded.
        (Spelman) **£45 [≈ $80]**

Ribot, Theodule A.
- Heredity: a Psychological Study of its Phenomena, Laws, Causes, and

Consequences. From the French ... London: Henry S. King, 1875. 1st edn in English. 8vo. x,393 pp. Orig cloth gilt.
        (Fenning) **£32.50 [≈ $59]**
- The Psychology of the Emotions. London: W. Scott, Contemporary Science Series, 1897. B'plate. Orig cloth. *(Caius)* **$75 [≈ £42]**

Ricci, James V.
- The Genealogy of Gynaecology. History of the Development of Gynaecology throughout the Ages 2000 B.C. - 1800 A.D. ... Phila: Blakiston, 1943. 8vo. xxi,578 pp. 54 figs. Orig cloth, some shelf wear.
        (Goodrich) **$150 [≈ £84]**

Richards, J.
- A Treatise on the Construction and Operation of Wood-Working Machines ... London: 1872. 4to. xx,283 pp. 117 plates. Occas sl foxing. Orig pict gilt cloth, t.e.g., some soiling, recased, reprs to spine.
        (Francis Edwards) **£100 [≈ $178]**

Richards, Richard Kohler
- Arithmetic Operations in Digital Computers. New York: Van Nostrand, 1955. 1st edn. 8vo. 398 pp. Ills. Lib pocket. Orig bndg, sm bump at hd.   *(Schoen)* **$85 [≈ £48]**

Richardson, Benjamin Ward
- Diseases of Modern Life. London: 1876. 1st coll edn. 8vo. 520 pp. Contemp half calf, sl rubbed.   *(Robertshaw)* **£25 [≈ $45]**
- Vita Medica. Chapters of Medical Life and Work. London: 1897. x,495 pp. Half-title sl foxed. Orig bndg, spine sl worn.
        (Whitehart) **£35 [≈ $62]**

Richardson, Charles
- The New Book of the Horse ... [with] an extensive Veterinary Section. London: Cassell, [1910]. 4to. xii,628 pp. 29 cold plates, num ills. Contemp half mor gilt, a.e.g., light paint splash on spine.
        (Fenning) **£48.50 [≈ $87]**

Richardson, Donald Elmer
- Electrical Network Calculations - Tabular Methods of Solution. New York: Van Nostrand, 1946. 1st edn. 8vo. xii,270 pp. Ills. Lib pocket. Orig bndg. *(Schoen)* **$110 [≈ £62]**

Richardson, G.F.
- An Introduction to Geology and its Associate Sciences Mineralogy, Fossil Botany, and Palaeontology. A New Edition, Revised and considerably Enlarged by Thomas Wright. London: Bohn, 1855. Sm 8vo. xvi,508,[32

advt] pp. Frontis, num figs. Occas sl mark.
Orig cloth, sl used.
(Bow Windows) £36 [≈ $64]

Richardson, Sir John, & others
- The Museum of Natural History ... London:
[1859-62]. 2 vols. 4to. Cold title, 136 plates
(21 hand cold). Contemp half calf.
(Wheldon & Wesley) £75 [≈ $134]
- The Museum of Natural History ... Glasgow:
Mackenzie, (1859-62). 2 vols in one. 4to.
Hand cold title, 70 (of 78) hand cold & 53 (of
58) plain plates. Occas sl foxing. Contemp
half calf, rubbed.   *(Egglishaw)* £52 [≈ $93]
- The Museum of Natural History ... Glasgow:
Mackenzie, n.d.. 2 vols. Sm folio. 65 + 71
plates, some cold. Occas sl foxing. Dec gilt
leather.   *(Carol Howard)* £130 [≈ $231]

Richardson, M.T.
- Practical Blacksmithing: a Collection of
Articles contributed by Skilled Workmen to
the columns of 'The Blacksmith and
Wheelwright' ... New York: 1889-95. 4 vols.
8vo. Num ills. Lib perf stamp through titles.
Orig dec cloth.   *(Weiner)* £100 [≈ $178]
- The Practical Horseshoer, being a Collection
of Articles which have appeared from time to
time in the columns of 'The Blacksmith and
Wheelwright' ... New York: 1897. 8vo. 283
pp. Num ills. Lib perf stamp through title.
Orig dec cloth.   *(Weiner)* £25 [≈ $45]

Richey, J.E., & others
- The Geology of Ardnamurchan, North-West
Mull and Coll. London: 1930. 8vo. xiii,393
pp. Cold map in pocket, 7 plates, 54 text figs.
Cloth gilt.   *(Henly)* £60 [≈ $107]

Ricketson, Shadrach
- Means of Preserving Health, and Preventing
Diseases ... New York: 1806. 1st edn. 300 pp.
Sm blank piece missing from title. Disbound,
lacks endpapers.   *(Fye)* $150 [≈ £84]

Rickman, Edwin
- Madness, or the Maniac's Hall; a Poem, in
Seven Cantos. London: Smith, Elder, 1841.
1st edn. 8vo. xiv,[ii],302,24 ctlg pp. Orig
cloth, rebacked, faded, rubbed. Anon.
(Burmester) £180 [≈ $320]

Rickman, Philip
- Sketches and Notes from a Bird Painter's
Journal. London: 1949. 4to. 2 cold & 42 plain
plates, num text ills. Orig cloth. Dw.
(Henly) £35 [≈ $62]
- Sketches and Notes from a Bird Painter's
Journal. London: RSPB, 1949. 4to. Cold

frontis, 1 cold & 42 plain plates, num text ills.
Cloth.   *(Wheldon & Wesley)* £28 [≈ $50]

Ridgway, R.
- A Nomenclature of Colors for Naturalists and
Compendium of Useful Knowledge for
Ornithologists. Boston: 1886. 8vo. 129 pp. 10
plates of colour patterns, 7 plain plates. Orig
cloth.   *(Wheldon & Wesley)* £75 [≈ $134]

Rigby, Edward
- Chemical Observations on Sugar ... London:
for J. Johnson, 1788. 1st edn. 8vo. [iv],112
pp. V sl browned. 19th c half calf.
(Finch) £240 [≈ $427]

Riley, Henry A.
- An Atlas of the Basal Ganglia, Brain Stem,
and Spinal Cord. Baltimore: 1943. 1st edn.
Oblong 4to. 708 pp. Plates. Orig cloth,
scuffed, backstrip relaid.
(Goodrich) $150 [≈ £84]

Rimmel, E.
- The Book of Perfumes. London: 1867. 5th
edn. 8vo. xx,266 pp. 13 plates (1 cold), num
text ills. Endpapers marked. Orig dec cloth,
faded, trifle used.
(Wheldon & Wesley) £50 [≈ $89]
- The Book of Perfumes. London: 1871. 7th
edn. xx,266 pp. 250 text ills. Occas sl foxing.
Orig cloth gilt, sl worn, inner hinge sl
cracked.   *(Whitehart)* £35 [≈ $62]

Ringwalt, John L.
- Development of Transportation Systems in
the United States ... Phila: J.L. Ringwalt,
1888. 1st edn. Folio. 398,7 pp. Ills. Name.
Orig cloth, spine ends & crnrs sl bumped, rear
inner hinge cracked.
(Argonaut) $350 [≈ £197]

Rinpoche, Rechung
- Tibetan Medicine, Illustrated in Original
Texts. London: 1973. 1st edn. 340 pp. Orig
bndg.   *(Fye)* $60 [≈ £34]

Ripley, S.D.
- Rails of the World. London: 1977. Roy 4to.
430 pp. 17 maps, 41 cold & 35 plain plates.
Cloth.   *(Wheldon & Wesley)* £80 [≈ $142]

Riverius, Lazarus
- The Universal Body of Physick, In five Books
... Translated by William Carr. London:
Henry Eversden, 1657. 1st edn. Sm folio.
[xiv], 1-236, 257-417,[4] pp, inc 2 fldg tables
(sl worn). Occas sl marks. Old calf, rebacked.
Wing R.1567.   *(David White)* £435 [≈ $774]

Rivers, Thomas
- The Orchard-House or the Cultivation of Fruit-Trees under Glass. London: Longmans, 1865. 12th edn, enlgd & improved. Half-title, final advt leaf. Ills. Orig cloth, spine sl faded. *(Jarndyce)* £38 [≈ $68]

Rivers, William Halse Rivers
- Conflict and Dream. London: Kegan Paul, 1932. xi,[1], 194,[2],[20 advt] pp. Orig cloth, leaning, spotted. *(Caius)* $50 [≈ £28]
- The Influence of Alcohol and Other Drugs on Fatigue. The Croonian Lectures ... London: 1906. 1st edn. Lge 8vo. vii,136,[8 advt] pp. Orig cloth. *(Francis Edwards)* £25 [≈ $45]

Riviere, B.B.
- A History of the Birds of Norfolk. London: Witherby, 1930. 1st edn. 8vo. xlviii,296 pp. Fldg map, sketch map, frontis, 21 plates. Orig pink cloth, faded. *(Gough)* £75 [≈ $134]

Roberts, A.
- The Mammals of South Africa. Cape Town: 1951. 4to. xlviii,700 pp. 24 cold & 54 plain plates. Cloth, spine partly faded.
(Wheldon & Wesley) £100 [≈ $178]

Roberts, J.A.F.
- An Introduction to Medical Genetics. London: 1963. 3rd edn. xiii,283 pp. 121 ills. Orig bndg. *(Whitehart)* £15 [≈ $27]

Roberts, John
- The Surgical Treatment of Disfigurements and Deformities of the Face. Phila: 1901. 2nd edn. 72 pp. Plates. Orig bndg.
(Fye) $250 [≈ £140]

Roberts, M.
- The Conchologist's Companion. London: 1834. Sm 8vo. ix,210,2 pp. Hand cold frontis, title vignette, 16 w'cut text engvs. Orig cloth, rebacked. *(Henly)* £36 [≈ $64]

Robertson, Alexander White
- Studies in Electro-Pathology. London: Routledge, 1918. 1st edn. 8vo. viii,304 pp. 2 cold plates. Orig cloth. Inscrbd by the author. *(Fenning)* £24.50 [≈ $45]

Robertson, C. Lockhart
- Notes on the Prognosis in Cases of Mental Disease. Exeter: William Pollard, 1859. 32 pp. Rec wraps. *(C.R. Johnson)* £60 [≈ $107]

Robertson, J.H.
- The Story of the Telephone. A History of the Telecommunications Industry of Britain.

London: 1947. viii,299 pp. Orig bndg, spine faded, back sl faded. *(Whitehart)* £15 [≈ $27]

Robertson, J.R.
- Wiesbaden, its Baths and Beauties. With Special reference to the effect of the Waters on Gout, Rheumatism, Paralysis and Spinal Irritation ... London: John Churchill, 1857. 1st edn. 8vo. viii,95,[1] pp. Orig cloth gilt.
(Fenning) £55 [≈ $98]

Robertson, James
- General View of the Agriculture in the County of Perth ... Perth: R. Morison ..., 1813. 2nd edn. 8vo. xxii,566,2 pp. Fldg cold map frontis, 5 plates, num tables (1 fldg). Mod half leather.
(Francis Edwards) £75 [≈ $134]

Robertson, John
- A Treatise of such Mathematical Instruments as are usually put into a Portable Case ... The Third Edition ... London: 1775. 8vo. xxiv,233,[3 advt] pp. Frontis, 11 fldg plates. Minor marks. Contemp sheep, rebacked & reprd. *(Bow Windows)* £185 [≈ $329]

Robertson, R.
- An Essay on Fevers ... and the Cure Established on Philosophical Induction. London: 1740. xvi,286 pp. Lib marks on title & endpaper. Sl foxing on endpapers & half-title. Contemp mrbld bds, sl marked, rebacked in cloth. *(Whitehart)* £90 [≈ $160]

Robinson, E. & Masson, A.E.
- James Watt and the Steam Revolution. A Documentary History. London: 1969. ix,229 pp. 8 dble sided cold plates. Orig bndg.
(Whitehart) £25 [≈ $45]

Robinson, E. Colpitts
- The Geology of Genesis, an Inquiry into the Credentials of the Mosaic Record of Creation. London: 1885. 8vo. 137 pp. Orig pict cloth gilt. *(Weiner)* £25 [≈ $45]

Robinson, H.C., & others
- The Birds of the Malay Peninsula. London: 1927-39-76. 5 vols. Imperial 8vo. 125 cold plates. Orig cloth.
(Wheldon & Wesley) £600 [≈ $1,068]

Robinson, Victor
- An Essay on Hasheesh. New York: 1930. 2nd edn. 91 pp. Dw. *(Fye)* $75 [≈ £42]

Robinson, William
- The English Flower Garden: Style, Position

and Arrangement; followed by a Description, alphabetically arranged, of all the Plants best suited for its Embellishment. London: 1883. 1st edn. 8vo. xii,cxxiv,303 pp. 274 plates of figs. Sl foxed. Calf, sl faded.
(Wheldon & Wesley) **£60 [≈ $107]**

- Flora and Sylva. A Monthly Review for Lovers of Garden, Woodland, Tree of Flower ... London: April 1903 - Dec 1905. All published. 3 vols. 4to. 66 cold plates, w'engvs in text. Orig bndgs, t.e.g.
(Hortulus) **$575 [≈ £323]**

- The Florist's Journal and Gardener's Record. A Practical Book of Reference for all who have Gardens. London: Groombridge, n.d. 8vo. 277,[xcviii] pp. Hand cold engvd title, 12 hand cold plates. Mod half mor gilt.
(Hollett) **£130 [≈ $231]**

- The Virgin's Bower. Clematis. Climbing Kinds and their Cultivation at Gravetye Manor. London: Murray, 1912. 1st edn. 8vo. 38 pp. Orig cloth gilt, extrs trifle worn.
(Hollett) **£110 [≈ $196]**

Robson, J., & others
- Canaries, Hybrids and British Birds in Cage and Aviary. Edited by S.H. Lewer. London: Waverley Book Co., (1911). Subscribers Edition (with the additional 8 plates). 4to. xii,424 pp. 26 cold plates, ills. Orig half mor, t.e.g.
(Egglishaw) **£80 [≈ $142]**

Rodd, Edward Hearle
- The Birds of Cornwall and the Scilly Islands by the late Edward Hearle Rodd. Edited by James Edmund Harting. London: Trubner, 1880. 1st edn. 8vo. lvi,320 pp. Port frontis, fldg map. Orig cloth gilt, extrs rubbed, spine ends worn & chipped. *(Hollett)* **£75 [≈ $134]**

Roe, F.G.
- The North American Buffalo, a Critical Study of the Species in its Wild State. London: 1972. 2nd edn. 8vo. xi,991 pp. Map. Good ex-lib. Cloth.
(Wheldon & Wesley) **£35 [≈ $62]**

Roemer, Ferd.
- The Bone Caves of Ojcow in Poland. Translated by J.E. Lee. London: 1884. 4to. xi,41 pp. Mtd photo frontis, 8 plates. Orig pict cloth gilt, rebacked.
(Weiner) **£65 [≈ $116]**

Rogers, Sir L. & Muir, E.
- Leprosy. Bristol: John Wright, 1925. 1st edn. 8vo. xii,301 pp. 32 plates, figs, tables. Lib stamps. Orig cloth, spine ends frayed.
(David White) **£28 [≈ $50]**

Roget, Peter Mark
- Animal and Vegetable Physiology considered with reference to Natural Theology. London: William Pickering, 1834. 2 vols. 8vo. Few lib marks. Leather, scraped.
(Key Books) **$110 [≈ £62]**

Rohault, Jacques
- System of Natural Philosophy illustrated with Dr. Samuel Clarke's Notes, taken mostly out of Sir Isaac Newton's Philosophy ... Second Edition. London: 1729-28. 2 vols. 8vo. 27 fldg plates. Contemp polished calf, backstrips relaid. *(Weiner)* **£200 [≈ $356]**

- A Treatise of Mechanics: or, the Science of the Effects of Power of Moving Forces, as apply'd to Machines ... [translated] by Thomas Watts. London: Symon, 1716. 1st English edn. 8vo. xii,160,[2] pp. 4 fldg plates. Contemp mor elab gilt, rather worn.
(Gaskell) **£550 [≈ $979]**

Rokitansky, Carl
- A Manual of Pathological Anatomy. London: Sydenham Society, 1854. 4 vols. 8vo. Foxed. Orig cloth, faded & sunned.
(Goodrich) **$250 [≈ £140]**

Rolleston, George
- Scientific Papers and Addresses. Edited by W. Turner and E.B. Tylor. Oxford: 1884. 2 vols. Frontis port, num w'cuts. Orig cloth.
(Whitehart) **£90 [≈ $160]**

Rolleston, Sir Humphry Davy
- Medical Aspects of Old Age. Being a Revised and Enlarged Edition of the Linacre Lecture. London: 1932. 2nd edn. x,206 pp. 7 figs. Orig bndg. *(Whitehart)* **£15 [≈ $27]**

- The Right Honourable Sir Thomas Clifford Allbutt K.C.B. A Memoir. London: 1929. vii, 314 pp. Port frontis. Sl foxing to endpapers. Pencil underlining. Cvrs marked.
(Whitehart) **£25 [≈ $45]**

- Some Medical Aspects of Old Age. London: 1922. 1st edn. 170 pp. Ex-lib. Orig bndg.
(Fye) **$75 [≈ £42]**

- Some Medical Aspects of Old Age. Being the Linacre Lecture, 1922 ... London: Macmillan, 1922. 1st edn. 9 plates. Orig cloth, water stained.   *(Caius)* **$50 [≈ £28]**

Rollin, Charles
- The History of the Arts and Sciences of the Antients. Translated from the French. London: for John & Paul Knapton, 1737-39. 4 vols. 8vo. 52 fldg plates. Few lib marks. Contemp calf gilt, some jnts split.
(Key Books) **$160 [≈ £90]**

Romanes, G.J.
- Jelly-fish, Star-fish and Sea-urchins. Being a Research on Primitive Nervous Systems. London: International Scientific Series, 1885. 1st edn. 8vo. Advt ff at ends. Orig cloth, spine ends sl rubbed. *(Bow Windows)* £30 [≈$53]
- The Life and Letters of George John Romanes. London: 1896. 2nd edn. 391 pp. Orig bndg. *(Fye)* $60 [≈£34]

Romayne, Nicholas
- An Address delivered at the Commencement of the Lectures, in the College of Physicians and Surgeons in the City of New York. New York: Collins & Perkins, 1803. 8vo. 39 pp. Browned. New wraps. By-laws not bound in.
(Goodrich) $95 [≈£53]

Ronalds, A.
- The Fly-Fisher's Entomology. London: 1868. 7th edn. 8vo. xvi,132 pp. 20 hand cold plates. Mod cloth.
(Wheldon & Wesley) £70 [≈$125]

Ronayne, Philip
- A treatise of Algebra in Two Books ... The Second Edition with Additions. London: Innys, 1727. 2nd edn. 8vo. [viii],v,[iii errata], 160; 177-461, [3 advt] pp. Contemp calf gilt, worn, upper jnt cracked.
(Gaskell) £375 [≈$668]

Ronsil, G.A.D.
- A Dissertation on Hernias, or Ruptures ... London: 1748. vii,[8],412 pp. Endpapers sl stained. Pp 413-439 (vocabulary of terms) never bound in. Orig leather, rubbed & worn, rebacked. *(Whitehart)* £65 [≈$116]

Rorschach, Hermann
- Psychodiagnostics. A Diagnostic Test based on Perception ... Editor, W. Morgenthaler. Berne: Hans Huber, (1942). 1st edn in English. 2 vols. Lge 8vo. Port. The 10 cards loose in fldg box, paper label. Orig yellow cloth, sl soiled. *(Karmiole)* $175 [≈£98]

Roscoe, E.
- Floral Illustrations of the Seasons consisting of Representations drawn from Nature of some of the most beautiful Hardy and Herbaceous Plants cultivated in the Flower Gardens. London: 1829. 4to. 55 hand cold plates. Later red mor gilt, a.e.g.
(Wheldon & Wesley) £3,000 [≈$5,340]

Rose, John
- The English Vineyard Vindicated, with an address, where the best Plants are to be had at

easie rates. London: 1672. Sm 8vo. 48 pp. Fldg plate. Lib stamps on title. Sl soiled. Later half calf, sl worn. Wing R.1937.
(Weiner) £150 [≈$267]

Rose, William
- On Harelip and Cleft Palate. London: 1891. 1st edn. 172 pp. 75 w'cut ills. B'plate removed. Orig bndg, sm mark on spine.
(Fye) $650 [≈£365]
- The Surgical Treatment of Neuralgia of the Fifth Nerve (Tic Douloureux). London: Bailliere, 1892. 8vo. viii,85 pp. Orig cloth, rebacked. *(Goodrich)* $295 [≈£166]

Rosen, M. & others (editors)
- The History of Mental Retardation. Collected Papers. Baltimore: 1976. 2 vols. xxvi,400; x,454 pp. Lib marks. Orig bndg, lib labels on front cvrs. *(Whitehart)* £35 [≈$62]

Rosenberg, C.E.
- The Cholera Years. The United States in 1832, 1849 and 1866. London: 1962. x,257 pp. Traces of label removal. Orig bndg.
(Whitehart) £15 [≈$27]

Rosenfeld, L.
- Nuclear Forces. Amsterdam: 1948. 8vo. xix, 543 pp. 4 fldg charts, tables, diags. Orig cloth. *(Weiner)* £40 [≈$71]

Rosenthal, M.
- A Clinical Treatise on the Diseases of the Nervous System. With a Preface by Professor Charcot. Translated ... by L. Putzel. New York: W. Wood, 1879. xv,[3],555 pp. Text ills. Names. Orig cloth. *(Caius)* $135 [≈£76]

Rosevear, D.R.
- The Carnivores of West Africa. London: BM, 1974. Roy 8vo. xii,548 pp. 11 cold plates, 172 ills. Cloth. *(Wheldon & Wesley)* £42 [≈$75]

Ross, F.W. Forbes
- Cancer. The Problem of Its Genesis and Treatment. London: Methuen, 1912. 1st edn. x,261 pp. Half-title. Orig green cloth, sl faded. *(Jermy & Westerman)* £20 [≈$36]

Ross, Sir John
- Considerations on the Present State of Navigation by Steam. Stockholm: 1845. 8vo. 29 pp. Some browning, title sl spotted. Cloth backed bds, sl soiled. Author's pres copy.
(Francis Edwards) £250 [≈$445]

Rossi, Bruno Benedetto
- Ionization Chambers and Counters -

Experimental Techniques. New York: McGraw Hill, 1949. 1st edn. 8vo. xviii,243 pp. Ills. Lib pocket. Orig cloth, sl rubbed.
(Schoen) **$65 [≈ £37]**

Roth, Bernard
- The Treatment of Lateral Curvature of the Spine. London: 1899. 2nd edn. 141 pp. Ills. Orig bndg. *(Fye)* **$100 [≈ £56]**

Rothschild, W.
- The Avifauna of Laysan and the Neighbouring Islands, with a Complete History of the Birds of the Hawaiian Possessions. London: 1893-1900. Text only. One of 250. 4to. xx,xiv,320 pp. New cloth.
(Wheldon & Wesley) **£250 [≈ $445]**

Rousseau, J.J.
- Letters on the Elements of Botany. Addressed to a Lady ... System of Linnaeus. Translated by T. Martyn. London: 1787. xxv, 500, [28] pp. Fldg table. Contemp calf, rebacked.
(Whitehart) **£85 [≈ $151]**

Row, T. Sundara
- Geometric Exercises in Paper Folding. Edited and Revised by W.W. Beman and David Eugene Smith. Chicago: 1901. 8vo. xiv,148 pp. Ills, diags. Orig cloth, sl string marked & soiled. *(Weiner)* **£25 [≈ $45]**

Rowbotham, G.F.
- Acute Injuries of the Head. Their Diagnosis, Treatment, Complications and Sequels. Edinburgh: 1945. xvi,424 pp. 201 ills (12 cold). Cloth sl marked.
(Whitehart) **£15 [≈ $27]**

Rowe, N.L. & Killey, H.C.
- Fractures of the Facial Skeleton. Edinburgh: 1955. xxxvi,923 pp. Num text ills. Orig cloth, sl marked. *(Whitehart)* **£35 [≈ $62]**

Rowland, Henry Augustus
- The Physical Papers of Henry Augustus Rowland. Baltimore: Johns Hopkins, 1902. 1st edn. 8vo. xi,704 pp. Port frontis. Lib pocket. Orig cloth gilt. *(Schoen)* **$125 [≈ £70]**

Rowland-Brown, H.
- Butterflies and Moths at Home and Abroad. London: 1912. 4to. 271 pp. 21 cold plates. Cloth, trifle foxed, back cvr sl damp stained.
(Wheldon & Wesley) **£25 [≈ $45]**

Royal Society ...
- Royal Society for the Encouragement of Arts, Manufactures, and Commerce. Transactions

... with the Premiums offered ... London: Dodsley ..., 1789-1804. Vols 1-4 2nd edn, rest 1st edn. 22 vols. Num plates. Occas browning & staining. Contemp calf, gilt spines, some worn. *(Frew Mackenzie)* **£260 [≈ $463]**

Royle, John Forbes
- An Essay on the Antiquity of Hindoo Medicine ... London: 1837. 8vo. iv,196,[16 ctlg] pp. Contemp cloth, ptd paper label, fine. Author's pres copy. *(Hemlock)* **$225 [≈ £126]**
- The Fibrous Plants of India fitted for Cordage, Clothing, and Paper ... London: Smith, Elder, 1855. 2 advt,16 ctlg pp. Orig dec cloth. *(Jarndyce)* **£85 [≈ $151]**
- Illustrations of the Botany and Other Branches of the Natural History of the Himalayan Mountains and of the Flora of Cashmere. London: 1839. 2 vols. Imperial 4to. Cold frontis, cold map, 97 cold & 3 plain plates. Title & 1 plain plate sl foxed. New half mor. *(Wheldon & Wesley)* **£3,000 [≈ $5,340]**

Rudiments of Conchology ...
- See Venning, M.A.

Ruffin, Edmund
- An Essay on Calcareous Manures. Petersburg, Va.: J.W. Campbell, 1832. 1st edn. 12mo. 242,[1] pp. Minor staining 1st ff. Contemp calf, rebacked.
(Bookpress) **$425 [≈ £239]**

Rundall, L.B.
- The Ibex of Sha-Ping and other Himalayan Studies. London: 1915. 1st edn. Lge 8vo. xiv,152 pp. 15 cold plates, ills. Occas marks. Orig cloth. *(Bow Windows)* **£65 [≈ $116]**

Rush, Benjamin
- An Account of the Bilious Remitting Yellow Fever, as it appeared in the City of Philadelphia, in the Year 1793. Phila: 1794. 8vo. x,363 pp. Sm ink spots on title. Contemp qtr calf, new endpapers.
(Goodrich) **$550 [≈ £309]**
- An Account of the Bilious Remitting Yellow Fever, as it appeared in the City of Philadelphia, in the Year 1793. Phila: 1794. 1st edn. 8vo. x,363 pp. Occas sl browning. Contemp calf, rubbed.
(Hemlock) **$825 [≈ £463]**
- Letters of Benjamin Rush. Edited by L.H. Butterfield. Princeton: 1951. 1st edn. 2 vols. 1295 pp. Orig bndg. *(Fye)* **£100 [≈ $56]**
- Medical Inquiries and Observations. Phila: Bennet & Walton ..., 1809. 3rd edn, enlgd. 4 vols. 8vo. Sl foxing. Contemp tree sheep, gilt spines, contrasting labels, traces of rubbing.

(Ximenes) **$1,500 [≈ £843]**
- Medical Inquiries and Observations upon the Diseases of the Mind. Phila: Greig, 1830. 4th edn. 8vo. 365,advt pp. Usual browning & foxing. Orig sheep. *(Goodrich)* **$195 [≈ £110]**

Ruskin, Arthur
- Classics in Arterial Hypertension. Springfield: 1956. 1st edn. 358 pp. Orig bndg. *(Fye)* **$100 [≈ £56]**

Russel, A.
- The Salmon. Edinburgh: Edmonston & Douglas, 1864. 8vo. viii,248,advt pp. New cloth. *(Egglishaw)* **£25 [≈ $45]**

Russell, F.S.
- The Medusae of the British Isles. Vol. 2. Pelagic Scyphozoa, with a Supplement to Vol.1. Cambridge: 1970. Roy 8vo. 296 pp. 17 plates (6 cold). Cloth.
  (Wheldon & Wesley) **£60 [≈ $107]**
- The Medusae of the British Isles. Volume II. Pelagic Scyphozoa, with a Supplement to the First Volume on Hydromedusae. Cambridge: 1970. 4to. xii,284 pp. 15 plates, 102 text figs. Orig bndg. *(Whitehart)* **£35 [≈ $62]**

Russell, Hon. Francis Albert Rollo
- Smoke in Relation to Fogs in London. A Lecture delivered ... under the auspices of the National Smoke Abatement Institution. London: published at the Offices, [1889]. 8vo. 40 pp. Orig ptd wraps. Inscrbd "From the Author.' *(Burmester)* **£45 [≈ $80]**

Russell, Joseph
- A Treatise on Practical and Chemical Agriculture ... Warwick: E. Foden, for the author, Kenilworth, 1831. 1st edn. 8vo. xvi, 396 pp. Some spotting. Orig bds, uncut, rebacked. *(Burmester)* **£120 [≈ $214]**

Russell, Richard
- A Dissertation on the Use of Sea-Water in the Diseases of the Glands. Particularly the Scurvy, Jaundice, Kings-Evil, Leprosy, and the Glandular Consumption. London: W. Owen, 1752. 1st edn. Fcap 8vo. xii,204 pp. Frontis. Contemp calf, jnt ends & hd of spine reprd. *(Spelman)* **£260 [≈ $463]**
- A Dissertation Concerning the Use of Sea Water in Diseases of the Glands, &c. To which is added An Epistolary Dissertation to R. Frewin, M.D. Oxford: 1753. xv,398 pp. 7 engvs. Occas foxing. Contemp leather.
  (Whitehart) **£180 [≈ $320]**

Russell, T.
- Meteorology Weather, and Methods of Forecasting Description of Meteorological Instruments and River Flood Predictions in the United States. New York: 1895. xxiii,277 pp. 50 maps, 29 text figs. Few pages sl nicked at top marg. Orig bndg.
  (Whitehart) **£25 [≈ $45]**

Russow, B.
- Bruno Liljefors, an Appreciation. Translated from the Swedish by A. Poignant. Stockholm: 1929. One of 1000. 4to. 190 pp. 24 cold plates, num ills. Inscrptn on half-title. Half mor. *(Wheldon & Wesley)* **£150 [≈ $267]**

Rutherford, Ernest
- History of the Alpha Rays from Radioactive Substances ... Worcester, Mass.: Clark UP, 1912. Orig bndg. *(Key Books)* **$60 [≈ £34]**
- Radioactive Substances and their Radiations. Cambridge: UP, 1913. 1st edn. Ills. Orig bndg. *(Key Books)* **$120 [≈ £67]**
- Radioactive Transformations. New York: Scribner, 1906. 1st edn. Diags. Few lib marks. Orig bndg. *(Key Books)* **$175 [≈ £98]**
- Radioactivity. Cambridge: UP, 1904. 1st edn. Few lib marks. Orig bndg.
  (Key Books) **$310 [≈ £174]**
- Radioactivity. Cambridge: UP, 1905. 2nd edn, enlgd. Orig bndg. *(Key Books)* **$150 [≈ £84]**

Rutherford, Ernest, & others
- Radiations from Radioactive Substances. Cambridge: UP, 1930. 1st edn. 8vo. xii,588 pp. 12 plates. Orig cloth.
  (Gaskell) **£100 [≈ $178]**

Rutter, J. & Carter, D.
- Modern Eden: or the Gardener's Universal Guide. London: 1769. 8vo. xiv,396 pp. Trifle foxed. Mod dec half mor.
  (Wheldon & Wesley) **£75 [≈ $134]**

Rutty, John
- Observations on the London and Edinburgh Dispensatories: with an Account of the Various Subjects of the Materia Medica, not contained in either of those Works. London: Dilly, 1776. 1st edn. 8vo. [ii],viii,208,[2] pp. Lacks half-title. Contemp sheep, jnts cracked.
  (Burmester) **£120 [≈ $214]**

Ryan, James
- A Letter from Mr. James Ryan ... (late of the Netherton Colliery, near Dudley;), on his Method of Ventilating Coal Mines ... London: 1816. 8vo. 31 pp. 4 plates. Plain wraps. *(Weiner)* **£225 [≈ $401]**

Rydberg, P.A.
- Flora of Colorado. Fort Collins: 1906. 8vo. xxii,448 pp. New cloth.
(Wheldon & Wesley) **£50 [≃ $89]**

Rye, E.C.
- British Beetles: An Introduction to our Indigenous Coleoptera. London: 1866. 1st edn. 8vo. xv,280,16 advt pp. 16 hand cold plates. Orig cloth, spine sl faded & worn.
(Henly) **£65 [≃ $116]**
- British Beetles. Second Edition. Edited by C. Fowler. London: 1890. 8vo. xii,288 pp. 16 cold plates. Cloth, trifle used.
(Wheldon & Wesley) **£28 [≃ $50]**

Ryle, Gilbert
- The Concept of Mind. London: Hutchinson's University Library, [1949]. 1st printing. 8vo. 334,[2] pp. Orig cloth. Dw (chipped).
(Gach) **$100 [≃ £56]**

Sachs, Edwin O. (editor)
- Facts on Fire Prevention: the Results of Fire Tests conducted by the British Fire Prevention Committee. London: 1902. 2 vols. 8vo. Num fldg plate & ills. Neat lib stamps. Orig cloth. *(Weiner)* **£75 [≃ $134]**

Sachs, Julius von
- Text-Book of Botany, Morphological and Physiological. Translated and annotated by A.W. Bennett ... Oxford: 1875. 1st English edn. Roy 8vo. xii,852,[2 advt] pp. 461 ills. Lib stamp title verso. Orig qtr calf, spine rubbed & chipped at hd.
(Fenning) **£24.50 [≃ $45]**

Sahli, H.
- A Treatise on Diagnostic Methods of Examination. London: 1906. 1008 pp. 12 plates, 383 text figs. Sl marg tears last few pp. Orig cloth. *(Whitehart)* **£25 [≃ $45]**

Sainbel, Charles Vial de
- Elements of the Veterinary Art ... prefixed, a Short Account of his Life. London: for J. Wright, 1797. 3rd edn. 3 parts in 1 vol. 4to. Port, frontis to Lectures on Farriery, 7 plates. Orig bds, uncut, jnts reprd.
(Burmester) **£650 [≃ $1,157]**
- Lectures on the Elements of Farriery ... London: for the author, 1793. 1st edn. 4to. xii,[iv],202 pp. Frontis, 2 plates. Orig bds, uncut, rebacked, new label.
(Burmester) **£400 [≃ $712]**

Sainte-Marthe, Scevole de
- Paedotrophia; or, the Art of Nursing and Rearing Children, a Poem ... Translated from the Latin ... Notes ... Life of the Author ... by H.W. Tytler. London: for the author, 1797. 8vo. cxci,224 pp. Subscribers. Name erased from title. Contemp half calf, sl worn.
(Weiner) **£150 [≃ $267]**

Sajous, Charles E.
- Lectures on the Diseases of the Nose and Throat. Delivered during the Spring Session Jefferson Medical College. Phila: 1889. 8vo. 439 pp. 10 chromolithos, 93 w'engvs. Orig cloth, front bd stained.
(Goodrich) **$75 [≃ £42]**

Sakai, T.
- The Crabs of Sagami Bay. Tokyo: 1965. 4to. xvi,206 pp. 100 cold plates. Cloth.
(Wheldon & Wesley) **£75 [≃ $134]**

Salmon, C.E.
- Flora of Surrey. London: 1931. 8vo. 688 pp. 2 cold maps, port, 8 plates. Cloth.
(Wheldon & Wesley) **£36 [≃ $64]**

Salmon, F.
- A Practical Essay on the Stricture of the Rectum. Illustrated by Cases ... London: 1828. xi,188 pp. Perf lib stamps on title. Old cloth backed bds, worn & torn at spine ends.
(Whitehart) **£70 [≃ $125]**

Salmon, William
- Doron Medicum; Or, a Supplement to the New London Dispensatory ... London: for T. Dawks ..., 1683. 1st edn. 8vo. xvi,720, [60],[4] pp. Contemp calf, reprd, jnts rubbed. Wing S.426. *(Hemlock)* **$675 [≃ £379]**
- Pharmacopoeia Londinensis. Or, The New London Dispensatory ... Translated into English ... Second Edition, corrected and amended ... London: 1682. 8vo. 8 ff, "877" [i.e. 909],[2] pp. Title washed. Contemp calf, sl dull, crnrs bumped.
(Hemlock) **$500 [≃ £281]**
- Pharmacopoeia Londinensis; or The New London Dispensatory. In Six Books. Eighth Edition, Corrected and Amended. London: 1716. 8vo. Title supplied in facs. Mod mor.
(Robertshaw) **£30 [≃ $53]**

Salmonia: or Days of Fly Fishing ...
- See Davy, Humphry.

Salter, J.
- A Treatise upon Bulbous Roots, Greenhouse Plants, Flower Gardens, Fruit Trees ... Bath: Wood & Co., 1816. 2nd edn. 12mo. iv,120 pp. 1st few crnrs sl worn. Orig pink ptd

wraps, rebacked. *(Burmester)* **£68 [≈$121]**

Salverte, A.J.E.B.
- The Philosophy of Magic, Prodigies and Apparent Miracles ... With Notes Illustrative, Explanatory, and Critical by Anthony Todd Thomson, M.D. London: Bentley, 1846. 1st edn in English. 2 vols. Sl browned. Mod cloth.   *(D & D Galleries)* **$275 [≈£154]**

Samouelle, G.
- The Entomologist's Useful Compendium. London: 1819. 8vo. 496 pp. 12 plates (11 cold), plain duplicates of plates 2-12. Trifle foxed. Orig bds, lower jnt torn.
        (Wheldon & Wesley) **£85 [≈$151]**

Sampson, H.C.
- The Coconut Palm. The Science and Practice of Coconut Cultivation. London: 1923. 1st edn. Lge 8vo. xiv,[2],262 pp. 46 plates, figs. Sl foxing. Orig cloth, sl rubbed.
        (Bow Windows) **£75 [≈$134]**

Samuelson, James
- The Honey-Bee; Its Natural History, Habits, Anatomy, and Microscopical Beauties. London: 1860. Cr 8vo. xvi,166,16 advt pp. Errata slip. 8 tinted plates. Orig cloth, spine worn.   *(Henly)* **£32 [≈$57]**
- The Honey-Bee; its Natural History, Habits, Anatomy, and Microscopical Beauties. With Tinted Illustrations ... London: 1860. 1st edn. Sm 8vo. xvi,166,[16 advt] pp. 8 tinted litho plates. Marg foxing. Orig cloth.
        (Bow Windows) **£40 [≈$71]**
- Humble Creatures. The Earthworm and the Common Housefly, in Eight Letters. London: 1858. 8vo. viii,78 pp. 8 plates. Cloth.   *(Wheldon & Wesley)* **£18 [≈$32]**

Sanborn, F.B. (editor)
- Memoirs of Pliny Earle, M.D., with Extracts from his Diary and Letters (1830-1892) and Selections from his Professional Writings (1839-1891). Boston: 1898. 409 pp. Unabused ex-lib. Orig bndg.
        (Fye) **$75 [≈£42]**

Sanders, James
- A Comprehensive View of the Small Pox, Cow Pox, and Chicken Pox. With a Concise History of their Different Stages and Terminations ... Edinburgh: L. Bryce, 1813. xvi,234,[2 advt] pp. Sl damp staining & foxing. New qtr calf. *(Goodrich)* **$150 [≈£84]**

Sansom, A.E.
- The Diagnosis of Diseases of the Heart and

Thoracic Aorta ... London: 1892. xxiv,568,36 pp. 186 figs. Orig bndg.
        (Whitehart) **£55 [≈$98]**

Sargent, C.S.
- Trees and Shrubs. Illustrations of New or Little Known Ligneous Plants prepared chiefly from Material at the Arnold Arboretum of Harvard University. Boston: 1902-13. 2 vols. Sm folio. 200 plates (lib stamps on reverse). Half calf, cloth.
        (Wheldon & Wesley) **£250 [≈$445]**

Sarton, George
- History of Science: Ancient Science through the Golden Age of Greece. Cambridge: Harvard UP, 1952. 1st edn. 8vo. xxvi,646 pp. Orig cloth. Dw (worn).
        (Gach) **$31.50 [≈£18]**
- History of Science: Hellenistic Science and Culture in the Last Three Centuries B.C. Cambridge: Harvard UP, 1952. 1st edn. 8vo. xxvi, 554 pp. Orig cloth. Dw (worn).
        (Gach) **$31.50 [≈£18]**
- A History of Science. Cambridge: 1959. 1st edn. 2 vols. 646; 554 pp. Orig bndg.
        (Fye) **$75 [≈£42]**

Saumarez, Richard
- A Dissertation on the Universe in General, and on the Procession of the Elements in Particular ... London: T. Egerton ..., 1795. 1st edn. 8vo. xxvii,266 pp. 3 ff sl stained in margs. Old calf, rubbed, label chipped.
        (Young's) **£110 [≈$196]**

Saunders, E.
- The Hemiptera Heteroptera of the British Islands. London: 1892. Roy 8vo. vii,350 pp. 1 plain & 31 hand cold plates. Occas sl foxing. Rebound in half mor.
        (Wheldon & Wesley) **£120 [≈$214]**
- The Hemiptera Heteroptera of the British Islands. London: 1892. 8vo. vii,350 pp. 1 plain plate. Cloth.
        (Wheldon & Wesley) **£20 [≈$36]**
- The Hymenoptera Aculeata of the British Islands. London: 1896. Large Paper. Roy 8vo. vii,391 pp. 51 hand cold & 3 plain plates. Orig cloth.
        (Wheldon & Wesley) **£200 [≈$356]**

Saunders, H.
- An Illustrated Manual of British Birds. London: Gurney, 1899. 2nd edn. 8vo. xl,776 pp. 3 cold maps, 384 ills. Orig cloth gilt.
        (Egglishaw) **£25 [≈$45]**
- Manual of British Birds. Third Edition, revised by W.E. Clarke. London: 1927. viii,

834 pp. 405 figs. New cloth, t.e.g.
(Whitehart) **£25 [≃ $45]**

Saunders, P.
- Edward Jenner. The Cheltenham Years, 1795-1823. Being a Chronicle of the Vaccination Campaign. London: 1982. xviii,469 pp. 11 ills. Orig bndg.
(Whitehart) **£18 [≃ $32]**

Saunders, William
- Treatise on the Structure, Economy and Diseases of the Liver ... Boston: W. Pelham, 1797. 1st Amer edn. 8vo. xx,231 pp. Lib stamp title verso. Contemp calf, upper hinge cracked. *(Hemlock)* **$125 [≃ £70]**
- A Treatise on the Structure, Economy and Diseases of the Liver. Walpole: 1810. 2nd Amer edn. 8vo. xix,20-173,[1] pp. 2 lib stamps. Contemp calf, rubbed, hinges cracked. *(Hemlock)* **$75 [≃ £42]**

Savage, C.
- The Mandarin Duck. London: 1952. 4to. ix,78 pp. 16 plates, 41 text figs. Cloth.
(Wheldon & Wesley) **£35 [≃ $62]**

Savage, Henry
- The Surgery, Surgical Pathology and Surgical Anatomy of the Female Pelvic Organs. In a Series of Plates taken from Nature ... Third Edition revised and greatly extended. New York: Wood Library, 1880. 32 plates, 22 w'engvs. 2 gatherings sprung. Orig cloth.
(Goodrich) **£125 [≃ £70]**

Savary, Jacques
- Universal Dictionary of Trade and Commerce ... see Postlethwayt, Malachy

Saville-Kent, W.
- A Manual of the Infusoria ... London: Bogue, 1880-82. 3 vols. Roy 8vo. Cold frontis, 52 plates. Orig cloth gilt.
(Egglishaw) **£195 [≃ $347]**
- A Manual of the Infusoria. London: 1881-82. 3 vols. Roy 8vo. Cold frontis, 52 plates. Half mor, trifle rubbed.
(Wheldon & Wesley) **£150 [≃ $267]**

Sawer, J.C.
- Odorographia, a Natural History of Raw Materials and Drugs used in the Perfume Industry, intended to serve Growers, Manufacturers, and Consumers. London: 1892-94. 2 vols. 8vo. Cloth.
(Wheldon & Wesley) **£120 [≃ $214]**
- Odorographia. A Natural History of Raw Materials and Drugs used in the Perfume

Industry ... London: 1912. 1st edn. 8vo. xxiii,383 pp. 13 ills inc fldg map. Orig cloth, worn, shaken, extrs rubbed.
(Francis Edwards) **£45 [≃ $80]**

Sawyer, J.
- Contributions to Practical Medicine. Birmingham: 1886. xi,127 pp. Orig cloth, sl faded & stained. Inscrbd by the author.
(Whitehart) **£15 [≃ $27]**

Saxby, Henry L.
- The Birds of Shetland ... Edited by his Brother, Stephen H. Saxby. Edinburgh: MacLachlan & Stewart, 1874. 1st edn. 8vo. xv, [ii],398 pp. 8 tinted lithos. Few spots to back of some plates. Orig pict cloth gilt.
(Hollett) **£275 [≃ $490]**

Say, Thomas
- American Entomology, or Descriptions of the Insects of North America ... Philadelphia Museum: Samuel Augustus Mitchell, 1824-25-28. 1st edn. 3 vols. 8vo. 54 hand cold plates. Contemp half mor, spines v sl rubbed.
(Chapel Hill) **$2,800 [≃ £1,573]**

Sayre, Lewis
- Lectures on Orthopedic Surgery and Diseases of the Joints. New York: 1879. 1st edn. 476 pp. 274 w'cut ills. Lib stamps on title. Rec qtr leather, new endpapers. *(Fye)* **$400 [≃ £225]**
- Lectures on Orthopedic Surgery and Diseases of the Joints. New York: 1885. 2nd edn, enlgd. 569 pp. 324 ills. Orig bndg.
(Fye) **$200 [≃ £112]**
- Spinal Disease and Spinal Curvature. Their Treatment, Suspension and the Use of Plaster of Paris Bandage. London: 1878. 1st edn. 121 pp. 21 mtd albumen photo prints. Lib perf stamp on title & 3 ff. Some wear & tear. Rebound. *(Fye)* **$750 [≃ £421]**

Scammon, Charles M.
- The Marine Mammals of the North-Western Coast of North America, described and illustrated, together with an Account of the American Whale-fishery. San Francisco: 1874. 4to. 319,v pp. 27 litho plates. Sm blind stamps on plates. New half mor.
(Wheldon & Wesley) **£800 [≃ $1,424]**

Scarpa, Antonio
- Engravings of the Cardiac Nerves, the Nerves of the Ninth Pair ... copied from the 'Tabulae Neurologicae' ... Edinburgh: 1829. 2nd edn. 4to. [52] pp. 14 plates. Occas sl foxing. New three qtr leather. *(Whitehart)* **£180 [≃ $320]**
- Engravings of the Cardiac Nerves, the Nerves

of the Ninth Pair ... copied from the 'Tabulae Neurologicae' ... Edinburgh: 1832. 3rd edn. 136 pp.. 23 cold & 7 other plates. Some foxing page edges. Mod half cloth.
(Whitehart) **£280 [≃ $498]**

Schachner, August
- Ephraim McDowell, "Father of Ovariotomy" and Founder of Abdominal Surgery ... Phila: Lippincott, 1921. 1st edn. Thick 8vo. xviii, 332 pp. Frontis port, 20 plates. Orig cloth.
(Karmiole) **$45 [≃ £25]**

Schall, W.E.
- Electro-Medical Instruments and their Management. London: 1952. [6],148 pp. Num ills. Orig linen backed ptd card cvrs.
(Whitehart) **£25 [≃ $45]**

Scheinker, I. Mark
- Neuropathology in its Clinicopathologic Aspects. Springfield: C.C. Thomas, [1947]. 1st edn. xvii,[1],306 pp. Cold frontis, ills. Orig cloth.
(Caius) **$100 [≃ £56]**

Scherf, D. & Schott, A.
- Extrasystoles and Allied Arrhythmias. London: 1973. 2nd edn. xiv,1041 pp. Text figs. Orig bndg.
(Whitehart) **£25 [≃ $45]**

Schimper, A.F.W.
- Plant Geography upon a Physiological Basis. English Translation by W.R. Fisher. Oxford: 1903. 1st edn. Roy 8vo. xxx,839 pp. Port, 4 maps, 502 plates & ills. Orig qtr mor, used, lower crnrs sl stained.
(Wheldon & Wesley) **£60 [≃ $107]**
- Plant Geography upon a Physiological Basis. English Translation by W.R. Fisher. London: 1977. Reprint of Oxford 1903 edn. Roy 8vo. 869 pp. 73 plates. Cloth.
(Wheldon & Wesley) **£76 [≃ $135]**

Schliepake, Erwin
- Short-Wave Therapy: the Medical Uses of Electrical High Frequencies. London: 1938. 2nd English edn. 8vo. [xviii],296 pp. Ills. Orig cloth.
(Weiner) **£25 [≃ $45]**

Schmeidler, C.
- Historical Survey of Pharmacy in Great Britain. London: [1944]. 92 pp. Endpapers foxed. Orig bndg, stained. Signed by the author.
(Whitehart) **£15 [≃ $27]**

Scholl, William
- The Human Foot: Anatomy, Deformities and Treatment. Chicago: 1920. 415 pp. 271 ills. Orig bndg.
(Fye) **$75 [≃ £42]**

Schorlemmer, Carl
- A Manual of the Chemistry of the Carbon Compounds: or, Organic Chemistry. London: 1874. 8vo. xii,512 pp. Ills. Good ex-lib. Orig cloth, discold, sl worn. *(Weiner)* **£40 [≃ $71]**

Schrodinger, Erwin
- What is Life? The Physical Aspect of the Living Cell. Cambridge: 1944. 8vo. viii,91 pp. 4 plates, diags. Name. Orig cloth. Dw.
(Weiner) **£20 [≃ $36]**
- What is Life? The Physical Aspects of the Living Cell. Cambridge: UP, 1945. 1st edn. 16mo. 91 pp. 4 plates. Orig cloth. Dw.
(Schoen) **$45 [≃ £25]**

Schroeder van der Kolk, J.L.C.
- On the Minute Structure and Functions of the Spinal Cord and Medulla Oblongata ... Translated ... by William Daniel Moore. London: New Sydenham Society, 1859. 1st edn in English. ix,[5],291 pp. 10 plates. Orig cloth, jnts cracking, sm tears spine ends.
(Caius) **$150 [≃ £84]**

Schuchert, C.
- Atlas of Palaeographic Maps of North America. New York: 1955. Lge 4to. 177 pp. Frontis port, 84 maps. Lib bndg.
(Whitehart) **£25 [≃ $45]**

Schullian, Dorothy M. & Sommer, Francis E.
- A Catalogue of Incunabula and Manuscripts in the Army Medical Library. New York: 1948. 8vo. 361 pp. Ills. Lib stamp on title, b'plate removed. Orig bndg.
(Goodrich) **$65 [≃ £37]**
- A Catalogue of Incunabula and Manuscripts in the Army Medical Library. New York: 1950. 1st edn. 361 pp. Orig bndg.
(Fye) **$90 [≃ £51]**

Schullian, Dorothy M. & Schoen, Max
- Music and Medicine. New York: 1948. 1st edn. 499 pp. Orig bndg. *(Fye)* **$85 [≃ £48]**

Scobee, R.G.
- The Oculorotary Muscles. London: 1952. 2nd edn. 512 pp. 159 ills. Review stamp on title. Orig bndg. *(Whitehart)* **£18 [≃ $32]**

Scoffern, John
- The Manufacture of Sugar, in the Colonies and at Home, chemically considered. London: Longman, Brown ..., 1849. 1st edn. 8vo. viii, 160 pp. Cold plate at end, text ills. Contemp green half roan, extrs rubbed.
(Finch) **£95 [≃ $169]**

Scoffern, John C.
- The Victoria Gold Valuer's Ready Reckoner and Assayer's Chemical Guide ... London & Melbourne: 1853. Sm 8vo. 115 pp, tables, ills. Possibly lacks 2 ff before title. Binder's cloth, worn & shaken. *(Weiner)* £30 [≈ $53]

Scot, John
- An Enquiry into the Origin of the Gout ... Third Edition, Corrected and Improved. London: J.P. Cooke, [ca 1783]. 8vo. [2],216 pp. Rebound in qtr calf, vellum tips. *(Spelman)* £120 [≈ $214]

Scott, D.H.
- Studies in Fossil Botany. London: 1909. 2nd edn. xxiv,683 pp. Fldg frontis, 213 ills. Cloth, sl marked, front inner hinge cracked. Signed by the author. *(Whitehart)* £18 [≈ $32]

Scott, J.A.
- The Butterflies of North America, a Natural History and Field Guide. Stanford: 1986. Roy 8vo. 632 pp. Num ills. Cloth. *(Wheldon & Wesley)* £35 [≈ $62]

Scott, Robert Forsyth
- A Treatise on the Theory of Determinants and their Application in Analysis and Geometry. Cambridge: UP, 1880. 1st edn. 8vo. xii,251,28 advt pp. Orig cloth. *(Gaskell)* £20 [≈ $36]

Scott, T. & Scott, A.
- The British Parasitic Copepods. London: Ray Society, 1913. 2 vols. 8vo. 74 plates (36 cold). Orig cloth, backstrips relaid. *(Henly)* £42 [≈ $75]

Scott-Brown, W.G.
- Diseases of the Ear, Nose and Throat. London: 1952. 2 vols. 27 cold plates, 598 text figs. Orig bndg. *(Whitehart)* £25 [≈ $45]

Scripture, Edward W.
- Thinking, Feeling, Doing. New York: Flood & Vincent, 1895. 1st edn. 304 pp. Cold frontis, num ills. Orig cloth. *(Caius)* $75 [≈ £42]

Scrivenor, J.B.
- The Geology of Malaya. London: 1931. xx,217 pp. Lge fldg cold map in pocket, 33 text figs. Orig cloth, sl marked. *(Whitehart)* £18 [≈ $32]

Scrope, G.P.
- The Geology and Extinct Volcanos of Central

France. London: 1858. 2nd edn. 8vo. xvii,258 pp. 2 cold maps, 17 plates. Orig cloth. *(Wheldon & Wesley)* £120 [≈ $214]

Scudder, S.H.
- Nomenclator Zoologicus: an Alphabetical List of all Generic Names that have been employed by Naturalists for Recent and Fossil Animals ... Washington: 1882. 2 parts in one vol. 8vo. 376; 340 pp. Cloth. *(Wheldon & Wesley)* £80 [≈ $142]

Seafield, Frank (pseudonym of Alexander H. Grant)
- The Literature and Curiosities of Dreams ... London: Chapman & Hall, 1865. 1st edn. 2 vols. xxiii,[1],360; viii,394,[2 advt] pp. Rec half calf. *(Caius)* $115 [≈ £65]

Seaman, V.
- A Dissertation on the Mineral Waters of Saratoga. New York: 1809. 2nd edn. 12mo. 131 pp. Fldg map. Browned. Blind stamp & name on title. Boards. *(Wheldon & Wesley)* £35 [≈ $62]

Searle, George Frederick Charles
- Experimental Optics. Cambridge: UP, 1925. 1st edn. 12mo. 357 pp. Num ills. Name. Orig cloth. *(Schoen)* $50 [≈ £28]

Sedgwick, Adam
- The Life and Letters of the Reverend Adam Sedgwick. By J.W. Clark and T.M. Hughes. Cambridge: 1890. 2 vols. 8vo. Num plates. Orig cloth. *(Wheldon & Wesley)* £50 [≈ $89]

Seebohm, Henry
- The Birds of Siberia. London: 1901. 8vo. xx,512 pp. Map, text figs. Last few ff sl stained. Orig dec cloth, rather worn, trifle loose. *(Wheldon & Wesley)* £45 [≈ $80]
- Coloured Figures of the Eggs of British Birds. Edited by R.B. Sharpe. London: 1896. Roy 8vo. Port, 60 cold plates (1-59,58a). Sl foxing. Orig cloth, trifle used, spine faded. *(Wheldon & Wesley)* £40 [≈ $71]
- A History of British Birds. With Coloured Illustrations of their Eggs. London: 1883-85. 4 vols. Roy 8vo. 68 cold plates. Minor foxing & dust soiling. Half mor, trifle used. *(Wheldon & Wesley)* £95 [≈ $169]

Seemann, B.
- Popular History of the Palms and their Allies. London: Reeve, 1856. Sm 8vo. xvi,359 pp. 20 cold litho plates. New qtr calf gilt. *(Egglishaw)* £90 [≈ $160]
- Popular History of the Palms and their Allies.

London: 1856. Cr 8vo. xvi,359 pp. 20 cold plates (4 foxed). Cloth, recased.
(Wheldon & Wesley) £50 [≈ $89]

Selby, P.J.
- A History of British Forest Trees, Indigenous and Introduced. London: 1842. 8vo. xx,540,16 pp. Text figs. Cloth.
(Henly) £80 [≈ $142]
- The Natural History of Pigeons. Edinburgh: Lizars, Jardine's Naturalist's Library, 1835. 1st edn. Cr 8vo. 228 pp. Port, cold vignette title, 30 hand cold plates by Edward Lear. New half calf. *(Egglishaw)* £85 [≈ $151]

Select Essays on Husbandry ...
- See Catesby, Mark

The Self-Instructor ...
- The Self-Instructor, or, Young Man's Best Companion ... Useful Learning and Knowledge ... added, The Artist's Assistant ... Medicinal Receipts: Nuttall ..., [ca 1814]. 8vo. [iv],593,[3] pp. Frontis, 6 plates. Some foxing, 2 tears. Contemp calf, rebacked. *(Burmester)* £75 [≈ $134]

Selwyn-Brown, Arthur
- The Physician throughout the Ages ... New York: 1928. 1st edn. 2 vols. 4to. 848; 854 pp. Ports. Orig bndg. *(Fye)* $100 [≈ £56]

Selye, Hans
- The Physiology and Pathology of Exposure to Stress ... Montreal: Acta Medical Publishers, [1950]. 1st edn. xx,822,203 pp. Orig cloth.
(Caius) $150 [≈ £84]

Senn, Nicholas
- Tuberculosis of Bones and Joints. Phila: 1892. 1st edn. 504 pp. 107 w'cut ills. Ex-lib. Orig bndg. *(Fye)* $75 [≈ £42]

Sennertus, D.
- The Institutions of the Fundamentals of the Whole Art, both of Physick and Chirurgery ... Also the Grounds of Chemistry ... London: 1656. 494 pp. Cambridge antique calf.
(Whitehart) £580 [≈ $1,032]

Seth-Smith, D.
- Parrakeets: a Handbook to the Imported Species. London: 1903. Roy 8vo. xix,281 pp. 20 cold plates (19 hand cold), 24 text figs. Half mor. *(Wheldon & Wesley)* £380 [≈ $676]

Shaffer, Newton
- Pott's Disease, Its Pathology and Mechanical Treatment with Remarks on Rotary Lateral

Curvature. New York: 1879. 1st edn. 82 pp. Orig bndg. *(Fye)* $125 [≈ £70]

Shankland, E.C.
- Dredging of Harbours and Rivers. A Work of Descriptive and Technical Reference ... Glasgow: 1931. xii,248 pp. Num figs. Orig bndg. *(Whitehart)* £25 [≈ $45]

Sharp, Archibald
- Bicycles & Tricycles. An Elementary Treatise on their Design and Construction ... London: Longmans, 1896. xviii,536 pp. Half-title. Ills. Crnr damp stain to a few pp. Orig green cloth. *(Jermy & Westerman)* £75 [≈ $134]

Sharp, Samuel
- A Critical Inquiry into the Present State of Surgery. London: for Tonson & Draper, 1750. 1st edn. 294 pp. Contemp half calf & bds. *(Goodrich)* $395 [≈ £222]
- A Critical Enquiry into the Present State of Surgery. Second Edition. London: Tonson, 1750. 8vo. [8],294 pp. Lacks front endpaper. Contemp calf. *(Spelman)* £160 [≈ $285]
- A Treatise on the Operations of Surgery, with a Description and Representation of the Instruments used in Performing them. London: 1761. 8th edn. 234 pp. Plates. Leather. *(Fye)* $350 [≈ £197]
- A Treatise on the Operations of Surgery, with a Description and Representation of the Instruments used in Performing them ... Eighth Edition. London: Tonson, 1761. 8vo. [viii], liv,234 pp. 14 plates. Contemp calf, spine sl rubbed & chipped at hd.
(Frew Mackenzie) £265 [≈ $472]

Sharpe, R.B. & Wyatt, C.W.
- A Monograph of the Hirundinidae, or Family of Swallows. London: 1885-94. 2 vols. 4to. 26 maps, 103 hand cold plates. Mod half mor.
(Wheldon & Wesley) £4,500 [≈ $8,010]

Sharpe, Samuel
- A Critical Enquiry into the Present State of Surgery. London: Tonson, Draper, 1750. 2nd edn. 8vo. [viii],294 pp. Sm blank piece cut from title crnr. Contemp calf, jnts sl tender, hd of spine sl worn. *(Burmester)* £95 [≈ $169]

Sharrock, R.
- The History of the Propagation and Improvement of Vegetables by the Concurrence of Art and Nature. Oxford: 1660. 1st edn. 8vo. [xviii],150 pp. Plate. Mod half calf, a.e.g.
(Wheldon & Wesley) £380 [≈ $676]

Shaw, Alexander

- Narrative of the Discoveries of Sir Charles Bell in the Nervous System. London: 1839. 8vo. 232 pp. 1 plate. Lib stamp on title. Orig cloth, uncut. "From the Author" on front blank.   *(Goodrich)* **$695 [≈ £390]**

Shaw, G.

- Zoological Lectures delivered at the Royal Institution in 1806 and 1807, with Plates from the First Authorities and most Select Specimens. London: 1809. 2 vols. Roy 8vo. 2 engvd titles, 167 plates. Contemp half calf.
(Wheldon & Wesley) **£150 [≈ $267]**

Shaw, J.

- Medical Priestcraft. A National Peril. London: 1907. xx,246 pp. Prelims foxed. Orig bndg.   *(Whitehart)* **£18 [≈ $32]**

Shaw, Peter

- Chemical Lectures publickly read at London in the years 1731 and 1732, and since at Scarborough in 1733 ... London: for Shuckburgh & Osborne, [1734]. 1st edn. 8vo. xxiv,478 pp. Tiny marg worm hole in title. Contemp calf, sl rubbed, rec label.
(Burmester) **£250 [≈ $445]**
- An Enquiry into the Contents, Virtues and Uses, of the Scarborough Spaw-Waters: with the Method of examining any other Mineral Water. London: for the author, 1734. 1st edn. 8vo. viii,[2],166 pp, advt leaf. Contemp calf, rebacked, crnrs reprd.
(Spelman) **£110 [≈ $196]**

Shaw, T.R.

- Lathes, Screw Machines, Boring and Turning Mills. Manchester: 1903. x,648,xv pp. 425 figs. Some soiling. Orig cloth, worn & dusty, spine ends sl defective, inner hinge sl cracked.   *(Whitehart)* **£25 [≈ $45]**

Shaw, W.F.

- Twenty-Five Years. The Story of the Royal College of Obstetricians and Gynaecologists 1929-1954. London: 1954. viii,192 pp. 12 plates. Orig bndg.   *(Whitehart)* **£15 [≈ $27]**

Shearman, William

- Essay on the Nature, Causes, and Treatment of Water in the Brain. London: Underwood, 1825. 8vo. xxii,123,[1] pp. Lib stamps on title. Orig bds, unopened, spine worn.
(Goodrich) **$495 [≈ £278]**

Sheehan, J. Eastman

- General and Plastic Surgery with emphasis on War Injuries. New York: 1945. 1st edn. 345 pp. 496 figs. Orig bndg. *(Fye)* **$100 [≈ £56]**
- A Manual of Reparative Plastic Surgery. New York: 1938. 1st edn. 311 pp. 314 ills. Orig bndg.   *(Fye)* **$150 [≈ £84]**
- Plastic Surgery of the Orbit. New York: 1927. 1st edn. 348 pp. Orig bndg.
(Fye) **$125 [≈ £70]**

Sheen, James Richmond

- Wines and other Fermented Liquors; from the Earliest Ages to the Present Time ... London: Robert Hardwicke, (1864). 2nd thousand. 7 advt pp. Orig cloth, dulled & rubbed, wear at ft of spine.
(Jarndyce) **£45 [≈ $80]**

Sheldon, H. Horton

- Space, Time, and Relativity. The Einstein Universe. New York: The University Society, 1932. 1st edn. 12mo. 104 pp. Frontis. Orig linen bds. Signed by the author.
(Schoen) **$65 [≈ £37]**

Shelley, G.E.

- A Handbook to the Birds of Egypt. London: Van Voorst, 1872. 1st edn. Lge 8vo. 14 hand cold litho plates. Name on title. Contemp half calf, gilt dec spine, cloth sides sl faded.
(Georges) **£400 [≈ $712]**
- A Handbook to the Birds of Egypt. London: 1872. Roy 8vo. ix,342 pp. 14 hand cold plates by Keulemans. Orig red cloth, trifle used, inner jnts strengthened.
(Wheldon & Wesley) **£380 [≈ $676]**

Shepard, J.A.

- Spencer Wells. The Life and Work of a Victorian Surgeon. Edinburgh & London: 1965. xii, 132 pp. Frontis port, 14 plates. Lib label & stamp. Orig bndg, spine faded, sl marked.   *(Whitehart)* **£15 [≈ $27]**

Shepherd, J.A.

- Simpson and Syme of Edinburgh. London: 1969. xv,288 pp. Frontis, 20 plates. Dw.
(Whitehart) **£15 [≈ $27]**

Sheppard, T.

- Geological Rambles in East Yorkshire. London: [1903]. 8vo. xi,235 pp. Map, 53 figs. Cloth, faded.
(Wheldon & Wesley) **£28 [≈ $50]**

Sherer, John

- Rural Life. London: London Printing & Publishing Co., [1868-69]. 5 vols. demy 4to. Num engvd plates. Orig dec cloth gilt, split in 1 spine.   *(Ash)* **£250 [≈ $445]**

Sherrington, Charles S.

- The Endeavour of Jean Fernel. Cambridge: 1946. 1st edn. 223 pp. Orig bndg. Dw.
  (Fye) **$60 [≈ £34]**
- The Endeavours of Jean Fernel. With a List of the Editions of his Writings. Cambridge: 1948. 8vo. 223 pp. Dw (worn).
  (Goodrich) **$75 [≈ £42]**
- The Integrative Action of the Nervous System. London: Constable, 1911. 1st edn. 2nd issue, with cancelled title-page. 8vo. 411 pp. Occas underlining. Later cloth.
  (Goodrich) **$395 [≈ £222]**
- The Integrative Action of the Nervous System. With a New Foreword by the Author and a Bibliography of his Writings. Cambridge: 1947. 8vo. 433 pp. Port. Orig bndg. *(Goodrich)* **$75 [≈ £42]**
- Man on his Nature. New York: Macmillan, 1941. 1st Amer edn. 8vo. 7 plates, 5 text ills. Orig cloth. *(Gach)* **$50 [≈ £28]**

Sherrington, Charles S., & others

- Reflex Activity of the Spinal Cord. London: 1938. 2nd printing. 8vo. Dw.
  (Goodrich) **$100 [≈ £56]**

Shirley, Evelyn Philip

- Some Account of English Deer Parks. With Notes on the Management of Deer. London: Murray, 1867. Sq 8vo. xiii,267 pp. Num ills. Orig green cloth gilt, a.e.g.
  (Lamb) **£125 [≈ $223]**

Shirley or Sherley, Thomas

- A Philosophical Essay: declaring the probable Causes, whence Stones are produced in the Greater World ... London: for William Cademan, 1672. 1st edn. 8vo. [xvi],143 pp. Worm track in upper crnr. Contemp sheep, spine & crnrs worn. Wing S.3523.
  (Gaskell) **£350 [≈ $623]**

Shock, Nathan

- A Classified Bibliography of Gerontology and Geriatrics. Stanford: 1951. 1st edn. 599 pp. Dw. *(Fye)* **$125 [≈ £70]**

Shoemaker, John

- Heredity, Health, and Personal Beauty. Phila: 1890. 1st edn. 422 pp. Orig bndg.
  (Fye) **$150 [≈ £84]**

Short, Thomas

- A Comparative History of the Increase and Decrease of Mankind in England and several Countries abroad ... General States of Health, Air, Seasons and Food ... London: 1767. 1st edn. 4to. [xii],213 pp. Title laid down, some soil. Mod half leather.
  (Whitehart) **£150 [≈ $267]**
- Discourses on Tea, Sugar, Milk, Made-Wines, Spirits, Punch, Tobacco, &c. with Plain and Useful Rules for Gouty People. London: Longman & MIllar, 1750. 1st edn. 8vo. vi,[iv],424 pp. Advt leaf before title. Occas sl browning. Old calf gilt, rebacked.
  (Hollett) **£650 [≈ $1,157]**
- The Natural, Experimental, and Medicinal History of the Mineral Waters of Derbyshire, Lincolnshire, and Yorkshire ... London: 1734. [xx],xxii,362 pp. 4 plates. Sl worm in last few ff. Reversed calf, v sl worn, inner hinges sl cracked. *(Whitehart)* **£250 [≈ $445]**

Shuckard, W.E.

- British Bees ... London: Reeve, 1866. 1st edn. 8vo. xvi,371 pp. 16 hand cold plates. Orig cloth, spine & part of cvr faded.
  (Egglishaw) **£34 [≈ $61]**
- British Bees. London: 1866. 8vo. xvi,371 pp. 16 hand cold plates. Orig cloth, sl worn, jnts splitting, spine faded.
  (Wheldon & Wesley) **£30 [≈ $53]**

Shuldham, E.B.

- Headaches: Their Causes and Treatment. London: E. Gould, 1876. 2nd edn, rvsd. 77,[3] pp. Orig dec cloth, sl worn.
  (Caius) **$85 [≈ £48]**

Sidgwick, N.V.

- The Chemical Elements and their Compounds. OUP: 1952. 2 vols. Lge 8vo. Inscrptns. Orig cloth, sl marked, minor stains vol 2. *(Francis Edwards)* **£30 [≈ $53]**
- Some Physical Properties of the Covalent Link in Chemistry. Ithaca, New York: 1933. 1st edn. [7],249 pp. Frontis port, text diags. Orig cloth, sl dusty. *(Whitehart)* **£30 [≈ $53]**

Siegel, R.E.

- Galen on Psychology, Psychopathology, and Function and Diseases of the Nervous System. Edited by R.E. Siegel. Basel: 1973. 310 pp. Dw. *(Goodrich)* **$75 [≈ £42]**
- Galen on Sense Perception. His Doctrines, Observations, and Experiments on Vision, Hearing, Smell, Taste, Touch and Pain, and their Historical Sources. Basel: Karger, 1970. 216 pp. Dw. *(Goodrich)* **$75 [≈ £42]**

Siemens, C.W.

- On the Utilisation of Heat and Other Natural Forces: a Lecture delivered in ... Glasgow. London & Glasgow: 1878. 8vo. 32 pp. Ills. Orig ptd wraps pasted into plain wraps.
  (Weiner) **£21 [≈ $37]**

Sigerist, Henry
- A Fifteenth Century Surgeon: Hieronymus Brunschwig and his Work. New York: 1946. 1st edn. 48 pp. Ills. Orig bndg.
(Fye) **$50 [≈ £28]**
- Landmarks in the History of Hygiene. London: 1956. ix,78 pp. 4 plates. Orig bndg.
(Whitehart) **£15 [≈ $27]**
- Man and Medicine: An Introduction to Medical Knowledge. New York: 1932. 1st English translation. 340 pp. Orig bndg.
(Fye) **$75 [≈ £42]**
- Man and Medicine. Translated by M.G. Boise. London: 1932. x,340 pp. Orig cloth, sl dusty, sm label ft of spine.
(Whitehart) **£15 [≈ $27]**

Sikes, Wirt
- British Goblins: Welsh Folk-lore, Fairy Mythology, Legends and Traditions. London: Sampson Low ..., 1880. 2nd edn. 8vo. xvi, 412,32 pp. Ills. Occas spotting. Orig pict cloth gilt, recased, new endpapers.
(Hollett) **£75 [≈ $134]**

Simmons, Owen
- The Book of Bread. London: (1903). 4to. 360 pp. 32 plates (inc 2 photos), ills. Lib stamp on title & plate versos). Orig dec cloth gilt.
(Weiner) **£100 [≈ $178]**

Simmons, Samuel
- Elements of Anatomy and the Animal Economy. From the French of M. Person. Corrected ... augmented with Notes. London: Wilie, 1775. 1st edn. xii,396 pp, errata leaf. 3 plates. Light pencilling. Old qtr calf, worn.
(Goodrich) **$75 [≈ £42]**

Simms, Eric
- Woodland Birds. London: New Naturalist, 1971. 1st edn. 8vo. xxii,391 pp. Ills. Dw (v sl browned).
(Francis Edwards) **£25 [≈ $45]**

Simms, Frederick Walter
- Practical Tunnelling ... London: 1844. 4to. xii,174 pp. Frontis, 12 fldg plates, w'engvs in text. Orig cloth.
(Whitehart) **£200 [≈ $356]**
- Practical Tunnelling. Fourth Edition, revised and greatly extended ... by D. Kinnear Clark. London: 1896. Lge 8vo. xxxii, 548 pp. 36 fldg plates, ills. Lib stamps on title & plate versos. Front free endpaper defective. Orig cloth.
(Weiner) **£75 [≈ $134]**

Simon, Andre L.
- Bibliotheca Bacchica. London: Holland Press, (1972). Reprint of 1927 edn. 2 vols in one. Lge 4to. Cloth. Dw.
(Bookpress) **$100 [≈ £56]**
- Bibliotheca Gastronomica. London: Holland Press, (1978). Reprint of 1953 edn. One of 750. 4to. Cloth. Dw. *(Bookpress)* **$85 [≈ £48]**

Simpson, John
- A Complete System of Cookery, on a Plan entirely new ... London: for W. Stewart, R. Lea ..., [1815?]. 4th edn "corrected and enlarged". 8vo. xx,696 pp. Half-title, tables. Contemp mrbld bds, blue paper spine, uncut, spine ends worn. *(Burmester)* **£350 [≈ $623]**

Simpson, N.D.
- A Bibliographical Index of the British Flora. Bournemouth: Privately Printed, 1960. One of 750. Imperial 8vo. xix,429 pp. Orig cloth, spine faded. *(Wheldon & Wesley)* **£48 [≈ $85]**

Simpson, R.R.
- Shakespeare and Medicine. Edinburgh: 1959. 1st edn. 267 pp. Orig bndg. *(Fye)* **$65 [≈ £37]**

Simpson, Thomas
- The Doctrine and Application of Fluxions ... Second Edition, Revised and Carefully Corrected. London: for John Nourse, 1776. 2 vols. 8vo. xii,274,[2 advt]; [ii],275-576 pp. Name torn from vol 2 title. Contemp sheep, rebacked, sides scuffed.
(Burmester) **£125 [≈ $223]**

Sims, J. Marion
- The Story of My Life. New York: 1885. 1st edn. 471 pp. Lacks port. Orig bndg.
(Fye) **$65 [≈ £37]**

Sinclair, J. & Freeman, J.
- A History and Description of the Different Varieties of the Pansey, or Heartsease, now in Cultivation in the British Gardens. London: 1835 [-38]. 8vo. 112 pp. 24 hand cold plates. Sl foxed. Half calf, trifle rubbed.
(Wheldon & Wesley) **£300 [≈ $534]**

Sinclair, Sir John
- The Code of Agriculture; including Observations on Gardens, Orchards, Woods and Plantations. London: for Sherwood, Neely & Jones ..., 1821. 3rd edn, enlgd. Lge 8vo. xv,593, 153,[i], [4 ctlg] pp. Port frontis, 9 plates. Some text browning. Bds, backstrip defective. *(Francis Edwards)* **£150 [≈ $267]**
- The Code of Health and Longevity; or, a Concise View of the Principles calculated for the Preservation of Health and the Attainment of Long Life. Second Edition. Edinburgh: 1807. 4 vols. 8vo. 3 frontis. Contemp calf, sl rubbed. ft of 2 spines sl

worn.   *(Robertshaw)* **£150 [≈ $267]**
- The Code of Health and Longevity ...
Edinburgh: Constable, 1807. Vol 1 2nd edn,
vols 2-4 1st edns. 4 vols. 8vo. Occas sl marks
& foxing. Period calf, red & green labels, v sl
cracking to spines.   *(Rankin)* **£250 [≈ $445]**

Singer, Charles
- The Discovery of the Circulation of the
Blood. London: 1922. 8vo. 80 pp. Ills. Orig
bndg.   *(Goodrich)* **$45 [≈ £25]**
- The Evolution of Anatomy. A Short History
of Anatomical and Physiological Discovery to
Harvey ... New York: Knopf, 1925. 8vo. 209
pp. 22 plates, 11 ills. Ex-lib. Sl wear to cloth.
            (Goodrich) **$75 [≈ £42]**
- From Magic to Science. Essays on the
Scientific Twilight. London: Ernest Benn,
1928. 1st edn. 14 cold plates, 108 figs. Few
lib marks. Mod cloth.
            (Key Books) **$50 [≈ £28]**
- From Magic to Science: Essays on the
Scientific Twilight. London: 1928. 1st edn.
253 pp. Ills. Orig bndg. *(Fye)* **$100 [≈ £56]**
- Greek Biology & Medicine. Oxford: 1922. 1st
edn. 128 pp. Orig bndg. *(Fye)* **$50 [≈ £28]**
- A History of Technology. London: OUP,
1957. Reprint. 5 vols. Num ills. Orig cloth.
Dws.   *(Schoen)* **$185 [≈ £104]**
- A Short History of Biology. A General
Introduction to the Study of Living Things.
Oxford: 1931. xxxv,572 pp. Frontis, 193 figs.
Orig bndg, front inner hinge cracked.
            (Whitehart) **£35 [≈ $62]**
- A Short History of Biology. Oxford: 1931.
8vo. xxxv,572 pp. 194 ills. Cloth, sl used.
            (Wheldon & Wesley) **£25 [≈ $45]**
- A Short History of Medicine ... OUP: 1928.
1st edn. xxiv,368 pp. Port frontis, 141 ills.
Endpapers sl spotted. Orig cloth, spine sl
rubbed.   *(Francis Edwards)* **£25 [≈ $45]**
- A Short History of Science to the Nineteenth
Century. London: (1941). 8vo. Cloth.
            (Wheldon & Wesley) **£18 [≈ $32]**

Singer, Charles (editor)
- Studies in the History and Method of
Science. Oxford: Clarendon Press, 1917-21. 2
vols. Roy 8vo. 2 cold frontis, 94 plates (11
cold). Unabused ex-lib. Orig cloth, spines
sunned.   *(Goodrich)* **$350 [≈ £197]**

Singer, Charles & Rabin, C.
- A Prelude to Modern Science, being
Discussion of the History, Sources and
Circumstances of the 'Tabulae Anatomica
Sex' of Vesalius. Cambridge: 1946. 1st edn.
4to. 144 pp. 6 fldg plates. Orig bndg.

            (Fye) **$275 [≈ £154]**
Siraisi, N.G.
- Taddeo Alderotti and his Pupils. Two
Generations of Italian Medical Learning.
Princeton: 1981. xxiv,462 pp. Orig bndg.
            (Whitehart) **£18 [≈ $32]**

**Sitwell, Sacheverell, Russell, J., & Blunt,
W.**
- Old Garden Roses. London: 1955-57. Special
Issue sgnd. 2 vols. Folio. 16 cold plates. Half
vellum.   *(Wheldon & Wesley)* **£225 [≈ $401]**

Skaife, S.H.
- African Insect Life. Cape Town: [ca 1953]. 70
photo plates, num text ills. Orig bndg.
            (Chalmers Hallam) **£36 [≈ $64]**
- African Insect Life. New revised edition by J.
Ledger. London: 1979. 4to. 279 pp. 147 cold
& 365 other ills. Cloth.
            (Wheldon & Wesley) **£30 [≈ $53]**

Skinner, Henry
- The Origin of Medical Terms. Baltimore:
1949. 1st edn. 379 pp. Orig bndg.
            (Fye) **$100 [≈ £56]**

Slack, H.J.
- Marvels of Pond Life. London:
Groombridge, 1889. 1st edn. 8vo. 7 cold
plates. Orig dec cloth, a.e.g., new endpapers.
            (Savona) **£20 [≈ $36]**

Slack, Thomas
- The British Negotiator; or, Foreign
Exchanges made perfectly easy ... The Fourth
Edition, Corrected and Enlarged. By S.
Thomas, Merchant. London: G. Robinson;
Newcastle: T. Slack, 1784. Tall 12mo. [xii],
323, [1 advt] pp. Browned, few ff frayed.
Contemp sheep, sl worn.
            (Gaskell) **£250 [≈ $445]**

Sladen, F.L.W.
- The Humble-Bee, its Life History and How
to Domesticate It, with Descriptions of all the
British Species of Bombus and Psithyrus.
London: Macmillan, 1912. 8vo. xiii,283 pp. 5
cold & 2 plain plates, 34 text figs. Name. Orig
cloth, t.e.g.   *(Egglishaw)* **£50 [≈ $89]**

Slater, C. & Spitta, E.J.
- An Atlas of Bacteriology ... London: 1898.
xiv, 120 pp. 111 plates. Occas foxing. Orig
bndg, discold & worn.
            (Whitehart) **£15 [≈ $27]**

Slater, J.W.
- Handbook of Chemical Analysis for Practical Men ... London: 1861. xvi,384 pp. 17 text diags. Endpapers foxed. Three qtr roan, rubbed.   *(Whitehart)* **£35 [≈ $62]**

Slaughter, F.G.
- Immortal Magyar. Semmelweis, Conqueror of Childbed Fever. New York: 1950. [ix],211 pp. Frontis, 2 dble-sided plates. Spine ends sl worn.   *(Whitehart)* **£18 [≈ $32]**

Smart, W.M.
- Celestial Mechanics. London: 1953. vii,381 pp. 35 figs. Orig bndg.
        (Whitehart) **£18 [≈ $32]**

Smeaton, John
- Experimental Enquiry concerning the Natural Powers of Wind and Water to turn Mills and Other Machines depending on a Circular Motion ... London: for I. & J. Taylor, 1794. 110 pp. 5 fldg plates. Qtr calf, mrbld bds.   *(C.R. Johnson)* **£260 [≈ $463]**

Smee, A.
- Elements of Electro-Biology, or, the Voltaic Mechanism of Man; of Electro-Pathology ... Electro-Therapeutics. London: 1849. xii,164 pp. 36 figs, 2 pp table. 2 sm lib stamps. Mor gilt, sl rubbed.   *(Whitehart)* **£150 [≈ $267]**
- Elements of Electro-Metallurgy. London: 1843. 2nd edn. xvi,338 pp. 37 ills. Some foxing prelims. Orig cloth, backstrip relaid.
        (Whitehart) **£60 [≈ $107]**

Smee, Alfred
- The Monogenesis of Physical Forces: a Lecture delivered at the London Institution ... London: 1857. 8vo. 24 pp. Faint lib stamps. Orig ptd wraps. *(Weiner)* **£50 [≈ $89]**
- Vision in Health and Disease: the Value of Glasses for its Restoration, and the Mischief caused by their Abuse ... London: 1847. 8vo. 64 pp. Frontis, w'cuts. Orig cloth.
        (Weiner) **£50 [≈ $89]**

Smellie, William
- The Philosophy of Natural History [vol 1]. Edinburgh: for the heirs of Charles Elliot ..., 1790. 1st edn. 4to. xiii,[3],547 pp. Contemp qtr calf, uncut, sl rubbed.
        (Heritage) **$450 [≈ £253]**
- The Philosophy of Natural History. Dover, N.H.: 1808. 4to. 551 pp. Contemp calf.
        (Hemlock) **$75 [≈ £42]**

Smiles, Samuel
- Industrial Biography: Iron Workers and Tool

Makers. London: 1863. xiv,342,[4] pp. Orig bndg, spine sl defective.
        (Whitehart) **£18 [≈ $32]**
- The Life of George Stephenson, Railway Engineer. London: Murray, 1857. 1st edn. 2 advt pp. Frontis. Orig maroon cloth, v sl rubbed.   *(Jarndyce)* **£120 [≈ $214]**
- The Life of George Stephenson, Railway Engineer. London: Murray, 1857. 1st edn. Demy 8vo. xvi,(518),[ii] pp. Port. Orig dec cloth, sl discold & soiled, endpapers cracked.   *(Ash)* **£75 [≈ $134]**
- The Life of George Stephenson, Railway Engineer. London: Murray, 1857. 4th edn, rvsd, with addtns. 2 advt pp. Frontis. Orig brown cloth, dulled, recased.
        (Jarndyce) **£48 [≈ $85]**

Smillie, I.S.
- Osteochondritis Dissecans. Loose Bodies in Joints. Etiology, Pathology, Treatment. Edinburgh & London: 1960. viii,224 pp. Num text ills. Orig bndg.
        (Whitehart) **£18 [≈ $32]**

Smit, Pieter
- History of the Life Sciences: An Annotated Bibliography. Amsterdam: 1974. 1st edn. 1071 pp. Dw.   *(Fye)* **$150 [≈ £84]**

Smith, Mrs.
- The Female Economist; or a Plain System of Cookery: for the Use of Families. Third Edition. London: Mathews & Leigh, 1810. 8vo. xxiv,330, vi,[iv] pp. Frontis. Some foxing & browning. Orig bds, spine worn, upper cvr nearly detached.
        (Frew Mackenzie) **£230 [≈ $409]**

Smith, Adam
- An Inquiry into the Nature and Causes of the Wealth of Nations ... The Third Edition, with Additions ... London: Strahan & Cadell, 1784. 3 vols. 8vo. Some faint marking. Contemp calf, rebacked to style, crnrs bumped, leather punctured on 1 bd.
        (Finch) **£1,150 [≈ $2,047]**
- An Inquiry into the Nature and Causes of the Wealth of Nations ... London: Strahan & Cadell, 1791. 3 vols. 8vo. Contemp tree calf, gilt spines, mor labels (sl defective), vol 2 hd of spine chipped.
        (Waterfield's) **£300 [≈ $534]**
- An Inquiry into the Nature and Causes of the Wealth of Nations. The Seventh Edition. London: Strahan & Cadell, 1793. 3 vols. 8vo. Occas sl foxing. Mottled calf gilt, dble labels.
        (Hartfield) **$850 [≈ £478]**
- An Inquiry into the Nature and Causes of the

Wealth of Nations ... With a Life of the Author ... Edinburgh: for Stirling & Slade ..., 1819. 3 vols. 8vo. Sl browning. Contemp polished calf, gilt spines, 1 hinge cracked, 2 with sm splits. *(Claude Cox)* **£110 [≈ $196]**

Smith, Annie Lorrain
- A Monograph of the British Lichens ... Second Edition. London: BM, 1918-26. 2 vols. 8vo. xxiv,519; ix,447 pp. 134 plates, text figs. Orig green cloth gilt.
(Blackwell's) **£100 [≈ $178]**

Smith, Cecil
- The Birds of Somersetshire. London: Van Voorst, 1869. 1st edn. 8vo. xii,643 pp. Orig cloth, sl rubbed & marked.
(Claude Cox) **£38 [≈ $68]**

Smith, David Eugene
- Rara Arithmetica. A Catalogue of the Arithmetics written before the Year MDCI ... Boston: Ginn & Co., 1908. 1st edn. Lge 8vo. xiv,[2],508 pp. 9 plates, 246 ills. Orig blue cloth, paper label, lower crnrs sl bumped.
(Karmiole) **$150 [≈ £84]**

Smith, E.
- The Life of Sir Joseph Banks President of the Royal Society with some Notices of his Friends and Contemporaries. London: 1911. 8vo. xvi,348 pp. 16 plates. Sl foxing. Orig cloth, spine faded.
(Wheldon & Wesley) **£50 [≈ $89]**

Smith, Edgar C.
- A Short History of Naval and Marine Engineering. Cambridge: 1937. xix,376 pp. 16 plates, 46 text figs. Orig cloth, sl stained.
(Whitehart) **£25 [≈ $45]**
- A Short History of Naval and Marine Engineering. Cambridge: 1937. 1st edn. Roy 8vo. xix,376 pp. 16 plates, 46 ills. Orig cloth, spine sl faded.
(Fenning) **£35 [≈ $62]**

Smith, Eliza
- The Compleat Housewife: or Accomplish'd Gentlewoman's Companion ... The Seventh Edition, with very large additions ... London: Pemberton, 1736. 8vo. [xvi],352,xv pp. 6 fldg plates. Occas soil & marg stains. Contemp style half calf. *(Burmester)* **£250 [≈ $445]**
- The Compleat Housewife: or, Accomplish'd Gentlewoman's Companion ... Receipts in Cookery ... Wines ... Seventh Edition, with very large Additions ... London: Pemberton, 1736. [xvi],352,xv pp. 5 plates (of 6). Crnr of plate 5 torn. 19th c cloth.
(Gough) **£195 [≈ $347]**

Smith, F.
- Catalogue of Hymenopterous Insects in the Collection of the British Museum. London: 1853-59. 7 parts. 12mo. 47 plates. Lib labels. Cloth backed bds, lib numbers on spines.
(Egglishaw) **£70 [≈ $125]**

Smith, F.J.
- Lectures on Medical Jurisprudence and Toxicology as delivered at the London Hospital. London: 1900. xii,396 pp. Orig bndg. *(Whitehart)* **£15 [≈ $27]**

Smith, Ferris
- Plastic and Reconstructive Surgery. Phila: 1950. 1st edn. 895 pp. 592 ills. Orig bndg.
(Fye) **$100 [≈ £56]**

Smith, George
- The Cassiterides: an Inquiry into the Commercial Operations of the Phoenicians in Western Europe, with particular reference to the British Tin Trade. London: 1863. 8vo. vii, 154 pp. Piece cut from title marg. Orig cloth, spine ends worn. *(Weiner)* **£40 [≈ $71]**
- A Complete Body of Distilling, explaining the Mysteries of that Science ... London: for Bernard Lintot, 1725. 1st edn. 8vo. Intl advt leaf. 24 ctlg pp at end. Contemp calf, rebacked, trifle rubbed.
(Ximenes) **$475 [≈ £267]**
- A Compleat Body of Distilling ... In Two Parts ... London: Printed in Fleetstreet, 1738. 3rd edn. 8vo. [vi],89,[3], 93-150,[2] pp. Frontis. Occas sl damp stains. Contemp bds, rec calf spine. *(Vanbrugh)* **£225 [≈ $401]**

Smith, Gerard Edward
- A Catalogue of the Rare or Remarkable Phaenogamous Plants, collected in South Kent ... London: Longman, Rees ..., 1829. 8vo. [iii], 76 pp. Subscribers list. 5 hand cold etchings, with tissue guards. Dust marks at hd of title. Orig ptd wraps, untrimmed.
(Blackwell's) **£350 [≈ $623]**

Smith, H.
- Flora Sarisburiensis; a Repository of English Botany, both General and Medical, the Arts and Agriculture. Salisbury: 1817. Parts 1-4 (of 5). Roy 8vo. 24 hand cold plates. Contemp half calf. *(Wheldon & Wesley)* **£200 [≈ $356]**

Smith, H.G.V. (editor)
- Insects and other Arthropods of Medical Importance. London: BM, 1973. 1st edn. 4to. xiv,561 pp. 12 plates, 217 text figs. Cloth. Dw. *(Savona)* **£20 [≈ $36]**

Smith, Homer William
- The Kidney: Structure and Function in Health and Disease. New York: OUP, 1951. 1049 pp. Frontis. Cloth sl faded.
(Goodrich) **$95 [≈ £53]**
- The Physiology of the Kidney. New York: 1937. 310 pp. 32 figs. Lib stamp on title, lib labels. Orig bndg, sl worn.
(Whitehart) **£15 [≈ $27]**

Smith, J.B.
- A Treatise upon Wire. Its Manufacture and Uses, embracing Comprehensive Descriptions of the Constructions and Applications of Wire Ropes. London: 1891. 4to. xxii,347 pp. 95 figs, 33 tables. Orig cloth, sl dust stained, sm nick to spine.
(Whitehart) **£25 [≈ $45]**

Smith, J.L.B.
- The Sea Fishes of South Africa ... South Africa: Central News Agency, 1949. 1st edn. 4to. xvi,550 pp. 2 pp subscribers. Cold frontis, num ills. Pict endpapers. Orig pict gilt cloth, upper hinge cracked.
(Francis Edwards) **£45 [≈ $80]**

Smith, J. Walker
- Dustless Roads Tar Macadam. A Practical Treatise for Engineers Surveyors and Others. London: 1909. 1st edn. 8vo. xii,225,[1],[66 advt] pp. 10 fldg tables, 24 figs (sev fldg). Orig cloth.
(Bow Windows) **£36 [≈ $64]**

Smith, James
- Researches in Newer Pliocene and Post-Tertiary Geology. Glasgow: 1862. 8vo. xi, 192 pp. 4 chromolithos, w'cuts. Sm lib stamp on title & endpapers. Orig cloth.
(Weiner) **£40 [≈ $71]**

Smith, Sir James Edward
- An Introduction to Physiological and Systematic Botany. London: Longman, 1825. 5th edn. 8vo. xxi,435 pp. 15 plates by James Sowerby. Occas sl foxing. Contemp half calf, spine ends worn.
(Egglishaw) **£30 [≈ $53]**
- A Selection of the Correspondence of Linneaus and Other Naturalists from the Original Manuscripts. London: 1821. 2 vols. 8vo. 10 plates (foxed) of 31 facss. Contemp half leather, rebacked.
(Wheldon & Wesley) **£185 [≈ $329]**
- Tracts relating to Natural History. London: 1798. xiv,[1],312 pp. 7 plates (6 cold). Calf, rebacked.
(Wheldon & Wesley) **£75 [≈ $134]**

Smith, Sir James Edward & Sowerby, J.
- Exotic Botany: consisting of Coloured Figures, and Scientific Descriptions of such

New, Beautiful or Rare Plants as are worthy of Cultivation in the Gardens of Britain. London: 1804-05. 2 vols. Roy 8vo. 120 hand cold plates. Half mor, practically uncut.
(Wheldon & Wesley) **£1,600 [≈ $2,848]**

Smith, John
- General View of the Agriculture of the County of Argyle ... London: Richard Phillips, 1805. 8vo. xvi,347,[i],[4 advt] pp. Fldg hand cold map, 3 plates. Orig bds, paper label, uncut.
(Spelman) **£180 [≈ $320]**

Smith, John, of Glasgow
- Monograph of the Stalactites and Stalagmites of the Cleaves Cove, near Dalry, Ayrshire. London: 1894. 1st edn. 4to. [iv],34 pp. 36 plates. Orig cloth.
(Bow Windows) **£55 [≈ $98]**

Smith, Joseph A.
- Productive Farming ... Edinburgh: William Tait, 1843. 2nd edn. Half-title. Intl 4 pp ctlg. Damp staining in prelims & on bds. Orig orange cloth, paper label rubbed.
(Jarndyce) **£38 [≈ $68]**

Smith, Joseph Mather
- Discourse on the Epidemic Cholera Morbus of Europe and Asia. New York: 1831. 8vo. 36 pp. Orig ptd wraps, uncut. Author's pres copy.
(Goodrich) **$95 [≈ £53]**

Smith, K.G.V. (editor)
- Insects and Other Arthropods of Medical Importance. London: BM, 1973. 1st edn. 4to. xiv,561 pp. 12 plates (2 cold), 217 text figs. Cloth.
(Savona) **£25 [≈ $45]**

Smith, L.B.
- The Bromeliaceae of Brazil. Washington: Smithsonian, 1955. 8vo. viii,290 pp. 128 ills. Wraps.
(Wheldon & Wesley) **£35 [≈ $62]**

Smith, Nathan
- Medical and Surgical Memoirs. Edited with an Addenda by Nathan R. Smith, M.D. Baltimore: 1831. 8vo. vii-374 pp. Errata. Port. Foxing. Orig bds, uncut, rebacked.
(Goodrich) **$195 [≈ £110]**
- Medical and Surgical Memoirs. Baltimore: 1831. 1st edn. 374 pp. Rec half leather.
(Fye) **$250 [≈ £140]**

Smith, Nathan Ryno
- Surgical Anatomy of the Arteries. Second Edition, much enlarged and corrected. Baltimore: Lucas & Wight, 1835. 2nd edn, enlgd. Folio. 133 pp. 20 cold plates, w'cut

text ills. Orig linen backed bds, upper hinge splitting. *(Hemlock)* **$275 [≃ £154]**
- Treatment of Fractures of the Lower Extremity by the Use of the Anterior Suspensory Apparatus. Baltimore: 1867. 1st edn. 70 pp. Orig bndg. *(Fye)* **$300 [≃ £169]**

Smith, Noble
- The Surgery of Deformities. London: 1882. 1st edn. 280 pp. 118 w'cut ills. Unabused ex-lib. Orig bndg. *(Fye)* **$200 [≃ £112]**

Smith, Robert, cook
- Court Cookery: or, The Compleat English Cook ... Second Edition, with Additions. London: for T. Wotton, 1725. 8vo. [viii], 218, [xiv] pp. Sm repr to title. Contemp calf, later labels. *(Gough)* **£450 [≃ $801]**

Smith, Robert, 1689-1768
- Harmonics, or The Philosophy of Musical Sounds ... The Second Edition, much improved and augmented. London: for T. & J. Merrill, Cambridge ..., 1759. 8vo. xviii,[ii], 280, [xiii] pp. 28 fldg plates. Orig bds, uncut, v sl soiled. *(Finch)* **£385 [≃ $685]**

Smith, S.
- Forensic Medicine. London: Churchill, 1931. 3rd edn. 8vo. 431 pp. 170 ills. Cloth. *(Savona)* **£20 [≃ $36]**

Smith, Samuel Stanhope
- An Essay on the Causes of the Variety of Complexion and Figure in the Human Species. To which are added Strictures on Lord Kaim's Discourse, on the Original Diversity of Mankind. Phila: Robert Aitken, 1787. 1st edn. 8vo. Sl foxing. Disbound. *(Ximenes)* **$500 [≃ £281]**
- An Essay on the Causes of the Variety, Complexion and Figure in the Human Species ... Second Edition ... enlarged and improved. New-Brunswick: A. Deare, 1810. 8vo. 411 pp. Contemp tree calf, front bd detached. *(Hemlock)* **$150 [≃ £84]**

Smith, W.
- A Synopsis of the British Diatomaceae; with Remarks on their Structure, Functions and Distribution ... London: Van Voorst, 1853-56. 2 vols. Roy 8vo. xxxiii,89,10 ctlg; xxix, 107,15 ctlg pp. 2 cold frontis, 67 plates (36 cold). Lib stamp on endpaper. Orig cloth, rebacked. *(Egglishaw)* **£160 [≃ $285]**

Smith, W.W., & others
- The Genus Primula, a Series of 22 Papers. London: (1929-50) 1977. 4to. iv,835 pp. Cloth. *(Wheldon & Wesley)* **£76 [≃ $135]**

Smith, William, Noble, John H., & others
- The Progress of Civil and Mechanical Engineering and Shipbuilding (Illustrated) ... Div. I. [all published]. London: Longmans, Green, 1877. 1st edn. Lge 4to. [2],ix, 119,[1 blank],[1] pp. 21 plates, some text ills. Orig brown cloth gilt, inner hinges weak. *(Fenning)* **£225 [≃ $401]**

Smuts, Jan Christian
- Holism and Evolution. London: Macmillan, 1926. 1st edn. 8vo. Orig cloth, jnts & edges sl rubbed. *(Gach)* **$65 [≃ £37]**

Smyth, Gonzalvo
- Medical Heresies Historically Considered. A Series of Critical Essays ... and Review of Homoeopathy, Past and Present. Phila: 1880. 1st edn. 228 pp. Orig bndg. *(Fye)* **$100 [≃ £56]**

Smyth, Henry
- Atomic Energy for Military Purposes. The Official Report on the Development of the Atomic Bomb. Princeton: 1945. 1st edn. 246 pp. Orig bndg. *(Fye)* **$50 [≃ £28]**
- Atomic Energy for Military Purposes. Princeton: UP, 1945. 1st hardbound edn. Orig bndg. Partial dw. *(Key Books)* **$100 [≃ £56]**
- Atomic Energy, for Military Purposes. Princeton: UP, 1945. 1st Princeton edn. 12mo. 265 pp. Orig wraps, taped lib number on spine. *(Schoen)* **$50 [≃ £28]**
- Atomic Energy, for Military Purposes. Princeton: UP, 1945. 1st edn. 12mo. 265 pp. Orig wraps, fine. *(Schoen)* **$150 [≃ £84]**
- A General Account of the Development of Methods of Using Atomic Energy for Military Purposes. 1945. 1st lithographed edn. Orig bndg. *(Key Books)* **$1,200 [≃ £674]**
- A General Account of the Development of Methods of using Atomic Energy for Military Purposes. Washington: GPO, 1945. 1st GPO edn. Orig bndg. *(Key Books)* **$400 [≃ £225]**
- A General Account of the Development of Methods of using Atomic Energy for Military Purposes. London: HMSO, 1945. 1st English edn. Orig bndg. *(Key Books)* **$190 [≃ £107]**

Smyth, James Carmichael
- The Effect of the Nitrous Vapour in Preventing and Destroying Contagion ... made chiefly by the Surgeons of His Majesty's Navy ... with an Introduction ... on Jail or Hospital Fever ... Phila: Dobson, 1799. 8vo. 174 pp. Fldg table. Sl wear, foxed. Sheep, rebacked. *(Goodrich)* **$165 [≃ £93]**

Smyth, William Henry
- A Cycle of Celestial Objects ... Observed, Reduced, and Discussed. London: 1844. 2 vols. 8vo. Ca 1100 pp. Ills. Lib marks. Orig cloth, worn.   *(Weiner)* **£100 [≃ $178]**

Smythies, Bertram E.
- The Birds of Borneo. London: 1960. 1st edn. Roy 8vo. xvi,562 pp. Map, 99 plates (52 cold). Cloth.
          (Wheldon & Wesley) **£100 [≃ $178]**
- The Birds of Borneo. London: 1968. 2nd edn. Roy 8vo. xx,593 pp. Map, 100 plates (51 cold). Cloth.
          (Wheldon & Wesley) **£90 [≃ $160]**
- Birds of Burma (Rangoon, 1940). Dehra Dun: 1984. Roy 8vo. xxix,[i],589 pp. Fldg map, 31 cold plates. Bds.
          (Wheldon & Wesley) **£71 [≃ $126]**
- The Birds of Burma. Second Edition. Edinburgh: Oliver & Boyd, 1953. xliii,668 pp. Frontis, fldg map, 30 cold plates. Extra plate pasted to half-title. Orig green cloth, gilt spine.   *(Gough)* **£90 [≃ $160]**

Snow, W.B.
- Currents of High Potential of High and Other Frequencies. New York: 1911. 2nd edn. xiv, 275 pp. Frontis, 63 text figs. New cloth.
          (Whitehart) **£25 [≃ $45]**

Sobotta, J.
- Atlas of Descriptive Human Anatomy. Edited by E. Uhlenhuth. New York: 1954. Vols 1 & 2 6th edn, vol 3 5th edn. 3 vols. Num plates, ills. Slipcases.   *(Whitehart)* **£40 [≃ $71]**

Soddy, Frederick
- The Chemistry of the Radioelements. London: 1911. 92 pp. Fldg chart. Orig bndg.
          (Key Books) **£40 [≃ $22]**
- The Interpretation of Radium ... London: Murray, 1908. 1st edn. Ills. Orig bndg, spine sl faded.   *(Key Books)* **£185 [≃ £104]**
- The Interpretation of the Atom. London: 1932. 1st edn. xviii,355 pp. 73 figs. Lib marks. Orig cloth, dusty.
          (Whitehart) **£40 [≃ $71]**

Solly, Samuel
- Surgical Experiences: The Substance of Clinical Lectures. London: 1865. 1st edn. 656 pp. Orig bndg, recased.   *(Fye)* **$175 [≃ £98]**

Solms-Laubach, H.
- Fossil Botany. Translated by H.E.F. Garnsey. Revised by I.B. Balfour. Oxford: 1891. Roy 8vo. xii,401 pp. Text figs. Buckram.   *(Wheldon & Wesley)* **£25 [≃ $45]**

Somerville, Mary
- On the Connexion of the Physical Sciences. London: Murray, 1834. 1st edn. Sm 8vo. Orig cloth backed bds, fine.
          (Ximenes) **$500 [≃ £281]**

Somerville, Robert
- General View of the Agriculture of East Lothian. London: Richard Phillips, 1805. 8vo. [4],326,[2] pp. Fldg hand cold map. Orig bds, paper label, uncut.
          (Spelman) **£150 [≃ $267]**

Soodak, Harry
- Elementary Pile Theory. New York: 1950. 1st edn. 16mo. 73 pp. Lib pocket. Orig cloth.
          (Schoen) **$45 [≃ £25]**

Soranus
- Soranus' Gynecology. Translated with an Introduction by Owsei Temkin. Baltimore: 1956. 1st English translation. 258 pp. Dw.
          (Fye) **$125 [≃ £70]**

Soroka, Walter W.
- Analog Methods in Computation and Simulation. New York: McGraw Hill, 1954. 1st edn. 8vo. 390 pp. Ills. Lib pocket. Orig cloth, sl rubbed.   *(Schoen)* **$45 [≃ £25]**

South, J.F.
- Household Surgery; or, Hints on Emergencies. London: 1847. xvi,340 pp. Plate, ills. Orig cloth, backstrip relaid, sl worn.   *(Whitehart)* **$35 [≃ $62]**

South, R.
- The Moths of the British Isles. London: (1939) 1946. 3rd edn. 2 vols. Cr 8vo. 191 cold & 127 plain plates. Cloth.
          (Wheldon & Wesley) **£22 [≃ $39]**

Southern, J.W.M.
- The Marine Steam Turbine. A Practical Illustrated Description of the Parsons and Curtis Marine Geared-Down Steam Turbines, etc. ... Glasgow: 1919. 6th edn, enlgd. Roy 8vo. xxxvi,790,[2 advt] pp. Over 750 ills. Orig cloth, soiled, extrs worn.
          (Francis Edwards) **£48 [≃ $85]**

Southey, H.H.
- Observations on Pulmonary Consumption. London: 1814. 174 pp. Lib marks on endpapers & title. Some marks on title. Contemp bds, rebacked.
          (Whitehart) **£60 [≃ $107]**

A Sovereign Remedy for the Dropsy ...
- A Sovereign Remedy for the Dropsy. Published by Desire, for Public Benefit. The Fourth Edition. London: for J. Triphook, 1805. 8vo. 15 pp. Half-title. Bulked out with blank paper. Contemp calf, rebacked.
(Spelman) **£75 [≈ $134]**

Sowerby, George Brettingham, the younger
- A Conchological Manual. London: 1842. 2nd edn. 8vo. vi,313 pp. 27 hand cold plates, 2 fldg tables. Polished calf gilt, trifle rubbed.
(Wheldon & Wesley) **£140 [≈ $249]**
- Illustrated Index of British Shells, containing Figures of all the Recent Species. London: Simpkin Marshall, 1859. 1st edn. Roy 8vo. xv,[48] pp. 24 hand cold plates, a.e.g. *(Egglishaw)* **£220 [≈ $392]**
- Illustrated Index of British Shells containing Figures of all the Recent Species. London: 1859. 1st edn. Imperial 8vo. xv,[48] pp. 24 hand cold plates. Orig cloth, sm repr to upper jnt. *(Wheldon & Wesley)* **£100 [≈ $178]**
- Popular British Conchology. London: 1854. Sq post 8vo. xii,304 pp. 20 hand cold plates. Orig cloth. *(Wheldon & Wesley)* **£50 [≈ $89]**

Sowerby, James, the elder
- British Mineralogy: or Coloured Figures intended to elucidate the Mineralogy of Great Britain. London: the author, 1804-11. 5 vols. 8vo. xii,223, 199,209, 184,281, xxiii pp. 550 hand cold plates. Some titles & indexes in facs. New leather.
(Gemmary) **$6,250 [≈ £3,511]**
- Coloured Figures of English Fungi or Mushrooms. London: 1797-1803. 3 vols in one. Folio. 400 hand cold plates. Contemp calf gilt, somewhat worn.
(Wheldon & Wesley) **£2,500 [≈ $4,450]**
- English Botany; or Coloured Figures of British Plants. Third Edition, edited by J.T. Boswell. London: 1877-86. Atlas of plates only, no text. 12 vols. roy 8vo. 1939 hand cold plates. Half calf.
(Wheldon & Wesley) **£425 [≈ $757]**

Sowerby, James, the elder, & Smith, J.E.
- English Botany ... London: 1841-44. 2nd edn. Vols 8-11 only. 4 vols. 892 hand cold plates. Half calf gilt, red & green labels.
(Egglishaw) **£530 [≈ $943]**

Sowerby, John Edward
- An Illustrated Key to the Natural Orders of british Wild Flowers. London: Van Voorst, 1865. 8vo. 42 pp. 9 hand cold plates. Occas sl foxing. Few sm ink notes. Orig cloth, a.e.g.
(Egglishaw) **£30 [≈ $53]**

Sowerby, John Edward & Johnson, C.P.
- British Wild Flowers, illustrated by John E. Sowerby. Described by C. Pierpoint Johnson ... With a Supplement. London: Van Voorst, 1863. 8vo. Hand cold frontis, 89 hand cold & 2 plain plates. Prize calf gilt, backstrip relaid.
(Egglishaw) **£160 [≈ $285]**
- The Ferns of Great Britain. London: 1855. 1st edn. 8vo. 87 pp. 49 partly hand cold plates. Orig cloth, spine sl faded.
(Henly) **£45 [≈ $80]**

Soyer, Alexis Benoit
- The Modern Housewife or Menagere ... Second Edition. London: Simpkin, Marshall, 1849. 8vo. xvi,442 pp. Port, engvd dedic, 3 plates (in the advts), w'cut text ills. Occas sl foxing. Orig green cloth, pict gilt spine, fine.
(Gough) **£125 [≈ $223]**
- The Pantropheon or, History of Food ... London: Simpkin, Marshall & Co., 1853. 1st edn. Roy 8vo. xvi,(470) pp. Port frontis, etched & engvd plates. Occas spotting. Later half mor gilt. *(Ash)* **£400 [≈ $712]**

Spallanzani, L.
- Tracts on the Natural History of Animals and Vegetables. Translated by J.G. Dalyell. Edinburgh: 1803. 2nd edn. 2 vols. 8vo. 11 plates. Contemp calf, vol 1 hd of spine defective. *(Wheldon & Wesley)* **£140 [≈ $249]**

Sparkes, John C.L.
- A Manual of Artistic Anatomy for the Use of Students of Art ... London: Bailliere, Tindall & Cox, 1888. 1st edn. 8vo. [iii],66 pp. 43 plates. Name on title. Orig cloth, recased.
(David White) **£35 [≈ $62]**

Spectacle de la Nature ...
- See Pluche, Antoine-Noel

Spencer, H.
- An Autobiography. London: 1904. 2 vols. 8vo. 10 ports, ills. Some foxing at ends & on edges. Orig cloth.
(Wheldon & Wesley) **£35 [≈ $62]**

Spencer, L.J.
- The World's Minerals. London: 1911. 1st edn. 8vo. xii,212 pp. 40 cold plates, 21 text diags. Orig cloth gilt.
(Bow Windows) **£55 [≈ $98]**

Spiers, W.
- Nature through the Microscope. London: Culley, [ca 1909]. 8vo. 355 pp. 99 plates. Occas sl foxing. Orig pict cloth, sl marked.
(Savona) **£30 [≈ $53]**

Spillane, John
- The Doctrine of the Nerves. Chapters in the History of Neurology. London: 1981. 1st edn. 467 pp. Dw.   *(Fye)* **$95 [≈ £53]**

Spink, W.W.
- Infectious Diseases, Prevention and Treatment in the Nineteenth and Twentieth Centuries. Minneapolis: 1978. xx,577 pp. 20 figs. Orig bndg.   *(Whitehart)* **£15 [≈ $27]**

Sprat, Thomas
- The History of the Royal-Society of London ... London: for Martyn & Allestry, 1667. 1st edn. 1st issue, 'of' repeated p 85 lines 6-7. 4to. [xvi],438,[1] pp. Frontis, 2 fldg plates. Faint water stain in upper marg. Contemp calf, rebacked. Wing S.5035.
                  (Gaskell) **£1,250 [≈ $2,225]**
- The History of the Royal Society of London, for the Improving of Natural Knowledge. London: T.R. for J. Martyn, Printers to the Royal Society, 1667. 438 pp, errata sheet. Frontis, fldg plate. Lib stamp on title. Leather gilt.   *(Key Books)* **$500 [≈ £281]**
- The History of the Royal-Society of London ... London: Rob. Scot ..., 1702. 2nd edn, crrctd. 4to. Imprimatur leaf. 2 fldg plates. Water stain at start. Contemp calf, rebacked.
                  (P and P Books) **£250 [≈ $445]**
- The History of the Royal Society of London for the Improving of Natural Knowledge. London: Knapton ..., 1722. 3rd edn. 4to. [xvi], 438 pp. 2 fldg plates. Contemp calf.
                  (Bookpress) **$375 [≈ £211]**

Spratt, George
- Obstetric Tables: Comprising Graphic Illustrations. With Descriptions and Practical remarks ... Subjects in Midwifery. Phila: Wagner & Guigan, 1847. 1st Amer edn. 4to. [100] pp. Frontis, 20 cold litho plates, moveable overlays. Orig cloth.
                  (O'Neal) **$500 [≈ £281]**

Sprengell, Sir Conrad
- The Aphorisms of Hippocrates and the Sentences of Celsus, with Explanations and References to the most considerable Writers in Physick and Philosophy ... Second Edition ... enlarged. London: 1735. 8vo. 435,index pp. Port. Marg worm index. Contemp calf, rebacked.   *(Robertshaw)* **£35 [≈ $62]**

Spry, W. & Shuckard, W.E.
- The British Coleoptera Delineated. London: Crofts, 1840. 1st edn. 8vo. viii,83 pp. 94 plates. Sl spotting. Half mor.
                  (Egglishaw) **£30 [≈ $53]**

Spurzheim, J.G.
- The Anatomy of the Brain, With a General View of the Nervous System. Translated from the Unpublished French Ms. by R. Willis ... Second American Edition, Revised by Charles H. Stedman. Boston: 1836. 8vo. 18 plates. Orig cloth, extrs sl chipped.
                  (Karmiole) **$75 [≈ £42]**

Squarrey, Charles
- A Popular Treatise on Agricultural Chemistry: intended for the Use of the Practical Farmer. London: James Ridgway, 1842. 1st edn. 8vo. iv,156,[16 ctlg] pp. Orig cloth, sl faded, hd of spine sl frayed.
                  (Burmester) **£48 [≈ $85]**

Squier, E.G.
- Tropical Fibres: their Production and Economic Extraction. London & New York: Madden & Scribner, 1863. 2nd edn. 8vo. 64 pp. 16 plates. Orig cloth, sl worn.
                  (Bookpress) **$235 [≈ £132]**

Stainton, H.T.
- British Butterflies and Moths. London: 1867. Post 8vo. xii,292 pp. 16 hand cold plates. Orig cloth, faded.
                  (Wheldon & Wesley) **£28 [≈ $50]**

Stainton, H.T., & others
- The Natural History of the Tineina. London: 1855-73. 13 vols. 8vo. 104 cold plates. Orig cloth.   *(Wheldon & Wesley)* **£275 [≈ $490]**

Stallybrass, C.O.
- The Principles of Epidemiology and the Process of Infection. London: 1931. xii,696 pp. 104 text figs. Occas sl foxing. Trace of label removal. Orig cloth, sl marked.
                  (Whitehart) **£15 [≈ $27]**

Standlee, Mary
- The Great Pulse. Japanese Midwifery and Obstetrics through the Ages. Tokyo: 1959. 192 pp. 58 ills. Dw. *(Goodrich)* **$45 [≈ £25]**

Stanhope, Charles, Earl
- Principles of the Science of Tuning Instruments with Fixed Tones. Stereotype Edition. London: stereotyped & ptd by A. Wilson, 1806. 1st edn. 8vo. 24 pp. Diags & tables. Orig wraps, v sl worn.
                  (Burmester) **£120 [≈ $214]**

Stanley, R.
- Text-Book on Wireless Telegraphy. New Edition. London: 1919-23. 2 vols. xiii,471; xi,394 pp. 2 frontis ports, fldg plate, ills. Orig

cloth, dusty.   *(Whitehart)* **£35 [≈ $62]**

Stanley, William Ford
- Experimental Researches into the Properties
and Motions of Fluids ... London: Spon,
1881. 1st edn. 8vo. xvi,550 pp. Ills. Mod
cloth. Inscrbd by the author.
        (Key Books) **$45 [≈ £25]**
- Surveying and Levelling Instruments
Theoretically and Practically Described ...
other Apparatus used by Civil Engineers and
Surveyors ... London: Spon, 1895. 2nd edn.
8vo. xiii,555 pp. 353 figs. Orig cloth gilt, sl
shaken.   *(Bates & Hindmarch)* **£30 [≈ $53]**

Stark, R.M.
- A Popular History of British Mosses.
London: Routledge, 1860. 2nd edn. Sm 8vo.
xx, 348 pp. 20 hand cold plates. Orig cloth, sl
loose.   *(Egglishaw)* **£16 [≈ $28]**

Starling, E.H.
- The Action of Alcohol on Man. London:
1923. viii,292 pp. Lib label. Sl foxing. Orig
bndg, worn, spine faded.
        (Whitehart) **£15 [≈ $27]**

Starobinski, J.
- A History of Medicine. New York: 1964. Roy
8vo. 108 pp. Ills. Dw. *(Goodrich)* **$45 [≈ £25]**

Starr, Louis (editor)
- An American Textbook of the Diseases of
Children ... by American Teachers ... London
& Phila: 1894. 2 vols. 8vo. 1195 pp. Lacks
front fly. Sheep, v worn, jnts split.
        (Goodrich) **$75 [≈ £42]**

Starr, M. Allen
- Familiar Forms of Nervous Diseases. New
York: Wood, 1890. xii,339 pp. 77 ills. Orig
blue cloth, rubbed esp spine ends.
        (Goodrich) **$150 [≈ £84]**

Staveley, E.F.
- British Insects. London: Reeve, 1871. 8vo.
xvi,392 pp. 16 hand cold plates, 73 figs.
Name. Orig cloth gilt.
        (Egglishaw) **£28 [≈ $50]**
- British Spiders: an Introduction to the Study
of the Araneidae. London: [1866]. Cr 8vo.
xvi,280 pp. 14 hand cold & 2 plain plates.
Orig cloth. *(Wheldon & Wesley)* **£35 [≈ $62]**

Stead, E.F.
- The Life Histories of New Zealand Birds.
London: 1932. Roy 8vo. xvi,162 pp. 93 photo
plates. Cloth, trifle used.
        (Wheldon & Wesley) **£35 [≈ $62]**

Stebbing, Edward Percy
- The Forests of India. London: John Lane,
1922-26. 3 vols. 8vo. 2 maps, 223 photo ills.
Orig cloth. Dws. *(Blackwell's)* **£250 [≈ $445]**

Stebbing, T.R.R.
- A History of Crustacea. London: Kegan Paul,
1893. 8vo. 466 pp. Plates, text figs. Orig dec
cloth, sm stain front bd. *(Savona)* **£20 [≈ $36]**

Steeds, W.
- A History of Machine Tools 1700-1910.
Oxford: 1969. xx,182 pp. 153 plates, 55 figs.
Occas lib stamps. Orig bndg. Dw taped to
endpapers.   *(Whitehart)* **£35 [≈ $62]**

Steers, J.A.
- The Sea Coast. London: Collins New
Naturalist, 1953. 1st edn. 8vo. Plates, maps,
diags. Orig cloth. Dw.
        (Egglishaw) **£25 [≈ $45]**

Steindler, Arthur
- Diseases and Deformities of the Spine and
Thorax. St. Louis, 1929. 1st edn. 8vo. Ills.
Orig bndg.   *(Fye)* **$200 [≈ £112]**
- Mechanics of Normal and Pathological
Locomotion in Man. Springfield: 1935. 1st
edn. 424 pp. Orig bndg. Signed by the author.
        (Fye) **$175 [≈ £98]**
- Orthopedic Operations: Indications,
Technique, and End Results. Springfield:
1940. 1st edn. 766 pp. Orig bndg.
        (Fye) **$150 [≈ £84]**
- Reconstructive Surgery of the Upper
Extremity. New York: 1923. 1st edn. 310 pp.
Ills. Orig bndg.   *(Fye)* **$175 [≈ £98]**
- The Traumatic Deformities and Disabilities
of the Upper Extremities. Springfield: 1946.
1st edn. 494 pp. Orig bndg.
        (Fye) **$125 [≈ £70]**

Steiner, Rudolf
- Occult Science. London: 1939. 1st edn. 8vo.
Orig dec cloth.   *(Deja Vu)* **£25 [≈ $45]**

Steinhaus, E.A.
- Principles of Insect Pathology. New York:
McGraw-Hill, 1949. 1st edn. 8vo. xi,757 pp.
219 text figs. Buckram. *(Savona)* **£25 [≈ $45]**
- Principles of Insect Pathology. New York:
McGraw Hill, 1949. 1st edn. 8vo. xi,757 pp.
219 text figs. Buckram. *(Savona)* **£30 [≈ $53]**

Steinmetz, Charles Proteus
- Elementary Lectures on Electric Discharges,
Waves and Impulses, and Other Transients.
New York: McGraw Hill, 1914. 2nd edn.

8vo. 156 pp. Ills. Orig bndg, upper jnt loose.
(Schoen) **$45 [≈ £25]**
- Four Lectures on Relativity and Space. New
York: McGraw Hill, 1923. 1st edn, 7th imp.
8vo. x,126 pp. Stereo views in pocket. Orig
bndg, spine sl faded. *(Key Books)* **$50 [≈ £28]**

Stensio, E.A.
- The Cephalaspids of Great Britain. London:
BM, 1932. 4to. xiv,220 pp. 66 plates, 70 text
figs. Cloth, trifle loose.
(Wheldon & Wesley) **£45 [≈ $80]**

Step, E.
- Bees, Wasps, Ants and Allied Insects of the
British Isles. London: 1932. Sm 8vo. xxv,238
pp. 108 plates (41 cold). Cloth.
(Wheldon & Wesley) **£25 [≈ $45]**
- Wayside and Woodland Blossoms. New
Edition. London: 1963. 3 vols. Sm 8vo. 396
plates. Orig cloth. Dw.
(Egglishaw) **£20 [≈ $36]**

Stephens, G.
- The Practical Irrigator and Drainer. London:
1834. 8vo. vii,195 pp. 9 plate & 4 text plans.
Orig cloth backed bds, uncut, recased.
(Henly) **£60 [≈ $107]**

Stephens, Henry
- The Book of the Farm ... Edinburgh:
Blackwood, 1850. 2 vols. Lge 8vo. xx,674;
xii,804,[i] pp. 24 ctlg pp. 14 steel engvs (damp
stained), 589 w'engvs in text. Vol 1 lacks half-
title. Rec binder's cloth.
(Blackwell's) **£85 [≈ $151]**

Stephens, J.W.
- Blackwater Fever. A Historical Survey and
Summary of Observations made over a
Century. Liverpool: 1937. 8vo. vi,727 pp.
Frontis, text ills. Orig cloth, rubbed.
(Goodrich) **$75 [≈ £42]**

Stephens, W.P.
- Canoe and Boat Building: a Complete
Manual for Amateurs. New York: 1895. 8vo.
263 pp. Diags. Perf lib stamp through title &
last leaf. Orig cloth, shaken.
(Weiner) **£20 [≈ $36]**

Stephens, William E., and others (editors)
- Nuclear Fission and Atomic Energy.
Lancaster, Pa.: The Science Press, 1948. 1st
edn. 8vo. x,294 pp. Lib pocket. Orig bndg.
(Schoen) **$75 [≈ £42]**

Stephenson, J.
- Medical Zoology and Mineralogy or

Illustrations and Descriptions of the Animals
and Minerals employed in Medicine.
London: 1838. Roy 8vo. vi,350 pp. 44 hand
cold & 2 plain plates (1-45, 29a). Sm stamp on
title & 2 plates. Binder's cloth, spine trifle
faded.   *(Wheldon & Wesley)* **£360 [≈ $641]**
- The Oligochaeta. Oxford: 1930. 1st edn. 8vo.
xvi,978 pp. 242 text figs. Tear in half-title.
Cloth, trifle loose, front cvr trifle faded.
(Wheldon & Wesley) **£50 [≈ $89]**
- The Oligochaeta. Oxford: 1930. Roy 8vo. xvi,
978 pp. 242 text figs. Orig cloth.
(Egglishaw) **£34 [≈ $61]**

Stephenson, T.A.
- The British Sea Anemones. London: Ray
Society, 1928-35. 2 vols. 8vo. 19 cold & 14
plain plates. Cloth.
(Wheldon & Wesley) **£85 [≈ $151]**
- The British Sea Anemones. London: Ray
Society, 1928-35. 1st edn. 2 vols. 33 plates,
107 text figs. Orig blue cloth gilt, fine.
(Gough) **£55 [≈ $98]**
- The British Sea Anemones. London: Ray
Society, 1928-35. 2 vols. 8vo. 19 cold & 14
plain plates. Orig cloth gilt.
(Egglishaw) **£75 [≈ $134]**

Stern, F.C.
- A Study of the Genus Paeonia. London:
1946. Imperial 4to. viii,155 pp. 8 maps, 15
cold plates, text ills. V sl foxing at ends. Orig
cloth gilt.   *(Henly)* **£245 [≈ $436]**

Sternberg, George M.
- Malaria and Malarial Diseases. New York:
Wood Library, 1884. 8vo. vii,329 pp. Orig
cloth.   *(Goodrich)* **$85 [≈ £48]**

Sterndale, R.A.
- Natural History of the Mammals of India and
Ceylon. Calcutta: 1884. 8vo. xxxii,540,xi pp.
Frontis, 169 text figs. Orig dec cloth.
(Wheldon & Wesley) **£48 [≈ $85]**

Steuart, Sir Henry
- The Planter's Guide; or, a Practical Essay on
the Best Method of Giving Immediate Effect
to Wood ... Edinburgh: Blackwood, 1828. 1st
edn. 8vo. [vi],xxii,473,8 advt pp. Frontis & 4
plates on india paper. Orig bds, green cloth
spine, uncut, sl worn. *(Rankin)* **£60 [≈ $107]**
- The Planter's Guide; or a Practical Essay on
the Best Method of Giving Immediate Effect
to Wood ... New York: 1832. 1st Amer edn.
8vo. 422 pp. Frontis, 3 plates. Occas foxing.
Cloth.   *(Henly)* **£65 [≈ $116]**
- The Planter's Guide; or, a Practical Essay on
the Best Method of Giving Immediate Effect

to Wood ... New York: G. Thorburn & Sons, 1832. 1st Amer edn. 8vo. xxxix,[2],42-422 pp. Frontis, 3 plates. Occas foxing. Orig glazed linen bds, black gilt label.
(Spelman) **£95 [≈ $169]**

Stevens, W.
- Observations on the Healthy and Diseased Properties of the Blood. London: 1832. xx,504 pp. Endpapers & title foxed. Contemp leather, rebacked, crnrs sl worn.
(Whitehart) **£150 [≈ $267]**

Stevenson, D. Alan
- The World's Lighthouses before 1820. OUP: 1959. 1st edn. 4to. xxiv,310 pp. 7 maps, 199 ills. Orig cloth, t.e.g. Dw (frayed).
(Francis Edwards) **£70 [≈ $125]**

Stevenson, Henry
- The Gentleman Gardener Instructed in Sowing, Planting, Pruning, and Grafting Seeds, Plants, Flowers, and Trees; also in the Management of Bees ... London: for James Hinton, 1764. 5th edn, enlgd. 12mo. Contemp sheep gilt, spine rubbed.
(Ximenes) **£175 [≈ £98]**
- The Young Gard'ners Director. London: 1716. Sm 8vo. vi,144 pp. Frontis. Calf, reprd. Anon.
(Wheldon & Wesley) **£100 [≈ $178]**

Stewart, C.
- Descriptive and Illustrated Catalogue of the Physiological Series of Comparative Anatomy contained in the Museum of the Royal College of Surgeons of England. Vol. III. London: 1907. 2nd edn. xiii,391 pp. Plates, text figs. Orig cloth, sl worn, dust stained.
(Whitehart) **£25 [≈ $45]**

Stewart, H.E.
- Diathermy. With Special reference to Pneumonia. New York: 1926. 2nd edn. xx,228 pp. 45 ills. Orig bndg. Signed by the author.
(Whitehart) **£15 [≈ $27]**

Stewart, Irvin
- Organizing Scientific Research for War; The Administrative History of the Office of Scientific Research and Development. Boston: Little, Brown, 1948. 1st edn. 8vo. xiv,358 pp. Lib pocket. Orig bndg.
(Schoen) **£100 [≈ £56]**

Stewart, J. & Campbell, B.
- Orchids of Tropical Africa. London: 1970. Roy 8vo. 128 pp. 45 cold plates. Cloth.
(Wheldon & Wesley) **£40 [≈ $71]**

Stewart, Matthew
- Tracts, Physical and Mathematical. Containing, an Explication of Several Important Points in Physical Astronomy ... Edinburgh: A. Millar ..., 1761. 1st edn. 8vo. viii,412 pp. 19 fldg plates. 19th c half calf, hinge cracked but sound.
(Karmiole) **$500 [≈ £281]**

Stewart, Samuel Alexander
- A Flora of the North-East of Ireland ... Belfast: Naturalists' Club, 1888. 8vo. xxxv, 331 pp. Orig cloth. *(de Burca)* **£68 [≈ $121]**

Stigand, C.H.
- The Game of British East Africa. London: 1909. 1st edn. 4to. 74 photos & ills. Occas sl foxing. Orig bndg, sl marked, recased.
(Chalmers Hallam) **£185 [≈ $329]**
- The Game of British East Africa. London: 1913. 2nd edn. Repr to 1 crnr. Occas sl foxing. Orig bndg, sl rubbed.
(Chalmers Hallam) **£120 [≈ $214]**

Still, George F.
- Common Disorders and Diseases of Childhood. London: Frowde, 1909. 1st edn. 8vo. 791,advt pp. Lib stamp on title. Orig cloth, sl shelf wear. *(Goodrich)* **$250 [≈ £140]**
- The History of Paediatrics: The Progress of the Study of Diseases of Children up to the End of the 18th Century. London: (1931) 1965. 526 pp. Orig bndg. *(Fye)* **$125 [≈ £70]**

Stillingfleet, Benjamin
- Miscellaneous Tracts relating to Natural History, Husbandry, and Physick ... The Second Edition ... London: 1762. 8vo. xxxi, 391 pp. 11 plates. Lib stamp on title. Contemp calf, rebacked. Author's pres copy.
(Goodrich) **$145 [≈ £81]**
- Miscellaneous Tracts relating to Natural History, Husbandry, and Physick. To which is added The Calendar of Flora. London: 1762. 2nd edn. xxxi,391 pp. 11 plates. Contemp sprinkled calf, spine gilt (sl rubbed).
(Whitehart) **£130 [≈ $231]**

Stillwell, Margaret B.
- The Awakening Interest in Science during the First Century of Printing 1450-1550. An Annotated Checklist ... New York: 1970. xxix, 399 pp. Orig bndg.
(Whitehart) **£25 [≈ $45]**
- The Awakening Interest in Science during the First Century of Printing 1450-1550. An Annotated Checklist of First Editions ... New York: 1970. Ltd edn. 4to. 399 pp. Orig bndg.
(Fye) **$100 [≈ £56]**

Stimson, Lewis
- A Practical Treatise on Fractures and Dislocations. Phila: 1905. 4th edn. 837 pp. Half leather, fine.   *(Fye)* **$75 [≈£42]**

Stirling, W.
- Some Apostles of Physiology being an Account of their Lives and Labours. London: 1902. v,130 pp. 32 plates, 30 ills. Sl foxing. Label on endpaper. Orig bndg.
     (Whitehart) **£60 [≈$107]**

Stirrup, Thomas
- Horometria: Or, The Compleat Diallist ... The Second Edition with Additions ... London: R. & W. Leybourn, for Thomas Pirrepoint, 1659. 4to. [iv],181, [xi],31,[i] pp. Lacks frontis & contents leaf. Sl wear & tear. Later half vellum, darkened. Wing S.5689.
     (Clark) **£150 [≈$267]**

Stokers and Pokers ...
- See Head, Sir Francis Bond

Stokes, George Gabriel
- Mathematical and Physical Papers. Cambridge: 1880-1905. 5 vols. 8vo. Frontis ports vols 4 & 5. Stamp on flyleaves. Orig cloth, 1 vol recased. *(Weiner)* **£225 [≈$401]**
- Memoir and Scientific Correspondence ... selected and arranged by Joseph Larmor. Cambridge: 1907. 2 vols. 8vo. 4 ports, diags. Orig cloth.   *(Weiner)* **£85 [≈$151]**

Stokoe, W.J.
- Butterflies and Moths of the Wayside and Woodland. London: 1939. 1st edn. Post 8vo. vi, 309 pp. 71 cold plates. Orig cloth.
     (Henly) **£21 [≈$37]**
- The Caterpillars of British Moths, including the Eggs, Chrysalids and Food-Plants. London: Warne, Wayside & Woodland Series, 1948. 2 vols. 8vo. 141 plates. Name. Orig cloth gilt.   *(Egglishaw)* **£38 [≈$68]**

Stone, Lee Alexander
- The Story of Phallicism with Other Essays on related Subjects ... Chicago: Covici, 1927. One of 1050. 2 vols. 8vo. Orig cloth gilt, t.e.g.   *(Karmiole)* **$50 [≈£28]**

Stone, W.
- The Plants of Southern New Jersey. Boston: 1973. 8vo. 828 pp. Port, map, 129 plates. Cloth, front bd cracked.
     (Wheldon & Wesley) **£35 [≈$62]**

"Stonehenge" (J.H. Walsh)
- The Dog in Health and Disease ... London:

Longman ..., 1859. 1st edn. Lge 8vo. xvi,468 pp. Num text engvs. Red qtr mor, gilt spine, sl frayed & faded.   *(Bookline)* **£50 [≈$89]**
- See also Walsh, John Henry

Stookey, Byron
- Surgical and Mechanical Treatment of Peripheral Nerves. With a Chapter on Nerve Degeneration and Regeneration by G. Carl Huber. Phila: Saunders, 1922. 8vo. [5]-475 pp. 2 cold plates, ills. Orig cloth, worn, lib number on spine. *(Goodrich)* **$185 [≈£104]**

Stopes, Marie Carmichael
- Birth Control Today. London: 1934. 1st edn. Sm 8vo. 237 pp. Plates, diags. Orig cloth.
     (Weiner) **£15 [≈$27]**
- Change of Life in Men and Women. London: 1936. 8vo. xv,282 pp. Orig cloth.
     (Weiner) **£15 [≈$27]**
- Contraception (Birth Control). Its Theory, History and Practice. A Manual for the Legal and Medical Professions. London: 1924. 1st edn, 3rd printing. 418 pp. Orig bndg.
     (Fye) **$100 [≈£56]**
- Married Love ... London: A.C. Fifield, 1918. 4th edn. xvii,[1],116,[2] pp. Orig cloth.
     (Caius) **$50 [≈£28]**

Storer, D.H.
- A Synopsis of the Fishes of North America. Cambridge: Memoirs Amer Acad, 1846. 4to. 298 pp. Cloth, trifle worn.
     (Wheldon & Wesley) **£80 [≈$142]**

Street, F.
- Rhododendrons. London: 1965. 1st edn. Cr 4to. xii,177 pp. 12 cold & 12 plain plates. Orig cloth. Dw.   *(Henly)* **£18 [≈$32]**

Strickland, F.
- A Manual of Petrol Motors and Motor Cars ... London: 1907. viii,376 pp. 329 ills, 15 tables. Occas soil. Orig cloth, sl stained, new endpapers.   *(Whitehart)* **£40 [≈$71]**

Strong, L.A.G.
- Dr. Quicksilver, 1660-1742. The Life and Times of Thomas Dover, M.D. London: 1955. 8vo. 184 pp. Frontis, 16 plates. Lib labels front endpaper. Orig cloth, sl marked.   *(Whitehart)* **£15 [≈$27]**

Strong, R.P., & others
- Trench Fever. Report of Commission Medical Research Committee American Red Cross. Oxford: 1918. viii,446 pp. 6 plates, 7 charts, 65 tables. Ink stamp. Orig bndg, worn.   *(Whitehart)* **£15 [≈$27]**

Strother, Edward
- Euodia: or, a Discourse on Causes and Cures. In Two Parts. Second Edition, carefully corrected, with additions. London: 1718. 8vo. 211,index pp. Lib stamp on title & at end. Contemp calf, upper cvr detached.
(Robertshaw) **£60 [≈$107]**

Strouts, C.R.N., & others
- Chemical Analysis. The Working Tools. Oxford: 1962. 3 vols. Plates, text figs. Orig bndgs.   *(Whitehart)* **£18 [≈$32]**

Strumpfell, Adolf
- A Textbook of Medicine ... Translated ... Notes by F.C. Shattuck ... New York: 1891. 981 pp. Ills. Sheep, worn, jnts weak.
(Goodrich) **£95 [≈$53]**

Strutt, Jacob George
- Sylva Britannica, or Portraits of Forest Trees. London: [1830-36]. Imperial 8vo. viii, 151 pp. Addtnl engvd title, 49 plates. Plate margs spotted. Qtr calf.   *(Henly)* **£60 [≈$107]**
- Sylva Britannica; or Portrait of Forest Trees distinguished for their Antiquity, Magnitude, or Beauty. Drawn from Nature. London: (1830). 4to. xvi,151 pp. 49 etched plates on india paper. Occas foxing. Orig bndg, gilt title chipped.   *(Hortulus)* **£320 [≈£180]**
- Sylva Britannica; or, Portraits of Forest Trees, Distinguished for their Antiquity, Magnitude, or Beauty, Drawn from Nature. London: [ca 1830-36]. Imperial 8vo. viii,151 pp. Addtnl illust title, 48 mtd plates. Orig cloth, hinges cracked.
(Francis Edwards) **£90 [≈$160]**

Strutt, Hon. R.J.
- See Rayleigh, Lord

Struve, Christian August
- A Practical Essay on the Art of Recovering Suspended Animation: together with a Review of the ... Means to be adopted in Cases of Imminent Danger. Albany: 1803. 1st Amer edn. 12mo. Contemp calf, jnts cracked.
(Goodrich) **£150 [≈£84]**

Sturges, O. & Coupland, S.
- The Natural History and Relations of Pneumonia. Its Causes, Forms and Treatment. London: 1890. 2nd edn. xv,452,[4] pp. 15 text ills. Orig bndg, sl faded & worn, sl stained. *(Whitehart)* **£18 [≈$32]**

Sudhoff, Karl
- Essays in the History of Medicine. Translated by various hands and edited .... by Fielding

H. Garrison. New York: Medical Life Press, 1926. 8vo. 397 pp. Port, plates. Dw.
(Goodrich) **$125 [≈£70]**

Sully, H.
- Observations on, and Plain Directions for, all Classes of People, to prevent the Fatal Effects of the Bites of Animals labouring under Hydrophobia. Taunton: 1828. viii,77,10 pp. 1 plate. Half leather. Inscrbd by the author.
(Whitehart) **£150 [≈$267]**

Sully, James
- The Human Mind: A Text-Book of Psychology. London: Longmans, Green, 1892. 1st edn. 2nd issue, with errata printed on p xvii. 2 vols. 8vo. Orig cloth, edges rubbed, vol 2 upper jnt frayed.
(Gach) **$100 [≈£56]**
- Illusions: A Psychological Study. London: Kegan Paul, 1881. 1st edn. xii,372,[34 advt] pp. Orig cloth.   *(Caius)* **$100 [≈£56]**
- Studies of Childhood. London, New York & Bombay: 1903. 2nd edn. viii,528,40 pp. 52 figs. Name. Orig bndg, worn.
(Whitehart) **£18 [≈$32]**

Summerhayes, V.S.
- Wild Orchids of Britain. London: Collins New Naturalist, 1951. 1st edn. 8vo. Ills. Endpapers trifle marked. Orig cloth. Dw.
(Wheldon & Wesley) **£30 [≈$53]**

Summers, Montague
- The Vampire: His Kith & Kin. London: Routledge, 1928. 1st edn. Thick 8vo. Ills. Inscrptn. Orig bndg. *(Deja Vu)* **£50 [≈$89]**

Suter, H.
- Manual of the New Zealand Mollusca. London: 1913-15. 2 vols. 8vo & 4to. xxiii, 1120 pp. Atlas of 72 plates. Atlas lacks front free endpaper. Cloth, atlas trifle marked.
(Wheldon & Wesley) **£175 [≈$312]**

Sutherland, George
- Australia or England in the South. London: Seeley & Co., 1886. 3 advt pp. Frontis, ills. Some spotting. Orig ptd wraps, dusty.
(Jarndyce) **£45 [≈$80]**

Sutherland, W.B.
- Blood Stains their Detecting and the Determination of their Source. A Manual for the Medical and Legal Professions. London: 1907. Sl sprung. Name. Orig bndg.
(Blakeney) **£95 [≈$169]**

Sutton, M.J.
- Permanent and Temporary Pastures with Descriptions ... London: Hamilton, Adams, 1886. 4to. xi,158 pp. 23 cold plates. Orig cloth, front hinge partly split.
(Egglishaw) **£40 [≈ $71]**
- Permanent and Temporary Pastures. London: 1887. 2nd edn. Roy 8vo. 23 cold plates. Cloth.
(Wheldon & Wesley) **£15 [≈ $27]**

Swainson, W.
- A Treatise on Malacology or Shells and Shell-Fish. London: 1840. Post 8vo. 419 pp. 130 text figs. Orig cloth, jnts cracked.
(Wheldon & Wesley) **£45 [≈ $80]**

Swan, M.E. & K.R.
- Sir Joseph Wilson Swan F.R.S. A Memoir. London: Benn, 1929. 1st edn. 8vo. 183 pp. 6 plates. Lacks front free endpaper. Orig cloth.
(Claude Cox) **£20 [≈ $36]**

Swayne, George
- Gramina Pascua: or, a Collection of Specimens of the Common Pasture Grasses, arranged in the Order of their Flowering ... Bristol: the author by S. Bonner, sold by W. Richardson, 1790. Folio. 6 plates displaying 19 mtd specimens. Orig bds, rebacked, reprd
(Blackwell's) **£750 [≈ $1,335]**

Swaysland, Edward J.C.
- Boot and Shoe Design and Manufacture. Northampton: 1905. 4to. 244,iv,14 pp. 120 plates. Orig cloth, worn.
(Weiner) **£125 [≈ $223]**

Swediaur, F.
- Practical Observations on Venereal Complaints. Edinburgh: 1787. 3rd edn. viii, 312 pp. Lib stamp on title. Old leather & mrbld bds, rebacked.
(Whitehart) **£85 [≈ $151]**

Sweet, R.
- Cistinae. The Natural Order of Cistus or Rock-Rose. London: 1825-30. Roy 8vo. 112 hand cold plates. 2 stamps on title. Contemp half calf.
(Wheldon & Wesley) **£1,350 [≈ $2,403]**
- Hortus Suburbanus Londinensis: or a Catalogue of Plants cultivated in the Neighbourhood of London: arranged according to the Linnaean System. London: 1818. 8vo. xi, 242 pp. Calf, rather used, lacks label.
(Wheldon & Wesley) **£55 [≈ $98]**

Swiggett, Robert L.
- Introduction to Printed Circuits. New York: John F. Rider, 1956. 1st edn. 12mo. 101 pp. Ills. Lib pocket. Orig dec wraps.
(Schoen) **$45 [≈ £25]**

Swingle, D.B.
- General Bacteriology. New York: Nostrand, 1940. 1st edn. 8vo. xii,313 pp. Frontis, 157 text figs. Cloth.   *(Savona)* **£25 [≈ $45]**
- General Bacteriology. New York: Van Nostrand, 1940. 1st edn. 8vo. xii,313 pp. Frontis, 157 text figs. Cloth. Dw.
(Savona) **£25 [≈ $45]**

Swinton, A.H.
- Insect Variety: its Propagation and Distribution ... London: [1880]. x,323,[4] pp. Frontis, 7 plates, text figs. Orig cloth, sl stained & worn, inner front hinge cracked but firm.   *(Whitehart)* **£20 [≈ $36]**

Switzer, S.
- The Nobleman, Gentleman, and Gardener's Recreation: or, an Introduction to Gardening, Planting, Agriculture and the other Business and Pleasures of a Country Life. London: 1715. 8vo. [vi],xxxiv, 266,[16] pp. Frontis. 3 sm ink marks frontis & title. Contemp calf, reprd.   *(Wheldon & Wesley)* **£200 [≈ $356]**

Sydenham, Thomas
- Anecdota Sydenhamiana. Medical Notes and Observations. Oxford: 1845. viii,80 pp. Occas marg pencil mark. Half leather antique, new endpapers.   *(Whitehart)* **£90 [≈ $160]**
- The Whole Works ... Translated from the Original Latin, by John Pechey. London: Richard Wellington, 1696. 1st edn in English. 8vo. [xxiv],248, 353-592 pp. Sl used. Rec half calf. Wing S.6305.   *(Clark)* **£380 [≈ $676]**
- The Works ... with a Life of the Author by R.G. Latham. London: 1848-50. 1st edn. 2 vols. 276; 394 pp. Buckram.
(Fye) **$200 [≈ £112]**

Sylvester, James Joseph
- The Collected Mathematical Papers. Cambridge: UP, 1904-12. 1st edn. 4 vols. Roy 8vo. Port. Orig cloth, sides v sl scuffed.   *(Gaskell)* **£150 [≈ $267]**

Syme, James
- Observations in Clinical Surgery. Edinburgh: 1862. 2nd edn. 217 pp. Orig bndg.
(Fye) **$250 [≈ £140]**
- Principles of Surgery. Edinburgh: 1842. 3rd edn. 508 pp. Lithos. Orig cloth, rebacked.
(Fye) **$250 [≈ £140]**

Syme, P.
- A Treatise on British Song-Birds ... Edinburgh: John Anderson, 1823. 8vo. [6 advt], 231 pp. 15 hand cold plates (backgrounds cold). Sl spotting. Inscrptn on frontis & title. Mor, spine & crnrs worn. Anon. *(Egglishaw)* **£145 [≈ $258]**

Symons, G.J.
- The Eruption of Krakatoa, and Subsequent Phenomena ... London: 1888. 1st edn. 4to. [ii],xvi, 494,[2] pp. Cold dble page frontis, 7 cold & 36 other plates, 2 fldg tables, 16 figs. Occas sl marks. Orig cloth, backstrip relaid. *(Bow Windows)* **£280 [≈ $498]**

Symons, William
- The Practical Gager ... New Edition ... London: for Wingrave & Collingwood, 1815. 8vo. xii,384 pp. Orig sheep, upper cvr held on cords. *(Claude Cox)* **£25 [≈ $45]**

Systema Agriculturae ...
- See Worlidge, John

Szent-Gyorgyi, A.
- Chemistry of Muscular Contraction. New York: 1951. 2nd edn, enlgd. x,162 pp. 55 figs. Orig bndg, worn & faded. *(Whitehart)* **£18 [≈ $32]**

Talbot, B.
- The New Art of Land Measuring; or, A Turnpike Road to Practical Surveying ... Wolverhampton: for the author, & sold by J. Smart ..., 1779. 1st edn. 8vo. xxiv,412 pp. 13 plates, fldg table. Contemp qtr calf, sl rubbed. *(Burmester)* **£325 [≈ $579]**

Talbot, C.H.
- Medicine in Medieval England. London: 1967. 222 pp. 4 dble-sided plates. Orig bndg. *(Whitehart)* **£15 [≈ $27]**

Talbot, C.H. & Hammond, E.A.
- The Medical Practitioners in Medieval England. A Biographical Register. London: Wellcome, 1965. 8vo. x,503 pp. Dw. *(Goodrich)* **$85 [≈ £48]**
- The Medical Practitioners in Medieval England. London: Wellcome Hist Med Library, 1965. 1st edn. 8vo. x,503 pp. Cloth. Dw (sl rubbed). *(Bookpress)* **$75 [≈ £42]**
- The Medical Practitioners in Medieval England. A Biographical Register. London: 1965. x,503 pp. Orig bndg. *(Whitehart)* **£40 [≈ $71]**

Tansley, A.G.
- The British Islands and their Vegetation. Cambridge: (1949). 2 vols. Roy 8vo. 970 pp. 162 plates, 179 text figs. Cloth. *(Wheldon & Wesley)* **£55 [≈ $98]**

Taplin, William
- The Gentleman's Stable Directory; or, Modern System of Farriery ... London: for G. Kearsley, 1788-91. 6th edn vol 1, 1st edn vol 2. 2 vols. 8vo. xxiii,448; viii,424 pp. Half-titles. Early 19th c calf, sometime rebacked. *(Young's)* **£110 [≈ $196]**
- The Gentleman's Stable Directory; or, Modern System of Farriery. The Sixth Edition, corrected, improved and considerably enlarged. London: for G. Kearsley, 1788. 8vo. Lacks free endpapers. Sm marg loss on T2. Contemp sheep, spine ends chipped, sm loss to leather of rear cvr. *(Waterfield's)* **£85 [≈ $151]**

Taylor, A.S.
- The Principles and Practice of Medical Jurisprudence. Vol. 1. London: 1873. 2nd edn. xvi,723 pp. 136 text figs. Sm lib stamps on title. Half mor, rubbed. *(Whitehart)* **£25 [≈ $45]**

Taylor, Charles F.
- Sensation and Pain. A Lecture ... March 21st, 1881 ... New York: Putnam, 1881. 1st edn. [2],77, [1],[2 advt] pp. Ills. Pencil notes. Orig cloth, some wear. *(Caius)* **$100 [≈ £56]**

Taylor, E.G.R.
- The Haven-Finding Art. A History of Navigation from Odysseus to Captain Cook. London: 1971. 3rd edn. xi,310 pp. Frontis, 24 plates, 27 ills. Orig bndg. *(Whitehart)* **£35 [≈ $62]**

Taylor, G.
- An Account of the Genus Meconopsis. London: 1934. Cr 4to. xxix,130 pp. 30 (on 25) plates, 12 maps. Green levant mor, a.e.g. Author's pres inscrptn. *(Wheldon & Wesley)* **£55 [≈ $98]**

Taylor, George H.
- Paralysis and Other Affections of the Nerves: Their Cure by Vibrationary and Special Movements. New York: S.R. Wells, 1871. 1st edn. vi,[5]-161 pp. Name on title. Orig cloth, sl faded, hd of spine chipped. *(Caius)* **$100 [≈ £56]**

Taylor, J.E.
- Flowers, their Origin, Shapes, Perfumes and

Colours. Edinburgh: 1906. 4th edn. Cr 8vo.
xxiv,347 pp. 8 cold plates, 143 text ills. Orig
dec cloth.   *(Henly)* **£24 [≈ $43]**

Taylor, Michael
- A Sexagesimal Table, exhibiting, at sight, the
Result of any Proportion, where the Terms do
not exceed Sixty Minutes ... London: 1780.
Roy 4to. xlvi,[2],316 pp. Fldg table, tables.
Inner marg of prelims water stained.
Contemp calf, worn, rebacked.
                             (Weiner) **£40 [≈ $71]**
- Tables of Logarithms of All Numbers, from
1 to 101000; and of the Sines and Tangents ...
Preface ... by Nevil Maskelyne. London:
1792. Thick folio. [xiv],64 pp. Subscribers.
Old mrbld bds, mod calf spine.
                             (Weiner) **£50 [≈ $89]**
- Tables of Logarithms of All Numbers, from
1 to 101000; and of the Sines and Tangents ...
Preface ... by Nevil Maskelyne. London:
1792. Thick folio. [xiv],64 pp. Subscribers.
Tables. Amateur cloth backed bds.
                             (Weiner) **£100 [≈ $178]**

Taylor, R. Tunstall
- Surgery of the Spine and Extremities. Phila:
1923. 1st edn. 550 pp. Num ills. Orig bndg.
                             (Fye) **$100 [≈ £56]**

Teale, Thomas Pridgin
- Dangers to Health: A Pictorial Guide to
Domestic Sanitary Defects. London: 1881.
3rd edn. xix,170 pp. 70 plates. Orig pict
cloth.   *(Whitehart)* **£28 [≈ $50]**
- Dangers to Health: A Pictorial Guide to
Domestic Sanitary Defects. Fourth Edition.
London: J. & A. Churchill, 1883. xvi,172,16
advt pp. Half-title. 70 plates. Orig brown
cloth.   *(Jermy & Westerman)* **£50 [≈ $89]**

Tebb, W.
- The Recrudescence of Leprosy and its
Causation. A Popular Treatise. London:
1893. 408 pp. Orig cloth, sl dust stained.
                             (Whitehart) **£25 [≈ $45]**

Tebb, William & Vollum, Edward Perry
- Premature Burial and How It May Be
Prevented ... Second Edition. London: Swan
Sonnenschein, 1905. Cr 8vo. Port, ills. Orig
cloth, t.e.g.   *(Georges)* **£75 [≈ $134]**

Tegetmeier, W.B.
- Pheasants: their Natural History and
Practical Management. London: Cox, 1881.
2nd edn, enlgd. 4to. v,142,advt pp. 13 plates,
text figs. Orig pict gilt cloth, a.e.g.
                             (Egglishaw) **£48 [≈ $85]**

Tesla, N.
- Colorado Springs Notes 1899-1900. Beograd:
1978. Lge 4to. 437 pp. Port frontis, num
plates, ills. Sm name. Orig bndg.
                             (Whitehart) **£55 [≈ $98]**

Thacher, James
- American Medical Biography ... prefixed a
Succinct History of Medical Science in the
United States ... Boston: 1828. 2 vols in one.
8vo. 436; 280 pp. 15 plates. Some browning
of text. Later half mor, rebacked.
                             (Goodrich) **$295 [≈ £166]**
- American Medical Practice: or, a Simple
Method of Prevention and Cure of Diseases
... Boston: 1817. 1st edn. 8vo. 744 pp. Some
foxing. Unabused ex-lib. Sheep.
                             (Goodrich) **$125 [≈ £70]**
- The American Orchardist; or a Practical
Treatise on the Culture and Management of
Apple and Other Fruit Trees ... Boston:
Joseph W. Ingraham, 1822. 1st edn. 8vo.
Some foxing. Contemp tree sheep, gilt spine.
                             (Ximenes) **$475 [≈ £267]**

Thackray, C.F.
- Catalogue of Aseptic Operating Theatre
Equipment, Ward Furniture and Sterilizing
Apparatus. London: [1935]. [8],1067-1366
pp. Hd of spine nicked.
                             (Whitehart) **£18 [≈ $32]**

Theakston, Michael
- British Angling Flies. Revised and Annotated
by Francis M. Walbran. Ripon: William
Harrison, [1888]. 2nd edn. Sm 8vo.
xv,145,[17 advt] pp. 8 plates, num w'cuts in
text. Orig gilt dec cloth.
                             (Blackwell's) **£75 [≈ $134]**

Thearle, Samuel J.P.
- The Modern Practice of Shipbuilding in Iron
and Steel. London & Glasgow: Collins'
Advanced Science Series, [1887]. 2 vols (text
& plates). 8vo & 4to. 34 plates, text ills. Orig
cloth, extrs sl worn.
                             (Francis Edwards) **£50 [≈ $89]**

Theobald, John
- Every Man his own Physician. Being a
complete Collection of Efficacious and
Approved Remedies, for every Disease
incident to the Human Body. New Edition.
London: 1766. 8vo. 61 pp. Engvd title. Lacks
final advt leaf. Mod qtr mor.
                             (Robertshaw) **£36 [≈ $64]**

Theophrastus's History of Stones ...
- See Hill, "Sir" John.

Thomas, Herbert (editor)
- Classical Contributions to Obstetrics and Gynecology. With a Foreword by Howard A. Kelly. Springfield: 1935. 265 pp. Orig bndg.
(Goodrich) **$50 [≈ £28]**

Thomas, K.B.
- The Development of Anaesthetic Apparatus. A History based on the Charles King Collection of the Association of Anaesthetists of Great Britain and Ireland. Oxford: 1975. x,268 pp. 257 plates. Dw (sl torn & dust stained). *(Whitehart)* **£48 [≈ $85]**

Thomas, O.
- Catalogue of the Marsupialia and Monotremata in the Collection of the British Museum. London: 1888. 8vo. xiii,401 pp. 28 litho plates (4 cold). Cloth, unopened.
(Egglishaw) **£95 [≈ $169]**

Thomas, Robert
- The Modern Practice of Physic ... Third Edition, corrected and considerably enlarged. London: Murray, 1810. 8vo. iv,672, v-x, [2], [16 advt] pp. Brown cloth, uncut.
(Hemlock) **$125 [≈ £70]**
- The Modern Practice of Physic ... London: 1834. 10th edn. xiv,1026 pp. Endpapers foxed. Contemp bds, v worn, rebacked in cloth. *(Whitehart)* **£80 [≈ $142]**
- The Modern Practice of Physic ... London: Longman, 1834. 10th edn. 8vo. xvi,1026 pp. Mid 19th c half leather, worn.
(Bates & Hindmarch) **£40 [≈ $71]**

Thomas, S.
- Britannicus Estimator: Or, the Trader's Complete Guide. In Two Parts ... London: for J. Wilson ..., 1764. 1st edn. 8vo. [vi], 13-262, [2] pp. Occas damp stains, sm marg hole. Old calf, rebacked.
(Young's) **£220 [≈ $392]**
- The British Negotiator ... see Slack, Thomas
- The Ready Calculator: or, Tradesman's Sure Guide ... Third Edition, Corrected. London: G. Robinson & T. Slack, 1777. 12mo. 251,[i] pp. No free endpapers. Minor soil. Contemp sheep, some wear, sm splits in jnts.
(Clark) **£25 [≈ $45]**

Thompson, Benjamin, Count Rumford
- The Complete Works. Published by the American Academy of Sciences. London: 1875-76. UK issue. 5 vols. Lge 8vo. Ports, fldg plates. Orig cloth.
(Weiner) **£195 [≈ $347]**
- Inventions, Improvements, and Practice of Benjamin Thompson, in the combined

Character of Colliery Engineer, and General Manager ... Watt's Steam Engine ... Newcastle: 1847. 8vo. viii,133 pp. 2 fldg plates. Occas sl foxing. Title sl soiled. New cloth. *(Weiner)* **£85 [≈ $151]**

Thompson, C.J.S.
- Alchemy: Source of Chemistry & Medicine. London: 1974. 1st edn thus. Ills. Dw.
(Deja Vu) **£25 [≈ $45]**
- The Chemist's Companion for Pharmacists, Medical Practitioners and Students. London: 1898. 2nd edn. viii,313 pp. Some dust staining. Orig rexine, worn & rubbed.
(Whitehart) **£15 [≈ $27]**
- The Mystery and Art of the Apothecary. London: 1929. 1st edn. viii,287,[4 advt] pp. Frontis, 9 plates. Endpapers sl browned. Cloth, spine sl discold.
(Francis Edwards) **£30 [≈ $53]**
- The Mystery and Lure of Perfume. London: 1927. 1st edn. 8vo. xvi,247 pp. 26 ills. Orig dec cloth. *(Hortulus)* **$45 [≈ £25]**
- The Mystery and Lure of Perfume. London: [1927]. xvi,247 pp. 26 plates. Occas foxing page edges. Orig cloth. Dw.
(Whitehart) **£25 [≈ $45]**
- Poisons and Poisoners. With Historical Account of Some Famous Mysteries in Ancient and Modern Times. New York: 1931. 392 pp. Frontis, 15 plates. Prelims foxed. Orig bndg, paper label, worn.
(Whitehart) **£25 [≈ $45]**
- The Quacks of Old London. London: 1928. 356 pp. Ills. Orig bndg. *(Fye)* **$75 [≈ £42]**

Thompson, Sir Henry
- Clinical Lectures on Diseases of the Urinary Organs. Fourth Edition. London: 1876. Lib marks on title. New cloth. Author's pres copy.
(Goodrich) **$65 [≈ £37]**
- Clinical Lectures on Diseases of the Urinary Organs ... Eighth Edition. London: Churchill, 1888. 8vo. xiv,470,[16 advt] pp. 121 ills. Orig cloth. *(Fenning)* **£24.50 [≈ $45]**

Thompson, J.J.
- Recollections and Reflections. London: 1936. 2nd edn. viii,452 pp. Frontis port, 2 plates. Name. Orig bndg. *(Whitehart)* **£25 [≈ $45]**

Thompson, John-Weeks
- The Poor Man's Medicine Chest; or, Thompson's Box of Antibilious Alterative Pills. With a few brief Remarks on the Stomach. London: for the author, 1791. 1st edn. 8vo. 36 pp. Mod cloth.
(Robertshaw) **£40 [≈ $71]**

Thompson, R.D.
- British Annual, and Epitome of the Progress of Science for 1838. London: 1838. 12mo. xii,387 pp. 28 plates & ills. Orig cloth, backstrip relaid.   *(Henly)* £18 [≈ $32]

Thompson, R.L.
- Glimpses of Medical Europe. Phila: 1908. 1st edn. 236 pp. Photo ills. Orig bndg.
        (Fye) $75 [≈ £42]

Thompson, Robert
- The Gardener's Assistant: Practical and Scientific ... Revised and extended by Thomas Moore. London: Blackie & Son, 1881. Sm 4to. lii,956 pp. 12 cold plates, num w'cut ills. Old half calf gilt, sl marked & worn.
        (Hollett) £85 [≈ $151]
- The Gardener's Assistant: Practical and Scientific. New Edition by T. Moore. London: 1884. Roy 8vo. 23,liii,956 pp. 32 plates (12 cold). Upper margs of 4 pp prelims frayed & soiled. Orig cloth, reprd.
        (Wheldon & Wesley) £50 [≈ $89]
- The Gardener's Assistant. A Practical and Scientific Exposition of the Art of Gardening ... New Edition Revised ... by William Watson. London: 1902. 2 vols. Sm thick 4to. 18 chromolitho & 30 b/w plates, num text figs. Orig qtr mor, sl worn.
        (Francis Edwards) £75 [≈ $134]
- Gardener's Assistant. New Edition edited by William Watson. London: 1913. 6 vols. 4to. 18 cold & 30 plain plates, num text ills. Sl foxed at ends. Orig dec cloth.
        (Henly) £75 [≈ $134]

Thompson, S.P.
- Dynamo-Electric Machinery: A Manual for Students of Electrotechnics. London: 1888. 3rd edn. xi,672 pp. 378 figs. Occas sl foxing. Orig bndg, spine defective.
        (Whitehart) £25 [≈ $45]

Thompson, William
- The Natural History of Ireland. Birds and Mammalia. London: Reeve, 1849-56. 4 vols. 8vo. Ex-lib. Orig cloth, rebacked.
        (de Burca) £450 [≈ $801]

Thoms, Herbert
- Classical Contributions to Obstetrics and Gynecology. Springfield: 1935. 1st edn. 265 pp. Dw.   *(Fye)* $100 [≈ £56]

Thoms, W.J.
- Human Longevity. Its Facts and Fictions ... London: 1873. xii,320 pp. Orig cloth, front inner hinge cracked, sm lib label on front cvr.
        (Whitehart) £25 [≈ $45]

Thomson, Anthony Todd
- The London Dispensatory. Second Edition. London: 1818. 8vo. 7 plates. Ex-lib. Contemp calf, bds loose.   *(Robertshaw)* £20 [≈ $36]

Thomson, A. Landsborough
- Britain's Birds and their Nests. London: Waverley / Chambers, [ca 1912]. Lge 8vo. xxviii, 340 pp. 132 cold plates. Orig blue cloth, gilt dec spine.
        (Bates & Hindmarch) £45 [≈ $80]

Thomson, A.T.
- The London Dispensatory containing I. The Elements of Pharmacy ... The Pharmaceutical Preparations of the London, Edinburgh, and Dublin Colleges of Physicians. London: Longman ..., 1811. 1st edn. 8vo. 5 plates. Some sl wear & tear. Contemp rough calf, rebacked.
        (David White) £125 [≈ $223]

Thomson, Adam
- Time and Timekeepers. London: T. & W. Boone, 1842. 1st edn. Sm 8vo. xii,195 pp. 54 text ills. Occas sl browning. Orig cloth gilt.
        (Fenning) £55 [≈ $98]

Thomson, Alexis
- On Neuroma and Neuro-Fibromatosis. Edinburgh: Turnbull & Spears, 1900. Lge 4to. viii-168 pp. 20 figs. Top of half-title cut away. Orig green cloth, edges worn.
        (Goodrich) $195 [≈ £110]

Thomson, Sir C. Wyville
- The Depths of the Sea. An Account of the General Results of the Dredging Cruises of H.M.SS. 'Porcupine' and 'Lightning' ... Second Edition. London: 1874. 8vo. [xxiv], 527, [1 blank],65 advt pp. 7 cold maps or charts, num ills. Orig cloth.
        (Bow Windows) £80 [≈ $142]
- The Depths of the Sea, an Account of the General Results of the Dredging Cruises of H.M.SS. 'Porcupine' and 'Lightning', 1868-70. London: 1874. 2nd edn. 8vo. xxiii,527 pp. 8 maps & plates, 84 text figs, 11 vignettes. Sl foxing. Orig dec cloth, sl used.
        (Wheldon & Wesley) £70 [≈ $125]
- The Voyage of the 'Challenger'. The Atlantic. A Preliminary Account of the General Results of the Exploring Voyage ... New York: 1878. 1st Amer edn. 2 vols. 8vo. Port, fldg map, 42 plates, 168 figs, 8 vignettes. Orig green cloth, fine.   *(Bow Windows)* £235 [≈ $418]

Thomson, George

- [Loimotomia, in Greek]: or the Pest Anatomised In these following particulars ... London: Nath. Crouch, 1666. Only edn. 8vo. [xvi], 189,[iii] pp. 3 advt pp at end. Frontis. Minor browning. Sm crnr repr. 19th c calf gilt, a.e.g., minor wear extrs. Wing T.1027.
(Clark) £780 [≈ $1,388]

Thomson, John

- Lectures on Inflammation, exhibiting a View of the General Doctrines, Pathological and Practical, of Medical Surgery. Phila: M. Carey & Son, 1817. 1st Amer edn. 8vo. vii, 8-509 pp. Contemp half calf, rubbed, upper cvr detached. *(Hemlock)* $325 [≈ £183]
- The Universal Calculator; or The Merchant's, Tradesman's, and Family's Assistant ... Edinburgh: Creech & Elliot, 1784. Tall 8vo. [viii],294 pp. Signed by the author on title verso as warranty. Period sheep, upper cvr sl scuffed.
(Rankin) £60 [≈ $107]

Thomson, Sir Joseph John

- Conduction of Electricity through Gases. Cambridge: 1903. 1st edn. 8vo. vi,[1],566,[2 blank] pp. Num ills. Orig cloth gilt.
(Fenning) £95 [≈ $169]
- Conduction of Electricity through Gases. Third Edition. Cambridge: 1928-33. 2 vols. Plates, diags. Lib b'plates. Orig cloth, vol 2 faded & worn. *(Weiner)* £40 [≈ $71]
- Notes on Recent Researches in Electricity and Magnetism. Intended as a Sequel to Professor Clerk-Maxwell's Treatise on Electricity and Magnetism. Oxford: Clarendon Press, 1893. 1st edn. 8vo. xvi,578 pp. Marg pencil notes. Orig bndg, spine rubbed. *(Key Books)* $190 [≈ £107]
- Rays of Positive Electricity and their Application to Chemical Analyses. With Illustrations. London: Longmans, Green, 1913. 1st edn. 8vo. viii,132 pp. 50 ills inc 5 plates. Orig blue cloth.
(Claude Cox) £65 [≈ $116]
- A Treatise on the Motion of Vortex Rings ... London: Macmillan, 1883. 1st edn. 8vo. xix, 124 pp. Text diags. Tear in 1 leaf without loss. Orig cloth, spine sl faded & rubbed, sl soiled.
(Key Books) $300 [≈ £169]

Thomson, T.

- Outlines of Mineralogy, Geology, and Mineral Analysis. Vol I. London: 1836. ix,726 pp. Crnr of title reprd, lib stamp on title verso. Binder's cloth.
(Whitehart) £25 [≈ $45]

Thomson, Thomas

- The History of Chemistry. Second Edition. London: [ca 1830]. 2 vols in one. Sm 8vo. [ii],xii, 349,[1 blank]; [ii],325,[1 blank] pp. Port dated 1830. Minor spots & sm tears. Lacks title to vol 2. Orig cloth, sl worn.
(Bow Windows) £55 [≈ $98]

Thomson, Sir William, Baron Kelvin

- Popular Lectures and Addresses. London: 1891. 2nd edn. 3 vols. Text ills. Orig cloth.
(Francis Edwards) £35 [≈ $62]
- See also Kelvin, Sir William Thomson, Baron

Thorburn, Archibald

- British Mammals. London: 1920-21. 2 vols. 4to. 50 cold plates. Orig red cloth.
(Wheldon & Wesley) £385 [≈ $685]
- British Mammals. London: 1920-21. 2 vols in one. Roy 4to. 50 cold plates. Rebound in red buckram to orig style.
(Wheldon & Wesley) £350 [≈ $623]
- British Mammals. London: 1920-21. One of 155 Large Paper. 2 vols. Imperial 4to. 50 cold plates, text ills. Orig red cloth.
(Wheldon & Wesley) £1,000 [≈ $1,780]
- A Naturalist's Sketch Book. London: 1919. Roy 8vo. viii,72 pp. 24 cold & 36 collotype plates. Sl foxing. Orig red cloth, trifle faded. *(Wheldon & Wesley)* £375 [≈ $668]
- A Naturalist's Sketchbook. London: Longmans, Green, 1919. 1st edn. 4to. 60 plates (24 cold). Unspotted. Orig cloth, t.e.g., spine sl darkened.
(Claude Cox) £450 [≈ $801]
- A Naturalist's Sketchbook. London: Longmans, Green, 1919. 1st edn. 4to. 60 plates (24 cold). Lib b'plate, lib stamps on title & verso, sm stamp on verso of plates. Contemp red buckram.
(Claude Cox) £150 [≈ $267]

Thorek, Max

- The Face in Health and Disease. Phila: 1946. 1st edn. 781 pp. 635 ills. Orig bndg.
(Fye) $250 [≈ £140]
- Modern Surgical Technic. Phila: 1939. 1st edn, 2nd printing. 3 vols. 2045 pp. 2174 ills. Orig bndg. *(Fye)* $175 [≈ £98]
- Plastic Surgery of the Breast and Abdominal Wall. Springfield: 1942. 1st edn. 446 pp. 458 ills. Orig bndg. *(Fye)* $300 [≈ £169]

Thorell, T.

- Descriptive Catalogue of the Spiders of Burma based upon the Collection made by E.W. Oates. London: BM, 1895. 8vo.

xxxvi,406 pp. Cloth, trifle used.
(Wheldon & Wesley) **£50 [≈ $89]**
- On European Spiders. Part I [all published]
Review of the European Genera. Uppsala:
1869-70. 4to. xxiv,242 pp. Wrappers (used).
(Wheldon & Wesley) **£45 [≈ $80]**

Thorndike, Augustus
- Athletic Injuries: Prevention, Diagnosis and
Treatment. Phila: 1938. 1st edn. 208 pp. Orig
bndg.   *(Fye)* **$200 [≈ £112]**

Thorndike, Lynn
- The Herbal of Rufinus. Edited from the
Unique Manuscript. By Lynn Thorndike,
assisted by Francis S. Benjamin, Jr. Chicago:
UP, 1949. 2nd imp. 8vo. Orig cloth, sl
sunned.   *(Georges)* **£25 [≈ $45]**
- A History of Magic and Experimental
Science. New York: Columbia UP, 1923-58.
Later printings. 8 vols. Orig buckram.
(Gach) **£350 [≈ £197]**
- A History of Magic and Experimental Science
... New York: Columbia UP, 1929-58. 8 vols.
Orig cloth. 6 vols with dws (2 defective).
(Frew Mackenzie) **£350 [≈ $623]**
- Latin Treatises on Comets between 1238 and
1368 A.D. Edited by Lynn Thorndike.
Chicago: UP, 1950. 8vo. Orig red cloth.
(Georges) **£35 [≈ $62]**
- The Sphere of Sacrobosco and its
Commentators. Chicago: UP, 1949. 8vo. Dw
(torn).   *(Georges)* **£35 [≈ $62]**
- The Sphere of Sacrobosco and its
Commentators. Chicago: UP, 1949. 1st edn.
8vo. Orig buckram.   *(Gach)* **£50 [≈ £28]**

Thornton, John
- John Abernethy. A Biography. London:
1953. 1st edn. 184 pp. Orig bndg. Dw.
(Fye) **£40 [≈ £22]**

Thornton, Robert John
- The British Flora ... London: J. Whiting,
1812. 5 vols. 8vo. 344 plates. Some browning
(esp edges). Contemp green straight grained
mor gilt extra, a.e.g., jnts sl rubbed.
(Blackwell's) **£275 [≈ $490]**
- Elements of Botany. London: for the author,
1812. 2 vols. 8vo. vi,90; 73 pp. 169 engvd
plates (sl offsetting). Lacks half-title.
Contemp mrbld calf, elab gilt spines, edges of
bds sl damaged. *(Blackwell's)* **£110 [≈ $196]**
- Elements of Botany. London: 1812. 2 vols in
one. Roy 8vo. viii,90,73 pp. 172 plates. Mod
half calf.   *(Henly)* **£70 [≈ $125]**
- Elements of Botany. London: 1812. 2 vols.
Roy 8vo. 173 plates. Sl foxing. Half calf,

uncut.   *(Wheldon & Wesley)* **£40 [≈ $71]**
- Elements of Botany. London: Whiting for the
author, 1812. Roy 8vo. 24 engvd sectional
titles, 171 engvd plates (3 hand cold).
Contemp calf gilt, rubbed.
(Egglishaw) **£68 [≈ $121]**
- A Grammar of Botany ... London: Phillips,
1811. 1st edn. 12mo. iv,238 pp. 45 hand cold
plates. Contemp calf gilt.
(Egglishaw) **£160 [≈ $285]**
- Temple of Flora; with Plates faithfully
reproduced from the Original Engravings and
the Work described by Geoffrey Grigson,
with Bibliographical Notes by Handasyde
Buchanan. London: Collins, 1951. One of
250 sgnd. Folio. 12 cold & 24 other plates.
Orig half mor slipcase.
(Gough) **£350 [≈ $623]**

Thorpe, C.
- British Marine Conchology ... Illustrated by
G.B. Sowerby and W. Wood. London:
Lumley, 1844. 8vo. lx,267 pp. 1 hand cold &
7 plain plates. Orig cloth, sm tears in jnts.
(Egglishaw) **£55 [≈ $98]**

Thorpe, T.E.
- Essays in Historical Chemistry. London:
Macmillan, 1902. 1st coll edn. 8vo. xii, 582,
[2 advt] pp. Orig cloth.
(Fenning) **£28.50 [≈ $52]**

Thwaites, G.H.K. & Hooker, J.D.
- Enumeratio Plantarum Zeylaniae: an
Enumeration of Ceylon Plants. London:
[1858-] 1864. 8vo. viii,483 pp. Some pencil
notes. Half mor, sl rubbed.
(Wheldon & Wesley) **£100 [≈ $178]**

Ticehurst, N.F.
- The Mute Swan in England and the Ancient
Custom of Swan-Keeping. London: 1957.
Roy 8vo. xiii,133 pp. 31 plates (4 cold).
Cloth.   *(Wheldon & Wesley)* **£30 [≈ $53]**

Tidswell, Herbert H.
- The Tobacco Habit its History and
Pathology; a Study in Birth-Rates ... An
Appeal to Medical Students. London: J. & A.
Churchill, 1912. Half-title. Orig cloth, v sl
rubbed. Inscrbd by the author.
(Jarndyce) **£30 [≈ $53]**

Tilbury, Farquhar T.
- On Certain Endemic Skin and other Diseases
of India and Hot Climates Generally ...
Including Notes on Pellagra, Clou de Biskra,
and Aleppo Evil by H. Vandyke Carter ...
London: Churchill, 1876. xi,[i],288 pp. 5 cold

plates. Sl lib marks. Orig half sheep, sl rubbed. *(Goodrich)* **$150 [≈ £84]**

Tilke, S.W.
- An Autobiographical Memoir with ... a Full Description of his Mode of Treating Diseases. London: for the author, 1840. 8vo. xli,399 pp. Frontis port. Orig cloth, spine faded & chipped at hd.
(Spelman) **£60 [≈ $107]**

Tiltman, R.F.
- Television Really Explained. London: [1952]. 128 pp. 2 dble sided plates, 12 ills. Page edges sl discold. Orig bndg.
(Whitehart) **£25 [≈ $45]**

Timbs, John
- Hints for the Table: or, The Economy of Good Living. With a Few Words on Wines. London: Kent & Co., 1859. 1st edn. Frontis. Advt endpapers. Orig cloth, spine rubbed.
(Jarndyce) **£68 [≈ $121]**
- Something for Everybody. London: Lockwood, (1861). 1st edn. Half title, 8 ctlg pp. Cold title. Orig brown cloth.
(Jarndyce) **£35 [≈ $62]**
- Stories of Inventors and Discoveries in Science and the Useful Arts. A Book for Old and Young. London: Kent & Co., 1860. 1st edn. 32 ctlg pp. Frontis, plates, ills. Orig dark brown cloth, spine faded.
(Jarndyce) **£25 [≈ $45]**
- Things not generally known ... Curiosities of Science, Past and Present. A Book for Old and Young. London: Kent & Co., 1858. 1st edn. 40 ctlg pp. Frontis. Advt endpapers. Intl advt leaf. Orig pink cloth, spine faded.
(Jarndyce) **£30 [≈ $53]**

Tinbergen, Niko
- The Herring Gull's World. London: New Naturalist Series, 1953. 1st edn. 8vo. xvi, 255 pp. 30 plates, text ills. Edges sl spotted. Dw (reprd with tape).
(Francis Edwards) **£30 [≈ $53]**

Tinney, J.
- Compendious Treatise of Anatomy, adapted to the Arts of Designing, Painting, and Sculpture ... London: Laurie & Whittle, 1808. Folio. 8 ff. 10 engvd plates. Some wear to text. Orig mrbld bds, new cloth spine.
(Goodrich) **$295 [≈ £166]**

Titford, W.J.
- Sketches towards a Hortus Botanicus Americanus; or Coloured Plates ... of new and valued Plants of the West Indies and North

and South America ... London: 1811 [-12]. 4to. Hand cold frontis, cold vignette, 17 hand cold plates. Title sl offset. Half mor, rubbed.
(Wheldon & Wesley) **£1,200 [≈ $2,136]**
- Sketches towards a Hortus Botanicus Americanus; or, Coloured Plates ... of New and Valuable Plants of the West Indies and North and South America ... London: 1811 [-12]. 4to. Hand cold frontis, cold vignette, 17 hand cold plates. Half mor, rubbed.
(Wheldon & Wesley) **£1,200 [≈ $2,136]**

Todd, Robert Bentley
- Clinical Lectures on Certain Acute Diseases. London: 1860. 8vo. xl,487 pp. Cloth, soiled.
(Goodrich) **$145 [≈ £81]**
- Clinical Lectures on Paralysis, Disease of the Brain, and Other Affections of the Nervous System. Phila: Lindsay & Blakiston, 1855. 1st Amer edn. 8vo. 311 pp. Lacks front fly, stamp on title, foxed. Orig cloth, faint lib numbers on spine, sunned. *(Goodrich)* **$295 [≈ £166]**

Todhunter, Isaac
- A Treatise on Analytical Statics with Numerous Examples. Cambridge: Macmillan, 1853. 1st edn. 8vo. [iv],318,[16 advt] pp. Text diags. Orig cloth gilt, sl frayed & rubbed. *(Hollett)* **£85 [≈ $151]**
- William Whewell, D.D. An Account of his Writings with Selections from his Literary and Scientific Correspondence. Farnborough: 1970. Reprint of 1876 edn. 2 vols. Orig bndg.
(Whitehart) **£40 [≈ $71]**

The Toilet of Flora ...
- See Buch'hoz, P.J.

Tomlinson, Charles (editor)
- Rudimentary Treatise on the Construction of Locks. London: 1853. Sm 8vo. vii,172 pp. Num ills. Good ex-lib. Orig limp cloth, sl worn. *(Weiner)* **£65 [≈ $116]**

Tonks, Edmund (editor)
- General Index to the Latin Names and Synonyms of the Plants depicted in the first 107 Volumes of Curtis's Botanical Magazine ... London: Quaritch, 1883. Tall 8vo. 264 pp. Interleaved. Few blind stamps. few sm marg reprs. Mod half mor gilt.
(Hollett) **£65 [≈ $116]**

Topley, W.W.C. & Wilson, G.S.
- The Principles of Bacteriology and Immunity. London: Arnold, 1938. 2nd edn. 8vo. xv,1645 pp. 276 text figs. Cloth, sl worn. *(Savona)* **£25 [≈ $45]**

Torriano, N.
- Compendium Obstetricii: or A Small Tract on the Formation of the Foetus and the Practice of Midwifery. London: 1753. 8vo. 80 pp. Lib stamp title verso. Contemp bds, uncut.   *(Hemlock)* **$375 [≈ £211]**

Townsend, Joseph
- The Physicians' Vade Mecum; being a Compendium of Nosology and Therapeutics, for the Use of Students. Second Edition. London: 1794. 2nd edn. Sm 8vo. 151 pp. Mod calf.   *(Robertshaw)* **£48 [≈ $85]**

Townshend, Chauncy Hare
- Facts in Mesmerism, with Reasons for a Dispassionate Inquiry into it. Second Edition, Revised and Enlarged. London: 1844. 8vo. Lacks free endpaper. Orig cloth, tear in spine.
                    (Robertshaw) **£38 [≈ $68]**

Tracts on Practical Agriculture and Gardening ...
- See Weston, Richard

Trade catalogues
- Allen & Hanbury: Catalogue of Surgical Instruments and Appliances, Ward Requisites, Hospital Furniture etc. London: [1908?]. Lge 8vo. [iii],1464,lxxii pp. Frontis, num ills (1 cold). Sl spotting on title & preface. Half mor, spine & crnrs rubbed.
                    (David White) **£85 [≈ $151]**
- Allen & Hanburys Ltd.: A Reference List of Surgical Instruments and Medical Appliances ... London: 1930. [xvi],1974,lxxxix pp. Plates, ills. Orig cloth, worn, sl marked.
                    (Whitehart) **£35 [≈ $62]**
- Allen & Hanburys Ltd.: Abridged Catalogue of Surgical Instruments and Appliances ... London: [1925]. xii,739 pp. Num ills. Cloth, dust stained, sl worn.
                    (Whitehart) **£55 [≈ $98]**
- Baird & Tatlock: Standard Catalogue Vol. 1. Chemistry including Apparatus for the teaching of an Research Work in Organic and Inorganic Chemistry. London: 1928. Abridged edn. 4to. [viii],75-544,xix pp. Num ills. Orig cloth, sl worn.
                    (Whitehart) **£25 [≈ $45]**
- Down Bros.: A Catalogue of Surgical Instruments and Appliances with Appendix ... London: July 1929. 3028,lxxvii pp. Num ills. Cloth, sl worn, spine dust stained.
                    (Whitehart) **£55 [≈ $98]**
- Fannin & Co. Ltd.: Surgical Instruments and Medical Appliances. London: 1926. xxvi, 415 pp. Num ills. Lacks price list from pocket. Orig cloth.   *(Whitehart)* **£40 [≈ $71]**

- Mayer & Phelps: An Illustrated Catalogue of Surgical Instruments and Appliances. London: 1931. xvi,568 pp. Num ills. Lib stamp. Spine sl faded with lib mark.
                    (Whitehart) **£28 [≈ $50]**
- McArthur Wirth & Co.: Butchers, Packers and Sausage Makers Fixtures, Tools, Machinery and Supplies ... Syracuse, New York: 1900. Thin 4to. 84 pp. Num ills. Margs sl browned. Orig wraps, spine ends sl chipped, upper wrapper creased.
                    (Francis Edwards) **£30 [≈ $53]**
- The Piston Freezing Machine and Ice Company: The Piston Process of Freezing. London: 1868. Sm 8vo. Orig cloth.
                    (Bookpress) **$150 [≈ £84]**
- Stanley Belcher & Mason Ltd.: Price List, of Chemical, Bacteriological, Botanical, Metallurgical, Apparatus and Chemicals. Microscopes and Accessories. Birmingham: [ca 1900]. Sm 4to. 325,43, xiv,[xx] pp. Num figs. Orig cloth, damp stained.
                    (Francis Edwards) **£40 [≈ $71]**
- Surgical Manufacturing Co. Ltd.: Illustrated Catalogue of Surgical Instruments and Appliances ... London: 1925. 6th edn. 1072 pp. Num ills. Cloth, v sl worn & marked.
                    (Whitehart) **£55 [≈ $98]**

Traill, C.P.
- Canadian Wild Flowers ... see Fitzgibbon, A.

Travers, Morris W.
- The Experimental Study of Gases ... London: 1901. xiii,323 pp. 130 text figs. Orig cloth, v sl marked & worn. *(Whitehart)* **£18 [≈ $32]**
- The Experimental Study of Gases ... London: 1901. xiii,323 pp. 2 fldg tables, num text ills. Endpapers & last page foxed. Orig cloth, hd of spine defective.
                    (Francis Edwards) **£25 [≈ $45]**

A Treatise on British Song-Birds ...
- See Syme, P.

Tredgold, Thomas
- Elementary Principles of Carpentry; a Treatise ... Second Edition; corrected and considerably enlarged. London: for J. Taylor, 1828. 4to. xx,280 pp, advt leaf. 22 plates, text ills. Occas sl spotting or soiling. New bds, uncut, orig cloth backstrip retained.
                    (Claude Cox) **£120 [≈ $214]**
- Elementary Principles of Carpentry. Revised from the Original Edition ... London: Spon; New York: Spon & Chamberlain, 1899. 10th edn. 4 advt,32 ctlg pp. 48 plates, ills. Orig cloth, with 1 scar.   *(Jarndyce)* **£40 [≈ $71]**
- A Practical Treatise on Rail-Roads and

Carriages, with the Theory, Effect, and Expense of Steam Carriages, Stationary Engines, and Gas Machines. London: 1835. 2nd edn. 8vo. xi,184 pp. 4 plates. Occas sl foxing. Few lib blind stamps. Orig cloth backed bds, rebacked.
(Weiner) **£135 [≈ $240]**

Trinder, William Martin
- The English Olive-Tree: or, a Treatise on the Use of Oil and the Air Bath: with Miscellaneous Remarks on the Cure of Various Diseases ... Third Edition ... London: for the author at Rowley Green, near Barnet, [1812?]. 8vo. 72 pp. New bds, uncut.
(Weiner) **£100 [≈ $178]**

Tripp, F.E.
- British Mosses, their Homes, Aspects, Structures and Uses. London: 1874. 2 vols. Roy 8vo. 39 cold plates. Orig cloth.
(Henly) **£120 [≈ $214]**

Trotter, Thomas
- A Proposal for Destroying the Fire and Choak-Damp of Coal-Mines ... Newcastle: 1805. 8vo. 47 pp. New cloth.
(Weiner) **£275 [≈ $490]**

Trousseau, Armand
- Lectures on Clinical Medicine, delivered at the Hotel-Dieu, Paris. Translated and edited ... by P. Victor Bazire. London: New Sydenham Society, 1869-82. 3rd rvsd & enlgd edn. 5 vols. 8vo. Sl marks. Orig cloth, hd of spines chipped.
(Frew Mackenzie) **£60 [≈ $107]**

Trowell, Samuel
- A New Treatise of Husbandry, Gardening, and other Matters relating to Rural Affairs ... London: Olive Payne, 1739. 164 pp. Contemp calf, sl worn. John Cator's b'plate.
(C.R. Johnson) **£220 [≈ $392]**
- A New Treatise of Husbandry, Gardening, and other Curious Matters ... London: for James Hodgson, 1739. 1st edn, 3rd issue. Post 8vo. [viii],164 pp. 1st few ff sl wormed in lower marg, few sl marks. Contemp gilt ruled sheep.
(Ash) **£125 [≈ $223]**

Truran, William
- The Iron Manufacture of Great Britain theoretically and practically considered ... London: 1855. 4to. x,176 pp. 23 plates. Orig dec cloth, dusty.
(Weiner) **£95 [≈ $169]**

Tryon, G.W.
- Structural and Systematic Conchology: an Introduction to the Study of the Mollusca.

Phila: 1882-84. 3 vols. 8vo. Map, 140 plates. Orig cloth, vol 2 sl bumped. Author's pres inscrptn. *(Wheldon & Wesley)* **£300 [≈ $534]**

Tubby, A.H.
- Deformities: A Treatise on Orthopaedic Surgery. London: 1896. 1st edn. 598 pp. Orig bndg.
(Fye) **$300 [≈ £169]**
- Deformities including Diseases of the Bones and Joints. London: 1912. 2nd edn. 2 vols. 883; 867 pp. Over 1000 ills. Orig bndg.
(Fye) **$175 [≈ £98]**

Tubby, A.H. & Jones, Robert
- Modern Methods in the Surgery of Paralyses with Special reference to Muscle-Grafting, Tendon Transplantation & Arthrodesis. London: 1903. 1st edn. 311 pp. Qtr leather.
(Fye) **$250 [≈ £140]**

Tugwell, G.
- A Manual of the Sea-Anemones Commonly found on the English Coast. London: 1856. [3],123 pp. 7 cold plates. Orig cloth.
(Whitehart) **£25 [≈ $45]**
- A Manual of the Sea-Anemones commonly found on the English Coast. London: 1856. 8vo. [vii],193,[1] pp. 7 plates (6 cold). Orig cloth. *(Wheldon & Wesley)* **£35 [≈ $62]**

Tuke, Daniel Hack
- Chapters in the History of the Insane in the British Isles. London: 1882. 8vo. xi,548 pp. 4 plates. Lib stamp on title. Frontis, title & blank crnr of 2 plates stained. Orig cloth, backstrip relaid. *(Weiner)* **£195 [≈ $347]**
- Illustrations of the Influence of the Mind upon the Body in Health and Disease ... London: J. & A. Churchill, 1884. 2nd edn. 2 vols. xxiv,335; viii,326,[2] pp. 2 frontis. Orig cloth, backstrips laid down.
(Caius) **$175 [≈ £98]**
- Sleep-Walking and Hypnotism. London: J. & A. Churchill, 1884. 1st edn. viii,119,[1], [4 advt], [16 ctlg dated 1884] pp. Orig brown cloth, somewhat worn. *(Caius)* **$250 [≈ £140]**

Tull, Jethro
- The Horse-Hoeing Husbandry ... Dublin: A. Rhames, 1733. 1st Dublin edn. 8vo. xvii, 417, [4] pp. 6 fldg engvs. Sl foxing at ends. New qtr calf over orig pink mrbld bds.
(Blackwell's) **£200 [≈ $356]**
- The Horse-Hoeing Husbandry ... Dublin: A. Rhames ..., 1733. 1st Dublin edn. 8vo. xvii, 417, [v] pp. 6 fldg plates. Few page edges dusty. Rec half calf, gilt spine.
(Clark) **£285 [≈ $507]**
- Horse-Hoeing Husbandry: or an Essay on the

Principles of Vegetation and Tillage ...
London: for A. Millar, 1762. 4th edn. 8vo.
xvi, 432 pp. 7 fldg plates. New half calf.
(Egglishaw) **£240 [≃ $427]**

Tully, J.D.
- The History of Plague as it has lately
appeared in the Islands of Malta, Gozo, Corfu
... London: Longman, Hurst ..., 1821. 1st
edn. 8vo. xi,292 pp. Orig bds, uncut,
rebacked.   *(Frew Mackenzie)* **£340 [≃ $605]**

Tunnicliffe, C.F.
- Shorelands Summer Diary. London: Collins,
1952. 4to. 160 pp. 16 cold plates, 180 ills.
Inscrptn. Orig cloth. Dw.
(Egglishaw) **£65 [≃ $116]**

Turner, A. Logan (editor)
- Joseph, Baron Lister. Centenary Volume,
1827-1927. Edinburgh: 1927. 1st edn. 182
pp. Ills. Orig bndg.   *(Fye)* **$50 [≃ £28]**

Turner, Daniel
- The Art of Surgery. The Fifth Edition,
Corrected. London: Rivington, 1736. 2 vols.
8vo. [16],576; iv,[8], 520,[28] index pp.
Frontis port vol 1, 1 fldg plate. Contemp calf,
reprd.   *(Spelman)* **£260 [≃ $463]**
- De Morbis Cutaneis. A Treatise of Diseases
incident to the Skin. In Two Parts ... London:
for R. Wilkin ..., 1736. 5th edn. 8vo.
[xvi],x,524 pp. Port frontis. Contemp calf,
gilt Victorian reback, front hinge cracked but
firm.   *(Vanbrugh)* **£275 [≃ $490]**

Turner, L.M.
- Contributions to the Natural History of
Alaska ... Washington: GPO, 1886. 1st edn.
4to. 226 pp. 26 plates (11 cold). Orig cloth.
(Walcot) **£65 [≃ $116]**

Turner, Richard
- An Easy Introduction to the Arts and
Sciences ... The Third Edition. With
Considerable Additions ... Physics ...
Electricity ... London: S. Crowder, 1791. xi,
[1], 248, [4] pp. Half-title. Contemp sheep,
rebacked.   *(C.R. Johnson)* **£125 [≃ $223]**
- Easy Introduction to the Arts and Sciences ...
Fifth Edition. London: 1795. 12mo. 251 pp.
8 plates, w'cuts in text. Hd of title cut with
loss of 1st word. Few sm stains. Contemp
sheep, jnts cracked. *(Robertshaw)* **£30 [≃ $53]**

Turner, W.
- Libellus De Re Herbaria Novus, originally
published in 1538, reprinted in facsimile,
with Notes, Modern Names and a Life of the

Author by D. Daydon Jackson. London:
Privately Printed, 1877. One of 100. 4to. xii,
xviii, [20],8 pp. Ex-lib, some use. Orig bds.
(Wheldon & Wesley) **£50 [≃ $89]**

Turner, William
- Atlas of Human Anatomy and Physiology.
Selected and arranged under the
superintendence of John Goodsir ...
Edinburgh & London: W. & A.K. Johnston,
1876. Lge folio. 8 dble-page cold plates. Orig
stiff cloth cvrs, rubbed & stained.
(David White) **£45 [≃ $80]**

Turnor, Hatton
- Astra Castra: Experiments and Adventures in
the Atmosphere. London: 1865. 4to. xxiii,
530 pp. Subscribers. 41 plates (2 more than
called for) & ports (sm stamp on rectos), ills.
Crnr of 1st few ff sl water stained. New cloth.
(Weiner) **£180 [≃ $320]**

Turton, William
- British Fauna. Vol. I [all published].
Swansea: 1807. 8vo. 230,viii pp. New bds.
(Wheldon & Wesley) **£60 [≃ $107]**
- A Conchological Dictionary of the British
Islands. London: 1819. 12mo. iii-xxviii, [ii]
,272 pp. Title vignette, 28 hand cold plates.
Some foxing of text. New cloth.
(Wheldon & Wesley) **£70 [≃ $125]**
- Conchylia Dithyra Insularum Britannicarum.
The Bivalve Shells of the British Islands.
London: Reeve, 1848. 4to. xlvii,279 pp. 20
hand cold plates. Orig cloth, unopened, fine.
(Egglishaw) **£320 [≃ $570]**
- A Manual of the Land and Fresh-Water
Shells of the British Isles. London: Longman
..., 1831. 1st edn. 12mo. viii,152,[12 advt] pp.
9 hand cold plates inc frontis. Orig blue cloth,
paper label, fine.   *(Gough)* **£48 [≃ $85]**
- A Manual of the Land and Fresh-Water
Shells of the British Islands. New Edition by
J.E. Gray. London: 1840. Post 8vo. ix,324
pp. 12 cold plates. Half calf.
(Wheldon & Wesley) **£45 [≃ $80]**
- Manual of the Land and Fresh-Water Shells
of the British Islands. London: Longman ...,
1857 [but advts dated 1860]. New edn. Cr
8vo. xvi, (336),24 pp. 12 hand cold plates,
text ills. Sl signs of use. Rec half mor, largely
unopened.   *(Ash)* **£100 [≃ $178]**

Tuson, Edward
- The Cause and Treatment of Curvature of
the Spine, and Diseases of the Vertebral
Column ... London: 1841. 1st edn. 283 pp. 26
plates. Orig bndg.   *(Fye)* **$500 [≃ £281]**
- Spinal Debility: Its Prevention, Pathology

and Cure ... London: 1861. 1st edn. 155 pp. Title chipped & detached. Lacks front endpaper. Paper brittle. Orig bndg, spine worn. *(Fye)* **$150 [≈ £84]**

Tusser, Thomas

- Five Hundred Points of Good Husbandry ... with an Introduction by Sir Walter Scott and a Benediction by Rudyard Kipling ... London: Tregaskis, 1931. One of 500. Cr 4to. xii, [ii], 336 pp. Dec title. Orig chestnut calf, uncut. Slipcase. *(Sotheran's)* **£235 [≈ $418]**

Tutin, T.G., & others (editors)

- Flora Europaea. Cambridge: 1964-80. 5 vols. 4to. Cloth. *(Wheldon & Wesley)* **£345 [≈ $614]**

Tutton, Alfred E.H.

- Crystals. London: Kegan Paul, Intl Scientific Series, 1911. 1st edn. 8vo. 25 plates, 120 ills. Orig cloth, tiny hole in spine. *(Fenning)* **£28.50 [≈ $52]**

Twamley, Louisa Anne

- See Meredith, Louisa Anne

Tweed, Isa

- Cow-Keeping in India. A Simple and Practical Book on their Care and Treatment ... Calcutta, Bombay & London: 1891. 1st edn. 8vo. xii,260,[32 ctlg] pp. 40 ills. Orig cloth, sl rubbed. *(Burmester)* **£58 [≈ $103]**

Tweedie, A. (editor)

- A System of Practical Medicine comprised in a Series of Original Dissertations. London: 1840. 5 vols. Contemp half roan, rubbed & worn. *(Whitehart)* **£35 [≈ $62]**

Tyas, Robert

- Popular Flowers: their Cultivation, Propagation and General Treatment ... London: Houlston & Stoneman, 1847. x,143, [2],[26] pp. 12 hand cold plates, tissue guards. Orig cloth gilt, a.e.g., jnt ends splitting, 1 hinge partly gone. *(Egglishaw)* **£68 [≈ $121]**
- Popular Flowers ... Second Series. London: Houlston & Stoneman, 1848. 12mo. vi,86 pp. 11 hand cold plates by James Andrews, tissue guards. Orig cloth gilt, a.e.g., spine ends sl worn. *(Egglishaw)* **£62 [≈ $110]**
- Popular Flowers. Their Propagation, Cultivation, and General Treatment in all Seasons. London: 1854. 3rd series. Lge 12mo. 12 hand cold plates. Sm blind stamp on endpaper. Orig cloth gilt, jnts splitting, minor soiling & fading. *(Francis Edwards)* **£50 [≈ $89]**

- The Wild Flowers of England, or Favourite Field Flowers Popularly Described. London: Houlston & Wright, 1859. 1st Series. Large Paper edn. 8vo. xi,196,[16 advt] pp. 12 hand cold plates. Orig green cloth gilt, spine darkened, cvrs sl marked. *(Egglishaw)* **£120 [≈ $214]**

Tyndall, John

- Essays on the Floating-matter of the Air in Relation to Putrefaction and Infection. London: Longmans, 1881. 1st edn. 8vo. xix,338 pp, advt leaf. Text diags. Orig plum cloth. *(Frew Mackenzie)* **£125 [≈ $223]**
- The Forms of Water in Clouds, Rivers, Ice, Glaciers. London: 1872. 1st edn. Orig cloth, marked. *(Wheldon & Wesley)* **£20 [≈ $36]**
- The Glaciers of the Alps. Being a Narrative of Excursions and Ascents, and Account of the Origin and Phenomena of Glaciers ... London: 1860. 1st edn. xx,444, [32 ctlg] pp. Frontis, 61 figs. Orig cloth, sl worn. *(Francis Edwards)* **£120 [≈ $214]**
- Heat Considered as a Mode of Motion. London: 1865. 2nd edn. 8vo. xx,532 pp. Num text ills. Occas foxing. New endpapers. Orig cloth, backstrip relaid. *(Francis Edwards)* **£25 [≈ $45]**
- Lectures on Light. Delivered in the United States in 1872-73. With an Appendix. New York: Appleton, 1873. 1st Amer edn. 8vo. 194, [10 advt] pp. Text ills. Orig cloth. *(Karmiole)* **$75 [≈ £42]**
- Notes on Light. London: 1869. 8vo. iv,74 pp. Half mor, worn. *(Weiner)* **£150 [≈ $267]**
- On Radiation. The "Rede" Lecture ... New York: Appleton, 1865. 1st Amer edn. 48 pp. Few lib marks. Orig wraps, spine reprd. *(Key Books)* **$60 [≈ £34]**

Tyson, Edward

- Orang-Outang, sive Homo Sylvestris: or, The Anatomy of a Pygmie compared with that of a Monkey, an Ape, and a Man ... London 1699. London: 1966. 4to. Port, 8 fldg plates. Orig cloth. *(Bow Windows)* **£35 [≈ $62]**

Tyson, Edward William

- Myology. Illustrated by Plates. In Four Parts ... Second Edition. London: Callow & Wilson, 1828. Elephant portfolio. 8 ff. 8 cold litho plates with flaps (sm lib stamps). Text sl browned. Orig bds, cloth spine, paper labels, rehinged internally, some wear. *(Goodrich)* **$2,500 [≈ £1,404]**

Ude, Louis Eustache

- The French Cook; A System of Fashionable and Economic Cookery adapted to the Use of

English Families ... Tenth Edition, thoroughly revised ... London: John Ebers, 1829. 8vo. lxxii,485,[i advt] pp. Port (sl foxed). 19th c green cloth, uncut.
                                (Gough) £165 [≈ $294]

Underwood, Arthur S.
- Studies in Comparative Odontology. London: 1903. 8vo. vii,152 pp. Ills. Orig cloth, v sl soiled.   *(Weiner)* £21 [≈ $37]

Ungewitter, Claus
- Science and Salvage from the German 'Verwertung des Wertlosen ...' London: 1944. 8vo. 183 pp. Orig cloth. *(Weiner)* £20 [≈ $36]

Ure, Andrew
- A Dictionary of Arts, Manufacture, and Mines: containing a Clear Exposition of their Principles and Practice. London: 1843. 3rd edn. vii,1334 pp. Half mor, v rubbed & worn. *(Whitehart)* £60 [≈ $107]
- The General Malaria of London and the Peculiar Malaria of Pimlico investigated ... London: 1850. 8vo. 39 pp. Old wraps.
                                (Weiner) £25 [≈ $45]
- A New System of Geology in which the Great Revolutions of the Earth and Animated Nature are reconciled at once to Modern Science and Sacred History. London: 1829. 1st edn. 8vo. 7 plates, text figs (2 hand cold). Some marks. Orig cloth backed bds, sl worn.
                        (Bow Windows) £185 [≈ $329]

Urey, H.C.
- The Planets. Their Origin and Development. New Haven: 1952. xvii,245 pp. 16 figs. Orig bndg.   *(Whitehart)* £18 [≈ $32]

Urquhart, B.L.
- The Camellia. London: 1956-60. 2 vols. Roy folio. 36 cold plates. Cloth, lower outer edge vol 2 sl water stained.
                    (Wheldon & Wesley) £95 [≈ $169]
- The Rhododendron. London: 1958-62. 2 vols. Folio. 36 cold plates. Cloth. Dws (that of vol 1 defective).
                    (Wheldon & Wesley) £135 [≈ $240]

Vallery-Radot, R.
- The Life of Pasteur. Translated from the French by Mrs. R.L. Devonshire. Westminster: Constable, 1902. 1st edn in English. 2 vols. 8vo. Port frontis. Orig cloth, recased, new endpapers.
                        (David White) £50 [≈ $89]
- The Life of Pasteur. Translated by R.L. Devonshire. London: 1902. 1st edn in English. 2 vols. vii,293; vii,336 pp. Port. Orig

qtr roan, spines v rubbed, hd of vol 2 spine defective.   *(Whitehart)* £18 [≈ $32]
- Louis Pasteur his Life and Labours ... Translated by Lady Claud Hamilton. London: Longman, 1855. 1st edn in English. 8vo. xlii, 300 pp. Inserted litho port laid down on half-title. Orig cloth, sl rubbed.
                        (Burmester) £50 [≈ $89]

Van't Hoff, J.H.
- Chemistry in Space, from 'Dix Annees dans l'Histoire d'une Theorie'. Oxford: 1891. 1st English edn. 8vo. vii,128 pp. Fldg plate. Orig cloth.   *(Weiner)* £40 [≈ $71]
- Studies in Chemical Dynamics. Translated by Thomas Ewan. Amsterdam: Frederick Muller, 1896. 1st edn in English. Ills. Few lib marks. Some browning. Orig bndg, partly uncut, spine ends worn.
                        (Key Books) $85 [≈ £48]

Van Butchell, S.J.
- Facts & Observations relative to a Successful Mode of Treating Piles, Fistula ... without Cutting or Confinement. Tenth Edition, Revised. London: Henry Renshaw, 1847. 8vo. [iv],iv, 198,[8] pp. Orig cloth, spine faded, upper cvr marked.
                        (Claude Cox) £30 [≈ $53]

Vancouver, Charles
- General View of the Agriculture of the County of Devon. London: Richard Phillips, 1808. 8vo. xii,479,[5] pp. Fldg hand cold map, 28 plates (2 hand cold). Orig bds, uncut, label reprd.   *(Spelman)* £180 [≈ $320]

Van Denburgh, J.
- The Reptiles of Western North America. Calif: 1922. 2 vols. Roy 8vo. 1028 pp. 128 plates. Few sm marg water stains. Orig wraps, trifle worn.
                    (Wheldon & Wesley) £90 [≈ $160]

Van der Ziel, Aldert
- Noise. New York: Prentice Hall, 1954. 1st edn. 8vo. 450 pp. Lib pocket. Orig cloth.
                        (Schoen) $65 [≈ £37]

Van Dyke, H.B.
- The Physiology and Pharmacology of the Pituitary Body. Chicago: 1936. 1st edn. Vol 1 (only, of 2). 8vo. 577 pp. Orig bndg.
                        (Goodrich) $95 [≈ £53]

Van Heurk, H.
- A Treatise on the Diatomaceae. Translated by W.E. Baxter. London: 1896. One of 300. Roy 8vo. xx,558 pp. Frontis, 35 plates, 291

text figs. Lib label. Orig buckram, t.e.g., sm tear to hd of spine. *(Egglishaw)* **£85 [≈$151]**

Van Swieten, Gerard
- The Commentaries upon the Aphorisms of Dr Herman Boerhaave ... Volumes I and II [only, of 14]. London: Knapton, 1744. 1st edns. 2 vols. 8vo. Contemp calf.
(Spelman) **£85 [≈$151]**

Van Wagenen, G. & Simpson, M.E.
- Embryology of the Ovary and Testis Homo sapiens and Macacac mulatta. New Haven: 1965. Folio. 225 pp. Ills. Bds warped. Dw.
(Goodrich) **$75 [≈£42]**

Varendonck, Julian
- The Psychology of Day-Dreams. With an Introduction by Sigmund Freud. London: Allen & Unwin, [1921]. 1st edn in English. 367,[1] pp. Foxed. Orig cloth, spine faded.
(Caius) **$150 [≈£84]**

Varley, D.
- Rudimentary Treatise on Mineralogy: for the Use of Beginners. London: 1849. 12mo. [iv],164,vi pp. 2 plates (1 hand cold), 60 text figs. Some crnrs creased. Lib marks on endpapers. Orig limp cloth, spine defective.
(Bow Windows) **£40 [≈$71]**

Varlo, Charles
- A New System of Husbandry. From Experiments never before made public. By C. Varley, Esq. [i.e. Varlo]. York: for the author by N. Nickson, 1770. 1st edn. 3 vols. 8vo. Fldg table, fldg plate. Contemp calf, gilt spines, mor labels, jnts trifle rubbed.
(Ximenes) **$900 [≈£506]**

Vaughan, Harold
- Congenital Cleft Lip, Cleft Palate and Associated Nasal Deformities. Phila: 1940. 1st edn. 210 pp. Orig bndg.
(Fye) **$125 [≈£70]**

Vavilov, N.I.
- Studies on the Origin of Cultivated Plants. Leningrad: 1926. 1st edn. Roy 8vo. 248 pp. 5 maps, 11 text figs. New cloth, orig wraps preserved. Inscrbd by the author.
(Wheldon & Wesley) **£100 [≈$178]**

Veitch, J., & Sons
- Manual of the Coniferae. A New and Enlarged Edition by A.H. Kent. London: 1900. 2nd edn. 8vo. 562 pp. Num plates, text figs. Orig cloth gilt. *(Henly)* **£60 [≈$107]**

Venning, M.A.
- Rudiments of Conchology. London: 1826. 12mo. vii,103 pp. 10 cold plates. Orig half roan, spine worn. Anon.
(Wheldon & Wesley) **£35 [≈$62]**

Verrier, E.
- Practical Manual of Obstetrics. Fourth Edition, Enlarged and Revised ... First American Edition ... New York: Wood Library, 1884. 8vo. 395 pp. Orig cloth.
(Goodrich) **$95 [≈£53]**

Vesalius, Andreas
- The Epitome of Andreas Vesalius. Translated from the Latin with Preface and Introduction by L.R. Lind. New York: 1949. xxxvi, 104,26 pp. Name & date. Dw (sl worn & torn).
(Whitehart) **£35 [≈$62]**

Veslingus, J.
- The Anatomy of the Body of Man. London: 1653. Translated by N. Culpeper. xii,194 pp. 22 engvs. Title & part of Table 1 supplied in facs. Leather antique.
(Whitehart) **£450 [≈$801]**

Vestiges of the Natural History of Creation ...
- See Chambers, Robert

View ...
- A View of Sir Isaac Newton's Philosophy ... see Pemberton, Henry

Vincent, Charles W. (editor)
- Chemistry, Theoretical, Practical, and Analytical, as Applied to the Arts and Manufactures. By Writers of Eminence. London: n.d. 2 vols bound in 8 divisions. Lge 8vo. 1048; 1008 pp. 53 plates. Tiny nick in foredge of a few ff. Orig dec cloth gilt.
(Bow Windows) **£105 [≈$187]**

Vincent, Ralph H.
- The Elements of Hypnotism ... London: Kegan Paul, International Scientific Series, 1897. 2nd edn, rvsd & enlgd. 17 ills. Orig cloth, soiled. *(Caius)* **$50 [≈£28]**

Virchow, Rudolph
- Cellular Pathology as based upon Physiological and Pathological Histology. Twenty Lectures ... New York: De Witt, [ca 1860]. 1st Amer edn. 8vo. xxvi,27-554 pp. 144 ills. Orig cloth, upper cvr detached.
(Hemlock) **$375 [≈£211]**

Virtue's Household Physician ...
- Virtue's Household Physician. A Twentieth Century Medica ... By a Corps of Eminent Specialists, Practising Physicians, and Surgeons. London: 1925. New & rvsd edn. 5 vols. 4to. Ills. Orig cloth bds, spine ends sl rubbed, edges rubbed.
(Francis Edwards) £25 [≈ $45]

Vleck, J.H. v.
- The Theory of Electric and Magnetic Susceptibilities. Oxford: 1932. xii,384 pp. Lib stamp. Orig bndg, sm repr to spine.
(Whitehart) £18 [≈ $32]

Voge, Cecil I.B.
- The Chemistry and Physics of Contraceptives. London: 1933. 8vo. 288 pp. Plates. Orig cloth.   *(Weiner)* £20 [≈ $36]

Vogt, Carl
- Lectures on Man: His Place in Creation, and in the History of the Earth. Edited by James Hunt. London: for the Anthropological Society ..., 1864. 1st edn in English. 127 text ills. Orig cloth.   *(Gach)* $125 [≈ £70]

Von ...
- For all surnames commencing with "von ..." see under the primary name.

Voyage ...
- A Voyage to the World of Cartesius ... see Daniel, Gabriel

W., C.
- Observations on Dr. Freind's History of Physick ... see Wentingham, Clifford.

W., G.
- A Rich Store-House or Treasury for the Diseased ... The eighth edition, augmented and enlarged, by D.B[order]. London: Clowse, 1650. Sm 4to. [22],274 pp. Sl marg water stains & reprs, sl marg worm at end. Rec half mor. Wing W.31.
(Spelman) £650 [≈ $1,157]

W., J.
- Systema Agriculturae ... see Worlidge, John

Wadd, William
- Nugae Chirurgicae; or, a Biographical Miscellany, Illustrative of a Collection of Professional Portraits. London: John Nichols, 1824. 8vo. ii,276 pp. Occas foxing. Rec cloth.
(Goodrich) $250 [≈ £140]

Wade, J.P.
- Select Evidences of a Successful Method of Treating Fever and Dysentery in Bengal. London: 1791. xi,336 pp. Pencil lib marks on title & endpaper. Some discoloration of endpapers. Contemp calf, rebacked.
(Whitehart) £180 [≈ $320]

Wade, W.
- Salices or an Essay towards a General History of Sallows, Willows, and Osiers, their Uses, and best Methods of Propagating and Cultivating Them. Dublin: 1811. 8vo. xxii, 406,56 pp. Fldg cold plate. 8 pp sl stained. Half calf gilt.
(Wheldon & Wesley) £80 [≈ $142]

Wagner, Albert F.
- Experimental Optics. New York: John Wiley, 1929. 1st edn. 8vo. xii,203 pp. Ills. Orig bndg.   *(Schoen)* $45 [≈ £25]

Wainewright, Jeremiah
- A Mechanical Account of the Non-Naturals: being a brief Explication of the Changes made in Humane Bodies, by Air, Diet, &c. The Third Edition, revis'd. London: J.H. for Ralph Smith, 1718. 8vo. [28],196 pp. Some browning. Contemp calf, jnts v sl reprd.
(Spelman) £160 [≈ $285]

Wait, W.E.
- Manual of the Birds of Ceylon. Colombo: 1931. 2nd edn. Roy 8vo. xxxiii,494 pp. Map. Orig cloth, trifle worn.
(Wheldon & Wesley) £30 [≈ $53]

Waite, A.E.
- The Secret Doctrine in Israel. London: 1913. 1st edn. Thick 8vo. Ills. Orig bndg.
(Deja Vu) £65 [≈ $116]

Wakefield, E. & Dennis, R.W.G.
- Common British Fungi; a Guide to the more common large Basidiomycetes of the British Isles. London: 1950. 1st edn. Roy 8vo. 290 pp. 111 cold plates, 6 text figs. Orig cloth. Dw.   *(Henly)* £24 [≈ $43]

Wakefield, Priscilla
- An Introduction to Botany in a Series of Familiar Letters. London: 1807. 5th edn. 12mo. xii,180 pp. 11 hand cold plates. Calf, jnts cracked.
(Wheldon & Wesley) £30 [≈ $53]
- An Introduction to Botany. London: 1818. 8th edn. 8vo. xii,187 pp. 9 plates. Bds, trifle used.   *(Wheldon & Wesley)* £20 [≈ $36]
- An Introduction to Botany, in a Series of

Familiar Letters. London: 1818. 8th edn. 12mo. xii,187 pp. Table, 9 cold plates. Orig bds, uncut, rebacked.
(Wheldon & Wesley) **£30 [≈ $53]**

Walcott, C.D.
- Fossil Medusae. Washington: 1898. 4to. ix, 201 pp. 47 plates (some cold). Good ex-lib. Few marg water stains. Cloth.
(Wheldon & Wesley) **£40 [≈ $71]**

Walcott, M.V.
- North American Wild Flowers. Washington: 1925. One of 500. 5 vols. Imperial 4to. 400 cold plates. Orig half mor portfolios.
(Wheldon & Wesley) **£450 [≈ $801]**

Walker, Alexander
- Intermarriage; or the Mode in which, and the Causes why, Beauty, Health and Intellect, result from certain Unions, and Deformity, Disease and Insanity, from Others ... London: 1838. 8vo. xxxiv,442 pp. 8 plates. Sl loose. Orig cloth, soiled. *(Weiner)* **£50 [≈ $89]**

Walker, E.A.
- William Fairlie Clarke. His Life and Letters. Hospital Sketches and Addresses. By E.A.W. London: 1885. 2nd edn. viii,297 pp. Port frontis. Orig cloth, dull, sl marked.
(Whitehart) **£15 [≈ $27]**

Walker, F.
- Catalogue of the Specimens of Neuropterous Insects in the British Museum. London: 1852-53. 4 parts. 12mo. Stamp on title. Cloth, orig wraps bound in. *(Egglishaw)* **£36 [≈ $64]**
- List of the Specimens of Homopterous Insects in the British Museum. London: 1850-58. 4 parts & Supplement, bound in 3 vols. 12mo. 1188,369 pp. 8 litho plates. Lib stamp on titles. Half calf, jnts & crnrs rubbed.
(Egglishaw) **£90 [≈ $160]**

Walker, Francis A.
- Political Economy. London: Macmillan, 1885. 1st edn. Contemp tree calf gilt, spine & jnts sl rubbed. *(Jarndyce)* **£45 [≈ $80]**

Walker, James
- The Analytical Theory of Light. Cambridge: UP, 1904. 1st edn. 4to. xvi,416 pp. Orig cloth. *(Gaskell)* **£20 [≈ $36]**

Walker, John
- The Philosophy of the Eye: being a Familiar Exposition of its Mechanism, and of the Phenomena of Vision, with a View to the Evidence of Design. London: 1837. 8vo. xii,

300 pp. Frontis, ills. Orig cloth.
(Weiner) **£65 [≈ $116]**

Walker, N.
- An Introduction to Dermatology. Bristol: 1899. xvi,247 pp. Frontis, 29 plates, 34 text ills. Orig cloth, sl marked, inner hinge sl cracked. *(Whitehart)* **£15 [≈ $27]**

Walker, R.
- The Flora of Oxfordshire and its Contiguous Counties ... according to the Linnean and Natural System. Oxford: 1833. 8vo. cxxxv,338 pp. Fldg table (torn), 12 plates (foxed). Few pencil notes. Orig cloth, trifle used. *(Wheldon & Wesley)* **£65 [≈ $116]**

Walker, Robert
- An Inquiry into the Small-Pox Medical and Political wherein a successful Method of treating that Diseases is proposed ... London: Murray, 1790. 8vo. xiv,499 pp. New cloth.
(Goodrich) **$150 [≈ £84]**

Walker, W.
- Memoirs of the Distinguished Men of Science of Great Britain living in the Years 1807-08. With an Introduction by Robert Hunt ... London: 1862. xii,228 pp. Frontis (creased). Orig cloth, sl worn, spine ends sl defective. *(Whitehart)* **£35 [≈ $62]**

Walkingame, Francis
- The Tutor's Assistant; being a Compendium of Arithmetic ... A New Edition with the Addition of Book-Keeping by Single Entry ... Revised ... by William Taylor. Birmingham: M. Swinney, 1797. Fldg table frontis. Contemp sheep, rebacked.
(C.R. Johnson) **£135 [≈ $240]**
- The Tutor's Assistant ... A New Edition, corrected ... by T. Crosby, mathematician. York: T. Wilson, 1835. 8vo. [4 Mozley ctlg], 199, [1] pp. Fldg plate. Orig sheep.
(Claude Cox) **£15 [≈ $27]**

Wall, E.J.
- A Dictionary of Photography for the Amateur & Professional Photographer. Second Edition revised. London: Hazell, Watson ..., 1890. Orig maroon cloth.
(Jermy & Westerman) **£30 [≈ $53]**

Wall, J.
- Plain Directions, &c. For the Cure of the Venereal Disease ... London: W. Griffin, 1764. Sm 8vo. [iv],45,[i] pp. Fldg leaf of Directions. V sl spotting. Qtr calf.
(Francis Edwards) **£80 [≈ $142]**

Wallace, Alfred Russell
- Darwinism. An Exposition of the Theory of Natural Selection with some of its Applications. London: 1889. 1st edn. 494 pp. Orig bndg.   *(Fye)* **$250 [≃ £140]**
- Darwinism: an Exposition of the Theory of Natural Selection with some of its Applications. London: Macmillan, 1889. 8vo. Orig green cloth, sl shaken.
          (Waterfield's) **£75 [≃ $134]**
- Darwinism. London: 1889. 2nd edn. 8vo. xvi, 494 pp. Port, map, 37 text figs. Cloth, trifle used.   *(Wheldon & Wesley)* **£35 [≃ $62]**
- Darwinism ... London: 1890. 2nd edn. 8vo. Port, fldg map, figs. Orig cloth.
          (Bow Windows) **£65 [≃ $116]**
- Darwinism. An Exposition of the Theory of Natural Selection with some of its Applications. London: 1890. Sm 8vo. xvi, 494, [1 advt] pp. Port frontis, fldg map, 37 ills. Orig cloth.
          (Francis Edwards) **£35 [≃ $62]**
- The Geographical Distribution of Animals, with a Study of the Relations of Living and Extinct Faunas. London: 1876. 2 vols. 8vo. 7 cold maps, 20 plates. Prize calf gilt, a.e.g., crnr of vol 1 bumped.
          (Wheldon & Wesley) **£220 [≃ $392]**
- Is Mars Habitable? ... London: 1907. 1st edn. 8vo. xii,110,[2 advt] pp. 2 plates. Orig cloth, v sl marked. *(Bow Windows)* **£105 [≃ $187]**
- Island Life: or, the Phenomena and Causes of Insular Faunas and Floras ... London: Macmillan, 1880, 1st edn. 8vo. xix,526,[3 advt] pp. 26 maps & ills. Name, label. Orig green cloth gilt. *(Blackwell's)* **£200 [≃ $356]**
- Island Life ... Second and Revised Edition. London: Macmillan, 1892. 8vo. xx,563 pp. 26 ills & maps. Early prize red calf gilt.
          (Frew Mackenzie) **£65 [≃ $116]**
- Miracles & Modern Spiritualism. London: Redway, 1896. Rvsd edn. Orig cloth gilt.
          (Deja Vu) **£45 [≃ $80]**
- Social Environment and Moral Progress. London: 1913. 1st edn. 8vo. Port. Orig cloth.
          (Bow Windows) **£35 [≃ $62]**
- The World of Life. A Manifestation of Creative Power, Directive Mind and Ultimate Purpose. Third Edition. London: 1911. 8vo. xvi,408 pp. 110 figs (some on plates). Occas pencil notes & spots. Orig cloth, marked, trifle rubbed.
          (Bow Windows) **£42 [≃ $75]**

Wallace, Anthony
- The Progress of Plastic Surgery: An Introductory History. Oxford: 1982. 1st edn. 184 pp. Ills. Dw.   *(Fye)* **$75 [≃ £42]**

Wallis, George
- The Art of Preventing Diseases, and Restoring Health ... London: Robinson, 1793. 8vo. xx,850,[12] pp. Tree calf, front jnt cracked.   *(Goodrich)* **$145 [≃ £81]**

Wallis-Tayler, A.J.
- Modern Cycles; a Practical Handbook on their Construction and Repair. London: 1897. 8vo. xvi,340,[8 advt] pp. Fldg plate, 304 ills. Orig cloth gilt, sl shaken.
          (Weiner) **£125 [≃ $223]**

Walmsley, R.M.
- The Electric Current. How Produced and How Used. London: 1894. xii,764 pp. 379 text figs. Endpapers marked. Cloth, sl marked.   *(Whitehart)* **£35 [≃ $62]**
- Electricity in the Service of Man. A Popular and Practical Treatise ... London: [1904]. viii,1208 pp. Frontis, 5 fldg plates, over 1200 ills. Occas sl foxing. Orig cloth, sl marked, inner hinges crudely reprd.
          (Whitehart) **£28 [≃ $50]**

Walsh, James J.
- The Popes and Science. The History of Papal Relations to Science during the Middle Ages and down to our own Times. New York: 1908. 8vo. 431 pp. Occas discoloration from tipped in cuttings. Orig bndg.
          (Goodrich) **$55 [≃ £31]**

Walsh, John Benn, Lord Ormathwaite
- Astronomy and Geology Compared. London: 1872. 8vo. 171 pp. Orig cloth, sl discold, hd of spine torn.   *(Weiner)* **£35 [≃ $62]**

Walsh, John Henry ('Stonehenge')
- The Horse, in the Stable and the Field: his Varieties, Management in Health and Disease, Anatomy, Physiology ... New Edition. London: Routledge, 1877. 8vo. x,622 pp. 170 ills. Name on title, cuttings on last page. New tan mor gilt.
          (Blackwell's) **£130 [≃ $231]**

Walshe, Sir Francis Martin Rouse
- Diseases of the Nervous System. Described for Practitioners and Students. Edinburgh & London: 1952. 7th edn. xvi,363 pp. 26 plates, 38 ills. Name. Orig bndg.
          (Whitehart) **£15 [≃ $27]**
- Diseases of the Nervous System. Described for Practitioners and Students. London: 1958. 9th edn. xvi,373 pp. 58 text figs. Orig bndg.   *(Whitehart)* **£15 [≃ $27]**

Walter, Richards
- S. Weir Mitchell, M.D. Neurologist. A
Medical Biography. Springfield: 1970. 1st
edn. 232 pp. Orig bndg. Dw.
(Fye) **$95 [≈ £53]**

Wang, Chung Yu
- Antimony: Its History, Chemistry,
Mineralogy, Geology ... London: 1909. 1st
edn. 8vo. x,217 pp. 1 plate, num figs. Name.
Orig cloth.   *(Bow Windows)* **£35 [≈ $62]**

Ward, The Hon. Mrs. Mary
- The Microscope. London: Groombridge,
1869. 3rd edn. 8vo. vi,154,[8 advt] pp. 8 cold
plates, 25 text figs. Orig dec cloth, rubbed,
new endpapers.   *(Savona)* **£25 [≈ $45]**
- The Microscope. London: Groombridge,
1876. 4th edn. 8vo. 8 cold plates, 25 text figs.
Orig pict cloth, a.e.g. *(Savona)* **£30 [≈ $53]**
- The Telescope: A Familiar Sketch. With a
special Notice of Objects coming within the
range of a Small Telescope. London:
Groombridge, 1870. 1st edn. 8vo. viii,150,2
pp. Ills. Orig cloth. *(de Burca)* **£90 [≈ $160]**

Ward, Robert Decourcy
- Climate especially considered in relation to
Man. New York: Putnam, 1908. 1st edn.
12mo. 372 pp. Ills. Sl foxing. Orig bndg,
upper jnt weak.   *(Schoen)* **$50 [≈ £28]**
- Practical Exercises in Elementary
Meteorology. Boston: Ginn & Co., 1899. 1st
edn. 8vo. 200 pp. Num ills, fldg tables. Orig
cloth, spine chipped. *(Schoen)* **$85 [≈ £48]**

Wardlaw, C.W.
- Diseases of the Banana, and of the Manila
Hemp Plant. London: 1953. 1st edn. 8vo. xii,
615 pp. Cold frontis, num ills & charts. Orig
cloth, some spotting.
(Francis Edwards) **£35 [≈ $62]**

Waring, Edward John
- Bibliotheca Therapeutica or Bibliography of
Therapeutics, chiefly in reference to Articles
of the Materia Medica. London: 1878. 1st
edn. 2 vols. 934 pp. Orig bndg.
(Fye) **$250 [≈ £140]**
- Pharmacopoeia of India. London: 1868. 1st
edn. 503 pp. Qtr leather, backstrip relaid.
(Fye) **$175 [≈ £98]**
- Pharmacopoeia of India, prepared under the
Authority of Her Majesty's Secretary of State
for India in Council. London: India Office,
1868. 8vo. xvi,502 pp. Orig cloth.
(Weiner) **£65 [≈ $116]**

Warltire, John
- Analysis of a Course of Lectures in
Experimental Philosophy ... The Sixth
Edition. London: for the author, 1769. 8vo.
31 pp. Rec wraps. *(Fenning)* **£185 [≈ $329]**
- Tables of the Various Combinations and
Specific Attraction of the Substances
employed in Chemistry ... London: for the
author, 1769. 1st (only?) edn. 8vo. 32 pp. Rec
wraps.   *(Fenning)* **£165 [≈ $294]**

Warman, Edward B.
- Telepathy: Mental Telegraphy - Thought
Transference - Mind Reading - Muscle
Reading. London: L.N. Fowler, 1910. 1st
English edn. Frontis port. Orig cloth backed
bds.   *(Caius)* **$60 [≈ £34]**

Warner, R.
- Select Orchidaceous Plants. Bath: 1970.
Folio. 10 cold plates. Wrappers.
(Wheldon & Wesley) **£25 [≈ $45]**

Warnes, John
- On the Cultivation of Flax, the Fattening of
Cattle with Native Produce ... London: W.
Clowes & Son, 1846. 1st edn. 8vo. xv,321 pp.
7 plates, text ills. Orig cloth, uncut.
(Claude Cox) **£35 [≈ $62]**

Warren, Erasmus
- Geologia: or, a Discourse concerning the
Earth before the Deluge ... London: 1690. Sm
4to. 8 ff, 359 pp. Ctlg. 4 engvd ills. Occas sl
marg water stain. Lib label. Contemp calf,
worn, loose, leather on back bd torn.
(Weiner) **£300 [≈ $534]**

Warren, J. Mason
- Surgical Observations, with Cases and
Operations. New York: 1867. 1st edn. 630
pp. Litho ills (some cold). Orig bndg, fine.
(Fye) **$700 [≈ £393]**

Wass, C.
- Introduction to Electronic Analogue
Computers. New York: McGraw Hill, 1955.
1st edn. 12mo. 237 pp. Ills. Lib pocket. Orig
bndg, hd of spine sl rubbed.
(Schoen) **$50 [≈ £28]**

Wasson, R. Gordon
- Maria Sabina and her Mazatec Mushroom
Velada. New York: Harcourt Brace
Jovanovich, 1975. 4to. Orig dec cloth.
Musical score in orig wraps. 4 cassettes in
box. In orig shrinkwrap, cardboard, mailing
box.   *(Frew Mackenzie)* **£100 [≈ $178]**
- The Wondrous Mushroom. Mycolatry in

Mesoamerica. New York: 1980. One of 501 signed by the author. 4to. xxvi,248 pp. 139 ills (52 cold). Qtr mor. Cloth slipcase.
(Wheldon & Wesley) **£200 [≈ $356]**

Waterhouse, Benjamin
- A Prospect of Exterminating the Small Pox ... Part II, being a Continuation of Facts concerning the Progress of the New Inoculation in America ... Cambridge: 1802. 8vo. 139 pp. V sm crnr defect 3 ff. Faint staining last 2 ff. Lib stamp on title. Mod half calf.   *(Hemlock)* **$1,200 [≈ £674]**

Waterman, T.H. (editor)
- The Physiology of Crustacea. New York: 1960-61. 2 vols. 8vo. 1351 pp. Cloth.
(Wheldon & Wesley) **£60 [≈ $107]**

Waters, T.H.
- On Diseases of the Chest: being Contributions to their Clinical History, Pathology, and Treatment ... London: 1868. 1st edn. 8vo. viii,418,[2 advt] pp. 9 plates. Orig cloth.   *(Fenning)* **£45 [≈ $80]**

Watson, Frederick
- The Life of Sir Robert Jones. Baltimore: 1934. 1st Amer edn. 327 pp. Orig bndg.
(Fye) **$50 [≈ £28]**

Watson, H.C.
- The New Botanist's Guide to the Localities of the Rarer Plants of Britain. London: [1835-] 1837. 2 vols in one. Post 8vo. xxv, 674 pp. Half mor. *(Wheldon & Wesley)* **£60 [≈ $107]**

Watson, James D.
- The Double Helix. A Personal Account of the Discovery of the Structure of DNA. London: 1968. 1st edn. xvi,226 pp. Ills. Dw.
(Francis Edwards) **£35 [≈ $62]**

Watson, John Selby
- Geology: a Poem in Seven Books. London: William Pickering, 1844. Sm 8vo. 213 pp. Orig cloth, paper label, sl worn. Inscrbd 'From the Author'.   *(Weiner)* **£40 [≈ $71]**

Watson, Ralph
- A Brief Explanatory Statement of the Principle and Application of a Plan for Preventing Ships Foundering at Sea ... London: A. Hancock, 1829. 1st edn. 8vo. 70, [2] pp. Middle Hill bds, spine worn. Author's pres inscrptn to Sir Thomas Phillipps on title.
(Burmester) **£120 [≈ $214]**

Watson, T.
- Lectures on the Principles and Practice of Physic: delivered at King's College, London. London: 1857. 4th edn. 2 vols. 2 plates. Few page edges sl water stained. 1 sm repr. New cloth.   *(Whitehart)* **£35 [≈ $62]**

Watson, W. & Bean, W.
- Orchids: their Culture and Management. London: 1890. 8vo. xi,554 pp. 52 plates (8 cold), 117 text figs. Sl foxing. Orig dec cloth gilt, trifle used, jnts loose.
(Wheldon & Wesley) **£60 [≈ $107]**
- Orchids: their Culture and Management ... Mew Edition by H.J. Chapman. London: 1903. 8vo. xi,559 pp. 20 cold plates, num ills. Fldg frontis sl defective at fold & taped in. Orig cloth gilt, trifle used.
(Wheldon & Wesley) **£65 [≈ $116]**

Watson, William
- An Account of a Series of Experiments, instituted with a View to ascertaining the most Successful Method of Inoculating the Small-Pox. London: J. Nourse, 1768. 1st edn. 8vo. [iv],58,[1] pp. Disbound.
(Bookpress) **$225 [≈ £126]**

Watt, Alexander
- The Art of Paper-Making. New York: Van Nostrand, 1907. 3rd edn. xii,260,64 pp. Name on half-title. Cloth.
(Bookpress) **$150 [≈ £84]**

Watt, George
- The Pests and Blights of the Tea Plant ... Calcutta: 1898. iii,467,xvii pp. Sev ills. Occas pencil notes. Half mor.
(Francis Edwards) **£40 [≈ $71]**

Watts, Isaac
- The First Principles of Astronomy and Geography ... London: for J. Clark & R. Hett, 1728. 2nd edn crrctd. 8vo. xii,222 pp. 6 fldg plates. Calf, spine & edges worn.
(Key Books) **$120 [≈ £67]**
- The Knowledge of the Heavens and the Earth made Easy; or the First Principles of Astronomy and Geography explain'd by the Use of Globes and Maps ... London: for J. Clark ..., 1726. 1st edn. 8vo. 6 fldg plates. Contemp calf, crnrs & spine ends worn, jnts cracked.   *(Gaskell)* **£300 [≈ $534]**

Webb, D.A. & Scannell, Mary J.P.
- Flora of Connemara and the Burren. Cambridge: UP, 1983. 8vo. xlv,322 pp. Maps, ills. Orig cloth. Dw.
(de Burca) **£60 [≈ $107]**

Webb, W.M. & Sillem, C.
- The British Woodlice. London: Duckworth, 1906. 1st edn. 8vo. x,54 pp. 25 plates. Orig cloth, spine faded, sl staining.
(Savona) **£28 [≈ $50]**

Webster, A.D.
- British Orchids. London: 1898. 2nd edn. 8vo. 132 pp. 40 ills. Cloth.
(Wheldon & Wesley) **£15 [≈ $27]**
- British Orchids. London: 1898. 2nd edn. 8vo. xii,132,3 pp. Frontis, 39 text ills. Cloth.
(Henly) **£36 [≈ $64]**

Webster, John
- Metallographia or, An History of Metals ... London: A.C. for Walter Kettilby, 1671. Only edn. 4to. [xvi],388 pp. Title soiled & mtd. Occas sl soil & damp stain. No advt ff. Rec half calf. Wing W.1231A.
(Clark) **£280 [≈ $498]**

Weinberger, Bernhard
- Pierre Fauchard, Surgeon-Dentist. A Brief Account of the Beginning of Modern Dentistry ... Minneapolis: 1941. 1st edn. 102 pp. Orig bndg.
(Fye) **$75 [≈ £42]**

Weismann, A.
- Essays upon Heredity and Kindred Biological Problems. Oxford: 1889. 1st edn. xii,455 pp. Half-title foxed, few pp at end creased. Orig cloth, worn, spine ends sl defective.
(Whitehart) **£38 [≈ $68]**
- The Evolution Theory. London: 1904. 1st edn in English. 2 vols. 131 ills. Orig cloth, sl marked.
(Whitehart) **£45 [≈ $80]**
- The Germ-Plasm: a Theory of Heredity. Translated by W.N. Parker and H. Ronnfeldt. London: 1893. 8vo. xxiii,477 pp. 24 text figs. Orig cloth, sl worn.
(Wheldon & Wesley) **£45 [≈ $80]**

Welch, J.J.
- A Text Book of Naval Architecture, for the Use of Officers of the Royal Navy. London: 1893. 3rd edn. Lge 8vo. 167 pp. 18 fldg plates, num text ills. Orig cloth, some soiling, spine sl chipped.
(Francis Edwards) **£60 [≈ $107]**

Welch, William
- Papers and Addresses. Baltimore: 1920. 3 vols. Tall 4to. Sm lib marks. Orig bndgs, uncut.
(Goodrich) **$195 [≈ £110]**
- Pathology and Preventive Medicine. Baltimore: 1920. 1st edn. 678 pp. Orig bndg.
(Fye) **$75 [≈ £42]**

Weld, Charles Richard
- A History of the Royal Society, with Memoirs of the Presidents ... London: John W. Parker ..., 1848. 1st edn. 2nd issue binding. 2 vols. 8vo. 14 plates inc frontis (6 included in pagination), w'engvd text ills. Orig brown cloth, sl worn.
(Gaskell) **£200 [≈ $356]**

Wellcome Historical Medical Library
- A Catalogue of Printed Books in the Wellcome Historical Medical Library. London: 1962-76. Vols 1-3 (all published to date). 3 vols. 4to. Orig buckram.
(Georges) **£450 [≈ $801]**

Wells, C.
- Bones, Bodies and Disease. Evidence of Disease and Abnormality in Early Man. London: Ancient People and Places Series, 1964. 288 pp. 88 plates, 33 ills. Orig bndg.
(Whitehart) **£18 [≈ $32]**

Wells, Edward
- The Young Gentleman's Astronomy, Chronology, and Dialling ... London: for James & John Knapton ..., 1725. 3rd edn. 3 parts in one vol. 8vo. [viii],148, [viii],86, [viii], 44 pp. 25 plates. Contemp panelled calf, sl worn.
(Young's) **£155 [≈ $276]**

Welwitsch, F.
- Catalogue of the African Plants collected in 1853-61. London: BM, 1896-1901. 6 vols. 8vo. Few lib stamps. Orig cloth & bds.
(Egglishaw) **£55 [≈ $98]**

Wendt, Edmund
- A Treatise on Asiatic Cholera. New York: 1885. 1st edn. 403 pp. Orig bndg.
(Fye) **$50 [≈ £28]**

Wentingham, Clifford
- Observations on Dr. Freind's History of Physick; Shewing, some False Representations of Ancient and Modern Physicians. By C.W., M.D. ... London: Strahan, 1726. 8vo. 65 pp. Period style qtr calf by Bernard Middleton. Anon.
(Goodrich) **$325 [≈ £183]**

West, Charles
- Lectures on the Diseases of Infancy and Childhood. London: Longmans, 1848. 8vo. 488, 16 advt pp. Orig cloth, backstrip relaid, new endpapers to style.
(Goodrich) **$495 [≈ £278]**
- Lectures on the Diseases of Infancy and Childhood. London: Longmans, Green, 1884. 7th edn, rvsd & enlgd. 8vo. xi,896,16

advt pp. Few pencil notes. Orig cloth, sl
shaken, hd of spine bumped.
(David White) **£44 [≃ $78]**
- Lectures on the Diseases of Women. London:
1858. xvi,672 pp. Orig cloth, backstrip relaid.
(Whitehart) **£90 [≃ $160]**
- On Some Disorders of the Nervous System in
Childhood: Being the Lumleian Lectures
delivered at the Royal College of Physicians
of London, in March, 1871. Phila: Lea, 1871.
1st Amer edn. 8vo. [5],131 pp. Cloth, wear to
spine ends, tear, stain ft of spine.
(Goodrich) **$135 [≃ £76]**

Westermarck, Edward
- The History of Human Marriage. London:
1894. 2nd edn. 644 pp. Orig bndg.
(Fye) **£100 [≃ £56]**
- The History of Human Marriage. New York:
Allerton Book Co., 1922. 5th edn, rvsd. 3
vols. Orig cloth gilt, lettering faded & inked
in.   *(Hollett)* **£120 [≃ $214]**

Weston, Richard
- The English Flora [with] The Supplement to
the English Flora. London: 1775-80. 2 vols in
one. 8vo. [xvi],259; [xii],120 pp. Contemp
calf.   *(Wheldon & Wesley)* **£80 [≃ $142]**
- The Gardener's Pocket-Calendar, on a New
Plan ... Nottingham: G. Burbage, 1797. 4th
edn, enlgd. 12mo. Engvd title & frontis.
Contemp sheep, spine worn.
(Ximenes) **$325 [≃ £183]**
- Tracts on Practical Agriculture and
Gardening ... By a Country Gentleman.
London: for S. Hooper ..., 1769. 1st edn. Lge
8vo. [viii], xxiii,277, [i],70,[xix],[i advt] pp.
Crnr stain at start. Edges worn & sl dog-eared.
Orig wraps, worn & soiled. Anon.
(Francis Edwards) **£60 [≃ $107]**

Westropp, Hodder M.
- A Manual of Precious Stones and Antique
Gems. London: 1874. 8vo. xvi,165 pp.
Frontis, ills. 1st few ff carelessly opened. Orig
cloth, shaken, sl soiled & cockled.
(Weiner) **£25 [≃ $45]**
- A Manual of Precious Stones and Antique
Gems. London: Sampson Low, 1874. 1st edn.
8vo. xvi,165 pp. Frontis, text ills. Orig cloth,
spine faded.   *(Burmester)* **£30 [≃ $53]**

Westwood, J.O.
- An Introduction to the Modern Classification
of Insects ... London: 1839-40. 1st edn. 2
vols. 8vo. Cold frontis, text figs. 1 leaf torn
across. Orig cloth.
(Bow Windows) **£150 [≃ $267]**

Wethered, H.N.
- The Mind of the Ancient World. A
Consideration of Pliny's Natural History.
London: 1937. xv,302 pp. Frontis. Cloth, sl
dull.   *(Whitehart)* **£18 [≃ $32]**

Wharton, Henry E. & Curtis, R. Farquhar
- The Practice of Surgery ... Revised Edition.
Phila: Lippincott, 1899. 1242 pp. Num ills.
Orig sheep, worn but firm, stain on rear cvr.
(Goodrich) **$125 [≃ £70]**

Wheatland, David P.
- The Apparatus of Science at Harvard
1765-1800. Assisted by Barbara Carson.
Collection of Historical Scientific
Instruments. Harvard: UP, 1968. 4to. xi,204
pp. 5 mtd cold plates, num ills. Endpaper
maps. Orig dec cloth.
(Francis Edwards) **£60 [≃ $107]**

Wheatstone, Charles
- The Scientific Papers. London: for the
Physical Society of London, 1879. 1st edn.
8vo. xvi,380 pp. 21 plates. Orig cloth,
unopened, v sl worn. *(Gaskell)* **£300 [≃ $534]**

Wheeler, James
- The Botanist's and Gardener's New
Dictionary ... London: Strahan, 1763. 8vo.
viii, xxxii, 480 pp. 2 plates. Contemp
sprinkled calf, label, sl rubbed.
(Blackwell's) **£150 [≃ $267]**

Whetham, William Cecil Dampier
- The Recent Developments of Physical
Science. London: Murray, 1904. 1st edn. 8vo.
xii,344 pp. 14 plates. Orig cloth.
(Gaskell) **£20 [≃ $36]**
- A Treatise on the Theory of Solution
including the Phenomena of Electrolysis.
Cambridge: UP, 1902. 1st edn. 8vo. x,488
pp. Orig cloth.   *(Gaskell)* **£20 [≃ $36]**

Whewell, William
- Astronomy and General Physics considered
with reference to Natural Theology. London:
William Pickering, 1833. 1st edn. 8vo. xvi,
381 pp. Leather, edges scuffed.
(Key Books) **$180 [≃ £101]**
- Astronomy and General Physics considered
with reference to Natural Theology. London:
1833. 1st edn. 8vo. xv,381 pp. Orig cloth,
paper label.   *(Weiner)* **£50 [≃ $89]**
- History of the Inductive Sciences, from the
Earliest to the Present Time. London: Parker
& Son, 1857. 3rd edn, rvsd & enlgd, 1st
printing. 3 vols. Sm 8vo. Orig cloth, fine.
(Gach) **$350 [≃ £197]**

- The Mechanics of Engineering intended for Use in Universities, and in Colleges of Engineers. Cambridge: UP for John W. Parker ... 1841. 1st edn. 8vo. xii,216 pp. Text diags. Lib stamps on title. Orig cloth backed bds, uncut, worn, spine frayed.
(Gaskell) **£175 [≈ $312]**

Whipple, G.C.
- The Microscopy of Drinking-Water. New York: Wiley, 1908. 2nd edn rvsd. 8vo. xiii, 323, [19 ctlg] pp. 19 plates, 23 text figs. Cloth, sl worn, new endpapers.
(Savona) **£30 [≈ $53]**

Whiston, William
- Astronomical Principles of Religion, Natural and Reveal'd. In Nine Parts ... London: for J. Senex ..., 1725. 2nd edn. 8vo. [iv], xxxii, 304,[4] pp. 7 engvd plates. Marg worm hole 1st 19 ff. Minor damp edges of endpapers. Contemp calf. *(Burmester)* **£120 [≈ $214]**
- A New Theory of the Earth ... [with his] A Vindication of the New Theory of the Earth ... [with his] A Second Defence of the New Theory of the Earth ... London: 1696-98-1700. 1st edns. 3 vols in one. Frontis & 7 plates in 1st work. Sl used. Old style calf. Wing 1696-8-7.
(P and P Books) **£680 [≈ $1,210]**
- A New Theory of the Earth, from its Original, to the Consummation of all Things ... Third Edition. London: 1722. 8vo. 95,460 pp. 8 plates (1 fldg). Occas sl spotting. Sm lib stamp title verso. Contemp calf, rebacked.
(Weiner) **£150 [≈ $267]**

White, A.
- A Popular History of Birds. London: Lovell Reeve, 1855. 1st edn. Sq 8vo. viii,347 pp. 20 hand cold litho plates. New cloth.
(Egglishaw) **£42 [≈ $75]**

White, Charles
- A Treatise on the Management of Pregnant and Lying-in Women, and the Means of Curing ... Preventing the Principal Disorders ... First Worcester Edition. Worcester, Mass.: Isaiah Thomas, 1793. 1st Amer edn. 8vo. [2], vii-xvi, 17-328 pp. 2 plates. Mod imitation leather. *(Hemlock)* **$375 [≈ £211]**

White, E. & Humphrey, J.
- Pharmacopoeia. A Commentary on the British Pharmacopoeia 1898. London: 1904. 4to. xxii, 692 pp. 46 plates. Reprs to title & half-title. Orig cloth, dull & faded, spine worn. *(Whitehart)* **£30 [≈ $53]**

White, F.B.W.
- The Flora of Perthshire. Edited by J.H.W. Trail. Edinburgh: 1898. One of 500. 8vo. lix, 407 pp. Port, cold map. Orig cloth.
(Wheldon & Wesley) **£45 [≈ $80]**

White, George R.
- Animal Castration. A Book for the Use of Students and Practitioners. Nashville: the author, 1914. 1st edn. Sm 4to. 228,[16],[4 advt] pp. 209 ills. Orig cloth, extrs frayed, sl soiled. *(Karmiole)* **$35 [≈ £20]**

White, Gilbert
- A Naturalist's Calendar, with Observations in Various Branches of Natural History ... London: 1795. 8vo. 176 pp. Cold plate. Orig bds, spine defective.
(Wheldon & Wesley) **£140 [≈ $249]**

White, James
- A Compendium of the Veterinary Art ... Canterbury: W. Bristow, for J. Badcock, 1802. 1st edn thus. 12mo. 20,232,[4 advt] pp. Hand cold frontis, 14 plates (3 hand cold). Clean tear in 1 leaf. Orig bds, uncut, rebacked. *(Burmester)* **£110 [≈ $196]**

White, P. Dudley
- Heart Diseases. New York: 1948. 3rd edn. xxviii,1026 pp. 138 ills. Sl foxing. Orig bndg, dust stained. *(Whitehart)* **£18 [≈ $32]**

White, R.P.
- Catarrhal Fevers commonly called Colds. Their Causes, Consequences, Control and Cure. London: 1906. viii,111 pp. 6 plates. Occas sl foxing. Orig cloth, marked & dust stained. *(Whitehart)* **£20 [≈ $36]**

White, T.
- A Treatise on the Struma or Scrofula, commonly called The King's Evil. London: 1787. 2nd edn. viii,100 pp. Lib marks on title. Some marg pencil lines. Mod half leather. *(Whitehart)* **£140 [≈ $249]**

Whitehead, Alfred North
- The Function of Reason. Princeton: UP, 1929. 1st edn. Sm 8vo. [vii],72 pp. Tape remnants to end ff. Orig ptd cloth.
(Gach) **£36.50 [≈ £21]**
- Process and Reality: An Essay in Cosmotology. New York: Macmillan, 1929. 1st Amer edn. 8vo. xii,546 pp. Orig cloth (dull, as usual). *(Gach)* **$50 [≈ £28]**
- Process and Reality: An Essay in Cosmotology. Cambridge: UP. 1st British edn. 8vo. Orig cloth, edges bumped. Author's

pres inscrptn (1930).   *(Gach)* $250 [≈ £140]
- Symbolism: Its Meaning and Effect. New York: Macmillan, 1927. 1st edn. Sm 8vo. Orig cloth.   *(Gach)* $50 [≈ £28]

Whitehead, G. Kenneth
- The Deer of Great Britain and Ireland. An Account of their History, Status and Distribution. London: Routledge & Kegan Paul, 1964. 1st edn. Lge thick 8vo. xv,597 pp. 95 plates. Orig cloth gilt. Dw.
          (Hollett) £85 [≈ $151]
- The Wild Goats of Great Britain and Ireland. London: 1972. 8vo. 184 pp. 6 maps, num photos. Cloth.
          (Wheldon & Wesley) £25 [≈ $45]

Whitehead, P.J.P.
- Forty Drawings of Fishes made by the Artists who accompanied Captain James Cook on his Three Voyages to the Pacific. London: BM, 1968. Folio.. 36 plates. Cloth. Dw.
          (Wheldon & Wesley) £100 [≈ $178]

Whitehurst, John
- An Inquiry into the Original State and Formation of the Earth deduced from Facts and the Laws of Nature ... Appendix ... On the Strata in Derbyshire. London: 1778. 1st edn. 4to. [xvi],iv,199 pp. Half-title. 9 plates (water stained) on 4 ff. Half calf, jnts worn.
          (Wheldon & Wesley) £325 [≈ $579]
- An Inquiry into the Original State and Formation of the Earth ... Appendix ... Strata of Derbyshire ... London: for the author, & W. Bent ..., 1778. Lge 4to. [xi], iv, 199 pp. Subscribers. 9 plates on 5 sheets. Orig bds, uncut, worn.   *(Weiner)* £500 [≈ $890]
- An Inquiry into the Original State and Formation of the Earth ... Appendix ... Strata of Derbyshire ... London: for the author, by J. Cooper, 1778. Lge 4to. Subscribers (reset). 9 plates on 4 sheets. Mod calf.
          (Weiner) £400 [≈ $712]
- The Works, with Memoirs of his Life and Writings. London: 1792. 4to. 10 plates (8 fldg). Lacks frontis port. Half calf, jnts cracking but firm.   *(Weiner)* £110 [≈ $196]

Whiting, Sydney
- Memoirs of a Stomach. Written by himself, that all who eat may read. Edited by a Minister of the Interior. London: W.E. Painter, (1853). 3rd edn. 4 advt pp. Frontis. Lacks free endpapers. Orig cloth, sl faded. Anon.   *(Jarndyce)* £38 [≈ $68]

Whitlaw, C.
- A Treatise on the Causes and Effects of

Inflammation, Fever, Cancer, Scrofula, and Nervous Affections ... London: 1831. xxxii, 304 pp. Occas foxing. Contemp linen cvrd bds, v worn.   *(Whitehart)* £90 [≈ $160]

Whittaker, Sir Edmund Taylor
- A History of the Theories of Aether and Electricity from the Age of Descartes to the Close of the Nineteenth Century. Dublin: UP, 1910. 1st edn. 8vo. xiii,[2],475 pp. 4 sm stamps. Orig cloth gilt.
          (Fenning) £75 [≈ $134]
- A History of the Theories of Aether and Electricity. The Classical Theories. London: 1951. 2nd edn. xiv,434 pp. Occas foxing. Dw.
          (Whitehart) £25 [≈ $45]
- A Treatise on the Analytical Dynamics of Particles and Rigid Bodies ... Cambridge: UP, 1904. 1st edn. Roy 8vo. xiv,414 pp. Orig cloth.   *(Gaskell)* £60 [≈ $107]

Whitteridge, G.
- William Harvey and the Circulation of the Blood. London: 1971. xiii,270 pp. Frontis port, 8 plates. Lib labels. Orig bndg.
          (Whitehart) £15 [≈ $27]

Whitwell, J.R.
- Historical Notes on Psychiatry (Early Times - End of 16th Century). London: 1936. 1st edn. 252 pp. Orig bndg, spine dull.
          (Fye) $75 [≈ £42]

Whymper, Charles
- Egyptian Birds for the most part seen in the Nile Valley. London: A. & C. Black, 1909. 1st edn. Lge 8vo. 51 cold plates. A few spots to foredge & prelims. Orig dec cloth gilt, t.e.g., upper jnt just cracking.
          (Hollett) £120 [≈ $214]

Wiener, Norbert
- Cybernetics or Control and Communication in the Animal and the Machine. New York: The Technology Press, (1948). 1st edn. Orig bndg.   *(Polyanthos)* $150 [≈ £84]
- Cybernetics, or Control and Communication in the Animal and the Machine. New York: John Wiley, (948) 1949. 1st edn, 5th printing. 12mo. 194 pp. Orig cloth.
          (Schoen) $45 [≈ £25]
- Extrapolation, Interpolation, and Smoothing of Stationary Time Series, with Engineering Applications. Cambridge: MIT; New York: John Wiley, 1949. 1st public edn. 12mo. ix, 163 pp. Lib pocket. Orig bndg.
          (Schoen) $125 [≈ £70]
- The Fourier Integral and Certain of its Applications. New York: Dover, 1951. 1st

US edn. 12mo. xi,210 pp. Lib pocket. Orig cloth. *(Schoen)* **$45 [≈ £25]**

Wildman, Thomas
- A Treatise on the Management of Bees ... London: for the author, & sold by T. Cadell, 1768. 1st edn. 4to. xx,169 pp. 3 fldg plates. Sl offsetting onto plates. Near contemp qtr calf & paper bds, crnrs trifle rubbed.
(Gough) **£250 [≈ $445]**
- A Treatise on the Management of Bees ... added the Natural History of Wasps and Hornets. London: 1768. 1st edn. 4to. xx, 169, [7] pp. 3 fldg plates (some offsetting). Contemp calf, rebacked.
(Wheldon & Wesley) **£200 [≈ $356]**
- A Treatise on the Management of Bees. London: 1770. 2nd edn. 8vo. xx,311, [8],16 pp. 3 plates. New half calf antique style.
(Wheldon & Wesley) **£85 [≈ $151]**
- A Treatise on the Management of Bees ... London: 1778. 3rd edn. xx,325,16 pp. 3 fldg plates. Occas foxing. Mod leather backed bds.
(Whitehart) **£140 [≈ $249]**

Wilkins, John
- The Mathematical and Philosophical Works ... London: for J. Nicholson ..., 1708. 1st coll edn. 8vo. viii,[vi],135, [iii],139-274, [x],90, [viii],184 pp. Plate, num w'cuts in text. Late 19th c calf, rubbed. *(Finch)* **£425 [≈ $757]**
- The Mathematical and Philosophical Works ... prefixed the Author's Life ... London: for J. Nicholson ..., 1708. 1st coll edn. 8vo. Port, 1 plate, num w'cuts in text. Occas sl foxing. Contemp panelled calf, jnts sl rubbed.
(Heritage) **$850 [≈ £478]**
- The Mathematical and Philosophical Works ... To which is prefixed the Author's Life, and an Account of his Works. London: 1802. 2 vols. 8vo. W'cuts. Sl foxing. Polished calf, spines worn, front bds detached.
(Weiner) **£125 [≈ $223]**
- Mercury, or the Secret and Swift Messenger; shewing how a Man may with Privacy and Speed communicate his Thoughts to a Friend at any Distance. London: 1641. 1st edn. 8vo. xiv,170 pp. Lacks A1 (blank?). Contemp sheep, backstrip relaid. Wing W.2202.
(Frew Mackenzie) **£400 [≈ $712]**

Wilkinson, Henry
- Engines of War: or, Historical and Experimental Observations on Ancient and Modern Warlike Machines and Implements ... London: 1841. 8vo. viii,268 pp. Sev lib blind stamps. Half calf, dec spine, upper jnt cracked, spine chipped, extrs sl rubbed.
(Francis Edwards) **£60 [≈ $107]**

Wilkinson, S.J.
- The British Tortrices. London: 1859. 8vo. 4 plates. Minor foxing. Cloth.
(Wheldon & Wesley) **£20 [≈ $36]**

Wilks, S. & Moxon, W.
- Lectures on Pathological Anatomy. London: 1889. 3rd edn. xx,672 pp. Cloth backed bds, sl worn. *(Whitehart)* **£25 [≈ $45]**

Willcocks, William
- Egyptian Irrigation. London: Spon, 1899. 2nd edn. xxvii,485,[34 advt] pp. Fldg maps, plates. Minor wear. *(McBlain)* **$125 [≈ £70]**

Willey, A.
- Zoological Results based on Material from New Britain, New Guinea, Loyalty Islands and elsewhere, collected 1895-97. London: 1898-1902. 6 parts. 4to. 830 pp. Map, 83 plates, text figs. Orig bds.
(Wheldon & Wesley) **£150 [≈ $267]**

Willi, Charles
- The Face and its Improvement by Aesthetic Plastic Surgery. London: 1949. 1st edn. 108 pp. Plates. Orig bndg. *(Fye)* **£150 [≈ £84]**

Williams, B.S.
- Choice Stove and Greenhouse Flowering Plants. Choice Stove and Greenhouse Ornamental-Leaved Plants. London: 1873-76. 2nd edn. 2 vols. 8vo. Num plates. Cloth, trifle worn, spines faded.
(Wheldon & Wesley) **£30 [≈ $53]**
- The Orchid Grower's Manual. London: 1894. 7th edn. Roy 8vo. xix,796 pp. Ca 300 ills. Endpapers sl browned. Orig dec cloth, trifle used. *(Wheldon & Wesley)* **£80 [≈ $142]**

Williams, Blanche
- Clara Barton, Daughter of Destiny. Phila: 1941. 1st edn. 468 pp. Orig bndg.
(Fye) **$40 [≈ £22]**

Williams, Butler
- Practical Geodesy: comprising Chain Surveying and the Use of Surveying Instruments ... London: 1842. 1st edn. 8vo. [iv],xvi, 273,[3 blank] pp. Errata slip. Fldg litho frontis (damp stained), fldg cold plate, text ills. Some marks & stamps. Orig cloth, sl worn. *(Bow Windows)* **£35 [≈ $62]**

Williams, C.B.
- The Migration of Butterflies. London: Oliver & Boyd, 1930. 8vo. xi,473 pp. 71 text figs. Cloth. *(Egglishaw)* **£26 [≈ $46]**

Williams, C.J.B.
- Principles of Medicine ... London: 1843. xxxvi, 390 pp. Orig cloth, rear hinge sl cracked.   *(Whitehart)* **£90 [≈ $160]**
- Principles of Medicine. An Elementary View of the Causes, Nature, Treatment, Diagnosis, and Prognosis of Diseases ... A New American from the Third London Edition. Phila: 1857. 8vo. 496 pp. Sheep, rubbed.
          (Goodrich) **$95 [≈ £53]**

Williams, C.W.
- A Speech on the Improvement of the Shannon ... giving a Comparative View of the Navigation of the Rideau Canal, in Canada, and the River Shannon ... London: 1835. 8vo. viii, (5-79) pp. Fldg map (sl cropped, split at fold). New card cvrs. *(Weiner)* **£65 [≈ $116]**

Williams, Frederick S.
- Our Iron Roads: Their History, Construction, and Administration. London: 1883. 2nd edn, rvsd. 8vo. xvi,514,[6] pp. Frontis, title vignette, text ills. Minor sl foxing. Orig gilt dec blue cloth, a.e.g.
          (Bow Windows) **£75 [≈ $134]**
- Our Iron Roads: Their History, Construction and Administration. London: 1885. 7th edn. 8vo. xvi,520 pp. Frontis, addtnl illust title, num ills. Minor browning. Mod buckram, orig spine & upper bd laid down.
          (Francis Edwards) **£25 [≈ $45]**

Williams, G.F.
- The Diamond Mines of South Africa. New York: 1906. 2 vols. Roy 8vo. xvii,359; xv,353 pp. 15 maps (4 cold), 28 plates (3 cold), num text ills. Rec half mor, largely unopened.
          (Henly) **£210 [≈ $374]**

Williams, J. Whitridge
- A Sketch of the History of Obstetrics in the United States up to 1860. Baltimore: 1903. 1st sep printing. 8vo. 55 pp. Orig bds.
          (Goodrich) **$75 [≈ £42]**

Williams, L.P.
- Michael Faraday. A Biography. London: 1965. xvi,531 pp. Frontis port, 18 dble sided plates, text figs. Lib stamps on title. Orig bndg. Dw. *(Whitehart)* **£35 [≈ $62]**

Williams, T.I.
- Howard Florey. Penicillin and After. Oxford: 1984. xvi,404 pp. Frontis port. Orig bndg.
          (Whitehart) **£18 [≈ $32]**

Williams, William Mattieu
- A Vindication of Phrenology. London: 1894.

1st edn. 8vo. xxii,428 pp. 9 plates, 44 ills. Orig cloth.   *(Fenning)* **£35 [≈ $62]**

Williamson, R.T.
- Diseases of the Spinal Cord. Oxford: 1908. xi, 432 pp. 7 plates, 183 text figs. 3 lib stamps. Orig cloth, spine sl marked.
          (Whitehart) **£25 [≈ $45]**

Willich, A.F.M.
- Lectures on Diet and Regimen: being a Systematic Enquiry into the most Rational Means of preserving Health and prolonging Life ... Second Edition, Improved and Enlarged. London: 1779. 8vo. 708 pp. Contemp calf, hd of spine sl worn.
          (Robertshaw) **£95 [≈ $169]**

Willis, Robert
- Servetus and Calvin: A Study of an Important Epoch in the Early History of the Reformation. London: 1877. 1st edn. 541 pp. Orig bndg.   *(Fye)* **$150 [≈ £84]**
- William Harvey: A History of the Discovery of the Circulation of the Blood. London: 1878. 1st edn. 350 pp. Lacks port. Orig bndg, minor tear hd of spine. Author's family inscrptn.   *(Fye)* **$250 [≈ £140]**

Willmott, E.
- The Genus Rosa. London: 1911-14. 2 vols. Imperial 4to. 132 chromolitho plates. A few tissue guards missing. Green qtr mor, the 25 orig wraps bound in at end.
          (Spelman) **£1,800 [≈ $3,204]**

Willoughby, Francis
- The Ornithology of Francis Willughby, In Three Books ... London: John Martin, 1678. 1st edn. Folio. x,448 pp. 78 plates of birds. 2 plates of traps in facs. Sm marg tear 1 plate. Contemp calf, rebacked.
          (Gough) **£595 [≈ $1,059]**

Willoughby, Robert
- Practical Observations upon Woods. Jersey: ptd by R. Payn, 1840. 12mo. 13 pp. Ink crrctns, cropped MS side notes. Disbound.
          (Jarndyce) **£25 [≈ $45]**

Wilson, A.
- The Illustrated Natural History, being a Systematic Arrangement of Descriptive Zoology. Edited by James Wylde. London: London Printing & Publishing, (1889). 4to. 847 pp. 36 cold plates, 2236 engvs. Half leather, gilt dec spine.
          (Egglishaw) **£75 [≈ $134]**

Wilson, A.P.
- An Essay on the Nature of Fever. Being an Attempt to Ascertain the Principles of Treatment. London: 1807. iv,210 pp. Half leather antique. *(Whitehart)* **£90 [≈ $160]**

Wilson, Albert
- The Flora of Westmorland ... Arbroath: privately printed, 1938. 8vo. 413 pp. Fldg map in pocket, 37 ills. Orig cloth gilt, trifle marked. *(Hollett)* **£75 [≈ $134]**

Wilson, Benjamin, & others
- Observations upon Lightning, and the Method of securing Buildings from its Effects, in a Letter to Sir Charles Frederick ... London: Lockyer Davis, 1773. 4to. [8],68 pp. Orig wraps, uncut, upper wrapper loose.
  (C.R. Johnson) **£325 [≈ $579]**

Wilson, E.H.
- The Conifers and Taxads of Japan. Cambridge, Mass.: Arnold Arboretum, 1916. 4to. xii,91 pp. 59 plates. Straight grain half mor. *(Wheldon & Wesley)* **£100 [≈ $178]**

Wilson, E.H. & Rehder, A.
- A Monograph of Azaleas, Rhododendron Subgenus Anthodendron. Cambridge, Mass.: Arnold Arboretum, 1921. 8vo. ix,219 pp. Sl foxing at ends. Mod half mor, uncut.
  (Wheldon & Wesley) **£100 [≈ $178]**

Wilson, Erasmus
- The Eastern, or Turkish Bath; with its History, Revival in Britain, and Application to the Purposes of Health ... New York: Miller, Wood, 1867. 8vo. 72 pp. W'engvd ill. Orig ptd wraps, spine sl stained.
  (Burmester) **£85 [≈ $151]**
- An Inquiry into the Relative Frequency, the Duration, and Cause of Diseases of the Skin. London: 1864. 8vo. 80 pp. Disbound.
  (Weiner) **£25 [≈ $45]**
- On Diseases of the Skin. Third American from the Third London Edition. Phila: Blanchard & Lea, 1852. Atlas 4th edn. 2 vols (text & plates). Half-title, xxxii-483, [32 advt] pp. 19 plates (12 cold). Plates damp stained. Later cloth. *(Goodrich)* **$125 [≈ £70]**

Wilson, Fred. J.F. & Grey, Douglas
- A Practical Treatise upon Modern Printing Machinery and Letterpress Printing. London: 1888. 8vo. vii,455,[24 advt] pp. Ills. Orig dec cloth, sl soiled.
  (Weiner) **£75 [≈ $134]**

Wilson, George
- The Life of the Hon. Henry Cavendish, including Abstracts of his more important Scientific Papers ... London: Cavendish Society, 1851. 1st edn. 8vo. xiv,478 pp. Frontis port, 2 w'engvs. Contemp prize calf gilt, hd of spine reprd. *(Claude Cox)* **£25 [≈ $45]**

Wilson, J.A.
- Memoir of George Wilson, M.D., F.R.S.E. Edinburgh: 1860. xii,536 pp. Frontis port (offset). Occas sl foxing. Orig cloth, sl stained, spine faded. *(Whitehart)* **£25 [≈ $45]**

Wilson, James
- The Water-Cure; its Principles and Practice. A Guide in the Preservation of Health, and Cure of Chronic Disease ... London: Trubner, 1857. 3rd edn. Frontis, ills. Orig cloth, faded. *(Jarndyce)* **£25 [≈ $45]**

Wilson, James C.
- A Treatise on the Continued Fevers. With an Introduction by J.M. da Costa. New York: Wood Library, 1881. 8vo. xviii,365 pp. Orig bndg. *(Goodrich)* **$65 [≈ £37]**

Wilson, John Charles
- Television Engineering. London: Pitman, 1937. 1st edn. 8vo. 492 pp. Fldg tables, ills. Orig cloth gilt, 2 tiny tears hd of spine.
  (Schoen) **$55 [≈ £31]**

Wilson, O.S.
- The Larvae of the British Lepidoptera and their Food Plants. London: Reeve, 1880. 4to. xxix, 367 pp. 40 cold plates. Orig cloth.
  (Egglishaw) **£150 [≈ $267]**
- The Larvae of the British Lepidoptera and their Food Plants. London: 1880. Roy 8vo. xxix, 367 pp. 40 cold plates. Sm stamp on endpaper.
  (Wheldon & Wesley) **£100 [≈ $178]**

Wilson, William
- Elements of Navigation: or the Practical Rules of the Art, plainly laid down ... Edinburgh: for the author ..., 1773. 1st edn. Lge 8vo. xvi,510 pp. Errata leaf pasted inside upper cvr. 14 fldg plates. Lacks half-title. Some signs of use. Contemp sheep, sl worn.
  (Burmester) **£150 [≈ $267]**

Wilson, William Rae
- Records of a Route through France and Italy; with Sketches of Catholicism. London: for Longman ..., 1835. 1st edn. 8vo. 4 uncold aquatint plates (sl stain in 2 crnrs). Orig cloth.
  (Ximenes) **$225 [≈ £126]**

Wilton, G.W.
- Fingerprints: History, Law and Romance. London: 1938. xix,317 pp. 2 ports, 8 plates. Orig bndg.   *(Whitehart)* **£25 [≈ $45]**

Wing, Vincent & John
- Geodaetes Practicus Redivivus. The Art of Surveying ... Now much augmented and Improv'd ... London: Matthews for Churchill, 1700. Folio. [viii],384, 134,[iv] pp. 6 plates. Occas sl marks to text. Contemp sheep, rebacked. Wing W.2991.
          (Vanbrugh) **£455 [≈ $810]**

Wingate, Edmund
- Mr. Wingate's Arithmetick ... The Seventh Edition, very much enlarged ... revised ... By John Kersey ... London: sold by J. Williams, 1678. 8vo. [xii],544 pp. Contemp calf, gilt dec spine, minor wear to extrs, sm splits in jnts. Wing W.3001.   *(Clark)* **£270 [≈ $481]**

Wingrove, Benjamin
- Remarks on a Bill now before Parliament ... regulating Turnpike Roads: in which are introduced Strictures on the Opinions of Mr. M'Adam ... Bath: 1821. 8vo. 35 pp. Mod bds, leather label.   *(Weiner)* **£75 [≈ $134]**

Winslow, Forbes Benignus
- On the Obscure Diseases of the Brain, and Disorders of the Mind. London: John Churchill, 1868. 4th edn, rvsd. 8vo. xxii,616 pp. Orig cloth, spine ends frayed.
          (David White) **£38 [≈ $68]**

Winslow, J.B.
- An Anatomical Exposition of the Structure of the Human Body. Translated from the French Original by G. Douglas. Edinburgh: 1772. 6th edn. 2 vols. xxxii,428; 470 pp. 4 engvs. Some ink scribbles on vol 2 title. Old calf, rather worn & torn in places.
          (Whitehart) **£150 [≈ $267]**

Winslow, Lyttleton Stewart Forbes
- Mad Humanity: Its Forms Apparent and Obscure. London: C.A. Pearson, 1898. 1st edn. xviii, [2],451 pp. Plates, ills. Orig dec cloth, somewhat worn. *(Caius)* **$115 [≈ £65]**

Wise, T.A.
- Commentary on the Hindu System of Medicine. Calcutta: Thacker, 1845. 8vo. xx, 431 pp. 2 plates. Contemp qtr calf.
          (Goodrich) **$395 [≈ £222]**

Wistar, Caspar
- A System of Anatomy ... Phila: Dobson,

1817. 2nd Amer edn. 2 vols. 8vo. 13 plates. Text foxed. Orig calf, rubbed, jnts cracked.
          (Goodrich) **$125 [≈ £70]**

Witham, Henry T.M.
- The Internal Structure of Fossil Vegetables found in the Carboniferous and Oolitic Deposits of Great Britain. Edinburgh: 1833. 4to. 84 pp. 16 plates (most cold). Orig half roan & ptd bds, sl marked.
          (Weiner) **£150 [≈ $267]**

Witherby, H.F., & others
- Handbook of British Birds. London: 1946. 5 vols. 8vo. 157 cold & other plates. Cloth.
          (Wheldon & Wesley) **£90 [≈ $160]**
- The Handbook of British Birds. London: Witherby, 1947. 4th impression. 5 vols. Lge 8vo. 157 plates, text figs, maps. Orig cloth.
          (Carol Howard) **£80 [≈ $142]**

Withering, W.
- An Account of the Foxglove and some of its Medical Uses (Birmingham 1785). Classics of Medicine Library: 1979. xi,207 pp. Fldg cold plate. Leather gilt, a.e.g.
          (Whitehart) **£75 [≈ $134]**
- An Arrangement of British Plants. London: 1830. 7th edn. 4 vols. 8vo. 35 plates. Some foxing. Calf, jnts sl weak.
          (Wheldon & Wesley) **£45 [≈ $80]**
- A Systematic Arrangement of British Plants. Edited by W. MacGillivray. London: 1841. 5th edn. 12mo. 414 pp. 10 plates (1 cold). Buckram. *(Wheldon & Wesley)* **£18 [≈ $32]**

Withers, Thomas
- Observations on Chronic Weakness. York: Ward, 1777. 8vo. ix,[1],169 pp. Rec contemp style bds.   *(Goodrich)* **$165 [≈ £93]**
- Observations on the Abuse of Medicine. London: 1775. 1st edn. x,356 pp. Title dusty, occas foxing. Three qtr calf & mrbld bds.
          (Whitehart) **£240 [≈ $427]**

Withers, W.
- The Acacia Tree, Robinia pseudo-acacia, its Growth, Qualities and Uses; with Observations on Planting, Manuring and Pruning. London: 1842. 8vo. xxxii,411, *363-393 pp. Orig cloth, recased.
          (Wheldon & Wesley) **£50 [≈ $89]**

Withington, Edward T.
- Medical History from the Earliest Times. A Popular History of the Healing Art. London: Scientific Press, 1894. 8vo. 424 pp. Lib stamps. Later cloth. *(Goodrich)* **$95 [≈ £53]**

Wittels, Fritz
- Sigmund Freud. His Personality, His Teaching & His School ... London: Allen & Unwin, [1924]. 1st edn in English. 287,[1] pp. Frontis port. Orig cloth.
(Caius) **$75 [≈ £42]**

Wittstein, G.C.
- An Explanation of Chemical and Pharmaceutical Processes, with the Methods of Testing the Purity of the Preparations ... London: 1853. Sm 8vo. [xiii],624 pp. Some figs. Cloth, faded & marked, spine reprd.
(Whitehart) **£18 [≈ $32]**

Wodarch, C.
- Wodarch's Introduction to the Study of Conchology ... Second Edition Revised and considerably Enlarged by J. Mawe. London: Longman, 1822. Sm 8vo. xv,152 pp. Hand cold frontis, 6 hand cold litho plates. New bds.
(Egglishaw) **£70 [≈ $125]**

Wodiska, J.
- A Book of Precious Stones ... Second Edition revised. New York & London: (1909). 8vo. xvi,365,[1 blank, 2 advt] pp. Num ills inc 4 cold plates. Orig cloth.
(Bow Windows) **£40 [≈ $71]**

Woglom, Gilbert Totten
- Parakites: a Treatise on the Making and Flying of Tailless Kites for Scientific Purposes and for Recreation. New York: 1896. 4to. xv,91 pp. Plates, ills. Orig pict cloth, sl soiled. Author's pres inscrptn.
(Weiner) **£85 [≈ $151]**

Woldman, Norman E. & Gibbons, Robert C.
- Machinability and Machining of Metals. New York: McGraw Hill, 1951. 1st edn. 8vo. 518 pp. Num ills. Lib pocket. Orig bndg.
(Schoen) **$65 [≈ £37]**

Wolf, Abraham
- A History of Science, Technology, and Philosophy in the 16th & 17th Centuries. New York: Macmillan, 1939. 1st edn, Amer issue. Lge 8vo. 63 plates. Orig cloth.
(Gach) **$60 [≈ £34]**

Wolf, Heinrich
- The Practice of Physical Medicine. Chicago: 1947. 1st edn. 322 pp. Orig bndg.
(Fye) **$50 [≈ £28]**

Wolf, S. & Wolff, H.G.
- Human Gastric Function. London: (1943)

1944. xv,195 pp. Cold frontis, 42 figs. Lacks front endpaper. Orig cloth, sl marked.
(Whitehart) **£18 [≈ $32]**

Wolfenden, R.N.
- Scientific and Biological Researches in the North Atlantic. London: [ca 1908]. 4to. v,234 pp. Fldg map, 7 plates, tables, text figs. Cloth.
(Henly) **£24 [≈ $43]**

Wollaston, T.V.
- Catalogue of Coleopterous Insects of Madeira. London: BM, 1857. 8vo. xvi,234 pp. Cloth, trifle used.
(Wheldon & Wesley) **£40 [≈ $71]**
- Catalogue of the Coleopterous Insects of the Canaries. London: BM, 1864. 8vo. xiii,648 pp. Cloth, crnrs bumped.
(Wheldon & Wesley) **£65 [≈ $116]**

Wolley-Dodd, A.H.
- Flora of Sussex. Hastings: 1937. 1st edn. 8vo. lxxiii,571 pp. 2 maps (1 in pocket), 6 plates. Cloth.
(Henly) **£36 [≈ $64]**

Wood, A.
- Thomas Young. Natural Philosopher 1773-1829. Completed by Frank Oldham. Cambridge: 1954. 1st edn. xx,355 pp. Frontis, 3 plates, 24 text ills. Orig bndg.
(Whitehart) **£35 [≈ $62]**

Wood, Casey A.
- An Introduction to the Literature of Vertebrate Zoology ... London: Humphrey Milford, 1931. 1st edn. Thick 4to. xix, 643, [1] pp. Orig cloth. prospectus loosely inserted.
(Oak Knoll) **$450 [≈ £253]**
- An Introduction to the Literature of Vertebrate Zoology (Oxford 1931). Hildesheim: 1974. Roy 8vo. xix,643 pp. Orig cloth.
(Wheldon & Wesley) **£55 [≈ $98]**

Wood, James
- The Elements of Algebra designed for the Use of Students in the University ... Eighth Edition. Cambridge: J. Smith, 1825. 8vo. Contemp diced calf, mor label sl chipped.
(Waterfield's) **£50 [≈ $89]**
- The Principles of Mechanics ... Eighth Edition. [Bound with] The Elements of Algebra ... Tenth Edition. Cambridge: 1830-35. 2 vols in one. 8vo. Pencil notes. Contemp half calf. *(Fenning)* **£32.50 [≈ $59]**

Wood, John
- A Supplement to the New Compendious Treatise of Farriery ... London: for the author ..., 1758. 1st edn. 8vo. [ii],88 pp. Contemp

sprinkled calf, gilt spine, labels, hd of spine chipped, extrs rubbed. *(Finch)* **£200 [≈ $356]**

Wood, John George

- The Common Objects of the Country. London: Routledge, 1858. 1st edn. Fcap 8vo. iv, 182, [vi] pp. Plates, text ills. Orig elab gilt cloth, v sl rubbed, sl shaken.
  (Ash) **£50 [≈ $89]**
- The Common Objects of the Sea Shore. London: Routledge, 1857. 1st edn. Sm 8vo. 204 pp. 12 cold plates. Orig gilt dec cloth, a.e.g., sl shaken. *(Carol Howard)* **£20 [≈ $36]**
- Homes Without Hands being a Description of the Habitations of Animals. London: 1866. 8vo. xix,632 pp. Calf gilt.
  (Egglishaw) **£26 [≈ $46]**
- Homes Without Hands. London: Longmans, Green, 1868. 632 pp. Engvs. Endpapers sl foxed. Orig gilt dec green calf, a.e.g., sl rubbed. *(Carol Howard)* **£29 [≈ $52]**
- Homes Without Hands, being a Description of the Habitations of Animals ... London: 1884. New edn. 8vo. xix,632 pp. Num ills. Half calf gilt.
  (Wheldon & Wesley) **£25 [≈ $45]**
- Natural History. London: [ca 1852]. 8vo. xx, 444 pp. Cold frontis, num text ills by William Harvey. Blue calf gilt, crnrs sl rubbed.
  (Francis Edwards) **£35 [≈ $62]**

Wood, T.W.

- Curiosities of Entomology. 64 pp. 10 cold plates. [Bound with] Curiosities of Ornithology. 64 pp. 10 cold plates. London: Groombridge, [1871]. 2 vols in one. 8vo. Minor foxing. Orig cloth gilt, spine faded. Anon. *(Wheldon & Wesley)* **£60 [≈ $107]**

Wood, William

- General Conchology: or, a Description of Shells, arranged according to the Linnean System. Volume 1 [all published]. London: 1815. 8vo. [iv],7,lxi,246 pp. 60 hand cold plates (1-59,4*). Half mor gilt.
  (Wheldon & Wesley) **£300 [≈ $534]**
- Index Entomologicus or a Complete Illustrated Catalogue ... of the Lepidopterous Insects of Great Britain. New and revised Edition, with Supplement by J.O. Westwood. London: 1854. Roy 8vo. viii, 21,ii pp. 59 hand cold plates. Half mor gilt.
  (Wheldon & Wesley) **£180 [≈ $320]**
- Index Entomologicus; or a Complete Illustrated Catalogue ... of the Lepidopterous Insects of Great Britain. New and revised Edition with Supplement by J.O. Westwood. London: Willis, 1854. Roy 8vo. viii, 298 pp. 59 hand cold plates. Half mor gilt.

(Egglishaw) **£170 [≈ $303]**

- Index Testaceologicus, or a Catalogue of Shells British and Foreign, arranged according to the Linnean System. London: for W. Wood, 1818. 1st edn. 8vo. viii,190 pp. 8 hand cold plates. New cloth.
  (Egglishaw) **£60 [≈ $107]**
- Index Testaceologicus ... London: 1825. xxxiv, 188,[2] pp. 38 hand cold plates. [With] Supplement to the Index Testaceologicus. London: 1828. v,59 pp. 8 hand cold plates. 2 vols. Orig cloth gilt.
  (Egglishaw) **£240 [≈ $427]**
- Index Testaceologicus: or a Catalogue of Shells, British and Foreign. New and entirely revised edition by S. Hanley. London: 1856. Roy 8vo. xx,234 pp. 46 hand cold plates. Half mor gilt. *(Wheldon & Wesley)* **£200 [≈ $356]**
- Zoography; or, the Beauties of Nature displayed in Select Descriptions from the Animal, and Vegetable, with Additions from the Mineral Kingdom, systematically arranged. London: 1807. 3 vols. 8vo. 60 plates by W. Daniell. Contemp calf, reprd.
  (Wheldon & Wesley) **£170 [≈ $303]**

Woodcock, H.B.D. & Stearn, W.T.

- Lilies of the World, their Cultivation and Classification. London: Country Life, 1950. 8vo. 431 pp. Ills. Name. Orig cloth. Dw.
  (Egglishaw) **£44 [≈ $78]**

Woodcroft, B.

- Brief Biographies of Inventors of Machines for the Manufacture of Textile Fabrics. London: 1863. xv,51 pp. Orig bndg.
  (Whitehart) **£25 [≈ $45]**

Woodforde, J.

- A Catalogue of the Indigenous Phenogamic Plants, growing in the Neighbourhood of Edinburgh ... Edinburgh: 1824. 12mo. xi,86 pp. Few lib stamps. Sl foxing. Orig bds, uncut, trifle worn, lacks backstrip.
  (Wheldon & Wesley) **£40 [≈ $71]**

Woodhouse, L.G.O.

- The Butterfly Fauna of Ceylon. Colombo: 1950. 2nd edn, abridged. 4to. xvi,133 pp. Map, 37 cold & 12 plain plates. Orig cloth, rebacked. *(Wheldon & Wesley)* **£50 [≈ $89]**
- The Butterfly Fauna of Ceylon. Second Complete Edition. Colombo: The Colombo Apothecaries' Co., [ca 1950]. Lge 4to. xxxii, 232 pp. Map, cold frontis, 55 plates (36 cold), text ills. Orig cloth. *(Karmiole)* **$175 [≈ £98]**
- The Butterfly Fauna of Ceylon. Colombo: 1950. 2nd (abridged) edn. 4to. xvi,133 pp. Map, 37 cold & 12 plain plates. Orig cloth,

crnr bumped.
(Wheldon & Wesley) **£50 [≈ $89]**

Woods, Henry, & others
- Geology of the Tertiary and Quaternary Periods in the North-West Part of Peru. London: 1922. 8vo. xxii,434 pp. 11 fldg maps, sections & panoramas, 26 plates, 150 ills. Sm repr 1 map. Orig cloth, sl used.
(Weiner) **£75 [≈ $134]**

Woodward, A.S.
- Catalogue of the Fossil Fishes in the British Museum. London: 1899-1901. 4 vols. 8vo. 70 litho plates, 138 w'cuts. Lib stamp on titles. Orig cloth.   *(Egglishaw)* **£160 [≈ $285]**

Woodward, Henry
- A Catalogue of British Fossil Crustacea, with their Synonyms ... London: B.M., 1877. 1st edn. 8vo. xii,155 pp. 2 lib stamps. Orig cloth.
(Bow Windows) **£40 [≈ $71]**

Woodward, Horace Bolingbroke
- The Geology of England and Wales: a Concise Account of the Lithological Characters, Leading Fossils ... London: 1876. xx, 476 pp. Fldg map, 28 w'cuts in text. Orig cloth, spine sl marked..
(Whitehart) **£18 [≈ $32]**
- The Geology of England and Wales: with Notes on the Physical Features of the Country. London: 1887. 2nd edn. xv,670 pp. Frontis, map (sl torn at creases), 101 ills. Orig cloth, dusty, sl worn, inner hinges sl cracked.
(Whitehart) **£25 [≈ $45]**

Woodward, John
- An Essay towards a Natural History of the Earth and Terrestrial Bodies, especially Minerals. London: 1702. 2nd edn. 8vo. xiv,277 pp. Contemp calf.
(Wheldon & Wesley) **£120 [≈ $214]**

Woodward, J.J., & others
- The Medical and Surgical History of the War of the Rebellion, 1861-1865. Washington: 1870-88. Mixed set with some 2nd issue vols. 6 vols. Lge 4to. Num photo ills. Some lib marks. Orig cloth, recased, some backstrips laid down.   *(Goodrich)* **$1,500 [≈ £843]**

Woodward, S.P.
- A Manual of the Mollusca, or Rudimentary Treatise of Recent and Fossil Shells. London: Weale, 1851-56. 1st edn. Parts 1-3. Cr 8vo. xvi, 486,24 pp. Fldg map, 25 plates, text figs. Orig cloth, sm piece missing from hd of spine.
(Egglishaw) **£24 [≈ $43]**

Woolnath, Thomas
- The Study of the Human Face. London: 1865. 1st edn. 260 pp. 26 steel engvd plates. Orig bndg.   *(Fye)* **$250 [≈ £140]**

Wooster, D.
- Alpine Plants: Figures and Descriptions of some of the most striking and beautiful of the Alpine Flowers. London: 1874. 2nd edn of vol 1. 2 vols. Roy 8vo. 108 cold plates. Endpapers v sl foxed, 1 or 2 spots. Half mor.
(Wheldon & Wesley) **£240 [≈ $427]**

Wootton, A.C.
- Chronicles of Pharmacy. London: 1910. 1st edn. 2 vols. 8vo. Num ills. Orig cloth, spines faded.   *(Bow Windows)* **£110 [≈ $196]**

Worlidge, John
- Systema Agriculturae; the Mystery of Husbandry ... added Kalendarium Rusticum ... Dictionarium Rusticum ... Second Edition ... Additions ... London: 1675. Folio. [32], 324, [4] pp. Engvd title, with explanatory leaf. Sl marg worm. Contemp calf, minor reprs. Anon.   *(Spelman)* **£480 [≈ $854]**
- Systema Agriculturae; the Mystery of Husbandry ... Fourth Edition ... Additions ... London: for Thomas Dring, 1687. Folio. xxiv, 326,[vi] pp. Engvd title, & Explanation, plate. Contemp calf, jnts v sl cracked.
(Gough) **£395 [≈ $703]**
- Systema Agriculturae; the Mystery of Husbandry Discovered ... By J.W. London: Nath. Rolls, 1697. 4th edn. Folio. [xxviii], 308, [iv],313-326, [327-332] pp. Addtnl engvd title, with explanation leaf. 1 plate. Contemp panelled calf, hinges cracked but firm. Wing W.3602.   *(Vanbrugh)* **£545 [≈ $970]**

Worster, Benjamin
- A Compendious and Methodical Account of the Principles of Natural Philosophy ... London: for the author ..., 1722. 1st edn. 8vo. xviii,[iv], 239,[1 advt] pp. Text diags. Some dust soiling & worm tracks in inner marg. Contemp calf, v worn, jnts cracked.
(Gaskell) **£450 [≈ $801]**
- A Compendious and Methodical Account of the Principles of Natural Philosophy ... London: for Stephen Austen, 1730. 2nd edn, rvsd. 8vo. xviii,[ii], 269,[3 advt] pp. Text diags. Some dust soiling & worm tracks in inner marg. Contemp calf, v worn, jnts cracked.   *(Gaskell)* **£300 [≈ $534]**

Worthington, A.M.
- A Study of Splashes. London: 1908. xii,129 pp. 197 ills. Orig bndg, sl rubbed.

(Whitehart) £35 [≈ $62]

Wrench, G.T.
- Lord Lister, His Life and Work. London: Fisher Unwin, 1913. 1st edn. 8vo. 384 pp. Frontis port, 3 plates. Few lib blind stamps.
(David White) £20 [≈ $36]
- Lord Lister. His Life and Work. London: 1913. 384 pp. Frontis port, 3 plates. Sm lib stamp on endpaper. Orig cloth, spine faded, crnr marked.   *(Whitehart)* £15 [≈ $27]

Wright, A.E. & Colebrook, L.
- Technique of the Teat and Capillary Glass Tube. Being a Handbook for the Medical Research Laboratory ... London: 1921. 2nd edn. xxvi,384 pp. Frontis, 3 plates, 151 text figs. Orig bndg.   *(Whitehart)* £18 [≈ $32]

Wright, Almroth
- Researches in Clinical Physiology. London: 1943. 1st edn. 163 pp. Ex-lib. Orig bndg.
(Fye) $75 [≈ £42]

Wright, G., & others (editors)
- Systemic Pathology. London: Longmans, Green, 1966. 1st edn. 2 vols. 4to. Num text figs. Cloth. Dw (sl torn).
(Savona) £40 [≈ $71]

Wright, Lewis
- The Illustrated Book of Poultry ... London: Cassell ..., [ca 1875]. 1st edn(?). 4to. viii,591, [1 blank,5 advt] pp. 50 chromolitho plates, 100 figs, num ills. Some foxing & other marks. Orig dec green cloth gilt, a.e.g.
(Bow Windows) £950 [≈ $1,691]
- Light. A Course of Experimental Optics chiefly with the Lantern. London: 1882. xxiv, 358,index pp. Cold frontis, 8 plates. Cloth, spine faded, jnts sl weak.
(Whitehart) £30 [≈ $53]
- The Microscope. A Practical Handbook. London: [1922]. 8vo. 293 pp. Cold frontis, 195 text ills. Half-title sl foxed. Orig cloth, stained.   *(Henly)* £18 [≈ $32]
- The New Book of Poultry. London: [1902]. 4to. viii,600 pp. 47 plates (30 cold). Extra plain plate of Frizzled Fowls. Half mor, trifle rubbed. *(Wheldon & Wesley)* £300 [≈ $534]

Wurtz, Adolphe C.
- An Introduction to Chemical Philosophy according to the Modern Theories, translated, by permission of the author, by William Crookes. London: Chemical News, 1867. Sm 8vo. viii, 192 pp. Orig cloth, rubbed.   *(Weiner)* £50 [≈ $89]

Wyeth, John A.
- A Text-Book on Surgery. General, Operative, and Mechanical. New York: Appleton, 1887. 777 pp. 771 text w'cuts (some cold). Orig sheep, rebacked. *(Goodrich)* $295 [≈ £166]

Wyld, Samuel
- The Practical Surveyor, or the Art of Land-Measuring made Easy ... Fifth Edition, corrected and enlarged by a Careful Hand. London: W. Johnston, 1764. 8vo. viii,191 pp. Frontis, 6 plates (1 with marg tear). Some soiling throughout. New qtr calf.
(Blackwell's) £125 [≈ $223]

Wylde, James (editor)
- The Circle of the Sciences; A Cyclopedia of Experimental, Chemical, Mathematical & Mechanical Philosophy, and Natural History ... London: [ca 1875]. 2 vols in 10 parts. 4to. 62 plates (inc 10 ports & 5 maps), num text ills. Orig cloth, sl worn.
(Bow Windows) £140 [≈ $249]

Wynter, Andrew
- The Borderlands of Insanity and other Allied Papers. London: 1875. 1st coll edn. 8vo. [2],vii, 314,[2 blank] pp. Stamp on title. Orig cloth.   *(Fenning)* £48.50 [≈ $87]

Wynter, H. & Turner, A.
- Scientific Instruments. London: Studio Vista, 1975. 239 pp. 28 cold & 270 b/w ills. Orig bndg.   *(Phillips)* £175 [≈ $312]

Y-Worth, William
- Introitus Apertus ad Artem Distillationis; or the Whole Art of Distillation Practically Stated ... London: Joh. Taylor, 1692. Only edn. 8vo. [xvi],189,[iii] pp. Frontis, 4 plates. Sl wear & marg worm. Contemp calf, crnrs worn, jnts split at ends. Wing Y.218.
(Clark) £500 [≈ $890]

Yarrell, W.
- A History of British Birds. London: Van Voorst, 1865. 2nd edn. 3 vols. 8vo. 535 w'engvs by the Thompsons after Alexander Fussell. Contemp half calf.
(Egglishaw) £68 [≈ $121]
- A History of British Fishes. London: Van Voorst, 1836. 1st edn. 2 vols. Nearly 400 w'engvs. Later half calf, extrs sl rubbed.
(Egglishaw) £65 [≈ $116]
- A History of British Fishes. London: Van Voorst, 1841. 2nd edn. 2 vols. 8vo. 500 w'engvs. Half calf. *(Egglishaw)* £75 [≈ $134]
- A History of British Fishes. Edited by Sir John Richardson. London: Van Voorst, 1859.

3rd edn. 2 vols. 8vo. Port, 522 w'engvs. Inscrptn. Orig cloth. *(Egglishaw)* £46 [≈ $82]

Yates, Frances
- The Art of Memory. London: 1966. 1st edn. Fldg chart, ills. Orig bndg.
(Deja Vu) £30 [≈ $53]
- Giordano Bruno and the Hermetic Tradition. Chicago: UP, [1964]. 1st edn. 8vo. Ills. Orig cloth. Price-clipped dustwrapper.
(Gach) $75 [≈ £42]

Yates, William & MacLean, Charles
- A View of the Science of Life; on the Principles established in the Elements of Medicine, of the late celebrated John Brown ... Phila: 1797. 232 pp. Foxing. Old bds, rebacked. *(Goodrich)* $65 [≈ £37]

Yonge, C.M.
- Oysters. London: Collins New Naturalist, 1960. 8vo. xiv,209 pp. 17 plates, 72 text figs. Sm label on endpaper. Cloth. Dw.
(Wheldon & Wesley) £45 [≈ $80]
- A Year on the Great Barrier Reef. London: (1930) 1931. Roy 8vo. xx,246 pp. Frontis, 6 maps, 69 plates, 17 diags. Cloth, somewhat spotted, spine faded.
(Wheldon & Wesley) £50 [≈ $89]

Yonge, Charlotte Mary
- The Instructive Picture Book or Lessons from the Vegetable World. By the Author of "The Heir of Redclyffe". Edinburgh: Edmonston & Douglas, 1858. Folio. 31 dble page cold plates. Sm repr 1 plate. Orig cold bds, sl worn. Anon. *(Egglishaw)* £450 [≈ $801]

Yorke, W. & Maplestone, P.A.
- The Nematode Parasites of Vertebrates. London: Churchill, 1926. 1st edn. 8vo. xi,536 pp. 307 text figs. New cloth.
(Savona) £25 [≈ $45]

Youatt, William
- Cattle; their Breeds, Management and Diseases ... London: 1867. 8vo. viii,600 pp. Num text ills. Some browning. Orig cloth, inner hinges torn.
(Bow Windows) £85 [≈ $151]
- The Horse. With a Treatise on Draught. New Edition, completely revised. London: 1846. 8vo. viii,581 pp. text figs. Calf.
(Wheldon & Wesley) £30 [≈ $53]
- The Horse. With a Treatise on Draught. Revised and Enlarged by E.N. Gabriel. London: Longman, Green ..., 1860. Lge 8vo. x,601,2 advt pp. W'cut ills. Pp 13-18 torn at top not affecting text. Orig cloth, spine sl

splitting. *(Bookline)* £45 [≈ $80]

The Young Gard'ners Director ...
- See Stevenson, H.

Young, Arthur
- The Farmer's Calendar ... London: for Richard Phillips ..., 1805. 6th edn, enlgd. Lge 8vo. xi,638,[2 advt] pp. Plate. Occas sl browning. Bds, jnts cracking, backstrip defective. *(Francis Edwards)* £150 [≈ $267]
- The Farmer's Guide in Hiring and Stocking Farms ... London: 1770. 1st edn. 2 vols. 8vo. [iv],viii, 458,[ii]; [iv],500 pp. Advt leaf in vol 1. 10 plates vol 2. Occas sl foxing. Contemp calf, gilt spines, rubbed, lacks secondary labels. Anon. *(Clark)* £250 [≈ $445]
- The Farmer's Guide in Hiring and Stocking Farms ... London: for W. Strahan ..., 1770. 1st edn. 2 vols. 8vo. Advt leaf end of vol 1. 2 fldg & 8 other engvd plates. Contemp calf, gilt spines, mor labels, fine. Anon.
(Georges) £300 [≈ $534]
- The Farmer's Letters to the People of England ... added, Sylvae; or, Occasional Tracts on Husbandry and Rural Oeconomics. London: for W. Nicoll, 1767. 1st edn. 8vo. [iv], 324 pp. Period calf, sl ink stains upper cvr, sm worm hole lower cvr. Anon.
(Rankin) £125 [≈ $223]
- The Farmer's Tour through the East of England ... By the Author of the Farmer's Letters ... London: for W. Strahan ..., 1771. 1st edn. 4 vols. 8vo. xlviii,495; [4],560; [4],483; [4],523,[4 advt] pp. Fldg table, 29 plates. Sl marg water stain. Contemp calf, rebacked. Anon. *(Claude Cox)* £275 [≈ $490]
- General View of the Agriculture of the County of Suffolk ... Third Edition. London: for Richard Phillips, 1804. 8vo. xv,432,[16 advt] pp. Fldg hand cold map, 2 fldg plates. Orig bds, uncut, fine. Anon.
(Gough) £245 [≈ $436]

Young, C.F.T.
- The Economy of Steam Power on Common Roads ... With its History and Practice in Great Britain ... and its Progress in the United States ... London: (1861). 8vo. xii,423 pp. Errata slip. Fldg frontis, plates, ills. Orig pict cloth gilt. *(Weiner)* £165 [≈ $294]

Young, David
- National Improvements upon Agriculture in Twenty-Seven Essays. Edinburgh: the author & John Bell, 1785. 403 pp. 3 plates. Contemp sheep, brown label.
(C.R. Johnson) £125 [≈ $223]

Young, E.H.
- A Bird in the Bush. London: 1936. One of 550 sgnd by author & artist, Peter Scott. 4to. viii,148 pp. 3 cold & 19 other ills. Orig cloth, front cvr sl spotted.
(Wheldon & Wesley) **£55 [≈ $98]**

Young, George
- A Geological Survey of the Yorkshire Coast ... assisted by John Bird, Artist. Second Edition, much improved and enlarged ... Whitby: 1828. Lge 4to. iv,367 pp. Subscribers. Frontis, cold map, cold plate of sections, 17 cold plates. Half calf, backstrip relaid. *(Weiner)* **£250 [≈ $445]**

Young, J.H.
- Caesarean Section: The History and Development of the Operation from Earliest Times. London: 1944. 1st edn. 254 pp. Orig bndg, sl damage to spine. *(Fye)* **$150 [≈ £84]**

Young, J.Z.
- A Model of the Brain. Being the William Withering Lectures ... 1960. Oxford: 1964. ix, 348 pp. Num ills. Orig bndg.
(Whitehart) **£15 [≈ $27]**

Young, James
- A Manual and Atlas of Orthopedic Surgery including ... Deformities. Phila: 1906. 1st edn. 4to. 942 pp. 720 ills. Orig bndg, fine.
(Fye) **$250 [≈ £140]**
- A Practical Treatise on Orthopedic Surgery. Phila: 1894. 1st edn. 446 pp. Orig bndg, front inner hinge cracked. *(Fye)* **$100 [≈ £56]**

Young, Morris N.
- Bibliography of Memory. Phila: Chilton, 1961. 1st edn. ix,[3],436 pp. Orig cloth.
(Caius) **$125 [≈ £70]**

Young, Thomas
- Elementary Illustrations of the Celestial Mechanics of Laplace. Part the First comprehending the First Book. London: Murray, 1821. 1st edn. All published. 8vo. [vi], vi, 344 pp. Text diags. Orig bds, uncut, cloth spine, paper label, crnrs & spine worn.
(Gaskell) **£200 [≈ $356]**
- An Introduction to Medical Literature, including a System of Practical Nosology ... London: 1823. 2nd edn. xxvi,660 pp. Occas foxing, lib stamp on title. Three qtr leather & watered silk, new label.
(Whitehart) **£250 [≈ $445]**
- Miscellaneous Works of the late Thomas

Young, M.D., F.R.S. Edited by G. Peacock. London: 1855. 3 vols. 15 + 3 + 5 plates. Occas lib stamps. Orig cloth, rebacked.
(Whitehart) **£250 [≈ $445]**
- Miscellaneous Works of the late Thomas Young. Edited by George Peacock. Volumes 1 and 2. London: 1855. 1st edn. 2 vols. 600; 623 pp. Rec leatherette. A further volume published later. *(Fye)* **$250 [≈ £140]**

Zeller, H.
- Wild Flowers of the Holy Land. With a Preface by H.B. Tristram. London: 1876. 2nd edn. Cr 4to. xiv pp. 54 cold plates. Sl foxing of text. Blue mor gilt, a.e.g.
(Wheldon & Wesley) **£75 [≈ $134]**
- Wild Flowers of the Holy Land. London: Nisbet, 1877. 3rd edn. Roy 8vo. 54 cold plates. New cloth, a.e.g.
(Egglishaw) **£60 [≈ $107]**

Zenneck, J.
- Wireless Telegraphy. New York: McGraw Hill, 1915. 1st edn. 8vo. 443 pp. Errata sheet. Orig bndg, worn & shaken.
(Schoen) **$60 [≈ £34]**

Zilboorg, Gregory
- A History of Medical Psychology. New York: Norton, 1941. 606 pp. Orig cloth. Dw.
(Goodrich) **$65 [≈ £37]**
- A History of Medical Psychology. New York: W.W. Norton, [1941]. 1st edn. 606 pp. Orig cloth, some wear. *(Caius)* **$100 [≈ £56]**
- Mind, Medicine, & Man ... New York: Harcourt, Brace, [1943]. vi,[2],344 pp. Orig cloth, worn. *(Caius)* **$75 [≈ £42]**

Zittel, K.A. von
- Text-Book of Palaeontology. English Edition, Revised and Enlarged by C.R.E. Eastman and A.S. Woodward. London: (1913-32) 1964. 3 vols. Roy 8vo. Cloth.
(Wheldon & Wesley) **£90 [≈ $160]**

Zworykin, Vladimir Koska
- Television; The Electronics of Image Transmission. New York: J. Wiley, 1940. 1st edn. 8vo. xi,646 pp. Ills. Orig bndg.
(Schoen) **$45 [≈ £25]**

Zworykin, Vladimir Koska, & others
- Electron Optics and the Electron Microscope. New York: Wiley, 1946. 2nd printing. 8vo. xi,766 pp. Num text figs. Cloth.
(Savona) **£25 [≈ $45]**

Catalogue Booksellers Contributing to IRBP

The booksellers who have provided catalogues during 1991 specifically for the purpose of compiling the various titles in the *IRBP* series, and from whose catalogues books have been selected, are listed below in alphabetical order of the abbreviation employed for each. This listing is therefore a complete key to the booksellers contributing to the series as a whole; only a proportion of the listed names is represented in this particular subject volume.

The majority of these booksellers issue periodic catalogues free, on request, to potential customers. Sufficient indication of the type of book handled by each bookseller can be gleaned from the individual book entries set out in the main body of this work and in the companion titles in the series.

Alphabet	=	Alphabet Bookshop, 145 Main Street West, Port Colborne, Ontario L3K 3V3, Canada (416 834 5323)
Antic Hay	=	Antic Hay Rare Books, P.O. Box 2185, Asbury Park, NJ 07712, U.S.A. (908 774 4590)
Any Amount	=	Any Amount of Books, 62 Charing Cross Road, London WC2H 0BB, England (071 240 8140)
Appelfeld	=	Appelfeld Gallery, 1372 York Avenue, New York, NY 10021, U.S.A. (212 988 7835)
Argonaut	=	Argonaut Book Shop, 786-792 Sutter Street, San Francisco, California 94109, U.S.A. (415 474 9067)
Armchair Traveller	=	The Armchair Traveller, 1 Sea View Terrace, Emsworth, Hampshire PO10 7EN, England (0243 371203)
Ars Libri	=	Ars Libri, Ltd., 560 Harrison Avenue, Boston, Massachusetts 02118, U.S.A. (617 338 5763)
Ash	=	Ash Rare Books, 25 Royal Exchange, London EC3V 3LP, England (071 626 2665)
Bates & Hindmarch	=	Bates and Hindmarch, Antiquarian Bookseller, Fishergate, Boroughbridge, North Yorkshire Y05 9AL, England (0423 324258)
Between the Covers	=	Between the Covers, 132 Kings Highway East, Haddonfield, NJ 08033, U.S.A. (609 354 7665)
Blackwell's	=	Blackwell's Rare Books, B.H. Blackwell Ltd., Fyfield Manor, Fyfield, Abingdon, Oxon OX13 5LR, England (0865 791438)
Black Sun	=	Black Sun Books, 157 East 57 Street, New York, NY 10022, U.S.A. (212 688 6622)
Blakeney	=	Adam Blakeney, Apartment 313, Butlers Wharf Building, 36 Shad Thames, London SE1 2YE, England (071 378 1197)
Book Block	=	The Book Block, 8 Loughlin Avenue, Cos Cob, Connecticut 06807, U.S.A. (203 629 2990)
Bookline	=	Bookline, 35 Farranfad Road, Downpatrick BT30 8NH, Northern Ireland (039687 712)
Bookmark	=	Bookmark, Children's Books, Fortnight, Wick Down, Broad Hinton, Swindon, Wiltshire SN4 9NR, England (0793 731693)
Bookpress	=	The Bookpress Ltd., Post Office Box KP, Williamsburg, Virginia 23187, U.S.A. (804 229 1260)
Bookworks	=	Bookworks, "Gernon Elms", Letchworth Lane, Letchworth, Hertfordshire SG6 3NF, England (0462 673189)
Bow Windows	=	Bow Windows Book Shop, 128 High Street, Lewes, East Sussex BN7 1XL, England (0273 480780)
Bromer	=	Bromer Booksellers, 607 Boylston Street, at Copley Square, Boston, MA 02116, U.S.A. (617 247 2818)

Burmester	=	James Burmester, Manor House Farmhouse, North Stoke, Bath BA1 9AT, England (0272 327265)
Chalmers Hallam	=	E. Chalmers Hallam, "Trees", 9 Post Office Lane, St. Ives, Ringwood, Hampshire BH24 2PG, England (0425 470060)
Chapel Hill	=	Chapel Hill Rare Books, P.O. Box 456, Carrboro, NC 27510, U.S.A. (919 929 8351)
Clark	=	Robert Clark, 6a King Street, Jericho, Oxford OX2 6DF, England (0865 52154)
Clearwater	=	Clearwater Books, 19 Matlock Road, Ferndown, Wimborne, Dorset BH22 8QT, England (0202 893263)
Claude Cox	=	Claude Cox, The White House, Kelsale, Saxmundham, Suffolk IP17 2PQ, England (0728 602786)
Dalian	=	Dalian Books, David P. Williams, 81 Albion Drive, London Fields, London E8 4LT, England (071 249 1587)
de Burca	=	de Burca Rare Books, "Cloonagashel", 27 Priory Drive, Blackrock, Co. Dublin, Eire (01 2882159)
Deja Vu	=	Deja Vu, 31 Trafalgar Street, Brighton BN1 4ED, England (0273 600400)
Dermont	=	Joseph A. Dermont, 13 Arthur Street, P.O. Box 654, Onset, MA 02558, U.S.A. (508 295 4760)
D & D Galleries	=	D & D Galleries, Box 8413, Somerville, New Jersey 08876, U.S.A. (201 874 3162)
Edrich	=	I.D. Edrich, 17 Selsdon Road, London E11 2QF, England (081 989 9541)
Francis Edwards	=	Francis Edwards, The Old Cinema, Castle Street, Hay-on-Wye, via Hereford HR3 5DF, England (0497 820071)
Egglishaw	=	H.J. Egglishaw, Bruach Mhor, 54 West Moulin Road, Pitlochry, Perthshire PH16 5EQ, Scotland (0796 2084)
Egret	=	Egret Books, 6 Priory Place, Wells, Somerset BA5 1SP, England (0749 679312)
Ellis	=	Peter Ellis, 31 Museum Street, London WC1A 1LH, England (071 637 5862)
Europa	=	Europa Books, 15 Luttrell Avenue, Putney, London SW15 6PD, England (081 788 0312)
Fenning	=	James Fenning, 12 Glenview, Rochestown Avenue, Dun Laoghaire, County Dublin, Eire (01 2857855)
Finch	=	Simon Finch Rare Books, 10 New Bond Street, London W1Y 9PF, England (071 499 0974)
Frew Mackenzie	=	Frew Mackenzie plc, 106 Great Russell Street, London WC1B 3NA, England (071 580 2311)
Fye	=	W. Bruce Fye, Antiquarian Medical Books, 1607 North Wood Avenue, Marshfield, Wisconsin 54449, U.S.A. (1 715 384 8128)
Gach	=	John Gach Books, 5620 Waterloo Road, Columbia, Md. 21045, U.S.A. (301 465 9023)
Gaskell	=	Roger Gaskell, 17 Ramsey Road, Warboys, Cambridgeshire PE17 2RW, England (0487 823059)
Gekoski	=	R.A. Gekoski, 33B Chalcot Square, London NW1 8YA, England (071 722 9037)
Gemmary	=	The Gemmary, Inc, PO Box 816, Redondo Beach, CA 90277, U.S.A. (213 372 5969)
Georges	=	Georges, 52 Park Street, Bristol BS1 5JN, England (0272 276602)
Glyn's	=	Glyn's Books, 4 Bryn Draw Terrace, Wrexham, Clwyd LL13 7DF, Wales (0978 364473)
Goodrich	=	James Tait Goodrich, Antiquarian Books and Manuscripts, 214 Everett Place, Englewood, New Jersey 07631, U.S.A. (201 567 0199)

Gough	=	Simon Gough Books, 5 Fish Hill, Holt, Norfolk, England (0263 712650)
Green Meadow	=	Green Meadow Books, Kinoulton, Nottingham NG12 3EN, England (0949 81723)
Hannas	=	Torgrim Hannas, 29a Canon Street, Winchester, Hampshire SO23 9JJ, England (0962 862730)
Hartfield	=	Hartfield, Fine and Rare Books, 117 Dixboro Road, Ann Arbor, MI 48105, U.S.A. (313 662 6035)
Hazeldene	=	Hazeldene Bookshop, A.H. & L.G. Elliot, 61 Renshaw Street, Liverpool L1 2SJ, England (051 708 8780)
Henly	=	John Henly, Bookseller, Brooklands, Walderton, Chichester, West Sussex PO18 9EE, England (0705 631426)
Heritage	=	Heritage Book Shop, Inc., 8540 Melrose Avenue, Los Angeles, California 90069, U.S.A. (213 659 3674)
Hermitage	=	The Hermitage Bookshop, 290 Fillmore Street, Denver, Colorado 80206-5020, U.S.A. (303 388 6811)
High Latitude	=	High Latitude, P.O. Box 11254, Bainbridge Island, WA 98110, U.S.A. (206 598 3454)
Hollett	=	R.F.G. Hollett and Son, 6 Finkle Street, Sedbergh, Cumbria LA10 5BZ, England (05396 20298)
Horowitz	=	Glenn Horowitz, 141 East 44th Street, Suite 808, New York, New York 10017, U.S.A. (212 557 1381)
Hortulus	=	Hortulus, 139 Marlborough Place, Toronto, Ontario, Canada (416 920 5057)
Carol Howard	=	Carol Howard Books, Jubilee Cottage, Leck, Cowan Bridge, Carnforth, Lancashire LA6 2JD, England (05242 71072)
James	=	Marjorie James, The Old School, Oving, Chichester, West Sussex PO20 6DG, England (0243 781354)
Janus	=	Janus Books, Post Office Box 40787, Tucson, Arizona 85717, U.S.A. (602 881 8192)
Jarndyce	=	Jarndyce, Antiquarian Booksellers, 46 Great Russell Street, Bloomsbury, London WC1B 3PA, England (071 631 4220)
Jermy & Westerman	=	Jermy & Westerman, 203 Mansfield Road, Nottingham NG1 3FS, England (0602 474522)
C.R. Johnson	=	C.R. Johnson, 21 Charlton Place, London N1 8AQ, England (071 354 1077)
Karmiole	=	Kenneth Karmiole, Bookseller, Post Office Box 464, Santa Monica, California 90406, U.S.A. (213 451 4342)
Key Books	=	Key Books, P.O. Box 58097, St. Petersburg, FL 33715, U.S.A. (813 867 2931)
King	=	John K. King, P.O. Box 33363, Detroit, Michigan 48232, U.S.A. (313 961 0622)
Lame Duck Books	=	Lame Duck Books, 90 Moraine Street, Jamaica Plain, MA 02130, U.S.A. (617 522 7827)
Larkhill	=	Larkhill Books, Larkhill House, Tetbury, Gloucestershire GL8 8SY, England (0666 502343)
Levin	=	Barry R. Levin, 726 Santa Monica Blvd., Suite 201, Santa Monica, California 90401, U.S.A. (213 458 6111)
Lewton	=	L.J. Lewton, Old Station House, Freshford, Bath BA3 6EQ, England (0225 723351)
Limestone Hills	=	Limestone Hills Book Shop, P.O. Box 1125, Glen Rose, Texas 76043, U.S.A. (817 897 4991)
Lopez	=	Ken Lopez, Bookseller, 51 Huntington Road, Hadley, MA 01035, U.S.A. (413 584 2045)
McBlain	=	McBlain Books, P.O. Box 5062 Hamden, CT 06518, U.S.A. (203 281 0400)

Mac Donnell	=	Mac Donnell Rare Books, 9307 Glenlake Drive, Austin, Texas 78730, U.S.A. (512 345 4139)
Martin	=	C.J. Martin, 76 Raylawn Street, Mansfield, Nottinghamshire NG18 3ND, England (0623 20691)
Meyer Boswell	=	Meyer Boswell Books, Inc., 2141 Mission Street, San Francisco, CA 94110, U.S.A. (415 255 6400)
Ming Books	=	Ming Books (UK) Ltd., 1 Penrose Avenue, Carpenders Park, Watford, Hertfordshire WD1 5AE, England (081 428 5034)
Moorhouse	=	Hartley Moorhouse Books, 142 Petersham Road, Richmond, Surrey TW10 6UX, England (081 948 7742)
Mordida	=	Mordida Books, P.O. Box 79322, Houston, Texas 77279, U.S.A. (713 467 4280)
Northern Books	=	Northern Books, PO Box 211, Station P, Toronto, Ontario M5S 2S7, Canada (416 531 8873)
Nouveau	=	Nouveau Rare Books, Steve Silberman, P.O. Box 12471, 5005 Meadow Oaks Park Drive, Jackson, Mississippi 39211, U.S.A. (601 956 9950)
O'Neal	=	David L. O'Neal, 234 Clarendon Street, Boston, Massachusetts 02116, U.S.A. (617 266 5790)
Oak Knoll	=	Oak Knoll Books, 414 Delaware Street, New Castle, Delaware 19720, U.S.A. (302 328 7232)
Parmer	=	J. Parmer, Booksellers, 7644 Forrestal Road, San Diego, CA 92120, U.S.A. (619 287 0693)
Petrilla	=	R & A Petrilla, Roosevelt, NJ 08555-0306, U.S.A. (609 426 4999)
Phillips	=	Phillips of Hitchin, (Antiques) Ltd., The Manor House, Hitchin, Hertfordshire, England (0462 432067)
Polyanthos	=	Polyanthos Park Avenue Books, P.O. Box 343, Huntington, NY 11743, U.S.A. (516 271 5558)
P and P Books	=	P & P Books, J.S. Pizey, 27 Love Lane, Oldswinford, Stourbridge, West Midlands DY8, England (0384 393845)
Quest Books	=	Quest Books, Harmer Hill, Millington, York YO4 2TX, England (0759 304735)
Rankin	=	Alan Rankin, 72 Dundas Street, Edinburgh EH3 6QZ, Scotland, Scotland (031 556 3705)
Reese	=	William Reese Company, 409 Temple Street, New Haven, Connecticut 06511, U.S.A. (203 789 8081)
David Rees	=	David Rees, 18A Prentis Road, London SW16 1QD, England (081 769 2453)
Robertshaw	=	John Robertshaw, 5 Fellowes Drive, Ramsey, Huntingdon, Cambridgeshire PE17 1BE, England (0487 813330)
Rostenberg & Stern	=	Leona Rostenberg and Madeleine, Stern, Rare Books, 40 East 88th Street, New York, N.Y. 10128., U.S.A. (212 831 6628)
Sanders	=	Sanders of Oxford Ltd., 104 High Street, Oxford OX1 4BW, England (0865 242590)
Savona	=	Savona Books, 9 Wilton Road, Hornsea, North Humberside HU18 1QU, England (0964 535195)
Schoen	=	Kenneth Schoen, Bookseller, One Cottage Street, Easthampton, MA 01027, U.S.A. (413 527 4780)
Sclanders	=	Andrew Sclanders, 73 Duckett Road, London N4 1BL, England (081 340 6843)
Sheppard	=	Roger Sheppard, 117 Kent House Road, Beckenham, Kent BR3 1JJ, England (081 778 0534)
Sklaroff	=	L.J. Sklaroff, The Totland Bookshop, The Broadway, Totland, Isle of Wight PO39 0BW, England (0983 754960)
Alan Smith	=	Alan Smith, 15 Oakland Avenue, Dialstone Lane, Stockport, Cheshire SK2 6AX, England (061 483 2547)

Sotheran's	=	Henry Sotheran Ltd., 2 Sackville Street, Piccadilly, London W1X 2DP, England (071 439 6151)
Spelman	=	Ken Spelman, 70 Micklegate, York YO1 1LF, England (0904 624414)
Monroe Stahr	=	Monroe Stahr Books, 166 1/2 S. Sycamore Ave., Los Angeles, CA 90036, U.S.A. (213 931 9919)
Stewart	=	Andrew Stewart, 11 High Street, Helpringham, Sleaford, Lincolnshire NG34 9RA, England (052 921 617)
Sumner & Stillman	=	Sumner & Stillman, P.O. Box 225, Yarmouth, ME 04096, U.S.A. (207 846 6070)
Terramedia	=	Terramedia Books, 19 Homestead Road, Wellesley, MA 02181, U.S.A. (617 237 6485)
Thelema	=	Thelema Publications, P.O. Box 1393, Kings Beach, California 95719, U.S.A.
Tiger Books	=	Tiger Books, Yew Tree Cottage, Westbere, Canterbury Kent CT2 0HH, England (0227 710030)
Trophy Room Books	=	Trophy Room Books, Box 3041, Agoura, CA 91301, U.S.A. (818 889 2469)
Turtle Island	=	Turtle Island Booksellers, 2067 Center Street, Berkeley, CA 94704, U.S.A. (415 540 5422)
Ulysses Bookshop	=	Ulysses Bookshop, 41 Museum Street, London WC1A 1LH, England (071 637 5862)
Vanbrugh	=	Vanbrugh Rare Books, 'Ruskin House', 40a Museum Street, Bloomsbury, London WC1A 1LT, England (071 404 0733)
Virgo	=	Virgo Books, Little Court, South Wraxall, Bradford-on-Avon, Wiltshire BA15 2SE, England (02216 2040)
Walcot	=	Patrick Walcot, 60 Sunnybank Road, Sutton Coldfield, West Midlands B73 5RJ, England (021 382 6381)
Washton	=	Andrew D. Washton, 411 East 83rd Street, New York, New York 10028, U.S.A. (212 751 7027)
Waterfield's	=	Waterfield's, 36 Park End Street, Oxford OX1 1HJ, England (0865 721809)
Weiner	=	Graham Weiner, 78 Rosebery Road, London N10 2LA, England (081 883 8424)
Wheldon & Wesley	=	Wheldon & Wesley Ltd., Lytton Lodge, Codicote, Hitchin, Hertfordshire SG4 8TE, England (0438 820370)
Whitehart	=	F.E. Whitehart, Rare Books, 40 Priestfield Road, Forest Hill, London SE23 2RS, England (081 699 3225)
David White	=	David White, 17 High Street, Bassingbourn, Royston, Hertfordshire SG8 5NE, England (0763 243986)
Nigel Williams	=	Nigel Williams (Books), 196 Court Lane, Dulwich, London SE21 7ED, England (081 693 0464)
Susan Wood	=	Susan Wood, 24 Leasowe Road, Rubery, Rednal, Worcestershire B45 9TD, England (021 453 7169)
Woolmer	=	J. Howard Woolmer, Revere, Pennsylvania 18953, U.S.A. (215 847 5074)
Words Etcetera	=	Words Etcetera, Julian Nangle, Hod House, Child Okeford, Dorset DT11 8EH, England (0258 860539)
Worldwide	=	Worldwide Antiquarian, Post Office Box 391, Cambridge, MA 02141, U.S.A. (617 876 6220)
Wreden	=	William P. Wreden, 206 Hamilton Avenue, P.O. Box 56, Palo Alto, CA 94302-0056, U.S.A. (415 325 6851)
Ximenes	=	Ximenes: Rare Books, Inc., 19 East 69th Street, New York, NY 10021, U.S.A. (212 744 0226)
Young's	=	Young's Antiquarian Books, Tillingham, Essex CM0 7ST, England (0621 778187)